D1090126

The Solution ˌ ˌ ˌ
'Son of Man' Problem

THE SOLUTION TO THE 'SON OF MAN' PROBLEM

MAURICE CASEY

t & t clark

Published by T&T Clark International
A Continuum imprint
The Tower Building, 11 York Road, London SE1 7NX
80 Maiden Lane, Suite 704, New York, NY 10038

www.tandtclark.com

First published in hardback as volume 343 of the Library of New Testament
Studies series, 2007

This edition published, 2009

British Library Cataloguing-in-Publication Data
A catalogue record for this book is available from the British Library

ISBN 10: 0567030709 (paperback)
ISBN 13: 9780567030702 (paperback)

Typeset by Free Range Book Design & Production Limited
Printed on acid-free paper in Great Britain by the MPG Books Group,
    Bodmin and King's Lynn

CONTENTS

PREFACE

This book was written in 2002–4. In 2001–4, I held a Leverhulme Major Research Fellowship awarded for me to complete all the necessary research and write the first draft of this book, as well as a small monograph on the *Similitudes of Enoch*. I am extremely grateful to the Leverhulme Trust for this award, which enabled me to complete this massive piece of research.

I am also grateful to all those who have discussed with me the problems of method and of detail which this work has entailed. I began research on some aspects of the Son of man problem by reading for a doctorate at Durham University under Professor C. K. Barrett, whose extraordinary combination of learning and helpfulness with lack of bureaucracy or interference remains a model to which one can only aspire. I would particularly like to thank also Dr A. Angel, Professor R. Bauckham, the late Professor M. Black, Professor B. D. Chilton, Dr. J. G. Crossley, Professor J. A. Fitzmyer, Professor D. R. A. Hare, Dr C. Fletcher Louis, Professor R. Kearns, the late Professor B. Lindars, Professor M. Müller, Professor C. M. Tuckett and Professor W. Walker. I would also like to thank members of the Aramaic Background and Historical Jesus seminars at SNTS, the Jesus seminar at meetings of British New Testament scholars, and an annual seminar on the Use of the Old Testament in the New now generally held at Hawarden, for what I have learnt from them. I alone am responsible for what I have said.

I would also like to thank my Nottingham colleague Dr R. H. Bell for help with the word processor on which this book was written: and the libraries of SOAS and the British Library for the facilities necessary for advanced scholarly work.

ABBREVIATIONS

AB	Anchor Bible
Adv. Haer.	Adversus Haereses
Adv.Mc.	Adversus Marcionem
Adv. Prax.	Adversus Praxeam
AGJU	Arbeiten zur Geschichte des antiken Judentums und des Urchristentums
Akk.	Akkadian
AnBib	Analecta Biblica
ANRW	H. Temporini and W. Haase (eds), *Aufstieg und Niedergang der römischen Welt* (many vols., Berlin: W. de Gruyter, 1972–)
Ant.	*Antiquities of the Jews*
A.Pers.	Aeschylus, *Persians*
ASTI	*Annual of the Swedish Theological Institute*
ATANT	Abhandlungen zur Theologie des Alten und Neuen Testaments
AThD	*Acta Theologica Danica*
AZ	'Abodah Zarah
b.	Babylonian Talmud
BaL	Bampton Lectures
2 Bar.	*2 Baruch*
Ber	Berakhot
BETL	Bibliotheca ephemeridum theologicarum lovaniensium
BGBE	Beiträge zur Geschichte der biblischen Exegese
Bib	*Biblica*
BibRes	*Biblical Research*
BJRL	*Bulletin of the John Rylands Library*
BJRLM	*Bulletin of the John Rylands Library of Manchester*
BNTC	Black's New Testament Commentaries
BSRel	Bibliotheca di Scienze Religiose
BTL	Benjamins Translation Library
BWANT	Beiträge zur Wissenschaft vom Alten und Neuen Testament
CBM	Chester Beatty Monographs
CBQ	*Catholic Biblical Quarterly*
CChr.SL	Corpus Christianorum, Series Latina
2 Clem.	2 Clement
ConBNT	Coniectanea biblica, New Testament

ConBOT	Coniectanea biblica, Old Testament
1 Cor.	1 Corinthians
CRINT	Compendia rerum iudaicarum ad Novum Testamentum
CSCO	Corpus Scriptorum Christianorum Orientalium
cur	Curetonian
Dan.	Daniel
Dec.	*De decalogo*
Dem.	*Demonstratio*
Deut.	Deuteronomy
Dial.	Dialogue
Dips.	Dipsades
DJD	Discoveries in the Judaean Desert
EBib	Etudes Bibliques
Ebr.	*De ebrietate*
EKKNT	Evangelisch-Katholischer Kommentar zum Neuen Testament
1 En.	*1 Enoch*
2 En.	*2 Enoch*
2 Esd	LXX Ἔσδρας Βʹ
Est.	Esther
Est.R.	Esther Rabbah
ETL	*Ephemerides theologicae lovanienses*
Eus.	Eusebius
Exod.	Exodus
ExpTim	*Expository Times*
Ezek.	Ezekiel
FRLANT	Forschungen zur Religion und Literatur des Alten und Neuen Testaments
FZPT	Freiburger Zeitschrift für Philosophie und Theologie
Gal.	Galatians
Gen.	Genesis
Gen.R.	Genesis Rabbah
Gitt.	Gittin
Gos. Thom.	Gospel of Thomas
H.A.	*Historia Animalium*
hark	Harklean
Hab.	Habakkuk
Hdt.	Herodotus
H.E.	*Historia Ecclesiastica*
Ḥag	Ḥagigah
Hos.	Hosea
HSM	Harvard Semitic Monographs
HTR	*Harvard Theological Review*
HTS	Harvard Theological Studies
IBS	*Irish Biblical Studies*

ICC	International Critical Commentary
IG	Inscriptiones Graecae
Isa.	Isaiah
Jas	James
Jer.	Jeremiah
JBL	*Journal of Biblical Literature*
JJS	*Journal of Jewish Studies*
Jn	John
Jon.	Jonah
Jos.	Josephus
Josh.	Joshua
JSJ	*Journal for the Study of Judaism in the Persian, Hellenistic and Roman Period*
JSNT	*Journal for the Study of the New Testament*
JSNTSup	*Journal for the Study of the New Testament*, Supplement Series
JSP	*Journal for the Study of the Pseudepigrapha*
JSP	*Journal for the Study of the Pseudepigrapha*, Supplement Series
JSS	*Journal of Semitic Studies*
JTS	*Journal of Theological Studies*
Jub.	*Jubilees*
Judg.	Judges
KAI	H. Donner and W. Röllig, *Kanaanäische und Aramäische Inschriften* (Wiesbaden: Harrassowitz, 2nd edn, 1966–9)
Ket.	Ketuboth
1 Kgdms	LXX 1 Kingdoms
2 Kgdms	LXX 2 Kingdoms
3 Kgdms	LXX 3 Kingdoms
4 Kgdms	LXX 4 Kingdoms
1 Kgs	1 Kings
2 Kgs	2 Kings
Kil.	Kilayim
Lam.	Lamentations
Lev.	Leviticus
LCL	Loeb Classical Library
LD	Lectio divina
Lk.	Luke
LXX	Septuagint
M.	Mishnah
1 Macc.	1 Maccabees
2 Macc.	2 Maccabees
3 Macc.	*3 Maccabees*
Mal.	Malachi
MekhY	Mekhilta de-Rabbi Ishmael
Mic.	Micah

Midr.Ps.	Midrash on Psalms
Mt.	Matthew
MQ	Mo'ed Qatan
MT	Massoretic Text
Nah.	Nahum
Naz.	Nazir
NCB	New Century Bible
Ned.	Nedarim
Neh.	Nehemiah
Neof	Neofiti
N.H.	Naturalis Historia
NHS	Nag Hammadi Studies
NovT	*Novum Testamentum*
NovTSup	*Novum Testamentum*, Supplements
NTOA	Novum Testamentum et orbis antiquus
NTS	*New Testament Studies*
Num.	Numbers
NumenSup	*Numen*, Supplements
Onq	Onqelos
OTP	J. H. Charlesworth (ed.), *The Old Testament Pseudepigrapha* (2 vols; New York: Doubleday, 1983–5)
palsyrlec	*palestinian syriac lectionary*
Pes.	Pesaḥim
Pesh	Peshitta
2 Pet.	2 Peter
Phil.	Philippians
PO	Patrologia orientalis
Prov.	Proverbs
Ps.	Psalm
Pss.	Psalms
Pss. Sol.	*Psalms of Solomon*
Ps-J	Pseudo-Jonathan
PTS	Patristische Texte und Studien
1QapGen.	Genesis Apocryphon
1QpHab	Qumran Commentary on Habakkuk
Qid	Qiddushin
11QTgJob	Job Targum from Qumran
R.	Rabbi
RB	*Revue biblique*
Ref.	*Refutatio Omnium Haeresium*
Rev.	Revelation
Rev Thom	*Revue thomiste*
Sam	Samaritan Targum
1 Sam.	1 Samuel

2 Sam.	2 Samuel
San.	Sanhedrin
SBL	Society of Biblical Literature
SBLDS	SBL Dissertation Series
SBLMS	SBL Monograph Series
SBT	Studies in Biblical Theology
SC	Sources Chrétiennes
SE	Studia Evangelica
Sem	Semaḥoth
Shabb.	Shabbat
Shevi.	Shevi'it
Shevu	Shevu'ot
sin	sinaitic syriac
Sir.	Sirach
SNTSMS	Society for New Testament Studies Monograph Series
Spec. Leg.	*De specialibus legibus*
ST	*Studia theologica*
Suk.	Sukkah
SUNT	Studien zur Umwelt des Neuen Testaments
Ta'an.	Ta'anith
TBü	Theologische Bücherei
TDNT	G. Kittel and G. Friedrich (eds), *Theological Dictionary of the New Testament* (trans. G. W. Bromiley; 11 vols; Grand Rapids: Eerdmans, 1964–76)
T.Ephraem	Testament of Ephraem
Ter.	Terumoth
Tg	Targum
Theod.	Theodotion
1 Thess.	1 Thessalonians
1 Tim.	1 Timothy
Thuc.	Thucydides
T.Jud.	Testament of Judah
T.Levi	Testament of Levi
Tob.	Tobit
TSAJ	Texte und Studien zum antiken Judentum
TT	*Theologisch Tijdschrift*
TU	Texte und Untersuchungen
TWNT	G. Kittel and G. Friedrich (eds), *Theologisches Wörterbuch zum Neuen Testament* (11 vols; Stuttgart, Kohlhammer, 1932–79)
TynBul	*Tyndale Bulletin*
TZ	*Theologische Zeitschrift*
v.	verse
Vit.Cont.	*De vita contempliva*
VTSup	*Vetus Testamentum*, Supplements

WBC	Word Biblical Commentary
Wis.	Wisdom of Solomon
WUNT	Wissenschaftliche Untersuchungen zum Neuen Testament
y.	Yerushalmi (= Jerusalem/Palestinian Talmud)
Yeb.	Yebamoth
Zech.	Zechariah
ZAW	*Zeitschrift für die alttestamentliche Wissenschaft*
ZNW	*Zeitschrift für die neutestamentliche Wissenschaft*
ZTK	*Zeitschrift für Theologie und Kirche*

Chapter One

THE STATE OF PLAY

The Son of man problem is one of the most difficult problems in the whole of New Testament Studies. Long after the two monographs of A. J. B. Higgins have ceased to be influential, many scholars still refer to the title of his article, 'Is the Son of man problem insoluble?'[1] The purpose of this chapter is to offer a critical *Forschungsberichte* to the whole problem. This is not a comprehensive catalogue of previous work: Mögens Müller has provided a comprehensive history of the interpretation of ὁ υἱὸς τοῦ ἀνθρώπου.[2] I offer a selective discussion of what advances have been made, what significant mistakes have been made, and the reasons for both of these. The role of the Aramaic term (א)שׁנ(א) בר has been crucial to this, and I argue that the absence of satisfactory discussion of it has been one major cause of this problem's apparent insolubility.

1. The Fathers

The earliest Fathers took important steps away from the historical Jesus, because they inherited ὁ υἱὸς τοῦ ἀνθρώπου in the Gospels in Greek, and were not generally aware of the Aramaic term (א)שׁנ(א) בר. We shall see that in the Fourth Gospel ὁ υἱὸς τοῦ ἀνθρώπου already refers to the humanity of God incarnate.[3] Here, and to a lesser extent in the other canonical Gospels, Jesus is also ὁ υἱὸς (τοῦ θεοῦ). As the Fathers developed the doctrine of Jesus' two natures, human and divine, they naturally interpreted ὁ υἱὸς τοῦ ἀνθρώπου as a reference to his human nature. For example, Tertullian, as part of a statement of faith, declares concerning the Son and Word through whom all things were made:

---

1.   A. J. B. Higgins, *Jesus and the Son of Man* (London: Lutterworth, 1964): 'Is the Son of Man Problem Insoluble?', in E. E. Ellis and M. Wilcox (eds), *Neotestamentica and Semitica: Studies in Honour of Matthew Black* (Edinburgh: T&T Clark, 1969), pp. 70–87: *The Son of Man in the Teaching of Jesus* (SNTSMS 39. Cambridge: CUP, 1980).

2.   M. Müller, *The Expression 'Son of Man' and the Development of Christology. A History of Interpretation* (forthcoming). Earlier, see also extensive parts of M. Müller, *Der Ausdruck 'Menschensohn' in den Evangelien. Voraussetzungen und Bedeutung* (AThD XVII. Leiden: Brill, 1984).

3.   See Ch. 12.

hunc missum a patre in virginem et ex ea natum hominem et deum, filium hominis et filium
dei, et cognominatum Jesus Christum.
… that he was sent by the Father into the virgin and born from her man and God, Son of man
and Son of God, and was named Jesus Christ. (*Adv. Prax.* 2)

Here the reference to the two natures of Jesus is clear from the context, which has
Jesus arrive on earth as man and God before using the two referential titles Son of
man and Son of God.

Considering further the term ὁ υἱὸς τοῦ ἀνθρώπου in Greek, the Fathers also
took ἀνθρώπου as a reference to a particular person. One major line of interpretation
took the reference to be to Mary. For example, Gregory of Nyssa quotes Eunomius
as follows:

αὐτὸς ὁ κύριος υἱὸς ὢν τοῦ θεοῦ τοῦ ζῶντος τὴν ἐκ τῆς παρθένου γένησιν οὐκ
ἐπαισχυνόμενος ἐν τοῖς ἑαυτοῦ λόγοις υἱὸν ἀνθρώπου πολλάκις ὠνόμασεν ἑαυτόν.
… the Lord himself, being the Son of the living God, not being ashamed of his birth from the
virgin, often called himself 'Son of man' in his own sayings. (*Against Eunomius* III,I,91)

Here the connection between 'Son of man' and the virgin birth is absolutely clear,
as is the reference to the doctrine of the two natures of Christ. There is also a very
clear reference to the sayings of Jesus, and hence to the Gospels, in which the term
is ὁ υἱὸς τοῦ ἀνθρώπου, with two articles. Here in the quotation from Eunomius,
however, υἱὸν ἀνθρώπου has no articles. Gregory of Nyssa does the same in his
following discussion of Eunomius:

ὡς γὰρ υἱὸς ἀνθρώπου λέγεται διὰ τὴν τῆς σαρκὸς αὐτοῦ πρὸς τὴν ἐξ ἧς ἐγεννήθη
συγγένειαν …
For as he is called Son of man because of the kinship of his flesh to her from whom he was
born …

Here too there is a clear reference to Jesus' birth from Mary, and to the title which in
the Gospels is ὁ υἱὸς τοῦ ἀνθρώπου. Here too, however, the term is simply υἱὸν
ἀνθρώπου. This is moreover widespread in the Greek Fathers. The reason for this
appears to be the doctrine of the two natures. The potential problem with ὁ υἱὸς τοῦ
ἀνθρώπου is that, in a culture where the Aramaic (א)שׁנ(א) בר has long since been
forgotten, ὁ υἱὸς τοῦ ἀνθρώπου refers especially to Jesus himself. The doctrine
of the two natures required clear reference to his humanity rather than simply to
himself, and this is easier to achieve with υἱὸν ἀνθρώπου without the articles.
The question of this difference did not arise for the Latin Fathers, since reasonable
literary Latin had no articles. Accordingly, *filius hominis* could function as a specific
title of Jesus and a reference to his general human nature even in the same context.

The interpretation with particular reference to Mary continued for centuries. It
began to wane under the criticism, first made during the Reformation period, that
the second article in ὁ υἱὸς τοῦ ἀνθρώπου is the masculine τοῦ rather than the
feminine τῆς. This criticism requires a more literal understanding of the reference
to Mary than is found for example in the above passages of Tertullian and Gregory.

This interpretation slowly died out, and never made it into critical scholarship of the modern period.

The other major line of interpretation which took ὁ υἱὸς τοῦ ἀνθρώπου to indicate Jesus' sonship of a particular person regarded it as a reference to Adam. Ps-Athanasius provides a clear example of this:

ὁ γὰρ τῶν ὅλων δημιουργὸς λόγος ὤφθη υἱὸς ἀνθρώπου, οὐχ ἕτερός τις γενόμενος, ἀλλὰ δεύτερος Ἀδάμ ... εἰ μὲν οὖν ἐπὶ γῆς γέγονεν υἱὸς ἀνθρώπου, καίτοι οὐκ ἐκ σπέρματος ἀνδρὸς, ἀλλ᾽ ἐκ πνεύματος ἁγίου γεννηθεὶς, ἑνὸς ὄντος τοῦ πρωτοπλάστου Ἀδὰμ υἱὸς νοηθήσεται.

For the Word, the artificer of the universe, appeared as Son of man, not as having become something different, but a second Adam ... If therefore he became Son of man on earth, yet was begotten of (the) holy spirit, not of the seed of man, he shall be considered son of one, the first-formed, Adam. (*On the Incarnation Against Apollinaris* I,8)

Here again the doctrine of the two natures underlies the whole discussion, the term λόγος being used with reference to the fully divine maker of the universe, and υἱὸς ἀνθρώπου referring to his existence as man during his incarnate life on earth. Here too it will be noted that υἱὸς ἀνθρώπου does not need the articles in Greek.

This line of interpretation did not merely continue for centuries, it is regrettably still with us.[4] It is accordingly to be noted that in the Greek Fathers it does not require any stress on the second article in ὁ υἱὸς τοῦ ἀνθρώπου, as if the expression itself required the incarnate Jesus to be son of a particular man. On the contrary, we have just seen in Ps-Athanasius that this interpretation was held with the articles omitted from υἱὸς ἀνθρώπου. This is again due to the overriding influence of the doctrine of the two natures.

Once the Fathers produced these interpretations which saw the term Son of man having some special reference to Mary or to Adam in this theological kind of way, there was nothing to stop a theologically minded Father from holding both interpretations at once. Gregory of Nazianzus provides a straightforward example of this, as he discusses the various names of Jesus:

Υἱὸς δὲ ἀνθρώπου, καὶ διὰ τον Ἀδάμ, καὶ διὰ τὴν Παρθένον, ἐξ ὧν ἐγενέτο· τοῦ μὲν, ὡς προπάτορος, τῆς δέ, ὡς μητρὸς νόμῳ, καὶ οὐ νόμῳ γεννήσεως.

Son of man both because of Adam and because of the virgin from whom he was born, the one as forefather, the other as mother, both according to and not according to the law of generation. (*Oration* 30, 21)

This is as clear as one could wish for in espousing both interpretations, and again in using υἱὸς ἀνθρώπου without the articles.

Another major trend which began in the patristic period was the view that the Gospel title 'Son of man' was derived from Daniel 7.13. Tertullian was the first Father to give expression to this view. He was not of course the first Father to interpret Dan. 7.13 with reference to Jesus. We find this already in Justin. For

---

4.   See pp. 32–3, 53–4 below.

example, at *Dial.* 31,1, Justin interpreted Dan. 7.13 with reference to the parousia, as the Gospel writers had done before him. At *Dial.* 76,1, he went further:

ὅταν γὰρ ὡς υἱὸν ἀνθρώπου λέγῃ Δανιὴλ τὸν παραλαμβάνοντα τὴν αἰώνιον βασιλείαν, οὐκ αὐτὸ τοῦτο αἰνίσσετα; Τὸ γὰρ ὡς υἱὸν ἀνθρώπου εἰπεῖν, φαινόμενον μὲν καὶ γενόμενον ἄνθρωπον αὐτὸν μηνύει, οὐκ ἐξ ἀνθρωπίνου δὲ σπέρματος ὑπάρχοντα δηλοῖ.

For when Daniel calls him who receives the eternal kingdom 'like a son of man', is he not hinting at the same thing? For to say 'like a son of man' means that he appeared to be and became man, but shows that he was not of human seed.

Here Daniel is held to have predicted the virgin birth of Jesus. Justin interpreted the Gospel title ὁ υἱὸς τοῦ ἀνθρώπου similarly at *Dial.* 100,3, citing it with the articles, and immediately discussing it without them. As in the Greek Fathers already discussed, the presence or absence of the articles in the expression 'Son of man' makes no apparent difference. Also, in ignorance of the Aramaic term (א)שׁנ(א) בר, both Daniel's ὡς υἱὸν ἀνθρώπου and the Gospel title ὁ υἱὸς τοῦ ἀνθρώπου can be interpreted with reference to the virgin birth in a way that the mundane (א)שׁנ(א) בר could not, because the latter was an ordinary term for any man, or even any person, and people are not born of virgins.

In the first major commentary on Daniel extant, Hippolytus took a similar approach at greater length. He refers for example to Jesus' two natures, and his function of judgement at his parousia:

... ἔνσαρκος δὲ θεὸς καὶ ἄνθρωπος, υἱὸς θεοῦ καὶ ἀνθρώπου ἀπ' οὐρανῶν κριτὴς τῷ κόσμῳ παραγινόμενος.
... God incarnate and man, Son of God and of man, come from heaven as judge for the world. (IV,10,2)

Hippolytus also uses the Gospel term ὁ υἱὸς τοῦ ἀνθρώπου with reference to the Danielic text, commenting on the manlike figure being brought before the Ancient of Days:

πρὸς τοῦτον προσηνέχθη ὁ υἱὸς τοῦ ἀνθρώπου ὑπὸ νεφέλης βασταζόμενος ...
The Son of man was brought to him, borne by a cloud ... (IV,11,3)

Here again we see a Greek Father apparently quite oblivious to the presence or absence of the articles in the expression 'Son of man'.

This is the western tradition of the interpretation of Dan. 7.13 which was carried so much further by Tertullian. I have already noted Tertullian's adherence to the doctrine of the two natures of Christ, and his interpretation of *filius hominis* as a reference to Jesus' human nature (*Adv. Prax.* 2).[5] At *Adv.Mc.* III,7, Tertullian expounds the idea of two advents of Christ, and assigns Dan. 7.13-14 to the second. His most extensive discussion is at *Adv.Mc.* IV,10. The context is the story in which

---

5.   See pp. 1–2 above.

Jesus pronounces the forgiveness of a man's sins, using the term 'Son of man' of himself at Luke 5.24. Tertullian argues that the term *filius hominis* must mean that Jesus had a human parent, and since God was his Father, that must mean his virgin mother. He then turns to Daniel with the following comment:

> Quid nunc, si ipso titulo filii hominis censetur Christus apud Danielem?
> What now if Christ is appreciated according to Daniel with the very title of Son of man?
> (*Adv.Mc.* IV,10,9)

This is the absolute centre of the line of interpretation which began here, and which is still with us. Here the actual title used by Jesus, *filius hominis* to Tertullian and to any other Latin Father, is seen to be present in the text of Daniel itself. The term (א)בר נש(א) was not known to Tertullian, so it cannot come into question. By the time that it did come into question, the tradition that the Gospel term 'Son of man' was derived from Dan. 7.13 was much too strong a tradition to be easily budged. In originating it, Tertullian was able to argue that Jesus was uniquely qualified to have both the name of Christ and the title of *filius hominis*.

> Nec alius erit capacior utriusque quam qui prior et nomen sortitus est Christi et appellationem filii hominis, Iesus scilicet creatoris.
> Nor will anyone be more capable of both than he who first received the name of Christ and the title of Son of man, namely the creator's Jesus. (*Adv.Mc.* IV,10,11)

The only other possible place where *filius hominis* could be found was in other passages of scripture. Tertullian unfortunately went for Dan. 3.25, a mistake which therefore never caught on. Otherwise, he saw fit to develop further his use of Dan. 7.13, commenting as follows:

> Idem ipsi Danieli revelatus directo filius hominis veniens cum caeli nubibus iudex, sicut et scriptura demonstrat.
> He was also revealed directly to Daniel himself as the Son of man coming with the clouds of heaven as judge, as scripture also demonstrates. (*Adv.Mc.* IV,10,12)

This interprets Dan. 7.13 as a direct revelation to Daniel of Jesus as Son of man coming with the clouds of heaven, so this is not only the standard western Christian interpretation of this text, it also includes the direct revelation of the title *filius hominis* to Daniel. Tertullian further derives Jesus' ability to forgive sins from his position as judge in the Danielic text. This kind of reasoning is also still with us.

Once this tradition of interpretation was properly established, it could be adhered to by Fathers who knew the 'son of' idiom perfectly well. For example, Theodoret explains it in commenting on Dan. 11.9-10:

> υἱοὺς δὲ αὐτοῦ καλεῖ τὴν στρατείαν πεπιστευμένους, ὡς υἱοὺς ἀνθρώπων τοὺς ἀνθρώπους, καὶ υἱοὺς τῶν προφητῶν τοὺς προφήτας· ἰδίωμα γάρ ἐστι τῆς Ἑβραίων διαλέκτου.
> He calls 'his sons' those entrusted with raising the army, as men (are called) sons of men, and the prophets (are called) sons of the prophets. For it is an idiom of the language of the Hebrews.

This did not prevent Theodoret from expounding a conventional western Christian view of Dan. 7.13 and of the Gospel title ὁ υἱὸς τοῦ ἀνθρώπου. Commenting on Dan. 7.13-14, he quotes Mt. 24.30 complete with both the articles of ὁ υἱὸς τοῦ ἀνθρώπου, and comments:

> τοῦτο σαφῶς ἡμᾶς ἐδίδαξεν ὁ μακάριος Δανιὴλ, τὴν δευτέραν σωτῆρος ἐπιφάνειαν προθεσπίζων ...
>
> The blessed Daniel clearly taught us this, foretelling the second appearance of the saviour ...

Having quoted Mt. 24.30, where ὁ υἱὸς τοῦ ἀνθρώπου has both the articles, to expound a text without them, Theodoret comments further on the meaning of the term:

> υἱὸν μὲν ἀνθρώπου σαφῶς ἀποκαλῶν, δι᾽ ἣν ἀνέλαβε φύσιν.
>
> clearly calling him 'Son of man', because of the nature which he took on.

Here the Gospels' use of ὁ υἱὸς τοῦ ἀνθρώπου as a title of Jesus alone, and the patristic doctrine of the two natures of Christ, are both paramount. There is no question of Theodoret being able to see past the evidence of the Gospels to an original Aramaic idiom in sayings of Jesus.

Gnostic use of the term 'Son of man' was even further removed from the ministry of the historical Jesus. According to different Gnostics, Man, or ἄνθρωπος, might refer not to humankind, but to an exalted syzygy, or even, apparently in partial dependence on Gen. 1.26, to God himself. The Son of man could then be an emanation from this being. In one version reported by Irenaeus, Christ united to Sophia descended on the virgin-born Jesus, who openly confessed himself as *filium primi hominis*, son of the first man (*Adv. Haer.* I,30,1 and 12-13). In due course, Eugnostos had as the first, second and third aeons, Immortal Man, Son of Man = First Begetter, and Son of Son of Man = Saviour (III,3,85, with V,13,12-13).[6] This reveals further remoteness from the Jesus of history, and no real connection with the Aramaic (א)שׁנ(א) בר.

Some gnostic documents show varying degrees of connection with the canonical Gospels. For example, the Gospel of Thomas, which has only some gnosticizing features, has a slightly elaborated version of Mt. 8.20//Lk. 9.58 as saying 86, without any indication as to how it was interpreted. The Peratae reported by Hippolytus had a version of Jn 3.14, including ὁ υἱὸς τοῦ ἀνθρώπου with both articles (Hipp. *Ref.* V,16,11). This reference has however nothing to do with the crucifixion of Jesus, an event with which Gnosticism could never properly come to terms. It concerns rather the exposition of the meaning of the serpent and the centrality of the Son for salvation.

---

6.   For an ET, D. M. Parrot, 'Eugnostos the Blessed (III,3 and V,1) and the Sophia of Jesus Christ (III,4 and BG 8502,3)', in J. M. Robinson (ed.), *The Nag Hammadi Library in English* (4th edn, Leiden: Brill, 1996), pp. 220–43. The text is still available only in Ms facsimile, which I regret that I do not read.

Thus, gnostic use of the term 'Son of man' is even more remote from the ministry of the historical Jesus than the comments of more orthodox Fathers. Moreover, specifically gnostic ideas about the 'Son of man' did not survive beyond the ancient period. Accordingly, they will not be further discussed in this book.

The comments of the Syriac-speaking Fathers might have been expected to be of especial interest, since they spoke and wrote in the same language as the historical Jesus. Unfortunately, however, they had no idea that Son of man sayings now found in the Gospels originated from Jesus using the ordinary Aramaic term בר (א)נש(א) with reference to himself. Their knowledge of Jesus was mediated through the Gospels. Initially, this knowledge came directly from the Diatessaron of Tatian, which represented ὁ υἱὸς τοῦ ἀνθρώπου with ברה דאנשא. For example, it has this partial version of Mt. 8.20//Lk. 9.58:

לתעלא נקעין אית להון ...ולברה דאנשא לית לה אתר דנסמוך רישה
(Ephraem, *Commentary on the Diatessaron* VI,24a,1-2.)[7]

Here ברה דאנשא is a Christological title which refers to Jesus alone, a translation of ὁ υἱὸς τοῦ ἀνθρώπου , not a reflection of any direct knowledge of the way in which Jesus referred to himself in Aramaic. It is a new term, not previously known in Aramaic, and invented as a strategy for dealing with a translation problem. In due course, other Fathers and translators used ברה דגברא (e.g. Lk. 7.34 sin cur), or ברה דבראנשא (e.g. Mark 2.28 palsyrlec). Neither of these alters the main point. Each is a translation of the Greek Christological title ὁ υἱὸς τοῦ ἀνθρώπου. Each is accordingly a neologism, an Aramaic Christological title which refers to Jesus alone.

Given that these were new titles, the fathers and translators naturally continued to use בר (א)נש(א) itself as a general term for humankind. So, for example, Tatian used בר אנשא for ἄνθρωπος at Mark 2.27, thereby correctly representing the sentiment of Mark and indeed of Jesus that the Sabbath was created for people in general (Ephraem, *Commentary on the Diatessaron* V,24,10-12).[8] With this as part of the everyday language, the Fathers made widespread theological use of בר (א)נשא with reference to Jesus' human nature. For example, Ephraem comments directly on Jesus during the Incarnation:

דאלהא הו אף בכסיא ובר אנשא הו בגליא ...
For he is/was God also in a hidden manner, and (son of) man visibly...(*Commentary on the Diatessaron* V,19,10-11.)

7.   I cite section, paragraph and line of paragraph from L. Leloir (ed.), *Saint Éphrem. Commentaire de L'Evangile Concordant. Texte Syriaque (Ms Chester Beatty 709)* (CBM 8. Dublin: Hodges Figgis, 1963); L. Leloir (ed.), *Saint Éphrem. Commentaire de L'Evangile Concordant. Texte Syriaque (Ms Chester Beatty 709). Folios Additionels* (CBM 8. Leuven/Paris: Peeters, 1990).

8.   See P. M. Casey, *Aramaic Sources of Mark's Gospel* (SNTSMS 102. Cambridge: CUP, 1998), pp. 158–68; pp. 121–5 below.

At the same time, somewhat similarly to the western Fathers, the Syriac-speaking Fathers also used their Gospel title 'Son of man' with reference to Jesus' human nature. For example, Philoxenus refers to the doctrine of Jesus' two natures:

וברה הו האלא שרירית באלהותה וברה הו דאנשא כינאית באנשוותא

and (his) Son of God truly in his deity, and (his) Son of man by nature in the humanity. (*Tractatus de Adversario* 32)

Here the two balancing Christological titles are interpreted by means of more general terms to give clear reference to the divine and human natures of Christ.

With some idea of the two natures in the background, חד בר (א)נשא or בר (א)נשא could be used to refer to Jesus as a human being, the reference being made clear by the context. For example, Narsai comments, חד בר (א)נשא גבא, 'he chose one (son of) man' (*Homily On the Epiphany of Our Lord*, 387). Here the lengthy contextual discussion makes it clear that the reference is to God's choice of Jesus for the incarnation, a situation to which his human nature was essential. Again, Jacob of Serug comments:

עמא סרב דלברנשא תלת על קיסא

the denying people who hung a/the (son of) man on a/the tree. (*Homily against the Jews* I,17)

In this case, the broad cultural context is as important as the immediately surrounding literary context in leaving no doubt that this refers to the crucifixion of Jesus by the Jews. Both these examples illustrate the massive gap between the kind of comments that could be made during the ministry of the historical Jesus and the advanced literary and theological environment of the Syriac-speaking church. The latter context permits even the simple בר (א)נש(א) to be used on its own with reference to Jesus himself alone, whereas attempts to reconstruct sayings of Jesus with similar reference result in confusion.

The use of Dan. 7.13 in the Syriac-speaking church was complicated by two factors. One was the extraordinary translation of the original בר אנש with בר אנשין, perhaps originally a deliberate attempt to avoid the interpretation of this figure as a direct prophecy of Jesus. The second factor, which may indeed have been involved in the first, was that the Syriac-speaking church preserved the original interpretation of כבר אנש as referring to the Saints of the Most High, interpreting these as Maccabean Jews or something close to this: they added a secondary reference, at the level of רז or the like, to Jesus. For example, Theodore bar Koni comments on בר אנשין at Dan. 7.13:

הנין דאף לזובנהין מתנסבן על מקביא אלא חתיתותהין במרן משיחא אשתמלית

In their historical context these words refer to the Maccabees, but their essential quality is fulfilled in our Lord the Messiah.[9]

9.   A. Scher (ed.), *Theodorus bar Kōnī – Liber Scholium* (2 vols; CSCO 55, 69: SS 19, 26, 1954), vol. 1, p. 344, lines 5–9.

Although this was the main interpretative tradition, it remained possible to use בר אנשין in an appropriately Danielic context with simple reference to Jesus. For example, Aphrahat turns down the interpretation of Dan. 7.27 with reference to Jewish triumph, and after supporting this with scriptural quotations, he comments:

ואתא בר אנשין דנחרר אנון ונכנש אנון והנון לא קבלוהי

And a son of men came to set them free and gather them, 'and they did not receive him'. (Jn 1.11) (Aphrahat, *Dem.* V, 21)

It was also possible to use בר אנשין and ברה דאנשא together, as in the following passage of Jacob of Serug:

והי דאתחוי איך בר אנשין הדא רמזת
דברה דאנשא אית לה דהוא לבר אלהא

That he appeared 'like a son of men', this is the sign that the Son of God could become the Son of man. (*Homily against the Jews* VI,173–4)

Here the second level of interpretation of בר אנשין at Dan. 7.13 is deliberately interpreted with the Gospel title ברה דאנשא. The difference is however so great that no Syriac Father has been recorded as arguing that the Gospel title 'Son of man' was derived from Dan. 7.13, as we have seen Tertullian do.

As in the West, the doctrine of the incarnation permitted especial reference to be made to Jesus' mother Mary, or to the first man Adam. For example, Jacob of Serug followed the above comment on Dan. 7.13 with a comment on the plural 'thrones' at Dan. 7.9:

לברנשא גיר כורסיא צידוהי לא מתקן הוא
אלא לברה דברה דאנשא הוא מן מרים.

For a throne was not placed beside him for a (son of) man,
But for his Son who became the Son of man from Miriam. (*Homily against the Jews* VI,175–6)

Here the underlying point, declared in the following two lines, is that neither angels nor mortals can sit in the presence of God. Hence the second throne must be for God's Son, and this contrast has led Jacob quite reasonably to make reference to the process of the incarnation, and hence to Jesus' birth from Mary. Jacob does not however say that אנשא in ברה דאנשא actually refers to her.

Isho'dad of Merw associated the term itself more closely with Adam. He commented on Mt. 16.13:

...אלא ברה דאנשא אמר דנשודע דלית לה אבא דיליניא באנשותה איך דשרכא אלא ברה דאנשא קדמיא הנו
דאדם אבא דגוא.

… but he said '(his) Son of (the) man', to make it known that He had in truth no personal father in his manhood, like the rest, but was (his) Son of the first Man, that is to say, of Adam the father of the (whole) community.

Here the term has been interpreted as 'the son of the man', and the man in question has been identified as Adam, so that in effect the term is held to mean 'son of Adam'.

It is clear that the interpretation of ברה דאנשא and the other expressions for the Gospel title ὁ υἱὸς τοῦ ἀνθρώπου in the Syriac-speaking churches is of limited value to a search for the original meaning of בר (א)נ(א)ש as used by the historical Jesus. There are three important points. One is that the invention of ברה דאנשא and two other similar expressions, all neologisms, was felt necessary by Tatian and by subsequent translators. This shows what a large shift in meaning had taken place between בר (א)נ(א)ש and ὁ υἱὸς τοῦ ἀνθρώπου. Secondly, the continued use of בר (א)נ(א)ש is instructive, both because there are a large number of examples in our relatively extensive primary sources, and because references to Jesus can be compared and contrasted with the use of בר (א)נ(א)ש during the historic ministry. Thirdly, as in the West, theological interpretations of Gospel titles for 'Son of man' continued in accordance with the theological traditions of the churches, not with any concerns about what the origins of the term might have been.

It was moreover the mainline interpretations of relatively orthodox western Fathers which dominated Christian theological comments on 'Son of man' for centuries. One major line of interpretation continues to be of central importance, that the term really derives from Dan. 7.13. A minority of scholars, on the other hand, still believe that it means 'son of Adam'. Interest in the origins of the term ὁ υἱὸς τοῦ ἀνθρώπου as seen in its relationship to the Aramaic term בר (א)נ(א)ש did not begin until the days of the Reformation and the Enlightenment, as the work of some learned men began the very slow process of heading towards critical scholarship.

2. *From Grotius to Meyer*

Among the earlier scholars, I cite Grotius, for he was to be one of the most influential. Commenting on Mt. 12.8 in 1641, Grotius set off with the main point:

> Errant qui υἱὸν τοῦ ἀνθρώπου [*filium hominis*] hoc loco Christum peculiariter intelligunt.
> Those who understand υἱὸν τοῦ ἀνθρώπου [*son of man*] in this passage as a reference to Christ in particular are mistaken.

This is one of the main points which has been central to the debate on this term ever since, and Grotius gave several reasons for his judgement. Of especial importance is this comment:

> Sed, ut dixi, notissimum est Hebraeis בן אדם [*filium hominis*] hominem quemvis significare
> ...
> But, as I said, it is quite clear that for the Hebrews בן אדם [*son of man*] meant 'any man'...[10]

---

10.   H. Grotius, *Annotationes in libros evangeliorum* (Amsterdam/Paris, 1641), ad loc. I had access to this as *Annotationes in quatuor Evangelia & Acta Apostolorum* in H. Grotii *Opera Omnia Theologica* (Amsterdam: Blaev, 1679), Tom II vol. I.

This comes close to a reason why ὁ υἱὸς τοῦ ἀνθρώπου could not be a Christological title on the lips of Jesus, but it leaves insoluble problems behind it. If we know only this, we cannot explain why Jesus used the Aramaic term (א)נשׁ(א) בר, nor how it came to be transmuted into a Christological title. The bible-centred nature of this limitation is especially obvious in Grotius, for he could read Aramaic and Syriac. Subsequent critics naturally fastened on the obvious fact that in the Gospels in general, ὁ υἱὸς τοῦ ἀνθρώπου is evidently a title of Jesus alone, and makes sense as such everywhere.

Grotius made another significant and complementary point in commenting on Mt. 12.32. With a reference back to Mt. 12.8, he now declared:

> ... idem hic observandum puto per υἱὸν ἀνθρώπου [*filium hominis*], quamvis addito articulo, non hic Christum solum intelligi, sed hominem quemvis, ne Christo quidem excepto. Est enim saepe articulus signum generalitatis, ut ὁ ἐθνικὸς [*Ethnicus*] infra XVIII.17, τῷ ἱερεῖ [*sacerdoti*] Marci I,44.
> ... likewise I think it must be observed that by υἱὸν ἀνθρώπου [son of man], although the article has been added, Christ alone is not to be understood, but any man, Christ not excepted. For the article is often a sign of generality, as with ὁ ἐθνικὸς [*a Gentile*] (Mt. 18.17), τῷ ἱερεῖ [*the priest*]. (Mark 1.44)

Behind Grotius' second point here lies a subsequently frequent objection to his interpretation of both these passages, that the first Greek article in ὁ υἱὸς τοῦ ἀνθρώπου entails a reference to a single person. Grotius already knew that it might be what I shall call generic.

One of the most extensive attempts at a linguistic explanation of ὁ υἱὸς τοῦ ἀνθρώπου in the pre-modern period was made by J. A. Bolten in 1792.[11] At Mt. 8.20, Bolten translates ὁ υἱὸς τοῦ ἀνθρώπου as 'ein Anderer', and explains:

> Ein ברנשא, womit Jesus hier auf sich selbsten zielt.
> A/one 'Son of man', with which Jesus here refers to himself.

Bolten offers cross-references to Mt. 5.16 and 7.9, and at 5.16, τῶν ἀνθρώπων, he translates 'andern', and offers more explanatory comments. He translates the 'Syrische' ברנשא, which he writes in Syriac script, 'wörtlich' as Menschensohn, and notes that it has a double meaning. Firstly, it means 'Mensch', like the Hebrew בן אדם. For this he compares the Arabic, the Samaritan 'Menschensohn', which he says is just like the Syriac, and the Ethiopic *walda eguala emmaḥeiaw*, which he translates 'Evensohn' and 'den Sohn des Geschlechts der Mutter der Lebendige', and notes as a translation of ὁ υἱὸς τοῦ ἀνθρώπου at Mt. 9.6, 12.8,32. Secondly, the Syriac ברנשא, like גברא, is used as an indefinite pronoun, like the German 'man, jemand, Einer, ein anderer'. Noting the use of ברנשא in the Syriac version, Bolten comments:

---

11. J. A. Bolten, *Der Bericht des Matthäus von Jesu dem Messia* (Altona: Staben, 1792).

Wenn also Jesus oft von sich selbsten in der dritten Person mit ברנשא geredet hat: so ist dieß
eben so viel, als wenn ein Deutscher so von sich mit Man sprache.
When therefore Jesus often spoke of himself in the third person with 'son of man', this is
very much like a German speaking of himself using 'Man'.

This attempt to explain the idiomatic use of (א)נש(א) בר with the German 'Man' was
a natural ploy, and Bolten's several different translations of ברנשא as an indefinite
pronoun show how hard he was trying to explain Syriac usage for German-speaking
scholars. However, Bolten went on to give most of the Matthean sayings as
examples. This combination made it almost inevitable that he would be interpreted
as giving (א)נש(א) בר too general a meaning, and that many of his examples would
be found unconvincing.

Bolten proceeded to another point which has been problematical ever since.
He suggested that the Greek translator did not understand the idiomatic usage of
ברנשא, and that he often translated it with ἄνθρωπος, but often, especially when
Jesus spoke of himself, with ὁ υἱὸς τοῦ ἀνθρώπου. This inability to understand
the translator(s) has continued to be a major weakness of linguistic approaches to
this problem until recently, and assumptions about the translation process remain a
weakness in the work of many scholars.

With these basic points made, Bolten offered similar comments and translations
for other passages. For example, at Mt. 10.23b he offers a translation 'daß man
schon ben euch gekommen ist': at Mt. 12.8, 'Und dem Menschen ist auch der
Sabbath untergeordnet': at Mt. 16.13, 'Wofür wird man von den Leuten gehalten?'.
At 17.12, he renders ὁ υἱὸς τοῦ ἀνθρώπου with 'ein Anderer', again noting the
Syriac ברנשא, and comments that this does not sound so good in German 'als in den
Morgenländischen Sprachen, in welchen man einer solchen Enallage personarum
mehr gewohnt ist'. Such comments were often made by scholars, but without any
sufficient justification. Bolten's attempts to translate ברנשא showed how difficult
it is to do so. His view that Jesus was speaking in the third person about himself
was based on only two factors, the general meaning of the Syriac ברנשא, and the
fact that some sayings are about Jesus himself. Evidence of Aramaic texts in which
(א)נש(א) בר was used by a speaker to refer to himself had to await the work of
Vermes. Without it, it is not surprising that scholars familiar with the Gospels in
Greek should argue that, like Grotius, Bolten had failed to make proper sense of Son
of man sayings in the Gospels.

Criticism of this linguistically based tradition was accordingly widespread.
Vigorous criticism of Grotius and others is found for example in the work of Gaillard
in 1684.[12] In the opening part of his treatise, he disputes the notion that ὁ υἱὸς τοῦ
ἀνθρώπου could mean simply 'man', citing Grotius on Mt. 12.8, and giving three
reasons for his judgement.[13] His first argument is that the Jews knew that Jesus was

---

12.   J. Gaillardus, *Specimen Quaestionum in Novum Instrumentum de Filio Hominis*
(Lugduni-Batavorum; Lopez, 1684).
13.   Gaillardus, *de Filio Hominis*, pp. 4–5.

human, so he did not have to tell them so. This argument would have some force against a view that Jesus was deliberately declaring his human nature, but it is not very well focused on the linguistic observations of Grotius and others. Gaillard's second argument is based on the articles in the Greek expression ὁ υἱὸς τοῦ ἀνθρώπου. He describes this as 'non ... simpliciter, sed emphaticus', contrasting the LXX occurrences of υἱὸς ἀνθρώπου without the articles. This argument has a main point which has been central in the debate down to present times. It effectively casts aside the Semitic evidence on the ground that the conclusions based on it are not consistent with the actual expression ὁ υἱὸς τοῦ ἀνθρώπου, read in accordance with Christian tradition as a title of Jesus alone. This was a much more reasonable approach in the time of Gaillard than it is now, for the transition from a Semitic expression such as בן אדם to the Greek ὁ υἱὸς τοῦ ἀνθρώπου had not been accounted for. Gaillard's third argument is that the interpretation of ὁ υἱὸς τοῦ ἀνθρώπου as a term for 'man' would not fit the context of Jn 1.51. This is true, and it should remind us that use of the Johannine sayings was to be expected throughout the pre-critical era. It also exemplifies the dependence of relatively conservative views of this problem on Christian tradition. It is also a major feature of Gaillard's positive argument that ὁ υἱὸς τοῦ ἀνθρώπου indicates the promised Messiah. This is based on a large number of prooftexts, the messianic interpretation of which is drawn from specifically Christian tradition.

This was a central feature of the argument of Scholten in 1809.[14] Scholten headed straight for Jesus as Messiah, and then to ὁ υἱὸς τοῦ ἀνθρώπου meaning that he was the Messiah prophesied by Daniel, as already observed by many interpreters. After going through all the biblical examples of בן אדם, and apocryphal examples of υἱὸς ἀνθρώπου too (*1 Enoch* had still not been published), he tabulated all the examples of Son of man sayings in the Gospels. It will be noted that at this stage Scholten did not discuss the everyday meaning of the Aramaic בר (א)נש(א) as well. The downplaying of this Aramaic expression has remained a feature of interpreters who focus on Dan. 7.13 for their interpretation of ὁ υἱὸς τοῦ ἀνθρώπου. This was much more natural for interpreters in the days of Scholten than it is now, because so much less was known about the usage of the Aramaic בר (א)נש(א), and because the work of Grotius, Bolten and others had so many obvious faults.

Scholten then proceeds to expound his main point:

Appellatio ὁ υἱὸς τοῦ ἀνθρώπου, quoties a Iesu fuit adhibita, toties indicat certum *illum hominem*, qui, forma humana, Danieli in viso symbolico (c.VII.13) fuit propositus; atque adeo Regem illum, a Deo constitutum, qui humane hominibus esset imperaturus, eundem, qui *Messiae* nomine indicatus fuit. Et ipse quidem Jesus, hoc enunciatio, de *se* locutus est, non de alio.[15]

14.   W. Scholten, *Specimen Hermeneutico-Theologicum, de Appellatione* τοῦ υἱοῦ τοῦ ἀνθρώπου *qua Iesus se Messiam professus est* (Paddenburg & Schoonhoven: Trajecti ad Rhenum, 1809).

15.   Scholten, *De appellatione* τοῦ υἱοῦ τοῦ ἀνθρώπου, p. 67.

> The term ὁ υἱὸς τοῦ ἀνθρώπου, as often as it was used by Jesus, so often refers to *that particular man* who, in human form, was shown to Daniel in a symbolic vision (Dan. 7.13); and so that king, established by God so that he might rule decently over people, the same who was revealed by the name of Messiah. And Jesus himself, indeed, by means of this expression spoke of *himself*, not of anyone else.

The first part of this, taking every reference to ὁ υἱὸς τοῦ ἀνθρώπου to be a reference to Dan. 7.13, is the tradition which I have traced back to Tertullian, as Scholten does himself, and which flourished in this renovated form throughout this period. The deliberate reference to the Messiah, so conspicuously absent from Son of man sayings and anything much like them in the Gospels, is also asserted, as it had been by Gaillard, and was by many others. It is associated with the messianic interpretation of כבר אנש in Dan. 7.13. Scholten asserts that this was the Jewish interpretation, citing only the work of Carpzov.[16] Lack of thorough comparative exegesis remained a widespread feature of scholarship until I rectified it.[17]

Section XXIX, 'quibus Jesus, de ΤΟΥ ΥΙΟΥ ΤΟΥ ΑΝΘΡΩΠΟΥ excelsa conditione, locutus est', sets off with Jn 1.51, the significant use of Johannine tradition which I have already noted in Gaillard. The following section, the title of which includes 'de humili Messiae conditione', justifies total departure from Jewish tradition about the Messiah by means of Jesus' own teaching that the Messiah would eventually come to his destined power not without suffering and dying.[18] The combination of this kind of argument with the kind of reference to Dan. 7.13 and other texts which I have just noted means that whenever Jesus' life and teaching fits into Jewish tradition about the Messiah, this shows that he was fulfilling that expectation: but when he differs from it, that does not count against his being the Messiah. This remained a feature of conservative Christian arguments, and Scholten fitted his interpretation of ὁ υἱὸς τοῦ ἀνθρώπου into this flexible framework without difficulty. An especially notable insertion of the Messiah where he is absent from the context of a Son of man saying is at Mk 9.11-13//Mt. 17.10-13, where Scholten comments on the view of the scribes:

> Eliam enim venturum, docebant, ante quam *Messias* veniret.[19]
> For they were teaching that Elijah would come before *the Messiah* came.

This caused a major problem for exegetes, especially when scholarship became sufficiently learned for the absence of such a view from Jewish sources to be

---

16.   Scholten, *De appellatione τοῦ υἱοῦ τοῦ ἀνθρώπου*, p. 92, citing I. B. Carpzov, *Dissertatio de filio hominis ad Antiquum Dierum delato, ad Dan. VII 13,14*, Ch. II.

17.   P. M. Casey, *Son of Man. The Interpretation and Influence of Daniel 7* (London: SPCK, 1980), revised and abbreviated from P. M. Casey, 'The Interpretation of Daniel VII in Jewish and Patristic Literature and in the New Testament: an Approach to the Son of Man Problem' (Diss. Dunelm, 1977).

18.   Scholten, *De appellatione τοῦ υἱοῦ τοῦ ἀνθρώπου*, p. 114.

19.   Scholten, *De appellatione τοῦ υἱοῦ τοῦ ἀνθρώπου*, p. 125.

considered important. We shall see that the scribes really believed that Elijah would come before the day of the Lord.[20]

In addition to putting forward his own opinions, Scholten made numerous criticisms of others. Many of these are very effective, and two of them are worthy of note at this point. One is his critique of the view that ὁ υἱὸς τοῦ ἀνθρώπου really means 'son of Adam'. Scholten pointed out that if this was what Jesus meant in Aramaic, the Gospel translators would have rendered it ὁ υἱὸς τοῦ Ἀδαμ. This is one of the decisive objections to this view, and it is regrettable that subsequent adherents of this view did not take more notice of it.[21] Secondly, Scholten criticizes the work of J. A. Bolten.[22] One of his objections is that the Gospels were not written in Syriac. This is not as significant as it looks at first sight, because the use of בר (א)נ(א)ש in Jesus' Aramaic was not seriously different from Syriac usage which Bolten tried so hard to present.

The importance of a Christian dogmatic framework for the complete derivation of ὁ υἱὸς τοῦ ἀνθρώπου from Dan. 7.13 was expressed with particular clarity by Schulze in 1867.[23] He begins with Mt. 16.13, treating it as literally a word of Jesus. Like the use of Johannine sayings already noted, such treatment of a completely unusual Matthean saying is to be expected in the pre-critical period, when the priority of Mark had not been established and the nature of Matthean editing had not been uncovered. After surveying Greek expressions such as υἷες Ἀχαιῶν, Schulze concludes that ὁ υἱὸς τοῦ ἀνθρώπου is not natural Greek. To explain it, he goes for the Hebrew בן אדם and the Aramaic בר אנוש. Nonetheless, he proceeds to argue very strongly that ὁ υἱὸς τοῦ ἀνθρώπου refers to Jesus alone at Mk 2.27f.//Mt.12.8.[24] Here he makes three main points. His first is the context. Christian scholars could generally do this in a plausible way, because most Son of man sayings in the Gospels really do refer primarily to Jesus. His second point concerns the first article, which he understands as a reference to a particular person. Thirdly, despite what he had just written about the Semitic background of ὁ υἱὸς τοῦ ἀνθρώπου, Schulze discusses it here primarily to argue that, whatever some of his predecessors had written, we must not forget the significance of the term as found in the Lord's usage. In practice, this means that he could argue from the surface meaning of Gospel texts in Greek, and largely ignore the question of how Jesus could mean this in Aramaic.

At this point, Schulze takes his next major step. He lists scholars who have seen the origin of ὁ υἱὸς τοῦ ἀνθρώπου in Dan. 7.13, quite a long list already in 1867.[25] He then argues for this view himself. He does so within a very strong framework, the Christian view of Jesus as Messiah. Hence he regards 'Son of man' as the equivalent

20. Casey, *Aramaic Sources of Mark's Gospel*, pp. 122–3; pp. 125–31 below.

21. Scholten, *De appellatione τοῦ υἱοῦ τοῦ ἀνθρώπου*, p. 163.

22. Scholten, *De appellatione τοῦ υἱοῦ τοῦ ἀνθρώπου*, pp. 174–9.

23. L. Th. Schulze, *Vom Menschensohn und vom Logos. Ein Beitrag zur biblischen Christologie* (Gotha: Perthes, 1867), pp. 1–80.

24. Schulze, *Vom Menschensohn*, pp. 12–15.

25. Schulze, *Vom Menschensohn*, pp. 20–21.

of 'Messiah', and sees the Old Testament as messianic throughout. This greatly facilitates seeing the origin of 'Son of man' in Dan. 7.13, for it was already seen as a messianic prophecy, as I noted in considering the work of Scholten. Schulze then has no difficulty in showing that some Son of man sayings in the Gospels are dependent on Dan. 7.13, for some of them really are, and Schulze sets his criteria rather loosely so that he increases this number. For example, in addition to texts such as Mk 13.26//Mt. 24.30, where the use of Dan. 7.13 is indeed obvious, he lists Mt. 13.37,41, under the general notion that Jesus' return for judgement is the basis of these verses.[26]

Schulze then proceeds to another major step. In discussing Mt. 8.20, which shows no sign of Dan. 7.13, he argues that it does have it in mind really because it is a *contrast* with this fundamental text.[27] With a criterion like that, the number of sayings dependent on Dan. 7.13 can be increased, completely contrary to the evidence. Together with all Schulze's main points, this criterion has been used by many scholars taking this view in the subsequent debate. The rest of Schulze's exposition is all along the same lines. His whole presentation presupposes that Jesus meant what the Greek text of the Gospels seems to say, when seen against a background of Christian dogma. This has remained a major feature of the debate ever since, despite the advent of more critical scholarship.

A major variation of this view was developed during the nineteenth century, following the rediscovery of *1 Enoch*. This was the development of the Son of Man Concept. This view was originally based on the occurrences of the term 'Son of man' in the *Similitudes of Enoch*, which survive only in the Ethiopic translation of *1 Enoch*. According to this view, Jews at the time of Jesus expected the coming of a glorious figure, 'the Son of man'. Jesus identified himself with this figure. The first three manuscripts of *1 Enoch* were brought to Europe in 1773, and the first translation, by R. Laurence, was published in 1821, followed by an edition of the Ethiopic version. A German translation soon followed and an improved text and German translation were provided by Dillmann.[28] I have already noted the lack of understanding of בר (א)נש(א) in attempts to understand the Gospel term ὁ υἱὸς τοῦ ἀνθρώπου, and the domination of scholarship by Christian tradition. The same trouble beset the *Similitudes*. In consequence, many scholars argued that the *Similitudes* were a Christian work, or that they had suffered from Christian interpolations. For example, in 1857 Hilgenfeld began his description of the main content of the *Similitudes* as the delineation 'des Auserwählten oder des

26.   Schulze, *Vom Menschensohn*, p. 33.

27.   Schulze, *Vom Menschensohn*, pp. 43–4.

28.   R. Laurence, *The Book of Enoch the Prophet ... now first translated from an Ethiopic manuscript in the Bodleian Library* (Oxford: Parker, 1821); idem, *Libri Enoch versio ethiopica* (Oxford: Parker, 1838); A. G. Hoffmann, *Das Buch Henoch in vollständiger Übersetzung mit fortlaufenden Kommentar ...* (2 vols; Jena: Croeker, 1833–8); A. Dillmann, *Liber Enoch aethiopice ad quinque codicum fidem editus* (Leipzig: Vogel, 1851); idem, *Das Buch Henoch übersetzt und erklärt* (Leipzig: Vogel, 1853).

29.   A. Hilgenfeld, *Die jüdische Apokalyptik in ihrer geschichtlichen Entwicklung* (Jena: Mauche, 1857), p. 152.

Menschensohns'.[29] The (already traditional) capitalization and comma are found in the translation of *1 En.* 46.3: 'Dies ist der Menschensohn, der die Gerechtigkeit hat …'[30] This makes 'der Menschensohn' look like a title, just as if it were a translation of ὁ υἱὸς τοῦ ἀνθρώπου. Hilgenfeld added a number of other points. He did not believe that a Jewish community could be described as Holy and Elect, nor that a Jewish figure could be described as the light of the nations (48.4) or 'der Sohn des Weibes' (corrupt available text of 62.5). All these made wonderful sense to him as a Christian work, with the Holy and Elect being the Christian community, and Jesus as the 'Son of man', the light of the nations and the son of Mary. The treatment of 'Son of man' as a title was central to this incorrect view.

Other scholars argued that this is a Jewish work, but they were still influenced by Christian conceptions of what the term 'Son of man' was. It did not at this stage occur to anyone that it might represent the ordinary Aramaic term בר (א)נשׁ(א). Hence it was capitalized and treated as a title. For example, in the first English translation of 1821, Laurence declares that *1 Enoch* repeatedly refers to the nature and character 'of the Messiah, thereby giving credible proof of Jewish opinions before the birth of Christ'. The terms for this exalted being include 'the Son of man'.[31] At 46.3, the translation capitalizes 'Son of man', and puts the definite article before it and a comma after it, so the identification of the figure is like this: 'This is the Son of man, to whom righteousness belongs;…'. Similarly, in the classic German translation and edition of 1853, Dillmann treated it as a Jewish work, listing the 'vorausgesetzt Begriffe des Himmelreiches, des Menschensohnes' among the things previously known from the New Testament and now known from books like this.[32] At 46.3, the translation identifies the figure as Laurence had done in English, with definite article, capital letter and comma: 'dieses ist der Menschensohn, der die Gerechtigkeit hat …'. It was this treatment of 'Son of man' as a title that led to the Son of Man Concept. Once this was seen in *1 Enoch*, it could be read into Dan. 7.13 too. It was also read into another well-known work, *4 Ezra* 13. These were the only significant sources of the Son of Man Concept until the late twentieth century, and they remain the most important.

In New Testament scholarship, this kind of development can be seen for example in Beyschlag's *New Testament Christology*, published in 1866.[33] Beyschlag begins like previous adherents of the tradition by heading straight for Dan. 7.13 as the origin of ὁ υἱὸς τοῦ ἀνθρώπου. To this end, he quotes the most obvious Gospel texts such as Mt. 24.30 and 26.64. The new variant is introduced by quite wild remarks about Jewish speculation, followed by more precise reference to *1 Enoch*. Here he regards the Son of man as a *Messiasbezeichnung*, and stresses that the term is 'der Menschensohn'.[34] Beyschlag goes on to criticize a variety of people

---

30.   Hilgenfeld, *jüdische Apokalyptik*, p. 155.
31.   Laurence, *The Book of Enoch the Prophet*, p. xl.
32.   Dillmann, *Das Buch Henoch*, p. lv.
33.   W. Beyschlag, *Die Christologie des Neuen Testaments. Ein biblisch-theologischer Versuch* (Berlin: Rauh, 1866), pp. 9–34, 'Die Idee des Menschensohnes'.
34.   Beyschlag, *Christologie*, pp. 14–16.

with a lower view of the title ὁ υἱὸς τοῦ ἀνθρώπου, referring to the heavenly ideal Man and Messiah of Dan. 7.13 with his *himmlische Herrlichkeit*. So even at Mt. 8.20//Lk. 9.58, the main point is said to be the great contrast between the *himmlische Herrlichkeit* of the *Menschensohn* and the context of the saying. This is further held to be what is important about the Son of man dying: it is the death of the Messiah that matters.[35] Thus Beyschlag's work indicates how the new work on the *Similitudes of Enoch* could be incorporated into a relatively conservative view of Dan. 7.13 as the origin of Jesus' use of the term 'Son of man'.

Towards the end of the nineteenth century, an important revival of the linguistic approach to this problem took place, with the application to it of much more information about the use of the Aramaic term (א)שׁנ(א) בר. In 1894, Eerdmanns again argued that the Aramaic (א)שׁנ(א) בר meant simply 'man', and was not a messianic designation in the teaching of Jesus, nor in Dan. 7.13, nor in the *Similitudes of Enoch*. His work was not as influential as it might have been because it was written in Dutch, and it did not carry work as far forward as three German scholars in the immediately succeeding period.[36]

In the same year, Wellhausen contributed an unduly famous footnote, in which he pointed out correctly that Jesus spoke Aramaic so he used *barnascha* rather than ὁ υἱὸς τοῦ ἀνθρώπου, and that the Aramaic *barnascha* means simply 'der Mensch'. This repeats what linguists had said before, and Wellhausen added that Christians, believing that Jesus was the Messiah,

> ... übersetzten es nicht mit ὁ ἄνθρωπος, wie sie gesollt hätten, sondern durchaus falsch mit ὁ υἱὸς τοῦ ἀνθρώπου ...[37]
>
> ... did not translate it with ὁ ἄνθρωπος, as they should have done, but quite wrongly with ὁ υἱὸς τοῦ ἀνθρώπου ...

This is a vigorous presentation of the continued inability of scholars to understand the translation process.

In 1896, two fundamental works were published. One was the first major monograph which attempted to see behind the Greek Gospels to the Aramaic sayings of Jesus: Meyer, *Jesu Muttersprache*.[38] Meyer assembled the main evidence for believing that Jesus spoke Aramaic, and supplied a sensible discussion of what

---

35.   Beyschlag, *Christologie*, pp. 17–22.

36.   B. D. Eerdmans, 'De oorsprong van de uitdrukking "Zoon des menschen" als Evangelische Messias-titel', *TT* 28 (1894), pp. 153–76: see further W. C. van Manen, 'Nachschrift', *TT* 28 (1894), pp. 177–87; B. D. Eerdmans, 'De uitdrukking "Zoon des menschen" in het boek "Henoch"', *TT* 29 (1895), pp. 48–71; W. C. van Manen, 'De "Zoon des menschen" bij Henoch', *TT* 29 (1895), pp. 263–7. I regret that I do not have access to this debate, as I do not read Dutch: I owe the latter references to Prof. M. Müller.

37.   J. Wellhausen, *Israelitische und Jüdische Geschichte* (Berlin: Reimer, 1894), p. 312 n.1.

38.   A. Meyer, *Jesu Muttersprache. Das galiläische Aramäisch in seiner Bedeutung für die Erklärung der Reden Jesu und der Evangelien überhaupt* (Freiburg i.B./Leipzig: Mohr (Siebeck), 1896). For a general assessment of Meyer's work, see Casey, *Aramaic Sources of Mark's Gospel*, pp. 12–15.

Aramaic sources should be used. He tried to go for Galilean Aramaic, since this was Jesus' dialect. For this purpose he used both the Jewish Aramaic of the Palestinian Talmud and Christian Palestinian Syriac. He stated openly that these sources were too late in date, but since earlier ones were not available, he used them all the same. The great advance which he made was to offer reconstructions of whole Aramaic sentences, which he located in their original cultural context. He was especially aware of the linguistic dimension of the Son of man problem. He proposed to put it on a new footing 'durch den Rückgang aufs Aramäische'.[39] Accordingly, he suggested this for Mk 2.27-28:[40]

שבתא בגין ברנשא איתעבידת ולא ברנשא בגין שבתא: בגלל כן מריה הוא דשבתא ברנשא.

The great advantage of this is that it enables the final example of ברנשא to appear as it must appear in Aramaic, as a normal term for man. Only a whole sentence can do this, and whole sentences cannot fail to do it. For this reason, the procedure as a whole was an essential step forward. This is a particularly good example, because the Son of man statement of Mk 2.28 is closely tied to the unambiguously general statement of 2.27. At the same time, the proposed reconstruction has problems. One is positing ברנשא behind both examples of ὁ ἄνθρωπος in 2.27. This made it difficult to understand the translator, and Meyer made no serious attempt to do so.

Meyer's reconstruction of Mt. 12.32[41] further illustrates these points:

כל דיימר מלא על ברנש ישתביק לה וכל דיימר על רוחא דקודשא לא ישתביק לה.

Here too, it is a great advantage that the complete sentence ensures that ברנש emerges as a normal term for man. It is also good that there are no problems with the late date of the Aramaic used. Moreover, this is a Q saying, and the proposed reconstruction permits the understanding of Lk. 12.10 as an alternative understanding of the same Aramaic. This might have led to important advances in our understanding of Q. Also helpful was Meyer's reference to Mk 3.28, πάντα ἀφεθήσεται τοῖς υἱοῖς τῶν ἀνθρώπων, where he saw a clear echo of ברנשא in the original saying. Nonetheless, he had insufficient appreciation of the need to understand the translator. The use of ברנש in the indefinite state, which is entirely reasonable on Aramaic grounds, requires an explanation of the consistent use of the articles in ὁ υἱὸς τοῦ ἀνθρώπου.

Meyer also offered an Aramaic reconstruction of Mk 2.10. He knew from his study of Aramaic, more extensive than that of any of his predecessors, that בר (א)נש(א) had to refer to 'man' in general, and he knew from his study of the Gospels that each Son of man saying had to refer to Jesus in particular. He had not however found Aramaic evidence that both things were possible at once. This led him to a conjecture which was to run fruitlessly for some time. He noted the use of the Aramaic ההוא גברא by a speaker in the third person to refer to himself, and announced that one would

---

39. Meyer, *Muttersprache*, p. 91.
40. Meyer, *Muttersprache*, p. 93.
41. Meyer, *Muttersprache*, p. 94.

also expect ההוא ברנשא. He could not however produce any evidence of this, and this was emphasized rather than mitigated by his bringing forward a little evidence which was not the same at all, such as the Christian Palestinian Syriac lectionary having גבר where other Syriac versions have ברנש.[42] He proceeded to offer Aramaic reconstructions of Mt. 8.20//Lk. 9.58 and of Mt. 11.18-19a//Lk. 7.33-34a, rendering ברנש as 'ein Mensch (wie ich)' and 'jemand' respectively.[43] The reconstructions themselves are quite plausible, which however underlines the fact that Meyer did not solve the problems which he raised so clearly.

Meyer also believed that in some passages ὁ υἱὸς τοῦ ἀνθρώπου is a messianic title, and he correctly noted that Dan. 7.13 had been used. It follows that his wonderful advances in our understanding of the Aramaic substratum of the synoptic Gospels did not lead him to solve the Son of man problem. There were two areas of it which were to need another century of study. One was an improved understanding of the idiomatic use of (א)בר נש(א) in sayings which have both a general level of meaning and a genuine reference to the speaker himself. This would necessarily entail the collection of much more Aramaic evidence. The other was the complete transition process, from the use of (א)בר נש(א) by Jesus in authentic sayings, through the translation process, to the creation of new sayings by the early church and the evangelists, sayings which never existed in Aramaic and which had no general level of meaning.

3. From Lietzmann to Vermes

Later in 1896, Lietzmann surveyed the use of (א)בר נש(א) in the Targums of Onkelos and Jonathan, the Palestinian Syriac Gospels, and several tractates of the Palestinian Talmud.[44] This survey of Aramaic source material was much more extensive than the work of his predecessors. It convinced him that בר נש was a straightforward term for a person, 'die farbloseste und unbestimmteste Bezeichnung des menschlichen Individuums'.[45] It is this part of Lietzmann's work that is of lasting importance, for it should have made it impossible to avoid the mundane nature of the expression (א)בר נש(א). He carried it through by arguing vigorously that (א)בר נש(א) was not a title in Dan. 7.13, *4 Ezra* 13 or the *Similitudes of Enoch*, though his ignorance of Ge'ez made the latter part of the argument a *tour de force* which would have to be completely redone. He concluded:

> Jesus hat sich selbst nie den Titel 'Menschensohn' beigelegt, weil derselbe im Aramäischen nicht existiert und aus sprachlichen Gründen nich existieren kann.[46]

42.   Meyer, *Muttersprache*, pp. 95–6.
43.   Meyer, *Muttersprache*, pp. 96–7.
44.   H. Lietzmann, *Der Menschensohn. Ein Beitrag zur neutestamentlichen Theologie* (Freiburg i.B./Leipzig: Mohr (Siebeck), 1896).
45.   Lietzmann, *Menschensohn*, p. 38.
46.   Lietzmann, *Menschensohn*, p. 85.

Jesus never conferred the title 'Son of man' on himself, for it does not exist in Aramaic and on linguistic grounds it cannot exist.

With this in mind, however, Lietzmann's consideration of the use of ὁ υἱὸς τοῦ ἀνθρώπου convinced him that it was a technical term of Hellenistic theology.[47] This was hardly a satisfactory conclusion for a term absent from Acts (except 7.56) and from the epistles. Where he did believe that בר נשא was original in a Son of man saying, Lietzmann did not offer reconstructions. On Mk 2.28 and Mt. 8.20// Lk. 9.58, for example, he simply translated with 'der Mensch' and treated both verses as general statements, with some reference back to the work of Meyer. In the latter case, he also conjectured that ὁ υἱὸς τοῦ ἀνθρώπου might have replaced אנא, a quite wild conjecture of no explanatory value.[48] His simple comments on the inappropriateness of ὁ υἱὸς τοῦ ἀνθρώπου rather than ὁ ἄνθρωπος as a translation also show that he belonged to a period of scholarship when translators could not be fully understood. It follows that, although part of Lietzmann's work was important, it could not lead to a complete solution to the problem.

There was very little positive development of this approach in the immediately succeeding years. In two contributions, Wellhausen again stated the main points asserted by this approach, but made no significant progress towards solving its outstanding problems.[49] In a good piece of independent critical scholarship, Dupont's 1924 monograph repeated many important points, but could not make further significant progress.[50] For example, he regards 'l'homme' as the original sense of בר (א)נש(א) at Mk 2.10, 2.28 and 3.28-29, and 'un homme' at Mt. 8.20// Lk. 9.58 and Mt. 11.19//Lk. 7.34. He could not however carry the discussion of the Aramaic level of the tradition any further forward, and his comments on the transition process to a 'titre messianique' show the same lack of understanding as his predecessors: 'sinon d'une erreur de traduction au moins d'une interprétation imparfaite'.[51] Other occasional contributions almost made significant progress. For example, in 1948, Black drew attention to an idiomatic use of בר (א)נש(א) which was later to be regarded as of fundamental importance.[52] This is at Gen.R. VII,2, where Jacob of Kefar Niburayya, ordered by R. Haggai to come and be beaten for ruling that fish should be ritually slaughtered, responded as follows:

בר נש דאמר מילה דאוריתא לקי אתמהא

A (son of) man who interprets the word of Torah is beaten! I am amazed.

47. Lietzmann, *Menschensohn*, p. 95.
48. Lietzmann, *Menschensohn*, pp. 89–90.
49. J. Wellhausen, *Skizzen und Vorarbeiten* VI (Berlin: Reimer, 1899), pp. 187–215, 'Des Menschen Sohn': *Einleitung in die drei ersten Evangelien* (Berlin: Reimer, 2nd edn, 1911), pp. 95–8, 123–30.
50. G. Dupont, *Le Fils de l'Homme: Essai Historique et Critique* (Paris: Fischbacher, 1924).
51. Dupont, *Le Fils de l'Homme*, pp. 41–60, 159.
52. M. Black, 'The Son of Man in the Teaching of Jesus', *ExpTim* 60 (1948–9), pp. 32–6 (34–5).

We should now be able to see that here the speaker uses a general statement to speak about himself. Black however was not able to see this, finding for example both that בר נש here refers unambiguously to the speaker, and that the Aramaic level of relevant sayings of Jesus is ambiguous. Significant progress on Aramaic sources had to wait until the seminal paper of Vermes in 1967, and progress on the question of ambiguity would hardly be possible until I offered a brief critical discussion of modern ambiguity research in 1985.[53]

A lot of other research was published from different perspectives. The basic view that the Gospel term ὁ υἱὸς τοῦ ἀνθρώπου was derived from Dan. 7.13 continued to flourish, albeit with several variations. In 1910, Abbott declared that the popular view in England was that 'the son of man' was a recognized messianic title derived from this passage.[54] In serious critical scholarship, this was often combined with the Son of Man Concept. For example, in his highly regarded 1959 monograph, Tödt entitled his Chapter I 'Die transzendente Hoheit der Menschensohngestalt in der spätjüdischen Apocalyptic'.[55] The discussion is carried through at the hand of German translations of Dan. 7.13f., *4 Ezra* 13 and the *Similitudes of Enoch*, the three major sources of the Son of Man Concept. There is no discussion of the Aramaic בר (א)נש(א), nor of the original text of any of these documents. The discussion of Dan. 7.13f. already introduces *die Gestalt eines transzendenten Vollenders*. Tödt bluntly casts aside the interpretative section of this chapter, interpreting the man-like figure in the light of the tradition of the Son of Man Concept. Having done so, he comments on the interpretative section:

> Schießlich beraubt die Deutung 7, 15ff. den 'der einem Menschen glich' seines Charakters als individueller Gestalt und setzt 'das Volk der Heiligen des Höchsten' an seine Stelle.
> The interpretation in vv. 15ff. robs him 'who is like a man' completely of his individuality and puts 'the people of the saints of the Most High' in his place.[56]

This arbitrarily removes the Jewish people from the original text of Daniel 7, and alters the interpretation of כבר אנש to the Son of Man Concept.

Tödt proceeds secondly to *4 Ezra* 13. He interprets the figure whom he calls 'the Man' from within the same tradition, even though he concedes that 'the Man' is not a title. He again interprets the vision as if it were a description of a real figure, and ignores the interpretative section of the chapter as secondary. Tödt then turns finally to the *Similitudes*, which he thinks provide the most detailed account of 'that Man' in late Jewish apocalyptic literature. He retails important facets of the Son of man figure, including for example his pre-existence and his function as the eschatological

---

53.   See pp. 33–5, 40–1 below.

54.   E.A. Abbott, *'The Son of Man' or Contributions to the Study of the Thought of Jesus* (Diatessarica VIII. Cambridge: CUP, 1910), p. xv.

55.   H. E. Tödt, *Der Menschensohn in der synoptischen Überlieferung* (Gütersloh: Gerd Mohn, 1959); *The Son of Man in the Synoptic Tradition* (trans. D. M. Barton; London: SCM, 1965).

56.   Tödt, *Menschensohn*, pp. 19, 21; *Son of Man*, pp. 22, 24.

judge. He does not however consider his identification as Enoch, nor does he discuss how the use of the Aramaic (א)בר נ(א)ש would affect his description of this figure. He does discuss briefly the considerable differences between the figures in his three chosen documents, but this does not cause him to consider seriously the possibility that this figure might be a modern construct.

This approach led to a major problem, for the Son of Man figure does not suffer and die, whereas in the Gospels ὁ υἱὸς τοῦ ἀνθρώπου is central to the major predictions of Jesus' suffering and death. This problem was usually met by resorting to another traditionally popular Christian text, Isaiah 53, interpreted in accordance with Christian tradition. This indicates how abstracted the Son of Man Concept had become, for death is a central characteristic of בר נ(א)ש(א).

Tödt made very little use of another major development, the attempt to see the Son of Man Concept against the background of a more general Near Eastern 'Man' concept. For example, in a 1951 book which became influential in its 1956 English translation, Mowinckel distinguished carefully between Jewish expectations of a national Messiah and the Son of man.[57] He offered a lengthy discussion of the Son of Man Concept. He began with Daniel 7. Although he accepted the interpretative section as what the author of the final form of the text intended, he argued on the basis of what he could not explain that 'about 200 B.C. or earlier there was in Judaism a conception of a heavenly being in human form ('one like a man'), who, at the turn of the age, the dawn of the eschatological era, would appear, and would receive from God delegated power and authority over all kingdoms and peoples'.[58] He argued from the plural 'thrones', which again he could not explain, that this figure 'was thought of as sharing God's throne, a divine being in human form'. Mowinckel then used the teaching of Jesus about the Son of man at Mk 13.26, 14.62 and parallels to argue that 'the conception of the Son of Man' was the traditional material which was reinterpreted by the seer of Daniel 7.[59] This is a particularly clear example of Christian tradition being used to form and expound 'the conception of the Son of Man', contrary to the text which is supposed to form the basis for the exposition.

Mowinckel proceeded to the *Similitudes of Enoch* and *4 Ezra* 13, the two other major sources of the Son of Man Concept. He added in several others, announcing for example the messianic interpretation of Ps. 8.5, without any discussion of texts which so interpret it, let alone their date.[60] He then provided a lengthy discussion of various features of the Son of Man, a composite character drawn from the various texts which Mowinckel considered to be relevant. Having formed this complex character from many different texts, Mowinckel found that his 'heavenly, pre-existent being, "the Man", of divine angelic character ... did not originally have any connexion with the Old Testament Messiah ...'[61] It is this which took him to 'the

57. S. Mowinckel, *Han som kommer* (Copenhagen: Gad, 1951): *He That Cometh* (trans. G. W. Anderson; Oxford: Blackwell, 1956).
58. Mowinckel, *He That Cometh*, p. 352.
59. Mowinckel, *He That Cometh*, pp. 352–3.
60. Mowinckel, *He That Cometh*, p. 357.
61. Mowinckel, *He That Cometh*, p. 420.

Primordial Man', conceptions of which he supposed to have been 'widespread in the ancient east'.[62] These are the two vital steps characteristic of this line of research. The first is to construct the Son of Man Concept from a variety of Jewish sources, some interpreted, and some drastically misinterpreted, from the perspective of this specific academic tradition. The second is to find that this cannot be explained on the basis of other aspects of Jewish culture, and to turn to another modern construct, 'the Primordial Man' or the like, for a proposed explanation. Mowinckel accordingly referred to extensive previous scholarship to back up his concept of this figure.[63] This scholarship drew on extremely variegated sources, and Mowinckel did the same.

For example, he begins with a cosmological conception from Norse mythology, 'the story of the giant Ymir, killed by the Aesir, who made the earth from his body, the sea, the lakes, and the rivers from his blood, the vault of heaven from his skull, the clouds from his brains, and so on.'[64] He switches straight to Iranian eschatology, where 'the eschatological saviour Saoshyant is regarded as an incarnation, both of Zarathushtra, the founder of the religion, and of Gayomart, the Primordial Man.'[65] Next comes an element of Indian religious speculation: 'At the beginning of each new age, it is the Primordial Man or god-Man (Purusha), who is incarnated in a new figure.' Mowinckel then shifts to the concept of the first man in time, noting Adam, as well as the Babylonian Oannes, who had previously been fundamental to Jansen's construction of a Man figure.[66] With much material of various kinds, Mowinckel puts together 'the most important features in the figure of Anthropos'. Before listing 14 such features, he actually notes that they 'recur with varying frequency in its different forms'. For example, his second feature is the name of this creature: 'He is called Man, the One like a man, Anthropos, the Primordial Man, Adam, Adamus, Adamanus, Anosh, Enosh, Mortal Immortality etc.'[67] One wonders what a complete list might have looked like!

---

62.   Mowinckel, *He That Cometh*, p. 422.
63.   Mowinckel, *He That Cometh*, p. 422, nn. 1–2, citing *inter alia* R. Reitzenstein, *Poimandres* (Leipzig: Teubner, 1904), pp. 81ff.; W. Bousset, *Hauptprobleme der Gnosis* (FRLANT 10. Göttingen: Vandenhoeck & Ruprecht, 1907), pp. 160ff.: A. Christensen, *Les types du premier homme et du premier roi dans l'histoire légendaire des Iraniens* (*Archives d'Etudes Orientales* 14. Stockholm: Norstedt, 1917); R. Reitzenstein, *Das mandäische Buch des Herrn der Grösse und die Evangelienüberlieferung* (Heidelberg: Winter, 1919); R. Reitzenstein, *Das iranische Erlösungsmysterium* (Bonn: Marcus & Weber, 1921); J. M. Creed, 'The Heavenly Man', *JTS* 26 (1925), pp. 113–36; C. H. Kraeling, *Anthropos and Son of Man* (*Columbia University Oriental Studies* 25. New York: Columbia U.P., 1927); W. Staerk, *Die Erlösererwartung in den östlichen Religionen. Untersuchungen zu den Ausdrucksformen der biblischen Christologie (Soter 2)* (Berlin/Stuttgart: Kohlhammer, 1938); H. L. Jansen, *Die Henochgestalt. Eine vergleichende religionsgeschichtliche Untersuchung* (Oslo: Dybwad, 1939).
64.   Mowinckel, *He That Cometh*, p. 423, citing V. Grønbech, *Nordiske myter og sagn*, pp. 23ff.
65.   Mowinckel, *He That Cometh*, p. 423, citing G. Widengren, *Religionens värld. Religionsfenomenlogiska studier och översikter* (Stockholm, 1945, ²1953), pp. 364f., 389f.
66.   Mowinckel, *He That Cometh*, pp. 423–4, citing Jansen, *Henochgestalt*, pp. 36f., 105ff.
67.   Mowinckel, *He That Cometh,* p. 427.

The main problem with this figure is that it never occurs anywhere. It is a modern construct, put together with no regard for space, time or culture. It is extraordinary that Mowinckel's comments on its different forms, and its massive variety of names and other qualities, did not alert him to this. Mowinckel then moves to 16 'most important features in the figure of the Son of Man', the similar faults of which I have already analysed. By this stage, it is doubly obvious that there is no real reason why this almighty construct should be called 'Son of Man', except when Mowinckel uses the *Similitudes of Enoch* to expound it. Nor is the result really all that like ὁ υἱὸς τοῦ ἀνθρώπου in the teaching attributed to Jesus. So the very short section on the 'Son of Man as Used by Jesus', after surveying briefly features of Jesus' ministry in which for example he does not come in glory, but is 'the preacher and mediator of God's forgiving grace, the friend of sinners and tax-collectors', assures us that '"The atmosphere about Him is different" from that in the usual ideas about the Son of Man.'[68] Mowinckel proposes two alternative understandings of the difference:

> Jesus may have meant that He was the heavenly Son of Man, who had come down in a mysterious manner, and now walked the earth. Or He may have meant that he was an elect man, who would be exalted to be what the initiated said that the Son of Man was in heaven.

It is striking that neither view is found in the teaching of Jesus.

Mowinckel proceeds to the problem which was by this stage traditional for the Son of Man Concept, commenting that 'there is another great and incomprehensible innovation in Jesus' view of Himself as the Son of Man.' To understand this 'incomprehensible innovation', Mowinckel turned to the Suffering Servant of Isaiah 53. 'Jesus was the first to take this prophecy seriously in its real meaning, and apply it to Himself.'[69] Contempt for Jewish use of scripture is thus combined with this proposed solution. What is so striking is that after the use of *two* modern constructs, the Son of Man Concept and the Primordial Man, Mowinckel totally failed to offer a proper explanation of the use of 'Son of man' in the teaching of Jesus. His whole approach indicates his membership of an academic Christian social subgroup, whose members devoted a massive amount of effort and learning to the further development of the work of their predecessors. Their efforts, learning and positions as distinguished professors served to conceal the decisive methodological weaknesses at the centre of their work.

In 1967, Borsch made another attempt at the problem from a similar perspective, but with much more extensive discussion of the New Testament material.[70] The first part of the book is similar in methodology to the work of Mowinckel, drawing on many diverse sources to put together an artificial construct. Borsch made more effort than Mowinckel to explain the specific term 'son of man'. For example, he

---

68. Mowinckel, *He That Cometh*, p. 447, quoting E. Sjöberg, 'Människosonen i judendom och urkristendom', in *28:e Svenska Läroverksläraröte i Stockholm*, p. 265.

69. Mowinckel, *He That Cometh*, pp. 448–9.

70. F. H. Borsch, *The Son of Man in Myth and History* (London: SCM, 1967).

used Psalm 8, treating this as a picture of the First Man ruling in paradise. He noted particularly the parallelism of 'Man' and 'Son of Man' suggesting that there is 'very real point in the second designation, for the reigning king was the representative of his ancestor the Man, the first king, in whose office he now serves, but he is also the *son* of that Man, his descendant and legitimate heir.'[71] This is however dependent on the artificial construct of 'his ancestor the Man, the first king', as well as on dubious interpretation of Psalm 8, and it cannot be reconciled with the mundane meaning of בר (א)נשׁ(א). For reasons of this kind, Borsch's first five chapters cannot be regarded as a significant improvement on the work of Mowinckel.

Borsch's relatively extensive comments on the New Testament material are also unsatisfactory as regards method. For example, he interprets John 3.13 in accordance with traditionally problematical exegesis, ending with the question as to what the Son of Man's previous ascent could have been. 'We would suggest that, according to the pattern of the rites and myths in which the Man ascends to heaven and is there shown divine secrets, the reference here is to the liturgical and/or mythical ascent of the one who was ordained to the function of the Son of Man.'[72] Here again the artificial nature of the Man construct makes this explanation untenable, even apart from the question of what the real interpretation of Jn 3.13 should be. Again, the Son of Man as lord of the sabbath (Mk 2.28//Mt. 12.8//Lk. 6.5) is associated with Adam, the coming of the new age, the ceremonial activity of the ruler and the coming of the Messiah. So Borsch comments on the Sabbath, 'In this sense, both in terms of its first purpose and its final purpose, it could be seen as the day of the Man.' As for Jesus' argument from the behaviour of David permitting his followers to eat the shewbread, 'it is possible to guess that there may once have been a profound relationship in the context of the Man speculations. David, as the anointed king, could well have been seen as a descendant of the Man and a type of the Son of Man on the basis of Ps. 80.17 or general tradition in this regard ... Thus it may once have been that, as Jesus acting as the Son of Man was lord over the sabbath, so he also was the Son of Man providing bread for his followers.'[73] Thus Borsch's strongly associative argument leaves the text behind altogether. This combination of artificial construct with associative reasoning could never lead to a successful solution to any problem.

So far, we have considered relatively conservative uses of the Son of Man Concept and the Primordial Man, in the sense that we have seen them used to inform our understanding of the teaching of Jesus about himself. Another major development was to suppose that, in using the Son of Man idea, Jesus predicted the coming of someone other than himself. This was generally associated with a radical view of sayings containing the term ὁ υἱὸς τοῦ ἀνθρώπου, for most of these were attributed to the early church. They resulted from the church's secondary identification of the Son of man with Jesus. The church then created sayings containing the term which corresponded with what they sought to believe about Jesus' historic ministry.

71.   Borsch, *Son of Man in Myth and History*, p. 114.
72.   Borsch, *Son of Man in Myth and History*, p. 273.
73.   Borsch, *Son of Man in Myth and History*, pp. 322–3.

One of the most influential figures was Bultmann, which is quite extraordinary in view of the brief and dogmatic nature of his published comments on this problem. Bultmann divided the Son of man sayings into three groups, (1) as coming, (2) as suffering death and rising again, and (3), as now at work.[74] This threefold classification was not new. For example, in 1900, Rose proposed the following: '(1) ceux qui se rapportent à la vie humaine et à l'apostolat du Sauveur, (2) les textes qui énoncent les souffrances et la passion du Sauveur, (3) ce titre est associé à la parousie et au triomphe final.'[75] Rose's work has however long since been forgotten, because his comments from a conservative Catholic perspective contained nothing new and memorable: for him this was simply a useful classification, which indicated 'les trois stages de la destinée et de la carrière du Fils de l'homme'. Bultmann's use of this threefold classification, on the other hand, was quite devastating.

Bultmann regarded his third group, the 'son of man as now at work', not as using a messianic title, 'Son of man', but as resulting from a misunderstanding of the Aramaic meaning 'man', or 'I'. This permitted the authenticity of a small group of sayings, but left standard difficulties over their meaning, and over the plausibility of the proposed misunderstanding. Bultmann further announced that the whole of his second group were *vaticinia ex eventu*. One reason was that they were separate from his first group, another that they are absent from Q, another that they were implicated in the interpretation of his death in the light of the early church's interpretation of scripture, since 'the idea of a suffering, dying, rising Messiah or Son of Man was unknown to Judaism'.[76] This is one of the points where Bultmann was dependent on the Son of Man Concept. It also presupposes that Q was not merely an entity from which things could be absent, but also so extensive that Matthew and Luke were bound to visibly reproduce from it things which they had already inherited from Mark. It does not really permit a proper explanation as to why these predictions contain the term ὁ υἱὸς τοῦ ἀνθρώπου. This is doubly so because Bultmann argued that they are 'probably later products of the Hellenistic Church',[77] even though the Hellenistic church as found in Acts and the Epistles shows no sign of them. The fact that the predictions of Jesus' resurrection are separate from the parousia predictions remains important. Bultmann thought his first group were old, and contained authentic predictions of the coming of the Son of man. This figure was not however identified with Jesus in these sayings, but only later by the church. Here again Bultmann was dependent on the Son of Man Concept, which is required for the belief that there was such a figure for Jesus to expect. Perhaps as a result of

74.   R. Bultmann, *Theology of the New Testament* (2 vols; trans. K. Grobel; London: SCM, 1952), vol. 1 p. 30; for convenience, I cite this systematic, if brief, discussion, rather than the remarks scattered throughout the several editions of *Die Geschichte der synoptischen Tradition* (FRLANT 29, N.F.12. Göttingen: Vandenhoeck & Ruprecht, 1921): *The History of the Synoptic Tradition* (trans. J. Marsh; Oxford: Blackwell, 1963).

75.   V. Rose, 'Études Évangéliques. III. Fils de l'homme et Fils de Dieu', *RB* 9 (1900), pp. 169–99 (172).

76.   R. Bultmann, *Theology*, p. 31.

77.   R. Bultmann, *Theology*, p. 30.

this, Bultmann made no attempt to explore how this expectation could be expressed in Aramaic.

This is the approach to the Son of man problem adopted by Tödt in his influential 1959 monograph.[78] I have already criticized his discussion of the Son of Man Concept. The remaining chapters of his book are organized around the threefold classification associated with Bultmann, beginning with Chapter II on the sayings about the coming Son of Man. Tödt does make a number of good points. Notably, following Bultmann, he makes it clear that Son of man sayings about the parousia cannot be fitted into indubitably authentic teaching of Jesus about the coming of the kingdom.[79] He also makes quite a lot of perfectly reasonable comments on the editorial work of Matthew and Luke.[80] The whole book is however fatally flawed by the Son of Man Concept, and by the associated absence of proper study of the Aramaic level of the tradition. For example, in dealing with sayings such as Lk. 12.8, Tödt argues on the same lines as Bultmann, 'Keineswegs wird die Identität Jesu mit dem Menschensohn behauptet'.[81] Thus such sayings are passed as authentic, but a figure other than Jesus is supposed to be referred to.

What is worse, this initial step of interpreting such sayings as sayings of Jesus about a figure other than himself led Tödt to suppose that all sayings which *do* identify Jesus with the Son of Man are secondary products of the early church. This had the devastating effect of attributing a massive proportion of Son of man sayings to the early church. These include all the predictions of Jesus' suffering, dying and rising again, together with predictions of his death such as Mk 10.45 and 14.21.[82] Unlike Bultmann, Tödt attributes this massive creativity to the Palestinian Christian community rather than the Hellenistic community, using comments by Jeremias which even include a little Aramaic.[83] This change is however of no real help, because the proportion of secondary sayings posited by Tödt is so great that he could not show why the church should have used ὁ υἱὸς τοῦ ἀνθρώπου in them, since the initial phase was simply Jesus talking about a figure other than himself. Sayings attributed to this community also include Mt. 8.20//Lk. 9.58 and Mt. 11.19//Lk. 7.34, 'their authenticity disproved by their dissimilarity from the authentic parousia sayings of the Son of Man'.[84] Despite many incisive comments, therefore, Tödt's basic approach to this problem ensured that he could not reach a correct solution of it.

At this stage of German scholarship, there seems to have been no limit to how radical an approach to the synoptic tradition might be favoured. The worst was

---

78.   Tödt, *Menschensohn*; *Son of Man*.
79.   E.g. Tödt, *Menschensohn*, p. 32; *Son of Man*, p. 35.
80.   Tödt, *Menschensohn*, pp. 62–104; *Son of Man*, pp. 67–112.
81.   Tödt, *Menschensohn*, p. 39; *Son of Man*, p. 42.
82.   Tödt, *Menschensohn*, Ch. IV; *Son of Man*, Ch. IV.
83.   E.g. Tödt, *Menschensohn*, p. 164, referring to Jeremias in *TWNT* V, p. 711 n. 32; *Son of Man*, p. 177, referring to J. Jeremias, *The Servant of God* (SBT 20. London: SCM, 1957), p. 102.
84.   Tödt, *Menschensohn*, p. 116; *Son of Man*, p. 125.

Vielhauer.[85] He picked up on the observation that while the kingdom of God and the Son of man both appear central concerns in the teaching of Jesus, they do not appear together in sayings that may reasonably be considered authentic.[86] Finding that the kingdom of God was indeed a central concept of the teaching of the historical Jesus, and accepting Bultmann's view that the group of sayings about the coming Son of man were the oldest layer of Son of man sayings, Vielhauer argued that *all* Son of man sayings originated in the early church. The problem is a real one, sufficient for me to label it in due course 'Vielhauer's dilemma'.[87] The use which Vielhauer made of this point, however, borders on the irrational. What stands against it are some of the most basic, important and thoroughly discussed points of Son of man research. For example, it does not enable us to see why the expression ὁ υἱὸς τοῦ ἀνθρώπου was used secondarily in a large number of sayings which were attributed to Jesus himself, when the term is virtually absent from the rest of the New Testament. Moreover, Vielhauer's dilemma appears serious because the Son of man element in the problem is the Son of Man Concept: 'der Menschensohn ist ein präexistententes Himmelswesen und gehört der Apokalyptik an …'[88] We shall see that the problem looks quite different when we consider why Jesus cannot be shown to have used the term (א)שׁנ(א) בר when teaching about the kingdom of God.[89]

It was natural that such destructive scholarship should produce criticism. Most of this will not be considered here, because it was of a conservative rather than incisive nature. In the 1960s, two scholars were especially prominent in serious criticism of the Son of Man Concept, the British and subsequently North American scholar Perrin, and the Scandinavian Leivestad.[90] Perrin discussed the three major sources of the 'apocalyptic Son of Man concept', Dan. 7.13, the *Similitudes of Enoch* and *4 Ezra* 13. He argued that the term 'son of man' is not a title in any of these three works. In particular, he noted that both the *Similitudes of Enoch* and *4 Ezra* 13 set off with careful reference back to Dan. 7.13, and each of them is using this text rather than using a title. He also noted that they are very different from each other.

85.　P. Vielhauer, 'Gottesreich und Menschensohn in der Verkündigung Jesu', in W. Schneemelcher (ed.), *Festschrift für Günther Dehn zum 75. Geburtstag* (Neukirchen: Kreis Moers, 1957), pp. 51–79. Reprinted in P. Vielhauer, *Aufsätze zum Neuen Testament* (TBü 31. Munich: Kaiser, 1965); 'Jesus und der Menschensohn: Zur Diskussion mit Heinz Eduard Tödt und Eduard Schweizer', *ZTK* 60, 1963, 133–77. Reprinted in Vielhauer, *Aufsätze*, pp. 92–140.

86.　Earlier, H. B. Sharman, *Son of Man and Kingdom of God* (New York: Harper, 1943), p. 89, which was not however available to Vielhauer ('Gottesreich und Menschensohn', p. 51 n. 5), who was much more influenced by German discussion in the Bultmann tradition.

87.　Casey, *Son of Man*, pp. 208–9.

88.　Vielhauer, 'Gottesreich und Menschensohn', p. 52.

89.　See pp. 234–5, 237–8 below.

90.　N. Perrin, 'The Son of Man in Ancient Judaism and Primitive Christianity: A Suggestion', *BibRes* 11 (1966), pp. 17–28: reprinted in N. Perrin, *A Modern Pilgrimage in New Testament Christology* (Philadelphia: Fortress, 1974), Ch. III; *idem*, *Rediscovering the Teaching of Jesus* (London: SCM, 1967), pp. 164–73; R. Leivestad, 'Der apokalyptische Menschensohn ein theologisches Phantom', *ASTI* 6 (1967–8), pp. 49–105; *idem*, 'Exit the Apocalyptic Son of Man', *NTS* 18 (1971–2), pp. 243–67.

Perrin's argument was not detailed enough to be altogether satisfactory, for he did not deal with either the Ge'ez text of the *Similitudes* or with the versions of *4 Ezra* 13. He nonetheless deserves credit for making one of the main points with great clarity.

Unlike Perrin, Leivestad was quite distressed by the destructive work of Vielhauer. His first main point was also that the term 'Son of man' is not a title in the main works used to develop the Son of Man Concept. Like Perrin, however, he did not discuss the Ge'ez text of the *Similitudes of Enoch*, and consequently his discussion of this work creaks and groans at significant points. He did also hit Vielhauer very hard with some of the most important standard points of Son of man research, such as that the term is used in the Gospels only by Jesus himself and is absent from Acts (except 7.56) and from the epistles. So when Vermes' seminal paper was published in 1967, the Son of Man Concept had been a little bit punctured, but it would need a lot more serious work to bring it to an end.

A different approach was offered by a small minority of scholars who argued that 'Son of man' was a corporate term. The most famous was T. W. Manson, though he was neither the first nor the last.[91] This approach was an offshoot of the traditional view that Jesus derived the term 'Son of man' from Dan. 7.13. One of the problems with the traditional view is that in that text, כבר אנש is not really an individual figure, but an abstract symbol of the Saints of the Most High, who are in effect the people of Israel.[92] This was the basis of the view that בר (א)נש(א) in the teaching of Jesus could have been a corporate term. After discussion of the Danielic text, Manson sought to impose this understanding on the use of this term in the *Similitudes of Enoch*. This was completely unconvincing.[93] Manson argued that the Son of man in the *Similitudes* is an idea: this idea existed in the mind of God before the creation of the world. It contains a double oscillation: the group idea finds expression in the concept of the elect and righteous ones, whereas the individual idea finds expression in two personalities – at the beginning of the course of events in Enoch, who is regarded as the first human individual to embody the Son of man idea, the nucleus of the elect and righteous ones; at the end it finds expression again in the figure of the Messiah who is to carry out the final vindication of the saints.

What is so remarkable is the remoteness of this abstract intellectualizing from the text and thought-world of the *Similitudes*. Already at *1 En*. 46.1-4, the first appearance of the figure usually described as 'that son of man', Manson considers him to be 'evidently' symbolic. This is a quite arbitrary interpretation of a vigorously presented individual who is finally identified as Enoch (*1 En*. 71.14). Manson tries to

---

91.   T. W. Manson, *The Teaching of Jesus* (Cambridge: CUP, 1931, 2nd edn, 1935), pp. 211–34, 259–84; 'The Son of Man in Daniel, Enoch and the Gospels', *BJRL* 32 (1949–50), pp. 171–93; reprinted in T. W. Manson (ed. M. Black), *Studies in the Gospels and Epistles* (Manchester: Manchester U.P., 1962), pp. 123–45; earlier, e.g. A. T. Cadoux, 'The Son of Man', *The Interpreter* 18 (1920), pp. 202–14.

92.   Casey, *Son of Man*, esp. Ch. 2; and further pp. 82–91 below.

93.   See especially Manson, 'Daniel, Enoch and the Gospels', 176–90, = *Studies*, pp. 128–42; and in response P. M. Casey, 'The Use of the Term "son of man" in the Similitudes of Enoch', *JSJ* 7 (1976), pp. 11–29 (11–13).

restrict the Son of man's righteousness and his position as a revealer of secrets: '…
what the Son of Man possesses and reveals is the hidden treasure of God's wisdom
and righteousness embodied in the Law'.[94] In fact the revelation is much broader
than this, including a multiplicity of cosmological, eschatological and other secrets,
in accordance with the tradition of Enoch as revealer. Hence the Law is not so much
as mentioned, for it does not cover the range of revelations which are central to this
work. Moreover the *Similitudes* provide no positive evidence of the Son of man as an
idea that is being actualized. This hypothesis is supposed to provide an explanation
for Enoch's identification with the Son of man: it provides no explanation of the
absence of similar remarks about other people who are supposed to actualize this
idea. The inclusion of 'divine vindication' as an element of the total conception
indicated by the term Son of Man enables Manson to overlook the fact that it is said
of 'that son of man' that he vindicates the righteous and elect by his condemnation
of kings and the mighty, whereas the righteous and elect are vindicated by this
process. Moreover 'that son of man' is the one who reveals, whereas the righteous
and elect are those who receive revelation. *1 En.* 48.4 also distinguishes between
'that son of man' and the righteous. The fact that the son of man figure and the
elect and righteous have in common certain basic qualities, those of election and
righteousness, should not be allowed to obscure these fundamental differences.
Finally, the use of the term 'corporate personality' gives the false impression that
a common feature of Israelite thought is being used, whereas it was as much an
artificial modern construct as the Son of Man Concept.[95]

Manson applied this understanding of the term to some but not all of the Gospel
texts. For example, he did not include Mk 2.10, 28, suggesting briefly on the basis
of previous scholarly discussion that in them the term 'Son of Man' 'represents a
misunderstanding of an original Aramaic *bar nāshā*', which should be rendered
'man'.[96] Where he did apply his corporate understanding of 'Son of man' to Gospel
texts, the result was quite disastrous. For example, in discussing Mt. 8.20//Lk. 9.58,
Manson declared that 'as an apocalyptic symbol the birds of the air stand for the
Gentile nations', and that in *1 En.* 89 '"foxes" is a symbol for Ammonites'. He
combined this with his corporate understanding of the term 'Son of man' to produce
his interpretation of the saying: 'everybody is at home in Israel's land except the
true Israel.'[97] This is completely remote from the Q text of which it is supposed to
be an interpretation.

All this also results from ignoring the normal use of the term (א)בר (א)נש. As
Manson himself put it so clearly, 'Jesus took the term Son of Man, and with it its
primary meaning, from Dan. vii … We have no good reason to suppose that he was

94.   Manson, 'Daniel, Enoch and the Gospels', p. 180, = *Studies*, p. 132.

95.   See especially J. W. Rogerson, 'The Hebrew Conception of Corporate Personality: a Re-
examination', *JTS NS* 21 (1970), pp. 1–16.

96.   Manson, *Teaching*, p. 214.

97.   T. W. Manson, *The Sayings of Jesus* (1937, as Part II of *The Mission and Message of
Jesus*, ed. H. D. A. Major *et al.* Reprinted separately, London: SCM, 1949), pp. 72–3.

aware of any other Son of Man than the Danielic.'[98] But we do! It was already well
known from the work of Meyer, Lietzmann, Wellhausen and others that בר (א)נש(א)
was an ordinary term for 'man'. It follows that Jesus could see several specimens of
בר (א)נש(א) by just walking down a Capernaum street, a lot more when he taught a
crowd, and thousands when on a visit to Jerusalem. It is a testimony to the inability
of Lietzmann and others to actually *solve* the Son of man problem that Manson
could make so little use of a piece of information which he knew perfectly well.

As well as these several different approaches to this problem, the traditional view
that the Son of man in the teaching of Jesus meant that he was in some special sense
the son of Adam continued to be put forward. The most extensive presentation was
that of Abbott.[99] Abbott believed that critics did not agree as to what the term for
Son of man was in the Aramaic of Christ's words.[100] He did not however discuss the
work of Lietzmann, Meyer and others who might be thought to have made a decisive
case for בר (א)נש(א). He regarded the Targum to Ezekiel, which always renders the
Hebrew בן אדם with בר אדם, as of decisive significance. This was not a satisfactory
move. It shows only that one translator overinterpreted the biblical בן אדם, which
was a term for 'man', 'human being'. It was not however so used in the translator's
environment, leaving the possibility for any exegete to interpret it literally as 'son of
Adam'. That the Targum to Ezekiel does this cannot possibly inform us about Jesus'
discourse in Aramaic. A decisive objection to this view is that it makes the behaviour
of the Gospel translators incomprehensible. If they found בר אדם in their sources,
they should have rendered it with ὁ υἱὸς τοῦ Ἀδαμ, a completely straightforward
equivalent. We have however seen that the translators were not properly understood
anyway, so it is perhaps not surprising that this objection seemed less important to
Abbott than it should do to us. Abbott saw significance in the fact that, while the
Targumist always used בר אדם, the LXX always used Υἱὲ ἀνθρώπου. He thought
this enabled him to equate the two to the point that this provided a precedent for
the Gospel translators to translate בר אדם with ὁ υἱὸς τοῦ ἀνθρώπου.[101] This is
not a legitimate move. The Targum and the LXX were two completely different
translators, and they interpreted בן אדם in Ezekiel differently from each other.
Nothing can equate the two quite different renderings.

Abbott's positive arguments were not strong enough. A lengthy series of
parallels between Ezekiel and Jesus are too general to give a reason for Jesus to use
בר אדם.[102] Against the conventional view that Jesus used בר (א)נש(א), Abbott held
the different Syriac renderings of ὁ υἱὸς τοῦ ἀνθρώπου in the Syriac gospels.[103]

98.   Manson, 'Son of Man', *BJRL* 32, 191, = *Studies*, p. 143; likewise, *The Servant-Messiah*
(Cambridge: CUP, 1953), p. 72.
99.   Abbott, *'The Son of Man'*; more briefly in previous years, *Notes on New Testament
Criticism* (Diatessarica VII. London: A & C Black, 1907), pp. 140–52, 'The Son of Man': *The
Message of the Son of Man* (London: Black, 1909).
100.   Abbott, *'The Son of Man'*, p. xi.
101.   Abbott, *'The Son of Man'*, pp. xxii–xxiii.
102.   Abbott, *'The Son of Man'*, pp. 82–107.

This is methodologically unsound, because it equates the difficulty of translating בר (א)נׁש(א) *into* Aramaic with what Aramaic might reasonably be *reconstructed* from ὁ υἱὸς τοῦ ἀνθρώπου as possible words of Jesus. Comparing בר (א)נׁש(א) with בר אדם, he argues that the latter 'covers more ground' and explains a variety of things such as Paul's mention of Christ as '"the last Adam" or second Man'.[104] This again shows the overweening influence of Christian tradition, according to which the actual *term* ὁ υἱὸς τοῦ ἀνθρώπου is of central importance. For people reading the Gospels in Greek, in the light of Christian tradition, this is a natural inference. We shall see however that in Jesus' own words it was the *content* of Son of man sayings which was of fundamental importance. The striving for an important *term* led Abbott astray, just as it did scholars who hardly ventured beneath the surface of the Gospels in Greek. At this level, presentation of the mundane nature of בר (א)נׁש(א) as an ordinary term for man was not helpful to scholars like Abbott, because it reinforced their natural feeling that this could not be the correct explanation of the important title ὁ υἱὸς τοῦ ἀνθρώπου.

These many different attempts on the Son of man problem underline how difficult it was to solve. Despite the earlier work of Lietzmann, Meyer and Wellhausen, the dominant tradition of German scholarship in the 1960s made little use of the Aramaic בר (א)נׁש(א), and believed in a *Menschensohnbegriff* artificially constructed from German translations of very few sources, two of which (*4 Ezra* and the *Similitudes of Enoch*) survived only in corrupt translations themselves. A fresh attempt on the Aramaic בר (א)נׁש(א) was overdue. It was natural that it should come from a Jewish scholar and be based on careful study of source material in the original Jewish Aramaic. I turn next to the seminal paper of Vermes.[105]

Vermes began with some brief comments on the history of scholarship. He then surveyed the use of בר נׁש(א) in Jewish sources as an ordinary term for 'man', and in references to a single individual, to 'everyone' and the like. This survey was broader than any which was previously available. It formed the background for the most important and influential section of his paper. Here Vermes brought forward Jewish Aramaic evidence of lasting importance, and interpreted it to mean that בר נׁש(א) was used as a circumlocution for 'I'. This aspect of his interpretation did not convince most scholars. Nonetheless, the primary source material used by Vermes required interpretation which has proved to be of vital significance. Moreover, some other aspects of his classification and interpretation have stood the test of time. In particular, it has been widely accepted that at least the majority of his examples are examples of the idiomatic use of בר (א)נׁש(א), and most of the argument has been about how to interpret the idiom found in most of these sayings. There has also been widespread acceptance of his interpretation of the circumstances

103.   Abbott, *'The Son of Man'*, pp. 108–9.
104.   Abbott, *'The Son of Man'*, p. 109.
105.   G. Vermes, 'The Use of בר נׁש/בר נׁשא in Jewish Aramaic', App. E in M. Black, *An Aramaic Approach to the Gospels and Acts* (Oxford: OUP, 3rd edn, 1967), pp. 310–28; reprinted in G. Vermes, *Post-Biblical Jewish Studies* (Leiden: Brill, 1975), pp. 147–65.

in which this idiom was used: 'In most instances the sentence contains an allusion to humiliation, danger, or death, but there are also examples where reference to the self in the third person is dictated by humility or modesty.'[106] This would also prove important in interpreting some sayings of Jesus.

The first passage discussed by Vermes was Gen.R. VII,2, to which Black had already drawn attention, and his comments enable the main issues to be seen especially clearly. Vermes presented the passage as follows:[107]

> Jacob of Kefar Nibburayya gave a ruling in Tyre that fish should be ritually slaughtered. Hearing this, R. Haggai sent him this order: Come and be scourged! He replied, Should בר נש be scourged who proclaims the word of Scripture?

Vermes' comments on this passage illustrate beautifully the strengths and weaknesses of his approach:

> Theoretically, of course, *bar nāsh* may be rendered here as 'one', but the context hardly suggests that at this particular juncture Jacob intends to voice a general principle. Hurt by his opponent's harsh words, he clearly seems to be referring to himself and the indirect idiom is no doubt due to the implied humiliation.

Here Vermes has correctly perceived that בר נש is a genuine reference to the speaker himself. In the state of scholarship as it was, that was an important advance. Vermes was also right in arguing that the idiom is an indirect one, used because of the implied humiliation of the speaker, and this has also proved important in understanding some Son of man sayings of Jesus.

What did not convince everyone was Vermes' attempt to remove the general level of meaning of this saying. As he showed so ably himself, בר (א)נש(א) is a general term for 'man', and this makes perfect sense here because Jacob was really appealing to a general principle that an interpreter of scripture should not be scourged, in order to avoid being scourged himself. What went wrong here was the question which Vermes asked. This was the traditional question as to whether the saying is intended to 'voice a general principle' *or* refer to the speaker himself. Vermes remained within the framework of this traditional question, and I was the only one of his supporters and critics not to do the same. Vermes was not helped by the fact that pragmatics, the study of language as a means of communication between people rather than a closed logical system, had still barely got off the ground. It was eventually to prove helpful in the understanding of this idiom. Vermes' adherence to the traditional question had a side effect which no one could possibly see at the time: it entailed that he did not admit as examples of this idiom sayings in which the general level of meaning was too obvious for him. This severely restricted the number of examples which he could find. Vermes' final comments on this saying contain another error of method within the framework of the same question. He

---

106. Vermes, 'Use of בר נש/בר נשא in Jewish Aramaic', p. 327.
107. Vermes, 'Use of בר נש/בר נשא in Jewish Aramaic', p. 321. For Black's comments, see pp. 21–2 above; and for my presentation of this passage, p. 75 below, passage 38.

claimed that his interpretation was 'further confirmed in the parallel text preserved in *Num.R.* xix.3', which he presented as follows:

Should בר נש be scourged who proclaims the word of Scripture? R. Haggai said, Yes, because *you* did not give the right ruling (לא הורית טב).

This presupposes that texts with variants may be interpreted as the same, when the main point may be that they are different. It also exemplifies again the restriction of Vermes' interpretative comment within the traditional question. This parallel does indeed show that בר נש in Jacob's saying is a proper reference to himself, but we should not follow Vermes in supposing that this undermines the general level of meaning.

Thus Vermes should be congratulated on writing a seminal paper. Much more research would however be necessary before his work could be fully utilized to put forward a complete solution to the Son of man problem.

4. After Vermes

The next event in scholarship was a magisterial and influential survey of the whole problem by Colpe.[108] Colpe's presentation of relevant Aramaic evidence included Sefire III,16, the oldest extant example of בר (א)נ(א)ש(א).[109] Referring to the evidence collected by Vermes and his predecessors, Colpe suggested that 'a speaker could include himself in ברנש as well as בר נשא, whose generic sense was always apparent, or he could refer to himself in either and yet generalise at the same time.'[110] This presentation of both levels of meaning at the same time pointed scholars in the right direction for future work. Colpe took the view that ὁ υἱὸς τοῦ ἀνθρώπου was a translation of the definite state בר (א)נ(א)שא, asserting that the definite state in Aramaic was already meaningless.[111] He thought this translation was 'not wrong', but 'when בר אנשא, which originally meant only a man in the everyday sense, is rendered ὁ υἱὸς τοῦ ἀνθρώπου in Greek, then this is misunderstood or rather deliberately interpreted along Messianic lines.'[112] A lot of progress was therefore still necessary on the state of בר (א)נ(א)ש(א) in this idiom and the translation process. Moreover, after defining the Aramaic evidence in this way, Colpe found only five examples in the teaching of Jesus (e.g. Mk 2.28: Matt. 8.20//Lk. 9.58). This was not enough to represent all the authentic sayings of Jesus.

Despite this presentation of the Aramaic evidence, Colpe proceeded to a lengthy argument that the Idea of the Son of Man (*Menschensohnvorstellung*) could not

---

108. C. Colpe, ὁ υἱὸς τοῦ ἀνθρώπου, *TWNT* VIII (1969), pp. 403–81 = *TDNT* VIII (1972), pp. 400–477.

109. *TDNT* VIII, p. 402, from *TWNT* VIII, p. 405. See further pp. 67–8 below, passage 20.

110. *TDNT* VIII, pp. 403–4, from *TWNT* VIII, p. 406.

111. *TDNT* VIII, p. 404, from *TWNT* VIII, pp. 406–7.

112. *TDNT* VIII, p. 405, from *TWNT* VIII, pp. 407–8.

have an Israelite genealogy. This has many of the problems which dogged the Son of Man Concept, including an inability to understand creative work using the ordinary term (א)שׁנ(א) בר within Israelite tradition. Nonetheless, Colpe offered a lot of useful criticism of proposed non-Israelite origins of this Idea, concluding without any apparent enthusiasm that the Canaanite hypothesis was the best available. Moreover, he did argue that 'Son of man' was not a title in Jewish sources, not even in the *Similitudes of Enoch*. Finally, he suggested that the synoptic Gospels displayed material of generally Jewish origin with such big differences from extant Jewish source material that they provided a fourth source for 'a Jewish Son of Man Tradition'.[113] This is methodologically a quite dubious move, which further underlined Colpe's inability to understand creative work, this time using ὁ υἱὸς τοῦ ἀνθρώπου within Jewish-Christian tradition.

Colpe then proceeded to a relatively detailed consideration of the Son of man material in the New Testament. He suggested that the synoptic Son of man sayings should be viewed as the result of a development which took place in three stages.

The first stage was the preaching of Jesus. Here Colpe included only three sayings which he understood in terms of his earlier discussion of the Aramaic expression (א)שׁנ(א) בר: Mk 2.10, Mt. 8.20//Lk. 9.58, and Mt. 11.19//Lk. 7.34. He offered no Aramaic reconstructions of these sayings, and his general comments in German (and likewise in English) showed that much more work was necessary. In considering the preaching of Jesus, Colpe added eight sayings about the coming Son of Man which 'yield a self-contained apocalyptic picture and seem to stand up to critical analysis'.[114] In discussing this group, Colpe made no attempt to consider the use of the Aramaic term (א)שׁנ(א) בר. This shows the continued strength of the *Menschensohnvorstellung*, which was still regarded as such an important entity that the use of (א)שׁנ(א) בר did not need to be brought to bear upon it. As to whether Jesus meant himself or not in this group of sayings, Colpe sat on the fence, unable to make up his mind.

Colpe's second stage of development was the oral tradition of the primitive community. Here Colpe argued that sayings about the coming Son of man were applied to the returning Jesus without actual change, and that this affected the interpretation of the other three authentic sayings. Then further Son of man sayings were formed by the community, and ὁ υἱὸς τοῦ ἀνθρώπου was added to existing sayings. Sayings attributed to this second stage included for example Mk 14.21, where Colpe supposed the term ὁ υἱὸς τοῦ ἀνθρώπου to be a secondary addition to a dominical saying, which originally began 'For I must go' in Aramaic. This extraordinary assertion was not however accompanied by proper discussion of any possible Aramaic original.[115] This was also one of several cases in which the criteria for considering sayings or expressions to be primary or secondary were not remotely adequate. Much further work would accordingly need to be done at points

113.   *TDNT* VIII, p. 429, from *TWNT* VIII, p. 432.

114.   *TDNT* VIII, p. 433, from *TWNT* VIII, p. 435.

115.   *TDNT* VIII, p. 446, from *TWNT* VIII, p. 449.

like this. Colpe's third stage was the literary tradition of the primitive community. Here he discussed the editorial work of Mark, Luke and Matthew. This was naturally dependent on the previous discussion of sayings which Colpe believed to have been spoken by the historical Jesus or produced within the oral tradition of the primitive community. All the incorrect decisions taken in the discussion of the first two stages accordingly entailed that the work on the third stage would need a complete overhaul.

Colpe's work was therefore a mixed blessing. On the one hand, he did draw careful attention to the Aramaic material, and this ought to have prevented future scholars from leaving it out. On the other hand, he made very little use of this material in his efforts to understand the teaching of the historical Jesus. Moreover, he still has an influential Son of Man Concept, and a variety of aspects of the Son of man problem remained unexplained. All this ensured that his extensive influence would not push scholarship in the direction of a solution to this problem.

Since then, the work of Vermes has led to further developments of a linguistic solution to some aspects of this problem, all of which has proved very controversial. I have been prominent in this aspect of the work, which reaches its culmination in this book. I now plot out the main points of development, and note the most important criticisms.

In a brief article in 1976, I proposed that the examples of the idiomatic use of בר (א)נ(א)שׁ(א) brought forward by Vermes have two levels of meaning. In discussing Tg. Gen. 4.14b as an example, I described the idiom as follows: 'in Aramaic, a speaker could use a general statement, in which the expression for 'man' was בר אנשׁ, in order to say something about himself'.[116] While I have been constrained by some regrettable criticism to describe this in different ways, the main point remains valid and is expounded in Chapter 2 of this book. I also argued that the translation with ὁ υἱὸς τοῦ ἀνθρώπου was natural and, noting other possibilities, virtually inevitable. Subsequent work has enabled me to further improve our understanding of the translation process. I also began to make use of Aramaic reconstructions of sayings of Jesus, and in so doing I noted that the impression that Son of man sayings might refer to someone other than Jesus 'is simply a function of the fact that Son of man sayings are translationese'.[117] This simple point is sufficient to demolish one of the main points of all the work in the Bultmann tradition. I proposed about a dozen examples of this idiom in authentic sayings of Jesus, all but one of which are found in Mark or Q. I also argued that this hypothesis would enable us to solve the classic problems of Son of man research, a contention which this book seeks to establish. In another article in 1976, I tackled the Ge'ez text of the *Similitudes of Enoch*.[118] I argued that its use of the term 'son of man' should be understood in the light of normal use of the Aramaic term בר (א)נ(א)שׁ(א), and that the Son of man figure was from the first intended to be understood as Enoch. I

---

116. P. M. Casey, 'The Son of Man Problem', *ZNW* 67 (1976), pp. 147–54 (147).
117. Casey, 'The Son of Man Problem', p. 150.
118. Casey, '"son of man" in the *Similitudes of Enoch*'.

concluded that the *Similitudes* should therefore be discounted as evidence of a special 'Son of man' concept in Judaism, which left very little evidence of any such thing.

I developed my hypothesis much further in a 1980 book.[119] This was the first attempt to offer a complete discussion of the comparative exegesis of Daniel 7, and hence to explore fully its significance for the Son of man problem in the New Testament. The discussion of Daniel 7 itself in Ch. 2, and of its use or absence in the Apocrypha and Pseudepigrapha in Ch. 5, demonstrated that there was no 'Son of Man Concept' in ancient Judaism. The discussion of the Gospels in Ch. 8 showed that the use of Dan. 7.13 was indeed important for understanding a small number of Son of man sayings attributed to Jesus. These were however too few to be the origin of the term. I argued that all of them were the work of the early church or of the evangelists. This was entirely consistent with seeing the origin of the term in the use of (א)נש(א) בר by the historical Jesus, in accordance with the idiom to which Vermes had drawn attention.

With all this in mind, I was able to draw up a table which showed how the development of Son of man sayings fitted into the development of Gospel traditions.[120] Genuine sayings of Jesus using the Aramaic term (א)נש(א) בר were almost all from our oldest sources, Mark and Q, and thus confined to the synoptic Gospels. Several further sayings resulted from developments of Jesus' genuine prediction of his death and resurrection: this fitted well into the needs of the evangelists as they composed their Gospels. There was also a group of sayings which used Daniel 7.13, in which ὁ υἱὸς τοῦ ἀνθρώπου clearly referred to Jesus alone at his second coming. These sayings too had an excellent *Sitz im Leben* in Mark and Matthew, where most of them were to be found, for they implied that Jesus would come very soon, a belief of fundamental importance to the earliest church including Mark and Matthew, but a problem by the time of Luke and John. There was then a penumbra of secondary sayings, and the sayings in the Fourth Gospel appeared to form a separate group which fitted into Johannine theology as a whole.

In 1983, Lindars offered a discussion of Son of man sayings in the Gospels on the basis of another modification of the evidence of the use of (א)נש(א) בר.[121] He proposed that the key to the Aramaic evidence was 'the idiomatic use of the generic article, in which the speaker refers to a class of persons, with whom he identifies himself ... It is this idiom, properly requiring *bar (e)nasha* rather than *bar (e)nash*, which provides the best guidance to the use of the Son of Man in the sayings of Jesus.'[122] There are two serious problems with this, as I pointed out in 1987.[123] One of these should have been obvious empirically at the time, though it was not fully understood until later. This is that examples of this idiom

---

119. Casey, *Son of Man*.

120. Casey, *Son of Man*, p. 236.

121. B. Lindars, *Jesus Son of Man. A fresh examination of the Son of Man sayings in the Gospels* (London: SPCK, 1983).

122. Lindars, *Jesus Son of Man*, p. 24.

123. P. M. Casey, 'General, Generic and Indefinite: The Use of the Term "Son of Man" in Aramaic Sources and in the Teaching of Jesus', *JSNT* 29 (1987), pp. 21–56 (27–34).

in fact vary as to whether they use the definite or indefinite state of בר (א)נשא. This is sufficiently striking to be inconsistent with Lindars' claim that this idiom properly requires the definite state (א)נש(א) בר. The second problem is that Lindars' reference to the 'generic article' is not a satisfactory description of the Aramaic definite state. Underlying this is the fact that neither articles nor generics were fully understood at the time, with the result that descriptions of the definite state in Aramaic were often misleading. This was especially regrettable in that Lindars was quite right to see that Son of man sayings might be true of a restricted social sub-group rather than of everyone. He appears to have thought that this was not consistent with my understanding of this idiom: I argue in Chapter 2 of this book that it is a major feature of it.

Responding to Lindars in 1985, Bauckham suggested that 'Jesus used *bar enash* (probably, rather than *bar enasha*) in the indefinite sense ('a man', 'someone'), which is itself a very common usage, but used it as a form of deliberately oblique or ambiguous self-reference.'[124] This has one of the same problems as Lindars' proposal, in that it implies that Jesus used only one state of (א)נש(א) בר, whereas extant examples vary. There is no difficulty in finding examples of this idiom in which בר נש is used in an indefinite sense: in 1987 I drew attention to what I now present as passages 24 and 29 in Chapter 2. But none of the examples provide an 'ambiguous self-reference'. All are intended to be true of more people than the speaker. Moreover, Son of man sayings in the Gospels are not generally presented as ambiguous. On the contrary, one of the major features of this problem is that the apparently unique and newly produced term ὁ υἱὸς τοῦ ἀνθρώπου causes no difficulty in understanding: everyone knows that it refers to Jesus, and apparently to him alone.[125] Bauckham's proposal should therefore not be accepted.

In 1984, M. Müller contributed a thorough survey of the whole problem.[126] In addition to discussing the relevant primary source material, Müller provided a massive amount of information about the history of scholarship, carefully classified into eleven excursuses.

The first two substantive chapters offer a very careful discussion of Daniel 7, especially v. 13, and of the *Similitudes of Enoch* and *4 Ezra* 13 – the three major sources of the Son of Man Concept. In Dan. 7.13, Müller interpreted כבר אנש as 'ein reines Symbol', a symbol for the 'Heiligen des Höchsten', and so 'ein Symbol des triumphierenden Israel in dessen Triumph'.[127] He noted the creative use of this text in both the other documents. While he did not himself discuss the text of the *Similitudes of Enoch* in Ge'ez, nor the versions of *4 Ezra* 13 in their original languages, he made careful reference to secondary literature which did. This led him to conclude that the use of Son of man at *1 En.* 46 is dependent on Dan. 7.13

124. R. J. Bauckham, 'The Son of Man: "A Man in my Position" or "Someone"?', *JSNT* 23 (1985), pp. 23–33 (28).

125. Casey, 'General, Generic and Indefinite', pp. 34–6.

126. Müller, *Der Ausdruck 'Menschensohn'*.

127. Müller, *Der Ausdruck 'Menschensohn'*, pp. 19, 23.

rather than the re-use of an existing Son of Man Concept. At *1 En.* 70.1, he noted the major textual variant then known, and translated 'Danach wurde der Name jenes Menschensohnes bei Lebzeiten fort von den Bewohnern des Festlandes zu dem Herrn der Geister erhöht.' At *1 En.* 71.14 he noted that the text was making careful reference back to 46.3, and accordingly the conclusion to this work 'handelt also nicht von Henochs Identifizierung mit einer bereits existierenden Erlösergestalt ... sondern sie verkünden, daß Henoch "jener Menschensohn" ist, den er geschaut hat.' Accordingly, after careful discussion of *4 Ezra* 13, he concluded, 'Die Untersuchung des Gebrauchs von Dan. 7,13 im. 1 Henochbuch und 4. Esrabuch bringt uns also zu dem Ergebnis, daß außerhalb des Neuen Testaments kein Zeugnis dafür gibt, daß der Audruck "Menschensohn" eine an sich verständliche Messiasbezeichnung gewesen sein sollte oder mit einer bestimmten Assoziationsreihe verbunden gewesen wäre.'[128] It was good to have this important result carefully presented in German, and highly regrettable that our German colleagues did not take more notice of it.

In his third chapter, Müller offered a thorough discussion of the possible influence of Dan. 7.13-14 in the New Testament. While he allowed more influence than I had done in my investigation, for he allowed more indirect or creative use in eschatological passages than I had done, he likewise concluded that its use came from the *Urgemeinde* rather than from Jesus himself. Moreover, he independently came to the important conclusion that 'Der Ausdruck "Menschensohn" kann nicht länger als sicheres Kennzeichen des Einflusses der Danielstelle gelten ...'[129]

This left one more substantial chapter on sayings of Jesus which were not dependent on Dan. 7.13-14. Here Müller worked systematically through all the Gospel Son of man sayings. He concluded his discussion of the remaining Markan sayings,

> Zusammenfassend läßt sich sagen, daß keines der in diesem Kapitel behandelten 11 Markinischen 'Menschensohn'-Worte es unmöglich macht, daß man den Gebrauch des Ausdrucks in dieser Evangelienschrift im Anschluß an oder von der aramäischen Redeweise her versteht, in der ein Sprecher aufgrund des besonderen Charakters der Aussage *bar nasch(a)* als Umschreibung für seine eigene Person benutzt.[130]

While this was a step in the right direction, further work would be needed on the Aramaic idiom itself, on reconstructions of proposed sayings of Jesus, and on the transition process from sayings of Jesus to sayings in the Gospels.

I made a number of contributions to these issues in the following years. In 1985, I offered a further refinement to our understanding of the Aramaic idiom discussed by Vermes. I proposed that it should not be regarded as ambiguous. In so doing, I offered a brief overview of work done in 'ambiguity research', and the more helpful

128. Müller, *Der Ausdruck 'Menschensohn'*, pp. 70, 72, 75, 88.
129. Müller, *Der Ausdruck 'Menschensohn'*, p. 154.
130. Müller, *Der Ausdruck 'Menschensohn'*, p. 187.

work of linguists such as J. R. Searle.[131] I also drew attention to the dire effects of the then common habit of treating sentences 'in isolation', drawing on the work of more linguists, and noting the fruitful influence upon them of children's specialists and ethnomethodologists.[132] I offered an Aramaic reconstruction of one saying, Mt. 8.20//Lk. 9.58. In explaining the meaning of this saying, I drew on existing scholarship about תעליא, a term which includes jackals as well as foxes, and on the known behaviour of jackals, and of birds which roost in the Capernaum area. I further noted the work of modern linguists on general statements, which may be restricted in scope but which may persuade if the general level of meaning is obvious enough.[133] The massive variety of work here drawn on should be carefully noted. One reason why the Son of man problem has been so difficult to solve is that many incorrect assumptions about the use of languages in general have been fed into New Testament scholarship, both from the inadequate work of previous generations, and from our own popular culture and use of language.

131.   P. M. Casey, 'The Jackals and the Son of Man (Matt. 8.20//Luke 9.58)', *JSNT* 23 (1985) pp. 3–22, at p. 7, with p. 18 n. 15, referring especially to J. R. Searle; 'Indirect Speech Acts', in P. Cole and J. L. Morgan (eds), *Syntax and Semantics. 3. Speech Acts* (London/New York: Academic Press, 1975), pp. 59–82, esp. 67–8.

132.   Casey, 'Jackals', pp. 19–20, n. 18, citing C. S. Smith, 'The Vagueness of Sentences in Isolation', *Papers from the Thirteenth Regional Meeting, Chicago Linguistic Society* (1977), pp. 568–77; H. H. Clark, 'Inferring what is meant', in W. J. M. Levelt and G. B. Flores d'Arcais (eds), *Studies in the Perception of Language* (Chichester: Wiley, 1978), pp. 295–322; J. R. Searle, 'Literal Meaning', *Erkenntnis* 13 (1978), pp. 207–24, reprinted in J. R. Searle, *Expression and Meaning. Studies in the Theory of Speech Acts* (Cambridge: CUP, 1979), Ch. 5; E. Ochs, 'Introduction. What Child Language Can Contribute to Pragmatics', in E. Ochs and B. B. Schieffelin (eds), *Developmental Pragmatics* (London/New York: Academic Press, 1979), pp. 1–17; A. L. Vanek, 'A Note on Context-Sensitive Grammar', *Papers in Linguistics* 12 (1979), pp. 271–92; R. D. van Valin, 'Meaning and Interpretation', *Journal of Pragmatics* 4 (1980), pp. 213–31.

133.   Casey, 'Jackals', p. 9, with p. 21 n. 23, citing R. P. Abelson and D. E. Kanouse, 'Subjective Acceptance of Verbal Generalization', in S. Feldman (ed.), *Cognitive Consistency* (London/New York: Academic Press, 1966), pp. 171–97; R. Revlis, S. G. Lipkin and J. R. Hayes, 'The Importance of Universal Quantifiers in a Hypothetical Reasoning Task', *Journal of Verbal Learning and Verbal Behaviour* 10 (1971), pp. 86-91; R. Revlis and J. R. Hayes, 'The Primacy of Generalities in Hypothetical Reasoning', *Cognitive Psychology* 3 (1972), pp. 268–90; H. Gollob, R. Rossman and R. P. Abelson, 'Social judgement as a function of the number of instances, consistency, and relevance of information present', *Journal of Personality and Social Psychology* 27 (1973), pp. 19–33; G. O. Klemp, 'The Influence of Selected Verb Characteristics on the Acceptance of Generic Assertions', *Journal of Verbal Learning and Verbal Behaviour* 13 (1974), pp. 355–64; G. Bear and A. Hodun, 'Implicational Principles and the Cognition of Confirmatory, Contradictory, Incomplete and Irrelevant Information', *Journal of Personality and Social Psychology* 32 (1975), pp. 594–604; D. M. Podeschi and R. S. Wyer, Jr., 'Acceptance of Generalizations Based on Inductive and Deductive Evidence', *Journal of Personality and Social Psychology* 34 (1976), pp. 496–509; Casey, 'Jackals', pp. 10–12 with pp. 21–2 nn. 24, 26, referring to H. Sacks, 'Everyone has to lie', in M. Sanches and B. G. Blount (eds), *Sociocultural Dimensions of Language Use* (New York: Academic Press, 1975), pp. 57–79; K. Wales, '"Personal" and "Indefinite" Reference: The uses of the pronoun *ONE* in Present-day English', *Nottingham linguistic circular* 9 (1980), pp. 93–117; *idem*, 'Exophora re-examined: the uses of the personal pronoun WE in present-day English', *UEA Papers in Linguistics* 12 (1980), pp. 12–44.

In 1987, I carried further the study of the idiomatic use of the Aramaic term בר (א)נש(א).[134] I noted the early example of it at Sefire III,16, long before the time of Jesus.[135] In discussing this and other examples, I argued that they all have a general level of meaning, but that this may be restricted to a small social subgroup. I also argued that examples of the idiom may use בר (א)נש(א) in the definite or indefinite state, and that the presence or absence of the prosthetic א makes no difference to the usage of the idiom. I presented Aramaic reconstructions of further sayings of Jesus, with brief discussions: Mt. 12.32//Lk. 12.10 (cf. Mk 3.28-29), Mk 2.27-28, Lk. 22.48, Mt. 11.19//Lk. 7.34, Mk 14.21, and 10.45. I also made a preliminary attempt to unravel the origin and secondary development of other Son of man predictions of Jesus' passion now found in the synoptic Gospels.

In 1988, I offered the first attempt at an Aramaic reconstruction of a whole Markan pericope, namely Mk 2.23-28, as then seemed possible in the light of modern discoveries of Aramaic documents, especially the Dead Sea scrolls.[136] The passage had often been split into small pieces by scholars who could not see the connection between the situation and Jesus' arguments, because they studied it in Greek against a background of Christian assumptions. After presenting the Aramaic reconstruction of the whole passage, I sought to understand it by means of Jewish assumptions which would have been common to Jesus, his disciples and his Pharisaic opponents. This enabled me to see the Son of man saying at Mk 2.28 in its original cultural context. This cultural context was in the life of the historical Jesus himself, so that the reconstruction of the Aramaic source of the whole pericope greatly increased the arguments for the historicity of the whole incident.

In 1994, I offered a more thorough survey of the use of בר (א)נש(א) in the Targums and Peshitta than had previously been attempted. In general, I concluded:

> בר (א)נש(א) is a normal Aramaic term for 'man'. Its semantic area corresponds approximately to that of the Hebrew בן אדם and the Aramaic אנשא. It overlaps greatly with the Hebrew אדם and אנוש, and to a lesser extent with the Aramaic בני (א)נש(א): it overlaps to some extent with the Hebrew איש, נפש and other words, and with the Aramaic גבר and נפש. Consequently, some translators used it frequently for אדם and אנוש, and occasionally for other words. Other translators used it less frequently, and some, faced with not more than one difficult example of בן אדם, did not use it at all. At least in documents which do not contain בן אדם, there is always an appropriate alternative.[137]

I also noted cases where בר (א)נש(א) is used with particular reference to Ezekiel, Daniel and Noah, and in general statements with particular reference to Adam, the chief butler, Joseph, Moses and Zerah and his army. I then brought forward a further six examples of its use in general statements which have particular reference to the

---

134. Casey, 'General, Generic and Indefinite'.

135. Now passage 20, pp. 67–8 below.

136. P. M. Casey, 'Culture and Historicity: The Plucking of the Grain (Mark 2.23-28)', *NTS* 34 (1988), pp. 1–23.

137. P. M. Casey, 'The Use of the Term בר (א)נש(א) in the Aramaic Translations of the Hebrew Bible', *JSNT* 54 (1994), pp. 87–118 (99).

speaker. Three of these were from the Targums (Neof I Gen. 2.23; Tg. Job 16. 20-21; 33.29-30), and three from the Peshitta (Job 16.20-21; Ps. 40.5; Ps. 94.12).

This new evidence contributed to the solution of the Son of man problem in three different ways. In the first place, passages in which (א)שׁנ(א) בר is used with particular reference to Ezekiel, Daniel and Noah clarified the fact that this term for 'man' can be used with reference to any particular individual precisely because it is a normal term for 'man'. It follows that bringing forward one or two passages in which it may be thought to refer especially to the messiah does not give it 'messianic overtones' or the like in passages where 'the Messiah' is not mentioned. Secondly, general statements in which (א)שׁנ(א) בר is used with particular reference to Adam, the chief butler, Joseph, Moses and Zerah and his army further clarified the fact that, again precisely because (א)שׁנ(א) בר is a normal term for 'man', it may be used in general statements which have particular reference to any particular individual. This forms essential background to its use in general statements which have especial reference to the speaker, or the speaker and others, made obvious by the context. Thirdly, it was useful to have more examples of this idiom. It should have become ever clearer that, when examples of it emerge from straightforward reconstructions of sayings of Jesus in their original Aramaic, they should be accepted as genuine examples of sayings of the historical Jesus.

In 1995, I brought forward new evidence from the fields of Bilingualism and Translation studies, and from study of translation techniques in the LXX and to some extent other Bible versions. My purpose was to illuminate further the process by which the Aramaic (א)שׁנ(א) בר was translated with some apparent consistency to produce the Gospel term ὁ υἱὸς τοῦ ἀνθρώπου.[138] There were two problems, both of which had been part of traditional scholarship for a long time. One was that some scholars could not see why the translator(s) had been literal enough to use υἱὸς at all. The other was that scholars could not understand how the consistent use of the first article, ὁ when in the nominative, perfectly comprehensible as deliberate reference to Jesus by Gospel writers writing freely in Greek, could have arisen from the process of translating (א)שׁנ(א) בר. In the immediately preceding years, for example, Hare had argued that the translator should have put ἄνθρωπος or υἱὸς ἀνθρώπου, A. Y. Collins ἄνθρωπος, and Ross ὁ ἄνθρωπος οὗτος, ἄνθρωπος, τις or ἄνθρωπος τις.[139] Hare was also among those scholars who approached the

138. P.M. Casey, 'Idiom and Translation. Some Aspects of the Son of Man Problem', *NTS* 41 (1995), pp. 164–82.

139. D. R. A. Hare, *The Son of Man Tradition* (Minneapolis: Fortress, 1990), pp. 249–50; A. Y. Collins, 'The Origin of the Designation of Jesus as "Son of Man"', *HTR* 80 (1987), pp. 391–407 (399); *idem*, 'Daniel 7 and Jesus', *Journal of Theology* 93 (1989), pp. 5–19 (14); *idem*, 'Daniel 7 and the Historical Jesus', in *Of Scribes and Scrolls: Studies on the Hebrew Bible, Intertestamental Judaism and Christian Origins presented to John Strugnell on the occasion of his Sixtieth Birthday* (ed. H. W. Attridge, J. J. Collins and T. H. Tobin; Lanham/NY/London: University Press of America, 1990), pp. 181–93 (190); J. M. Ross, 'The Son of Man', *IBS* 13 (1991), pp. 186–98 (191).

question of the first article by effectively translating ὁ υἱὸς τοῦ ἀνθρώπου *back into* Aramaic, commenting:

> That Aramaic-speaking Christians did not perceive the phrase as generic … is adequately demonstrated by the consistent choice of *ho huios tou anthrōpou* as its Greek equivalent. The articles indicate that the tradents regarded the Aramaic phrase as referring to a single individual, Jesus.[140]

In this situation, I brought to bear on this problem our greatly increased knowledge of the habits of translators, and especially the massive variety in the degree of literalism which their works exhibit. I showed that the translation of (א)נֹש(א) בר with ὁ υἱὸς τοῦ ἀνθρώπου falls within the range of normal behaviour by translators. I noted that all translators suffer from interference, both as bilinguals and doubly so from the text in front of them. The degree of literalism in this case is consistent with the known behaviour of the translators of the Hebrew Bible into the LXX. I also argued that, given the variation in the state of (א)נֹש(א) בר in this idiom, it was entirely reasonable of the translators to consistently use the first article in ὁ υἱὸς τοῦ ἀνθρώπου. This ensured the reference to Jesus remained clear, and could be perceived by bilingual translators as both generic and particular, so that the phrase ὁ υἱὸς τοῦ ἀνθρώπου as a whole was as nearly accurate a translation of (א)נֹש(א) בר as was in practice possible.

In 1998 and 2002, I carried this work further in two monographs, one on Aramaic sources of Mark's Gospel, and the second on Aramaic traditions behind the Q material.[141] There were three main points at which I sought to go further than had previously been possible. First, I sought to advance further the methodology of doing Aramaic reconstructions of whole passages. I argued that more work had become possible following the discovery of more Aramaic, especially the Dead Sea Scrolls. Secondly, this meant that it was now possible to reconstruct far more Aramaic sources than had previously been feasible, at points where the existing Greek text of the Gospels had been literally translated. In particular, some Son of man sayings could now be reconstructed within a complete narrative context. For example, Mk 10.45 could be seen to conclude Mk 10.35-45, and to draw together the whole pericope with reference back to its opening, and the whole pericope could consequently be set within the ministry of the historical Jesus. An even more remarkable example is the Son of man saying found at Mk 9.12. This has always been part of the small narrative now found at Mk 9.11-13. This does not make proper sense in Greek. The proposed Aramaic reconstruction, however, makes excellent sense, and can also be set within the ministry of the historical Jesus.

My discussion of Mk 9.11-13 made particular use of the third major advance which I sought to make in these two monographs, to carry further the insights into bilingualism and the processes of translation which continued to come from our

---

140. Hare, *Son of Man*, p. 249.
141. Casey, *Aramaic Sources of Mark's Gospel*; *An Aramaic Approach to Q: Sources for the Gospels of Matthew and Luke* (SNTSMS, 122; Cambridge: CUP, 2002).

colleagues in these fields and in the study of the LXX. I particularly drew attention to the use by the Gospel translators of a translation *strategy*:

> The only clear strategy in the synoptic Gospels concerns the translation of בר (א)נשׁ(א). We shall see that we must infer the following strategy: we use ὁ υἱὸς τοῦ ἀνθρώπου for בר (א)נשׁ(א) when it refers to Jesus, and not otherwise ... This is very important for understanding the whole of the synoptic tradition, for a translation strategy can only be employed when extensive portions of the literature in which it is found are in fact translated.[142]

This accounts both for the occurrences of ὁ υἱὸς τοῦ ἀνθρώπου as a translation of בר (א)נשׁ(א), and for the complete absence of anything like a translation of בר (א)נשׁ(א) when it does not refer to Jesus, and for the virtual absence of the plural. Mk 9.12 shows that this strategy was occasionally difficult to apply, because here there was a genuine reference to the death of Jesus, but reference to the death of John the Baptist was necessary to make sense of the saying. Hence the unsatisfactory result, which led me to quote from modern work on translation strategies:

> If the first article were taken as generic, as the second must be, bilinguals could see the original idiom. The translator had therefore done as well as possible. We may feel that his work illustrates a general observation made by modern students of translation: 'Strategies do not solve translation problems – they are merely plans that can be implemented in an attempt to solve problems.' This further illustrates the normality of the processes by which Mark's text was produced.[143]

In an article published in 2002, I made two further points.[144] One is that the Aramaic language was relatively stable for a period of centuries. Consequently, it is in principle legitimate to use the Aramaic of different times and places in order to reconstruct Jesus' sayings, and stories about him, in the language in which they were originally transmitted. Secondly, I laid out the optional use of the definite and indefinite states in generic nouns, and in some unique ones. For this purpose, I studied all the nouns in Aramaic down to the time of Jesus. A very clear pattern emerged in generics: the definite or indefinite state may be used. This is entirely logical because the use of either state cannot affect the meaning and use of such nouns. The same is true of the small number of nouns for unique items such as the earth. This is very important for understanding the variation in the state of בר (א)נשׁ(א) in the idiomatic usage central

---

142. Casey, *Aramaic Sources of Mark's Gospel*, p. 103.

143. Casey, *Aramaic Sources of Mark's Gospel*, p. 132, quoting H. G. Hönig, 'Holmes' "Mapping Theory" and the Landscape of Mental Translation Processes', in K. M. van Leuven-Zwart and T. Naaijkens (eds), *Translation Studies: The State of the Art.* Proceedings of the First James S. Holmes Symposium on Translation Studies (Amsterdam, 1991), pp. 77–89 (85), quoting D. C. Kiraly, 'Toward a Systematic Approach to Translation Skills Instruction', (Ph.D. thesis, Urbana, Illinois, 1990), p. 149.

144. P. M. Casey, 'Aramaic Idiom and the Son of Man Problem: a Response To Owen and Shepherd', *JSNT* 25 (2002), pp. 3–32.

to this book. The older scholarship debated whether the force of the definite state had already been removed in first-century Galilee, which we are in no position to know. Variation in the state of generic nouns had however certainly been normal for centuries, and this is the pattern into which the variation in the state of בר (א)נשׁ(א) in its idiomatic usage could now be fitted.

This book seeks to carry forward all this work to a complete solution of the Son of man problem. In the process, I hope to have answered all the major criticisms of this approach, many of which have been uncomprehending, or answered by subsequent research. I propose however to list some main points here, with brief responses, to make quite clear what my overall response to these criticisms is.

One set of criticisms results from taking my description of the idiom using the term 'general statement' too literally, and treating my suggestions in English or German rather than Aramaic. For example, Hooker, apparently referring to my interpretation of Mt. 8.20//Lk. 9.58, included 'a man has nowhere to lay his head' among sayings which, if so understood, are 'manifestly untrue'.[145] She did not however attempt to interpret the proposed Aramaic reconstruction, and interpreted part of my English translation in much too universal a sense.

Similar problems appear to lie behind the objections of those scholars who consider my exegesis to be wrong. For example, Kümmel commented in general:

> Die exegetischen Gewaltstreiche, zu denen sich CASEY und LINDARS gezwungen sehen, um Jesu Rede vom 'Menschen' als eine besondere Art der üblichen Verwendung dieses Wortes zur Umschreibung von 'ich' zu erweisen, zeigen zusammen mit der sprachlichen Fragwürdigkeit dieser These, daß das Rätsel dieser Redeform Jesus auf dies Weise nicht zu lösen ist.[146]
> The exegetical violence, to which Casey and Lindars appear forced, so as to understand Jesus' talk of 'man' as a special kind of ordinary employment of this word as a circumlocution for 'I', shows together with the linguistic questionability of this hypothesis, that the problem of this speech-form of Jesus cannot be solved in this way.

This objection was not founded on discussion of my proposed Aramaic reconstructions. Kümmel supported his assertion with brief comments on four examples, which he discussed entirely in German. On Mt. 11.18-19//Lk. 7.33-34, he commented:

> Das ist nun zweifellos keine *allgemeine* Aussage über menschliches Verhalten, wie CASEY annimt, sondern ein Tadel, den man ausschließlich gegen Jesus vorbringen konnte.[147]
> Now that is unquestionably no *general/universal* statement about human behaviour, as Casey supposes, but a reproach which people could bring exclusively against Jesus.

---

145. M. D. Hooker, 'Is the Son of Man problem really insoluble?', in E. Best and R. McL. Wilson (eds), *Text and Interpretation. Studies in the New Testament presented to Matthew Black*, (Cambridge: CUP, 1979), pp. 155–68 (158).

146. W. G. Kümmel, 'Jesus der Menschensohn?' *Sitzungsberichte der Wissenschaftlichen Gesellschaft an der Johann Wolfgang Goethe-Universität Frankfurt am Main* XX,3 (Stuttgart: Steiner, 1984), pp. 147–88 (159).

147. Kümmel, 'Jesus der Menschensohn?', p. 158.

This is simply repetition of standard Christian tradition, according to which all statements about ὁ υἱὸς τοῦ ἀνθρώπου in the Gospels are supposed to be about Jesus alone. Kümmel did not engage with the proposed Aramaic reconstruction, and consequently he did not even seek to discuss how a general level of meaning could be absent from it. His comments have in common with those of Hooker that he has exaggerated *how* general the general level of meaning needed to be.[148]

For the supposed linguistic questionability of this hypothesis, Kümmel referred back to some comments of Fitzmyer.[149] Fitzmyer's original argument was that examples of the idiomatic use of בר (א)נש(א) collected by Vermes should not be accepted because they do not have the prosthetic א. I have noted subsequent work showing that the semantic area of בר (א)נש(א) is not affected by whether it has the prosthetic א, and it is in any case entirely possible that the prosthetic א was not pronounced by Galileans.[150] It should also be noted that Fitzmyer's original criticism was a reaction to Vermes' interpretation of the idiomatic use of בר נש as a simple substitute for 'I', a very large change from otherwise-known usage of this term, and an interpretation which excludes Sefire III, 16 from serious consideration as an example. If all examples are seen as general statements, and Sefire III, 16 is taken into account, the shift is very small and one of the examples is early.

An extraordinary effect of the massive bureaucratization of scholarship has been a number of allegations that I am really discussing secondary literature when I have been trying to interpret primary sources. For example, in an article which explicitly discussed several attempts which I made to carry forward our understanding of this problem, Marshall claimed that in discussing my own proposed Aramaic reconstruction of Mt. 11.18-19, 'Casey simply takes over the view of Colpe without apparently realizing that it is not the same as his own'.[151] I was not taking over the view of Colpe: I was trying to explain how my proposed Aramaic reconstruction should be understood.

The same process of bureaucratization of scholarship has led to the presentation of my proposed hypothesis as if it were really the same as earlier scholarship. For example, Burkett described my view of authentic sayings such as Mt. 8.20, and

---

148. See further P. M. Casey, 'Method in our Madness, and Madness in their Methods. Some Approaches to the Son of Man Problem in Recent Scholarship', *JSNT* 42 (1991), pp. 17–43 (19–21).

149. Kümmel, 'Jesus der Menschensohn?', p. 157, referring to J. A. Fitzmyer, 'The New Testament Title "Son of Man" Philologically Considered', in J. A. Fitzmyer, *A Wandering Aramean. Collected Aramaic Essays* (SBLMS 25. Missoula: Scholars, 1979), pp. 143–60 (154); *idem*, 'Another View of the "Son of Man" Debate', *JSNT* 4 (1979), pp. 58–68 (62).

150. Cf. further G. Vermes, *Jesus the Jew* (London, 1973), pp. 188–91; *idem*, 'The Present State of the "Son of Man" Debate', *JJS* 29 (1978), pp. 123–34 (127–30); *idem*, 'The "Son of Man" Debate' *JSNT* 1 (1978), pp. 19–32 (23–5); Fitzmyer, 'New Testament Title "Son of Man"', pp. 149–53; Fitzmyer, 'Another View', esp. pp. 61–4; G. Schwarz, *Jesus 'der Menschensohn'. Aramaistische Untersuchungen zu den synoptischen Menschensohnworten Jesu* (BWANT 119, = VI, 19; Stuttgart: Kohlhammer, 1986), pp. 71–3, 84; Casey, 'Use of the Term בר (א)נש(א) in the Aramaic Translations of the Hebrew Bible'.

151. I. H. Marshall, 'The "Son of Man" Sayings in the Light of Linguistic Study', in T. E. Schmidt and M. Silva (eds), *To Tell the Mystery. Essays on New Testament Eschatology in Honor of R. H. Gundry* (JSNTSup 100; Sheffield: JSOT Press, 1994), pp. 72–94 (84).

then commented that in my view 'the general reference was misunderstood as a title referring to Daniel 7.13'. Then, classifying me together with Lindars, Bauckham and Fuller, he declares, 'They have to assume that the Aramaic has been mistranslated.'[152] We have seen what a serious problem the whole question of translation of this idiom and the shift from an Aramaic term to a Greek Christological title posed for all the earlier scholarship. We have also seen that I took a different view, and especially that, in a 1995 article listed in Burkett's bibliography, I used insights from colleagues working in Translation Studies and on the LXX to propose a new understanding of the translation process. Burkett has assumed that I must nonetheless believe what dead professors had written long ago. I hope this book will be read with more care, and that it will be assessed in its own right.

Other attempts have been made to approach this problem from a linguistic perspective. The most notable is that of Kearns.[153] In the first of several exceptionally learned volumes devoted to this problem, Kearns argued that ברנש is a four-letter word derived from Ugaritic.[154] This is not a probable derivation, in the first place because all the earliest examples of this term are of the form בר אנ(ו)ש. The form ברנש is first found in relatively late sources which drop the prosthetic א from other words too. Accordingly, it cannot reasonably be regarded as the earliest form. Secondly, even if the usually accepted etymology of בר (א)נ(א)ש as a combination of two words, בר 'son' and (א)נ(א)ש 'man', were shown to be secondary, the effect of the usual etymology would still be decisive. Kearns agrees that בר (א)נ(א)ש was understood as a combination of these two separate words in the Aramaic of our period. This etymology must therefore be taken into account in interpreting Aramaic texts from any environment where such an etymology was perceptible.

Kearns also argues that ברנש had several 'Bedeutungen', including for example vassal, citizen, smallholder, and Lord (Herr).[155] This view involves confusion

152. D. Burkett, *The Son of Man Debate. A History and Evaluation* (MSSNTS 107. Cambridge: CUP, 1999), pp. 90, 93.

153. R. Kearns, *Vorfragen zur Christologie*. Vol. 1. *Morphologische und Semasiologische Studie zur Vorgeschichte eines christologischen Hoheitstitels* (Tübingen: Mohr (Siebeck), 1978); Vol. 2. *Überlieferungsgeschichtliche und Rezeptionsgeschichtliche Studie zur Vorgeschichte eines christologischen Hoheitstitels* (Tübingen: Mohr (Siebeck), 1980); Vol. 3. *Religionsgeschichtliche und Traditionsgeschichtliche Studie zur Vorgeschichte eines christologischen Hoheitstitels* (Tübingen: Mohr (Siebeck), 1982); *Das Traditionsgefüge um den Menschensohn. Ursprünglicher Gehalt und älteste Veränderung im Urchristentum* (Tübingen: Mohr (Siebeck), 1986); *Die Entchristologisierung des Menschensohnes. Die Übertragung des Traditionsgefüges um den Menschensohn auf Jesus* (Tübingen: Mohr (Siebeck), 1988); *Mutmaßungen zur Christologie*. Part 1, *Der gewaltsam getötete und nach dem Tod verherrlichte Gerechte* (Tübingen: Gulde-Druck Gmbh, 2002); Part 2. *Ο υἱὸς τοῦ ἀνθρώπου als hoheitstitulares Wortgebilde* (Tübingen: Gulde-Druck Gmbh, 2003); Part 3. *Die Epiphanie des Menschensohnes in der Welt: Die transzendent-eschatologische Epiphanie des Menschensohnes* (Tübingen: Gulde-Druck Gmbh, 2003); Part 4. *Ο κύριος als Hoheitstitel* (Tübingen: Gulde-Druck Gmbh, 2004); Part 5. *Der Allherr und die Übrigbleibenden* (Tübingen: Gulde-Druck Gmbh, 2004).

154. Kearns, *Morphologische und Semasiologische Studie*, pp. 9–88; and for further development, esp. *Ο υἱὸς τοῦ ἀνθρώπου als hoheitstitulares Wortgebilde*.

155. See especially Kearns, *Morphologische und Semasiologische Studie*, pp. 98–182; *Ο κύριος als Hoheitstitel*, pp. 2–9.

between meaning and reference. In all the texts cited by Kearns, בר (א)נש(א) makes sense *meaning* 'man', though it does *refer* to vassals, smallholders and all sorts of other people. It is a result of this confusion that the number of proposed meanings is too great for the expression to function without additional qualification. Some passages also do not make very good sense when interpreted in this way. This may be illustrated from 1QapGen. XXI,13.[156] Kearns finds this passage problematical because he proposes that בר אנוש here should mean 'smallholder' rather than 'man'.[157] God's promise to Abraham, whose seed is to be like the dust of the earth which no man can number, is given in Hebrew at Gen. 13.16, where the word for 'man' is איש. The author of the Genesis Apocryphon represented איש with בר אנוש, a fact which shows clearly that בר (א)נש(א) was already a normal term for 'man'. But for Kearns, the author has to be supposed to have God declaring that Abraham's seed will be like the dust of the earth which no *smallholder* can number. Kearns does not explain why the hyperbole 'no man can number' should be rendered so peculiarly 'no smallholder can number', when אנש and גבר were readily available to the midrashic author.

Kearns also constructs a number of traditions, most of which are no more convincing than the Son of Man Concept and the Primordial Man. These include, for example, the tradition of the returning Elijah, from which Kearns derives μετὰ τρεῖς ἡμέρας in the Markan passion predictions.[158] At least in this case there was a tradition of Elijah's return, utilized by Jesus at Mk 9.11-13 and Mt. 11.13-14.[159] This did not however contain μετὰ τρεῖς ἡμέρας, which Kearns draws from very late sources such as the Gospel of Nicodemus and Lactantius. For the clouds of heaven, Kearns goes right back to the formula *rkb 'rpt* from the cultic-mythic Hadadtradition.[160] Kearns suggests that Hadad might have been translated into western Aramaic as ברנש rather than בעל. He takes ענני, quoted from Dan. 7.13 but described as the vehicle of the Lord of the World (*Weltenherr*) in the *apokalyptic Traditionsgefüge*, as the equivalent of *'rpt*.[161] The problem with all arguments of this type is that they *construct* from diverse primary sources extant centuries apart discrete traditions which are suppposed to have been available to Jesus and the Gospel writers. The strength of Kearns' belief in the traditions which he has constructed is especially well illustrated by his suggestion that Mk 13.26 is not dependent on Dan. 7.13, but rather on Kearns' tradition.[162]

---

156. See pp. 61–2 below.

157. Kearns, *Morphologische und Semasiologische Studie*, p. 135 n. 181 from p. 134.

158. Kearns, *Traditionsgefüge*, pp. 146–54, 167–70; *Entchristologisierung*, p. 43; *Epiphanie*, p. 4. n. 10.

159. Casey, *Aramaic Sources of Mark's Gospel*, pp. 121–37; *Aramaic Approach to Q*, pp. 105–7, 125–9.

160. Kearns, *Religionsgeschichtliche und Traditionsgeschichtliche Studie*, pp. 3–82; *Epiphanie*, pp. 1–2, 13–16.

161. Kearns, *Religionsgeschichtliche und Traditionsgeschichtliche Studie*, pp. 106–7; *Traditionsgefüge*, pp. 66–7; *Epiphanie*, pp. 13–16.

162. Kearns, *Traditionsgefüge*, pp. 66–8. nn. 220, 230; *Entchristologisierung*, pp. 67–8, n. 16; *Epiphanie*, pp. 16–17, n. 47.

Kearns also suffers from some of the standard faults of traditional German *überlieferungsgeschichte* and *redaktionsgeschichte*. For example, referring back to the work of Colpe, he supposes that the original saying behind Mk 10.45 had an implicit or explicit first person pronoun which was replaced with ברנש during the history of its development. This is as arbitrary as Colpe's work on this verse.[163]

For all these reasons, Kearns' attempt to solve this problem should not be accepted.

Throughout this period, traditional approaches also continued to be reworked and presented afresh. Perhaps the outstanding attempt to argue again for the crucial influence of Dan. 7.13 was that of Otto Betz.[164] Betz begins with a description of Son of man sayings as 'Hoheitssagen, die auf eine einzigartige Vollmacht weisen', and he argues that 'deutete Jesus mit der Selbstbezeichnung "der Menschensohn" seine besondere, singuläre, Sendung und Vollmacht an'.[165] This fits in with Betz's convictions about the meaning of Son of man sayings in the Gospels, but it is very difficult to reconcile with the usage of the Aramaic term (א)בר נש(א). Betz's discussion of Aramaic source material is very meagre. The bulk of the book is devoted to discussion of the influence of Dan. 7.13-14 and some other Old Testament passages on Son of man sayings attributed to Jesus, with a final chapter on aspects of the teaching of St Paul. Betz presents his final conclusions about Jesus in a postscript:

> Jesus hat den formalen Begriff 'Menschenähnlicher, Menschensohn' in Dan 7,13 inhaltlich näher bestimmt. Er tat dies, indem er ihn mit anderen Vorstellungen aus Schriftworten verband, die für seine Zeitgenossen wichtig waren, so mit der Messiaserwartung (Gen 49,10; 2. Sam 7,12-14; Ps 110,1) und mit dem Gottesknecht (Jes 42; 43; 53) oder mit Ps 103. Aus solcher Zusammenschau ergab sich eine Art Dienstanweisung für helfendes Handeln. Dabei wurde die Vollmacht des Menschensohns, von der Dan 7,14 spricht, zu einer Bevollmächtigung für den Gesandten Gottes umgewandelt, der die Heiligen Gottes, das Volk des Neuen Bundes, beruft und sammelt und die helfende Gerechtigkeit des Gottesreiches aufrichtet.[166]
>
> With regard to its content, Jesus ascertained the formal concept, 'One like a Son of man, Son of man' in Dan. 7.13. He did this, while he combined it with other concepts from scriptural passages which were important for his contemporaries, so with the Messianic expectation (Gen. 49.10; 2 Sam. 7.12-14; Ps. 110.1) and with the Servant of God (Isa. 42; 43; 53) or with Ps. 103. From such a combination came a sort of service instruction for helpful use. Thereby the power of the Son of man, of whom Dan. 7.14 speaks, was transformed into an empowerment for the One Sent of God, who calls and gathers the Holy Ones of God, the people of the New Covenant, and sets up the succouring righteousness of the kingdom of God.

This approach is methodologically unsound. In the first place, as well as failing to offer proper discussion of the Aramaic term (א)בר נש(א), which was already well known to be an ordinary term for 'man', Betz never deals with Aramaic reconstructions of

---

163. Kearns, *Entchristologisierung*, p. 74; p. 36 above.
164. W. Grimm and O. Betz, *Jesus und das Danielbuch* (2 vols; Frankfurt am Main: Lang, 1985); Vol. 2, O. Betz, *Die Menschensohnworte Jesu und die Zukunftserwartung des Paulus (Daniel 7,13-14)*.
165. Betz, *Menschensohnworte Jesu*, p. 15.
166. Betz, *Menschensohnworte Jesu*, p. 175.

sayings of Jesus. This means that he never discusses the general level of meaning of authentic sayings of Jesus, the main point which cannot be reconciled with his convictions that the term simply refers to Jesus (*Selbstbezeichnung*), and that all the sayings are sayings of majesty (*Hoheitsaussagen*) which point to a unique power.

Secondly, Betz's arguments for the use of scriptural texts proceed by weak connections and loose associative links. For example, at the beginning of his discussion, Betz considers Mk 2.10. He asserts:

> Denn gerade die große Vollmacht, die Jesus in den Menschensohnworten bekundet, hat ihren biblischen Bezugspunkt in der von Daniel geschauten Einsetzung des Menschensohns in die Würde des Endzeitkönigs.[167]
> For exactly the massive power, which Jesus bears witness to in the Son of man sayings, has its biblical reference point in the placement of the Son of man into the majesty of the eschatological king pictured by Daniel.

Yet, apart from the question as to what an Aramaic reconstruction of Mk 2.10 might mean, Dan. 7.13-14 cannot be seen as a reasonable source of it for three reasons. Firstly, there are too few connecting links, a fact obscured by Betz's failure to discuss the Aramaic term (א)שׁנ(א) בר as an ordinary term for 'man'. This omission makes the use of בר אנשׁ appear to be a much stronger connection than it is. Secondly, the man-like figure of Dan. 7.13, and Saints of the Most High symbolized by him, were not given the power to forgive sins or anything of that kind. Thirdly, there is no sign in the New Testament that anyone placed the fulfilment of Dan. 7.13-14 at the time of Jesus' earthly life, whereas there is very clear evidence that it was interpreted of his parousia, as most obviously at Mk 13.26//Mt. 26.64//Lk. 21.27; Mk 14.62//Mt. 26.64. I had moreover already made these points, in a discussion to which Betz makes no reference.[168]

Finally, even the brief summary which I quote above contains items notoriously absent from the teaching of Jesus. These include the Servant of God, the people of the New Covenant, and the association between the Son of man and the kingdom of God. These things are however very important to German Lutheran academics, and that locates Betz's book where it belongs. It distorts the evidence from beginning to end in the service of the social subgroup of which Betz is a member. After the work of Vermes and myself which had already been published, this shows a degree of blindness to evidence and argument which the Dan. 7.13 hypothesis had not needed in earlier times.

Despite the criticisms of the Son of Man Concept, it did not die out. For example, in 1984 Kümmel continued to base it primarily on the *Similitudes of Enoch*.[169] He dealt with this difficult text entirely in German. He added some discussion of Dan. 7.13 and *4 Ezra* 13, together with *Sib. Or.* V.414-6 and a saying of R. Aqiba at bT Ḥag 14a. Despite the ample citation of secondary literature in his footnotes,

---

167. Betz, *Menschensohnworte Jesu*, p. 16.
168. Casey, *Son of Man*, pp. 92–8, 165–84.
169. Kümmel, 'Jesus der Menschensohn?', pp. 162–6.

Kümmel's brief comments on those who disagreed with him consist of authoritative contradiction rather than genuine engagement.

As recently as 2001, U. B. Müller took the existence of the *Menschensohnbegriff*, or *Menschensohnvorstellung* for granted.[170] Seeing that 'der frühjüdische Menschensohn' (p.4) does not come with the clouds of heaven, as indeed the Son of man figure in the *Similitudes of Enoch* does not, he devoted a whole article to arguing that the Menschensohn was secondary to early Christian expectation of the second coming of Jesus, as this is found in *maranatha* (1 Cor. 16.22) and elsewhere. He also cited Dan. 7 for 'das Stichwort Menschensohn'.[170] He still has Lk. 12.8f. distinguish between 'dem Ich Jesus im Vordersatz und Menschensohn im Nachsatz'.[172] Müller's footnotes are full of references to German secondary literature, but there is no mention of Vermes, Lindars or myself, or indeed of anyone else who does not agree with his presuppositions. This illustrates the regrettable insularity which is increasingly affecting German scholarship.

There were however two changes to the Son of Man Concept among scholars more affected by criticisms of it. One was the demise of the Primordial Man, as I have noted it in the work of Mowinckel and Borsch.[173] As J. J. Collins put it in 1992, 'The notion that the Son of Man was a variant of a widespread myth of the Primordial Man has been laid to rest with no regrets.'[174] The second change was the effective replacement of the Son of Man Concept with views about the messianic overtones of בר נש. These views were generally connected with messianic interpretation of כבר אנש in Dan. 7.13, but some scholars brought forward a considerable variety of other passages in support of this kind of view. Collins himself concluded that there were 'common assumptions about the interpretation of Daniel 7 in first century Judaism…', so that anyone 'who spoke of one in human form riding on the clouds, or appearing with an Ancient of Days, or in any terms reminiscent of Daniel 7, would evoke a figure with distinct traits which go beyond what was explicit in the text of Daniel's vision.'[175] This conclusion was based on his discussion of the three major texts previously used to form the Son of Man Concept, Daniel 7, the *Similitudes of Enoch*, and *4 Ezra* 13. In a revised version of this essay, published in 1995, he also offered some discussion of 4Q246 and three passages of *Sib. Or.* V, and concluded that '"Davidic Messiah" and "Son of Man" were not mutually exclusive concepts. Each involves a cluster of motifs, which could be made to overlap'.[176]

In the light of some change in what was being looked for, more and more passages could be considered as supporting this kind of view. The most extensive survey was

---

170.   U. B. Müller, 'Parusie und Menschensohn', *ZNW* 92 (2001), pp. 1–19.

171.   Müller, 'Parusie und Menschensohn', p. 2.

172.   Müller, 'Parusie und Menschensohn', p. 13.

173.   See pp. 23–6 above.

174.   J. J. Collins, 'The Son of Man in First Century Judaism', *NTS* 38 (1992), pp. 448–66 (449).

175.   Collins, 'Son of Man in First Century Judaism', pp. 465–6.

176.   J. J. Collins, 'The Danielic Son of Man', Ch. 8 of *The Sceptre and the Star* (New York: Doubleday, 1995), pp. 173–94 (189).

that of Horbury in 1985. In an article entitled 'The Messianic Associations of "The Son of Man"', Horbury brought forward passages including for example Tg. Ps. 80.18, where בר נש is used with reference to מלכא משיחא, and Ezekiel the Tragedian, where Moses sits on a throne in heaven, and Horbury suggested that Ezekiel's presentation was in part formed by Dan. 7.[177] There are two problems with this kind of view. One is that it is difficult to see how the mundane use of the Aramaic term בר (א)נש(א) can be reconciled with such views except where the context makes clear a reference to Dan. 7.13. The second is that the exegesis of many of the passages brought forward does not seem to me to be convincing. Two such passages are discussed in Chapter 3.[178]

A much older traditional approach which supposed that ὁ υἱὸς τοῦ ἀνθρώπου referred to Jesus as 'son of Adam' has continued to find the occasional adherent. There were two notable ones during this period, Cortés and Gatti in 1968, and Marcus as recently as 2003.[179] In discussing the patristic view that ὁ υἱὸς τοῦ ἀνθρώπου referred to Jesus as son of Adam, I noted that the Fathers were simply not aware of the normal usage of the Aramaic בר (א)נש(א).[180] Both Cortés and Gatti and Marcus set aside our knowledge of the use of this term, which was unsatisfactory in 1968, and almost beyond belief in 2003, when we know so much more about it. They each make a number of other moves which the Fathers did not make, and which are contrary to results agreed in this and other fields of study on the basis of a massive amount of evidence put together over a period of years with careful argument. For example, both of them stress the second article, τοῦ, as if it should mean that Jesus was the son of a particular man. In so doing, they do not take proper account of the generic use of this article, and ignore the problem of interference which is important for understanding bilinguals and doubly so in understanding the work of bilinguals as translators. They both also prefer to suppose that ὁ υἱὸς τοῦ ἀνθρώπου must somehow mean *exactly* what Jesus said. This was culpable in 1968 when we had significant knowledge of interference and shifts in meaning which take place during the translation process. In 2003, Marcus had to cast aside all the knowledge of these matters achieved by our colleagues in the fields of bilingualism, translation studies and the study of the LXX, even though he had access to work in which I had pointed out what these results are and what they might signify for this problem. We must conclude that the continued presentation of this proposal is regrettable, and can only be understood as attempted continuation of ancient tradition.

---

177. W. Horbury, 'The Messianic Associations of "The Son of Man"', *JTS NS* 36 (1985), pp. 34–55 (48–9 and 42–3).

178. See pp. 112–4 below.

179. J. B. Cortés, and F. M. Gatti, 'The Son of Man or The Son of Adam', *Bib* 49 (1968), pp. 457–502; J. Marcus, 'Son of Man as son of Adam', *RB* 110 (2003), pp. 38–61, 370–86.

180. See pp. 3, 9–10 above.

5. Conclusions

The history of scholarship shows abundantly how and why the solution to this problem has been so excruciatingly difficult to find. Two problems have been so colossal that we are only now beginning to recover from them.

One massive problem has been the influence of existing traditions. The notion that ὁ υἱὸς τοῦ ἀνθρώπου is derived from Dan. 7.13 is as old as Tertullian. Every serious scholar who has espoused this view has made reference to some of their predecessors. Not only is this view traditional in itself, but Dan. 7.13 is part of scripture, and thus part of the traditional sacred text of the traditional religion to which these scholars have belonged. Moreover, some New Testament texts which use the term ὁ υἱὸς τοῦ ἀνθρώπου genuinely do make use of Dan. 7.13 (most obviously Mk 13.26//Mt. 26.64//Lk. 21.27; Mk 14.62//Mt. 26.64), so the use of Dan. 7.13 as the apparent origin of ὁ υἱὸς τοῦ ἀνθρώπου is also part of the traditional sacred text of the traditional religion to which these scholars have belonged. Moreover, messianic interpretation of Dan. 7.13 fits very well into Christian messianic interpretation of many passages of the Old Testament. It is that massive weight of tradition which has been so difficult to overcome.

Similar comments apply to the interpretation of ὁ υἱὸς τοῦ ἀνθρώπου as 'son of Adam'. Though less common in the modern period than reference to Dan. 7.13, this was also originally a patristic view, and this tradition has been of obvious importance in its recent emergence. It originated with western Fathers who did not know about the Aramaic בר (א)נש(א). Of late, however, it has become increasingly reliant on refusing to know about recent advances in knowledge about בר (א)נש(א) and numerous other things. Here again we can see the importance of its being an old tradition. The material about Adam used in this view is also part of theological tradition, and the theological tradition can be seen already in Paul's view of Christ as the second Adam. These general traditions about Adam have been just as important as the more specific ones about the interpretation of ὁ υἱὸς τοῦ ἀνθρώπου. Here too the interpretation can be seen as part of ancient tradition which goes back ultimately to scripture. This massive weight of tradition helps to explain why so implausible a view is still with us.

A more modern and academic tradition is the Son of Man Concept. This began in the nineteenth century, when the traditional Christian interpretation of ὁ υἱὸς τοῦ ἀνθρώπου was important in the first attempts to understand the terms for 'son of man' in the difficult Geʻez text of the newly discovered *Similitudes of Enoch*. This concept was further developed and carried forward during the twentieth century. It was read into Dan. 7.13, which we have already seen to have been scriptural, and thus part of the traditional sacred text of the traditional religion to which most scholars have belonged. It was found primarily in these two texts and in *4 Ezra* 13. Both the *Similitudes of Enoch* and *4 Ezra* were in some people's Bibles, and they both became part of the sort of informal canon of works seen fit for detailed study by Christian academics. They usually studied them within the traditions of their own languages, leaving study in their extant languages, and translation into

English, German and other languages, to a small number of traditional specialists who were considered safe to repeat. In the early to mid-twentieth century, the Son of Man Concept was amplified with the Primordial Man concept. This involved the use of sources which belonged to the traditions of religious studies rather than New Testament studies, so this is probably why it died out. One would like to believe that it died out because of the criticisms made of it as a modern construct, but that should have led to the demise of the Son of Man Concept itself, whereas this has continued to the present day, especially in Germany.

The second massive problem which has made the Son of man problem difficult to solve has been scholarly ignorance, especially of Aramaic and of bilingualism and translation studies. I have observed the lack of knowledge of בר (א)נש(א) among the western Fathers, and how it was not seen as a Christological title among the Syriac Fathers, because ὁ υἱὸς τοῦ ἀνθρώπου was translated into Syriac with ברה דאנשא and other terms which did function as a Christological title. When serious study of the Semitic background to ὁ υἱὸς τοῦ ἀνθρώπου got under way with scholars such as Grotius, and בר (א)נש(א) with Bolten, scholarly ignorance was still so serious that a proper presentation of all the relevant evidence was not remotely possible. Nor did either of them understand the translation process. This greatly helped the comments of scholars who came in from a more traditional perspective to seem entirely reasonable. Even after Meyer and Lietzmann increased our knowledge of Aramaic and of how to use it, our knowledge of בר (א)נש(א) was still insufficient to lead to a solution of this problem. Nor did any scholar fully understand the translation process. This led to Aramaic evidence continuing to be ignored, not only by conservative scholars who preferred a traditional solution to this problem, but also by radical critics. Of particular importance was the misinterpretation of Lk. 12.8 as distinguishing between Jesus and the Son of man. This led many scholars to argue that any saying in which ὁ υἱὸς τοῦ ἀνθρώπου clearly is Jesus cannot be authentic.

The seminal paper of Vermes, published in 1967, was important in starting a new phase of research with new evidence of the interpretation and usage of בר (א)נש(א). In itself, however, it did not offer an altogether correct understanding of the usage of בר (א)נש(א), nor did Vermes or anyone else fully understand the translation process. In the succeeding years, I made a number of contributions which sought to bring to bear on this problem evidence drawn from more Aramaic sources, and the results of the work of our colleagues in other fields, especially linguistics, bilingualism and translation studies. Thus I have gradually sought to undermine the deleterious effects of scholarly ignorance on our understanding of this problem. Criticisms of my work have all suffered from the first major problem, scholarly membership of existing traditions. Accordingly, this book is intended to be a decisive contribution to the solution of the Son of man problem. I propose to bring all available and relevant knowledge to bear on this problem, regardless of the field of study from which significant insights can be gained. In this way, I propose to undermine attempted solutions which are essentially the continuation of old traditions, and to present a proof that my solution is correct.

Chapter Two

THE USE OF THE ARAMAIC TERM בר (א)נשׁ(א)

The main purpose of this chapter is to survey the idiomatic use of the Aramaic term בר (א)נשׁ(א). This lays the foundations for arguing in Chs 4–10 that this is the idiom which was used by the historical Jesus in those Son of man sayings which he actually spoke and which have survived in Greek translation in the synoptic Gospels. For this purpose I use Aramaic of different dates and dialects, because hardly any first century Galilean Aramaic has survived. This is legitimate because Aramaic was such a stable language, the vocabulary and syntax of which changed relatively slowly over a period of many centuries. I therefore begin by illustrating this.

1. The Stability of the Aramaic Language

Aramaic was a particularly stable language after it was spread in standard form by the Persian bureaucracy.[1] Even before this, it had features which are found later in the Talmuds and in Jewish midrashim. For example, the Sefire inscriptions, three steles set up *c.* 750 BCE, contain words still found more than a millennium later in Talmud and midrash, including אב, 'father', בין, 'between', גבר, 'man', (א)דם, 'blood', and הוי, 'to be'. Linguistic features in use for more than a millennium include the construct state. The term בר (א)נשׁ(א) belongs here, for it occurs already at Sefire III,16 and it was still in use centuries later.

Such evidence reflects the fact that Aramaic was the *lingua franca* of the Assyrian empire as early as the eighth century BCE, especially in the provinces 'Beyond the River'. It superseded Akkadian as the main language of communication even internally during the period of the Babylonian empire, when many Jews were exiled to Babylon. Aramaic was also the *lingua franca* of the whole Persian empire. This is the cultural background of the replacement of Hebrew by Aramaic as the normal language of communication between Jewish people. By the time of Jesus, Aramaic had for a long time been the *lingua franca* of Jewish people in Israel and round the fertile crescent to Babylon.

---

1.   On the emergence of distinctive Aramaic features, and standardization through Official Aramaic, see especially J. Huehnergard, 'What is Aramaic?', *Aram* 7 (1995), pp. 261–82.

This situation continued for centuries. This is reflected in the fact that many words found at Qumran before the time of Jesus were still in use in the Talmuds and in rather late Jewish midrashim. As well as those already mentioned, such words include זער, 'seed', חבר, 'companion', טלל, 'to cover', ידע, 'to know', and כל, 'all, every'. Syntactic features common for centuries include the narrative use of the participle. The term בר (א)נש(א) belongs here too, for it occurs at Qumran in both singular and plural, and it is quite normal in more extensive documents of later date. Similarly, many words found in the Qumran texts are attested abundantly centuries later in Syriac. As well as those already mentioned, these include לא, 'not', מלך, 'king', נפל 'to fall', סוף, 'end', and עלל, 'enter'. The placement of a suffix on a noun before the particle ד or די, 'of', followed by the noun anticipated by the suffix, is also found at Qumran and common in Syriac. The term בר (א)נש(א) belongs here too, for it occurs at Qumran in both singular and plural, and it is quite normal in more extensive Syriac documents of later date, just as in later Jewish sources.

As far as the development of Aramaic is concerned, the importance of the Qumran discoveries is to make this stable situation clearer. This also means that, as far as it goes, Qumran Aramaic can safely be used in the reconstruction of sayings of Jesus. It does not however go far enough, for the Dead Sea scrolls do not contain enough Aramaic to form a language. If therefore we confine ourselves to them, we do not have enough Aramaic to reconstruct the whole language of anyone. Accordingly, we must make careful use of later Aramaic sources too. I illustrate this with some examples from the synoptic Gospels.

At Mk 5.41, we have Jesus' words in the original Aramaic transliterated into Greek letters, and translated into Greek:

Ταλιθα κουμ, ὅ ἐστιν μεθερμηνενόμενον Τὸ κοράσιον, σοὶ λέγω, ἔγειρε.

The first word, טליתא, is properly attested both in later Jewish Aramaic and in Syriac. It is in the emphatic state because it is a form of address, overliterally translated with the Greek definite article. Would anyone seriously suggest that Jesus did not say this because טליתא is not found in the Dead Sea scrolls or in earlier Aramaic? One hopes not: it is straightforward evidence that Jesus' speech included words not found in earlier Aramaic because there is so little earlier Aramaic extant. The words σοὶ λέγω are simply explicitative. The next interesting point is the form κουμ. The verb קום is widely attested both before and after the time of Jesus. Its 2.f.sg.imp. is written קומי (e.g. Dan. 7.5), to which some MSS of this verse have corrected it. There is however ample evidence that final vowels after the tone syllable, including this one, were quiescent in Syriac and in Christian Palestinian Aramaic, though they are written down in standard texts and textbooks.[2] This is accordingly straightforward evidence that Jesus' idiolect, and therefore surely his Galilean dialect, had this particular isogloss in common with these later dialects.

2.   Th. Nöldeke, *Compendious Syriac Grammar* (trans. J. A. Crichton; London: Williams & Norgate, 1904), pp. 35–6, 103–4; F. Schulthess, *Grammatik des christlich-palästinischen Aramäisch* (Tübingen: J. C. B. Mohr (Paul Siebeck), 1924), pp. 16, 62.

At Mk 7.34, another of Jesus' words is transliterated and translated:

Εφφαθα, ὅ ἐστιν, Διανοίχθητι.

Here the form Εφφαθα caused scholars much trouble, and before we learnt from the Dead Sea scrolls how much Hebrew influenced the Aramaic of our period, it was frequently suggested that this form was Hebrew, not Aramaic. More recently, Wilcox has shown that the ת of the 2 m.sg.imp.Ithpe'el of פתח has been assimilated to the following פ, just as in the later source Vat.Ebr.440 of Gen. 49.1.[3] It follows that Jesus' Galilean dialect had this feature in common with some later Jewish Aramaic.

An important loanword not found in the scrolls or in earlier Aramaic is φαρισαῖοι, representing פרישין or פרושין. It is absent from early sources because there were no Pharisees before the second century BCE. It is absent from a few Dead Sea scrolls for the same reason and from the others for two different reasons. Many of the scrolls do not concern such sectarian matters, and Hebrew ones which do call them by the polemical term דורשי החלקות. This is another important word which requires us to study later source material, including in this case Josephus, who also uses it as a loanword.

The Greek text of the Gospels also shows interference from Aramaic found only in later sources. For example, at Lk. 14.18 the expression ἀπὸ μιᾶς is not satisfactory Greek. It is a literal translation of the idiomatic Syriac expression מן חדא, which means 'all at once', and which is found also in Christian Palestinian Aramaic. We must infer that מן חדא was in use in the Aramaic of our period.[4] In some cases, a word which Jesus must have used occurs in earlier Aramaic sources, but is only found in later sources with a metaphorical meaning required by a Gospel passage. For example, at Mk 14.21 ὑπάγει is used with reference to Jesus' forthcoming death. The Greek word ὑπάγω was not a normal term for dying, whereas the equivalent Aramaic אזל was used with this reference. There are plenty of examples of this in later Jewish Aramaic (including passage 27 below), and in Syriac, and the word itself occurs in earlier sources with the mundane meaning 'go'. We must infer that this word was already used as a metaphor for death in first century Galilee.[5]

Finally, some words are standard but rare because they refer to things which are not normally discussed in extant texts. These words include נגעא, 'mint', שבתא, 'dill', שברא, 'rue', כמונא, 'cummin', which we need in order to understand the Aramaic background of Mt. 23.23//Lk. 11.42. In each case, the word ought not to be in doubt, because there is only one Aramaic word extant. None of them occurs at anything like the right period because sources such as the Dead Sea scrolls do not contain any discussions of herbs.[6]

---

3.   M. Wilcox, 'Semitisms in the New Testament', ANRW II.25.2 (1984), pp. 978–1029 (998–9).

4.   See further Casey, *Aramaic Sources of Mark's Gospel*, pp. 42–3, 53–4.

5.   See further Casey, *Aramaic Sources of Mark's Gospel*, pp. 233–6.

6.   See further Casey, *Aramaic Approach to Q*, pp. 57, 72–3.

Although the term בר (א)נש(א) is attested in earlier Aramaic, its frequency belongs with this class of evidence. Ὁ υἱὸς τοῦ ἀνθρώπου occurs no less than 14 times in Mark, and 8 times in Q: there are 69 occurrences in the synoptic Gospels as a whole, and when all parallels are discounted, this still leaves no less than 38 independent sayings. It follows that בר (א)נש(א) was as normal in first century Galilean Aramaic as it is in later Jewish sources and in Syriac. It also follows from the stability of the Aramaic language that we are perfectly entitled to use later sources to help us understand how it was used.

2. Generic and Optional Use of the Emphatic State

Like all Aramaic nouns, בר (א)נש(א) may be used in the emphatic or definite or determined state, בר (א)נשא, or it may be in the absolute or indefinite state, בר (א)נש. To some extent this is related to dialect. In Syriac, and in some late texts in Jewish Aramaic, the difference between the states broke down. This breakdown took the form of increased use of the emphatic state, so that in Syriac this is the normal form of the noun. Equally, in generic and some other uses, optional use of either state is found throughout the whole Aramaic corpus down to the time of Jesus, and in some later documents in Jewish Aramaic too. This is central to the use of בר (א)נש(א), because it is a generic term in all its uses, including the particular idiomatic use of it employed by the historical Jesus. We must therefore consider next the optional use of the emphatic state in generic expressions, as well as with some unique items such as the heavens and the earth, where also the meaning cannot be affected by which state of the noun is employed.

Some variation is found even before the Persian period.[7] For example, in a letter of 605 BCE, we find שמיא וארקא for 'heaven and earth' in line 2: one line later, however, שמין is used for 'heaven'. This shows the emphatic state already in use for the earth, and optional for the heavens. Among abundant examples of the generic use of the emphatic state from before the time of Jesus, we find in the proverbs of Ahiqar דגנא וחנטתא for 'grain and wheat', רשיעא for a generically wicked person, and עתירא for a generically rich person (Ahiqar lines 129, 171, 207). Likewise, in biblical Aramaic the vessels of the house of God were די דהבה וכספא, 'of gold and silver' (Ezra 5.14), and before he sent for them, Nebuchadnezzar drank חמרא, 'wine' (Dan. 5.1). Similarly at Qumran, we find ימא for the sea at 11QTgJob XXX,6, where MT (Job 38.8) has the bare ים; ארעא for the earth at 11QTgJob XXXI,2, where MT (Job 38.24) has the bare ארץ; נשרא, 'the eagle', at 11QTgJob XXXIII,8, where MT (Job 39.27) has the bare נשר; כפנא, 'famine' at 1QapGen XIX,10, which is based on Gen. 12.10 where we find the bare רעב; חזוא for a vision at 1QapGen XXI,8; צדקתא, 'righteousness' at 4Q542 I i 12; and חמסה, 'violence' at 4Q En[a] 1 iv 8 (*1 En.* 9.1).

---

7.   On the origin of the emphatic state, or postpositive article, see J. Tropper, 'Die Herausbildung des bestimmten Artikels im Semitischen', *JSS* 46 (2001), pp. 1–31, with bibliography.

The emphatic state was however optional for such expressions. So we find in the proverbs of Ahiqar מלך for a generic king, and צדיק for a generically righteous person (lines 107-8, 126): and at the end of the fifth century BCE, דהב and כסף for 'gold' and 'silver' (Cowley 30, line 28).[8] Similarly in biblical Aramaic, we find דהב and כסף for 'gold' and 'silver' (Dan. 2.32), and צדקה for 'righteousness' (Dan. 4.24). At Qumran, Noah's vineyard produces חמר (1QapGen XII,13), and חכמה is used in the absolute state for 'wisdom' (11QTgJob XXX,2, MT Job 38.4 בינה).

As far as we can tell, usage changed over time, with increasing use of the emphatic state. This does not however mean that the emphatic state lost its force in all kinds of expression, nor that it became necessary even in generic expressions. It is especially important that there are documents which have similar usages of both emphatic and absolute states, some of them in close proximity. This leaves no doubt about the optional nature of the use of the emphatic and absolute states in some kinds of expression.

For example, both קרב and קרבא are used for 'war', 'battle', in the opening lines of the Aramaic translation of the Bisitun inscription of Darius I; in a letter of 407 BCE, we find pillars of אבנא, 'stone', and gateways of אבן in the very next line (Cowley 30, lines 9-10). In biblical Aramaic, we find דהב 'gold', and נחש, 'bronze' at Dan. 2.32, and דהבא and נחשא at Dan. 2.38-39; even more strikingly, in Daniel 7 the first beast was given לבב אנש, a human heart (Dan. 7.4), whereas the little horn was given eyes כעיני אנשא, 'like the eyes of a man' (Dan. 7.8). Similarly at Qumran we find בקושטא at 1QapGen II,5 and בקושט at 1QapGen II,10, both meaning 'in truth': שמחא, 'joy', at 4Q542 I i 3, and שמח at line 11; קשט, 'truth' at 4Q212 iv.12 al (*1 En.* 93.10) and קושטא at ii.20 (*1 En.* 91.19).

In 11QTgJob, we find אנש רשעין (11QTgJob XI,3) for אדם רשע (Job 27.13), as well as אנש רשיעיא (11QTgJob XXV,6) for אדם חנף (Job 34.30). A particular decision was required by the translator whenever a one-consonant preposition was attached directly to the front of a noun, because in such cases the presence or absence of the article is not marked in a consonantal Hebrew text. In a devastating review of scholarship on the Hebrew article, Barr showed that the vocalization of the MT produced far more occurrences of the article in some texts than their authors had written in front of nouns without attached prepositions.[9] It follows that the vocalization of the MT is no guide to how our translator understood the text. It is accordingly significant that there are several cases where he took different decisions about the same or similar generic nouns. So we find מטר (11QTgJob XXVIII,5) for מטר (Job 36.27), and למטרא (11QTgJob XXXI, 3 and 5) for לשטף (Job 38.25) and for למטר (Job 38.28); ערפלין (11QTgJob XXX,7) for ערפל (Job 38.9) and ערפלא (11QTgJob XXIX,8) for לשחקים (Job 37.18); כ]רוח (11QTgJob XVI,4) for כרוח (Job 30.15) and לרוחא (11QTgJob XIII,6) for לרוח (Job 28.25); כענן (11QTgJob XVI,4) for כעב (Job 30.15) and לעננא (11QTgJob III,8) for לעב (Job 20.6).

8.   A. Cowley, *Aramaic Papyri of the Fifth Century B.C.* (Oxford: Clarendon, 1923).
9.   J. Barr, '"Determination" and the Definite Article in Biblical Hebrew', *JSS* 34 (1989), pp. 307–35 (325–33).

All this evidence shows that in generic and some other expressions, the use of either state was optional. It is therefore natural to find that בר (א)נש(א) may be used in either state, since it is a generic expression.

3. *The Meaning and Use of* בר (א)נש(א)

Being written in Greek for Greek-speaking Christians, the Gospels use ὁ υἱὸς τοῦ ἀνθρώπου in sayings of Jesus. There should be no doubt that, in authentic sayings of Jesus, this represents his use of בר (א)נש(א). The following reasons should be regarded as decisive. Firstly, there are abundant reasons for supposing that Jesus spoke Aramaic.[10] Secondly, the Greek expression ὁ υἱὸς τοῦ ἀνθρώπου is not normal monoglot Greek, and could be understood as a literal translation of a Semitic expression. Thirdly, the Greek υἱὸς overlaps greatly in semantic area with the Aramaic בר and the Hebrew בן. It is extensively used in the LXX to render בן, in both literal and figurative senses, including expressions which are not normal monoglot Greek, but literal translations (e.g. υἱὸν δυνάμεως for בן־חיל, 1 Sam. 14.52).[11] Fourthly, the Aramaic (א)נש(א) overlaps extensively in semantic area with the Greek ἄνθρωπος. Fifthly, the Hebrew בן אדם, the philological equivalent of the Aramaic בר (א)נש(א), is normally rendered υἱὸς ἀνθρώπου in the LXX, by several different translators. Sixthly, the Gospel expression ὁ υἱὸς τοῦ ἀνθρώπου evidently did not cause difficulty in understanding at the time. It must therefore represent a normal Aramaic expression rather than an unusual one. This requirement is satisfied by בר (א)נש(א). Seventhly, some Gospel sayings (notably Mk 13.26; 14.62) make use of Dan. 7.13, where בר אנש is certainly the underlying Aramaic expression.[12] I therefore proceed with the known use of the Aramaic term בר (א)נש(א).

In the first place, בר (א)נש(א) was a normal term for 'man'. Examples of this include many general statements, such as passage 1.

1. 1QapGen. XXI,13: MT שיא (Gen. 13.16).

ואשגה זרעך כעפר ארעא די לא ישכח כול בר אנוש לממניה
And I will multiply your seed like the dust of the earth which no son of man can count …

---

10.   These have been repeatedly surveyed. See especially J. T. Marshall, 'The Aramaic Gospel', *The Expositor*, 4th series, 3 (1891), pp. 1–17, 109–24, 275–91; Meyer, *Jesu Muttersprache*, esp. pp. 35–72; G. H. Dalman, *Die Worte Jesu*. Bd I. *Einleitung und wichtige Begriffe* (Leipzig: Hinrichs, 1898), pp. 1–72; *idem*, *The Words of Jesus. I. Introduction and Fundamental Ideas* (trans. D. M. Kay; Edinburgh: T&T Clark, 1902; 2nd edn, 1930), pp. 1–88; *idem*, *Jesus-Jeschua. Die drei Sprachen Jesu* (Leipzig: Hinrichs'sche, 1922), pp. 6–25; *idem*, *Jesus-Jeshua. Studies in the Gospels* (trans. P. P. Levertoff; London: SPCK, 1929), pp. 7–27; J. Jeremias, *New Testament Theology* (trans. J. Bowden; London: SPCK), pp. 3–29; J. A. Fitzmyer, 'The Languages of Palestine in the First Century A.D.', *CBQ* 32 (1970), pp. 501–31, rev. *Wandering Aramean*, pp. 29–56; G. Schwarz, *Und Jesus sprach. Untersuchungen zur aramäischen Urgestalt der Worte Jesu* (BWANT 118 = VI,18. Stuttgart: Kohlhammer, 1985, 2nd edn 1987), esp. pp. 5–48; Casey, *Aramaic Sources of Mark's Gospel*, esp. pp. 76–9, 83–8; Casey, *Aramaic Approach to Q*, pp. 53–6.
11.   See further pp. 256–61 below.
12.   Casey, *Son of Man*, Ch. 8; pp. 215–6, 242–5 below.

Here the fact that בר אנוש represents the Hebrew איש must mean that it was felt to be especially suitable for a general statement. This would surely not be the case if (א)נש(א) בר also brought to mind a resplendent heavenly figure, the Son of Man Concept beloved of too much scholarship.[13] This passage was written as near to the time of Jesus as we can get with Aramaic source material.

Since the term (א)נש(א) בר was a general term for 'man', it is used in tractates about humankind, and in the most general references to the composition of human beings and the variety of our life experiences. This is illustrated in passage 2.

> 2. Bardaisan, *The Book of the Laws of the Countries*, p. 559 lines 11–14.
>
> כינה דברנשא הנו דנתילד ונתרבא ודנקום באקמא ודנולד ודנקש כד אכל וכד שתא וכד דמך וכד מתתעיר ודנמות.
>
> This is the nature of (the son of) man, that he should be born and grow up and reach his peak and reproduce and grow old, while eating and drinking and sleeping and waking, and that he should die.

Passage 2 is the oldest general discussion of humankind extant in Aramaic sources. This is the only reason why it is the earliest text in which (א)נש(א) בר has all the most basic human experiences, including death. It is not however true of everyone. When it was written, many children died before they were grown up, some people had no children, and relatively few grew old. This was not considered relevant to this general description of human life.

Death is such a natural part of life that the death of the son of man is found in Jewish Aramaic sources as soon as they are sufficiently extensive. Passage 3 is a general statement inserted into the story of how Ḥaninah ben Dosa was bitten by a snake when he was praying, with the result that the snake died. I quote MS Leiden Or.4720: those texts which transmit בר נש in the indefinite state do not offer any difference in meaning.

> 3. y. Ber 5,1/26 (9a).
>
> כד הוות נכית לבר נשא אין בר נשא קדים למיא חברברא מיית ואין חברברא קדים למיא בר נשא מיית.
>
> When it bites a/the (son of) man, if the (son of) man reaches (the) water first the snake dies, and if the snake reaches (the) water first, the (son of) man dies.

Since (א)נש(א) בר is a normal term for 'man', the minimal requirements for its use are that human beings are referred to, and that there is a general level of meaning. We have however already seen that it is not necessary for son of man statements to be literally true of all people. This is further illustrated by passage 3, which is false and refers only to people who have been bitten by a snake. It is conspicuously not true of Ḥaninah ben Dosa, who survived through his prayerful relationship with God, not by making a rapid dash for the nearest pond. Passage 4 further illustrates the kind of limited references which are quite normal in the use of son of man statements:

---

13.   See further pp. 16–18, 22–30 above; pp. 82–115 below.

4. John of Dalyatha, *Letters* 49, 13.

מן בתר הנא שוחלפא אתא בתרה שוחלפא אחרנא דלבשא לה לברנשא נורא מן פסת רגלה ועמדא למוחה דמא
דחאר ברנשא הו בה לא חזא לפגרא מרכבא אן להד נורא דלביש.

After this transformation, there follows another transformation in which fire clothes the (son of) man from the soles of his feet up to his brain, so that when the (son of) man looks at himself he does not see his composite body, but only the fire with which he is clothed.

This is part of an account of an experience of ascetic visionaries, not part of the normal experience of everyone.

The term בר (א)נש(א) is also used in the plural with reference to people in general. This is illustrated by passages 5 and 6.

5. Dan. 2.37-38.

אנתה מלכא מלך מלכיא די אלה שמיא מלכותא חסנא ותקפא ויקרא יהב־לך ובכל די דארין בני־אנשא חיות ברא
ועוף־שמיא יהב בידך והשלטך בכלהון אנתה־הוא ראשה די דהבא.

You, king, king of kings, to whom the God of heaven has given the kingdom, power, might and glory, and has given into your hand the sons of men, the beasts of the field and the birds of the air, wherever they live, and has given you power over all of them – you are the head of gold.

This is the opening of Daniel's interpretation of King Nebuchadnezzar's dream. Here בני אנשא is a general term for people, in contrast to animals and birds. At the same time, the statement containing this expression is not true of everyone, but applies only to people in the Babylonian empire. This does not matter, for the four kingdom theory forms the general context, within which the statement is perceived to be true.

6. *1 Enoch* 22.3.

נפש]ת כל בני אנשא

the soul]s of all the sons of men

The context of this small Aramaic fragment is supplied by the Greek and Ethiopic versions. This is a place where the souls of all people are kept after their deaths until the final judgement. This time בני אנשא, combined with כל, really does refer to everyone. It is closely associated with death, one of the major facts of life.

These two passages exemplify the fact that, given the generic nature of the expression בר (א)נש(א), it has some overlap in semantic area with its own plural, בני (א)נשא, but the two forms are by no means interchangeable.

Naturally, the term בר (א)נש(א), being normal in natural Aramaic, was used in translation Aramaic as well. This is illustrated in passages 7 and 8.

7. Pesh Gen. 8.21: MT האדם (twice).

ואמר מריא בלבה לא אוסף תוב למלטה לארעא מטל בר אנשא מטל דיצרא דלבה דבר אנשא ביש מן טליותה.

And the Lord said in his heart, 'I will never again curse the ground because of (the son of) man, for the inclination of (the son of) man's heart is evil from his youth.'

Here בר אנשא is used twice for people as a whole, rendering the equally general האדם.

8. Tg. Jer. 51.43: MT בן אדם.

ארעא לא יתיב בה כל אנש ולא יעבר בה בר אנש
… a land in which no man lives, and which no son of man passes through.

Here בר אנש is used with the negative לא to mean no one, a standard usage with so general a term for people. It renders its nearest etymological equivalent in Hebrew, בן אדם. It is in parallel with the simple אנש, which translates the Hebrew איש. There is a massive overlap in semantic area between בר (א)נש(א) and the simple (א)נש(א). In the most straightforward usages, the decision between them is often a matter of sociolect or idiolect. Many authors used both. It is all the more striking that the idiomatic usage of בר (א)נש(א) which is the focus of the next section of this chapter has not been recorded with examples of the simple (א)נש(א).

Two examples of בר אנש in translation Aramaic, rendering the Hebrew בן אדם, have been found in the Job Targum from cave 11 at Qumran. These are presented as passages 9 and 10.

9. 11QTgJob IX,9 (MT Job 25.6 בן אדם).

וב]ראנש תולע[
How much less a mortal, a maggot, and a s]on of man, a wor[m!

Here, although just enough of the term survives at the edge of a small fragment, it is evident that בראנש has been used to translate בן אדם in a very general comparison of people to worms, in contrast with God. It has been written as a single word, as often later in both Jewish Aramaic and in Syriac.

10. 11QTgJob XXVI,2-3 (MT Job 35.8 בן אדם).

… ך חטיך ולבר אנש צדקתך […
Your sin [affects a man like yo]u, and your righteousness a son of man.

Here בר אנש has been used to translate בן אדם in a very general comment on the effect of Job's behaviour on other human beings.

The broad range of בר (א)נש(א) in natural Aramaic is reflected in the different Hebrew words which it is used to translate in the Aramaic translations of the Hebrew Bible. In addition to בן אדם as in passages 8–10, I have noted it used twice for האדם in passage 7, and in place of איש in the very midrashic passage 1. Passages 11–15 further illustrate its range.

11. Tg. Ps. 104.14-15: MT האדם, אנוש, אנוש:

דמרבי עסבא לבעירי וירקי לפולחנא דבר נשא למיפק לחמא מן ארעא וחמרא דמחדי ליבא דבר נשא לאנהרא
אפיא מן משחא ולחמא ליבא דבר נשא יסעד.
Who increases the grass for the cattle, and greens for the service of (the son of) man, to bring forth bread from the earth and wine which gladdens the heart of (the son of) man, to make his face shine with oil, and bread satisfies the heart of (the son of) man.

Here בר נשא is generic in all three examples of the definite state. As well as rendering האדם as in passage 7, it renders אנוש twice.

12. Ps-J Exod. 31.14: MT הנפש.

כל מאן דיעבד בה עיבידתא וישתיצי בר נשא ההוא מעמיה

… whoever does work on it, that (son of) man shall be destroyed from his people.

Here the context is working on the Sabbath day. The Hebrew הנפש is effectively used to mean any person. The translator found בר נשא a suitable rendering, because it is a general term for any person. The translator naturally also used ההוא to render the Hebrew ההוא. The result is no special idiom, but a normal anaphoric use of ההוא, so that בר נשא ההוא refers back to the person who works on the Sabbath. The next verse makes it clear that he is to be put to death, so this is another of the many examples of the association of (א)בר (א)נש(א) with death, an association which reflects the universality of human mortality.

13. Ps-J Lev. 13.24: MT בשׂר.

או בר נש ארום יהי במשכיה כואה דנור ...

Or if a (son of) man has a fiery burn in his skin …

Here the context is one of various kinds of skin disease. The Hebrew text uses בשׂר because the symptom is found in the flesh of the body. The translator has preferred to render it with בר נש because this is a general term for any person, and thus suitable for this completely indefinite reference.

14. Tg. Ps. 88.5: MT גבר.

הוית היך בר נש דלית לה חילא.

I have been like a (son of) man who has no strength.

The Hebrew גבר is usually rendered with the Aramaic (א)גבר, because this is the same word. In this case, however, the psalmist has made a completely generalized comparison of himself to people who are weak to the point of death. This comparison to anyone of a particular kind, or anyone in a particular situation, explains the translator's choice of the very general term בר נש to render גבר. The context shows a close, if metaphorical, association with death.

In view of the normal use of (א)בר (א)נש(א) both as a general term in natural Aramaic, and to render several different terms in Aramaic translations of the Bible, it is natural that we should also find it used in those Targums which add pieces to the translation of the Hebrew text. This is illustrated by passage 15.

15. Neof I, in an insertion at Gen. 49.22.

דין הוא יוסף גברא חסידא דלא אזל בתר חיוזי עייניה ולא בתר הרהורי לבוי אינון דמובדין לבר נשא מן עלמא.

This is Joseph, the pious man who has not gone after the impressions of his eyes nor after the imaginations of his heart. These are what destroy a(/the son of) man from the world.

Here, following on the description of Joseph, the targumist has added a general statement about the effects of certain human faults, and has used בר נשא because it is a normal term for people in general.

As a term for human beings, בר (א)נ(א)ש may also be used in the singular for a single individual, whether anonymous, generic or specific. This is illustrated in passages 16–19.

16. *y. Demai* 2, 1/17 (22d).

חד בר נש אייתי חדא אשפלה דקפלוטין לר׳ יצחק בר טבליי.

A (son of) man brought a basket of leeks to R. Isaac son of Tablai.

This is one of over 100 stories in the Yerushalmi which begin חד בר נש. Its point is to set up a situation so that a legal decision can be taken. In this case, a decision has to be taken as to whether some produce is liable to be tithed as doubtful produce. It is to be considered whether the nature of a given load can lead the matter to be settled, on the ground that such a load of produce would or would not be likely to have been produced locally or outside Israel. It matters who the rabbi is, but it does not matter who the person bringing the load is. It does have to be a person, however, so that a decision on his case can be taken. Hence it is appropriate to use a generic term for 'person' which could nonetheless refer to anyone.

17. *y. Shabb.* 1,7/10 (3c).

כן הוה ר׳ יונתן עבד כד הוה חמי בר נש רב עליל לקרתיה הוה משלח לה איקרין.

Thus R. Jonathan used to do. When he saw an important (son of) man entering his town, he used to send him a gift.

The general context concerns relationships with Gentiles on the Sabbath, and this shifts into this anecdote about R. Jonathan. The result of his behaviour is said to be that he found favour when a case involving an orphan or a widow came to court. Here בר נש is a generic indefinite expression, and qualified by רב it refers to any important person.

18. Narsai, *Homily on the Translation of Enoch and Elijah*, line 75.

חד ברנשא נטר בזהירא דלא חובלא

He preserved one (son of) man securely without corruption.

Here God has been clearly set up in the preceding context as the subject. The explanation of this sentence follows immediately, with Enoch being mentioned by name in line 77. The general background is the drastic corruption of most people at the time. Accordingly, חד ברנשא is in the first instance an indefinite generic, to indicate that when everyone else was corrupt, God preserved one being of the same species without corruption. At the same time, the context unfolds a reference to one single individual, Enoch.

19. Narsai, *Homily on the Translation of Enoch and Elijah*, line 425.

חד ברנשא משיחא דמנן על לה לוקדם

One (son of) man, the Messiah, who is of us, entered it first ...

The context makes clear that this is Jesus, shortly after his death and resurrection, entering the garden of Eden, where Enoch and Elijah already were. He then went on up to heaven. There is no problem in the collocation of son of man and Messiah. The Aramaic term משיחא could be used to indicate Jesus in the Syriac-speaking church in a way that was not possible during the ministry of Jesus. This is because of a major cultural change. At the time of Jesus the high priest was the most important anointed figure, as a king might also be. More would therefore be needed than the simple term משיחא to refer to a figure who might be thought of as anointed metaphorically because God had appointed him for an important prophetic task. In the Syriac-speaking church however, משיחא had become a term for Jesus alone, translating the Greek ὁ χριστός, and there was no other significant anointed figure in view. In these circumstances משיחא could function perfectly as a title, much like ὁ χριστός in Greek. This figure is referred to as חד ברנשא because his humanity was important. This was also much less likely to happen during the historic ministry, when Jesus' humanity was taken for granted by everyone, and no thought of his divinity had yet been entertained.

In general, therefore, בר (א)נש(א) was a general term for humankind. It could be used for everyone in general, or for a more restricted group of people. It could be used in the singular of a single individual person, whether anonymous, generic or specific. This forms the cultural background for the particular idiom central to this book, whereby a speaker might use a general statement containing the term בר (א)נש(א) to say something about himself, or himself and others, or about whoever was clearly from the context, particularly in mind.

4. *The Particular Idiomatic Use of* בר (א)נש(א)

I now present the known examples of this particular idiom. It will be noted that בר (א)נש(א) may be in either the definite or indefinite state. This is especially clear in Jewish Aramaic, where it is due to the more general custom that generic expressions might be in either state. The Syriac examples are however all in the definite state, except in passage 47 where ברנש follows כל, because in Syriac the definite state was the normal state of the noun. The earliest example is from long before the time of Jesus.

20. Sefire III.14–17.

והן יסק על לבבך ותשא על שפתיך להמתתי ויסק על לבב בר ברך וישא על שפתוה להמתת בר ברי או הן יסק
על לבב עקרך וישא על שפתוה להמתת עקרי והן יסק על [ל]בב מלכי ארפד בכל מה זי ימות בר אנש שקרתם
לכל אלהי עדיא זי בספרא זנה.

And if you think of killing me and you put forward such a plan, and if your son's son thinks of killing my son's son and puts forward such a plan, or if your descendants think of killing my descendants and put forward such a plan, and if the kings of Arpad think of it, in any case that a (son of) man dies, you have been false to all the gods of the treaty which is in this inscription.

This example, with בר אנש in line 16, was written *c.* 750 BCE, in the name of Bar-ga'yah, king of Kittik.[14] It uses בר אנש in a general statement. In view of the cultural

---

14.   E. Lipiński, *The Aramaeans. Their Ancient History, Culture, Religion* (OLA 100. Leuven: Peeters, 2000), Ch. IX, 'Kittik or Bēt-Ṣullul'.

context, it is most unlikely that it was intended to refer to the death of anyone other than people on the side of the king of Kittik, and it probably refers only to the king and his descendants. Precise description is not part of this idiom, the effectiveness of which depends on the plausibility of the general level of meaning. When this passage is taken together with many later passages, it should be obvious that dying is a universal experience characteristic of בר (א)נש(א), and that this was already so long before the time of Jesus.

21. y. Ber. 1,5/10 (3b) (//y. Shabb. 1,5/14 (3b)).

הוינא מתבעי קומוי קומוי רחמנא דיתברי לבר נשא תרין פומין, חד דהוה לעי באוריתא וחד דעביד ליה כל צורכיה.

... I would have asked the Merciful that two mouths should be created for (the son of) man, one to study the Law and one to see to all his (other) needs.

This is the first of several examples from the Yerushalmi. In all cases I quote Leiden Or. 4720 from the synoptic edition of the Yerushalmi, and comment on significant variants. Here, where Leiden Or. 4720 has בר נשא, the other extant MS which is neither corrupt nor mutilated, the London MS BL Or. 2822, has the indefinite state בר נש. This makes no difference. The saying is attributed to R. Simeon son of Yohai, who flourished in the first half of the second century CE. The general level of meaning does not refer to all people, for most Gentiles did not study the Law, and R. Simeon is not likely to have asked for an extra mouth for them for such a purpose. Rather, this shows that the general level of meaning of בר (א)נש(א) in this idiom may apply to a social subgroup to which the speaker belongs. Equally, R. Simeon will have had himself especially in mind, so this is a straightforward example of a general statement made with reference to a particular person. The parallel at y. Shabb. 1,5/14 (3b) has להדן לבר נשא. This changes the reference of the term בר נשא. It is here a reference to R. Simeon son of Yohai alone, and no longer has the general level of meaning.

Another example of the idiomatic use of a general statement with בר (א)נש(א) made to refer especially to the speaker, or the speaker and someone else, is attributed to R. Simeon son of Yohai in passage 29. It is significant that two examples should be attributed to an early rabbi, who lived some of his life in Galilee.

22. y. Ber. 2,8/3 (5b).

תלמידיה דבר נשא חביב עליה כבריה

The disciple of a (son of) man is as dear to him as his son.

In this passage, two other MSS have בר נשא: Vat. Ebr. 133 has בר נשה, a different spelling of the emphatic state. Thus all four manuscripts have the emphatic state in this example of the idiom. It is a general statement in which בר נשא refers especially to R. Ḥiyya bar Adda. In its context, it explains why he was so dear to Resh Laqish that when he died Resh Laqish received condolences for him and did his eulogy. It is obviously not true of everyone, for most people do not have disciples, and some people do not have sons. This does not in any way inhibit the use of בר נשא, which is frequently used like this with reference to a limited group of people. Moreover, this general term does provide a genuine reference to R. Ḥiyya bar Adda, since without this the passage would not make sense.

23. y. Ber. 2,8/10 (5c).

בר נש דאימיה מבסרא ליה ואיתתיה דאבוהי מוקרא ליה להן ייזל ליה

A (son of) man whose mother despises him and a(nother) wife of his father honours him, where shall he go?

This is a general statement referring especially to the speaker, R. Kahana. It is an unusual example in that it might reasonably be described as ambiguous, or perhaps rather deceptive. The ambiguity in this deceptive statement is produced mainly by the allegorical concealment of Israel by 'mother', and of 'Babylon' by 'a wife of his father', rather than by the use of בר נש. The result is quite different from the result of any son of man saying in the Gospels. R. Johanan answered the question at the level of a purely general statement, and when R. Kahana acted by applying this to himself and going to Babylon, R. Johanan made it clear that he did not understand why he had gone. Accordingly, from the perspective of the speaker, R. Kahana, the general comment really did apply to himself, even if R. Johanan did not realize this. Johanan's disciples then explained the self-reference to him. This is the necessary result of the kind of ambiguous sentence that this idiom can be used to produce, and it is not a reaction found in the Gospels. It is the only ambiguous example so far recorded from our Aramaic sources, and the Gospel evidence also does not imply ambiguity in the usage of Jesus, which therefore corresponds to normal Aramaic usage.

24. y. Ber. 2,8/12 (5c).

רבנן, מה ביש מנהגא דהכא דלא אכיל בר נש ליטרא דקופד עד דמחו ליה חד קורסם.

Rabbis, how evil is the custom of this land, that a (son of) man cannot eat a pound of meat until they have given him a lash!

This is a general statement referring especially to the speaker, R. Ze'ira. The general context is that of a group of stories about rabbis who immigrated to Israel from Babylon, a situation in which anyone is liable to be unaware of local customs. R. Ze'ira went to buy a pound of meat from a butcher. When he asked the price, he was told '50 minas and a lash'. He offered more and more money to get his pound of meat without suffering a lash, but when his offer of 100 minas was still refused, he gave in with the words עביד כמינהגך, 'Do according to your custom'. Passage 24 is a comment which he made to his colleagues in the evening.

R. Ze'ira's colleagues did not accept that this was a custom in Israel, and made enquiries as a result of which it emerged that the butcher was already dead. R. Ze'ira refuted any idea that he was responsible for divine vengeance on his behalf by saying that he was not really angry with the butcher because סברת דמנהגא כן, 'I thought that the custom (was) like that'. It is clear from the reactions of R. Ze'ira's colleagues, and from his own final admission, that he was the only person who was lashed by the butcher when he bought his pound of meat, but this does not diminish the general nature of the statement using the general term בר נש. In relating a humiliating incident, R. Ze'ira deliberately used a general statement in order to avoid referring directly to himself. His three references to local custom show that he did not believe that he was the only person to be treated like this. Since however he was wrong about the custom in a place with which he was not familiar, it is clear that he felt able to use a general statement by generalizing from his own experience. At one level, therefore, this is on an extreme wing of the use of these statements, in that the majority of them are true at least of a social subgroup of people.

Although this example is in Jewish Aramaic which has no particular Babylonian features, and in particular does not have the Babylonian spelling בר אינש, it should be noted that it is attributed to a rabbi who had just come from Babylon.

25. y. Ber. 3,1/12 (6a).

אמר לון, רבנן, אכן בר נש עביד לחבריה.

He said to them: Rabbis, does a (son of) man treat his colleague like this?

This is a saying of R. Isaac. It is difficult to know which R. Isaac because of textual variants: most probably he was son of R. Hewa the scribe. The situation arose when R. Isaac was bereaved of a close relative, so R. Mana and R. Judan went to call on him. And there was good wine, and they drank a lot and laughed. This was within the parameters of permissible customs in cases of bereavement, with the obvious intention of trying to make the bereaved person feel valued and a little less miserable.

Next day, however, R. Mana and R. Judan wanted to call on R. Isaac again! It is this which led R. Isaac to make the above comment. He concluded by reminding them that the previous day they had done everything but get up and dance. Clearly, therefore, the above question is a general question expecting an answer on the lines of 'not really', or 'one shouldn't' or the like. The term בר נש has a general level of meaning which does not however refer to all people, but rather to rabbis with colleagues who are also rabbis. At the same time, בר נש refers primarily to R. Mana and R. Judan, as is obvious from the context.

26. y. Ber. 8,1/11 (12a).

רבי אבהו כד הוה אזיל לדרומה הוה עבד כרבי חנינא וכד הוה נחית לטיבריא הוה עבד כרבי יוחנן דלא מפלג על בר נש באתריה.

When R. Abbahu went to the south, he did according to R. Haninah, and when he went to Tiberias, he did according to R. Johanan, so that he might not differ from a (son of) man in his place.

Here בר נש refers especially to R. Haninah and R. Johanan. The narrator makes a general statement which presupposes that one should follow the halakhah of the local rabbi, which also conforms one's behaviour to that of the local Jewish community. Thus the general level of meaning is central in providing an explanation of R. Abbahu's behaviour. The general level of meaning does not refer to all people, but rather to rabbis in charge of communities.

27. y. Kil. 9,4/4 (32b)//y. Ket. 12,3/4 (35a)//Ber.R. 100,2.

לא כמה דבר אינש אזיל הוא אתי

It is not as a son of man goes that he comes (again).

The *editio princeps* follows Leiden Or. 4720 with the Babylonian spelling of the absolute state אינש. MS Vat. Ebr. 133 has בר נשה, a western spelling of the emphatic state: Paris Bib.Nat.Heb.1389 has בר נש, the standard Yerushalmi spelling of the absolute state: and the London MS. Or.2822 has בר אנש. The parallel passage y. Ket. 12,3/4(35a) is less well attested. Here Leiden Or. 4720 has בר נשא, the standard Yerushalmi spelling of the emphatic state, and it is followed by the *editio princeps*. It is difficult to sort out the text of passages like this. It is however surely probable that the distinctive Babylonian spelling בר אינש is secondary, and that the prosthetic א in בר אנש of London Or. 2822 is due to it. Since the following saying of the rabbis has בר נש in the absolute state in most witnesses including Leiden Or. 4720 of both passages, with only Vat.Ebr.133 having the emphatic state בר נשה, it is surely more probable than not that the original text of the first saying had the emphatic state בר נשה in both passages. It is however much more important that the meaning of this saying, and its usage of בר (א)נש(א), is not affected by these variations. This idiomatic usage is simply not dependent on spelling, and not altogether on dialect.

The saying is attributed to Rabbi. He is recorded to have been buried in a single sheet on account of his use of this saying. This means that the general statement was applied directly to him. It is one of a number of sayings about burial, and our sources show so great an interest in the general level of meaning that they contradict it:

ורבנין אמרין כמה דבר נש אזיל הוא אתי

And the rabbis say: as a son of man goes so will he come (again).

This express interest in the general level of meaning is quite unusual in extant sources. It in no way undermines the practical way in which it was applied to Rabbi in particular.

28. y. Kil. 9,4/19(32c)//y. Ket. 12,3/19(35b)//Ber.R.100,2//b. Suk. 53a.

רגליי דבר נשא ערבתי ביה למיקמתיה כל הן דהוא מתבע

The feet of a son of man are his surety to bring him to wherever he is wanted.

The Babylonian version, which naturally has the Babylonian spelling בר אינש, is the clearest, so I begin with it.

28a. b. Sukkah 53a.

רגלוהי דבר איניש אינון ערבין ביה לאתר דמיתבעי תמן מובילין יהית.

The feet of a son of man are a surety for him. To the place where he is wanted, there they take him.

This saying occurs twice. In the first instance, it is attributed to R. Joḥanan, and it appears to be quite general. It is followed by a story of two Ethiopians who attended Solomon, and who died when they reached the appointed place. The story ends with Solomon applying this general statement to the two Ethiopians. This is accordingly another example of the Aramaic term 'son of man' in a general statement applied to people made obvious by the context. It is the only version in which this is absolutely clear. In both Yerushalmi versions the connection is more tenuous, and Ber.R. 100,2 does not have this story, to the point where the saying in these versions can barely be regarded as an example of this idiom.

It is therefore especially useful to have this Babylonian example, which is clear and which indicates that the idiom was more widely used than has sometimes been thought. It is also important that, however general the statement may be perceived to be, it really does apply to the two Ethiopians. At one level, it is on the extreme end of this idiomatic usage, in that it is clear from the parallels that the saying could circulate independently.

29. y. Shevi. 9,1/12 (38b)//Ber.R. 79,6.

ציפור מבלעדי שמיא לא יבדא. כל שכן בר נשא.

A bird does not perish without the will of Heaven. How much less a (/the son of) man.

This is from the story of R. Simeon, son of Yohai, holed up in a cave on the run from the Roman authorities after the Bar Kokhba war. He was wondering whether it was safe to come out. He saw some birds being hunted: some were captured, while others escaped, and the fate of all of them depended on the judgement of a heavenly voice which he heard. He made the above comment, and then emerged from the cave. It follows that he intended to apply the statement to himself. At the same time, each of the sentences is a general statement. The comment on the birds is obviously a general comment on the fate of several birds. Equally, the son of man statement which balances it cannot lose its general level of meaning, which would be entirely acceptable in R. Simeon's culture.

This version of the story uses the definite state בר נשא. Among the variants in the parallel at Ber.R. 79,6 are the use of the indefinite state בר נש. This in no way affects the meaning. The parallel at Ber.R. 79,6 also tells the story somewhat differently, in that R. Simeon has his son with him. Thus the general statement applies both to R. Simeon and his son, who emerges from the cave with him. This illustrates the flexibility inherent in this idiomatic usage, the reference being determined by the context. At the same time, the emergence of R. Simeon and his son from the cave shows that, in this version of the story, R. Simeon really did intend the statement to be about both of them.

30. y. 'Erub 9,3/1(25c)//y. Yeb. 4,7/4 (5d).

ולית בר נש הוי שמע מילה דלית חברה שמיע לה.

Is there no (son of) man who hears something which his colleague does not hear?

This saying occurs at y. 'Erub 9,3/1 in a complex debate in which different opinions are expressed about the liability or otherwise of someone who carries from one domain to another if a courtyard is breached to a public way. R. Ze'ira and R. Ila offer a different opinion from R. Zeriqan and R. Jacob bar Bun in the name of R. Ḥaninah. R. Zeriqan says that he spent a lot of time with R. Jacob bar Bun in legal discussion, but never heard this matter from him. One of the others replies with the above saying. Here בר נש is the speaker, who did hear this from R. Jacob bar Bun, and his colleague is R. Zeriqan, who did not. Thus this is a general statement, in which בר נש refers especially to the speaker.

The parallel at y. Yeb. 4,7/4 has a very similar comment attributed to different rabbis debating a different topic, but with a very similar disagreement about the transmission of an opinion, this time an alleged opinion of R. Hoshaiah. R. Johanan comments that he sat before R. Hoshaiah many times and never heard this from him. The response is a similar sentence to the one given above. This time בר נש refers especially to R. Abbahu and R. Eleazar, and חבריה refers especially to R. Johanan.

At one level this is on an extreme end of the usage of this idiom, in that once it was being transmitted the saying could be reapplied to different rabbis in the same situation.

31. y. Pes. 6,3/3 (33c).

ואית בר נש אמר לרבי או חליף.

And does a (son of) man say to his master, 'Or the opposite!'?

This is from a complex discussion of whether aspects of Passover celebrations override the sabbath. A dispute between R. Eliezer and R. Aqiba is taken over from the mishnah. It seems clear from the context that בר נש is not any person, but any rabbi, and that the general statement applies especially to R. Aqiba.

32. y. Ta'an. 1,1/15 (63d).

בעי בר נשא ייחון מיתייא כל אימת. לא בעי בר נשא ייחות מיטרא כל אימת.

A (/the son of) man asks at any time that the dead should rise. A (/the son of) man does not ask at any time that the rain should come down.

Here are two examples of the definite state בר נשא in sayings of Rabbi Jose. The general context is one of fasting for rain. The prayer for rain could be included in the prayer for the resurrection of the dead, so there are comparisons of the coming of rain and the resurrection of the dead. R. Jose objects to one of these on the ground that they are not comparable events. Here בר נשא refers to observant Jews rather than to all people, and R. Jose can hardly have excluded himself. The general level of meaning is more important here than in some examples.

33. y. MQ 3,5/40 (82d)//Ber.R. 100,7.

לא ילפין עובדא מן בר נש זעיר.

We do not learn the decision from an inferior (son of) man!

The context is a series of stories about what lesser figures did on the sabbath during the seven-day fasting period. It ends with R. Yona saying to R. Guryon, what do we learn from you about such a thing, and the answer to this is nothing, and the above saying is given as the reason for this. It is accordingly a general statement which has especial reference to R. Guryon. The general level of meaning of בר נש concerns Jewish rabbis rather than people in general.

34. y. Ter. 8,9/5(46a)//y. Shabb. 2,3/5(4d)//y. Shabb. 19,3/4(17b)//y. Pes. 1,8/11(28a)//y. Sukk. 1,2/2(52b)//y. Sukk. 3,4/2(53c)//y. Yeb. 8,1/21(9a)//y. Ḥag. 1,1/12(76a)//y. Gitt. 9,7/5(50c).

ולית בר נש אמר אינה אלא דהוא מודי על קדמייתא.

And no (son of) man says that's not the case unless he agrees with the first (opinion).

All the versions of this saying have an identical *Sitz im Leben* in rabbinical debates. In each case an attempt is made to derive a rabbi's opinion from his other known opinions. A general statement like this concludes the argument, whether with the negative אינה, as here and at y. Pes. 1,8/11(28a), or in its place the positive אף (y. Shabb. 19,3/4(17b); y. Yeb. 8,1/21(9a); y. Ḥag. 1,1/12(76a), or אפילו (y. Shabb. 2,3/5(4d); y. Sukk. 1,2/2(52b); y. Sukk. 3,4/2(53c); y. Gitt. 9,7/5(50c). For example, at y. Ter. 8,9/5(46a)//y. Pes. 1,8/11(28a) the context is a dispute about the effect of unclean ordinary stuff in the same vat as a priestly offering. The general level of meaning of בר נש is not that of all people, but of all debating rabbis. In this particular case, בר נש refers especially to R. Jose, whose opinion the rabbis were attempting to derive. The general level of meaning is the same in every example. At y. Shabb. 2,3/5(4d), with אפילו, בר נש refers especially to R. Eliezer. At y. Shabb. 19,3/4(17b)// y. Yeb. 8,1/21(9a)//y. Ḥag. 1,1/12(76a), with אף, בר נש refers especially to R. Judah. At y. Sukk. 1,2/2(52b), with אפילו, בר נש refers especially to a certain elder before R. Zeira. At y. Gitt. 9,7/5(50c), with אפילו, בר נש refers especially to R. Meir.

At one level, this is an extreme example, in that the general statement is applied in different passages to different rabbis. This is instructive for understanding the nature of the idiom. On the one hand, the general level of meaning illustrates what all the examples have in common, and indicates with especial clarity that the general level of meaning of בר נש may refer to a social subgroup, not to everyone. On the other hand, not one single example makes sense unless the point of using the idiom is to say something quite precise about a particular rabbi. Even in these examples, therefore, the particular reference to a single individual is essential to the use of this idiom.

35. y. Ned. 5,4/3 (39b).

וכן בר נש עביד דילמא בקביוסטיסא.

And a (son of) man does so that he may not be a gambler!

The discussion of vows has turned to the case of a man (חד בר נש) who vowed not to make a profit. He came before R. Judan bar Salom, who responded with the above general statement. The general level of meaning concerns observant Jews who vow not to make a profit. The particular reference of בר נש is to the anonymous subject of the story.

36. y. San. 7,2/3 (24b).

לית אורחא דגברא רבא מהלך עם בר נש פחות מתלתין שנין.

It is not the way of a great man to walk with a (son of) man who is less than thirty years old.

The general context is that of capital punishment, and the discussion has come to the question as to how you burn a person. This proceeds with the story of R. Eleazar ben Zadok riding on his father's shoulders and seeing a priest's daughter burnt. It goes on to say that he was more than ten years old at the time, and adds that he was not less than thirty years old when he left home to study with his master. The above general statement is given as an indication of his age when he saw the event. Thus it applies to R. Eleazar in particular.

37. y. San. 10,2/47 (29a).

הדא היא דמתלא אמרה צריק בר נש חשיש על לווטייה דרבה אפילו על מגן.

This is what the proverb says: a (son of) man needs to be careful of his master's curses, even if in vain.

The context is a series of stories about people who have no portion in the world to come, and this saying ends a story about Ahitophel. David is said to have declared that anyone who could have stopped up a flood and did not do so would in the end be strangled. Ahitophel stopped up the flood, but died by strangulation anyway. This leads R. Jose to apply this proverb to Ahitophel. This example is on the extreme wing of the use of this idiom, in that the general statement is explicitly said to be a proverb. Even so, בר נש in this context clearly applies especially to Ahitophel.

38. Gen. R. 7,2 (/ /Num.R. 19,3//Pes. 4,30).

בר נש ראמר מילה ראוריתא לקי אתמהא.

Shall a (son of) man who interprets the word of Torah be beaten?

This is from a story in which Jacob of Niburayya was ordered by R. Haggai to come and be beaten for ruling that fish should be ritually slaughtered. The son of man saying is Jacob's first response. He used a general statement because he was in a very humiliating situation. It was at the same time important to him that it really applied to him, so that he could try to avoid being beaten (he did not succeed). A second example follows, in which he gives another ruling, which was deemed equally inadequate, and his first response is the same son aof man saying.

With so many examples of this idiom to be found in natural Jewish Aramaic, it was to be expected that some examples could be found in translation Aramaic. This involves somewhat different problems of method. In lengthy speeches, examples of a general statement applied to the speaker himself might be unconscious, and appear with בר נש in translation because a particular translator considered בר נש to be the most natural translation of a given word for 'man' in the Hebrew Bible. Accordingly, one or two examples are less than certain. Others are straightforward, either because they are unambiguous translations, or because the rendering with בר (א)נש(א) is not to be expected, especially not when it is a rendering of גבר (ה).

39. Neof I Gen. 1.26-27: MT אדם and האדם.

ואמר ייי נברא בר נש בדמותן ... ובְרא ממרה דייי ית בר נשא בדמותיה ...

And the Lord said, 'Let us create (a son of) man in our image ...' and the Word of the Lord created (the son of) man in his image ...

This is a somewhat doubtful, or perhaps better, extreme example of this idiom, in that God created both Adam and thereby humankind at the same time. I propose it as an example, however, because God clearly did not create the whole of humankind at once. Accordingly, while the statement has a general level of meaning, it does refer to a particular person, Adam, so I propose that it should be regarded as an example of this idiom. This probability is increased by noting the efforts of the other written Aramaic translations of this verse: Onk, Ps-J and Pesh all have אדם, and Sam has האדם. All four translations have gone for the obvious fact that God created Adam at the time. This increases the probability that, in using בר נשא, the author of Neof I was making deliberate use of this idiom, and declaring that in creating a particular person, Adam, God was creating humankind.

40. Neof I Gen. 2.23, Insertion.

הדא זמנא ולא עוד תתברא אתה מן בר נשא. היך מה דאתחרית דא מני גרם מן גרמי ובשר מן בשרי. להדא יאי
למתקריה אתה ארום מן גבר אתבריית דא.

This time and not again a woman is created from a (/the son of) man. As this one has been created from me, she is bone of my bone and flesh of my flesh. So it is fitting that she should be called woman, since she was created from man.

This is part of a speech by Adam. Most of it is in the first person, like his speech in MT. The opening part of this insertion is a more general statement, as is clear both from the sense and from the use of the generalizing expression בר נשא. Thus Neofiti I has a general statement about what should not happen, and one which has especial reference to Adam, who is in this version the speaker.

41. Leningrad, Saltykon-Schedrin, MS Antonin Ebr III B 739v, at Gen. 4.14.[15]

הא טרדת יתי יומה הדן מן עלוי אפי ארעא ומן קדמיך אדני לית אפשר לברנש למטמרה.

Look! You have banished me this day from upon the face of the earth, and from before you, Lord, it is not possible for a (son of) man to hide.

Here the meaning of the Hebrew text was not acceptable to some Aramaic translators, for they believed that Cain could not be hidden from God because no one can be hidden from God. They therefore expanded their translations to mean the opposite of what the text said.[16] It is useful to compare here the translation found in Neofiti I.

41a. Neof I, Gen. 4.14.

הא טרדת יתי יומא דין מעילוי אפי דארעא ומן קדמ[י]ך לית אפשר לי למטמרה.

Look! You have banished me this day from upon the face of the earth, and from before you it is not possible for me to hide.

Here the Targumist has altered the text simply to say that Cain himself could not hide from God. With its use of בר נש, passage 40 has generalized. Unlike passage

15.   For the text, M. L. Klein, *Genizah Manuscripts of the Palestinian Targum to the Pentateuch* (2 vols; Cincinatti: Hebrew Union College Press, 1986), p. 9.
16.   On translations which contradict the sacred text, see M. L. Klein, 'Converse Translation: A Targumic Technique', *Bib* 57 (1976), pp. 515–37.

41a, therefore, passage 41 is an example of the idiom which is central to this chapter. It has provided us with a general statement, in which בר נש nonetheless refers especially to one individual, Cain.

42. Ps-J Gen. 40.14. Insertion.

שבק יוסף ית רוחצניה דלעיל ונקט רוחצניה דבר נש ואמר לרב מזוגיא ...

Joseph abandoned his trust which is from above and put his trust in a (son of) man, and said to the chief of the butlers ...

Here the Targumist has inserted a general statement, in which בר נש refers especially to the chief butler. The contrast with 'from above' intensifies the general level of meaning, while Joseph's speech makes the particular reference of בר נש to the chief butler equally unambiguous.

43. Neof I Gen. 40.23 (רבגה from Jer. 17.5).

שבק יוסף חסדא דלעל וחסדא דלרע ... ואתרחיץ ברב מזוגיה בבשר עביר ... ולא אדכר כתבא דכתיב בספר
אוריתא דייי ... לייט יהוי בר נשא די תרחץ בבשרא ...

Joseph abandoned the grace which is from above and the grace which is from below ... and he put his trust in the chief of the butlers, in flesh which passes away ... and he did not remember the scripture which is written in the book of the Law of the Lord ... 'Cursed be the son of man who puts his trust in flesh ...'

Here Neof I uses בר נשא to render הגבר from Jer. 17.5, thus inserting a general statement which applies particularly to Joseph. The rendering of הגבר, normally rendered with גבר(א) in the Aramaic translations of the Hebrew Bible,[17] with the general term בר נשא indicates the Targumist's deliberate intention to make a general statement, and Joseph's action again shows that בר נשא in the translation of the scriptural text has been deliberately applied to him at the same time.

44. Neof I Exod. 33.20. MT האדם.

לא תכל למחמי אפי ארום לית אפשר דחמי יתי בר נש וייחי.

You cannot see my face because a (son of) man cannot see me and live.

Here the MT has a general statement using האדם referring particularly to Moses, who is told not to look directly at the face of God. We cannot be quite certain that the Targumist deliberately used בר נש to bring about the idiomatic usage central to this investigation, because this rendering is normal for him. However, the fact that there is heavy editing in this context because of the sensitivity of the Targumist to the central issue of whether one can see God, together with the fact that, like the marginal gloss, the Targumist has used the indefinite state despite the presence of the article in the MT, makes it more probable that the Targumist was thinking carefully about what he was doing. This makes it more probable that the use of בר נש is due to deliberate use of this idiom.

17.   See Casey, '(א)בר נש(א) in the Aramaic Translations', pp. 113–16.

45. Tg. Job 16.21. MT גבר.

אפשר דמכסן בר נש עם אלהא והיך אינש עם חבריה.

Can a (son of) man rebuke God, even as a man (rebukes) his fellow?

Here I leave aside the second half of the verse, in which ובן־אדם appears to have been rendered with והיך אינש, whether this was due to corruption of the text or difficulties with the sense, or more probably both. The important point is the rendering of גבר with בר נש. This is similar to the rendering of הגבר with בר נשא in passage 43. As I pointed out in discussing that passage, the normal rendering of גבר in the Aramaic translations of the Hebrew Bible is with גבר(א). This is so marked that the rendering of גבר with בר נש is sufficient to indicate the deliberate use of a general statement which has especial reference to the speaker, Elihu.

46. Tg. Job 33.29-30. MT גבר.

הא כל אילין יעביד אלהא תרי זמנין ותלת עם בר נש, מטול לאתבא נפש מן שוותא לאנהרא בניהור חייא.

Look, God does all these things two times and three with a (son of) man, to bring back his soul from the pit, to lighten him with the light of life.

As in passage 45, the rendering of גבר with בר נש is sufficient to indicate the deliberate use of a general statement which has especial reference to the speaker, Elihu.

47. Tg. 2 Chron. 14.10: MT אנוש.

ייי אלהנא אנת לא ישלט עמך בר נש

Lord, you are our God! Let not a (son of) man prevail over you!

This is from a prayer by Asa, King of Judah, directly to God. The context is an attack on Judah by Zerah the Ethiopian with an army of a million men and three hundred chariots. The use of בר נש has a general level of meaning contrasting people with God himself. At the same time, בר נש refers especially to Zerah and his army: Asa prays that they will not triumph over God, his interpretation of what would happen if they won the forthcoming battle with him and his army. The rendering of the Hebrew אנוש with בר (א)נש(א) is not unusual in the Aramaic translations of the Hebrew Bible, but this is the only Targumic example outside Job and Psalms.[18] It is therefore very probable that the Targumist was making deliberate use of this known idiom.

I have also found a few examples of this idiom in Syriac.

48. Testament of Ephraem, lines 121-6.

מן דסאם לי בגו היכלא　　לא נחזא היכל מלכותא
דלא מותר שובחא סריקא　　לברנשא דלא שוא לה
דכל ברנש ערטלאית　　עאל יהב פתגמא

Whoever lays me in the church, may he not see the Church of the kingdom!
For empty praise is no use to the (son of) man who is not worthy of it.
For every (son of) man goes in naked and gives an account.

18.　　For a more complete presentation of the evidence, see Casey, '(א)נש(א) בר in the Aramaic Translations of the Hebrew Bible', pp. 96–8.

Lines 121–2 belong to a whole section which uses the first person singular. It is consequently clear that the son of man statement in lines 123–4 also refers to Ephraem, writing *c.* 370 CE and contemplating his forthcoming death. He asks not to be buried in church because he is unworthy of empty praise. At the same time, the use of ברנשא ensures that a general level of meaning is retained. Similar remarks apply to the son of man statement in lines 125–6. The use of כל with בר נש shows that the general level of meaning is intended to be true of absolutely everyone, and this makes good sense in Ephraem's culture, where people believed in a Final Judgement for everyone. At the same time, it is used because Ephraem applied it to himself. The use of the definite state בר נשא, the normal state of the noun in Syriac, in line 124, and the indefinite state בר נש in line 125, following כל, makes no difference to the meaning and use of this idiom.

49. Testament of Ephraem, lines 297–304.

297–8　דמלתא אית לי עם אלהא　דעם אכסניא אתעפא
299–300　אכסניא אנא אכותהון　עמהון אחי סימוני
301–2　דכל עופא לגנסה רחם　וברנשא לדדמא לה
303–4　בקימטרין סימוני　איכא דאית תבירי לבא

297–8 I have given an undertaking to God that I shall be buried with the strangers.
299–300 I am a stranger like them: put me with them, my brethren,
301–2 for every bird loves its species, and a (/the son of) man loves him who is like him.
303–4 Put me in the cemetery where the repentant of heart are.

As in passage 48, the context makes it absolutely clear that the general statement of line 302 is made because of the particular reference to the author himself, with explicit instructions about him in the preceding and following lines. At the same time, this does not undermine the general level of meaning of line 302. As in passage 29, the general statement about birds underlines the general nature of the son of man statement.

As well as these three examples in natural Syriac, I have noted four examples in the Peshitta.

50. Pesh Exod. 33.20: MT האדם.

ואמר לא משכח אנת למחזא אפי מטל דלא חזא לי ברנשא וחיא.
And he said, 'You cannot see my face, because a (/the son of) man does not see me and live.'

This is very similar to passage 44. The MT has a general statement using האדם referring particularly to Moses, who is told not to look directly at the face of God. Again we cannot be quite certain that the Peshitta deliberately used ברנשא to bring about the idiomatic usage central to this investigation, because this rendering is found elsewhere. However, it is a relatively unusual rendering for the Peshitta, so it is more probable that this is a deliberate use of the idiom which is central to this chapter.

51. Pesh Job 16.21. MT גבר.

לוי דין נכס בר אנשא לאלהא איך גברא לחברה.
Would that a (son of) man might reprove God, as a man (reproves) his neighbour!

This is very similar to passage 45. The very unusual rendering of גבר with בר אנשא is sufficient to indicate the deliberate use of a general statement which has especial reference to the speaker, Job.

52. Pesh Ps. 40.5. MT הגבר.

טבוהי לבר אנשא דעל שמה דמריא תכיל ...
Blessed is the (son of) man who trusts in the name of the Lord.

Psalm 40 begins in the first person. This is used again in vv. 6-7, and the subject of vv. 8-11 is also in the first person. It is natural to take v. 5 as a general statement which refers especially to the speaker, and we must infer from the rendering of הגבר with בר אנשא that the Peshitta has done this.

53. Pesh Ps. 94.12. MT רבגה.

טבוהי לברנשא דתרדיוהי אנת מריא ומן נמוסך תלפיוהי.
Blessed is the (son of) man whom you chasten, Lord, and teach from your Law.

The first few verses of Ps. 94 are about God, and in vv. 16-19 the psalmist refers to himself in the first person. It is a reasonable perception that v. 12 is a general statement which refers especially to the speaker, and we must infer from the rendering of הגבר with בר אנשא that the Peshitta translator took this view.

5. *Conclusions*

The following conclusions should therefore be drawn. Aramaic was an exceptionally stable language in its development over a period of centuries. While in most usages, nouns in the definite or determined state were used in a significantly different way from those in the indefinite or indetermined or absolute state, in generic and some other cases the matter was quite different. The use of either state was optional, for the very good reason that the use of one state or the other cannot affect the meaning of nouns which are being used generically, nor can it affect the meaning of some unique items such as the sun and the moon. The term (א)נש(א) בר is a very general term for man, so many general statements using (א)נש(א) בר may have it in either the definite or indefinite state.

Since (א)נש(א) בר is a general term for human beings as a whole, it may be used with reference to all basic human experiences, including death. (א)נש(א) בר may also be used indefinitely with reference to a particular individual. This use is not however recorded with reference to the speaker, and the only general level of meaning is that the individual is a human being, which may be of central importance or somewhat incidental.

I have found over 30 examples of general statements using (א)נש(א) בר with reference to the speaker, or a group of people including the speaker, or someone else made obvious by the context. The majority of examples are in Jewish Aramaic from Israel, and most of these concern rabbis who have some connection with Galilee. There is also one very early example (passage 20 above), which is important because it establishes the use of this idiom long before the time of Jesus. There is also one Babylonian example (passage 28a above), and a handful of examples have been noted in Syriac. It follows that when examples of this idiomatic usage emerge from the reconstruction of Aramaic sources from our Gospel sayings, they should be accepted as genuine examples of this idiom. This will entail that they have to some extent a kind of general level of meaning. It does not however in any way undermine the fact that most of these sayings are obviously and primarily about Jesus.

Chapter Three

THE 'SON OF MAN CONCEPT'

We have seen from the history of scholarship in Chapter 1 that for many years scholars believed in a Son of Man Concept, or *Menschensohnbegriff*, or *Menschensohnvorstellung*. Sharp criticism of such views began some 40 years ago, but some scholars still believe in it. The purpose of this chapter is to show that no version of this view should be regarded as tenable. The foundational documents on which this view was based were Daniel 7, the *Similitudes of Enoch* and *4 Ezra* 13. Accordingly, I discuss these documents first. Long after this view was considered by some scholars to have been established, a number of other documents were brought forward as evidence of it. I discuss two of these to illustrate that they should not be accepted as evidence of it either.

1. Daniel 7

I have discussed this document, and the history of its interpretation, at length elsewhere.[1] Accordingly, I repeat here only the main points necessary to determine the correct interpretation of it.

Daniel 7 is an apocalyptic chapter which consists of a vision and its interpretation. It was written in Israel, *c.* 166–5 BCE. In the visionary section of this chapter, four extraordinary beasts, each partly like a real ferocious animal but with features that make all of them *Mischwesen*, come up from out of the big sea, the normal term for the Mediterranean. The most ferocious is the fourth, which is not said to be like a real animal, though Jews of the period would surely have recognized a caricature of a Seleucid elephant.[2] It has more features than the other animals, most notably a little horn, which puts down three of the ten horns before it, and has eyes like the eyes of a man and a mouth speaking big things.

The vision continues with a judgement scene. Thrones are placed, and one Ancient of Days takes his seat. His throne and its wheels are flames of fire, and he has thousands of attendants. The court sits, and the books are opened. The fourth beast is immediately put to death, and its body destroyed. This is evidently the first

1.   Casey, *Son of Man*.
2.   U. Staub, 'Das Tier mit den Hörnern: Ein Beitrag zu Dan 7.7f', *FZPT* 25 (1978), pp. 382–96.

major event of the judgement. The other beasts have their power taken away, but are allowed to live for a time.

The next event of the judgement scene is the one central for present purposes. One like a son of man, כבר אנש, is brought before the Ancient of Days. He is given power and glory and kingship, all nations will serve him, and his power and kingship are eternal and indestructible.

There is then a small interlude in which Daniel asks one of those standing by for the interpretation of his vision. It follows that the interpretation takes place within the vision, which is important for understanding the addition to the visionary part at v.21. Otherwise, the interpretation takes up the rest of the chapter. All the problems encountered by scholarship flow from not taking this interpretative section seriously enough, problems compounded by replacing it with tradition, most commonly Christian tradition.

The first interpretative section makes two main points. The first main point is that the four big beasts are four kings (מלכין), a normal cipher for kingdoms, who shall arise on the earth (Dan. 7.17). The second is that the Holy Ones of the Most High (קדישי עליונין) will receive the kingdom/kingship (מלכותא) for ever and ever (Dan. 7.18). As was customary in apocalyptic visions, the interpretative section has already made absolutely clear the main points for contemporary Jews. The four kingdoms were already well enough known for their identity to be clear for Jews at the time, especially those who suffered under Antiochus Epiphanes and hoped for deliverance. The Syrian tradition preserved the original interpretation of the four kingdoms.[3] As Ephraem put it, commenting on the four kings of Dan. 7.17:

בבליא הלין דהא קימין, ומדיא ופרסיא ויוניא.
These are the Babylonians who will arise, and the Medes and the Persians and the Greeks.

That will have been obvious to everyone at the time. So will the interpretation of the Holy Ones of the Most High as the Jewish people, whose hopes for deliverance are so vigorously expressed in this book. The surviving authors of the Syrian tradition, writing much later, tend to be quite specific about the Jews of this period. So, for example, Galipapa comments on Dan. 7.18:

אמר גם כן כי נאמר על החשמונים
He expresses himself like this because he is referring to the Hasmoneans.[4]

This is a little more specific than the original authors will have intended, because the Syrian tradition saw the fulfilment of Daniel's predictions in the Maccabean victory over the Seleucids. Otherwise, however, it is quite right. Some readers may have imagined that angels on the Jewish side were included, but no one will

3.   On the Syrian tradition, see Casey, *Son of Man*, Ch. 3.
4.   For the text, see Joseph Albo, *Sepher Ha-'Ikkarim, Book of Principles*. Critically edited, with a translation and notes by I. Husik (5 vols.; Philadelphia: Jewish Publication Society of America, 1929–30), IV,42, pp. 418–20.

have imagined that the Holy Ones of the Most High were really angels, because that would have eliminated the Jewish people from the triumph, whereas God's forthcoming deliverance of them is the main point of the book.

With the two main points of the interpretation of the vision settled by the summary interpretation, Daniel asks the interpreting angel for more details. In particular, he homes in on details of the fourth beast, asking especially about its horns, above all the additional horn. It is at this point that Daniel sees the additional horn making war on the Holy Ones, and wearing them down (Dan. 7.21). This is a very clever piece of arrangement, though it is one with which modern scholars have not generally sympathized. Its effect is that the authors can continue to use their symbolism to portray the Seleucid attacks on Israel. To have done so in the main visionary section would have caused problems with the symbol of the man-like figure, which they kept as a symbol of Israel in triumph. The horn's war on the Holy Ones, however, represents the existential main point of their current experience. The Syrian tradition preserved this too. Aphrahat clearly set up the situation in the Maccabean war before alluding to this verse (Dem. V,20)[5]:

... וכד יהודה ואחוחי מתכתשין הוו על אפי עמהון כד עמרין הוו בטשיתא. בהו זבנא עבדת קרנא קרבא עם קדישא ואתמצית חילהון.

... and when Judah and his brothers were fighting for their people and were living in secret places (cf. 2 Macc. 5.27). At that time the horn made war with the Holy Ones, and their forces prevailed.

The very end of this looks forward to Dan. 7.22, the next statement of Jewish triumph. This mentions the coming of the Ancient of Days, so obvious to Jews who expected God to come in judgement that it was taken for granted in the first picture of judgement at Dan. 7.9-10. We are then told that judgement was given for the Holy Ones of the Most High and, for the second time, that they received the kingdom/kingship (מלכותא).

The interpreting angel continues with a much longer account of the interpretation of the fourth beast as the fourth kingdom, concluding with a more detailed interpretation of the additional horn. He will be a king who will speak against the Most High, wear out the Holy Ones of the Most High, and seek to change times and law: they will be given into his hand for a time, times and half a time (Dan. 7.25). This is evidently the detailed interpretation of the additional horn of Dan. 7.8 in terms of the activities of Antiochus Epiphanes during the Maccabean period. Then the court sat, for the sitting of the heavenly court is part of reality, not the kind of symbolism that we see in the four beasts. The power of the king will be taken away, and he will be destroyed. There is then a third announcement of the final triumph, this time of the people of the Holy Ones of the Most High who will have eternal kingship and who will be served by other nations.

Here too an outline of the original interpretation was preserved in the Syrian tradition. For example, Ephraem comments:

5.   For the text, ed. I. Parisot, see R. Graffin (ed.), *Patrologia Syriaca* vol. I (Paris: Firmin-Didot et Socii, 1894).

... עדן עדנין ופלגות עדן. הו תלת שׁנין ופלגה. הו דינא יתב. הו למתבל עירתא דאולצניהון דקדישׁא, הו דכהנא
דנטרי נמוסה דמרימא, ודנחבל ונובד לאנטיוכוס קרנא זעותא דאלץ ורדף אנון לטננא דבית מקבי. ולה מן
לעולא אריס מן חיא, ולהון יהב שׁולטנא ורבותא.

'... a time, times and half a time' (Dan. 7.25). That is, three years and a half. 'And the court sat' (Dan. 7.26). That is, to exact vengeance for the suffering of the Holy Ones, that is, the priests who kept the Law of the Most High, and to destroy and eliminate Antiochus, the little horn, who oppressed and persecuted them, the zealots of the house of Maccabees. Him, because of his wickedness, He removed from life, and to them He gave dominion and greatness.

Apart from overprecise interpretation of the Holy Ones, this transmits the original and correct interpretation of several main points of the most detailed part of the interpretative section of Daniel 7.

The end of Ephraem's comment refers briefly to Dan. 7.27, which is crucial to this investigation, because of its close correlation with 7.14. It is this close correlation which makes it absolutely clear that 'the people of the Holy Ones of the Most High', that is, Israel, *are* the interpretation of the man-like figure (כבר אנשׁ) at 7.13-14. In Dan. 7.13, the man-like figure comes on the clouds of heaven and is brought before the Ancient of Days. This is simply part of the narrative of the vision, and consequently it has no direct equivalent in the interpretative section. In 7.14, he is given שׁלטן ויקר ומלכו: in 7.27, the people of the Holy Ones of the Most High are given מלכותא ושׁלטנא ורבותא. In 7.14, his שׁלטן is eternal (עלם), and his kingdom/ kingship (מלכותה) will not be damaged: in 7.27, the people's kingdom/kingship (מלכותה) is eternal (עלם). In 7.14, all peoples, nations and tongues will serve him (לה יפלחון): in 7.27, all dominions will serve and obey it (לה יפלחון וישׁתמעון). These considerations ought to be regarded as decisive: the man-like figure (כבר אנשׁ) is a symbol for Israel, who is described in the interpretative section as 'the Holy Ones of the Most High', 'the Holy Ones', and 'the people of the Holy Ones of the Most High'.

This interpretation was also preserved in the Syrian tradition, but it has been more difficult to realize this, because of the influence of specifically Christian tradition. Christians believed that the Son of man in the New Testament was Jesus, and a small number of Son of man sayings in the New Testament clearly refer to Dan. 7.13. In the west, therefore, the man-like figure was interpreted as Jesus. This appealed to Syrian exegetes too, and some of them appropriated it by means of what I call the 'typological interpretation of prophecy', what French scholars call 'prophéties à double visée'. This supposes that a prophet predicts a future event: this future event really occurs: it is also a type of another event in the more distant future, which also occurs, or will occur in due course.[6] The interpretation of Dan. 7.13 attributed to Ephraem is an example of this method:

6.   See further P. M. Casey, 'The Fourth Kingdom in Cosmas Indicopleustes and the Syrian Tradition', *Rivista di Storia e Letteratura Religiosa* 25 (1989), pp. 385–403 (396–9), with bibliography.

חזא הוית איך ברנשין על ענני שמיא. הו אפן ראזה דהדא בבני עמא דשבעדו ליונא ולכל מלכון דחדריהון
אתתציר הוא,אלא שולמה במרן אשתכלל הו.

'I was watching one like a son of men on the clouds of heaven' (from Dan. 7.13). That is,
even if the significance of this was shown forth in the sons of the people, who subdued the
Greeks and all the surrounding kingdoms, its consummation was perfected in Our Lord.

Here Dan. 7.13-14 has been interpreted with two levels of meaning. One is the
Christian level of meaning, at which the man-like figure is the Son of man, Christ
Jesus our Lord, however any exegete chooses to put that. The even older traditional
level of meaning is one which Ephraem had no reason to invent, and must therefore
have inherited. This clearly refers to the Jews of the Maccabean period as 'the sons
of the people', and refers to their victories over the Seleucids and others as the
fulfilment of the prophecies of Dan. 7.14. The terms in which this is put make sense
only if the man-like figure is a symbol of the Holy Ones of the Most High, and they
are the Jewish people. It will be noted that even while Ephraem's comments cannot
be interpreted in any other way, he did not find it necessary to write anything on the
lines of 'now one like a son of men, this is the holy ones of the Most High, who are
the sons of the people'. No ancient commentator shows any signs of difficulty over
the fact that the interpretative section does not say anything like 'now one like a son
of man, this is the Holy Ones', nor does anything lead any of them to imagine that
the man-like figure might be an angel.

I have noted already the interpretation of the man-like figure found in Theodore
bar Koni, who comments on בר אנשין at Dan. 7.13:

הנין דאף לזבנהין מתנסבן על מקביא אלא חתיתותהין במרן משיחא אשתמלית

In their historical context these words refer to the Maccabees, but their essential quality is
fulfilled in our Lord the Messiah.[7]

This has the same two levels of meaning as the comment of Ephraem. Despite its
brevity, it implies without any doubt that the man-like figure is a symbol of the
Holy Ones of the Most High, and that this term refers to the Jews of the Maccabean
period.

Some exegetes were not happy with this interpretation, but their comments
make clear that it was a flourishing tradition to which they objected. For example,
Aphrahat has some Syrian and some western comments. I have noted him setting
up the Maccabean situation before quoting Dan. 7.21. He was less happy with such
an interpretation of the victory of the Holy Ones of the Most High, and in quoting
Dan. 7.18 at Dem. V,21, he argues against such an interpretation:

דלמא בני איסריל קבלו מלכותא דמרימא: חס. או דלמא הו עמא אתא על ענני שמיא: הדא עברת לה מנהון.

Have the children of Israel received the kingdom of the Most High? Certainly not! Or has
that people come on the clouds of heaven? That has passed away from them.

The force of the first objection is brought out by other exegetes who stress Jewish
defeats by the Romans, on account of which they cannot have received the kingdom

---

7.   See p. 8 above.

'for ever', so that the Maccabean victories cannot be the correct interpretation of the triumphs set out in Daniel 7. It is the other objection which is more interesting for present purposes. It clearly refers to Dan. 7.13, and takes it very literally on the assumption that the man-like figure might be the children of Israel. It therefore bears witness to the corporate interpretation of the man-like figure as the people of Israel, even as it turns this down.

Another major witness to the Syrian tradition was the Greek philosopher Porphyry. It is a great pity for scholarship that all copies of his work 'Against the Christians' were destroyed by Christians, with the result that his comments have to be recovered from the severe polemic of Jerome's commentary on Daniel. There should be no doubt about Porphyry's basic adherence to the Syrian tradition. For example, at Dan. 7.7-8, Jerome comments:

> Frustra Porphyrius cornu parvulum, quod post decem cornu ortum est, Ἐπιφανήν Antiochum suspicatur ...
> In vain Porphyry imagines that the little horn, which arose after the ten horns, is Antiochus Epiphanes ...

Again, at Dan. 12.11, Jerome comments:

> Hos mille ducenti nonaginta dies Porphyrius in tempore vult Antiochi, et in desolatione templi esse completos
> Porphyry wants these 1290 days to have been fulfilled in the time of Antiochus, and in the desolation of the temple ...

Such comments are typical of the Syrian tradition. The dependence of the Neoplatonist philosopher on Christian tradition is especially well shown by Porphyry's exegesis of Dan. 11.40–12. Here the book of Daniel leaves pseudo-prophecy of known history for genuine prophecy, complete with the resurrection of the dead at Dan. 12.2-3. Porphyry and the rest of the Syrian tradition, however, believed the whole account referred to the final campaigns and ultimate victory of the Jews under the Maccabees over Antiochus Epiphanes and the Greeks and others. This is not the mistake of an anti-Christian Neoplatonist philosopher, who would have been only to happy to point out that this was an inaccurate pseudo-prophecy. It is the mistake of the Judaeo-Christian tradition which he used, which inherited mostly correct exegesis, and which knew that the account at the end of the book must be true because it was the Word of God.[8]

Jerome knew perfectly well that Porphyry's opinions were held by other interpreters. For example, he comments on Dan. 7.18:

> Si hoc de Machabaeis intelligitur, doceat, qui ista contendit, quomodo regnum eorum perpetuum sit.
> If this is understood to be about the Maccabees, let he who strives for such an opinion show how their kingdom might be eternal.

---

8.   P. M. Casey, 'Porphyry and the Origin of the Book of Daniel', *JTS* NS 27 (1976), pp. 15–33: 'Porphyry and Syrian Exegesis of the Book of Daniel', *ZNW* 81 (1990), pp. 139–42.

This is another clear indication of the Syrian tradition, and an obvious objection which indicates that the Syrian tradition originated before the defeats of the Jews in which Christians took such delight. The 'if' clause, like the pejorative use of 'ista', is part of Jerome's polemic, but the objection is a real one, from which we should infer that Jerome did not know what representatives of the Syrian tradition would do with this particular point.

With Porphyry's membership of the Syrian tradition in mind, we must turn to Jerome's comments on Dan. 2.34-35 and 7.13-14 in his commentary at Dan. 11.44-45. Jerome patiently catalogued the Syrian tradition's historical interpretation of this part of Daniel, together with his own western tradition which interpreted it of Antichrist in the future. At 11.44, his patience ran out. I quote in the first instance just a little of his polemic:

> Et in hoc loco Porphyrius tale nescio quid de Antiocho somniat … pone enim haec dici de Antiocho, quid nocet religioni nostrae? … Dimittat itaque dubia et manifestis haereat …
> In this passage too Porphyry dreams I know not what about Antiochus … for suppose these things were said about Antiochus, what harm would be done to our religion? … So let us put doubtful things on one side, and stick to what is clear …

The first of these comments shows little more than Jerome's impatience, though he had more reason here than sometimes: it is precisely about here that the Syrian tradition left behind historical facts in the guise of a pseudo-prophecy, and wrongly believed that Daniel's account gave a genuine account of further historical facts, when it was really a prophecy which was never fulfilled. Jerome's second point is probably due to his awareness that some Christians adhered to the tradition which he has treated as that of Porphyry. They believed that Daniel was a genuine prophecy which was already fulfilled, and the Christian religion really is just as easy to support with the Syrian tradition's view of fulfilled prophecy, as it is with the western view that this was a prediction of what would take place in the last times. This makes Jerome's third point all the more interesting. In the first place he admits that the difference between the Syrian and western traditions of interpretation is up to a point doubtful. What Jerome considered clear rather than doubtful leads directly to matters more central to this investigation:

> Qui sit ille lapis qui, de monte abscisus sine manibus, creverit in montem magnum et orbem impleverit et quadriformem imaginem contriverit? Qui sit ille filius hominis qui cum nubibus venturus sit et staturus ante vetustum dierum et dandum sit ei regnum quod nullo fine claudatur omnesque populi, tribus ac linguae ipsi servituri sint?
> Who is that stone which, cut from the mountain without hands, grew into a great mountain and filled the world and shattered the four-part statue? Who is that Son of man who will come with the clouds and stand before the Ancient of Days, and to whom a kingdom is to be given which will not be completed with any ending, and all peoples, tribes and tongues themselves will serve?

The interpretation of both the stone of Dan. 2 and the man-like figure of Dan. 7.13-14 as Jesus is taken to be so obvious that Jerome, having said so in his comments on those passages, felt no need to repeat these interpretations here. He calls these interpretations 'obvious' again in the next sentence, in which he retails the view of Porphyry:

> Haec quae manifesta sunt praeterit, et de Iudaeis asserit prophetari quos usque hodie servire cognoscimus.
> He passes over these points which are obvious, and maintains that the prophecy concerns the Jews, whom we know to be enslaved until the present day.

Three points are crucial here. One is the clarity of Jerome's evidence that Porphyry believed that both the man-like figure of Dan. 7.13-14 and the stone of Dan. 2 symbolized the Jews. A second major point is the nature of Jerome's objection, that the Jews are enslaved until the present day. This is a very good objection to the historicizing interpretation of the man-like figure as a symbol of the Jews winning a victory for ever in the Maccabean period. The third point is that Jerome accuses Porphyry of passing over the main points which Jerome has just made. We must infer that Porphyry did not interpret the man-like figure as an individual.

Before proceeding to Jerome's comments at Dan. 7.14, we must consider his comment on the stone at Dan. 2.35:

> ... quod Iudaei et impius Porphyrius male ad populum referunt Israel, quem in fine saeculorum volunt esse fortissimum et omnia regna conterere et regnare in aeternum.
> ... which the Jews and wicked Porphyry wrongly refer to the people of Israel, whom they imagine will be the most powerful at the end of the ages, and will shatter all the kingdoms and reign for ever.

In the first place, this comment shows that Jerome was perfectly well aware that this tradition was held by Jewish exegetes as well as by Porphyry. It is indeed Jewish in spirit, looking forward to the eventual triumph of the Jewish people. This eschatological interpretation is not at all met by Jerome's objection at 11.44-45, that the Jews are still in servitude. It follows that it must be the man-like figure of Dan. 7.13-14 which Porphyry regarded as a symbol of the Jewish people at the time of the Maccabean victory. This eschatological interpretation of the stone in Dan. 2 is in perfect accord with the interpretation of the Peshitta, ביומתא אחריא, and of the LXX, ἐπ' ἐσχάτων τῶν ἡμερῶν, at Dan. 2.45. We must conclude that while Porphyry held both the stone of Dan. 2 and the man-like figure of Dan. 7.13-14 to be symbols of the Jews, he interpreted them differently in this one respect, that the stone symbolized the eschatological victory of the Jews, whereas the man-like figure represented the Holy Ones of the Most High, the Jews at the time of the Maccabean victory.

We are now almost in a position to interpret Jerome's comment on Porphyry at Dan. 7.14, a point at which his polemic has misled most scholars. To do this, however, we must also consider Jerome's own interpretation. At 7.13, he refers back to the stone of Dan. 2, which he interpreted as *Dominus et Salvator*.

> ... nunc sub persona filii hominis introducitur, ut assumptio carnis humanae significetur in Filio Dei ...
> ... (he) is now introduced under the name of the Son of man, so that the assumption of human flesh in the Son of God might be indicated ...

Jerome supports this by quoting Acts 1.11, and for the reception of power from the Ancient of Days he adds Phil. 2.6-8. He therefore clearly and repeatedly interpreted the man-like figure as Jesus, his Lord and Saviour, Son of man and Son of God, and his comments at 11.44 show that he regarded his interpretation as obvious.

It is in this light that we must consider his polemic against Porphyry at 7.14:

> Hoc cui potest convenire, respondeat Porphyrius, aut quis iste tam potens sit qui cornu parvum – quem Antiochum interpretatur – fregerit atque contriverit. Si responderit Antiochi principes a Iuda Machabaeo fuisse superatos, docere debet quomodo cum nubibus caeli veniat quasi filius hominis, et offeratur vetusto dierum, et detur ei potestas et regnum, et omnes populi ac tribus serviant illi, et potestas eius aeterna sit quae nullo fine claudatur.
> Let Porphyry reply by telling us to whom this can refer, or who is that man who is so powerful that he can break and crush the little horn, which he interprets as Antiochus. If he replies that Antiochus' generals were defeated by Judas Maccabaeus, he must show how he comes on the the clouds of heaven like a son of man, and is presented to the Ancient of Days, and power and kingship is given to him, and all peoples and tribes serve him, and his power is eternal and is not brought to any end.

In a classic article published in 1897, Loisy made the classic mistake:

> Il semble que P. ait appliqué à Judas Machabée ce qui est dit du 'fils d'homme' qui arrive sur les nuées du ciel.[9]
> It appears that Porphyry applied to Judas Maccabaeus what is said of the 'son of man' who comes on the clouds of heaven.

Most scholars have followed this, many of them apparently not reading Jerome's commentary on Daniel, but Harnack's collection of the fragments of Porphyry, which left out Jerome's comments on Dan. 7.13 made in his commentary at Dan. 11.44-45.[10] Thorough examination of all Jerome's comments on Porphyry should make it clear that this is quite wrong.

The first major point is the comment of Jerome at Dan. 11.44-45. I have noted that Jerome sets up both the stone of Dan. 2, and the son of man (ille filius hominis) from Dan. 7.13, and says quite clearly that Porphyry maintains that these prophecies concern the Jews. This is very straightforward evidence that Porphyry believed that the man-like figure was a symbol of the Holy Ones of the Most High, who were the Jewish people. After considering Jerome's other comments in detail, I concluded, again on the basis of very clear evidence, that Porphyry belonged to the Syrian tradition, and interpreted the man-like figure as a symbol of the Jews at the time of the Maccabean victory. The second major point is the grammar and syntax of Jerome's comments at Dan. 7.14, which make clear that Porphyry did *not* believe that the man-like figure was Judas Maccabaeus. The request for a response

9.   A. Loisy, under the pseudonym of J. Lataix, 'Le Commentaire de s. Jérôme sur Daniel', *Revue d'histoire et de littérature religieuses* II (1897), pp. 164–73, 268–77 (168).

10.   A. von Harnack (ed.), *Porphyrius, 'Gegen die Christen', 15 Bücher. Zeugnisse, Fragmente und Referate* (Abhandlungen der königlich preussischen Akademie der Wissenschaften, Phil-hist Klasse, Nr. 1, 1916. Berlin: Verlag der königlichen Akademie der Wissenschaften), esp. pp. 71–2, Frg. 43.

from Porphyry to the question posed by Jerome is in the subjunctive: *respondeat* Porphyrius, *Let* Porphyry reply …. This must mean that Porphyry had not already answered Jerome's question as to which individual the man-like figure represented. We know why because of Jerome's comments at Dan. 11.44-45: Porphyry did not believe that the man-like figure was any particular individual, because he did believe that it was a symbol of the Holy Ones of the Most High, the Jews. Jerome, certain as he was that the man-like figure was an individual, namely Jesus, made up the most appropriate answer he could for Porphyry in order to demonstrate that the objections which he then offers are decisive objections to the Syrian tradition. This is why he introduces his answer with a conditional clause: *si* responderit …, *If* he replies. This is because, as Jerome knew perfectly well, Porphyry had never said anything of the kind.

There is accordingly only one reasonable conclusion. Porphyry belonged to the Syrian tradition, and held that the man-like figure was a symbol of the Holy Ones of the Most High, the Jewish people at the time of the Maccabean victory. In this matter the Syrian tradition preserved the original interpretation of the author(s) of this document, as we know from the close correlation between what is said of the man-like figure in the visionary section, and what is said of the Holy Ones of the Most High in the interpretative section.

The man-like figure is however described in such a way that he might have been an individual rather than a symbol, and there have been numerous attempts to identify him on the assumption that he must be an individual really. Two have been especially important. One is the traditional Jewish and Christian interpretation of him as the Messiah, and so in the Christian tradition more specifically as Jesus Christ. This is a traditional piece of eisegesis. The figure of 'the Messiah' had not crystallized out at the time when the book of Daniel was written, and consequently he is not mentioned in the book as a whole, nor in the interpretative section of this vision. These points should be regarded as decisive. The other major interpretative gambit is more academic. This regards the man-like figure as an angel, most often Michael. At least Michael does occur in the book of Daniel, as the major figure who stands up for Israel in the last times (Dan. 12.1). At the same time, however, the absence of any such figure from the interpretative section of Daniel 7 should be regarded as decisive. Moreover, it is difficult to explain his absence from the Syrian tradition, within which he was a well-known angel who would have served perfectly well as a type of Christ.[11]

It follows that Daniel 7 itself does not provide any kind of evidence of the existence of a Son of Man Concept in Second Temple Judaism.

2. *The Similitudes of Enoch*

In the nineteenth century, the publication of the recently rediscovered *Similitudes of Enoch* was of central importance to the formation of the Son of Man Concept.

11. On these interpretations, see further Casey, *Son of Man*, pp. 24–40.

It has not however been sufficiently realized that Christian use of the term 'Son of man' was of central importance to this interpretation of the terms for 'Son of man' in the *Similitudes*. For example, in the first English translation in 1821, Laurence expressed the opinion that this work repeatedly refers to the nature and character of 'the Messiah', even though the term *mas(h)iḥu* occurs only twice (*1 En.* 48.10; 52.4).[12] This was because the term 'Messiah' was so widespread in the Judaeo-Christian tradition that it was the natural term for scholars such as Laurence to use when they sought to label this figure. Laurence also translated the most important part of Enoch's crucial question at 46.2, '... concerning this Son of man; who he was ...', and likewise the opening of the angel's reply, 'This is the Son of man, to whom righteousness belongs ...' (46.3). In both cases 'Son of man' has been capitalized in accordance with Christian usage, without any discussion of the term 'son of man' in Aramaic. Moreover, the second example has a comma put after it. The combination of capitalization and comma creates a title, 'the Son of man', without any attempt to consider whether a Jewish Aramaic text might mean this. Again, this is due to the influence of Christian tradition.

Similarly, in the first German translation, Hoffmann rendered the most important part of Enoch's question '... in Betreff dieses Menschensohnes: wer er sey, woher er sey ...' (46.2): he commented on 'die Erscheinung des Menschensohnes', and on the limited occurrences of 'Der Name *Menschensohn*': and began the angel's response 'Dieses ist der Menschensohn, dem Gerechtigkeit ist ...' (46.3).[13] The capitalization is doubly natural in German, a language in which the capitalization of proper nouns is universal. Nonetheless, the combination of capitalization with the comma gives the impression that Menschensohn is a title, an impression which Hoffmann carried through in translation and discussion alike.

A similar impression permeates the classic editions, translations and commentaries of Dillmann and Charles, both of which remain influential more than a century after they were written. Dillmann's opening description of the *Bilderreden* has in the second one 'der Messias' and 'das messianisch Gericht', and the 'messianische Reich' features in his description of the third parable and of the ending of the whole work.[14] Among the New Testament concepts now known to us from Jewish documents, Dillmann lists 'vorausgesetzen Begriffe des Himmelreiches, des Menschensohnes'.[15] Here the *Menschensohn* is clearly a *Begriff* in accordance with German Christian tradition, and has little connection with an ordinary Aramaic term for 'man'. At the most important part of 46.2, Enoch asks 'über jenen Menschensohn, wer er sei ...', and the angel's response begins, '... diess ist der Menschensohn, der die Gerechtigkeit hat ... (46.3). Here again, the combination of capitalization with the comma reinforces the impression that *Menschensohn* is a title, an impression which Dillmann does not seem to have seriously questioned.

---

12.   Laurence, *Book of Enoch the Prophet*, p. xl.
13.   Hoffmann, *Das Buch Henoch*, pp. 346–7.
14.   Dillmann, *Das Buch Henoch*, p. III. For the text, Dillmann, *Liber Henoch Aethiopice*.
15.   Dillmann, *Das Buch Henoch*, p. lv.

Charles went further. In his standard 1893 translation and commentary, he declared that 'Christ', or 'the Anointed One', was now for the first time 'applied to the ideal Messianic king that is to come'. He was entirely confident that 'The Son of Man' was 'a definite title', and 'the source of the New Testament designation'.[16] In his translation of the angel's question at 46.2, he put '... concerning that Son of Man, who he was, and whence he was ...': the angel's reply begins, 'This is the Son of Man who hath righteousness, with whom dwelleth righteousness ...' (46.3). The slight differences from his predecessors indicate the independence of mind for which this great scholar was famous, but the capitalization of Son of Man expresses his view that this was already a title, a view derived from Christian tradition. This view was reinforced by his extraordinary comment, 'the Ethiopic translator can only have had one and the same phrase before him, i.e. ὁ υἱὸς τοῦ ἀνθρώπου.'[17] This conjecture attributes a major Christian Christological title to the author(s) of a Jewish work. Charles found nothing odd in this. On the contrary, he went further: 'As the *Similitudes* are pre-Christian, they furnish the first instance in which the definite personal title appears in literature ... The Son of Man as portrayed in the Similitudes is a supernatural being and not a mere man ... This title with its supernatural attributes of superhuman glory, of universal dominion and supreme judicial powers, was adopted by our Lord.'[18] This leaves an obvious problem with Jesus' suffering and death, which Charles approached with another piece of Christian tradition, one for which there is not adequate historical support in the oldest traditions of the synoptic Gospels. He argued that the 'title "the Son of Man" assumed a deeper spiritual significance' in the ministry of Jesus, when this 'transformed conception of the Son of Man is thus permeated throughout by the Isaiah conception of the Servant of Jehovah.'[19]

There is however no evidence that there ever was a Greek version of the *Similitudes of Enoch*. This notion seems to have got into scholarship because there really are Greek versions of some other parts of *1 Enoch*. At no stage did Charles explain how the Aramaic term (א)שׁנ(א) בר could have functioned as 'the definite personal title', nor did he offer a proper explanation as to why it should be translated with the Greek term ὁ υἱὸς τοῦ ἀνθρώπου. He simply continued and intensified the scholarly habit of reading the *Similitudes* against an assumed backdrop of Christian tradition.

As this tradition of scholarship sought to interpret the *Similitudes*, it was faced with a major fact which may have pushed it in this direction. One of the three terms for Son of man in the Ethiopic text of the *Similitudes* is *walda 'eguala 'emmaḥeiāw* (*1 En.* 62.7,9,14; 63.11; 69.26,27; 70.1; 71.17). In the four Gospels,

---

16.   R. H. Charles, *The Book of Enoch: Translated from Professor Dillmann's Ethiopic Text, emended and revised ...* (Oxford: Clarendon, 1893), p. 51: and for his still essential edition of the text, R. H. Charles, *The Ethiopic Version of the Book of Enoch, Edited from Twenty-three mss. together with the fragmentary Greek and Latin Versions* (Oxford: Clarendon, 1906).

17.   Charles, *Book of Enoch*, p. 128.

18.   Charles, *Book of Enoch*, p. 315.

19.   Charles, *Book of Enoch*, pp. 315–16.

the Ethiopic translation of ὁ υἱὸς τοῦ ἀνθρώπου is *always* precisely the same expression, *walda 'ĕguala 'ĕmmaḥĕiāw*: Charles indeed noted that 'it is found throughout Ezekiel, in Dan. vii.13, and universally in the N.T.'[20] It was therefore natural that Christian scholars who were familiar with the Ethiopic Gospels long before the methodology of reconstructing original sources had made any significant progress, should jump to this conclusion, and infer that as *walda 'ĕguala 'ĕmmaḥĕiāw* represented ὁ υἱὸς τοῦ ἀνθρώπου in the Christian Gospels, so it must have done in *1 Enoch*. Such a conclusion would be reinforced by any contact with Ethiopian Christian tradition, according to which Enoch's comments on *walda 'ĕguala 'ĕmmaḥĕiāw* were wonderful prophecies of Christ Jesus.

If this were so, however, it would be difficult to explain why the Ethiopic translators should ever have used *walda sab 'ĕ* (*1 En.* 46.2,3,4; 48.2) or *walda bĕ'ĕsī* (*1 En.* 62.5; 69.29 (*bis*); 71.14). Charles, using Latin rather than Ethiopic for these two terms, commented lamely: 'Hence *filius viri* and *filius hominis* in the Ethiopic text may be synonymous and the variation may be due to the carelessness of the translator.'[21] This exemplifies the lack of understanding of translators which was a feature of scholarship until very recently, and it in no way solves the problems produced by positing the Christian title ὁ υἱὸς τοῦ ἀνθρώπου as the underlay of these three Ethiopic terms. Another major problem caused by this hypothesis arises from the demonstratives normally used with all three of these expressions in the *Similitudes*, whereas *walda 'ĕguala 'ĕmmaḥĕiāw* as a translation of ὁ υἱὸς τοῦ ἀνθρώπου in the four Gospels does not have a demonstrative with it once. In the first English translation, Laurence simply put 'the Son of man' all four times at the end of Ch. 69. Hoffmann, criticizing him for often omitting the demonstrative, announced that the demonstrative 'von dem κατ' ἐξοχὴν sogennanten Menschensohne verstehen müssen', but he did not explain how any original text could be understood like this.[22]

Thirdly, at *1 En.* 71.14 Enoch is greeted, 'You are the son of man who is born to righteousness ...'. If *walda bĕ'ĕsī* here is taken to be a careless translation of the major title ὁ υἱὸς τοῦ ἀνθρώπου, this is quite impossible to explain. Indeed, it has caused endless trouble to scholarship. In 1893, Charles used this as an argument that this part of the *Similitudes* was of different authorship from the rest, and his comparison with *1 En.* 60.10 notably did not cause him to consider that anything might be wrong with his overall understanding of the three Ethiopic phrases as representing a title of majesty.[23] In 1912, he proposed a notorious textual emendation, producing the following translation:

This is the Son of Man who is born unto righteousness,
And righteousness abides over him,
And the righteousness of the Head of Days forsakes him not.[24]

20.   Charles, *Book of Enoch*, p. 128.
21.   Charles, *Book of Enoch*, p. 128.
22.   Laurence, *Book of Enoch*, at his 68.26-29, subsequently numbered 69.26-29; Hoffmann, *Das Buch Henoch*, p. 579.
23.   Charles, *Book of Enoch*, p. 183, referring back to p. 156.
24.   Charles, *Book of Enoch* (2nd edn, 1912), ad loc.

This simply alters the text to what Charles thought it should have said.

All these problems resulted from the basic notion that 'son of man' was a title of majesty, as it is in Christian tradition, both in Ethiopia and elsewhere. This influence was so pervasive that scholars did not really try to explain how the Aramaic (א)נשׁ(א) בר could have functioned in this way, not even if they really believed in an original Aramaic text. I have noted that at about the same time as Charles was working, the dominant view was challenged by Lietzmann.[25] This was primarily because of his excellent knowledge of Aramaic, but neither he nor his critics were competent in Ge'ez, and this was at least partly why he made no impression on the dominant view.

In 1946, Sjöberg was learned enough to mount a challenge to the dominant view, but he did so only tentatively.[26] For example, he noted the demonstrative in *zĕku walda sab'ĕ* at *1 En.* 46.2, and commented, 'Hier ist der Ausdruck "Menschensohn" selbstverständlich kein Titel.'[27] He was not however able to carry this through as far as it should go. For example, in commenting on 46.3, he did offer a partial Aramaic reconstruction:

דְּנָה הוּא בַר נָשָׁא דִּי צִדְקָא לֵהּ

This is reasonable in itself, but Sjöberg also offered a conjectural Hebrew version with בֶּן הָאָדָם, and a proposed Greek with ὁ υἱὸς τοῦ ἀνθρώπου! He almost took the major step forward which was needed when he commented on the Aramaic, 'Man kann בר נשא als Titel, man kann es aber auch als Appellativum, das durch den Relativsatz näher bestimmt wird, auffassen.'[28] Sjöberg did not however explain how בר נשא could function as a title, nor did he carry through properly the potential insight shown in the second half of this sentence. Rather he argued that even if it were not a title, which ὁ υἱὸς τοῦ ἀνθρώπου in any case surely must be, 'der Ausdruck doch einen besonderen Klang hat', and the being seen by Enoch is in any case 'der ganze besondere *himmlische Mensch*'.[29]

I have noted that Perrin and Lievestad became prominent in scholarly attacks on the Son of Man Concept, but that neither they nor those New Testament scholars who ignored them were properly competent in Ge'ez.[30] In 1976, I did tackle the Ge'ez text of the *Similitudes*, and used it to argue that in the original text the term 'son of man' was an ordinary word for man.[31] It is this work which now needs to be carried much further, by reconstructing and interpreting the original source which was once translated into Ge'ez.

There should be no doubt that this source was in Aramaic. We now know from the Dead Sea Scrolls that most of *1 Enoch* was written in Aramaic, because this is

---

25. See pp. 20–21 above.
26. E. Sjöberg, *Der Menschensohn im äthiopischen Henochbuch* (Lund: Gleerup, 1946).
27. Sjöberg, *Menschensohn*, p. 49.
28. Sjöberg, *Menschensohn*, p. 50.
29. Sjöberg, *Menschensohn*, p. 50.
30. See pp. 29–30 above.
31. Casey, 'Use of the Term "Son of Man" in the *Similitudes*'.

the language of the extant fragments. This demonstrates the fragility of arguments to the contrary based on one-word naughty tricks. For example, at *1 En.* 6.6, the Ethiopic is obviously corrupt, and the Greek text of Syncellus reads as follows:

ἦσαν δὲ οὗτοι διακόσιοι οἱ καταβάντες ἐν ταῖς ἡμέραις Ἰάρεδ ...
Now these were two hundred who descended in the days of Jared ...

Hallévi reconstructed this in Hebrew, and argued that this must be the original language because of the pun on the name Jared and the Hebrew word ירד, which means 'to descend' in Hebrew, but not in Aramaic, and in this he was followed by Charles:[32]

וַיֵּרְדוּ בִימֵי יֶרֶד עַל ראשׁ הַר חֶרמוֹן ...

Now, however, 4QEnᵃ has provided a fragmentary but continuous text of the whole of *1 En.* 6.4–8.1 in Aramaic, 4QEnᵇ provides a fragmentary text of *1 En.* 5.9–6.4 and 6.7–8.1, and all the surviving fragments are in Aramaic rather than Hebrew. Milik[33] suggested the following reconstruction:

...[והוו כלהן מאתין די נחתו]
ביומי ירד על [ראש הרמו]ן

It will be clear from this that ירד has survived as the name of Jared, but that the word for 'descend' has not survived. Milik has used the ordinary Aramaic נחתו. This would mean that the pun, which will have been found in Hebrew at *Jub.* 4.15, would not have been used in the Aramaic text. That is entirely reasonable: the older scholarship was far too inclined to posit puns and wordplays whenever older scholars could make them up, but the mere fact that they can be conjectured never showed that they were originally there. Knibb, on the other hand, noted that an occasional Hebrew word might have been used in this Aramaic text.[34] In general, we now know that Hebrew penetrated Aramaic at this time much more than we knew before the discovery of the Dead Sea scrolls, and it is entirely plausible that ירד was used in the Aramaic text at this point.

The important point here is that an occasional conjecture about a single word does not tell us the original language of a text. Moreover, the older scholarship suffered from being understood to mean 'Hebrew' when it really meant 'Hebrew or Aramaic'.[35] Similar comments apply to the text of the *Similitudes*, where scholars

32.   J. Hallévi, 'Recherches sur la langue de la rédaction primitive du Livre d'Énoch', *Journal Asiatique*, Sixième Série, 9 (1867), pp. 352–95 (356–7), followed by Charles, *Book of Enoch*, p. 63.
33.   J. T. Milik, *The Books of Enoch. Aramaic Fragments of Qumran Cave 4* (Oxford: Clarendon, 1976), pp. 150, 152.
34.   M. Knibb, *The Ethiopic Book of Enoch. A New Edition in the Light of the Aramaic Dead Sea Fragments* (2 vols; Oxford: Clarendon, 1978), vol. 2, pp. 68–9.
35.   For more detailed discussion of the older scholarship, see N. Schmidt, 'The Original Language of the Parables of Enoch', in R. F. Harper *et al.* (eds), *Old Testament and Semitic Studies in Memory of W. R. Harper* (2 vols; Chicago: Univ. of Chicago, 1908), vol. 2, pp. 327–49 (329–36).

have not produced any reasonably convincing arguments for either a Hebrew original or for a Greek version. The Greek versions of some parts of *1 Enoch* are very valuable, but there is no trace of a Greek version of the *Similitudes*. To give a detailed example, Black notes the peculiarity of *yaḥarri* at *1 En.* 45.3, which says that the Elect One sitting on his glorious throne will 'choose' their works.[36] After a brief review of the older scholarship, Black posits this as a direct translation of the Greek ἐκλέξει, and seems inclined towards ברר in a Hebrew *Grundschrift*. But he notes older scholarship conjecturing a misunderstanding of the Aramaic בחר, which means 'choose' as well as 'test, try', an entirely plausible conjecture as to the meaning of the original text. Moreover, בחר could have been *directly* translated with *yaḥarri*. All our evidence is accordingly consistent with the Ethiopic text being a direct translation from an Aramaic original.

There are two further points in favour of this. First, I have noted that the fragments of *1 Enoch* from Qumran are in Aramaic. The *Similitudes* contain a further development of the figure of Enoch, going significantly further than other material in *1 Enoch*. The central focus of the *Similitudes* lies in the figure of Enoch and the deliverance of the elect from oppression by the wicked. The differences between these different groups are quite basic. For example, the opponents may be described as 'the kings and the powerful', and they will be cast down because 'they do not exalt and do not praise him and do not confess from whom the kingdom was given to them' (*1 En.* 46.4-5). They are not at any stage accused of detailed legal offences, such as for example having sex with a woman during her menstrual period. This is forbidden at Ezek. 18.6, a prohibition violated by people at *Pss. Sol.* 8.12, who then further proceeded to eat sacrificial meat in the Temple. The descriptions of the Elect are equally basic. They are not said to do anything exceptionally righteous, such as living in a state of purity: indeed they are nowhere said to keep all the details of the Law, though it is assumed that they are basically observant. They are said, for example, to be 'the faithful who hang upon the name of the Lord of Spirits' (*1 En.* 46.8). This means that the authors of the *Similitudes* had no reason to change from Aramaic to Hebrew, the language of learned students of the Law. On the contrary, writing for a group of faithful Jews distinguished by their development of Enoch traditions, they had every reason to keep to Aramaic, the *lingua franca* of Judaism in general in Israel, and the language of their own traditions.

Thirdly, the main son of man passages make excellent sense in Aramaic. When they are properly reconstructed, we find that בר (א)נש(א) emerges as a normal term for 'man', as it is in all extant Aramaic sources. I propose to illustrate this here by reconstructing some of the main passages, leaving more extensive discussion of more complete reconstructions to a future monograph, which is necessary for such detailed discussion. I begin with the opening of the first son of man passage, *1 En.* 46.1-3.

---

36. M. Black, *The Book of Enoch or 1 Enoch. A New English Edition with Commentary and Textual Notes* (Leiden: Brill, 1985), p. 185.

1. .תמן חזית דלה ראש יומין וראשה כעמר נקא, ועמה אחרן דאנפוהי כחזו אנש ומלא חן אנפוהי כעיר וקדיש.

2. ובעית מן חד מן מלאכיא, הוא דאזל עמי וכל מסתרתא חויני,על בר אנשא דכן מן הוא ומן הן הוא למא עם ראש יומיא אזל הוא.

3. וענא ואמר לי, דנה הוא בר אנשא דאיתי לה קושטא וקושטא עמה יתב וכול גנזיא דמסתרתא הוא יגלא כי מרא דרוחיא בחרה וחלקה מכול תקף קדם מרא דרוחיא בקושטא לעלם.

1. There I saw one who had a head of days, and his head was like pure wool, and with him was another whose face was like the appearance of a man, and his face was full of grace like a Watcher and a Holy One.

2. And I asked one of the angels, he who went with me and showed me all the mysteries, about that (son of) man, who he was and where he was from, why he was going with the Head of Days.

3. And he answered and said to me, 'This is that (son of) man who has righteousness, and righteousness dwells with him, and he reveals all the treasures of the mysteries, for the Lord of Spirits has chosen him, and his lot is stronger than all before the Lord of Spirits in truth for ever.'

The expression 'head of days' has caused great difficulty to scholars. It is generally agreed that it is derived from the description of God, עתיק יומין, at Dan. 7.9, and this should be accepted. The precise form of the description is simply due to an author who was bowled over by the description of God in this very verse, ושער ראשה כעמר נקא. He thus had a vision of God with a quite remarkable head, the head of a remarkable old man with flowing locks. He made use of this vision of God again at *1 En.* 71.10, where again he selected his head for particular description, and declared it white and pure like wool. This creative re-use of imagery from a well-known text explains why Enoch does not need to ask the angel who this being is, he simply refers to him as ראש יומיא in the next verse, and subsequently.

At the end of v.1, the עיר וקדיש is obviously a good being, as so often in this literature (e.g. Dan. 4.10). The translators sometimes replace this expression with 'angel' or 'holy angel' (e.g. *1 En.* 93.2). When we reconstruct a possible original text, therefore, we have to use our discretion on a foundation of Intrinsic Probability, as I have done here. It is of course possible that I should have reconstructed more literally כחד מן מלאכיא קדישיא. It is important that this degree of uncertainty affects only this expression, and does not mean that the rest of this reconstruction is uncertain.

In v. 2, בר אנשא דכן is used with reference to the being whom Enoch saw with God, and it is used before this being is identified. It follows that בר אנשא cannot be a title here, because Enoch in asking the question is making clear that he does not know who this being is, and this question is not answered until the following verse. Thus בר אנשא is an ordinary term for man, as it is in all surviving Aramaic texts. The demonstrative דכן is entailed by the Ethiopic demonstrative *zĕku*. In each language, this demonstrative is anaphoric, that is to say, it refers back to the figure seen in the first verse. This anaphoric demonstrative is necessary precisely because בר (א)נש(א) is an ordinary term for 'man'. It would not have been necessary if it had been possible to use בר (א)נש(א) as a title, which also would not make sense because it was an ordinary term for man. If the authors had wanted a title for the figure mentioned after God in the first verse, בר (א)נש(א) would accordingly have been a very unsuitable choice.

It follows that בר אנשא is not a title in v. 3 either. The following relative clause defines which (son of) man Enoch has seen. The following description is a covert description of Enoch himself, seen from the perspective of the devotees of Enoch who wrote this document. It would not be clear to outsiders, who would need the dénoument at *1 En.* 71.14-17, a dénoument which will have delighted audiences who were this interested in the figure of Enoch. There are four points:

1. Righteousness is his outstanding characteristic. While other major figures in Second Temple Judaism might be regarded as especially righteous, in the Enoch literature this is particularly true of Enoch himself. In the opening of the whole book, he is described as a righteous man (ἄνθρωπος δίκαιος, *bě'ěsī ṣādĕq*), and the context implies that this was necessary for his visionary experiences. At 12.4, when he is called by God's own Watchers to go from the divine presence and convey the divine judgement to the wicked Watchers, he is addressed as scribe of righteousness (ὁ γραματεὺς τῆς δικαιοσύνης, *ṣaḥāfē ṣĕdĕq*). At 14.1, the account of Enoch's vision and reprimand of the Watchers has a title which begins 'The book of the words of righteousness/truth': the Greek has Βίβλος λόγων δικαιοσύνης, the Ethiopic *maṣḥaf qāla ṣĕdĕq*, and this time we have some of the Aramaic, ספר מלי קושט] (4Q204 vi 9). It is especially important that קושט] rather than צדק(ה) is the underlying term. It is characteristic of the Aramaic fragments, and consequently I have used it in the above reconstruction of *1 En.* 46.3. It has connotations of 'truth' as well as 'righteousness', and both are appropriate for the figure of Enoch. At *1 En.* 15.1, God himself, commissioning Enoch to take the news of his judgement to the Watchers, addresses him as righteous/true man and scribe of righteousness/truth (ἄνθρωπος ἀληθινὸς καὶ γραμματεὺς τῆς ἀληθείας, *bě'ěsī ṣādĕq waṣaḥāfē ṣĕdĕq*). It is likely that we have here two alternative translations of some form of קושטא. Regardless of this detail, it follows from all this evidence that, when the *Similitudes of Enoch* were written, the righteousness of Enoch had been a well-established feature of his character for more than a century. At a similar time, the book of Jubilees opined that because of his righteousness, Noah's life on earth was more excellent than any of the sons of men *except* Enoch (*Jub.* 10.17). Much later, two passages of the *Testaments of the Twelve Patriarchs* refer back to the book of Enoch the righteous (*T. Levi* 10.5 βίβλος Ἐνὼχ τοῦ δικαίου, and likewise *T. Dan* 5.6), and Judah is likewise said to have read aspects of the future ἐν βίβλοις Ἐνὼχ τοῦ δικαίου (*T. Jud.* 18.1).

It follows that when a devotee of Enoch wrote the opening part of *1 En.* 46.3, 'This is that (son of) man who has righteousness, and righteousness dwells with him', other members of the group would have instantly recognized Enoch, long before the recognition scene at *1 En.* 71.14, which clearly picks up this description.

2. 'He reveals all the treasures of the mysteries.' A major function of Enoch throughout the Enoch literature is that of revelation, a function in which he clearly exceeds all the other luminaries of Jewish tradition. A list of his revelations is also provided as early as *Jub.* 4.17-24, where it already includes a vision of human history until the day of judgement. It follows that, from the perspective of the Enoch

devotees for whom the *Similitudes* were written, the second point in the description of this figure would again identify him as Enoch himself.

3. The reason for this figure's position is that God himself has chosen him. The choice of Enoch for the function of revelation is also explicitly mentioned at *2 En.* 64.5. It is implicit in the whole of the Enoch literature, and in the context of the *Similitudes* it identifies him as the Elect One.

4. '… his lot is stronger than all before the Lord of Spirits in truth for ever.' This identifies the figure as the most outstanding human being ever, and from the perspective of Enoch circles this identifies him as Enoch himself.

All these points will have been decisive in the social context within which this document was written. It also makes perfect sense of the opening description of him, 'another whose face was like the appearance of a man, and his face was full of grace like a Watcher and a Holy One' (*1 En.* 46.1). Enoch's translation is recorded already at Gen. 5.24. It is described more fully at the end of the Similitudes, where he himself says 'all my flesh melted and my spirit was transformed' (*1 En.* 71.11). At *2 En.* 22, Enoch is taken before God himself, and is given clothes of glory in place of his earthly clothing. Then he declares, 'I looked at myself, and I had become like one of his glorious ones' (*1 En.* 22.10).[37] This tradition entails that some of the audience will have recognized Enoch already at *1 En.* 46.1, even the first time that the document was read.

The rest of this passage expounds the role of this figure as eschatological judge. Together with his role as the revealer, this is Enoch's most important role in the Similitudes. We must also look in detail at the next verse.

4. ובר אנשא דנה דחזית ינסא מלכיא ותקיפיא מן משכביהון וחסיניא מן כרסיהון ויפתח חרציהון דחסיניא
ויתבר שניהון דחיביא.

4. And this son of man whom you have seen will remove the kings and the powerful from their beds and the strong from their seats, and he will open the loins of the mighty and break the teeth of the sinners.

Here it is most important to note the care with which this figure is described. Once again, the Ethiopic *walda sab'ĕ*, the same term as at *1 En.* 46.2 and 46.3, must represent the Aramaic בר (א)נש(א). Most MSS have before it the Ethiopic demonstrative *zĕntū*. I have accordingly reconstructed the Aramaic demonstrative דנה. Tana 9 however omits this demonstrative, so a small degree of uncertainty is unavoidable. It is all the more important that a relative clause follows immediately. The Ethiopic *zar'īka* entails דחזית. In each language, we have a straightforward relative clause saying which son of man is referred to, the one 'whom you have seen'. This is a clear reference back to the figure seen in the previous verses, and this

---

37.   For *2 Enoch*, I follow the translation of F. I. Andersen in *OTP* II, as I regret that I do not read Old Slavonic.

reference is essential precisely because (א)בר נ(א)ש(א) is an ordinary term for 'man', not a title. This is why we need to be told which son of man is being referred to. The following verses clarify this figure's role as the eschatological judge.

The eschatological setting continues through the following verses to the next occurrence of the term 'son of man', at 48.2.

2. ובה בשעתא אתקרי בר אנשא דכן לות מרא דרוחיא ושמה קדם ראש יומיא.
3. ומן קדם דאתבריו שמשא ואתיא, מן קדם דאתעבדו כוכבי שמיא, שמה אתקרי קדם מרא דרוחיא.
4. והוא להוא לשבטא לקשיטיא דיסמכון עלוהי ולא ינפלון והוא לנהור דעממיא והוא לסברא לתבירין בלבא.
5. ינפלון ויסגדון קדמוהי כל דיתבין על יבשתא וישבחון ויברכון ויזמרון לשמה דמרא דרוחיא.
6. כל קבל דנה הוה בחיר וטמיר קדמוהי מן קדם דאתברי עלמא ועד עלמא.
7a. וגליתה לקדישיא ולקשיטיא חכמתא דמרא דרוחיא כי אזדהר בחלקה דקשיטיא.

2. And in that hour this son of man was designated to the Lord of Spirits, and his name before the Head of Days.

3. And before the sun and constellations were created, before the stars of heaven were made, his name was called before the Lord of Spirits.

4. And he will be a staff to the righteous that they may lean on him and not fall, and he (will be) the light of the Gentiles and hope to the broken-hearted.

5. All those who live on the dry ground will fall down and do obeisance before him, and they will praise and bless and sing to the name of the Lord of Spirits.

6. For this reason he was chosen and hidden before him before the world was created and for ever.

7a. And the Wisdom of the Lord of Spirits revealed him to the holy and the righteous, for he has guarded the lot of the righteous.

In the opening of this passage, we are given the information that in these last times the son of man figure whom we have met in Ch. 46 is named to the Lord of Spirits and before the Head of Days, parallel expressions which have him named to God. The term for 'son of man' is again *walda sab'ĕ*, the same term as at *1 En.* 46.2-4, and here again it must go back to the Aramaic (א)בר נ(א)ש(א). As at 46.2, the Ethiopic *walda sab'ĕ* is accompanied by the demonstrative *zĕku*, for which I have again reconstructed the Aramaic דכן. The function of this demonstrative is unambiguous. It is again anaphoric, and refers back to the figure already seen and expounded in Ch. 46.

Verse 3 then conveys another piece of information, that 'this son of man' was already named before God before the creation of the universe. It is not yet clear whether he was pre-existent or more simply foreknown. At v. 6, the fact that he was hidden before God before the creation of the world strongly implies his pre-existence. At v. 7, we are told how the Wisdom of God revealed him to the holy and the righteous. We are not given a time for this event. It must be after the creation of the world for there to be people for him to be revealed to. On the other hand, it does not seem to be in the eschatological period either. It is therefore the same time as v. 4, which is during normal human history. This makes excellent sense of the position of Enoch in the devotions of this social subgroup. From their perspective, Enoch really had been revealed to them, 'the holy and the righteous', as he had not been revealed to the rest of the Jewish people.

Enoch's extraordinarily elevated position in the belief and experience of this group is further shown by the functions which he is given. As a 'staff to the righteous' and 'hope to the broken-hearted' (v. 4), as well as the person who 'guarded the lot of the righteous' (v. 7a), he must have been central to the religious experience of this group. It is even more extraordinary that he shoud be presented as 'the light of the Gentiles'. While this is from Isaiah (42.6; 49.60), in our period it must be the work of people favourably disposed towards the large number of Gentile Godfearers found throughout the diaspora.

The immediately following part of the *Similitudes* returns to eschatological events. At Ch. 52, however, Enoch resumes his journeys, interspersed with events which happen in the places which he sees. At Ch. 56, this shifts to Israel, and at Ch. 57 the second similitude ends with people falling down and worshipping the Lord of Spirits. Chapter 58 marks the beginning of the third and final similitude. Again, however, we find Enoch seeing things, and at 60.1 there is a very strange date, in the 500th year of the life of Enoch, who did not live that long. At Gen. 5.32, this is a date in the life of Noah, and at *1 En.* 60.8 the speaker refers to 'my great-grandfather, the seventh from Adam', being taken to the garden of Eden. Scholars have therefore reasonably seen this chapter as a Noah apocalypse which has been edited in. At 60.10, the speaker is addressed as *walda sab'ĕ*. This is the same term for 'son of man' as before. It must again represent בר (א)נשׁ(א). This is an ordinary term for 'man', used as a form of address. There is accordingly no problem in its having no further connection with the use of 'son of man' in the rest of the *Similitudes*.

In Ch. 61, the main narrative of the *Similitudes* appears to resume, with the eschatological judge being described as 'the Chosen One'. The Ethiopic is *ḫĕruy*, which must represent the Aramaic בחירא. At the beginning of Ch. 62, God himself invites the kings and the mighty and the exalted and the landowners to see if they can recognize the Chosen One. The setting is evidently eschatological, and the term 'son of man' is used several times in the description of the 'Chosen One'. I propose the following Aramaic reconstruction of these verses.

5. ויחזון מנהון למנהון וידחלון ויאמכון אנפיהון ותאחד המון עקה כדי יחזון בר אנשׁא דכן דיתב בכרסי יקרה.
6. ויברכונה וישבחונה וירימונה מלכיא וגיבריא וכל דאחדין ארעא להוא דמלך על כולא דאתכסי.
7. כי מן עלמא מתכסא הוא בר אנשׁא ונטרה עליא קדם חילה וגליה לבחיריא.
8. ותתזרע חבורה דקדישׁיא ויקומון קדמה כל בחיריא ביומא הוא.
9. וינפלון כל מלכיא וגיבריא ועליא ואלין דמלכין על יבשׁתא ויסגדון ויסכון לבר אנשׁא דכן ויתחננו לה ויבעון רחמין מן קדמה.

5. And they will look at each other and be afraid and lower their countenances and distress will seize them, when they see that son of man sitting on his glorious throne.
6. And the kings and the mighty and all the landowners will bless and praise and magnify him who rules over everything, he who was hidden.
7. For from of old that son of man was hidden, and the Most High kept him before his host, and revealed him to the elect.
8. And the community of the holy ones will be sown, and all the chosen will stand before him on that day.
9. And all the kings and mighty and exalted and those who rule the dry ground will fall down and worship, and they will set their hope on that son of man, and they will beseech him and seek mercy from him.

Given the context, it is clear that throughout this passage the term 'son of man' refers to the 'Chosen One'. At 62.5, the Ethiopic term for 'son of man' is *walda bě'ěsī*, a change from the use of *walda sab'ě* in the previous examples. It is difficult to see any significance in this change. Both expressions mean 'son of man' in the sense of 'human being', and must go back to an original Aramaic (א)נש(א) בר. We should infer that, after a gap of several chapters, one or another translator simply went for an established alternative phrase. Nonetheless, this change caused trouble. Ethiopian Christians came to believe that this is a wonderful prophecy of Christ Jesus, and some of them perceived *walda bě'ěsī* as a son of a man in the sense that he was born, as we all are, with a human father. Accordingly, all late MSS read *walda bě'ěsit*, 'son of a woman', with the virgin birth of Jesus in mind. This reading must accordingly be regarded as secondary. It may be for the same reason that Tana 9 reads *walda sab'ě*. Before the term 'son of man', all MSS have a demonstrative, almost all of them *zěku*. I have accordingly reconstructed דכן, as before. The demonstrative is again anaphoric. It refers back directly to the 'Chosen One', and to the earlier occurrences of (א)נש(א) בר in Chs 46 and 48. This figure is still sitting on his glorious throne as the eschatological judge, who now receives adoration from the wicked kings and mighty.

At 62.7, the Ethiopic text has the first occurrence of *walda 'ěguala 'ěmmaḥěiāw*. This is the second change in three verses. It strongly suggests a translator who did not like *walda sab'ě*, and who did not know quite what to do. It is difficult to imagine anything other than (א)נש(א) בר in an Aramaic source text. In the Ethiopic text, the immediately preceding word is *kōna*, which must be taken in the meaning 'was' with the preceding participle *ḥěbū'*, 'hidden', to give the meaning 'the son of man was hidden'. The Aramaic underlying *kōna* must however be הוא, or הוה. This may also be part of the past tense of the verb 'to be', as the translator has interpreted it, but הוא may equally well be the demonstrative pronoun, 'that'. I propose that this makes much better sense, as in the above reconstruction. This is anaphoric, and refers back to the immediately preceding figure, previously known as the 'Chosen One', and of whom the term (א)נש(א) בר has been used several times already. The existence of this figure 'from of old' is consistent with the story of Enoch, who was thought to have been with the angels for three hundred years (*Jub.* 4.21, cf. Gen. 5.22), which could reasonably be interpreted as God keeping him 'before his host'. The revelation to the elect is given no time indication, but it is clearly neither in primordial time nor in the last times. As at 48.4,7a, this reflects the situation of Enoch as revealed to his adherents, including the author(s) of the *Similitudes*.

The following verses look forward to the last times. At v. 9, the kings and mighty will set their hope on 'that son of man'. The term for 'son of man' in the Ethiopic text is again *walda 'ěguala 'ěmmaḥěiāw*, and here it is preceded by the demonstrative *zěku*. I have accordingly reconstructed בר אנשא דכן. In both languages the demonstrative is again anaphoric. It looks back to the figure already under discussion, and this defining particle is again needed precisely because (א)נש(א) בר on its own is not fit to be a title or a precise term. The hope of the wicked is in vain.

The next few verses describe the final punishment of the oppressive wicked. The righteous and chosen will of course be saved on that day. Part of the description of their salvation, at *1 En.* 62.14, again uses the term 'son of man'.

14. ומרא דרוחיא ישכן עליהון ועם בר אנשא דכן יאכלון וישכבון ויקומון עד עלם עלמיא.

14. And the Lord of Spirits will abide over them, and they will eat and lie down and rise up with that son of man for ever and ever.

Here again the Ethiopic text has *walda 'ĕguala 'ĕmmaḥĕiāw* for 'son of man', preceded by the demonstrative *zĕku*. I have accordingly reconstructed once more בר אנשא דכן. In both languages the demonstrative is again anaphoric. It looks back to the figure already under discussion, and this defining particle is again needed precisely because בר (א)נ(א)ש on its own is not fit to be a title or a precise term.

The following chapter continues with the eschatological theme, and returns to the fate of the kings and the mighty and the landowners. They attempt a somewhat belated repentance, which is much too late to prevent their punishment. One verse again uses the term 'son of man':

11. ובאתר דנה יתמלון אנפיהון בהתא הוא בר אנשא קדם הוא בר אנשא ויתרדפון מן קדם אנפוהי וחרבא יתב קדם אנפוהי לותהון.

11. And after this their faces will be filled with shame before that son of man, and they will be driven from before his face, and the sword will dwell with them before his face.

The term for 'son of man' in the Ethiopic text is again *walda 'ĕguala 'ĕmmaḥĕiāw*, preceded by the demonstrative *zĕku*. This time I have reconstructed הוא בר אנשא. In both languages the demonstrative is again anaphoric. It looks back to the mighty figure expounded in the previous chapter as well as earlier in the book, and the demonstrative is again needed precisely because בר (א) נ(א)ש on its own is not fit to be a title or a precise term.

This chapter ends this whole section of the *Similitudes*. The next section shifts right back to the sins of the angels who descended to earth and caused people to sin, with the subsequent judgement of people in the Flood, and of the wicked angels in torments which are somehow supposed to be related to the waters taken by the kings and mighty. The names of the major wicked angels follow, and then an account of an extraordinary oath by which the universe was created and is sustained. This leads to praise of the Lord of Spirits by the stars, winds and so on, and that shifts into joy at the revelation of the name of that son of man. The text appears to have been put together by a final redactor who thought associatively about the different kinds of judgement and salvation, not by someone with a keen sense of logic. The end of the third similitude, still concerned with the eschatological fates of the righteous and the wicked, follows at the end of Ch. 69.

26. והוה להון חדוא רבה וברכו ושבחו ורוממו כי אתגלי להון שמה די הוא בר אנשא.

27. ויתב בכרסי יקרה וראש דינא דינא אתיהב להוא בר אנשא ולא יחלף ולא יאבד מן אנפי ארעא.

28. ואלין דאטעיו עלמא באסורין יתאסרון ובכנישת אבדון יתחבשון וכל עבדיהון יחלפון מן אנפי ארעא.

29. ומן אדין לא להוא דיתחבל כי הוא בר אנשא אתחזי ויתב בכרסי יקרה וכל רשעא מן קדם אנפוהי יחלף.
ויאזל ויאמר להוא בר אנשא ויתקף קדם מרא דרוחא.
דנה הוא מתל תליתי דחנוך.

26. And they had great joy, and they blessed and praised and extolled, because the name of that son of man was revealed to them.

27. And he sat on his glorious throne, and the sum of judgement was given to that son of man. And he will not pass away and he will not perish from the face of the earth.

28. And those who led the world astray shall be bound with chains, and they shall be imprisoned

in an assembly of destruction, and all their deeds will vanish from the face of the earth.
29. And from then onwards there will not be anything corruptible, for that son of man has appeared and has sat on his glorious throne, and all evil will vanish from before his face. And He will go and speak to that son of man, and he will be strong before the Lord of Spirits.
    This is the third parable of Enoch.

This section is the end of the third parable. This parable began at Ch. 58. I have noted that additional material has been interpolated into it, and we cannot tell whether anything was lost in the process, only that the transitions are very uneven. The changes of tense in this section are due to changes of perspective. In vv. 26-27a, the perfect tense is used to narrate what Enoch saw in his vision. The major event here is the revelation of the name of 'that son of man'. This is clearly the same major figure as before, otherwise the 'Chosen One', and referred to with the term 'son of man' since Ch. 46. The term for 'son of man' in most MSS of the Ethiopic text of v. 26 is again *walda 'ĕguala 'ĕmmaḥĕiāw*. It is difficult to know what to make of the omission of *walda* in a few relatively good MSS (Knibb lists BM 491, Abb 35, Abb 55 and Tana 9). This may be due to homoioarcton after the preceding demonstrative *wĕ'ĕtu*. I have presupposed this in reconstructing הוא בר אנשא. Here again the demonstrative is anaphoric, referring back to the figure of the previous chapters, and presumably it was originally much closer to the end of Ch. 63 than it is now. It is however possible that the omission of *walda* is original, and that it was added to conform the expression to the one which is commonest in the *Similitudes*. In this case the translator was even more inconsistent than we now suppose, for Intrinsic Probability favours the view that *'ĕguala 'ĕmmaḥĕiāw* would be a translation of בר (א)נ(א)שׁ rather than of anything else.

    The name of 'that son of man' is known to us from the end of the *Similitudes* as 'Enoch', and we have seen that this was known to the chosen already in Ch. 62. He sits on his glorious throne to carry out his role as the eschatological judge. In v. 27a, the term for 'son of man' in the Ethiopic text is again *walda 'ĕguala 'ĕmmaḥĕiāw*. This time it is preceded by the Ethiopic *lōtū 1*. Literally, this means that the sum of judgement was given 'to him, to the son of the offspring of the mother of the living'. This is an alternative to the demonstrative, another way of making clear that the figure referred to is the same figure as was referred to previously. I have attributed this change to the translator, and I have reconstructed להוא בר אנשא. There should be no doubt about בר (א)נשׁ(א), but one or two other details are necessarily uncertain. For example, the Aramaic might have been closer to the present Ethiopic, reading perhaps לה לבר אנשא. Such possibilities do not affect the meaning of the text.

    Verse 27b makes an important point about 'that son of man', namely that he will not die, despite being human, the only possible interpretation of his being a (son of) man. This interpretation results from following the reading of Tana 9, with some varying degree of support from other MSS which sometimes preserve old readings. It prepares the way for his identification as Enoch himself in the following account of his translation. This is contrary to Ethiopian Christian tradition, which interpreted *walda 'ĕguala 'ĕmmaḥĕiāw* as Jesus Christ, and which held the atoning death of Jesus to be important, as have most strands of Christian tradition. Hence the corruptions in later MSS, which drop the *'ī*, 'not', before both verbs, change their aspect and give them an object, 'sinners', which enables v. 27b to be taken into the picture of the destruction of the wicked in v. 28. The reading of Tana 9 has a perfect *Sitz im Leben* in the original text of the *Similitudes*, and the above Aramaic reconstruction from it is unproblematical. The very phrase (א)נש(א) בר implies that this being is human, and will therefore die. Enoch, almost uniquely among human beings, did not die, and it was accordingly very important to the Enoch devotees who wrote this document to declare his immortality at this point. His name has just been revealed to people in the last days at v. 26, and v. 27 further confirms to anyone in the know that his name is indeed Enoch, as they will to varying degrees have known or suspected since Ch. 46.

In v. 28, the imperfect is used with a future sense to predict the final punishment of the wicked. In the first sentence of v. 29, the imperfects are used as in v. 28 to predict future events, and the two perfects both hark back to Enoch's vision and relate an event, the appearance of 'that son of man', which takes place before the destruction of the wicked. Here the term for 'son of man' is *walda bĕ'ĕsī*, as at 62.5, preceded by the demonstrative *wĕ'ĕtu*. The demonstrative is unproblematic, as is the reconstruction הוא בר אנשא. The demonstrative is again anaphoric, referring back to the central figure of the previous verses, and of the *Similitudes* as a whole. The reasons for the translators' change from *walda 'ĕguala 'ĕmmaḥĕiāw* back to *walda bĕ'ĕsi*, however, remain puzzling. We can only infer that since both expressions begin with 'son of', and mean one single man, the translators considered them both equivalent to the Aramaic (א)נש(א) בר, and did not mind which they used as much as we think they should have done.

The final sentence of the narrative of v. 29 has been found so difficult that it is customary to alter the text. We should not do this. We should rather follow the reading of Tana 9, with support from Bodl 4. These MSS read the singular verb *wayĕnagĕr*, 'and he will speak'. I have accordingly reconstructed ויאמר. I have also taken ואזל with it, and I propose that the subject is God. This kind of unmarked change of subject is quite normal in Aramaic texts. The term for 'son of man' is again *walda bĕ'ĕsī*, as in the earlier part of this verse, and it is again preceded by the demonstrative *wĕ'ĕtu*. The demonstrative is again anaphoric, referring back to the central figure of this and previous verses, and of the *Similitudes* as a whole. We can now see that this sentence looks forward to *1 En.* 71.14, where God does speak to Enoch, who is strong before him. Thus when the oldest available text of these final verses of the last similitude is used to reconstruct a possible Aramaic source, they look forward unambiguously to the dénouement of this work in the final chapter.

The very last sentence of v. 29 announces the end of the Parables as such. This clears the way for the story of Enoch's removal, which was already old, and of his translation, which was part of the oldest traditions about him. It follows that these chapters should not be seen as a later addition. We have seen that the very first comments to make use of the term 'son of man' (*1 En.* 46.1-3) look forward very clearly to 71.14. We should now see that the concluding passage was deliberately designed to do the same.

The final two chapters have caused terrible problems to scholars, who have misunderstood them in a variety of ways. The problems have been both textual and conceptual, and to some degree these two different kinds of problems have been related. I begin with *1 En.* 70.1-4, for which I propose the following reconstruction.

1. והוה באתר דנה אתרומם שמה חיא להוא בר אנשא לות מרא דרוחיא מן אנון דיתבין על יבשא.
2. ואסתלק במרכבה דרוחא ונפק שמה ביניהון.
3. ומן יומא הוא לא אתחשבת ביניהון. ואותבני בין תרתין רוחין בין צפונא ומערבא, דסלקו חבלין מלאכיא לתמן דימשחון לי אתרא לבחיריא ולקשיטיא.
4. ותמן חזית אבהתא קדמיא וקשיטיא דמן עלמא בהוא אתרא יתבון.

1. And it came to pass after this that the living name of that son of man was exalted with the Lord of Spirits more than those who dwell on the dry ground.
2. And he was taken up in a chariot of the spirit, and his name went out among them.
3. And from that day I was no longer counted among them. And he settled me between two winds, the North and the West, where the angels took ropes to measure for me the place for the elect and the righteous.
4. And there I saw the first fathers and the righteous, who from of old will dwell in that place.

The most serious problem occurs in the opening verse. Here the corrupt texts used by older scholars resulted in Enoch being exalted to 'that son of man', which made hopeless nonsense of his identification with this figure at *1 En.* 71.14. I began to sort this problem out in 1976, when I pointed out that Intrinsic Probability favoured the reading of one of the earliest and best manuscripts, labelled U by Charles, with support from V and W, both of which were known to have preserved some old and sound readings.[38] This removed the main problem by having the name of 'that son of man' raised aloft to the Lord of Spirits, so this seemed to be the old story of the translation of Enoch, which made perfect sense of 71.14, where he is finally greeted by God. This work was carried much further by Olson in 1998, in the light of further discoveries of older manuscripts.[39] My reconstruction is based on these more ancient readings, and owes much to Olson's exegesis, which has caused me to change other aspects of my interpretation.

The opening phrase is unproblematical: it simply locates the events about to be described later than the visions of Enoch which have been described already. The next word, *tala'āla*, may reasonably be reconstructed as אתרומם. Some kind of exaltation is evidently referred to, but I follow Olson in seeing this not as the beginning of Enoch's exaltation, but an indication of his reputation. The next two words, *sĕmu ḥĕyāw*, have also been a major cause of trouble. The proposed reconstruction, however, שמה חיא, is not problematical. I have followed Olson in

38. Casey, 'Use of the Term "son of man" in the *Similitudes*', pp. 25–7. Cf. also A. Caquot, 'Remarques sur les chapitres 70 et 71 du livre éthiopien d'Hénoch', in *Apocalypses et Théologie de l'Espérance. Congrès de Toulouse (1975)* (LD 95. Paris: Cerf, 1977), pp. 111–22 (113); Kearns, *Überlieferungsgeschichtliche und Rezeptionsgeschichtliche Studie*, p. 102 n. 27; Black, *Enoch*, p.250.

39. D. C. Olson, 'Enoch and the Son of Man in the Epilogue of the Parables', *JSP* 18 (1998), pp. 27–38.

taking these two words closely together, and in supposing that Enoch's 'living name' refers to his great reputation.

Next comes a crucial aspect of the readings of UVW, now found also in EMML 1768 and 7584, both fifteenth century MSS, and the oldest of all MSS only more difficult to read just here, EMML 2080, which is certainly at least as old as the fifteenth century, and may be even older. They are supported by EMML 2436 and 6974, which have in common with VW that, while later in date, they have preserved some old and sound readings. All these MSS crucially omit *baḥabēhū* between *sěmu ḥěyāw* and *lawě'ětū walda 'ěguala 'ěmmaḥěiāw*. It follows that this shorter reading has massive Weight of Attestation among the oldest and best manuscripts in its favour, as well as Intrinsic Probability. I have followed it in the above reconstruction, where it means that the words שמה חיא להוא בר אנשא can all be taken together, to mean 'the living name of that son of man'.

In the light of the above reconstruction, I follow the main lines of Olson's comments on the Ethiopic translation as my interpretation of the original text. The first verse refers to Enoch's outstanding reputation before God. At v. 2, Enoch really is taken up, but this is not his translation either: it is his removal to the place designated in v. 3. Olson also correctly saw, as Black had done, that the end of the verse refers to his fame, not to his disappearance. I have readily reconstructed an Aramaic source which also refers to his fame, for in Aramaic as in Ge'ez this is the meaning of an idiom according to which a person's name going out refers to their fame. At Lev.R. 619:2, for example, שמך נפיק בעלמא means 'you will be famous'. This is in accordance with traditions about Enoch. At *Jub.* 4.23, for example, he is taken from among the children of men and conducted to the garden of Eden 'for greatness and honour'.

At v. 3, the text says in a different way that he was removed from among people, and this time it says where he was put. There is a deliberate reference to *1 En.* 61.1, where the angels head for the north with their measuring ropes. Enoch is therefore in the 'garden of righteousness', the name for Eden at *1 En.* 32.3, where it is placed in the north-east (*1 En.* 32.1-2, cf. 77.3).

Chapter 71 really does give an account of Enoch's translation. In the opening of v. 1, we must reconstruct אתלקח for the Ethiopic *tětkabat*, using the same word as at Gen. 5.24. This gives us the following blunt statement right at the beginning:

1. והוה באתר דנה דאתלקח רוחי וסלק לשמיא.

1. And it came to pass after this that my spirit was translated and ascended to the heavens.

A detailed account of Enoch's traditional translation follows. He sees many angels, and traditional imagery of fire, light and the like are much used. When he falls on his face, Michael pulls him up, and shows him secrets of the universe again. A landmark is reached at v. 5, ולקח רוחי לשמי שמיא, 'And he translated my spirit to the heaven of heavens …'. This is evidently further up. Here Enoch sees God's house, the Seraphin, Cherubin and Ophannin who guard his glorious throne, and myriads of angels including Michael, Raphael, Gabriel and Phanuel. At v. 10, he sees God himself, and this leads to the next landmark.

11. ונפלת על אנפי וכל בשׂרי אתמסי ורוחי אשׁתני ...

11. And I fell on my face, and all my flesh melted and my spirit was transformed.

Now Enoch has been completely translated, and he is effectively just like a heavenly being. I have noted the close parallel to this at *2 En.* 22, where Enoch is also taken before God himself, and is given clothes of glory in place of his earthly clothing. Then he declares, 'I looked at myself, and I had become like one of his glorious ones' (*1 En.* 22.10). This explains why the figure whom he saw in his vision at *1 En.* 46.1 looked so much like a heavenly being.

Enoch then utters blessings which please God, who comes to him with Michael, Gabriel, Raphael, Phanuel and myriads of lesser angels. The dénouement of the whole work follows. There is a slight textual problem at the beginning of v. 14, where we should follow four of the oldest MSS in omitting 'angel'. This will have been a gloss, caused by God speaking of himself in the third person. There is no such problem with what God says to Enoch, the words which have caused so much trouble to scholars. I offer the following reconstruction and translation of the closing verses of this work.

14. ואתא עלי ובקלו נשׁקני ואמר לי אנתה הוא בר אנשׁא די יליד לקושׁטא וקושׁטא עלך יתב וקושׁטא לראשׁ יומיא לא ישׁבקנך.

15. ואמר לי, יקרא לך שׁלם בשׁם עלמה דאתי כי מן תמן נפק שׁלם מן בריתא דעלמא וכן להוה לך לעלם ולעלם דעלמין.

16. וכל יהלכון על אורחך כדי קושׁטא לא ישׁבקנך לעלם. עמך להוה מדורהון ועמך חולקהון ומנך לא יתפרשׁון לעלם ולעלם דעלמין.

17. וכדנא להוה ארך יומין עם הוא בר אנשׁא ושׁלם להוה לקשׁיטיא ואורח קשׁט לקשׁיטיא בשׁם מרא דרוחיא לעלם דעלמין.

14. And he came to me and kissed me with his voice and said to me, 'You are the son of man who is born to righteousness, and righteousness dwells with you, and the righteousness of the Head of Days will not leave you.'

15. And he said to me, 'He will proclaim peace for you in the name of the world to come, for peace has come out from there since the creation of the world, and so shall it be for you for ever and for ever and ever.

16. And everyone will walk according to your way inasmuch as righteousness will not forsake you for ever. With you will be their dwelling and with you their lot, and they will not be separated from you for ever and for ever and ever.'

17. And thus there will be length of days with that son of man, and there will be peace for the righteous, and a righteous way for the righteous, in the name of the Lord of Spirits for ever and ever.

At v. 14, the term for 'son of man' is *walda bĕ'ĕsi*, as at 62.5 and 69.29 (bis). We have already seen that the use of three different terms for 'son of man' in this text is puzzling, but does not seem to be of any significance. The underlying Aramaic can again only be בר (א)נשׁ(א), which makes excellent sense. It must be taken closely with the following relative clause, which defines which (son of) man is referred to. It looks back to Enoch's vision at *1 En.* 46.3, where he saw 'that (son of) man who has righteousness, and righteousness dwells with him'. In the light of the *Similitudes* as a whole, this also identifies Enoch with the Chosen One, and as the eschatological judge who will vindicate the righteous and condemn the wicked. We have also seen that *1 En.* 69.29 looks forward to this scene. It follows that this dénouement is an integral part of this work, not some kind of late addition. Finally, it should be noted that הוא, like *wĕ'ĕtū* in the Ethiopic text, could be taken as a demonstrative rather than as the copula, which is not strictly speaking necessary. We could then translate, 'You are that (son of) man who is born to righteousness ...'. This would not significantly affect the meaning, since it would still be a reference back to *1 En.* 46.3, and with all the overtones which I have described.

The final use of the term 'son of man', at *1 En.* 71.17, must be interpreted as a closing comment by the author. For the expression 'son of man' itself, the translator has gone back to *walda 'ĕguala 'ĕmmaḥĕiāw*. Again this change is puzzling, but does not seem to be significant. It must again represent בר (א)נש(א), as in the above reconstruction. This final comment is a highly integrative use of הוא בר אנשא, for it is the precise expression used for the central figure throughout the *Similitudes*, and it is used here straight *after* his explicit identification as Enoch at 71.14.

It follows that, throughout the visions which made up the bulk of the *Similitudes*, Enoch saw visions of himself as he would be after his translation. Many scholars have refused to believe this.[40] The main point should however now be clear: this is what the text clearly implies, and only this view makes sense of the ending of this document. We must therefore make greater efforts to understand it. In 1972, Caquot noted a helpful parallel in the *Testament of Levi*.[41] In a vision at Bethel (*T. Levi* 7.4–8.1), Levi sees in the future seven men telling him to put on the robe of the priesthood and other things associated with it. They then anoint him and effectively initiate him into the priesthood. Finally they prophesy the future after Levi's earthly life. This is as clear a parallel as one could wish for. It is too Jewish to have originated when this document was rewritten by Christians. We may therefore safely consider this phenomenon as native to Second Temple Judaism. Moreover, it should not be difficult to see how it arose. There are numerous documents from this period in which people foresee the future in visions. Those who do so are always great figures of the past. All that has to happen is that the sage himself must belong to the distant past, and later perform functions of exceptional importance. This is what led the author of the *Testament of Levi* to portray Levi having a vision of the future in which he was inaugurated into the priesthood, a Jewish institution of exceptional importance of which he was perceived as a founding father. The *Testaments of the Twelve Patriarchs* also have several references to the book of Enoch the righteous as an authoritative work (e.g. *T. Levi* 10.5), so the visionary traditions of Enoch and

40.   E.g. C. C. Caragounis, *The Son of Man* (WUNT 38; Tübingen: Mohr (Siebeck), 1986), pp. 110–12, n. 121, puts forward all kinds of reasons for rejecting the text, and at p. 115 n. 126 comments, apparently on 71.14, 'that miserable blunder of Ethiopic transcription'; J. J. Collins, *The Scepter and the Star. The Messiahs of the Dead Sea Scrolls and Other Ancient Literature* (New York: Doubleday, 1995), pp. 177–82 offers a complex discussion because he does not accept this main point.

41.   A. Caquot, 'La Double Investiture de Lévi (Brèves remarques sur *Testament de Lévi, VIII*)', in C. J. Bleeker *et al.* (eds), *Ex orbe religionum. Studia Geo Widengren* (2 vols; NumenSup 21–2. Leiden: Brill, 1972), vol. 1, pp. 156–61.

of the twelve patriarchs evidently emanated from Jewish traditions of a generally similar kind.

Moreover, there is another parallel in the older Enoch traditions themselves. At the close of the massive vision of the future generally known from its imagery as the *Animal Apocalypse* (*1 En.* 85–90), Enoch comments, 'And this is the vision which I saw while I was asleep' (*1 En.* 90.40). Between the two parts of the final judgement, however, we find that three angels and 'that ram' (? Elijah) take Enoch up and put him down 'among those sheep' (*1 En.* 90.31). Here, therefore, Enoch, while asleep, saw himself in a vision at the last judgement. The *Animal Apocalypse* was written *c.* 165–60 BCE. This means that, when the *Similitudes* were written, the idea of Enoch seeing himself in a vision at the last judgement had been around among Enoch devotees for generations. His position in the *Similitudes*, where Enoch sees himself not merely *at* the last judgement, but as the eschatological judge himself, is a vigorous development of existing Enochic traditions. We should therefore see this as a creative literary and religious achievement: we should not refuse to follow the only natural interpretation of the text.

The following conclusions may therefore be drawn. The *Similitudes of Enoch* were written in the form of a revelatory work. They belong to a very old tradition of Enoch as a visionary, and as a scribe who wrote down the condemnation of wicked beings, and the salvation of the righteous. In this work, Enoch sees visions of the eschatological judge who will carry out the judgement, of the salvation of the righteous and the punishment of the wicked. In the vision of Ch. 46, Enoch sees this figure and describes him in such a way that Jewish devotees of Enoch would recognize him. In Ch. 69, at the end of the third vision, there are deliberate pointers to Enoch's translation in Ch. 71. In Ch. 70, after the visions, Enoch is taken to the garden of Eden. In Ch. 71, there is a narrative of his translation, in accordance with old tradition about him. This narrative has the further development of a recognition scene, in which God identifies Enoch in terms strongly reminiscent of Ch. 46. It follows that Enoch in a vision actually saw himself in the future, in accordance with old tradition about him.

In the vision of Ch. 46, before the description which would alert devotees of Enoch to the identity of the son of man figure, he is first of all described in more mysterious terms with some reminiscences of Dan. 7.13. This is where the term (א)שׁנ(א) בר was originally drawn from. Throughout the *Similitudes*, this term (א)שׁנ(א) בר was used in accordance with normal Aramaic usage as an ordinary term for 'man'. In every case, something makes clear a reference back to the original appearance of this figure at the beginning of Ch. 46. Much the commonest device is the anaphoric use of a demonstrative. It follows that this work does not provide evidence of a Son of Man Concept. It is however the central work on which the existence of this figure has been based. It follows that, after finding no such concept in this work or in Daniel 7, I have come most of the way towards showing that there was no such concept in Second Temple Judaism. This demonstration must be completed by discussing a small selection of other works in which this Concept has been found.

3. *4 Ezra 13*

The third work which was traditionally used as evidence for a Son of Man Concept is a single chapter in *4 Ezra*. This work must be dated *c.* 100 CE, so it requires the support of earlier works to be taken seriously as evidence of a Son of Man Concept being in existence by the time of Jesus. It has not survived in its original language, which was probably Hebrew. Of the major versions, the Latin and the Syriac form one textual tradition which the older scholarship took most notice of, and these versions were certainly made from a lost Greek translation. Another major textual tradition is formed by the Ge'ez and the Georgian versions.[42]

The chief character in this chapter is the figure of a man. It is unfortunate that there is a lacuna in the Latin at his first appearance, where the Syriac reads איך דמותא דברנשא. This use of ברנשא was important in leading some traditional scholarship to the view that here was further evidence of a Son of Man Concept, and more recently Caragounis has found it decisive.[43] This view should not be accepted. In this first occurrence, the Latin has *homo* and the Ge'ez has *bě'ěsī*. In the subsequent descriptions of the man-like figure in the vision (13.3b,5,12), the Latin always has *homo*, the Syriac ברנשא and the Ge'ez *bě'ěsī* (the Georgian is not extant). In the interpretative section (13.25,32,51), the Latin always has *vir*, the Syriac גברא, and the Ge'ez *bě'ěsī*. It follows that the Latin and Syriac translated ἄνθρωπος from the Greek version in the visionary section, and that this, like the Ge'ez *bě'ěsī*, represents אדם in the original Hebrew text. Similarly in the interpretative section, the Greek translation used ἀνήρ, representing איש in the original text. The use of the Syriac ברנשא to translate the Greek ἄνθρωπος is entirely natural, because it was so common. Consequently, it is also found where the Latin has *homo* in several passages of *4 Ezra*, both in the singular (e.g. 6.10 (bis), 7.29, 8.6) and in the plural (e.g. 3.36, 5.12, 6.26).

It follows that the term 'son of man' was not used in the original text of *4 Ezra 13*. It should not therefore be used as evidence of a Son of Man Concept in Judaism.

4. *Other Passages*

Once the Son of Man Concept was found in these three passages, it was read into many others. It was not however normally founded on them. I have not found any of them remotely convincing. I therefore discuss only two such passages, as a sample of what has been attempted, with a view to indicating why I have found all such attempts unconvincing.

A vigorous attempt to use Tg. Ps. 8 as evidence that בר (א)נש(א) was a messianic term was made by Moloney.[44] The most important part of it is v. 5.

---

42. For recent discussion of the text and versions, see M. E. Stone, *Fourth Ezra. A Commentary on the Book of Fourth Ezra* (Hermeneia. Minneapolis: Fortress, 1990), pp. 1–11.

43. Caragounis, *Son of Man*, pp. 127–8.

44. F. J. Moloney, 'The Targum on Ps. 8 and the New Testament', *Salesianum* 37 (1975), pp. 326–36; 'The End of the Son of Man?', *Downside Review* 98 (1980), pp. 280–90 (284–5); 'The Re-Interpretation of Psalm VIII and the Son of Man Debate', *NTS* 27 (1981), pp. 656–72 (665–6).

Tg. Ps. 8.5: MT אנוש and בן אדם.

מה בר נשא מטול תדכר עובדוי ובר נשא מטול תסער עלוי.

What is (the son of) man that you remember his works, and (the son of) man that you visit him?

One of Moloney's main points is that 'the generic term "man" (MT: אנוש) is individualized to a specific "the Son of Man"'.[45] This is untrue. The definite state had lost its force by the time that the Targum to Psalms was written down. Moloney's suggestion that the context is more important, and indicates an exception to this general rule, is contrary to the nature of exhausted features of languages. Once any feature of a language has lost its force, something else has to be used if its function is to be replaced. The generic use of בר נשא is quite common in late Targums. Examples include Ps. 104.14-15 (passage 11 above), where Tg and Pesh both use the definite בר נשא three times, once for האדם where the Hebrew article is generic, and twice for anarthrous אנוש, as at Tg. Ps. 8.5.

11. Tg. Ps. 104.14-15: MT האדם, אנוש, אנוש:

דמרבי עסבא לבעירי וירקי לפולחנא דבר נשא למיפק לחמא מן ארעא וחמרא דמחדי ליבא דבר נשא לאנהרא
אפיא מן משחא ולחמא ליבא דבר נשא יסעד.

Who increases the grass for the cattle, and greens for the service of (the son of) man, to bring forth bread from the earth and wine which gladdens the heart of (the son of) man, to make his face shine with oil, and bread satisfies the heart of (the son of) man.

Here בר נשא is generic in all three examples of the definite state. It follows from many examples of this kind that the definite state of בר נשא at Tg. Ps. 8.5 does not show that אנוש has been individualized to a specific 'the Son of Man'. Moloney also sees significance in the fact that at Tg. Ps. 8.5 בר נשא occurs twice, rendering two different expressions. Tg. Ps. 104.14-15 is a good example of this happening with בר נשא in a generic sense, having three occurrences for two different expressions. I have shown elsewhere that בר נש(א) is the normal rendering of בן אדם, and that it renders אנוש many times in the major Aramaic versions of the Hebrew Bible, including 6 of the other 11 examples in the Targum to Psalms.[46] Tg. Ps. 104.14-15 provides two examples of the generic use of the definite state בר נשא for the anarthrous אנוש. Occurrences of the anarthrous אנוש are rendered with the definite בר נש(א) 4 out of 7 times in Lagarde's edition of the Targum to Psalms, and 8 times out of 8 in the Peshitta. This illustrates the incorrect nature of Moloney's argument.

Moreover, Moloney did not consider the rendering of two terms with בר נשא in the light of similar renderings of other words. For example, Tg. Mic. 2.2. renders both גבר and איש with גבר; Tg. Ps. 9.9 renders both ישפט and ידין with ידין: Pesh Job 35.8 renders both איש and בן אדם with נפש; LXX Prov. 2.13 renders both ארחות and דרכי with ὀδοί, and LXX Prov. 2.20 renders both דרך and ארחות with τρίβοι. These examples illustrate the fact that ancient translators, including Tg. Pss., did in fact use one term twice where the Hebrew text has two. This again shows Tg. Ps. 8.5 to

45. 'Re-Interpretation of Psalm VIII', p. 662.
46. Casey, 'Use of the Term בר נש(א) in the Aramaic Translations'.

be normal, for this is particularly liable to happen when the translator's term is his normal translation of both the terms in the text, as בר נשא is normal for both בן אדם and אנוש.

It follows that Moloney's arguments should not be accepted. The Aramaic term (א)נש(א) בר is used perfectly normally in Tg. Ps. 8, as an ordinary term for humankind.

A number of other passages were suggested by Horbury as evidence that the term 'son of man' picked up 'messianic associations'.[47] For example, he suggests that pre-Christian currency for messianic interpretation of the man-like figure in Dan. 7.13 is supported by the evidence of Ezekiel the Tragedian, *Exagoge* 68–89.[48] There are several problems with this. First, the date of Ezekiel's work is uncertain, and may be earlier than that of the book of Daniel. Second, the term for 'man' at line 70 is φώς, and the being in question on the throne is God himself. Third, despite the plural θρόνων at line 76, only one throne is clearly described in Moses' dream, the throne of God himself. Moses mounts this when God has left it. There is then a metaphorical use of the term 'throne' in the interpretative section carried through by Moses' father-in-law, and this indicates Moses' future sovereignty. Finally, the term 'son of man' is not used in this passage. Horbury's arguments should accordingly not be accepted. This passage provides important evidence of how high the position of Moses as an intermediary figure could be presented. It is not however connected with the use of the term 'son of man'.

These two passages indicate quite how far-fetched the scholarly discussion of the Son of Man Concept has been. Its existence is in a real sense dependent on the first two passages discussed in this chapter, and if these are found wanting, other passages like those discussed in this section cannot make up for them.

5. *Conclusions*

The following conclusions should therefore be drawn. There was no Son of Man Concept, or *Menschensohnbegriff*, in Second Temple Judaism. The scholarly view that there was such a concept has been based on inadequate study of the primary source material. In the foundational source, Dan. 7.13, כבר אנש, 'one like a son of man', is a pure symbol of the Saints of the Most High, a description of the people of Israel. He is not a separate figure, and he is merely likened to a man. The study of the *Similitudes of Enoch* has been made very difficult by the fact that it has survived only in Ge'ez, and in a very corrupt textual tradition at that. Careful study of Aramaic source material which can be recovered from the oldest manuscripts has shown that (א)נש(א) בר was used in the original text of this work in the same way as it is used in extant Aramaic texts, as a normal term for 'man'. The man in question was Enoch, first described in Ch. 46 in a mysterious way which would be

---

47.   Horbury, 'Messianic Associations of "The Son of Man"'.
48.   Horbury, 'Messianic Associations of "The Son of Man"', pp. 42–3.

recognizable to members of the Enoch group, and then revealed in all his glory in the recognition scene at the end of the work. Other sources studied either do not use the term 'son of man', or use it normally. Accordingly, this scholarly construct is largely ignored in subsequent chapters of this book, and chapters concerned with the historical Jesus use the Aramaic material studied in Ch. 2.

Chapter Four

SIX AUTHENTIC SAYINGS

The main purpose of this chapter is to present Aramaic reconstructions of six authentic sayings of Jesus which I have presented in more detail elsewhere, and to update these discussions in the light of the evidence presented in Chs 1–3. I begin with the methodology presupposed in the detailed discussions of individual sayings.

1. Method

Aramaic was the *lingua franca* in Israel at the time of Jesus.[1] Consequently, Jesus will have been brought up with Aramaic as his native tongue, and he will have had to use Aramaic to teach normal Jews in Galilee and in Judaea. The Gospels provide direct and indirect evidence of Jesus' use of Aramaic, despite the fact that they were written in Greek for Greek-speaking churches. For example, Mk 14.36 records Jesus' prayer in the garden of Gethsemane. The first word is ἀββα, the Aramaic אבא, 'Father'. It is the fact that Jesus taught in Aramaic which makes it desirable that we should study his sayings in the original Aramaic, if only we can reconstruct them.

The most outstanding feature of the indirect evidence is the idiomatic use of the term 'son of man'. The Greek ὁ υἱὸς τοῦ ἀνθρώπου is not known in texts previously written by monoglot Greeks. It can only be understood as a translation of the Aramaic בר (א)נש(א), for the following combination of reasons. First, Jesus spoke Aramaic. Second, the Greek expression ὁ υἱὸς τοῦ ἀνθρώπου is not normal monoglot Greek, and it makes perfect sense as a literal translation of a Semitic expression.[2] Third, the Greek υἱός overlaps greatly in semantic area with the Aramaic בר and the Hebrew בן. It is extensively used in the LXX to render בן, in both literal and figurative senses, including expressions which are not normal monoglot Greek, but literal translations (e.g. υἱὸν δυνάμεως for בן־חיל, 1 Sam. 14.52).[3] Fourth, the Aramaic (א)נש(א) overlaps extensively in semantic area with the Greek ἀνθρώπος. Fifth, the Hebrew בן אדם, the equivalent of the Aramaic

---

1. Casey, *Aramaic Sources of Mark's Gospel*, pp. 76–9; and for further bibliography, p. 61, n. 10 above.
2. On the translation process, see pp. 246–66 below.
3. For thorough discussion, see pp. 256–61 below.

בר (א)נש(א), is normally rendered υἱὸς ἀνθρώπου in the LXX, by several different translators. Sixth, the Gospel expression ὁ υἱὸς τοῦ ἀνθρώπου evidently did not cause difficulty in understanding at the time. It must therefore represent a normal Aramaic expression rather than an unusual one. This requirement is satisfied by בר (א)נש(א). Seventh, some Gospel sayings (notably Mk 13.26; 14.62) make use of Dan. 7.13, where בר אנש is certainly the underlying Aramaic expression. This combination of arguments is decisive. Authentic Son of man sayings must be reconstructed with בר (א)נש(א) where the Greek text of the Gospels has ὁ υἱὸς τοῦ ἀνθρώπου in order that we may correctly understand them. We have seen in Ch. 2 that בר (א)נש(א) is well enough attested for this purpose, so the present chapter can be devoted to discussing the reconstructed sayings in the light of earlier discussion of the idiomatic uses of this phrase.

Other signs of interference include the use of certain words. For example, at Mk 14.21 ὑπάγει is used with reference to Jesus' forthcoming death. The Greek word ὑπάγω was not a normal term for dying, whereas the equivalent Aramaic אזל was used with this reference. There are plenty of examples of this in later Jewish Aramaic and in Syriac, and the word itself occurs in earlier sources with the mundane meaning 'go'. We must infer that this word was already used as a metaphor for death in first-century Galilee, and interpret this as a piece of evidence that Mk 14.21 is indeed a translation of an Aramaic source.[4]

Sometimes the different forms of a saying should be explained as a result of transmission in Aramaic or translation from Aramaic into Greek. For example, at Mk 3.28 the only occurrence of ὁ υἱὸς τοῦ ἀνθρώπου in the plural in the Gospels is evidently due to the translator. He did not like the sense of a genuine saying of Jesus, which can be recovered with the help of Mt. 12.32//Lk. 12.10.[5]

The sort of Aramaic that may reasonably be used for reconstructing sayings of Jesus has been controversial. We must suppose that Jesus spoke Galilean Aramaic, but hardly any Galilean Aramaic of the right period survives. This difficult situation has been quite transformed by the discovery of the Dead Sea scrolls, which provide us with a large slice of Aramaic vocabulary, and standard syntax, from shortly before the time of Jesus. These words and constructions are virtually all found in other dialects too. We have seen in Ch. 2 that we now know what a stable language Aramaic was over a period of centuries. Consequently, we can use material from other dialects with caution. The probability of words extant in old sources still being extant is high, even when they do not survive in later material. Similarly, we should not hesitate to use later sources with care. The most important single source is the Palestinian Talmud. This is the right language and culture, only somewhat later in date. It contains many words which are also extant in the Dead Sea scrolls and earlier sources, and many sayings which are attributed to rabbis long before the final date of its composition. Finally we may turn to other later sources, including the Syriac versions of the Gospels.

4.   See further Casey, *Aramaic Sources of Mark's Gospel*, pp. 233–6.
5.   For detailed discussion, see pp. 140–43, 254–5 below.

I have noted the importance of later Aramaic in discussing the idiomatic use of
(א)נ(א)שׁ בר throughout Ch. 2. We saw that the term (א)שׁנ(א) בר itself is sufficiently
well attested in the (still) meagre sources from before the time of Jesus for us to
be confident that it was in normal usage. I noted one example of its idiomatic use
as early as 750 BCE.[6] For more details of this idiomatic usage, however, we need
later sources because they are comparatively extensive. The Yerushalmi alone has
more than 280 examples of the simple (א)שׁנ(א) בר, and the careful use of this and
other later sources has enabled me to find some 30 examples of its idiomatic use
with particular reference to the speaker or to whoever else is especially in mind.
Accordingly, I make careful use of later sources whenever this is necessary.[7]

Intimately interwoven with this process of reconstructing sayings of Jesus is that
of uncovering the work of the people who translated them into Greek. One major
result of the variety of problems which face a normal translator is important at this
point: they may adopt strategies. To translate freely, or literally, can be adopted as
a strategy. A strategy may be undertaken at a verbal level, as for example Aquila's
decision to render the Hebrew את with the Greek σύν + Acc., when את means that
the next word will be the object of the previous verb. The result of this is not normal
Greek at all. We may feel that it illustrates a general observation made by modern
students of translation: 'Strategies do not solve translation problems – they are
merely plans that can be implemented in an attempt to solve problems.'[8]

The only clear strategy in the synoptic Gospels concerns the translation of
(א)שׁנ(א) בר itself. The positive half of this strategy was to use ὁ υἱὸς τοῦ ἀνθρώπου
for (א)שׁנ(א) בר when it refers to Jesus. This follows from the above comments on
its appropriateness, from the fact that all the Son of man sayings in the Gospels
are clearly intended to refer to Jesus, and from the absence of other terms for him
which might reasonably represent (א)שׁנ(א) בר. The negative half of the translator's
strategy follows from the absence of the term from most of the synoptic Gospels,
in which it is never used of anyone except Jesus, and only once in the plural. On
general grounds, if the tradition contained (א)שׁנ(א) בר as a reference to Jesus, it will
have contained it when it was not a reference to him as well, and it will have had
it in the plural too. In attempting to avoid confusion, other words have been used
instead, surely including ἄνθρωπος both in the singular and the plural. The few
exceptions (Mk 3.28; 9.12; Mt. 10.32-33) are responses to particular problems.[9]
This is very important for understanding the whole of the synoptic tradition, for a
translation strategy can only be employed when extensive portions of the literature
in which it is found are in fact translated. This strategy alone enables us to infer
substantial translated sources used by Matthew, Mark and Luke, whether translated
by them personally, or by their sources, or by assistants. It provides the general
context in which we must view genuine Son of man sayings.

6.   See passage 20, pp. 67–8 above.
7.   See further, pp. 56–9 above; Casey, *Aramaic Sources of Mark's Gospel*, pp. 89–93;
Aramaic Approach to Q, pp. 56–60; 'Aramaic Idiom and the Son of Man Problem'.
8.   Hönig, 'Holmes' "Mapping Theory"', p. 85. For detailed discussion, see pp. 253–66
below.
9.   See pp. 130–1, 140–3, 254–5 below.

We are now in a position to outline the principles and procedures to be followed when reconstructing genuine sayings of Jesus. In two previous books, I have sought to lay down methodological principles for uncovering some written Aramaic sources of Mark's Gospel, and for approaching the Aramaic dimension of Q.[10] The Son of man sayings discussed in this chapter were included in these two books. I have offered reconstructions of other Son of man sayings in earlier publications, before the most fruitful methodology for reconstructing Aramaic versions of sayings of Jesus had been completely worked out. I now offer a modified version of the basic principles of reconstructing sayings of Jesus with a view to the discussion of Son of man sayings in the rest of this book.

1. An attempt should be made to reconstruct all Son of man sayings in the four Gospels. This is because the very presence of ὁ υἱὸς τοῦ ἀνθρώπου is evidence of literal translation of an Aramaic expression, בר (א)נשׁ(א). We shall find that all the sayings discussed in Chs 4–8 can be satisfactorily reconstructed. This is because in each case a genuine attempt has been made to translate the saying literally, in accordance with the strategy discussed above. In Ch. 9, I make a more complex attempt to recover one or more genuine predictions of Jesus' death and resurrection. This is because one or more genuine sayings have not only been literally translated, but also subjected to heavy editing in accordance with the early church's need to understand Jesus' atoning death and to hold an increasingly literal form of belief in his resurrection. In Chs 10–12, I discuss sayings most of which cannot be satisfactorily reconstructed, and none of which should be regarded as genuine sayings of the historical Jesus. By this stage, ὁ υἱὸς τοῦ ἀνθρώπου was an important Christological title in Greek, and the evangelists produced sayings which conspicuously satisfied the current needs of the church.

2. For the majority of words in the proposed reconstructions, we must use, in the first instance, the Aramaic of the Dead Sea scrolls. We have seen that it is close to the right date and cultural environment, which is of central importance. It is the wrong dialect for Jesus' speech, but this is much less important than has generally been thought.

Where words are not found in the scrolls, we must use other Aramaic with care. This is most obviously the case with the idiomatic use of the central expression בר (א)נשׁ(א), only one example of which occurs in earlier Aramaic. The judicious use of Aramaic of earlier and later date enables us to recover a good approximation to the language of the historical Jesus, despite the fragmentary nature of early remains. It is only at this stage that we should use the Syriac versions. We should never begin with them, because they are translations *into* the wrong dialect. This is especially obvious with the secondary renderings of ὁ υἱὸς τοῦ ἀνθρώπου.[11] At a late stage, however, they may alert us to possibilities for other words, because they are in the right language and derive from a significantly similar culture.

---

10.   Casey, *Aramaic Sources of Mark's Gospel*, pp. 107–10; *Aramaic Approach to Q*, pp. 60–63.

11.   See pp. 7–10 above.

3. As we proceed, we must continually check that the draft reconstructions are sufficiently idiomatic. Some specifically Aramaic locutions are bound to have been removed during the process of translation into Greek, and we have to recreate them. For example, confronted with the quite Greek ἔχει ποῦ at Mt. 8.20//Lk 9.58, I have suggested לא איתי לה אן ד ... בה.[12] We cannot normally infer that such suggestions are accurate verbatim. What we should claim is that Jesus must have spoken, and our sources must have written, idiomatic Aramaic. If therefore this is what we reconstruct, we will obtain an accurate impression of the source even where details are uncertain. My fifth procedure is a particularly important check and balance against too much creativity.

4. We must interpret the resulting reconstructions from a first-century Jewish perspective. We must pay particular attention to any respect in which they differ from their Greek translations. This is most striking with בר (א)נש(א) itself, a normal term for 'man' with a general level of meaning, significantly different from ὁ υἱὸς τοῦ ἀνθρώπου, a Christological title of Jesus alone. Again and again we will see unexpected levels of meaning appearing from straightforward reconstructions. Sometimes it is later exegetical tradition which has to be removed. For example, at Mt. 8.20//Lk. 9.58, I have suggested משכנין for Q's κατασκηνώσεις, and discussed the alternative possibilities מטללין and מדרין.[13] This permits consideration of the natural provision of roosts for birds, instead of being hidebound by the traditional translation 'nests': in Aramaic this would be קנין, which would have given rise to the precise Greek equivalent νοσσιάς.[14] The erroneous nature of traditional exegesis should however already have been clear from Q's κατασκηνώσεις.

5. We must go through all the reconstructions from the perspective of an ancient translator. If s/he was faced with the proposed reconstruction, might s/he reasonably have put what we have got? We must pay careful attention both to the overall sweep of the translation, and to all the small details. In doing this, we must make use both of research into the known habits of ancient translators, and modern insights into the nature of the translation process itself. We shall feel happiest when our translator could *only* have done what we posit, but we must not impose this as a general standard of judgement, because there are many situations in which translators have a genuine choice. We must be on the look-out both for consistent habits and for strategies, but we must be careful not to invent either of them. We have already seen that the central strategy in translating Son of man sayings was to render בר (א)נש(א) with ὁ υἱὸς τοῦ ἀνθρώπου when it refers to Jesus, and to use something different in both the singular and the plural whenever the reference was to other people.

6. We must isolate as far as possible deliberate editing by the Gospel writers themselves. It is fortunate that this is not of great importance in dealing with the majority of genuine sayings discussed in Chs 4–8, because the Gospel writers did not feel a need to alter these sayings to any considerable degree. We shall see that

12.   Casey, 'Jackals', p. 7; pp. 168, 178 below.
13.   Casey, 'Jackals', pp. 8, 20–1; pp. 173–4 below.
14.   See further, Casey, *Aramaic Sources of Mark's Gospel*, pp. 21, 50, 61, 69–71.

it does matter for a minority of sayings, which however survive in enough different forms for us to be able to distinguish the original sayings from the evangelists' editing. Detecting their editing is quite crucial to sorting out the predictions of Jesus' death and resurrection in Ch. 9. We must also uncover the creativity of the evangelists in the production of secondary sayings. This is crucial to Chs 10–12.

7. Finally, the results must be written up in a way that is as reader-friendly as possible. It should be obvious that this does not entail following the order of events in which the investigation was conducted. In this chapter, I have presented the reconstruction of Son of man sayings at or near the beginning of each section, recalling the context from previous discussions. I have followed the same basic order in Chs 5–9, but with the presentation of the whole context in the case of Mk 2.10, which is firmly embedded in Mk 2.1-12. I have discussed any Aramaic words which might be considered difficult or controversial, the proposed behaviour of the translators in difficult or controversial circumstances, not least in their treatment of בר (א)נש(א), and significant editorial behaviour by Matthew and Luke. I have not however given the attestation of every Aramaic word, nor every detail of the behaviour of the translators, as this would make this book even more lengthy and very tedious. In Chs 10–12, I have discussed significant points which show that Aramaic originals should not be posited for secondary sayings. I have devoted most of these chapters to detailed consideration of the creativity and editing of each of the evangelists.

I turn next to the six genuine sayings which I have reconstructed in two relatively recent books. Each of these sayings is part of a larger passage, for which I have reconstructed the whole of the context.[15] I do not repeat here either the reconstructions or the discussions of these larger contexts, but simply refer to my previous discussions, sometimes adding responses to critical discussions of my earlier proposals. It is of fundamental importance that these sayings are all embedded in contexts where there is good reason to infer that our evangelists are reproducing literal translations of Aramaic sources which gave abbreviated accounts of genuine incidents. This adds cumulative weight to the arguments for the genuineness of the reconstructed Son of man sayings.

2. Mark 2.27-28

These two verses form Jesus' second argument in response to criticism of his disciples' behaviour by some Pharisees.[16] The disciples had been going along a path through other people's cornfields plucking ears of corn on the sabbath. The Pharisees criticized them for doing so on the sabbath, but not for stealing other people's corn. It follows that the disciples were taking *Peah*, the grain left for the

---

15. See Casey, *Aramaic Sources of Mark's Gospel*; *Aramaic Approach to Q*.
16. For detailed discussion of the whole pericope, Casey, *Aramaic Sources of Mark's Gospel*, pp. 138–73.

poor on the borders of people's fields, accessible from the paths through the fields. This is the only legitimate reason for them to be able to pluck ears of other people's corn.

Mark's account of this incident shows clear indications of literal translation from a written Aramaic source, as does Jesus' first argument. So also does the following incident, in which Jesus heals a man on the sabbath, as a result of which the Pharisees take counsel with the Herodians to put him to death. Mark's accounts of both incidents also take for granted several Jewish assumptions, so they must be of early date.[17]

Jesus' second argument may be reconstructed as follows:

שבתא בדיל אנשא אתעבדת ולא אנשא בדיל שבתא.

שליט נא הוא בר נש אף בשבתא.[28]

The sabbath was made for man, and not man for the sabbath.
[28]Surely, then, a/the (son of) man is master even of the sabbath.

The general background is that of conventional Jewish thought about the creation, especially the view that man was intended to dominate the created world. The classic texts are Gen. 1.26,28 and Ps. 8.6-9, and two pseudepigraphical expressions of this belief are especially relevant. The orthodox author of *4 Ezra* concludes his account of creation, 'And over these (*sc.* created beings) Adam, whom you appointed as ruler (ducem, מדברנא) over all the works which you had created' (*4 Ezra* 6.54). The author of *2 Baruch* similarly looked back to the divine intention at creation: 'And you said that you would make for your world (a/the son of) man (ברנשא) as the manager (מפרנסנא) of your works, to make it clear that he was not made for the world, but the world was made for him' (*2 Bar.* 14.18). These passages show how observant Jews could declare man's lordship over creation.

A second factor is the idea of the sabbath as a great gift of God. This is biblical, 'for YHWH has given you the sabbath' (Exod. 16.29), and of the massive later evidence it is sufficient to quote *Jubilees*: 'And he gave us a great sign, the sabbath day, that we should work six days, but keep sabbath on the seventh day from all work' (*Jub.* 2.17). This is the sense in which the sabbath was made for humankind. That it was given at the time of the creation is straightforward OT belief, and continued to be felt so strongly that the rabbis could call the weekly sabbath 'the sabbath of creation' to distinguish it from the sabbath year (e.g. MekhY Kaspa III, Exod. 23.12).

Jewish sources use words for 'man' in many general statements about sabbath observance. This is well illustrated in Greek by Philo, *Dec.* 99. Here Philo declares that God once for all made a final use of six days for the completion of the world and had no further need of periods of time. Contrast ἀνθρώπων δ' ἕκαστος:

---

17.   See further in general, J. G. Crossley, *The Date of Mark's Gospel. Insight from the Law in Earliest Christianity* (JSNTSup 266. London: T&T Clark International, 2004).

ἀνθρώπων δ'ἕκαστος ἅτε θνητῆς φύσεως μετέχων καὶ μυρίων ἐνδεὴς ὢν πρὸς τὰς ἀναγκαίας τοῦ βίου χρείας ὀφείλει μὴ κατοκνεῖν ἐκπορίζειν τὰ ἐπιτήδεια μέχρι τελευτῆς τοῦ βίου διαναπαυόμενος τὰς ἱερὰς ἑβδομάδας.

But each man, since he shares in mortal nature and needs masses of things for the necessities of life must not slacken in providing for his needs to the end of his life, but should rest on the sacred seventh days.

Here the use of 'each man' with reference to the specifically Jewish sabbath arises naturally from the context of the creation of humankind. Only observant Jews are in mind, a fact which must be inferred from the cultural context as a whole. The Jewish context of Mk 2.27-28 should be taken full account of in a similar way.

Many Hebrew examples are found in legal judgements in orthodox Jewish sources.

> Clothes vendors who go out on the sabbath with cloaks folded (and) lying on their shoulders are liable to a sin-offering. And they [*sc.* the sages] said this not of clothes vendors alone but of every man (כל אדם), but that it is in the nature of merchants to go out like that (b. Shab 147a).

Here the cultural context of Talmudic Law makes it so obvious that observant Jews are referred to that the description כל אדם can safely be used of them without confusion. A more extreme example is found at m. Shab 6,6:

> Arabian women go out veiled and Median women with cloaks looped up over their shoulders. And so everyone (כל אדם), but the sages spoke about normal customs.

Here the cultural assumptions of the document are so strong that observant Jewish women in Arabia and Media can be referred to as Arabian women and Median women, and observant Jewish women as a whole as כל אדם.

These examples illustrate the basic fact that the level of generality intended in general statements is limited by the cultural as well as the literary context. It is this which restricts the reference of Mk 2.27-28 to observant Jews. The passage makes perfect sense against the background of a standard Jewish theology of creation, and the use of words for 'man' is all the more natural in the context of a dispute which hinges partly on the importance of bodily needs which are common to all people. An additional reason for Jesus to use these words is that it enabled him to utilize the Aramaic idiom of Mk 2.28 and thus declare his authority to ward off hostile sabbath *halakhah* by associating himself with the mastery of humankind in the created world in general.

At 2.28, the term ὁ υἱὸς τοῦ ἀνθρώπου represents (א)בר(א)נש(א), used idiomatically in a general statement which refers particularly to the speaker and a larger group of people. It does not, however, tell us whether (א)נש(א) was in the absolute or emphatic state, for two reasons. First, examples of the idiom in Aramaic texts show no difference in meaning according to the use of the absolute or emphatic state.[18]

18.   See pp. 67–81 above.

Second, the behaviour of the translator continues to follow the strategy of using ὁ υἱὸς τοῦ ἀνθρώπου whenever s/he thought that examples of this idiom referred to Jesus. It follows that we can never infer the state of (א)נש(א) from the translator's use of ὁ υἱὸς τοῦ ἀνθρώπου.

The next problem is κύριος. An obvious possibility is מרא, which was naturally used by the Syriac versions to translate κύριος, and by Meyer in his attempt at a reconstruction.[19] Wellhausen's שליט is however greatly to be preferred,[20] because it fits so well both with the general level of meaning and with the earlier part of the dispute. It is the same word as in the Pharisees' question, and it had already been used in Jesus' first argument. It is likely that it had already been used on an earlier occasion, as we shall see in a detailed discussion of Mk 2.10.[21] שליט takes ב to give the sense of mastery over, so we can write בשבתא for τοῦ σαββάτου. אף is straightforward for καί. It follows from v. 27, which stated the purpose of the creation of the sabbath as being for man's benefit, that man is master on the sabbath, as well as in respect of the shewbread and the forgiveness of sins, and therefore entitled to eat of the fruits of God's creation. בשבתא means 'on the sabbath' as well as 'over the sabbath', so that the sentence declares the authority of humankind, from which the authority of Jesus and the defence of the disciples are derived, in an indirect way. For ἐστιν we may reasonably write הוא, bearing in mind that its semantic area normally and conventionally includes a copulative usage approximately equivalent to the Greek εἰμι.

We may now consider the nature of the idiomatic use of (א)נש(א) בר in the Aramaic sentence underlying Mk 2.28. This sentence runs smoothly as an example of the idiom whereby a speaker used a general statement to refer to himself, or himself and a group of associates. Moreover, the general level of meaning follows necessarily from the general statement of 2.27. Consequently, these two verses form an excellent example of the absolute chaos that would be involved in any attempt to use (א)נש(א) בר as a title while it was still a normal term for 'man'. Jesus thus claimed for himself only what is potentially the case for other people too. The reference to the speaker however, combined with the vigour of his comments, means that at the same time Jesus took responsibility for his disciples' actions, as the Pharisees assumed that he would by directing their question to him in the first place. At this level, his final sentence says that he, as a (son of) man, is master on/over the sabbath. The ambiguity of ב in בשבתא further ensures the indirectness of the expression, but there is no doubt about its thrust. Jesus claimed the authority to ward off Pharisaic criticism and allow his poor and hungry disciples to pluck grain on the sabbath. The ground which he gave for this authority is the theological statement of 2.27, in accordance with which anyone who is obedient to God has the mastery over the sabbath which God made for him at the creation. The general nature of the statement also implies that Jesus' disciples in some sense have mastery on/over the sabbath, and the sense in which this is true may be deduced from the context.

19.   Meyer, *Jesu Muttersprache*, p. 93.
20.   Wellhausen, *Skizzen und Vorarbeiten* VI, p. 203.
21.   See pp. 162–6 below.

First, in a theological sense, they have the mastery given to them by God at creation because they are obedient to their heavenly Father. Second, in a practical sense, they are entitled to feed themselves on the sabbath, taking advantage of the provisions deliberately laid down by God for the poor and hungry in the Law of Moses.

Finally, this is a perfect example of the idiomatic use of בר (א)נ(א)ש in a genuine statement by Jesus himself. As we work through genuine sayings of Jesus, we shall see that sayings with an excellent *Sitz im Leben* in his life and teaching can be properly reconstructed in their original Aramaic. In subsequent chapters, we shall see that most sayings which have their *Sitz im Leben* in the early church rather than in the teaching of Jesus cannot be so reconstructed. This is surely not coincidental, but rather a significant indication of which sayings are genuine and which are not.

3. Mark 9.11-13

The Son of man saying at Mk 9.12 has caused great difficulty to interpreters. The reconstruction of all three verses in the original Aramaic is essential to the task of seeing what Jesus originally meant.

11 שאלין לה ואמרין, למה אומרין ספריא דאליה עתיד למאתא לקדמין?

12 ואמר להון, אתה אליה לקדמין ומתיב כולא, והיכה כתיב על בר אנש דיכאב שגיא ואתבסר.

13 ואמר אנה לכון דאף אליה אתה ועבדו לה דצבו כדי כתיב עלוהי.

And (they were) asking him and saying, 'Why do (the) scribes say that Elijah is going to come first?' [12]And he said to them, 'Elijah comes first and turns back all, and how is it written of (a/the son of) man that he suffers much and is rejected! [13]And I tell you that, moreover, Elijah has come, and they did in the case of him whom they desired according as it is written concerning him/it.'[22]

The disciples' question presupposes Jewish expectation that Elijah would come. Both known examples of this expectation (Sir. 48.10; 4Q558) take up the text of Mal. 3.23-24, according to which Elijah will come before the day of the Lord. Jesus was well known for preaching the imminent coming of the kingdom of God. We must infer that scribes hostile to the movement had resorted to the scriptures, and had argued that God could not be about to establish his kingdom, because the scriptures said that Elijah would come first.

I have again reconstructed עתיד as the Aramaic word which caused a translator to use δεῖ in v. 11. The word עתיד means 'ready, prepared', and it is extant in Aramaic before the time of Jesus at Dan. 3.15, where Shadrach, Meshach and Abednego will be let off if they are 'ready', 'prepared' to worship Nebuchadnezzar's image (LXX and Theod. ἔχετε ἑτοίμως for איתיכון עתידין). In its take-up of Malachi, the Geniza text of Sir. 48.10 has נכון, the semantic area of which includes 'ready'. In later Aramaic, דיתע is used idiomatically to indicate the future, even the remote future. It was therefore very suitable to indicate the future event of Elijah's coming, and its use in the Peshitta of Sir. 48.10 illustrates what a suitable word it is to take up in

---

22. For detailed discussion, see Casey, *Aramaic Sources of Mark's Gospel*, pp. 121–37.

Aramaic the prophecy of Mal. 3.23-24. This range of meaning made it difficult for the translator to proceed without making a conscious decision. He took the same kind of option as the translator of Dan. 2.28-29 LXX and Theod., where δεῖ is part of an explicitative translation of an Aramaic imperfect. He thus indicated the certainty of the scribes that the scriptural prediction will be fulfilled, and thereby correctly represented them.

This proposal has been rejected by Aitken,[23] partly on the ground that the idea of necessity is not conveyed with עתיד in my reconstruction. This argument is faulty in method: it presupposes that I should have translated δεῖ *back into* Aramaic, so as to produce a sentence *identical* in meaning to Mark's Greek sentence. This is not however possible, because there is no sufficiently literal equivalent of δεῖ in Aramaic, and in any case we should not be translating anything *back into* Aramaic. We should be reconstructing Aramaic which could have given rise to Mark's Greek. This is especially clear in this passage, because taken as a whole it does not make proper sense in Greek. This is why we have to look for something which Aramaic speakers might use which would cause a translator to put δεῖ.

Aitken's second argument is that there was a real Aramaic equivalent to δεῖ. 'In Aramaic there do exist, however, the noun צְרִיכָא, which can be found in clauses meaning "it is necessary" (e.g. *b.Ber* 10a, 21a), and (in the Talmud) the corresponding verb צְרַך "to need"'.[24] Aitken was not however able to make the case for this. There is no early evidence of it, and late Talmudic evidence shows that צריך began to approximate to δεῖ in the context of detailed legal discussions, none of which is quite parallel to what we find in Mark. Aitken's criticisms, and his attempt to argue that the Aramaic equivalent for δεῖ was צריך must therefore be rejected. There was no such equivalent at the time of Jesus, and developments in that direction were specific to Jewish legal discussion at a later time.[25]

I turn to Jesus' reply, the Son of man saying which has traditionally been the main cause of difficulty. Jesus' opening comment accepts that the prophecy in the book of Malachi is to be fulfilled. He naturally used the Aphel of תוב to recall the Hiphil of שׁוב. The Aramaic מתיב כולא cannot however be accurately and completely translated, for any translation into Greek or English loses the cultural resonances present in Jesus' deliberate reference to the text of Mal. 3.23-24, probably to Sir. 48.10, and certainly to the tradition which Sir. 48.10 represents. The role of Elijah is described at Mal. 3.24:

והשיב לב אבות על בנים ולב בנים על אבותם.

And he will turn back the heart of the fathers to the children and the heart of the children to the fathers.

23.   J. K. Aitken, 'The proposed Aramaic background to Mark 9:11', *JTS* NS 53 (2002), pp. 75–80.

24.   Aitken, 'Proposed Aramaic background to Mark 9:11', pp. 76–7.

25.   For detailed discussion, see P. M. Casey, 'The Aramaic Background of Mark 9:11: A Response to J.K. Aitken', *JTS NS* 55 (2004), pp. 92–102.

The original text of Sir. 48.10 has not survived. It is nonetheless clear from the surviving versions that the hope of Malachi was repeated, and interpreted with something about preparing/restoring the tribes of Israel/Jacob.

Jesus believed that these prophecies were fulfilled in the ministry of John the Baptist. He used מתיב because Mal. 3.24 used השיב, and he used כולא as a summary of both texts and/or of the tradition which Sir 48.10 represents. Aramaic-speaking Jews who knew their scriptures would have no difficulty in interpreting his comment as a reference to the comprehensively successful popular ministry of John the Baptist. John the Baptist, however, had been arrested and executed by Herod Antipas, and the prophecies of Elijah said nothing about that. Jesus therefore combined general statements in the scriptures with specific references to John the Baptist.

Mal. 3.1 says of the messenger whom Jesus interpreted as John the Baptist:

הנני שלח מלאכי ופנה דרך לפני
Look! I am sending my messenger and he will prepare the way before me …

The same exegesis of Mal. 3.1 as a prediction of John the Baptist is found in the Q passage Mt. 11.10//Lk. 7.27.[26] Sooner or later, this was bound to make Jesus think of Isa. 40.3, which he would interpret likewise of John the Baptist.

קול קורא במדבר פנו דרך יהוה
A voice crying in the wilderness, 'Prepare the way of the Lord …'

The remains of this exegesis is found in the composite quotation of Mal. 3.1 and Isa. 40.3 at Mk 1.2-3. Once Jesus had got to Isa. 40.3, he could hardly fail to read the rest of the passage, going past the prophecy of John's successful ministry preparing the way of the Lord to a metaphorical presentation of the transitory nature of human life:

כול הבשר חציר וכול חסדיו כציץ השדה ...
All flesh (is) grass and all their acts of kindness like the flower of the countryside.

Isa. 40.6-8 must then surely remind him of the classic presentation of the suffering of man in Job 14.

Job 14 begins with a blunt general statement about man:

אדם ילוד אשה קצר ימים ושבע רגז.
Man who is born of woman is shortlived and full of turmoil.

The rabbinical Targum has בר נש for אדם. This Targum is too late in date to have influenced Jesus, but the rendering is a common one because of a genuine overlap in semantic area,[27] and this is significant because it means that Jesus might have used בר (א)נש(א) in a general statement based on this text, even without the further reasons which he had for doing so.

26.　Casey, *Aramaic Approach to Q*, pp. 118–21.

27.　Casey, '(א)נש(א) בר in the Aramaic Translations of the Hebrew Bible', pp. 93–5.

The next verse is equally important:

כציץ יצא וימל ויברח כצל ולא יעמוד.

Like a flower he comes out and withers, and he flees like a shadow and will not stay.

The word ציץ is the same as at Isa. 40.6,7,8, and the whole context is similar. This is the link which a faithful Jew, learned in the scriptures, could not fail to make. In the middle of the chapter, we read at some length of man's death, essential for understanding the death of John the Baptist. The last verse is also especially significant:

אך בשׂרו עליו יכאב ונפשׁו עליו תאבל.

Indeed his flesh suffers upon him, and his soul mourns over him.

Here the word בשׂר forms another verbal link with Isa. 40.6, and כאב is the word which Jesus used for 'suffer'. The noun מכאב is now extant at 4Q541 4 ii +6, lines 2 and 4, with … מכאב] at 2 ii 3, so there should be no doubt that כאב could be used in the Aramaic of our period, and meditation on this Hebrew scripture is precisely what would make Jesus choose it.

Mal. 3 would also remind Jesus of Jer. 6.27ff. Mal. 3.2-3 says of the messenger, identified at 3.23 as Elijah:

כי־הוא כאשׁ מצרף וכברית מכבסים: וישׁב מצרף ומטהר כסף וטהר את־בני־לוי וזקק אתם כזהב וככסף והיו ליהוה מגישׁי מנחה בצדקה.

For he is like a refiner's fire and like fullers' lye, and he will sit refining and purifying silver, and he will purify the sons of Levi and he will refine them like gold and like silver and they will bring an offering to the LORD in righteousness.

At Jer. 6.27-30 this process seems to have begun but not finished. The piece may be perceived as addressed to John the Baptist/Elijah, and it ends with the wicked still unremoved, and the word מאס is used, and could be interpreted either of the wicked or the people:

לשוא צרף צרוף ורעים לא נתקו: כסף נמאס קראו להם כי מאס יהוה בהם.

Refining he refines in vain, and the wicked are not drawn off: they shall be called rejected silver, for the LORD has rejected them.

This leads into Jer. 7, of which Jesus made vigorous use when he cleansed the Temple (Mk 11.17).[28] It contains a conditional threat to the whole Jewish people, and to the Temple. Jer. 7.29 uses מאס again:

כי מאס יהוה ויטשׁ את־דור עברתו.

For the LORD has rejected and abandoned the generation of his fury.

The rejection of the people in Jer. 6–7 is quite sufficient to justify the general statement בר (א)נש(א) … אתבסר, made as an interpretation of scripture. It was this

---

28.   P. M. Casey, 'Culture and Historicity: the Cleansing of the Temple', *CBQ* 59 (1997), pp. 306–32.

rejection which required John the Baptist's death, and would require Jesus' death also, with whoever would die with him. I have suggested אתבסר as the word which Jesus used to pick up מאס, and which the translator rendered ἐξουδενηθῇ. It has the right semantic area. It occurs before the time of Jesus at 4Q542 1 i 6, and subsequently in several dialects, including Jewish Aramaic.

We have now recovered some of Jesus' biblical exegesis. He interpreted Mal. 3 and Isa. 40 of the successful ministry of John the Baptist; Isa. 40 and Job 14 of the death of man; Job 14 of the suffering of man; and Jer. 6–7 of the rejection of the Jewish people. We now have a second reason why he should use the term בר נש(א)(א) in a general statement which had particular reference to John the Baptist/ Elijah: his suffering and rejection is written in the scriptures in general statements, not in specific references. The idiomatic use of בר נש(א)(א) is the third reason. His Aramaic-speaking disciples would know as they listened that John the Baptist was being particularly referred to, because he was the main figure under discussion. At the same time, Jesus predicted his own death during the ministry.[29] Since the disciples' question reflects a scribal reaction to the position of Jesus at the centre of a popular and successful Jesus movement, we should infer that he had already done so, as in the Marcan narrative. He will therefore have included himself in this general statement, and his disciples could hardly fail to realize this. If the Marcan narrative is in the right order, this will have been especially obvious after Peter's objection (Mk 8.32-33). It would become even more so after the discussion of Jacob and John's request to sit on his right and left in his glory (Mk 10.35-45).[30] This passage is permeated by the perception that some of the disciples would die with him, and Jacob and John's immediate acceptance of their fate (Mk 10.39) shows that they had learnt much from something, surely including Jesus' rebuke of Peter and the present incident.

Jesus saw his own fate in the scriptures in the same kind of way, in passages such as Pss 41; 118.22-23 referring to him individually (Mk 12.10-11; 14.18,20) and in general statements such as Ps. 116.15 (cf. Mk 14.21).[31] Verbal links with the passages just discussed include מאס again at Ps. 118.22, מות at Job 14.10,14 and Ps. 41.6; 116.3,15; 118.17-18, and קום at Job 14.12 and Ps. 41.9,11. We must add Ps. 116.15 to the general statements which helped Jesus to understand the death of John the Baptist.

Why then does Mk 9.12 not actually mention death? Because John the Baptist's death was not the main problem. All people die, and if John the Baptist's successful ministry had prepared the way for Jesus, and John had died a natural death when his ministry had been complete, his death could have been seen unproblematically at Isa. 40.6; Ps. 116.15; Job 14.10,14 and elsewhere. The *problem* was the rejection of John by many of Israel's leaders, and his suffering at their hands. That is why כאב and בסר were used to reflect scriptural texts in the source of Mk 9.12. John

29. See Ch. 9.
30. For detailed discussion of the Aramaic source of this whole passage, see Casey, *Aramaic Sources of Mark's Gospel*, Ch. 5; on Mark 10.45, see pp. 131–4 below.
31. See pp. 134–6 below.

the Baptist's death was accordingly different from the death of Jesus, mentioned literally by him at Mk 8.31; 10.34,45, and metaphorically at Mk 10.38-39; 12.7-8; 14.8,21,24; Lk. 13.32-33. Jesus' death was seen by him as an important event which would enable God to redeem Israel. Positive assessment of his death was always necessary to the early church, doubly so when Gentiles entered the churches without becoming Jews, and this explains both the preservation of his predictions and the extension and editing of one of them through the centre of Mark's Gospel.[32] The source of Mk 9.12 was primarily about the fate of John the Baptist, and John's death had no such function.

What Jesus meant is now clear. It faced the translator with a very difficult problem. He had a strategy, to use ὁ υἱὸς τοῦ ἀνθρώπου as a translation of בר (א)נשׁ(א) when it referred to Jesus, and not otherwise.[33] That strategy is however difficult to apply to this passage, because the primary reference was to John the Baptist, but there was a genuine reference to the fate of Jesus too, together with anyone who might die with him. As a committed Christian, the translator believed that Jesus' death was more important than that of John the Baptist, so he decided that reference to it must be retained. He did this as he had previously agreed to do, by translating בר (א)נשׁ(א) with ὁ υἱὸς τοῦ ἀνθρώπου. If the first article is taken as generic, as the second must be, bilinguals could see the original idiom, and the reference to Jesus' atoning death is also perfectly clear. In his own view, therefore, the translator had done as well as possible. From the perspective of monoglot Greeks, however, the result is quite confusing, as the history of exegesis bears witness. This is a perfect illustration of the fact that strategies are devices to enable translators to continue. They are not necessarily successful in transmitting the original meaning of a text in the target language. This is especially so in a case like this, where the source language has an idiom not found in the target language, and the target culture has significantly different beliefs from the source culture.

The final verse is also more lucid in Aramaic than it can have been for monoglot Greeks. The Aramaic צבו, which gave rise to ἤθελον, will have been a deliberate reference to Mal. 3.1. Here John the Baptist/Elijah could be seen predicted as מלאך הברית אשׁר־אתם חפצים, 'the messenger of the covenant in whom you delight'. This takes us on to the scriptures referred to in this verse – they are the same as the ones in the previous verse. People delighted in John the Baptist, who carried through the successful popular ministry prophesied in Mal. 3, and referred to more briefly at Isa. 40.3 and Sir. 48.10. The generalized plural also refers to the other scriptures discussed above. He suffered and died like all men in Job 14. Since the people were not sufficiently refined as in Jer. 6–7, they were rejected, and some of them shed the innocent blood of John the Baptist.

Mark's source was accordingly a perfectly lucid passage of Aramaic, which concerns primarily the death of John the Baptist. Jesus saw John as the fulfilment of Malachi's prophecy that Elijah would come before the day of the Lord. When John was put to death by Herod Antipas, Jesus meditated on the scriptures, and applied

32.   See Ch. 11 below.
33.   See pp. 44–5, 118 above; pp. 253–66 below.

to John a number of general statements about the fate of humankind, to which John was not an exception. This is what the crucial v. 12 refers to. In Aramaic it makes perfect sense as a general statement which applies primarily to John the Baptist, but with a general level of meaning which applies to Jesus and to other people as well. The difficulties of translating this idiom account for the confusion which has descended upon people who have read it only in Greek. It is accordingly a classic case of a passage which has to be reconstructed in Aramaic to make proper sense at all. It is therefore a very strong argument for this part of my solution to the Son of man problem.

4. Mark 10.45

The next Son of man saying concludes another passage which traditional exegesis has found difficult. I have sorted out these difficulties in a detailed discussion which includes a reconstruction of the Aramaic source of the whole of Mk 10.35-45.[34] I summarize the main points, because they are essential for understanding the resonances of the Son of man saying.

The passage begins with a request of Jacob and John, sons of Zebedee, to sit on Jesus' right and left in his glory. This would effectively put them in charge of the twelve in the last days, when they would sit on twelve thrones judging the twelve tribes of Israel (Mt. 19.28//Lk. 22.30). Jesus' response was to ask, in a very metaphorical way, whether they would share in his death. Jacob and John immediately gave an affirmative answer to Jesus' question. They must therefore have understood the metaphorical references to Jesus' death. It follows that Mark is right to place this incident after some of the passion predictions. Jacob and John must also have understood that to sit on Jesus' right and left in his glory would entail suffering and death for them.

Jesus responded by declaring that Jacob and John would indeed share his fate. His affirmation of this is as straightforward as possible, and shows that, at this stage of his ministry, he expected others to die with him. It follows that his understanding of his forthcoming death must have been rooted in the function of the deaths of righteous Jews, as well as in his personal uniqueness. Nonetheless, Jesus did not grant Jacob and John places on his right and left, not even if they died with him. He believed that these places were for those whom God had chosen to be there.

When Jesus had finished this speech, the other ten of the twelve were annoyed with Jacob and John. Jesus responded by calling the twelve to him. He defined service rather than lordship as characteristic of leadership in the Jesus community, contrasting this with the unsatisfactory behaviour of Gentile rulers. This led to a more precise comment on service in the Son of man saying, which draws the whole incident together.

34.   Casey, *Aramaic Sources of Mark's Gospel*, Ch. 5.

ואף בר אנשא לא אתא להשתמשא אלא לשמשה ולמנתן נפשה פורקן חלף שגיאין.

What is more, a/the son of man does not come to be served but to serve, and to give his life/soul/self as a ransom for many.

The first part of the saying continues the theme of service, already stated as a requirement for leaders of the Jesus community. The term (א)בר נ(א)שׁ(א) cannot lose its general level of meaning, and it is the general level of meaning which continues the instruction of the immediately preceding part of the passage. It follows that אתא does not refer to the incarnation alone, but more generally to the purpose of all their lives. Jesus' assertion that the purpose of life is service is not an empirical statement, but a declaration of God's purpose which the disciples are thereby ordered to carry out.

The second part of the saying carries the nature of service in the Jesus community to the point of death. There should be little doubt that פורקן was the original Aramaic underlying λύτρον. The verb פרק is extant at 11QTgJob XXVII,9, where it renders חלץ, apparently meaning 'set free, rescue, deliver'. It should be restored at 11QTgJob XXIII,6, which has פר]: this renders פדה (LXX σώσον) of God's redeeming/rescuing a man's soul from the Pit. At Dan. 4.24, it is used of Nebuchadnezzar doing something to his sins by righteousness: LXX and Theodotion both translate it as λυτρώσαι (Dan. 4.27), so an interpretation close to 'redeem' and analogous to λύτρον at Mk 10.45 was established long before the time of Jesus. פרק also occurs in Nabatean Aramaic at pap 5/6ḤevA nab I,10 in the first century CE, and later in both Jewish Aramaic and in Syriac. We should infer that פורקן was already in existence for Jesus to use, in an appropriate sense. The overlap in semantic area is so obvious that it is used to translate λύτρον by palsyrlec, sin, pesh, hark.

The correct cultural background for understanding the death of Jesus, together with disciples who should have been prepared to die with him, must be existing thought about the atoning deaths of people.[35] This underlines the unity of the passage, for the connection between the question of Jacob and John and the son of man saying is the general level of meaning in the son of man saying. The main group of people involved are the Maccabean martyrs. When faithful Jews were put to death during the Maccabean period, other faithful Jews needed to understand their deaths within the context of the purposes of God. We can see this being done already in the book of Daniel. In Dan. 7–9, this goes only so far as reassurance that God will bring triumph after persecution. Towards the end of the vision which concludes the book, two additional developments are found. The first (Dan. 11.35) refers again to these martyrs:

ומן המשכילים יכשלו לצרוף בהם ולברר וללבן עד־עת קץ כי־עוד למועד

35.   C. K. Barrett, 'The Background of Mark 10.45', in A. J. B. Higgins (ed.), *New Testament Essays: Studies in Memory of T.W. Manson*, (Manchester: Manchester University Press, 1959), pp. 1–18; M. D. Hooker, *Jesus and the Servant* (London: SPCK, 1959); J. Downing, 'Jesus and Martyrdom', *JTS* NS 14 (1963), pp. 279–93; C. K. Barrett, 'Mark 10.45: a Ransom for Many', *New Testament Essays* (London: SPCK, 1972), pp. 20–6; M. De Jonge, 'Jesus' death for others and the death of the Maccabean martyrs', in T. Baarda *et al.* (eds), *Text and Testimony. Essays on New Testament and Apocryphal Literature in Honour of A.F.J. Klijn* (Kampen: Kok, 1988), pp. 142–51.

This text evidently supposes that the deaths of the righteous will have a beneficial effect. The second development is their reward at Dan. 12.2-3, where they must be among those who rise from the dead and shine like the stars of heaven.

This was elaborated in subsequent literature. There is some material in *1 Maccabees*, where Mattathias urges his sons, δότε τὰς ψυχὰς ὑμῶν ὑπὲρ διαθήκης πατέρων ἡμῶν (*1 Macc.* 2.50), and again ἀνδρίζεσθε καὶ ἰσχύσατε ἐν τῷ νόμῳ, ὅτι ἐν αὐτῷ δοξασθήσεσθε (*1 Macc.* 2.64). This has the central notions of giving one's life for the will of God, and being glorified as a result. The accounts of martyrdoms in *2 Macc.* 6–7 have several references to resurrection. For example, the fourth brother at the point of death declares it right τὰς ὑπὸ τοῦ θεοῦ προσδοκᾶν ἐλπίδας πάλιν ἀναστήσεσθαι ὑπ᾽ αὐτοῦ (7.14): Antiochus however will have no resurrection to life. The last brother prays that in him and his brothers the wrath of God, justly brought upon the whole nation, may cease:

ἐγὼ δέ, καθάπερ οἱ ἀδελφοί, καὶ σῶμα καὶ ψυχὴν προδίδωμι περὶ τῶν πατρίων νόμων ἐπικαλούμενος τὸν θεὸν ἵλεως ταχὺ τῷ ἔθνει γενέσθαι καὶ σὲ μετὰ ἐτασμῶν καὶ μαστίγων ἐξομολογήσασθαι διότι μόνος αὐτὸς θεός ἐστιν, ἐν ἐμοὶ δὲ καὶ τοῖς ἀδελφοῖς μου στῆσαι τὴν τοῦ παντοκράτορος ὀργὴν τὴν ἐπὶ τὸ σύμπαν ἡμῶν γένος δικαίως ἐπηγμένην (7.37-8).

This also has the expression ψυχὴν προδίδωμι, used of what the martyr does. Following a similar prayer, Judas and his army are successful, because the wrath of God had turned to mercy. The prayer is said to have included a plea to God τῶν καταβοώντων πρὸς αὐτὸς αἱμάτων εἰσακοῦσαι (8.3). Thus the martyrs were bearing the wrath of God.

The fourth book of Maccabees comes from faithful Jews in the tradition of these earlier works, and it provides dynamic parallels to the situation of Jesus and those who might have died with him. At 6.28-29, one of the martyrs prays to God to be merciful to the whole people, and says, καθάρσιον αὐτῶν ποίησον τὸ ἐμὸν αἷμα καὶ ἀντίψυχον αὐτῶν λαβὲ τὴν ἐμὴν ψυχήν. At 17.20-22, the author even more clearly attributes the deliverance of Israel to the sacrificial death of the martyrs. He describes them as ὥσπερ ἀντίψυχον γεγονότας τῆς τοῦ ἔθνους ἁμαρτίας, and writes of τοῦ ἱλαστηρίου τοῦ θανάτου αὐτῶν. This type of development was just as likely to take place in Aramaic-speaking Judaism, given the view of these martyrs already noted from earlier sources.

What about the reference of שֹׁגיאין? This must be deliberately generalized. If Jesus had wanted to say ישׂראל, he could have said it: and if he had wanted to declare that their deaths would atone for the sins of the world, he could readily have said לכ עממיא or כל בני אנשׁא or the like. To interpret שֹׁגיאין, we must therefore consider the parameters of the ministry as a whole. His death would atone for Israel. Scribes and Pharisees who had counted themselves out of the kingdom of God were out, and Gentiles who would worship in the cleansed court of the Gentiles were in. Basically, however, the covenant was between God and Israel, and that is the context in which Jesus himself saw his atoning death.

We can now see how effectively Mk 10.45 draws the whole passage together. It follows directly on from the immediately preceding teaching on service, for it carries the service required of leaders of the Jesus movement to the very point of death. This links up with Jesus' debate with Jacob and John. The general level of meaning of the term (א)נשׁ(א) בר further reinforces Jesus' assertion that they will share his fate, and it is clear that death is included. The general level of meaning is also sufficiently loose to include the other members of the twelve. At the same time, it idiomatically refers primarily to the speaker, whose leadership in the whole incident was decisive. This general level of meaning is not only unavoidable in Aramaic, it is available only in Aramaic. This saying also takes for granted that Jesus will be in glory, and the Twelve knew when they heard him give this teaching that they would rise from the dead and be with him in glory, whether or not they already expected to judge the twelve tribes of Israel.

Finally, we must consider the work of the translator of this saying. He had a familiar problem, the translation of (א)נשׁ(א) בר. He followed his strategy. He knew that it referred to Jesus, so he used ὁ υἱὸς τοῦ ἀνθρώπου. The reference to Jacob and John, and less directly to the others, would be lost on uninstructed monoglot Greeks, but that could not be helped. From a literal point of view, the translator could not have done better with an impossible problem. From a religious point of view, he used a major Christological title which highlighted the centrally important role of Jesus himself. What about אתא? It can be read as a perfect, or as a participle with present force, and either could be used in a general statement. The translator carried on with the reference to Jesus, whose death was a past event, and rendered the possible perfect with an aorist, as translators from Aramaic into Greek must be in the habit of doing. His behaviour was entirely reasonable. It is unfortunate that New Testament scholars read this translation as if it were the creation of a monoglot speaker of Greek. This ensures a meaning referring to Jesus alone in accordance with later Christian tradition, but the resonances with Jesus' own Jewish traditions and the connection with the rest of the passage have been lost.

Once again, therefore, the reconstruction of the Aramaic level of the tradition has proved essential in working out the original teaching of Jesus. Its *Sitz im Leben* is in the ministry of Jesus, not in the early church. With the original meaning of (א)נשׁ(א) בר clearly in view, the passage makes perfect sense as a whole. This is another strong argument for the correctness of the solution to the Son of man problem proposed in this book.

5. Mark 14.21

The next Son of man saying belongs to Mark's account of Jesus' final Passover with his disciples. I have offered elsewhere a complete reconstruction of the Aramaic source of Mk 14.12-26.[36] I presuppose this, and offer discussion only of the points necessary for understanding the crucial verse.

The introductory verses (Mk 14.12-16) show that this was a Passover meal, and this is supported by several details in the rest of the account, beginning with the

---

36.   Casey, *Aramaic Sources of Mark's Gospel*, Ch. 6.

arrival of Jesus and the Twelve after dark. We do not know how big the company was, but it was certainly much bigger than the traditional 13, and it will have included women who were important for the ministry, not just men. The first verse central for our understanding of this Son of man saying is Mk 14.18. This is a prediction of Jesus' betrayal in terms which recall Ps. 41. When we consider Ps. 41, from this perspective, we can recover Jesus' exegesis of it. The betrayal of Jesus by Judah of Kerioth could be seen at Ps. 41.7: 'And if he comes to see me, his heart speaks falsehood, he gathers wickedness, he goes outside, he speaks of it.' This gets Judah to the chief priests and scribes, who may be seen at v. 8, 'All those who hate me whisper together against me, they devise evil against me.' Their intention is given in v. 9, together with their denial of Jesus' resurrection: 'A thing of Belial will constrain him, and when he lies down, he will not rise again.' Then Judah of Kerioth at v. 10, 'Yes, a man of my peace, in whom I trusted, who eats my bread, has made great his heel against me.' There follows a plea for resurrection in v. 11, 'And you, LORD, be gracious and raise me up.'

All this is too simple, and too extensive, to be unintentional. We must infer that everyone knew Ps. 41, and that the betrayal of Jesus was written in scripture. This must therefore be one of the scriptures referred to at Mk 14.21. No one suggested that they could prevent him from being handed over. At the same time, the prediction saddened the disciples, and each of them affirmed that s/he personally would not betray him. Jesus responded by narrowing down the group from whom the traitor came to the inner circle of twelve. It is at this point that Jesus used the Son of man saying to refer indirectly but clearly to his forthcoming betrayal and death:

אזל בר נש ככתיב עלוהי, ואוי לאנשא הוא דבר נש מתמסר בידה. טב לה אן לא יליד גברא הוא.

A/The (son of) man goes as it is written concerning him, and woe to that man by whose hand a/the (son of) man is betrayed/handed over. (It would be) good for him if that man had not been born.

The first part of this saying carries further the reference to scripture. The Aramaic word אזל was in normal use as a metaphor for death, as the Greek ὑπάγω was not. Like the use of (א)נש(א) בר itself, this is part of the evidence that it is right to reconstruct an Aramaic source. The Aramaic (א)נש(א) בר cannot lose its level of generality, though this is not the main point of the saying. Jesus expected to suffer a humiliating death, but this was to have a fundamental redemptive function. He therefore had good reason to state the prediction of his death in scripture, and the doom awaiting the traitor, by means of a general statement. At the same time, no one will have been left in doubt that Jesus' own death was primarily referred to. Ps. 41 is one scripture clearly in mind. Others must have included the second group of Hallel psalms. These include the clear general statement of Ps. 116.15, 'Glorious in the eyes of the Lord is the death of his pious ones'. Surely none of them could sing that verse without thinking of the importance of Jesus' death. They could also include themselves, in so far as they formed any intention to die with him. Jesus himself will have seen the general level of meaning in passages such as Job 14.1-2 and Isa. 40.6-8, since he had already applied these passages to John the Baptist, himself and others (Mk 9.12-13).[37] Creative exegesis could lead to more precise references. Part of the final Hallel psalm, Ps. 118.14-17, could easily be read like this: 'The LORD is my strength and song, and he is for me, for Jesus … The right hand of the LORD raises up … I shall not die because I shall live.' The doom pronounced on the traitor was also made by means of general statements. The first is at one level a condemnation of traitors, and hence universally acceptable. This made it feasible for Jesus to proceed with the condemnation of the traitor. This is in accordance with scriptural passages such as Ps. 40.15-16; 41.11; 118.7f.

We must therefore conclude that this is another genuine saying of Jesus, with a double use of בר (א)נש(א). The circumstances of Jesus' forthcoming betrayal and death explain why he should use this idiom. The general level of meaning is essential to the idiom, but it was not the point of the saying, which was to predict Jesus' death and condemn the man who brought it about.

6. Mt. 11.19//Luke 7.34

This Q saying comes from a collection of sayings about John the Baptist and Jesus. I have reconstructed an Aramaic source of these sayings elsewhere, distinguishing them from editorial comments by Matthew and Luke.[38] The Son of man saying is part of Jesus' final comments in this passage (Mt. 11.16-19//Lk. 7.31-35). He began with a metaphorical comparison of his generation to awkward children, and ended with a sentence which is very difficult to understand.[39] I leave these matters aside here, and discuss the substantive comparison, which includes the Son of man saying. I number the verses as is conventional for Matthew. I present the proposed Aramaic source of this piece, an English translation of it, and the single Greek translation of the Aramaic source which both evangelists used:

.18 אתה יוחנן לא אכל ולא שתא ואמרין: שיד איתי לה.

.19 אתה בר אנש אכל ושתה ואמרין: הא אנש זולל וסבא, חבר למכסין ולחטיין.

[18]John has come not eating and not drinking and they say, "He has a demon." [19]A/the (son of) man comes eating and drinking and they say, "Look, a man 'glutton and drunkard', an associate of tax-collectors and sinners."

18. ἐλήλυθεν γὰρ Ἰωάννης μήτε ἐσθίων μήτε πίνων, καὶ λέγουσιν, Δαιμόνιον ἔχει·
19. ἐλήλυθεν ὁ υἱὸς τοῦ ἀνθρώπου ἐσθίων καὶ πίνων, καὶ λέγουσιν, Ἰδοὺ ἄνθρωπος φάγος καὶ οἰνοπότης, φίλος τελωνῶν καὶ ἁμαρτωλῶν.

The first comment describes one feature of John the Baptist's lifestyle and quotes a criticism of him by opponents of John and Jesus. The use of אתה in v. 18 refers to John arriving on the scene, and does not imply his pre-existence. The word אתה is abundantly attested in early sources with a very broad semantic area, so that this

---

37.   See pp. 127–30 above.

38.   Casey, *Aramaic Approach to Q*, Ch. 4.

39.   Cf. now S. Gathercole, 'The Justification of Wisdom (Matt 11.19b/Luke 7.35)', *NTS* 49 (2003), pp. 476–88.

usage should not be regarded as problematical. Later sources with a similar use of התא include b. San. 107b.

עד אלישע לא הוה איניש חליש דמיתפח ואתא אלישע ובעא רחמי ואיתפח

Until Elijah, there was not a man sick who recovered. And Elisha came and sought mercy and recovered.

I have supposed that Matthew's μήτε ἐσθίων μήτε πίνων reproduces his Greek source, which was a literal translation of לא אכל ולא שתא. This brief phrase is a perfectly good picture of John's ascetic lifestyle. In that sense it is confirmed by Mark, who reports him eating a diet of locusts and wild honey (Mk 1.6). John was very unconventional. He lived in the wilderness, away from cities, as demoniacs sometimes did too. He dressed and ate unconventionally. The accusation that he had a demon will have come as naturally to his opponents as it did to scribes and Pharisees who accused Jesus of casting out demons by the prince of demons.[40]

The statement about Jesus is put indirectly, using the key term בר (א)נש(א). The idiomatic use of בר (א)נש(א) was due to Jesus being in the humiliating situation of being falsely accused of a serious offence. The use of this idiom in a general statement does not imply that the statement was thought to be true of everyone. The first part of it is however true of everyone:

אתה בר אנש אכל ושתה

Everyone does come eating and drinking, otherwise they die! It should be clear that אתה has this very general level of meaning, as in the previous sentence about John the Baptist: it does not refer to Jesus' pre-existence, a piece of Christian doctrine which had not yet been invented. This very general statement provides the cover for the more precise comments which follow. These reflect the criticisms of Jesus made by his opponents. Jesus has used the term בר (א)נש(א) because it was a normal Aramaic way of saying something indirectly in humiliating circumstances. For the idiom to be effective, it is necessary for the rest of the statement to be true of more people than of Jesus, but not of everyone.

The subject of the next verb is left open. This is commoner in Aramaic than in Greek, German, English and the like. We must therefore reconstruct אמרין behind Matthew's λέγουσιν, and Luke's λέγετε must be regarded as an editorial alteration. The effect is to include anyone who makes this kind of criticism, not just the opponents of Jesus, so a general level of meaning is maintained. The reconstruction of φάγος καὶ οἰνοπότης is at first sight very difficult, since the nearest expression in Aramaic is אכל ושתה, which we must reconstruct behind ἐσθίων καὶ πίνων. We cannot posit this expression twice, since it would not make very good sense either of the sentence or of the translator. I therefore suggest that φάγος καὶ οἰνοπότης translates a quotation of the Hebrew זולל וסבא from Deut. 21.20.

The Hebrew words זולל וסבא conclude the description of the rebellious son. Jesus' opponents were scribes and Pharisees, who will have read the scriptures in Hebrew,

---

40. Casey, *Aramaic Approach to Q*, pp. 158–61.

as Jesus did himself. They could therefore use these Hebrew words, and Jesus could reproduce them. Jesus' relationship with his family was evidently difficult at times: on one occasion, they came out to seize him, an incident which Mark associates with his being accused of exorcising by the power of the devil (Mk 3.20-30), a very similar accusation to that thrown at John the Baptist and recorded in the previous verse.[41] This is the cultural background for Jesus' opponents to have resorted to this passage of scripture. There is also criticism of Jesus for feasting with the wrong people, and Mark represents Jesus' opponents describing these people as τῶν τελωνῶν καὶ ἁμαρτωλῶν (Mk 2.16). This too is the same criticism as we have here. The criticism of people for similar behaviour is also attested elsewhere. It is found in scripture at Prov. 23.20-21. Some passages of literature from about the time of Jesus take up this theme too (cf. *T. Jud.* 14; Philo, *Spec. Leg.* 4,97-104; *Ebr.* 206-24; Jos. *Apion* II.195). It follows that people who feasted will have been accustomed to criticism from stricter Jews. It is that criticism which makes the general level of meaning of the son of man statement plausible. It is a generalization from his own experience of being called a זולל וסבא, which will have struck a chord with people sympathetic to him partly because strict Jews were liable to say it of some of the people with whom he associated as well.

For φίλος I have suggested חבר, which is rendered with φίλος three times by Theodotion (Dan. 2.13,17,18). The word is very well attested in earlier and Qumran Aramaic. It means any sort of associate or companion. In rabbinical literature, in both Aramaic and Hebrew, it is the word used for groups of orthodox Jews who kept purity laws more strictly than most people did. Since the *halakhah* of the orthodox was stricter in the Second Temple period than it was later, it is probable that this sense of the term was already in use. It makes a very sharp piece of polemic. It presupposes that, as a significant Jewish teacher, Jesus should have been a חבר to ספרין ופרישׁין. He is accused of being a חבר to quite the wrong sort of people, מכסין וחטיין. From the perspective of his opponents, this was also a very serious accusation.

For ἁμαρτωλῶν I have suggested חטיין, a somewhat Hebraizing word used in Aramaic, properly corresponding to ἁμαρτωλῶν in its semantic area and corresponding also to the English term 'sinners'. It is possible that Jesus' opponents used the native Aramaic חיבין, and that it was translated fluently with ἁμαρτωλῶν (rather than literally with ὀφειλέτων, cf. Mt. 6.12//Lk. 11.4). This makes no significant difference. The reference of all these words is to people who committed sins. It is at this point that more than one perception of many people is possible. We must infer that this term is a hostile description of people who were not fully observant. The word מכסין is our next clue. There is nothing to indicate that the tax-collectors stopped collecting taxes. The only approach to an exception is Zacchaeus, who was at least rich enough to make reparations, so the story from unsupported Luke (Lk. 19.1-10) is untypical even if perchance it be true, and even it does not say that Zacchaeus would stop being an ἀρχιτελώνης. We should infer that, in general,

41.   Casey, *Aramaic Approach to Q*, pp. 150–61.

tax-collectors who followed Jesus did not stop collecting taxes. If they had, Jesus would have become famous overnight for this too, and scribes and Pharisees would have had reason to honour his achievement, rather than criticize him. Another clue comes from Jesus' saying at Mt. 21.31-2. Here tax-collectors are associated with prostitutes. We are first told that they will both precede 'you' into the kingdom of God. It follows that prostitutes will enter the kingdom of God. What happens in the meantime? Do they cease to be prostitutes? Surely not! The teaching of Jesus does not require that oppressed people shall starve because they abandon their only means of making a living. Moreover, the saying does not even make sense if applied to people who *used to be* tax-collectors and prostitutes. Whereas 'you' did not believe John the Baptist, 'the tax-collectors and prostitutes' did believe him. Even more striking is the accusation that 'you' did not repent when they saw this, and believe him. The whole situation does not make sense if the tax-collectors and prostitutes had ceased to be so.

It follows that tax-collectors and prostitutes repented in the manner represented by the Aramaic word תוב and the Hebrew שׁוב. They returned to the Lord. Like most faithful Jews, they will then have proceeded to keep the Law as best they could. That would not be enough for Jesus' opponents. From an orthodox perspective, other followers of Jesus will have committed other sins too. For example, they are not likely to have gone to Jerusalem for major festivals three times a year. Consequently, they are not likely to have offered the prescribed sacrifices every time they sinned.

We now have enough to understand these accusations against Jesus. At Mk 2.16 Pharisaic scribes merely ask why Jesus eats and drinks with tax-collectors and sinners. The description 'sinners' means that they did not keep the whole Law. Pharisees regarded themselves as guardians of the Law, and there is sufficient evidence that they did not eat with other people if that could be achieved. They therefore merely asked the disciples why Jesus did so. The accusation at Mt. 11.19// Lk. 7.34 is a more serious development of the same thing. Jesus has been described as a חבר of such people because he associated with them, and even ate with them. This is condemnation, not a question. It reflects the success of his ministry among Jews who were not fully observant, in circumstances where it was very difficult for them to be so.

We must therefore conclude that, faced with condemnation by his opponents, Jesus defended himself by associating himself with John the Baptist, as he was to do when he had cleansed the Temple (Mk 11.27-33). In this case, he portrayed their opponents with an unfavourable image, and retailed their accusations as if to show that they were obviously foolish. In his own case, he also resorted to the idiomatic use of a general statement with בר (א)נשׁ(א). One of the major situations in which this idiom was used was in humiliating situations, of which this is obviously one. The reality of the general level of meaning in no way detracts from the genuine and clear reference to Jesus himself.

7. Matthew 12.32//Luke 12.10, with Mark 3.28-29

The next saying is one of the most remarkable in the whole synoptic tradition. In general, where there are alternative versions of a saying in Mark and in Q, they cannot be regarded as alternative translations of a single Aramaic underlay. In this case, however, there are good reasons for such a view. Moreover, the Matthean version is part of a continuous series of sayings, as though Q had the saying in the same position in a collection of sayings in the same order as Mark. I have accordingly reconstructed the whole of both series elsewhere.[42] The Lukan version of this saying, however, is in a different place, quite out of common order, and may reasonably be treated as a third translation of the same Aramaic saying. It belongs in a collection of sayings, preceded by two genuine sayings both of which originally used the term (א)בר (א)נש.

I begin with the common Aramaic underlay to Mt. 12.32 and Lk. 12.10.

וכל די ימלל מלה לבר אנשא ישתביק לה, ומן דמלל מלה על רוחא קדישתא לא ישתביק לה לעלמין.

And everyone who speaks a word against a/the (son of) man, it shall be forgiven him, and whoever speaks/has spoken a word against the Spirit of Holiness, it shall not be forgiven him forever.

This saying has an excellent *Sitz im Leben* in the context in which it now occurs in Matthew, concluding Jesus' response to the accusation that he cast out demons by Beelzebul. The first part of it is a general statement decreeing forgiveness to people who oppose or even slander other people. The use of בר (א)נש(א) is the particular idiom whereby the statement refers especially to Jesus himself. The saying therefore appears at first sight to grant forgiveness to Jesus' opponents. The sting is in the second half. The Holy Spirit is a metaphor for God in action. Nowhere is the action of God to be seen more vigorously and obviously than in Jesus' exorcisms. The accusation that he cast out demons by Beelzebul is accordingly an unforgivable sin. What Jesus seems to concede in the first part of the saying is thus quite removed in the second part. This polemic, like the content of the saying, accordingly has an excellent *Sitz im Leben* where the Matthean and Markan sayings are now to be found, in the dispute over Jesus' exorcisms. The idiom is also specifically Aramaic. Once again, we certainly have a genuine word of Jesus.

The Matthean translation of this saying is reasonably clear and straightforward. ὃς ἐάν for כל די will have been done with ὃς δ' ἄν for ומן ד already in mind: it gives an excellent balance to both language and meaning in the resulting piece, and it is not beyond the parameters of what an ancient translator might do. The words εἴπῃ λόγον, with Luke's alternative ἐρεῖ λόγον, establish the original wording ימלל מלה ל, which we shall see lies behind Mark's highly explicitative rendering, and which is also essential for establishing the original wording of the opening of the second half of the saying. The potentially ambiguous לעלמין at the end has been translated explicitatively with οὔτε ἐν τούτῳ τῷ αἰῶνι οὔτε ἐν τῷ μέλλοντι.

---

42.   Casey, *Aramaic Approach to Q*, Ch. 5.

Lk. 12.10 is equally comprehensible as an alternative translation. Luke's πᾶς ὃς is more literal than Matthew's ὃς ἐάν, with ἐρεῖ as literal as possible for י_מלל. The preposition εἰς is an obvious possible alternative to Matthew's κατά with the genitive. In the second half of the saying, Luke's τῷ βλασφημήσαντι is a particularly interesting difference from Matthew's ὃς δ᾽ ἂν εἴπῃ, which presupposes λόγον from the first half. It must surely be an alternative rendering of מלל מלה על. This is the same basic clarification as used by Mark's translator, and an entirely appropriate one when it is the Holy Spirit which is being spoken against, since this is a metaphor for God himself in action. The potentially ambiguous לעלמין at the end has been omitted rather than expanded. The Lukan context is however one of collected sayings which are not in common order and which provide other evidence of more than one translation of an Aramaic original. We must conclude that Lk. 12.10 was collected with the sayings which surround it on the catchword principle. This caused the original context of Jesus' saying to be lost, and without its context its original meaning could never survive intact.

It is remarkable that Mk 3.28-29 can be understood as an alternative translation of exactly the same Aramaic words, except that it began with the additional introductory לכון אנה אמר אמן. This is likely to be authentic. Jesus had good reason to use an emphatic expression characteristic of his idiolect, because of the importance of the sentiments expressed in this saying, and the background of an extremely threatening situation. Matthew had Mark in front of him, but preferred διὰ τοῦτο λέγω ὑμῖν as he conflated his Markan and Q material. His Q may therefore have read לכון אנה אמר אמן. Luke has many fewer examples of ἀμήν than Matthew and Mark, and it might well get lost in a collection of sayings made on the catchword principle. We should conclude that Mark has probably preserved the original opening of Jesus' saying.

Apart from the opening, the translator was worried about the sense of the saying. This is shown by the use of τοῖς υἱοῖς τῶν ἀνθρώπων, the only use of the plural of ὁ υἱὸς τοῦ ἀνθρώπου in the whole of the Gospels. This diverges from the detectable strategy of translating בר (א)נ(א)ש with ὁ υἱὸς τοῦ ἀνθρώπου when it refers to Jesus, and with something else when it does not, including when it is plural.[43] The translator's concern about the sense also provides a good explanation of his explicitative additions. We must infer that he did not believe that speaking against Jesus was forgivable. This is entirely reasonable for someone who lived in the early church, who knew Jesus' polemic against his opponents and who periodically suffered damage from the outside world which included vilification of Jesus. It is also an entirely reasonable interpretation of the immediate context. Speaking against the Holy Spirit is said to be unforgivable, and Mark locates this correctly in its original context by interpreting it with reference to the accusation that Jesus had an unclean spirit. The translator was therefore certain that אנשא לבר could not follow immediately after מלה יאמר. Accordingly, he took אנשא לבר closely with הל ישתביק, and regarded לה as simply picking up אנשא לבר before the verb. He

---

43.   See p. 118 above; and for more detailed discussion, pp. 253–66 below.

also took בר אנשא as a collective term for people in general, and, like לה, it told him who would be forgiven – everyone in general, which fits the teaching of Jesus perfectly well.

The translator now took כל to mean everything, and the object rather than the subject of the verb of saying. The term מלה, no longer controlled by its context, is altogether too general a term – it means any thing, not only a word. The Greek term λόγος must surely have occurred to the translator, but he must surely have felt that it was not specific enough. Taking מלה ... כל to mean everything except blasphemy against the Holy Spirit, he has therefore translated explicitatively. His addition, τὰ ἁμαρτήματα καὶ αἱ βλασφημίαι ὅσα ἐὰν βλασφημήσωσιν, is phrased in such a way as to make clear that what very sinful people usually do is forgivable, a sentiment in accordance with the teaching of Jesus and the needs of formerly sinful converts in the early church.

In the second half of the saying, ὃς δ' ἂν βλασφημήσῃ εἰς is a perfectly reasonable rendering of ומן דמלל מלה על, with the verb βλασφημέω being a particularly natural choice in view of the wording which the translator had just thought of for his explicitative addition to the first half of the saying. Mark ends with a very determined piece of explicitation. Verse 30 declares the connection between the accusation and the incident, which Mark evidently felt might get lost if it were not explicitly stated. Equally, he has clarified the refusal of forgiveness for ever by adding ἀλλὰ ἔνοχός ἐστιν αἰωνίου ἁμαρτήματος. This ensures that לעלמין cannot be regarded as just a metaphor. Mark may also have used εἰς τὸν αἰῶνα as a relatively conventional rendering of לעלמין, or it may have been added by a scribe, for it is absent from D W Θ 565 569 and other manuscripts. Fortunately this does not affect the exegesis of the original saying nor appreciation of the behaviour of the translator, who was determinedly explicitative, whether or not he added εἰς τὸν αἰῶνα.

The Markan version of this saying is at first sight seriously divergent from the versions which we now find in Matthew and Luke. The way in which it can be understood as an alternative translation of the same Aramaic original is a very strong argument for the accuracy of the Aramaic original reconstructed above. That original Aramaic saying fits perfectly into the context in which two of the differing translations are now found in Matthew and Mark. I have expounded this controversy in detail elsewhere, and summarize only the main points now.[44] The Marcan version provides a coherent argument. After a question formulating his basic premise that Satan cannot cast out Satan, Jesus proceeded with two analogical arguments from a kingdom and a house. He inferred that Satan would be finished if he rose up against himself, from which it follows that Satan cannot have done any such thing. His next argument was another analogy, referring to the real experience of conflict with the devil before an exorcism. Having thus made absolutely clear that his exorcisms were done by the power of God, Jesus finally accused his opponents of the unforgivable sin of opposing the power of God. That completes a logical progression of arguments, provided that the final argument is read in Aramaic and

44.   Casey, *Aramaic Approach to Q*, Ch. 5.

all the arguments are seen in their original cultural context. Those sayings which are found in Q only fit perfectly well into this context, though Jesus may have said them on a separate occasion.

Thus this Son of man saying fits its original context perfectly. The context provided a natural situation for using this idiom. Jesus was in the humiliating situation of being accused of casting out demons by the power of the devil himself. The saying accordingly has a general level of meaning. Anyone who speaks against another person will be forgiven, a sentiment wholly in accordance with the teaching of Jesus. At the same time, this part of the saying refers especially to Jesus himself. The second part of the saying is equally indirect. Speaking against the Holy Spirit is unforgivable. Mark found this so indirect that he carefully added in the reference to this controversy, a reference which will have been blindingly obvious to anyone in the middle of it.

Once again, therefore, a Son of man saying makes even better sense when reconstructed in the original Aramaic than it does otherwise. It also fits perfectly into the context in which it is now found in both Mark and Matthew. It has a perfect *Sitz im Leben* in the teaching of Jesus in general, and in this context in particular. It has no reasonable *Sitz im Leben* in the early church. The arguments for this being an authentic saying of Jesus which should be understood as I have suggested are accordingly overwhelming.

8. Conclusions

Every one of the Son of man sayings discussed in this chapter belongs to an overall context, the whole of which I have been able to reconstruct in Aramaic in two previous books.[45] Every one of them has an excellent *Sitz im Leben* in the life and teaching of Jesus in general, and in the context in which they are now found (except Lk. 12.10, which has been removed from the context known to us from Mark and Matthew). When the Aramaic original of each saying is considered, none of them has a satisfactory *Sitz im Leben* in the early church. One saying, Mk 9.12, belongs to a context in which it makes sense only when the original Aramaic of the passage has been reconstructed. One saying, Mk 10.45, fully belongs to its context only when it has been reconstructed in Aramaic. One saying, Mk 2.28, follows properly from the immediately preceding verse only when it is reconstructed in Aramaic, so much so that Matthew and Luke independently omitted the previous verse. One saying, Mt. 12.32//Lk. 12.10 and Mk 3.28-29, is intelligible as three different translations of an original Son of man saying.

This is a quite remarkable set of results. It forms an overwhelming argument of cumulative weight for this part of my solution to the Son of man problem. So far, however, we have only six authentic sayings, containing seven uses of the term בר (א)נש(א). I have briefly proposed further examples, which I discuss in the following chapters.

---

45. Casey, *Aramaic Sources of Mark's Gospel; Aramaic Approach to Q.*

Chapter Five

THE HEALING OF A PARALYTIC (MARK 2.1-12)

The Son of man saying at Mk 2.10 is embedded in a complete narrative about the healing of a paralytic. This story has suffered very badly at the hands of scholarly dissection. In his classic work, Bultmann divided it into two, classifying vv. 5b-10 as 'a secondary interpolation', and for this he could already call upon predecessors.[1] Some recent scholars continue to follow this view, and commentators who do not follow it still feel obliged to discuss it.[2] We shall see that there is good reason to find some secondary glossing, mostly centred on the words which the scribes are explicitly reported *not* to have spoken. Nonetheless, one purpose of this chapter is to reconstruct Mark's Aramaic source for a single incident. In particular, I argue that, when the narrative is seen from a first-century Jewish perspective, Jesus' forgiveness of the man's sins was an essential part of the healing process, not a separate issue. Accordingly, I suggest that the most extensive insertion is much shorter than critical scholars have generally supposed.

1. The Original Story

I begin with a reconstruction and a literal translation of Mark's proposed Aramaic source. I keep the conventional verse numbers for convenience.

1. ועל עוד לכפר נחם בתר יומין. ואשתמיע דבבית הוא.
2. ואתכנשו שגיאין וממלל להון מלתא.
3. ואתין לה מיתין משרי וארבעה שקלין לה.
4. ולא יכלו למקרב עלוהי בדיל כנשתא וארימו טלולא דתמן הוא וחפרוהי. ואחתו ערסא דמשריא רבע עלוהי.
5. וחזא ישוע הימנותהון ואמר למשריא, טליא,אשתבקו חוביך.
6. ואיתיהון מן ספריא יתבין תמן.
8. ואמר להון, למה אנתון חשבין אלין בלבביכון?
9. המ קליל, למאמר אשתבקו חוביך או למאמר קום ושקל ערסך והלך?
10. ודתנדעון דשלטן לבר אנשא על ארעא למשבק חובין,

---

1.   Bultmann, *Synoptic Tradition*, pp. 14–15, citing *inter alia* the regrettably seminal study of W. Wrede, 'Zur Heilung des Gelähmten (Mc 2,Iff)', *ZNW* 5 (1904), pp. 354–8.
2.   E.g. J. Gnilka, *Das Evangelium nach Markus* (EKKNT. 2 vols.; Düsseldorf/Neukirchen-Vluyn: Benziger/Neukirchener, 4th edn, 1994), p. 96, explicitly following Bultmann and others; R. H. Gundry, *Mark. A Commentary on His Apology for the Cross* (Grand Rapids: Eerdmans, 1993), pp. 121–2, for critical discussion.

11. קוּם, אמר אנה לך, שׁקל ערסך ואזל לביתך.

12. וקום ומיד שׁקל ערסא ונפק מן קדם כלהון ותמהו כלא והדרו לאלהא ואמרין דכדן לא חזינא.

[1]And he entered Capernaum again after some days. And it was heard that he was at home. [2]And many (people) gathered together, and he was giving them a speech. [3]And they came to him bringing a paralytic, and four were carrying him. [4]And they were not able to approach him because of the gathering. And they took off the roofing where he was and dug it out. And they lowered the mattress on which the paralytic was lying [5]And Jesus saw their faith and said to the paralytic, 'Child, your sins have been forgiven/undone/released.' [6]And some of the scribes were sitting there. [8]And he said to them, 'Why are you considering these things in your hearts? [9]Which is light, to say "Your sins have been forgiven/undone/released", or to say "Get up and take up your mattress and walk"? [10]And so that you may know that a/the son of man on earth has power/authority to forgive/undo/release sins, [11]"Get up, I tell you, take up your mattress and go to your house."' [12]And he got up, and at once he took up his mattress and went out in front of all of them. And everyone was amazed and glorified God. And (they were) saying, 'We have not seen (anything) like this.'

2. The Setting

The story begins with the setting in Capernaum, the small town in which Mk 1.21-34 was set. The precise form אשׁתמיע is found already at *Ahiqar* 70, and this explains why the translator put ἠκούσθη, its very precise equivalent. He will not have noticed that the result is quite awkward Greek. That this news should spread in a small town is unproblematic, especially if Jesus is the subject of Mk 1.45, and if this was genuinely a recent event. More specifically, the incident is set in a house. It is difficult to know whether to read ἐν οἴκῳ or εἰς οἶκον. Either expression would be a translation of בבית, 'in a house'. The common conjecture that this would be the house of Simeon and Andrew[3] is possible, but cannot be verified.

I cannot find any reasonable Aramaic that would cause a reasonable translator to put ὥστε μηκέτι χωρεῖν μηδὲ τὰ πρὸς τὴν θύραν. I therefore suggest that this has been added in Greek, with a view to explaining the extraordinary behaviour of the men who carried the paralytic. Whether or not one of the houses excavated in Capernaum is really the house of Simeon and Andrew, it is clear that a normal house was not all that big. It is accordingly quite reasonable to suppose that there was a crowd round the outside of the door as well as in the house, and that Jesus was able to teach from his position inside the house. The setting is completed by וממלל להון מלתא, which simply means that Jesus spoke to the crowd, teaching them in his customary manner.

With the setting complete, the healing incident begins with the arrival of four people carrying a man described as 'paralytic'. It is evident that he could not or would not walk. What was wrong with him?

---

3.   E.g. V. Taylor, *The Gospel According to St. Mark* (London: Macmillan, 1959), p. 193.

3. Paralysis and Healing

In general, some kinds of paralysis come within the realm of illnesses which have psychological causes and may be subject to spontaneous remission and/or therapy. Hence this is within the area of illnesses which people in the ancient world might think were curable by deities and/or healers. So for example Jablensky includes 'problems with movement, paralysis' among the World Health Authority's classification of 'narrowly defined somatoform symptoms'.[4] Murphy likewise includes 'paralysis' as one of the examples of 'conversion disorder' which 'suggest neurological disease'. He notes that 'an episode of conversion is usually of short duration with sudden onset and resolution'.[5] In discussing paralysis among 'disorders of hysterical conversion', Toone notes that hysterical weakness 'involves principally the extremities, and the legs more than the arms'. It is 'usually a paralysis of movement rather than a weakness of individual muscles'; in these cases, strength is retained in the muscles.[6]

Hooker retails in anecdotal form the story of a woman who was paralysed for two years after seeing a violent crime. 'Reassurance that she was in no way responsible for the crime resulted in a cure as instantaneous and dramatic as the paralysis.'[7] More tightly controlled evidence is available from the occurrence and cure of hysterical paralysis in late nineteenth- and early twentieth-century Europe. Hysteria was a fashionable illness at the time, so it was a natural choice for people who needed to be patients but who had nothing else wrong with them. Equally, hypnotism was a culturally acceptable form of manipulating people. Consequently, we have a number of accounts of hysterical paralysis,[8] some cases of which were curable under hypnosis. The culturally determined nature of these cases is especially well illustrated by those who could move their limbs under hypnosis, but who could no more do so afterwards than they had done before. All such cases belong to the much larger phenomenon of somatized illness behaviour. They should be carefully distinguished from diseases, and their cure is not necessarily accompanied by what western biomedicine would regard as a change in symptomatology.[9]

---

4.   A. Jablensky, 'The Concept of Somatoform Disorders: A Comment on the Mind-Body Problem in Psychiatry' in Y. Ono *et al.* (eds), *Somatoform Disorders. A Worldwide Perspective* (Tokyo: Springer, 1999), pp. 3–10 (7).

5.   M. R. Murphy, 'Classification of the Somatoform Disorders', in C. Bass (ed.), *Somatization: Physical Symptoms and Psychological Illness* (Oxford: Blackwell, 1990), pp. 10–39 (25).

6.   B. K. Toone, 'Disorders of Hysterical Conversion', in Bass (ed.), *Somatization*, pp. 207–34 (217).

7.   M. D. Hooker, *The Gospel According to St Mark* (BNTC. London: Black, 1991), p. 85.

8.   Cf. A. R. G. Owen, *Hysteria, hypnosis and healing: the work of J.-M. Charcot* (London: Dobson, 1971), esp. pp. 68, 124ff.

9.   Cf. E. M. Pattison, N. A. Lapins and H. A. Doerr, 'Faith Healing. A Study of Personality and Function', *Journal of Nervous and Mental Disease* 157 (1973), pp. 397–409; A. Kleinman, *Patients and Healers in the Context of Culture. An Exploration of the Borderland between Anthropology, Medicine and Psychiatry* (Berkeley/LA: Univ. of California, 1980), pp. 311–74; R. Totman, *Social Causes of Illness* (London: Souvenir, 2nd edn, 1987), pp. 39–40, citing L. Rose, *Faith Healing* (London: Penguin, 1971).

Shorter has contributed a very useful history of psychosomatic illnesses in the modern world. In his chapter on 'Motor Hysteria' he notes that recorded instances of paralysis increased greatly after 1800, and he gives many useful examples. In particular, what was known as hysterical paralysis increased as the century passed. It could be very difficult for conventional doctors to cure, and it was susceptible to other kinds of treatment. Shorter quotes Osler declaring in 1892, 'Perhaps no single affection has brought more discredit upon the profession, for the cases are very refractory, and finally fall into the hands of a charlatan or faith-healer, under whose touch the disease may disappear at once.'[10] At this stage, the majority of cases were Victorian women, and the work of J.-M. Charcot was especially important in the classification and popularity of this illness. As a result of this popularity, hysterical paralysis was the illness suffered by many men who could not cope with being soldiers in the First World War.

This was part of a massive increase in psychosomatic illnesses during that war. Much study of psychosomatic illnesses followed. In the light of this, Micklem wrote a classic work in which he suggested that the paralytic in Mk 2.1-12 suffered from hysterical paralysis, which Jesus was able to cure.[11] When the First World War was over, instances of hysterical paralysis soon underwent a drastic decline, with Charcot's particular form of hysteria disappearing within a decade of his death. This further clarifies the culturally oriented nature of this illness. It is natural that this has also led to some criticism of 'hysterical paralysis' as a diagnosis of an illness. It is accordingly very important that it is only the extent and classification of this illness that are culture-specific to the late nineteenth and early twentieth century. The illness itself is much more widely attested. Shorter has a nice example of psychogenic paralysis from 1682.[12] A detailed report on several recent cases studied together was published in 1987: it includes one paralysed man who responded to the injunction 'get up'.[13] Attempts to *explain how* people with psychosomatic illnesses mimic diseases which result from neurological damage continue.[14] I respond to all this by treating Mk 2.1-12 as a report of Jesus' healing a man whose paralysis was of psychosomatic origin: I do not use anything specific to the late nineteenth and early twentieth century.[15]

10.　　E. Shorter, *From Paralysis to Fatigue. A History of Psychosomatic Illness in the Modern Era* (New York: Free Press, 1992), especially Ch. 5, 'Motor Hysteria': on p.125, he has the above quotation from W. Osler, *The Principles and Practice of Medicine* (New York: Appleton, 1892), p. 974.

11.　　E. R. Micklem, *Miracles and the New Psychology* (London: OUP, 1922), esp. pp. 85–91.

12.　　Shorter, *From Paralysis to Fatigue*, p. 7.

13.　　J. H. Baker and J. R. Silver, 'Hysterical paraplegia', *Journal of Neurology, Neurosurgery and Psychiatry* 50 (1987), pp. 375–82.

14.　　E.g. P. W. Halligan and A. S. David (eds), *Conversion Hysteria: Towards a Cognitive Neuropsychological Account* (Hope: Psychology Press, 1999).

15.　　For detailed discussion of this story in the light of modern medical knowledge, see J. Keir Howard, *Disease and Healing in the New Testament. An Analysis and Interpretation* (Lanham: University Press of America, 2001), pp. 75–80.

Paralysis is a well-attested illness in the ancient Greco-Roman world. Moreover, the cure of limbs is attested in pagan votive offerings. At Epidaurus, for example, Hermodikas of Lampsacus is said to have been paralysed of body (ἀκρατής τοῦ σώματος). He was healed in his sleep, and is said to have carried a large stone into the sanctuary the following morning. Kleimenes of Argos was also paralysed (ἀκρατής). He was cured after a night in which he had a vision (ὄψις) of Asclepius.[16]

Healing was a well-known activity in the Jewish world. Noah was supposed to have been taught healing by an angel, and transmitted his knowledge to Shem (*Jub.* 10.10-14). This story makes sense only if we assume that this knowledge was transmitted right down to the time of this account, in the second century BCE. Solomon was also believed to have been a remarkable healer, and Josephus' account shows that his knowledge was still in use (*Ant.* VIII,45-9). Exorcism is prominent in both these reports, as it was in the life of Jesus. Healing was also a feature of the Therapeutae (Philo, *Vit Cont* 2). Philo says that they cured not only bodies, but also souls oppressed with various things, including λῦπαι καὶ φόβοι. Whether or not the word Essene means 'healer', and whether or not the Therapeutae were a branch of them, some Essenes were certainly involved in healing, and Josephus' report explicitly says that they were concerned with the welfare ψυχῆς καὶ σώματος (Jos. *War* II, 136). These reports indicate serious and prolonged interest in healing what is known in our culture as psychosomatic illness.

It has been thought significant that we have no Jewish reports of the curing of any kind of lameness or paralysis.[17] The evidence just surveyed, however, entails that a lot of healing was done, whereas we have very few stories of actual healing events. We simply do not know whether, let alone how often, what was regarded as paralysis was perceived to have been cured by a healer. This is partly why we must attach fundamental importance to the cross-cultural evidence that paralysis may be of psychosomatic origin, and consequently curable at a healing event. There is also ample evidence that Jesus was the best-known and most remarkable healer of his day. It follows that he was able to cure illnesses which could not be cured by other healers who were around at the time. This is implied by Mk 2.12, but perhaps contradicted by Mk 3.1-6.[18]

There are also a few passages in Jewish sources which indicate knowledge that some sort of paralysis might result from fear. In Jer. 6, God threatens to bring a merciless people against Zion because so much wrong has been done in the city. The people's reaction to this news includes the following (Jer. 6.24):

---

16.   E. J. Edelstein and L. Edelstein, *Asclepius. A Collection and Interpretation of the Testimonies* (2 vols; Baltimore: Hopkins, 1945), pp. 224, 228, no. 423 (=IG IV, 1, nos. 121–2), XV and XXXVII: these texts may be more readily available in L. R. LiDonnici, *The Epidaurian Miracle Inscriptions. Text, Translation and Commentary* (Scholars: Atlanta, 1995), pp. 96–7 (A15), 112–13 (B37).

17.   A. E. Harvey, *Jesus and the Constraints of History* (BaL 1980. London: Duckworth, 1982), p. 100.

18.   Casey, *Aramaic Sources of Mark's Gospel*, pp. 176–80.

רפו ידינו צרה החזיקתנו
παρελύθησαν αἱ χεῖρες ἡμῶν, θλῖψις κατέσχεν ἡμας

For רפו, the Targum has אתרשלא, Pesh אתרפי. Both the context and the parallelism indicate that paralysis of the hands has resulted from fear among sinful people. A similar situation is found at Ezek. 21.12, where water is used for the state of the knees, so this is somewhat more extensive paralysis of the limbs. For the MT רפו, the Targum has יתרשלן, and Pesh מתרשלן. There is a more personal example at Jer. 50.43, where the king of Babylon cannot use his hands (MT רפו, LXX Jer. 27.43 παρελύθησαν, Tg. and Pesh 50.43 אתרשלא), again in a context of fear and anguish for political reasons. More personal still is Sir. 25.23, where feeble hands and knees are caused by a ghastly wife (LXX χεῖρες παρειμέναι καὶ γόνατα παραλελυμένα), not the sinfulness of the afflicted man. At Isa. 35.3, the prayer for eschatological deliverance of the nation includes an order to strengthen hands and knees (LXX ἰσχύσατε χεῖρες ἀνειμέναι καὶ γόνατα παραλελυμένα): this is in parallel with an instruction not to be afraid. For רפות used of the hands, the Targum has רשלן, Pesh מרפין. At *1 Macc.* 9.54-55, Alcimus begins the obviously sinful action of tearing down the wall of the inner court of the sanctuary. Consequently, ἀπεφράγη τὸ στόμα αὐτοῦ καὶ παρελύθη, a condition so serious that he died. In the opening chapter of *3 Maccabees*, Antiochus is on the verge of the obviously sinful act of entering the sanctuary. In response to prayers led by Simon the high priest, he is struck down by God, with the result that he ends up on the ground, ἔτι καὶ τοῖς μέλεσιν παραλελυμένον μηδὲ φωνῆσαι (*3 Macc.* 2.22). He was taken away by friends and bodyguards, and in due course recovered, being no longer in danger of committing this particular sinful act. At Wsd. 17.18, the Egyptians at the time of the Exodus, having already been labelled as sinful, are paralysed with fear (παρέλυεν αὐτοὺς ἐκφοβοῦντα).

None of this is the *same* as Mk 2.1-12. It is however sufficient to indicate that paralysis might be included among the illnesses which might result from sin, and that it might be thought of as temporary or terminal. Moreover, at least four of these passages were part of the text held sacred by all the characters in Mark's story. This is accordingly the first part of the Explanatory Model according to which the paralysis of the man in Mark's story might be thought of as caused by sin, and as something from which he could recover, provided that his sins were forgiven.

The absence of early Aramaic stories about paralysis means that there is some uncertainty about the exact word used by Mark's source. For παραλυτικόν I have used משרי, as do pesh hark. There is no doubt that this is the right word in Syriac. The underlying root שרי is well attested in Aramaic from before the time of Jesus. Its wide semantic area includes 'undo', 'unloose', and there is a particularly relevant example at Dan. 5.6. Here Belshazzar is terrified by the writing on the wall, with the result that his hip joints משתרין, Theod διελύοντο. This is accordingly the right general area for the paralysis of limbs through fear. The root שרי also continued in general use in Jewish Aramaic as in Syriac. This is much more probable than מרשל, which is used for 'paralysed' in Christian Palestinian Aramaic. We have seen the root רשל used in relevant texts of the Targums and the Peshitta, but there is no early attestation of it at all.

4. Getting to Jesus

The next remarkable event in the Marcan narrative is the digging through the roof. We must infer that the house had only one storey, at least in the part where Jesus was teaching. It is clear from archaeological evidence that Capernaum houses could not generally support a second storey. The walls of houses were generally constructed with pieces of black basalt held together with clay, and these were not strong enough to stand the weight of a second storey.[19] It was normally possible to have a ladder to the roof, so, assuming that the paralytic was not malingering, the four men must have carried him up to the roof on his mattress. Roofs were normally made from wooden beams, placed at intervals, covered with branches or reeds which were plastered with clay. This is a kind of roof which could be dug through, and the gaps between the beams might well be large enough for a sort of mattress with a man on it to be lowered between them. There is accordingly nothing implausible in the story, remarkable though it be. We are not told the mechanics of lowering the man, just as we are not told how they carried him up the ladder.

The digging of a hole big enough for this might well lead to debris descending on Jesus and others below. The Greek ἀπεστέγασαν τὴν στέγην ... καὶ ἐξορύξαντες looks like a deliberate attempt to avoid this impression. The Aramaic which I have proposed makes this a colourful Greek translation of more mundane Aramaic. For taking the roof off, I have proposed ארימו, using a common word which correctly describes what they did. Rather than go for the literalistic αἴρω, the translator has chosen the more colourful but absolutely clear and unambiguous ἀπεστέγασαν. This verb is rare in extant literature, but this is surely because we do not have lots of ancient Greek accounts of people removing roofs: it is not likely to have caused problems to Greek-speakers familiar with ἀπό and στέγη. Similarly, I have used the mundane word חפרוהי. Of course, when digging a normal hole the debris has to be taken *up* away from the hole. In this case, however, careless digging could lead to the debris going *down* and landing on Jesus and the others below. The translator has accordingly clarified the situation, not rendering with the simple and obvious equivalent ὀρύσσω, but with the clearer compound. He has thereby achieved an excellent explicitative translation, within the parameters normal among very good translators.

This hypothesis accounts for all our evidence. It is of methodological importance that we do not make either of two mistakes, each of them tempting enough to require discussion. We might argue that there was no original Aramaic source, because no reconstruction can quite represent ἀπεστέγασαν and ἐξορύξαντες. This would remove from the historical record everything which has not been translated absolutely literally, including cases where an absolutely literal translation would not be sensible.[20] This is the general reason why we should not do this. In this particular

19.   J. L. Reed, *Archaeology and the Galilean Jesus. A Re-examination of the Evidence* (Harrisburg: Trinity Press International, 2000), p. 159.

20.   For an important example, see P. M. Casey, 'The Original Aramaic Form of Jesus' Interpretation of the Cup', *JTS* NS 41 (1990), pp. 1–12.

case, it would also remove details which would appeal to people who were close to the original situation, but not to later Christians, as is illustrated by Matthew's omission of this process, and Luke's incorrect rewriting complete with tiled roof. The second mistake is illustrated by Wellhausen's conjecture that ἀπεστέγασαν τὴν στέγην is a mistranslation of the Aramaic '*schaqluhi*' or '*arimuhi leggara*', which really meant 'they brought him to the roof'.[21] The main point is that we should not conjecture misreadings in texts which are perfectly intelligible, especially not when we ourselves find them implausible because they come from a culture unlike ours. We must therefore follow my proposals above, which fit the incident into its first-century Jewish surroundings, and make perfect sense of a very good translator making an explicitative translation of a sound Aramaic text.

The real importance of this remarkable episode is that it shows that the five men had a very strong investment in the success of the healing event. They must have been determined to get the paralytic healed, and they would have suffered from severe cognitive dissonance if this had not happened. Assuming that they were not quite mad, this means that the paralytic himself was ready to be healed. The next part of the Explanatory Model follows accordingly. The narrator tells us that Jesus saw their faith. Attempts to exclude the paralytic himself from this miss the point completely.[22] It is precisely his faith which was most essential for the healing to take place. For it to be a permanent healing, however, this extraordinary support from his friends would be very helpful, as they could subsequently support him as a healed person, just as they had previously treated him as a paralytic.

5. *The Explanatory Model and the Healer*

Jesus responded in accordance with the first part of the Explanatory Model of this man's illness, according to which it was caused by his sin. Jesus did so by announcing that the man's sins were forgiven. This has caused endless trouble to interpreters. Some discussion is therefore necessary, beginning with the Explanatory Model which attributes sickness to sin. This is sufficiently well attested in the Hebrew Bible. For example, Psalm 32 has a man who was ill when he did not confess his sins to God, and who recovered when he did. Psalm 38 has a very ill-sounding man confess his sins and ask for God's help. Psalm 41 has a man asking God to heal him, and he attributes his need for healing to his sinning. Ps. 103.3 has God forgiving a person's iniquities, and healing his diseases, in parallelism. In a personal case, the thanksgiving psalm at Isa. 38.10-20 has God casting Hezekiah's sins behind his back when he was healed. All these passages were part of the sacred text of all first-century Jews, so there should be no doubt that this part of the Explanatory Model, which attributed illness to sin, was generally available. It is further attested in later sources. Sir. 38.1-15, which

---

21.   J. Wellhausen, *Das Evangelium Marci*, (Berlin: Reimer, 1903), p. 16; 'sie brachten ihn zum Dach hinauf.'

22.   Taylor, *Mark*, pp. 194–5, traces this view right back to Victor and Ephraem, but prefers to include the paralytic, with Lagrange and most modern commentators.

makes a strong plea for the acceptance of physicians, still associates illness and sin, and advocates prayer by the sick and by physicians. This part of the Explanatory Model continued into the rabbinical period. A saying of R. Alexandri in the name of R. Ḥiyya bar Abba puts it bluntly: 'A sick person does not arise from his sickness until they forgive him all his sins (עד שמוחלין לו על כל עונותין)' (b. *Ned* 41a). This is followed by a quotation from Ps. 103.3. The idiomatic use of the plural participle must be noted. It is often translated with an English passive, because it is approximately equivalent to an English passive. This idiomatic use of the participle is not specific to the Babylonian dialect, and it is already found in the book of Daniel (Dan. 4.22). It is noteworthy that the compilers of the Talmud did not take this saying so literally as to consider it inappropriate on the grounds that only God can forgive sins. They took it for granted that only God could forgive a person all his sins, and used normal Aramaic idiom as a way of saying so.

The first part of the Explanatory Model is accordingly clear. The man's illness has been attributed to his sins. Jesus therefore began the healing process by reassuring him that his sins had been forgiven. The passive אשתבקו, like Mark's Greek, presupposes that his sins have been forgiven by God, as always. There are some detailed problems over the exact word for this. I have resisted the temptation to posit אשתרי, which is the same root as the word for paralytic, משריא, because we should not multiply wordplays on principle. It is not however impossible, and we shall have to consider its implications further when we reach Mk 2.10. In either case, we should read the well-attested perfect ἀφέωνται in the text of Mk 2.5, with א A C D, as well as the majority of manuscripts. It is the most natural translation of any feasible Aramaic. We should attribute the much less well-attested present ἀφίενται (B 33 565 al) to a copyist who wanted to make it clear that Jesus was performing the act of forgiveness at that moment. The copyist may also have been assimilating to Mt. 9.2. The perfect אשתבקו reassures the man that God has forgiven his sins, and in accordance with the Explanatory Model used in this narrative, it prepares the way for the healing.

The next question is that of which human intermediaries may be involved in a healing. The commonest traditional person in the Hebrew Bible is a 'prophet', for whom the term 'man of God' may be used.[23] In Gen. 20, God appears to Abimelech in a dream, and tells him to return Sarah to Abraham. His life and the ability of his wife and female slaves to have children are said to be dependent on Abraham's praying for them, and God explains this by calling Abraham a prophet (נביא, Gen. 20.7). In 1 Kgs 17, Elijah prays to God, and the son of the widow of Zarephath is brought back to life. This causes the widow to say that she now knows that he is a 'man of God'. In 2 Kgs 4, the Shunammite woman sends for Elisha when her son dies, and he comes and heals him. In 2 Kgs 5, Naaman is cured of his skin disease when he follows the procedure laid down by Elisha. He is said to have done so because he was advised by a Jewish captive who thought the prophet would cure

---

23.　For more detailed discussion, see H. Avalos, *Illness and Health Care in the Ancient Near East. The Role of the Temple in Greece, Mesopotamia and Israel* (HSM 54. Atlanta: Scholars, 1995), pp. 260–77.

him, though not before he had made the serious mistake of approaching the king of Israel instead. The story clearly implies that Elisha had greater powers to cure people than the number of stories in the Bible would suggest. In 2 Kgs 20// Isa. 38, Isaiah is involved in the healing of Hezekiah, when Hezekiah has prayed to God. At the time of Jesus, all these stories were part of the sacred text. It follows that a prophet was an appropriate person to be involved in healing events. Jesus himself was known as a prophet, and performed many other healings. All this evidence is thus coherent and consistent.

Regardless of when they were written down, all these stories are set in the pre-exilic period or even earlier. In the post-exilic period, healing seems to have become the province of healers and/or exorcists, rather than prophets. I have noted some examples of both. In addition to these, a number of New Testament passages attest the existence of exorcists, who were favourably regarded by Jesus himself (Mt. 12.27//Lk. 11.19).[24] The expanded version of the story of the Pharaoh taking Abram's wife (1QapGen XIX–XX) illustrates the overlap between the two. It has Pharaoh and his household afflicted by an evil spirit (רוח באישא). It lists the Egyptians who could not cure them as healers, magicians and sages (כול אסיא ואשפיא וכול חכימיא, 1QapGen XX,20). Abram expels the evil spirit by prayer, and by the laying on of hands on Pharaoh himself. In the extant part of the text, this does not cause the narrator to give Abram any special label to indicate his role.

The prayer of Nabonidus (4Q242) is of especial interest because it has a similar Explanatory Model of illness to Mk 2.3-12. The context of this very fragmentary document is evidently that of Nabonidus praising God by writing the story of his cure from a lengthy illness. At the crucial point, Nabonidus declares that a Jewish man forgave/undid his sins: וחטאי שבק לה גזר. Since the influential work of Dupont-Sommer,[25] the man, here called a גזר, has often been thought to have been an exorcist, but this should not be accepted. The word גזר has a basic meaning of 'cut', and through the process of making decrees, it came to mean 'decree', or 'determine'. This meaning is found at 4Q197 4 ii 2 (Tob. 6.13), and it is common in later Aramaic. The actual noun occurs four times in the book of Daniel (Dan. 2.27; 4.4; 5.7,11), in a list of people whose function should evidently include providing the interpretation of dreams and of the writing on the wall. They are therefore some kind of wise men, sages or diviners. This meaning is suitable for the healer who pronounced the forgiveness of sins in 4Q242, whereas 'exorcist' is the wrong Explanatory Model for him. An exorcist drives out a demon. As an approach to someone who is behaving strangely, driving out a demon is quite different from the forgiveness of sins.

There have been numerous attempts to argue that the text cannot mean that this person forgave Nabonidus' sins, the most basic ground for this being that only God can forgive sins.[26] This is true, but we should not overturn the most natural

---

24. Casey, *Aramaic Approach to Q*, pp. 164–7.

25. A. Dupont-Sommer, 'Exorcismes et guérisons dans les récits de Qoumrân', in G. W. Anderson *et al.* (eds), *Congress Volume Oxford 1959* (VTSup 7. Leiden: Brill, 1960), pp. 246–61.

26. Cf. L. P. Hogan, *Healing in the Second Temple Period* (NTOA 21. Freiburg/Göttingen: Universitätsverlag/Vandenhoeck & Ruprecht, 1992), pp. 149–57.

interpretation of this passage with so literal an understanding of the different ways in which forgiveness might or might not be put. We should rather infer that the assumption that only God could forgive sins was so secure that, in a passage deliberately written to praise God for his cure, Nabonidus could be presented as expressing an important facet of his cure by saying that a diviner or the like forgave his sins. What he will have meant is precisely that the diviner pronounced the forgiveness of his sins. This entails the same Explanatory Model of illness as Mk 2.3-12, by having a particular illness be caused by sin.

This more varied material does nothing to undermine the importance of the material about prophets. This was still in the sacred text, so the stories were told and retold. A prophet was basically someone who spoke the word of God and acted on it. It is entirely reasonable for this to include a ministry of exorcism and other healings. Hence the stories of Jesus' healing ministry do not lead people to give him a special label such as 'healer' or 'exorcist'. This was rather subsumed under the general term 'prophet', to which was added 'teacher', a term denoting his other major role.

One negative piece of evidence is also important: priests were not involved in the healing process. They had two major functions. One was to keep people with some kinds of illness away from the Temple, or even out of society altogether. So, for example, if a person has a certain sort of skin disease, the priest's task is to declare him unclean (Lev. 13.42-44). The person is then supposed to live alone, 'outside the camp' (Lev. 13.46). Some of the Qumran documents have strict rules not found in the Hebrew Bible. For example, 11Q19 XLV,12-14 bans blind people from the city of Jerusalem forever. It should be obvious that where priests were involved in incidents like the one at Lev. 13.42-44, they did not forgive the sins of the person involved. Their purpose was to get the sick person out of the way, not to do anything to cure them.

If the sick person was excluded from the Temple, but not from society as a whole, they would be cared for at home. So, for example, Peter's mother-in-law was lying down with a fever (Mk 1.30), and Jairus' daughter was asleep at home when she was taken for dead (Mk 5.22-24, 35-41). There was no equivalent in Israel to the temples of Asclepius in the Greco-Roman world, where people might go for therapy and cure.[27] At home in Israel, people might or might not be looked after as well as was possible at the time. For example, Amnon trapped Tamar by claiming to be ill and thereby getting her alone to prepare food for him in his house where he was lying down (2 Sam. 13.1-14), and when Jesus raised up Jairus' daughter, he ordered that she be given food (Mk 5.43). In neither case is there any mention of anything which we would recognize as medication. The author of Sir. 38 was clearly concerned to make the case for having physicians at all, when this basic case might evidently be rejected. Moreover, ancient medicine was not always very helpful. As Mark says of one woman who is said to have been sick for twelve years, καὶ πολλὰ παθοῦσα ὑπὸ πολλῶν ἰατρῶν καὶ δαπανήσασα τὰ παρ' αὐτῆς πάντα καὶ μηδὲν ὠφεληθεῖσα ἀλλὰ μᾶλλον εἰς τὸ χεῖρον ἐλθοῦσα (Mk 5.26).

---

27.   See further Avalos, *Illness and Health Care*, Ch. 1, with bibliography.

Even this level of care was not available to people who were thrown out of the community altogether. How often regulations such as Lev. 13.46 were applied to ordinary towns and villages, and carried out literally, we have no idea. What we do know is that we have texts in which priests declare such people unclean. They declared them unclean and were responsible for their being thrown right out, in so far as this happened. They did not forgive their sins or cure them.

The second stage at which priests were involved was after people thought they were cured of sicknesses which had made them unclean, and unfit to enter the Temple and perhaps other places. There is an example of this at Lev. 14. Here a man who has had a skin disease is brought to the priest for examination, and the priest finds that the disease is healed (נרפא נגע־הצרעת מן הצרוע, Lev. 14.3). The text then gives detailed orders for the rituals to be carried out on such occasions. During these, the priest is said to 'cleanse' (הכהן המטהר, Lev. 14.11), and when he comes to offer the sin offering at the end of these proceedings, he is said to 'make atonement' (כפר, Lev. 14.18-19). When he has finished making all the offerings and everything, the text summarizes its regulations by saying that in this way the priest shall make atonement on the man's behalf and he shall be clean (וכפר עליו הכהן וטהר, Lev. 14.20). Not a single text ever says that the priest forgives the man's sins. This is entirely logical, for two reasons. One is that the priest's function was not to heal the patient. On the contrary, his function was to send the patient away until he became well again, and, if the patient recovered when he was somewhere else, to carry out the necessary rituals to enable him to declare the healthy man now clean enough to enter the Temple. Secondly, the Explanatory Model according to which illness is caused by sin is not explicitly mentioned in passages like Lev. 14. In so far as it is implied by the use of אשם and חטאת, it is all the more striking that the priest is not involved in pronouncing forgiveness, but only in the prescribed rituals to be followed when a person has recovered. Equally, I have noted Pss 32, 38, 41 and 103 which explicitly use this Explanatory Model and do not mention the Temple.

The priests were concerned for the removal of sin only when they had to offer prescribed sacrifices in the Temple. There are examples of this in Leviticus 4. This deals with the removal of guilt for unintentional sins. The first example is the anointed priest, for whom the text describes in detail the sacrifice of a bull as a sin-offering (Lev. 4.3-12). The second example is the congregation of Israel, for whom the sacrifice of a bull as a sin-offering is also prescribed. The text comments that with this the (anointed) priest shall make atonement for them and they shall be forgiven (וכפר עלהם הכהן ונסלח להם, Lev. 4.20). The passive meaning of the Niphal נסלח is clearly intended to refer to their being forgiven by God. There is no connection with illness, and the detailed regulations for the priest do not require him to *pronounce* the forgiveness of sins. Similar comments conclude the regulations for the sacrifice of sin-offerings for unintentional sins by a ruler (נשיא), and then by one of the ordinary people (עם הארץ), at Lev. 4.26,31,35. No such regulations deal with the cure of disease, and no such texts mention the pronouncement of the forgiveness of sins by the priest. We must infer that the priests made no such pronouncements.

It is thus entirely reasonable that when Jesus cured a man with skin disease, he told him to go and show himself to a priest and offer the prescribed offering (Mk 1.41-44): he did not pronounce the forgiveness of sins. Equally, at Mk 2.5 he begins the healing of a paralytic by reassuring him that his sins are forgiven. After the healing, he tells him to go home, which he does (Mk 2.11-12): there is no mention of priests or Temple. It follows that Jesus was not doing anything to subvert the activity of priests in the Temple.[28] He was carrying out a healing which they never had anything to do with.

The Hebrew Bible contains one example of a prophet announcing the forgiveness of a person's sins. This is the story of David sending Uriah the Hittite into the front line of battle, and marrying Uriah's wife Bathsheba when Uriah was killed. David was exposed by Nathan the prophet, to whom he confessed that he had sinned (חטאתי ליהוה, 2 Sam. 12.13). The penalty was the death of the first son of David and Bathsheba (2 Sam. 12.14-23). It was not however the death of David who had committed this sin. As Nathan put it, גם יהוה העביר חטאתך לא תמות (2 Sam. 12.13). This clearly means that David's own death would have been a possible penalty for his sin, but that it is not the penalty because God himself overlooked (העביר) his sin. This cannot be interpreted too literally, in view of the death of David's son. The limitation is nonetheless real and important. In practice, David was then able to go back to make love with Bathsheba, who in due course gave birth to Solomon. What is important for present purposes is that Nathan the prophet was the person required by God to deliver these verdicts on David's sin. They include both the penalty for this sin, and the overlooking of it. Moreover, this story was part of the sacred text of all first-century Jews. It follows that the remission of sins could be part of a prophet's interpretation of the will of God, just as much as the announcement of the destruction of a city, which Jesus is also credited with (e.g. Mk 13.2; Mt. 11.20-24//Lk. 10.13-15).

We now have all the information that we need to interpret what Jesus has done so far in the story. He was confronted with a paralytic, someone who would not make proper use of his limbs. He could see from the extreme actions of the four men with him, and perhaps from the man himself, that there was a very strong expectation that he would heal the man. He believed that, in this particular case, the man's inability to move his limbs was due to a sense of his own sinfulness. The Explanatory Model according to which illness was caused by sin was available to him from scripture and tradition. He therefore began by reassuring the man that his sins were forgiven. This was a pronouncement that God had forgiven the man's sins. Accordingly, this pronouncement lay within the range of what a prophet might declare the will and judgement of God to be.

28.   Cf. e.g. J. Marcus, *Mark 1-8. A New Translation with Introduction and Commentary* (AB 27. New York: Doubleday, 2000), p. 216.

6. Objection and Response

It is accordingly quite extraordinary that anyone should object to this. It follows that, having sorted out the story so far, we run into even greater difficulties with the next part. Hooker put one of the main points, and a possible deduction from it, with clarity:

> The sudden introduction of these men into the story appears artificial: why should they be present? The fact that their criticism is unspoken suggests that it was made on a later occasion.[29]

The *unspoken* nature of the criticism is surely very strange, and it is severely exacerbated by the improbable nature of the objection. The notion that what Jesus has already said is blasphemous is barely plausible. If, however, Mk 2.10 is interpreted literally in Greek as a reference to Jesus alone, then hostile opponents might well consider it blasphemous in the popular rather than strictly legal sense of such terms. Moreover, Jesus' ministry did in fact suffer from exceptionally hostile opposition from scribes. In the next chapter, we find scribes from Jerusalem accusing Jesus of being possessed by the devil and of casting out demons by means of his power (Mk 3.22-30).[30] In the end, it was scribes who gathered together with chief priests and elders to bring about his death. It is noteworthy that the specific accusation of blasphemy recurs only in the quite unconvincing account of Jesus' trial before Joseph Caiaphas (Mk 14.64). This means that it cannot have been a common accusation during the historic ministry. It follows that it makes best sense as a genuine reaction to Mk 2.10, which has been written up later because no objection was made at the time, as the Marcan narrative indicates.

It would help if we could settle the original language of this part of the story. Carmignac suggested a Hebrew wordplay, יושבים וחושבים, underlying καθήμενοι καὶ διαλογιζόμενοι.[31] This is not remotely sufficient. The creation of occasional wordplays in texts which are not properly reconstructed is a regrettable feature of the older scholarship, which underestimated the ability of scholars to produce rather than recover them. Much more than an occasional wordplay is necessary before we should believe in a Semitic source.[32] In the Aramaic reconstruction proposed above, I have omitted v. 7, for reasons which I have taken from Hooker and will shortly develop. It would however be possible to follow Black's development of Wellhausen's interpretation of the first half of Mk 2.7, מה הוא כדן ממלל מגדף.[33] This can be translated as idiomatic Aramaic, 'What is he thus saying, blaspheming?' However, this is not sufficient to show that there was an Aramaic source for this

---

29.   Hooker, *Mark*, p. 86.

30.   For detailed discussion, see Casey, *Aramaic Approach to Q*, Ch. 5.

31.   J. Carmignac, 'Studies in the Hebrew Background of the Synoptic Gospels', *ASTI* 7 (1968–9), pp. 64–93 (70).

32.   Casey, *Aramaic Sources of Mark's Gospel*, pp. 31, 59–63; *Aramaic Approach to Q*, pp. 10–12.

33.   Black, *Aramaic Approach* (³1967), pp. 65–6, following Wellhausen, *Einleitung*, p. 14.

part of the story. Mark's Greek makes perfect sense of a slightly different kind, as traditionally understood: Τί οὗτος οὕτως λαλεῖ; βλασφημεῖ. 'What is this man saying like this? He is blaspheming!' A lot of evidence of idiomatic Aramaic emerging like this would be decisive. The difficulty of trying to make a decision about such a short passage is greatly increased by the fact that one such piece of evidence could be coincidental, whereas the passage is too short for much more to be realistically expected.

Evidence of the opposite kind appears at first sight in v. 9, where there is no literal Aramaic equivalent of the comparative εὐκοπώτερον. It follows that traditional exegesis which tried to discover which Jesus might have meant was easier, forgiving the man's sins or getting him to walk, was based on a false premise. In Aramaic, Jesus could not have posed the question as it stands. When there is no literal Aramaic equivalent of a Gospel term or construction, however, another possibility must always be considered: perhaps Jesus, or Mark's Aramaic source, said something which was difficult to translate into Greek, and our text is the result. I have accordingly suggested קליל.

The word קליל means literally 'light'. Like its opposite, חומר, literally 'heavy', קליל was used metaphorically with regard to commandments, or legal judgements. It meant that they were comparatively of lesser importance. Thus the 'light of lights' (קלה שבקלות) may be the prohibition of taking a mother bird at the same time as her young or eggs (Deut. 22.6-7: Abba bar Kahana at y. Qid I,7/22(61b)). On the other hand, a heavy commandment might be an important one. So the heavy of heavies (מן מחורה החמורות) may be 'Honour thy father and mother' (Abba bar Kahana as above), or the commandment isolated as חמירא may be 'Thou shalt not take the name of the Lord thy God in vain' (b. Shevu 39a).

The word קליל is derived from the Akkadian *qallilu*, which means 'small', 'unimportant'. It is therefore obviously old, and it is duly attested in early Aramaic. It is found in the Dea Sea scrolls, and it is common in later Jewish Aramaic and in Syriac. The verb קלל is common already in biblical Hebrew, which also has the adjective קל. The attestation of this term is accordingly not in doubt. The semantic area of קליל extends further to 'lenient', 'insignificant'. It is its legal usage which is of particular interest here, partly because it makes excellent sense of Jesus' comments, and partly because, after all the problems we have noted in what the scribes did *not* actually *say*, it makes excellent sense of their *presence*. Jesus used a conventional legal term to ask which of his proposed actions, pronouncing the forgiveness of sins or telling the man to get up and walk, was 'light', that is to say, a matter of no great significance. It will be noted that at the present stage the forgiveness of sins is still in the passive: ἀφέωνταί σου αἱ ἁμαρτίαι, for which I have again reconstructed אשתבקו חוביך. This is important, because the passive shows that Jesus is still pronouncing the forgiveness of sins by God. The answer to his question was, from his perspective, 'neither'. The pronouncement of the forgiveness of sins by God was a matter of the greatest importance because it enabled the cure to go ahead in accordance with the will of God. The cure itself was of central importance, because the healing ministry was at the centre of Jesus' ministry as a whole.

The translation of מה קליל into Greek was difficult, because terminology of this significance was not available in Greek. The translator must have thought of something like τί ἐλαφρόν, a rather literal translation which would have proved difficult to understand. It is useful to compare Mt. 23.23//Lk. 11.42. Here the translators were faced with חומריא. The Matthean translator went for τὰ βαρύτερα, adding the explicitative τοῦ νόμου to try to make his meaning clear. Luke, writing for Gentiles, left it out.[34] This shows how difficult the translation was, and how the permanent comparison between 'light' and 'heavy' might lead a translator to use a Greek comparative. Moreover, 'light' commandments are by their nature easier to observe than heavier ones. Hence our translator has gone for εὐκοπώτερον. He will have agreed with Jesus that neither matter was a light one. We might render his translation very explicitatively into English: 'Which is an easier task rather than a more important and difficult one?' This sets up the following words of Jesus as he intended them, the answer again being 'neither'. The translator is not likely to have noticed that he could be interpreted to have Jesus asking which of these two things was easier than the other one. This is too far removed from the text which he was interpreting to have come to mind.

We should infer that with קליל in Mark's source, and with the clearly passive formulation אשתבקו חוביך, we have returned to a real incident in the life of the historical Jesus. We have further reasons to suppose that Hooker was partly right about what has gone wrong: the unspoken words of the scribes are in fact spurious, and have been written into the story at a later date. We should however accept that scribes were present. Jesus' use of קליל, and the attacking nature of v. 9 as a whole, cannot be explained without their presence.

The next question is how far the secondary insertion goes. There have been many previous suggestions, most of them more extensive than a shift from v. 6a to 9. We have now however seen good reason to include the forgiveness of sins in v. 5, and the presence of the scribes in v. 6a, as part of the original incident. We have also seen good reason to keep v. 9, and we shall see reason to interpret v. 10 in this light as part of the original incident too. The unspoken words of the scribes are secondary, for the Markan narrative tells us that they were unspoken, and that means they must be secondary. Secondly, we have seen that the words of v. 7 are intelligible as a reaction to v. 10 in Greek, but not as a reaction to the pronouncement of God's forgiveness of the man's sins at the end of v. 5. If v. 7 is secondary, the end of v. 6 is almost certainly secondary too.

What about v. 8? This is very difficult to determine. On the one hand, it looks like a follow-through from the secondary v. 7: on the other, something must have sparked the aggressive nature of Jesus' comments in vv. 9-10. In the above draft, I have omitted v. 8a, attributing it to the same redactor as v. 7. I have however kept Jesus' words in v. 8b. The change of subject, without any repetition of Jesus' name, is characteristic of Aramaic narratives. The resulting piece gives an excellent rationale for the editor who made the additions. Jesus' opening comments to the

---

34. Casey, *Aramaic Approach to Q*, pp. 74–6.

scribes are so hostile as to require explanation: this has been rationally supplied by an editor who already knew v. 10 in Greek. The Aramaic source, however, also makes excellent sense in its own terms. I have argued elsewhere that Mark's Aramaic sources were abbreviated. They will have been written on wax tablets, or single sheets of papyrus, or the like. I have also argued that brief accounts were possible because these sources were of early date. Consequently, many assumptions could be taken for granted, both about first-century Judaism in general and about the ministry of Jesus in particular. At an early date, everyone knew these assumptions: later, they would need to be explained, or Jewish things would need to be left out, as we can see with particular clarity in the editorial work of Luke.[35]

The next question must accordingly be whether we can reconstruct an assumption which the author of Mark's source might take for granted, and which would make sense of Jesus' suddenly aggressive comments. I suggest that the answer to this question is very straightforward: the extraordinary hostility between Jesus and his orthodox opponents had already started before this event took place. This is in no way improbable. As the Marcan narrative stands, we find a plot to bring about his death already at Mk 3.6. This was caused by two supposed violations of sabbath law so dubious that even these opponents turned to the secular authority of Herod Antipas rather than to a court of law.[36] After one supposed violation, they watched for another, and they were sufficiently inhuman to count healing on the sabbath as such a violation. They will have expected him to heal on the sabbath because he had successfully done so already (Mk 1.23-31), in a community observant enough to bring other people to him only when the sabbath was clearly over (Mk 1.32). They were already complaining at his eating with 'tax-collectors and sinners'[37] at Mk 2.16, a behavioural difference of the utmost seriousness. Another behavioural difference is already indicated by the Marcan narrator as early as Mk 1.22, where inhabitants of Capernaum were astonished at his teaching in the synagogue: ἦν γὰρ διδάσκων αὐτοὺς ὡς ἐξουσίαν ἔχων καὶ οὐχ οἱ γραμματεῖς.

These differences are such as to make early conflict unremarkable. Moreover, reasons have often been given for supposing that the Marcan narrative is not altogether in chronological order. Papias is supposed to have noticed already that it is not in an original order (Eus. *H.E.* III,39,15). Mark does not appear to have known the length of the historic ministry, a defect which Luke the historian was unable to correct. If they did not know the length of the ministry, they are not likely to have got everything in chronological order. Several aspects of Jesus' ministry are accordingly arranged topically, rather than in an historical order. In Mark, the proportion of parables in Ch. 4, and of eschatological teaching in Ch. 13, cannot reasonably be regarded as a reflection of two single occasions in the life and teaching of Jesus.

35.   Casey, *Aramaic Sources of Mark's Gospel*; *Aramaic Approach to Q*; Crossley, *Date*.
36.   For detailed discussion of Mark 2.23–3.6, see Casey, *Aramaic Sources of Mark's Gospel*, pp. 138–92.
37.   On these terms, see Casey, *Aramaic Approach to Q*, pp. 137–42.

The same has often been remarked of the conflict-stories at Mk 2.1–3.6. Too many of them are in a single place for us to believe both that they all happened at once, and that there was relatively little conflict with his most serious opponents for the rest of the ministry, with just the one more really serious incident in the relatively near future (Mk 3.22-31). There are moreover some signs of concentric arrangement in this collection. The collection begins and ends with the healing of a paralytic, which in both cases involves argument with opponents. In the present state of the collection, the first story also includes an allegation of blasphemy (Mk 2.7), which as a technical legal offence carried the death penalty, a view of blasphemy which scribes might be expected to hold: the last story ends with counsel to put Jesus to death (Mk 3.6).

We now have enough to understand the composition of the proposed Aramaic source of Mk 2.1-12. It was brief, because of the conditions under which it was written down. It explicitly portrays Jesus' extreme hostility to his most serious opponents (vv. 8b-9). It does *not* say that this is the *beginning* of this hostility. It was *not* written in its present position in Mark's Gospel. Consequently, its author(s) assumed that everyone would know about this serious quarrel, and took this quarrel for granted. Once we do the same, the presence of the scribes, and the shift from v. 6a to v. 8b, become intelligible. The scribes were there to see what Jesus was up to, like the Pharisees at Mk 3.2. Their hostility was blindingly obvious, which is how Jesus came to let fly at them with vv. 8b-9.

We must now return to the content of v. 9. We have already seen that קליל, 'light', was used to mean 'unimportant', and that it could be used in a legal sense as the opposite of חומר, 'heavy', of judgements which were relatively lenient, or regulations which were of relatively less importance. We have also seen that, from Jesus' perspective, the answer to his question was 'neither'. The first point is a repetition of what he had already done, pronounced the forgiveness/removal of the man's sins. The passive אשתבקו is used indirectly of the action of God, the author of the forgiveness/removal of the man's sins. I discuss the broader semantic area of this word in considering the original interpretation of v. 10. The second point tells everyone, and most notably the paralytic, what Jesus is going to do next. He is going to tell the man to get up, take up his mattress and walk. This prepared the man for the centre of the healing event, when he would actually do so. The pressure on the man to do as he was told was now extremely strong. He had been brought to Jesus in extreme circumstances, carried on his mattress by four people who dug through the roof of the house. They must therefore have been convinced that Jesus could heal him, and would now be around him, expecting the healing to happen. The man would hardly have agreed to this process, unless he believed this too. Jesus' assurance that God had forgiven his sins, which is effectively repeated in this verse, will have taken the necessary weight off his mind. He now knew what he would have to do next: get up, take up his mattress and walk, when Jesus told him to do so.

7. *The Son of Man Saying*

The hostile scribes have also been told what Jesus will do next, and it is this which explains the form and mode of expression of v. 10. There is no very precise Aramaic equivalent of ἵνα δέ. My reconstruction ודתנדעון uses the ubiquitous ו and ד, and would lead a normal translator to put ἵνα δέ. The Aramaic ודתנדעון is still strong enough to imply that the healing will demonstrate that the man's sins have been forgiven. At one level, that is directed at hostile scribes. At the same time, this sentence is also powerfully directed at the man himself. It tells him *for the third time* that his sins have been forgiven. This, in a drastically short narrative, underlines the profundity of Jesus' belief in the Explanatory Model expounded above: he perceived that this man was paralysed because he was overburdened by his sins.

The way that Jesus put it this third time has caused interpreters endless trouble, centred on the term 'Son of man', generally treated as a title of Jesus alone. For example, Gnilka declares: 'Der Menschensohntitel rückt dann deshalb hier ein, weil Jesus an die Stelle Gottes tritt und – vom Standpunkt dieser Überlieferung aus – göttliche Privilegien am ehesten mit diesem Prädikat zu verbinden waren.'[38] This has often been read back into the passive declarations of the forgiveness of the man's sins in vv. 5 and 9. For example, in showing knowledge of the divine passive, Marcus seeks to undermine it here:

> But 'are forgiven' is probably not just a divine passive in the Markan context … the scribes interpret 'your sins are forgiven' as a claim that Jesus himself has the power of absolution, and angrily reject this claim … The Markan Jesus does not draw back from the implication of near-divinity that gives rise to this objection.[39]

The use of the Son of Man Concept has the further problem that Jewish documents which use the term 'Son of man' of an exalted figure do not mention his forgiving sins. Scholars have frequently sought to meet this difficulty by referring to Dan. 7.13.[40] But in this text 'one like a son of man' is given authority as a symbol of God granting victory to the Jewish people and power over their enemies. There is nothing in it to cause Jesus to use the term בר (א)נ(א)ש(א) in respect of the forgiveness of sins. If he had been so peculiar, no one would have caught the reference, but as usual there is no sign of puzzlement as to what he said. This line of interpretation has also caused problems over the position of this verse in the Gospel of Mark. It has often been argued that it comes too early in this Gospel. This view presupposes that 'Son of man' is a messianic title. It should therefore not be used before Peter's confession at Caesarea Philippi, when some scholars believe that Jesus began to reveal his messiahship to his disciples. It has also been argued that it is doubly problematic that Jesus uses the term here in public. Mk 2.28 is equally problematical for this view, and for the same reasons. This view also generally presupposes that Peter's confession was a real event, despite the problems which this entails for the use of

---

38.   Gnilka, *Markus*, p. 101.
39.   Marcus, *Mark*, pp. 216, 222.
40.   E.g. Gundry, *Mark*, p. 119; Marcus, *Mark*, pp. 222–3.

the actual word 'messiah'. Similar concerns have led some scholars to believe that this is not a saying of Jesus, but a comment by Mark to the reader.[41] This despite the fact that Mark never addresses the reader in this extraordinary way elsewhere (Mk 13.14, the nearest parallel, is infinitely clearer): and that vv. 9 and 11 are sayings of Jesus, and Mark gives no indication that v. 10 involves such an abrupt change.

All these problems arise from studying this verse in Greek, in the light of Christian tradition. From these habits comes the whole idea that 'Son of man' is a messianic title in this verse, and refers to Jesus alone. All the other problems flow from these assumptions. To recover what Jesus originally meant, we must set Christian tradition aside, and study the saying in Aramaic:

ודתנדעון דשלטן לבר אנשא על ארעא למשבק חובין,
11. קום, אמר אנה לך, שקל ערסך ואזל לביתך.

The saying ends with Jesus' orders to the man to get up, take up his mattress and go home, where he had recently been cared for as a paralytic. It follows that there is a sense in which v. 10 refers to the power of Jesus in particular. At the same time, we have seen that this idiomatic use of (א)נש(א) בר also has a general level of meaning. This has been at the centre of traditional objections to any Aramaic explanation of the meaning of this sentence.[42] We have however seen that it cannot be gainsaid, so we must work out what the general level of meaning can have been. Two points are crucial. One is the general level of meaning, which may be both secondary and limited. The other is the semantic areas of שבק, שרי, and ἀφιέναι, none of which is a precise term equivalent to the English 'forgive'.

Firstly, then, the limited nature of the general level of meaning. We have seen that this can be very general, and that people and texts may be interested partially or primarily in this general level of meaning. This is however very unusual. Many examples of this idiom are primarily about the speaker, or about other people made clear by the context. We have seen that, at the extreme end of the spectrum, a speaker may generalize from his own experience, and imagine that what is true for him must be true for at least some other people too.[43] The majority of examples lie between these two extremes. They are primarily about the speaker, and they assume a general level of meaning which includes a social subgroup of people, not the whole of humanity. This example is normal, but heading towards one extreme end of the spectrum. It is primarily about Jesus, as his healing of the man demonstrates. It also includes a restricted group of people who may also pronounce the forgiveness of sins. In the nature of the case, these people are not defined. When I have discussed the semantic areas of שבק, שרי, and ἀφιέναι, we shall see that to some extent healers must be included, for only so could they perform healings

---

41.   For all these points, see e.g. W. L. Lane, *The Gospel of Mark* (London: Marshall, Morgan & Scott, 1974), pp. 96–7.

42.   E.g. H. Anderson, *The Gospel of Mark* (NCB. London: Oliphants, 1976), p. 102; Hooker, *Mark*, p. 87.

43.   See pp. 69–70 above.

for which this was the appropriate Explanatory Model. We have seen this already at 4Q242.[44] This is quite sufficient for the general level of meaning assumed by the idiomatic use of (א)שׁנ(א) בר. We must note also the vigorous way in which this power is asserted in the middle of a conflict situation. Jesus was not saying something which he expected everyone to know and accept already.

I turn to the semantic areas of these three words. The Greek word ἀφιέναι has a large semantic area: it is not primarily an equivalent of the English word 'forgive'. In the New Testament alone, there are texts in which it approximates to English words such as 'allow', 'permit' (e.g. Mt. 3.15), 'leave' (e.g. Mk 1.18,20), 'abandon' (e.g. Mk 14.50), 'send away', 'dismiss' (e.g. Mt. 13.36), 'divorce' (e.g. 1 Cor. 7.11). It is as part of this massive semantic area that it is appropriate for cancelling a loan (Mt. 18.27) or debt (Mt. 18.32), including cancelling debts as a metaphor for the forgiveness of sins. It is used in this way in the Lord's prayer, where we ask God to forgive/undo/remove our sins, and declare that we similarly forgive/undo/remove those who are indebted to us, a metaphor for other people who have done us wrong (Mt. 6.12//Lk. 11.4). Similar comments apply to the Aramaic שבק. This is well attested long before the time of Jesus. It approximates to English words such as 'allow', 'permit' (Cowley 30 line 23), 'leave' (Ahiqar 175), 'abandon' (Ahiqar 176), 'let alone' (Ezra 6.7). Within this broad semantic area it can mean to remit a debt (ATNS 35.5), and it is used twice in the Dead Sea scrolls of the forgiveness of sins (4Q 242; 11Q10 XXXVIII.2). It is abundantly attested in later Aramaic and Syriac with a large semantic area on the same lines. In Syriac, it continued to be used on its own of the forgiveness of sins. It is naturally used in this way here by pesh hark, as it is used in the Lord's prayer (Mt. 6.12 cur pesh hark; Lk. 11.4 sin cur pesh hark) and elsewhere. Hence I have used it here, for it is abundantly attested before and after the time of Jesus, and it is used of removing sins, twice in the Dead Sea scrolls and abundantly later.

In later Jewish Aramaic it is attested of the forgiveness of sins in particular only together with שרי, to which I turn next. This is attested before the time of Jesus with the meaning 'release' (Sefire III,18), 'undo' (4Q 203 viii 14) and hence 'solve' (Dan. 5.12,16), as well as to 'dwell', both literally (1QapGen XXII,13) and metaphorically (Dan. 2.22). It is abundantly attested in later Jewish Aramaic, where its even broader semantic area occasionally includes reference to the forgiveness of sins. For example, at y. Shevi 4,2/12 (35b) it is used twice with reference to R. Tarphon forgiving people who struck him, once when they ask him to and once when he says he has done so. It continued in widespread use in Syriac, including references to the absolution of sins.

It will be evident from the above distribution of these two words that שבק is much the more likely word to have been used by Jesus in first-century Galilee. Its broad semantic area is of fundamental importance. How could a healer heal someone suffering from paralysis of psychosomatic origin? Only by doing something to relieve the psychosomatic cause of this illness. What then if the Explanatory Model

44.   See pp. 153–4 above.

discussed above was the appropriate one, and the man was overburdened with a consciousness of sin? Somehow or other, that burden had to be lifted. Jesus has already attempted this twice, with the reassuring אשתבקן חוביך, directed first at the man and subsequently at Jesus' opponents. As we have seen, the passive refers to the action of God in forgiving the man's sins. At the same time, the broader semantic area of שבק prepares for the more self-centred statement of Mk 2.10. I have already noted that the forgiveness of sins by God could be referred to in a context of this same Explanatory Model of illness with an active participle in the plural (b. *Ned* 41a).[45] We now have a third attempt to express God's activity, with the idiomatic use of (א)בר (א)נש. The reason for putting it this way was Jesus' central role in the healing event, which he was about to demonstrate. It gave very powerful reassurance to the man that he had done the right thing in coming to Jesus personally, since Jesus had the power to undo his sins himself, as he and the man must now demonstrate. The term שבק facilitates this way of putting it, because of its broad semantic area. It also permits the general level of meaning which is an essential facet of this idiom.

This general level of meaning assumes that more people than Jesus should have had the ability to undo the effects of sin in the case of psychosomatic illnesses for which the Explanatory Model used here was appropriate. This must to some extent have been the case, because, as we have seen, both Essenes and Therapeutae were involved in the healing of what we would call psychosomatic illness, and the Explanatory Model according to which illness was caused by the sick person's sins was a biblical and well-known model. How well aware Jesus was of the detailed behaviour of other healers we do not know. He may have been generalizing from his own experience. In that case, the aggressive way he expressed himself was due to his abilities being denied by his opponents, and perhaps not generally accepted by other people. We know that he accepted the ability of other exorcists, even though he was the most able exorcist of his time known to us.[46] He may well have deliberately sought to demonstrate that God enabled people to undo the effects of sin upon illness to a much greater degree than people realized. This is explicit in the editorial work of Matthew, who has the crowds glorify God because he had given such power to men (τοῖς ἀνθρώποις, Mt. 9.8). However secondary this editing was at a literary level, it is culturally accurate in recognizing the general level of meaning implied by Mk 2.10. It is also implicit in sending the disciples out on a healing ministry (Mk 6.7,13,30), since cases of illness for which the same Explanatory Model was appropriate are likely to have been encountered. In due course the power to forgive sins was taken over by the church, without any particular connection with the healing of illness (John 20.23, cf. Lk. 24.47).

The phrase ἐπὶ τῆς γῆς has been troublesome. It is omitted by W b q, and it is in a different place in different manuscripts, so it might be a gloss. I have followed the order of words in P[88] א C D and several other manuscripts: ἐπὶ τῆς γῆς ἀφιέναι ἁμαρτίας. This is a good combination of ancient witnesses. Metzger prefers ἀφιέναι ἁμαρτίας ἐπὶ τῆς γῆς with B Θ *pc*, commenting that this 'represents the primitive,

45. See p. 152 above.
46   Casey, *Aramaic Approach to Q*, pp. 164–73.

Aramaic order of words, which was rearranged, perhaps for subtle exegetical reasons, by copyists who produced the other readings.'[47] He does not however specify reasons for regarding this as the primitive Aramaic order of words, nor does he explain the subtle exegetical reasons. It is in fact difficult to account for all the scribal changes as deliberate, whereas they might all represent reasonable reactions to a marginal gloss the position of which was not obvious. I have reconstructed my preferred reading as follows: שלטן לבר אנשא על ארעא למשבק חובין. Here it is most natural to take על ארעא closely with בר אנשא. Everyone agreed that God in heaven could remove sins as he saw fit: Jesus asserted that in these circumstances a human being on earth could remove sins as well. I cannot see anything wrong with this Aramaic. Metzger's comments imply the following Aramaic: שלטן לבר אנשא למשבק חובין על ארעא. This is perfectly satisfactory Aramaic which contrasts God forgiving sins in heaven with the healing activities, including the removal of sins, taking place down here on earth. If we do follow the order of words which I have proposed, we could treat the reading of B Θ *pc* as assimilation to Matthew, though this makes it difficult to see why Matthew altered the order of words.

8. The Healing Event

The word of command is then given to the man at v. 11. I have supposed that the words λέγει τῷ παραλυτικῷ, which have so often been used to carve the whole narrative into two pieces, are a secondary gloss. They were intended to mark the point at which Jesus turned from addressing people in general and his opponents in particular, and addressed the paralysed man in particular. The word of command requires him to use all his main limbs, since he has to walk and carry something. This is the point of getting him to go home, rather than to sit and join the crowd. The crowd reacts in a standard Jewish way to a healing event, by being amazed and glorifying God. This implies that events of this kind had not been taking place in Capernaum much in recent times, which is reasonable enough. It is sometimes considered problematic that the hostile scribes should be suddenly converted, and then relapse without warning in the following story.[48] We should not interpret the word 'all' so literally. It obviously means most people, in Aramaic or in Greek, and no other possibility will have occurred to Mark or to his brief source.

It is more important that there is no follow-up report, as always in our Gospels. Some people with psychosomatic ailments suffer relapses. We have no idea whether this man's cure was permanent, or not.

Two negative points must be made. Firstly, the general level of meaning of the Son of man saying does not imply that Jesus was an ordinary person just like any other. The social subgroup of people who might exercise this power was obviously

47.   B. M. Metzger, *A Textual Commentary on the Greek New Testament* (Swindon: UBS, 1971), p. 78.
48.   E.g. Marcus, *Mark*, p. 219.

very small. Jesus was concerned to demonstrate that a human being could exercise this power, not to expect everyone to exercise it. The general level of meaning does however imply that Jesus was a human being, not God. This is natural within Jewish monotheism. Secondly, Jesus' use of the Explanatory Model according to which this man's illness was due to his sin does not imply that Jesus believed that all illnesses were due to sin. This is especially clear in the case of his exorcisms. These assume a quite different Explanatory Model, according to which a person's strange behaviour was due to possession by one or more demons, not to their sins.

9. Conclusions

The following conclusions may therefore be drawn. The Son of man saying at Mk 2.10 is part of a true narrative of a real healing event. In its present form, the Marcan narrative has some secondary glosses, which I have been able to remove. The combination of our increasing modern knowledge of psychosomatic illness with some details of Mark's story enable us to infer that the man was suffering from paralysis of psychosomatic origin. The Explanatory Model used by Jesus in this case was a normal biblical one, according to which the man's illness was caused by his sins. Jesus therefore began with the forgiveness of sins. The narrative is secondary at the point where the scribes are supposed to have objected to this in their hearts, but the whole story makes sense only if there were hostile scribes really present. The Son of man saying comes at the climax of the story. It is the standard idiom of a general statement which refers especially to the speaker. The general level of meaning assumes that Jesus' power was at least potentially available to other human beings. At the same time it was a real reference to himself in particular, and it was he who actually exercised the power to heal. The narrative ends by recording the success of the healing event.

It follows that this Son of man saying must be classified with those already studied in Ch. 4, as a genuine saying of Jesus in which he used a particular Aramaic idiom.

Chapter Six

JACKALS HAVE HOLES (MATTHEW 8.19-20//LUKE 9.57-58)

The Son of man saying at Mt. 8.20//Lk. 9.58 is verbally identical in Matthew and Luke. It follows that it was taken from Q material which was transmitted in Greek. It has a brief introduction, the first part of which varies considerably between Matthew and Luke, who have in common the important point that someone else began the conversation by addressing Jesus. Apart from the address διδάσκαλε, which is found only in Matthew, the man's declaration is also verbally identical in Matthew and Luke. It too, therefore, was part of the Q material which was transmitted in Greek. I have also reconstructed most of the opening of Mt. 8.19, and I defend the probability that this too was part of Q, and was edited by Luke.

The immediately preceding context of these two verses is quite different in the two evangelists. Each of them has evidently edited this Q material into its present positions, which are also quite different in Matthew and Luke. The next saying and another introductory declaration from another person (Mt. 8.21-22//Lk. 9.59-60) are sufficiently similar in Matthew and Luke for us to infer that this too was part of the Q material in Greek. The two incidents have in common a comment by a potential disciple and an offputting or critical response by Jesus. Luke has a third such incident (Lk. 9.61-62). These three incidents are not organically connected, and the immediately following contexts in Matthew and Luke are completely different from each other. It follows that the broader context in the two evangelists is irrelevant to the original interpretation of these incidents, and that the collection of them into one Q passage is probably secondary. While all three might possibly have belonged to a period immediately preceding one migratory mission, only this very general point unites the meaning of the three sayings. Accordingly, I reconstruct and discuss in detail the Aramaic source of Mt. 8.19-20//Lk. 9.57-58 alone.

I propose the following reconstruction of this part of the Aramaic source of the Q passage:

ואמר לה חד ספר, רבי, אתא בתרך לאן דתאזל. ואמר לה ישוע, לתעליא איתי להון חורין ולצפרי שמיא משכנין ולבר אנש לא איתי לה אן דיסמוך רישה בה.

And a scribe said to him, 'Rabbi, I will come after you to wherever you go.' And Jesus said to him, 'Jackals have holes and the birds of heaven/the sky have roosts, and a (/the son of) man has nowhere to lay his head.'

The openings of these incidents have evidently undergone secondary editing by the evangelists. Luke's πορευσμένων αὐτων is an especially clear example of this.

Here Luke uses a word which is very common in this Gospel (πορεύομαι no less than 50 times) with the deliberate aim of integrating his Q source into his narrative of the extraordinarily lengthy and static journey which begins at Lk. 9.51. Equally, Matthew has προσέρχομαι no less than 52 times, including other Q passages where it introduces a person and is absent from Luke (Mt. 4.3; 8.5; 18.21; 25.20,22,24), and passages where it has been edited into Markan narratives for the same purpose (Mt. 8.2; 17.14; 19.16; 20.20; 27.58; 28.2). The probability that this part of his introduction is also secondary is therefore very strong.

I have however reconstructed חד ספר from Matthew's εἷς γραμματεύς. Matthew normally takes γραμματεύς from tradition. Luke never uses γραμματεύς in the singular: he sometimes removes it from Mark (Lk. 4.32; 18.31; 20.41; 23.35), or replaces it with νομικός (Lk. 10.25, possibly from Q), and sometimes he does not have γραμματεύς in Q passages where Matthew does (Lk. 11.39,42,44,47,49), and once more he has νομικός instead (Lk. 11.52). Luke might well therefore omit γραμματεύς from his Q source, leaving him with three analogous incidents concerning potential disciples who are responded to somewhat sharply at the beginning of Jesus' lengthy journey. Moreover, חד ספר has an excellent *Sitz im Leben* here. A sedentary scribe is a very suitable person to feel a need to make this declaration, and that a scribe should do so would be remarkable enough to be transmitted. The word חד is simply the Aramaic word for 'one' used as an indefinite article, which was conventional. It has been translated naturally with εἷς, which is not only its permanent equivalent as the numeral 'one', but also used occasionally as the equivalent of an indefinite article.

The scribe might well also use the term רבי. Matthew retains ῥαββι only to criticize its use (Mt. 23.7-8), or to record it used by Judas looking forward to his betrayal of Jesus and carrying it out (Mt. 26.25,49). Matthew would therefore be well motivated to alter it to διδάσκαλε, which he otherwise has both redactionally (Mt. 12.38), from Mark (Mt. 19.16; 22.16,24), and probably from Q (Mt. 22.36). Luke never uses ῥαββι. When he copies a Markan passage containing ῥαββι or ῥαββουνι, he either omits it (Lk. 22.47, possibly choosing to use a different source), or alters it to ἐπιστάτα (Lk. 9.33) or κύριε (Lk. 18.41). He would therefore be well motivated to alter or omit ῥαββι, if he read it in his source. He would be less well motivated to omit διδάσκαλε. He uses it 11 times, both redactionally (Lk. 11.45; 20.39) and in special Lukan material (Lk. 3.12; 7.40; 12.13; 19.39); one example has probably been retained from Q (Lk. 10.25). He retains from Mark its use by outsiders (Lk. 9.38; 18.18; 20.21,28), and alters it to ἐπιστάτα only when it is used by Jesus' disciples in general (Lk. 8.24), or by John in particular (Lk. 9.49). He omits it only at Lk. 18.21, abbreviating a speech by an outsider who has already used διδάσκαλε at Lk. 18.18, and at Lk. 21.5, where he completely removes unwanted direct speech by a disciple. We should infer that the Q source probably read ῥαββι. It follows that the Q opening edited by Matthew and Luke probably read as follows: καὶ εἷς γραμματεύς εἶπεν αὐτῷ ῥαββι, ἀκολουθήσω σοι ὅπου ἐὰν ἀπέρχῃ.

The scribe's declaration is an open profession of would-be discipleship. It is significantly more than the average profession of discipleship to a rabbi as we find it in later rabbinical literature. Someone who decided to be a disciple of a particular rabbi, and who was accepted as such, would expect to sit at that rabbi's feet, learn a great deal and put it into action. They would not however normally expect to have to follow their rabbi from place to place. Here is the importance of the end of the scribe's declaration: לאן דתאזל, correctly translated as ὅπου ἐὰν ἀπέρχη. This shows a clear awareness that the ministry was to some extent migratory, so that more was involved than listening to and accepting the teaching of Jesus. The scribe must have been aware that, in addition to Capernaum, Jesus had an extensive ministry in Chorazin and Bethsaida (Mt. 11.21//Lk. 10.13), and that he went throughout the towns and villages of Galilee (e.g. Mk 1.38-39; 6.6,56). Jesus' response, however, suggests that the scribe took it for granted that those whom they visited would give them some basic accommodation, as in Jesus' instructions to disciples whom he sent out on mission (Mk 6.10//Mt. 10.11//Lk. 9.4). Jesus denied this, making clear the fragile nature of daily life on the migratory ministry. The Son of man saying with which he said this has however proved difficult to interpret. I turn therefore to detailed discussion of the proposed Aramaic reconstruction, the only way in which to fit the saying into its original *Sitz im Leben* in the ministry of the historical Jesus.

I begin with the first animal. Both Matthew and Luke have αἱ ἀλώπεκες. The article is generic, and the animals referred to are foxes. There is however no doubt that the underlying Aramaic must have been תעליא, used here by the Syriac versions and in the reconstructions of Meyer, Burney, Jeremias, Hampel and Schwarz.[1] In 1985, I pointed out that תעליא includes jackals, members of the species *canis aureus*, supporting this with secondary literature to both biblical animals and to the behaviour of foxes and jackals.[2] Subsequently, however, most New Testament scholars have ignored this,[3] even though it is the unanimous view of scholars who have done serious research into the identification and behaviour of biblical

1.   Meyer, *Muttersprache*, p. 96; C. F. Burney, *The Poetry of Our Lord* (Oxford: Clarendon, 1925), pp. 132, 169; J. Jeremias, *New Testament Theology* vol. I, *The Proclamation of Jesus* (trans. J. Bowden; London: SCM, 1971), p. 23; V. Hampel, *Menschensohn und historischer Jesus. Ein Rätselwort als Schlüssel zum messianischen Selbstverständnis Jesu* (Neukirchen-Vluyn: Neukirchener, 1990), p. 227; Schwarz, *Menschensohn*, p. 191.

2.   Casey, 'Jackals', pp. 8, 20 n. 19, citing H. B. Tristram, *The Natural History of the Bible* (London: Christian Knowledge Society, 1867; 10th edn 1911), pp. 85–8, 109–11; R. Burrows, *Wild Fox* (London: David and Charles, 1968); *Encyclopaedia Judaica, s.v.* 'Animals of the Bible and Talmud', 'Jackal'; F. S. Cansdale, *Animals of Bible Lands* (Exeter: Paternoster, 1970), pp. 124–6; B. Grzimek, *Grzimek's Animal Life Encyclopaedia*, vol. 12, *Mammals III* (London/New York: Van Nostrand, 1972), pp. 195–9 (Introduction to canids, by H. Wendt), 236–43 (Jackals, by D. Müller-Using, B. Grzimek and H. Wendt), 243–56 (Foxes, by A. Pedersen, H. Dathe, D. Müller-Using and H. Wendt); H. F. Ewer, *The Carnivores* (London: Weidenfeld and Nicolson, 1973), pp. 253–61; E. P. Walker *et al.*, rev. J. L. Paradiso, *Mammals of the World* (London/Baltimore: Johns Hopkins, 1975) vol. II, pp. 1148ff., 'Carnivora; Family: CANIDAE'.

3.   E.g. D. A. Hagner, *Matthew 1-13* (WBC 33A. Dallas: Word Books, 1993), pp. 216–17; Davies and Allison, *Matthew*, vol. 2; p. 42, even while noting תעלא; J. Nolland, *Luke 9:21-18:34* (WBC 35B. Dallas: Word Books, 1993), p. 541, even while noting Casey, 'Jackals'.

animals. Moreover, M. H. Smith, in rejecting this suggestion, quite misrepresented it, commenting, 'Casey blurs behavioural distinctions to make both appear a single species to the Semitic mind'.[4] I did not use this antique concept of 'the Semitic mind'. I gave sufficient bibliographical data to indicate that 'jackals' were included in the Hebrew שׁועל and the Aramaic תעל. I did not blur any behavioural distinctions, any more than speakers of English blur them when they refer to Alsatians and Pekes as 'dogs', or to foxes, jackals, hyenas, wolves and the like as 'wild dogs'. Speakers of all languages use socially convenient classifications, and we may not assume that those of Aramaic speakers were the same as ours. In view of these points, I present more of the evidence than I did previously, and hope that scholars will be persuaded to look at important secondary literature rather than ignoring or misrepresenting main points.

Smith also refers to the Hebrew תנים as 'jackals', but he does not justify his assumption that its semantic area was confined to jackals and did not include wolves, nor does he give reason to believe that it was in use in Aramaic, which it was not. Whether there was already a precise Aramaic word for jackals is uncertain. The Hebrew תנים is normally rendered with some form of ירור in both Peshitta and Targum (Isa. 13.22; 34.13; 43.20: Jer. 9.10; 10.22; 49.33; 51.37; Mic. 1.8; also Tg. Ps. 44.20; pesh Lam. 4.3). This means that the translators knew what they were doing, which is more than can be said for the LXX, whose translators had the difficult task of translating into a language which had no normal word for 'jackal', presumably because there were no jackals in Greece: so δράκοντες Jer. 9.10; Lam. 4.3; Mic. 1.8: ἐχῖνοι Isa. 13.22; κακώσεως Ps. 43.20 (MT 44.20); σειρῆνες Isa. 34.13; 43.20; Job 30.29; στρουθοί Jer. 10.22; 30.28 (MT 49.33). It may therefore be that ירורין was the term for jackals in Aramaic already at the time of Jesus. This does not undermine the identification of תעליא as including both foxes and jackals. As Tristram noted: 'The Hebrew word undoubtedly includes the jackal (*Canis aureus*), as well as the fox (*Vulpes vulgaris*). Indeed, in most of the passages where it occurs, the jackal rather than the fox is intended, as may be seen from the context. The Hebrew *shu'al*, Arabic *jakal*, the Persian *shagul*, and the English *jackal*, are all the same word … But the two animals are commonly confounded by the natives of Syria, though they are perfectly aware of their distinctness … The natives of the East discriminate very little between the two animals, or rather look on the fox as a small and inferior species of jackal. Indeed their appearance to a cursory observer is very similar, the jackal having its fur of paler colour, or yellowish rather than reddish in hue.'[5] A similar situation is likely to have obtained in the ancient period.

The main point essential for identifying the biblical שׁועלים, the Hebrew equivalent of the Aramaic תעליא, is the major behavioural difference between these two animals: jackals hunt in packs, and foxes do not. The biblical שׁועל is always plural except at Neh. 3.35, and sometimes in considerable numbers. For

---

4.   M. H. Smith, 'No Place for a Son of Man', *Forum* 4 (1988), pp. 83–107 (89).
5.   Tristram, *Natural History*, pp. 85, 110.

example, Samson is said to have used three hundred of them (Tg. pesh תעלין, LXX ἀλώπεκας) to set fire to the Philistines' crops (Judg. 15.4-5). The story is not very plausible, but its author and audience are likely to have had jackals in mind because they can be found in packs. Again, the psalmist declares that his enemies מנת שעלים יהיו (Ps. 63.11). The image is of a pack of jackals eating carrion (Tg. תעלייא, pesh תעלא, LXX Ps. 62.11 ἀλωπέκων). It is also probable that jackals were commoner than foxes in the ancient Near East in general, and in Israel in particular.

The important point for understanding Jesus' use of this image is that these animals were well enough known, and that they have relevant behavioural characteristics in common. In particular, they hunt at night, and take cover during the day. It is when they take cover during the day that they use all sorts of caves, thickets and crannies to rest in. Thus God's natural creation provides חורין for תעליא all the time. When both animals mate and have their young, they frequently take over the burrows of other animals to create dens for this temporary period. Thus even these חורין could readily be thought of as provided by nature for תעליא. It makes no difference that there is some uncertainty over the Aramaic word for these holes. The word חור is found in biblical Hebrew for hole, including a lions' den at Nah. 2.13. It is derived from Akk. *ḫurru*, and used in Syriac. It is therefore a reasonable possibility, and was used here by Jeremias and Hampel, as by palsyrlec at Mt. 8.20. The term בורין was used by palsyrlec Lk. 9.58, and in the reconstruction of Burney, but it seems to have been more commonly used of wells, cisterns and other pits. Another possibility might be נקעין, used by sin cur pesh hark in both texts, and common in Syriac. This is used in the reconstruction of Schwarz, who quotes also Tg. Ezek. 28.13, but this reference appears incorrect, so this word appears to be Syriac-specific. Whichever word gave the translator reason to put φωλεούς, Jesus' image certainly referred to the holes provided by nature for foxes and jackals to use as a permanent part of their daily lives.

While תעליא included jackals as well as foxes, the translation with ἀλώπεκες was almost inevitable. Foxes were well known in Greece, and the ἀλώπηξ was the subject of many proverbs and fables. When viewed from a Greek perspective, Jesus' saying fits into this very general category. The Greek ἀλώπηξ is also the only rendering of the Hebrew שועל in the LXX. Furthermore, there was no popular Greek term for 'jackal', for there were no jackals in Greece. The most canvassed suggestion is θώς, on the ground that some comments on this animal fit the jackal. Some comments, however, do not: for example, Aristotle describes them as φιλάνθρωποι (H.A. IX,44,630a), which jackals are not. Hence suggestions such as 'stoat', or 'civet'.[6] All this evidence fits together perfectly: ἀλώπεκες was a good translation of תעליא, and there was no reasonable alternative.

<hr>

6.   A. L. Peck (ed. and trans.), *Aristotle. Historia Animalium* (LCL 3 vols.; London/ Cambridge, Massachusetts: Heinemann/Harvard University, 1965), vol. 2; pp. 377–8; D. M. Balme (ed. and trans.), *Aristotle. History of Animals, Books VII–X* (Cambridge, Massachusetts: Harvard University, 1991), p. 387.

The next creatures referred to are birds. They are a quite different class of creature, massively common, and conventionally described with reference to שׁמיא, where from an earthbound perspective they could reasonably be perceived to belong. Schwarz omits this word, which is absent from Thomas 86, to give him a 'Zweiheber' appropriate to his 'Klagelied-Rhythmus (3 + 2 Hebungen)'.[7] This reasoning should not be accepted. The term שׁמיא has an excellent *Sitz im Leben* here, where it prepares for the fact that this massive number of creatures who do not even live on the earth are still provided by nature with somewhere to go. The absence of the term from a Coptic version of this saying written so much later is too weak as textual evidence to be of any real significance. The assertion that we have a 'Klagelied-Rhythmus (3 + 2 Hebungen)' is quite arbitrary, and contrary to the text as it stands.

We then come to a quite crucial word, κατασκηνώσεις in Greek, for which I have reconstructed מַשׁכְּנִין in Aramaic. The major point which is easy to verify is that κατασκηνώσεις are *not* 'nests'. The Aramaic for 'nests' would be קִנִין, for which any reasonable translator would have put νοσσιάς, using the standard and straightforward Greek word for nests. It is therefore quite extraordinary that Burney, Jeremias and Schwarz should all have used קינין, that Hampel should have continued with it five years after I had pointed this out, and that Smith, after quoting my reconstruction, should nonetheless make the nesting of birds important for his interpretation.[8]

Whether מַשׁכְּנִין is exactly the correct word to reconstruct is subject to slight uncertainty, but makes no significant difference. It is a well-attested word both in biblical Hebrew and in later Aramaic. At Ezra 7.15 it refers to God's dwelling in Jerusalem, and it has been restored as מׁשכן at *1 En.* 89.36, where it refers to the Tabernacle. In the Hebrew Bible, the singular מׁשכן is almost always used of God's dwelling, but this is probably due to the content of the Hebrew Bible, that is to say, the reference of the word rather than its meaning in either Hebrew or Aramaic. The same factor will have affected the usage of the LXX, which normally renders it with σκηνή or σκήνωμα, both of which are from the same root as κατασκήνωσις. κατασκηνόω in the LXX almost always renders the Hebrew שׁכן (more than 50 times), and likewise the Aramaic שׁכן at Dan. 4.19 Theod. מׁשכן is rendered with κατασκήνωσις at Ezek. 37.27 LXX, and by Symmachus at Ps. 45(46).5 and Ps. 48(49).12. Thus it seems to me to be the best choice, and its translation with κατασκήνωσεις in this context is sound and comprehensible.[9]

It is however possible that מׁשכן was too closely associated with God's dwelling and not in normal usage in a general sense, and it is not the only word which Jesus might have used here. מטללין is used here at Mt. 8.20 by pesh sin cur, at Lk. 9.58 pesh cur, and suitably elsewhere in later Aramaic, and Meyer used it in his reconstruction.

7.   Schwarz, *Menschensohn*, p. 190.
8.   Burney, *Poetry*, pp. 132, 169; Jeremias, *New Testament Theology*, p. 23; Hampel, *Menschensohn*, p. 227; Schwarz, *Menschensohn*, p. 191; Smith, 'No Place', esp. p. 89.
9.   This seems to have been accepted e.g. by Davies and Allison, *Matthew*, vol. 2; p. 42; Nolland, *Luke*, p. 538.

The singular מטלל is used in the sense of 'roof' in a document of 408 BCE.[10] The verb טלל is found at Dan. 4.9, and the noun טלל (or possibly the verb) at 11QTg Job XXVIII.7 (Job 36.29) and probably at *1 En.* 4. At Dan. 4.9 Theodotion rendered טלל with κατασκηνόω (LXX σκιάζω). It is therefore possible that מטלל was in use in the Aramaic of our period with the required meaning, and if this was the case, the rendering κατασκηνώσεις would have been sound. Another possibility is מדרין. This is used at Dan. 2.11; 4.22,29; 5.21 and 11QTg Job XXXII.5 (Job 39.6), where it renders the Hebrew משכן, as well as in later Hebrew and Targumic Aramaic. In this context a translator might have used κατασκηνώσεις rather than the perhaps more likely κατοικίαι used by Theodotion (Dan. 2.11; 4.22,29; 5.21: of these examples, the LXX translates the equivalent of our MT only at Dan. 2.11, where it has the similar κατοικητήριον).

These details are not significant. The important point is that κατασκηνώσεις cannot be nests, that this word is a translation of משכנין or just possibly one of these other Aramaic words, and that this makes excellent sense with reference to the places where birds roost, as they do all the time, not just their nests, where they spend a relatively limited period of their lives rearing their young. It is at this point that the behaviour of birds in Israel becomes important. Palestine was a major flyway for centuries before and after the time of Jesus. Most of the birds seen there were migratory – they stopped on their way over to roost, not to build nests and rear their young. Among the many species native to Israel, Cansdale noted the Lesser Kestrel, which 'travels in large flocks and roosts in hundreds, in such conspicuous places as the trees round Capernaum.'[11] Here again, what the birds have got was provided by God in the ordinary course of nature, and it was provided for them as they moved about the countryside. All this will have been a matter of common everyday observation for the Jews in Jesus' environment, and it is this which provides the situational background against which we can see both the general level of meaning of the saying and the application of it to his migratory ministry. At the general level, the provision of resting-places for foxes/jackals and birds is contrasted with the lack of such provision for people, who have to build houses to have anywhere to stay.

A similar perspective on the divine provision for animals is found in a saying attributed to R. Simeon, son of Eleazar, at M. Kidd. IV,14:

> R. Simeon, son of Eleazar, says, Have you ever seen a wild animal or a bird practising a craft – yet they are sustained without care, and were they not created for no other purpose than to serve me? But I was created to serve my maker. How much then ought I to be sustained without care? But I have done evil, and forfeited my sustenance.

In the expanded version of this saying at b. Kidd. 82b, R. Simeon declares that he has never seen a שועל (fox/jackal) as a shopkeeper. The common element here is the notion that animals are directly provided for by God, whereas in some respects people are not – they have to provide for themselves. The function of the general

---

10.   Cowley, *Aramaic Papyri* 30, line 11// 31, line 10.
11.   Cansdale, *Animals of Bible Lands*, p. 140.

statement in the teaching of Jesus is however different from that of the abstract reflection of R. Simeon. Jesus was not concerned with the theological problem which could be seen here – indeed on another occasion he felt able to illustrate God's overall care of people by means of analogy with his care for the natural world (Mt. 6.25ff.//Lk. 12.12ff.). Jesus was not even making an assertion about animals and man, for in this idiom the general level of meaning is usually functional rather than substantive. Hence some of the general statements used in this idiom are obvious, as this one should probably be seen to be from the perspective of people who lived in Galilee. This will have assisted the application of the saying to the speaker, the scribe and all the disciples.

The choice of jackals, foxes and birds for this general level of meaning is natural enough. Birds were as obvious a large class of animate beings then as now, and a good deal more ubiquitous – hence their use in R. Simeon's saying, as elsewhere. They were especially suitable here because they were so migrant, and so obviously had the normal resting-places which they needed in the branches of the local trees. The choice of תעליא is perhaps less inevitable. They were however a sound choice because they were notorious, unclean and noisy animals which moved in and out of areas of human habitation, always finding somewhere to lay up as they moved about. Some of these factors also account for the selection of שועל in the expanded version of R. Simeon's saying at b.Kidd. 82b. While this explains the use of these particular items in this particular sentence, the appropriateness of the idiomatic use of בר (א)נש(א) is due to the humble situation in which Jesus found himself of having no accommodation for either himself or his disciples. It is not in any way ambiguous, for in the context of the migratory ministry to which it belongs, it will have applied rather obviously to Jesus himself, to the scribe who had offered to follow him *anywhere*, and to the general company of disciples who did follow Jesus on the actual migratory ministry.

It follows that this saying has an excellent *Sitz im Leben* in the historic ministry of Jesus. Moreover, it does not have a *Sitz im Leben* in the early church in the strong sense, that is to say, it cannot possibly be a community product. The early church shows no interest whatever in comparing Jesus to other creatures like this, nor in making negative assertions about him, nor did it have reason to use the indirect idiom which emerges when the saying is reconstructed in Aramaic. The view that the saying is secondary has usually taken the form of supposing that it is a proverb secondarily attributed to Jesus, a view particularly associated with Bultmann, who described it as 'presumably an old proverb which tradition has turned into a saying of Jesus'.[12] This view has never been supported with satisfactory empirical evidence of the existence of such a proverb, nor has the supposedly secondary attribution of it to Jesus ever been given a proper rationale. We must note the 'parallel' often cited from Plutarch's life of Tiberius Gracchus:

τὰ μὲν θηρία τὰ τὴν Ἰταλίαν νεμόμενα καὶ φωλεὸν ἔχει καὶ κοιταῖόν ἐστιν αὐτῶν ἑκάστῳ καὶ καταδύσεις, τοῖς δὲ ὑπὲρ τῆς Ἰταλίας μαχομένοις καὶ ἀποθνῃσκουσιν

12. Bultmann, *Synoptic Tradition*, p. 28.

ἀέρος καὶ φωτός, ἄλλου δὲ οὐδενὸς μέτεστιν, ἀλλ᾽ ἄοικοι καὶ ἀνίδρυτοι μετὰ τέκνων πλανῶνται καὶ γυναικῶν (ΙΧ,5,828c).

The wild beasts which roam over Italy have each of them a hole and place to lie down and they have hiding-places, but those who fight and die for Italy have a share in air and light but nothing else, but they wander homeless and unsettled with children and women.

These two passages, in different languages and from different cultural situations more than a century apart, do not constitute evidence of a proverb. What the Plutarch passage does do, with a saying which may well have originated with Tiberius Gracchus, is to illustrate the fact that when people's living conditions are harsh enough for social rather than environmental or climatic reasons, the lot of animals can appear to be better than ours.

As a Greek saying about other people, the saying of Gracchus is also too precisely expressed to be misunderstood in the way that the saying of Jesus has been. For example, in contemplating the possibility that Jesus' saying was a proverb, Manson commented that 'this proverb is required to say that man, in contrast to foxes and birds, has no home; which is plain nonsense'.[13] The possibility that this saying might be a proverb led Manson to contemplate an interpretation of it which is as general as possible and quite remote from its context. This is such a natural way for speakers of English to treat general statements that Manson did not even consider the possibility that the saying of Jesus might be a general statement in any other sense, nor did he consider the tradition in Aramaic form. He then suggested what is virtually an allegorical interpretation of the saying with the Roman overlords as the birds of the air, and the foxes as Edomite interlopers (noting Lk. 13.32), both making their position secure. The saying might then mean that 'everybody is at home in Israel's land except the true Israel'.[14] Allegorical interpretation of this kind should have been left behind with the advent of critical scholarship. It illustrates only too well the problems that scholars can create for themselves by ignoring the language and context of sayings of Jesus.

The recent trend for interpreting sayings within the literary framework of a Gospel can also have damaging effects. Kingsbury argues that 'scrutiny of Matthew rules out the argument that one is to understand Jesus' reference to "homelessness" in 8.20 in strictly literal terms'. In support of this, Kingsbury cites passages of Matthew's Gospel in which Jesus lives in a residence, starting with Nazareth (Mt. 2.11,23) and moving to Capernaum (Mt. 4.13). He particularly stresses that 'at 9.1, a passage in the immediate context of 8.20, Capernaum is even described as Jesus' "own city"'. He then suggests that 'the house there in which he frequently stays is to be distinguished from that of Peter (8.14) and regarded as belonging to himself (9.10,28; 13.1,36; 17.25)'.[15] This is an example of using the study of one Gospel to remove the Jesus of history. It presupposes the study of this saying in the Greek language of Matthew instead of the Aramaic language of Jesus, with the

13.   Manson, *Sayings*, p. 72.
14.   Manson, *Sayings*, pp. 72–3.
15.   J. D. Kingsbury, 'On Following Jesus: the "Eager" Scribe and the "Reluctant" Disciple (Matthew 8.18-22)', *NTS* 34 (1988), pp. 45–59 (50).

result that the general level of meaning is ignored. Kingsbury then proceeds with the assumption that the question is whether Jesus ever lived in a house, a question which completely ignores the context of the migratory ministry. When he argues that Jesus had his own house in Capernaum, he makes use of passages which are either Matthean redaction or special Matthean material. This is not a satisfactory way of treating a Q passage which has an excellent *Sitz im Leben* in the ministry of the historical Jesus.

With the situation in Jesus' ministry removed, so that Jesus' supposed 'homelessness' 'cannot simply be understood literally', Kingsbury leads into his creative redaction criticism with his question 'which shade of metaphorical meaning suits it best?' To answer the question which he has invented, he heads straight for the centre of his own frame of reference: 'scrutiny of Matthew itself suggests that it makes allusion to Israel's "repudiation" of Jesus.' To support this, Kingsbury cites passages from all over Matthew which relate Jesus' moving away from any kind of problem, beginning with Joseph taking him from Egypt (Mt. 2.13-14).[16] None of these passages mention either (א)נשׁ(א) בר having 'nowhere to lay his head', or Kingsbury's 'homelessness'. In short, having ignored the language and setting of this saying in the ministry of Jesus, Kingsbury has created his own Matthean world. This does not tell us what even Matthew thought of the fragmentary piece which he fitted into part of the ministry when Jesus was travelling about (Mt. 8.18,23,28), before he returns to 'his own city' at 9.1. It employs a methodology which can only lead to serious distortion of the life and teaching of Jesus.

Both these suggestions illustrate how far we can get from the life and teaching of Jesus if we do not study his sayings in the language in which he spoke them against the background of his culture in general and his ministry in particular. Having done so, I turn finally to the process of translation from Aramaic into Greek, for this must be comprehensible if the proposed reconstruction is to stand. We have already seen that, despite the shift in meaning which took place, ἀλώπεκες was the only reasonable possibility for תעליא. The word φωλεούς was equally clear for חורין, and ἔχουσιν is no more than idiomatic for אית להון: similarly, τὰ πετεινὰ τοῦ οὐρανοῦ is an obvious rendering of צפרי שמיא. The translator may have had a bit of a problem over משכנין, but we have seen that κατασκηνώσεις is a good solution, and it may not have taken long to think of.

As often, (א)נשׁ(א) בר is potentially problematic because it has a general level of meaning, referring to the scribe and the disciples, as well as a specific reference to Jesus. We have seen that the translators responded to this by adopting a strategy, using ὁ υἱὸς τοῦ ἀνθρώπου whenever (א)נשׁ(א) בר refers to Jesus. This is a perfect example of the shift in meaning which may result from this strategy. The translators have used ὁ υἱὸς τοῦ ἀνθρώπου because there was a genuine reference to Jesus, as he led a migratory phase of his ministry. This was the best that they could do, and as proper bilinguals, they could still see the original idiom in the Greek version of the saying, for they could read the first article in ὁ υἱὸς τοῦ ἀνθρώπου as generic, as

---

16.   Kingsbury, 'Following Jesus', p. 50.

we should all read the second in every occurrence. In the finished Gospels, however, ὁ υἱὸς τοῦ ἀνθρώπου often refers to Jesus alone. It can be so read here, and in that case the general level of meaning is lost. This reduces the effectiveness of the saying as a direct response to the scribe, and removes the general level of application to the disciples on the migratory ministry. It was still the best strategy that the translators could find, especially as it retained clear reference to Jesus, the leader of the disciples during the migratory ministry and the centre of the faith of the Christians for whom the Gospels were written. We shall see that this strategy was a central factor in the transition from בר (א)נֹשֹׁ(א) to the use of ὁ υἱὸς τοῦ ἀνθρώπου as a Christological title.

The rest of the saying was straightforward. The ו was correctly rendered with δέ placed after the first article. The negative לא has the straightforward equivalent οὐ(κ), ἔχει for לה איתי is the same idiomatic rendering as in the previous line, and ποῦ is correct for אן ד. τὴν κεφαλὴν is inevitable for רישׁה, κλίνη is a sound rendering of יסמוך and correctly placed at the end of the sentence, and בה should be omitted because it is redundant in Greek. Thus the translation was an excellent piece of work, and it is fortunate that it was literal enough for us to reconstruct Jesus' saying and part of the introduction to it in its original Aramaic.

The following conclusions may therefore be drawn. This Q saying and part of the introduction to it can be reconstructed from the Greek versions in Matthew and Luke. It was transmitted with the very small number of sayings which follow it, but otherwise it was transmitted in isolation from the rest of the Gospel traditions. While both evangelists edited their introductions to fit it into different parts of their narrative, part of the introduction and the whole of Jesus' saying are verbally identical in Greek. The same is true of the next saying. It follows that this part of the Q material was transmitted to the evangelists in Greek. The translation was however literal enough for us to be able to reconstruct the original Aramaic. What emerged was a genuine incident from the life of Jesus. On the verge of a migratory phase of his ministry, Jesus was confronted with a potential disciple who promised to follow him wherever he went. Jesus responded with a general statement comparing the lot of human beings in such conditions, and therefore particularly the situation of himself and his disciples, including the scribe if he joined them, with that of jackals/ foxes and birds. This functioned as a warning to the scribe. It was sufficiently memorable to be transmitted, partly because of the dramatically parlous conditions of life on the migratory ministry, and perhaps also because it was written down at once or very soon thereafter.

Chapter Seven

THE SON OF MAN IN THE HEAVENLY COURT
(LUKE 12.8-9// MATTHEW 10.32-33; MARK 8.38)

The purpose of this chapter is to consider two or more sayings which have been transmitted in more than one version. Two extant sayings use the term ὁ υἱὸς τοῦ ἀνθρώπου (Lk. 12.8; Mk 8.38), and three do not (Mt. 10.32-33; Lk. 12.9), but it is arguable that two or three original sayings used the term בר (א)נׁש(א), and that the other versions are due to the translation process and the editing of the evangelists. I begin by suggesting a possible Aramaic substratum for two original sayings which were subsequently edited. These might be reconstructed as follows:

1. כל די יודי בי קדם בני אנשא
2. אף בר אנש יודי בה קדם מלאכיא די אלהא
3. ומן דיכפר בי קדם בני אנשא
4. אף בר אנש יכפר בה קדם מלאכיא די אלהא

Everyone who confesses me before (the sons of) men,
a/the son of man will confess him (/her) too before the angels of God.
And whoever denies me before (the sons of) men,
a/the son of man will deny him (/her) before the angels of God.

I begin with the first saying, which I have reconstructed from Mt. 10.32//Lk. 12.8. In both Greek versions, there is one clear and undisputed Aramaism, the use of ἐν following all four occurrences of ὁμολογέω. This does not occur elsewhere in the New Testament, notably not at the closely related Rev. 3.5, where the heavenly Christ says of the victorious Christian from Sardis, ὁμολογήσω τὸ ὄνομα αὐτοῦ ἐνώπιον τοῦ πατρός μου καὶ ἐνώπιον τῶν ἀγγελων αὐτοῦ. Nor is this Aramaism found in the alternative version of the Gospel saying at 2 Clem. 3.2: τὸν ὁμολογήσαντά με ἐνώπιον τῶν ἀνθρώπων, ὁμολογήσω αὐτὸν ἐνώπιον τοῦ πατρός μου. This underlines the fact that this is a clear Aramaism, which implies a written source which caused such straightforward interference in the translators. The reconstruction of יודי ב in line 1 is accordingly very straightforward.

Conventional scholarship has sought to establish from Mt. 10.32//Lk. 12.8 an original version of this saying in Greek, to be ascribed to Q. I have previously suggested that the versions of the two evangelists make good sense as translation variants.[1] I therefore explain the saying from this perspective as a saying of the

---

1.   Casey, *Son of Man*, pp. 193–4, 232.

historical Jesus, and point out the faults of alternative suggestions. I have treated the connecting links of each evangelist as their own editorial work. Matthew uses οὖν no less than 57 times, and it cannot reasonably be regarded as a translation of an Aramaic word, so it must be excluded. Luke's λέγω δὲ ὑμῖν can be more reasonably defended, and Pesch went so far as to suggest that it is an abbreviation of ἀμὴν λέγω ὑμῖν.[2] This conjecture would permit the reconstruction of a characteristic of Jesus' speech, as I have done on the basis of sound evidence at Mk 3.28; 14.18, 25: אמן אמר אנה לכון.[3] This is however most improbable here. Matthew has such expressions some 30 times, and neither he nor his translator (if they were different people) would have reason to remove it from a saying of such social and existential importance. Luke however has other such expressions in this group of sayings, and all are absent from Matthew: λέγω δὲ ὑμῖν τοῖς φίλοις μου (Lk. 12.4), ὑποδείξω δὲ ὑμῖν (12.5), ναί, λέγω ὑμῖν (12.5). We should therefore conclude that Luke's λέγω δὲ ὑμῖν is due to his editorial work.

For כל, each evangelist has πᾶς, which is virtually inevitable. For די יודי, they have different constructions. Matthew employs ὅστις with the future indicative, whereas Luke has ὃς ἄν with the aorist subjunctive. Both renderings are excellent Greek, and within the usual stylistic parameters of each evangelist. For קדם, both evangelists have ἔμπροσθεν in this verse, whereas in the next verse, Matthew continues with ἔμπροσθεν, while Luke has ἐνώπιον twice. Again, both renderings are sound Greek, and within the normal habits of each evangelist. For τῶν ἀνθρώπων in both evangelists, I have reconstructed בני אנשא, because this fits the saying as a whole better than the simple אנשא, and in particular makes a beautiful contrast with בר אנש in the next line. At first sight, it might seem unduly coincidental that two different translators might render it with the simple τῶν ἀνθρώπων, neither of them going for the more literal τῶν υἱῶν τῶν ἀνθρώπων. We have however seen that this is in accordance with the translators' common strategy of rendering בר (א)נ(א) with ὁ υἱὸς τοῦ ἀνθρώπου when it refers to Jesus, and of rendering both בר(א)נ(א)ש, when it does not refer to Jesus, and its plural בני (א)נ(א)שא, with something else.[4] While we cannot be quite certain that Jesus used בני (א)נשא rather than the simple אנשא, this passage when reconstructed in this way illustrates perfectly how the translators' strategy worked. On general grounds, the plural בני (א)נשא must have been used by Jesus and in the transmission of the Gospel traditions. This passage, with the proposed reconstruction, illustrates how the translators normally handled this.

Near the beginning of the second line is the most important variant in this saying, where Luke has ὁ υἱὸς τοῦ ἀνθρώπου, and Matthew has the first person pronoun instead. I discuss other details first, so as to discuss the meaning of בר (א)נ(א)ש in Jesus' original saying in the context of a complete reconstruction. This difference is

2.   R. Pesch, 'Über die Autorität Jesu. Eine Rückfrage anhand des Bekenner und erleugnerspruchs Lk 12,8f par.', in R. Schnackenburg *et al.* (eds), *Die Kirche des Anfangs. Für Heinz Schürmann* (Leipzig: St Benno, 1978), pp. 25–55 (30–5).

3.   Casey, *Aramaic Sources of Mark's Gospel*, pp. 219, 220; *Aramaic Approach to Q*, p. 148.

4.   See p. 118 above; pp. 253–66 below.

closely associated with what is consequently the most remarkable similarity between the two versions, Luke's καί before ὁ υἱὸς τοῦ ἀνθρώπου before ὁμολογήσειι, and Matthew's καί in crasis with ἐγώ to produce κἀγώ after ὁμολογήσω. Both are perfectly normal Greek, but καί as an approximate equivalent of the English 'also', 'too', rather than 'and' is unusual enough to give us pause. That two translators should do this independently might seem sufficiently improbable for us to shift to a model of a single Greek Q in this passage. I have however proposed אף in the Aramaic source. The Greek καί in the sense 'also', 'too', is an excellent rendering of this, to the point where it could well be done by two independent translators, just as the equally normal but relatively uncommon καὶ γάρ at Mk 10.45 may be considered a sound translation of ואף.[5]

Apart from the change of person, יודי בה is translated in a similar way to the rendering in the previous line. Its nature as a simple future is properly rendered with a Greek future in both Gospels, and בה has been translated with ἐν αὐτῷ, repeating the clear Aramaism ἐν. I have already noted ἔμπροσθεν for קדם in both versions of this verse.

This brings us to the other major variant at the end of the verse, where Luke has τῶν ἀγγελων τοῦ θεοῦ, and Matthew has the significantly different τοῦ πατρός μου τοῦ ἐν οὐρανοῖς. I have reconstructed מלאכיא די אלהא from Luke. This makes excellent sense. It utilizes the traditional concept of God's council. This is especially clearly put at 1 Kgs 22.19-22, where Micaiah son of Imlah sees God sitting on his throne, with all the host of heaven (כל־צבא השמים) standing beside him. There is a discussion with several participants. At Job 1.6-12 and 2.1-6 the sons of God (בני האלהים) come before God and there is a debate between God himself and Satan. At Dan. 7.9-10,26 thrones are placed, and in addition to God taking his seat with myriads of standing attendants, we find the court (דינא) sitting in judgement, and books are opened before judgement is passed. These are the kinds of pictures of the angels which formed the tradition which Jesus used when he foresaw himself and others bearing witness before them. He will have taken it for granted that God would be in charge of his own council. Matthew did not however take this for granted, for he had a picture of Jesus in charge of the judgement (Mt. 16.27; 25.31-46), and another of the twelve judging the twelve tribes of Israel (Mt. 19.28). He is not likely to have envisaged the situation any differently from the way that it was imagined by Jesus, but simply sought to clarify it by making clear that God himself was the judge on this occasion when Jesus bore witness. The secondary nature of τοῦ πατρός μου τοῦ ἐν οὐρανοῖς has been widely recognized because from a redactional perspective it is so Matthean.[6]

Another common suggestion is that Luke's τοῦ θεοῦ is also secondary, and there are bad and good reasons for this. The most widespread reason is a mistake which goes back at least to Dalman. Dalman suggested that the angels were a secondary periphrasis for God, and that consequently τοῦ θεοῦ should be erased as an addition

---

5.   Casey, *Aramaic Sources of Mark's Gospel*, p. 194.
6.   See especially J. Jeremias, *The Prayers of Jesus* (London: SCM, 1967), I. 'Abba', pp. 29–35, 44–5.

which partially defeats the intention of introducing the angels.[7] This view is partly based on his extraordinary conviction that Jewish people avoided the term אלהא because they avoided the divine name. Dalman carried this so far that he attributed to Jesus the use of מלכותא דשמיא rather than מלכותא דאלהא on the ground that he was avoiding the divine name.[8] But אלהא is not the divine name! It was the ordinary Aramaic term for 'God'. It was not the only term for 'God', and some texts do use other expressions (e.g. מלך שמיא, Dan. 4.34), but it continued in use, whereas the Tetragrammaton could be lawfully used only by the high priest on Yom Kippur. Later scholars have treated the text in the same way. For example, Tödt comments that 'In Q the phrase "before the angels" may have been used to avoid the name of God ...'[9] We should not accept this approach, because the angels were believed to be real beings, not a periphrasis for God, and אלהא was a normal term for God, whose angels they really were.

Fleddermann provided a better reason for a similar conclusion. He pointed out that Luke adds a clarifying τοῦ θεοῦ elsewhere too, citing notably Lk. 9.20 (cf. Mk 8.29); Lk. 8.11 (cf. Mk 4.14); Lk. 11.42 (cf. Mt. 23.23); Lk. 22.69 (cf. Mk. 14.62); and Lk. 23.35 (cf. Mk 15.32).[10] There is however a significant difference between this case and the others. In this case, אלהא has an excellent *Sitz im Leben* in the teaching of Jesus. He must have used the term אלהא a great deal, in the standard expression מלכותה דאלהא, in similar expressions such as גבורה דאלהא (cf. τὴν δύναμιν τοῦ θεοῦ, Mk 12.24), and in many other ways, such as his reference to God instituting indissoluble marriages in the process of creation (Mk 10.9). Moreover, Jesus' use of אלהא could well have given rise also to the editorial use of τοῦ πατρός in the parallel version of these sayings (Mt. 10.32-33: Mk 8.38). The context of Luke's occasional addition of a clarifying τοῦ θεοῦ is his inheritance of the centrality of God in the teaching of Jesus. The angels however are not very common in the authentic teaching of Jesus, and the complete expression מלאכיא די אלהא makes an excellent contrast with בני אנשא in the previous line. While absolute certainty cannot be obtained, the balance of probability is strongly in favour of the originality of אלהא, which I have accordingly used in the proposed reconstructions.

Vos proposed that the original form of the end of the saying was reserved at Rev. 3.5, ἐνώπιον τοῦ πατρός μου καὶ ἐνώπιον τῶν ἀγγέλων αὐτοῦ.[11] His argument is of methodological interest, and should not be accepted. He suggests that it is rather unlikely that John produced this ending by bringing together individual elements from the Matthean and Lucan accounts of the saying, and that

---

7.   Dalman, *Worte*, pp. 161, 172; *Words of Jesus*, pp. 197, 210.

8.   Dalman, *Worte*, pp. 75–7; *Words of Jesus*, pp. 91–4; and the same mistake at *Worte*, pp. 75–9, 159–62, 223; *Words of Jesus*, pp. 91–4, 194–7, 272.

9.   Tödt, *Son of Man*, p. 56 n. 4, from *Menschensohn*, p. 52, n. 60.

10.   H. T. Fleddermann, 'The Q Saying on Confessing and Denying', *SBL Seminar Papers* 26 (Atlanta: Scholars, 1987), pp. 606–16 (611); *Mark and Q. A Study of the Overlap Texts* (BETL 122. Leuven: Leuven University Press, 1995), p. 147, with n. 56.

11.   L. A. Vos, *The Synoptic Traditions in the Apocalypse* (Kampen: Kok, 1965), pp. 91–2.

this is entailed by holding that Luke contains the more primitive tradition of this saying and Matthew represents a later alteration of it. The assumption that the alternative to Vos's suggestion is that only the Gospel versions of the saying could be known is an arbitrary restriction. John's first language was Aramaic, and he might well have known the *original* saying and Matthew's alteration of it. He has τοῦ πατρός μου used by the heavenly Christ of his Father in the letters to Thyatira and Laodicea (Rev. 2.28; 3.21), and he uses τοῦ πατρός αὐτοῦ similarly (Rev. 14.1, cf. 1.6). If he knew the original version which eventually gave rise to Lk. 12.8, he might have been affected by the Matthean version. Moreover, Rev. 3.5 is a saying of the heavenly Christ. John might have freely rewritten it himself, and added τοῦ πατρός μου without being dependent on Matthew.

This brings us to the main difference between the Matthean and Lukan versions of the saying, ὁ υἱὸς τοῦ ἀνθρώπου with ὁμολογήσει in Luke, and the emphatic first person singular ὁμολογήσω κἀγώ in Matthew. Conventional scholarship has supposed that one of these represents a Greek Q, and that the other has resulted from changes made deliberately by one of the evangelists. This has however made it extremely difficult to explain the behaviour of whichever evangelist be thought to have made the required changes. Attempts to understand the supposedly original saying without proper attention to its Aramaic idiom have also been disastrous, with widespread acceptance of spurious arguments in favour of or against the authenticity of the saying. For example, scholars who argue for the originality of ὁ υἱὸς τοῦ ἀνθρώπου usually content themselves with direct arguments for the originality of Luke, and the perfectly true fact that from a strictly linguistic point of view κἀγώ is typically Matthean.[12] This does not however explain the behaviour of Matthew, who uses the term ὁ υἱὸς τοῦ ἀνθρώπου no less than 30 times, and, as we shall see in detailed discussion, shows every appearance of loving it and using it creatively in eschatological contexts.[13] Tödt did attempt a proper explanation. He suggested that the problem from Matthew's point of view was that he regarded the Son of man's function as being that of the judge, whereas this saying implies that the Son of man is acting not as the independent judge but as an intercessor or guarantor before the assize.[14] There are two things wrong with this. One is that if ὁ υἱὸς τοῦ ἀνθρώπου is kept as a Greek title of Jesus alone, as Matthew often uses it with reference to the final events including the final judgement (see notably Mt. 16.27-28; 25.31-46), the saying does not tell us whether the Son of man is the judge or an intercessor or guarantor, because ancient judges might confess or deny people before the courts over which they had charge. The second is that Matthew's picture of the Son of man as the eschatological judge would be just as much affected by the image of Jesus as witness using the first person pronoun as by his using the title ὁ υἱὸς τοῦ ἀνθρώπου. It follows that Tödt's explanation is spurious.

12.   E.g. W. G. Kümmel, *Promise and Fulfilment: The Eschatological Message of Jesus* (trans. D. M. Barton; SBT 23; London: SCM, 2nd edn, 1961), pp. 44–5; Davies and Allison, *Matthew*, vol. 2, p. 16.

13.   See pp. 212–22, 230–39 below.

14.   Tödt, *Son of Man*, pp. 89–90, from *Menschensohn*, pp. 83–4.

Arguments for the originality of the Matthean version have been equally unsatisfactory. The most extensive is that of Hoffmann.[15] In the first place, the Matthean καγώ is blatantly redactional, so Hoffmann conjectures that it is an alteration of καὶ ἐγώ.[16] Like τοῦ πατρός μου τοῦ ἐν οὐρανοῖς, καγώ underlines the fact that some redaction must be postulated to explain the origin of the Matthean version. This is why it is so important that it is precisely at this point that it is difficult to explain why Luke should interpolate ὁ υἱὸς τοῦ ἀνθρώπου. Hoffmann refers forward to Acts 7.56, but this is not a comparable case.[17] In Acts, Luke is writing freely and has used ὁ υἱὸς τοῦ ἀνθρώπου in line with his editing of the Son of man saying at Lk. 22.69 in circumstances where he had a free choice of how to write Stephen's short speech. At Lk. 12.8, however, we would have to suppose that he deliberately altered a clear reference to Jesus, and in the next verse altered it to a different construction again. Thirdly, we would have to suppose that just at the point where Luke altered a very Matthean expression to a phrase which he did not want in the next verse, he coincidentally ended up with an edited version of a saying which is perfectly comprehensible as a translation of a saying which conforms to Aramaic idiom. Hoffmann could not see this because he did not correctly understand the Aramaic idiom.[18] This forms a very strong argument of cumulative weight against the possibility that καγώ represents an original feature of Jesus' saying, while ὁ υἱὸς τοῦ ἀνθρώπου is due to secondary Lukan redaction.

It follows that the *Sitz im Leben* of the variations between the Matthean and Lukan versions of this saying are to be found in the translation process, not in the editing of either evangelist. To understand this, we must first recall the nature of the idiom itself. Two points about it are important: the term (א)שׁנ(א) בר must have a general level of meaning, and at the same time it may refer to one or more people of especial importance. It is regrettable that we do not have the context of any of the sayings in this group, so that we do not know whether particular people other than Jesus himself were in view, as Jacob and John were especially in view at Mk 10.45, and John the Baptist at Mk 9.12.[19] What we can be sure of is that there is a general level of meaning, and that there is a particular reference to Jesus himself. The general level of meaning presupposes that 'the angels of God' form a heavenly court, and that witnesses can confess people before this court, just as in the next saying they can deny them. The idea of the heavenly court is based on an earthly court, so the notion that it should have witnesses is a natural one. A few Jewish texts have survived in which it is clear that the righteous dead will have a role in the condemnation of the wicked at some form of final judgement. The most striking is

15.   E.g. P. Hoffmann in C. Heil, P. Hoffmann *et al.*, *Documenta Q. Q 12:8-12. Confessing or Denying: Speaking against the Holy Spirit: Hearings before Synagogues* (Leuven: Peeters, 1997), pp. 210–38.

16.   Hoffmann, *Q 12:8-12*, p. 230.

17.   Hoffmann, *Q 12:8-12*, pp. 228–30.

18.   Hoffmann, *Q 12:8-12*, pp. 210–13.

19.   Casey, *Aramaic Sources of Mark's Gospel*, pp. 125–33, 211–18; pp. 127–34 above.

the Wisdom of Solomon. Here we are assured that the souls of the righteous are in the hand of God (Wis. 3.1): so when the righteous person has been put to an early death, they will condemn the impious who are still alive (Wis. 4.16). Finally they will take their stand to condemn those who oppressed them during their earthly lives (Wis. 5.1-16).

A similar role for people in the last times is found in the teaching of Jesus at Mt. 12.41-42//Lk. 11.31-32. Here a large number of people, Gentiles at that, will condemn the generation of Jesus' contemporaries in the final judgement. This presupposes a very large number of witnesses. A somewhat different image is found at Mt. 19.28//Lk. 22.30, where the twelve will sit on twelve thrones judging the twelve tribes of Israel. In our society, a judge is very different from a witness, but in theirs a judge might confess or deny a person on trial. We must conclude from all this evidence that the above Aramaic reconstruction of Mt. 10.32//Lk. 12.8 has an entirely satisfactory level of meaning. People's view of Jesus while he is here on earth will determine whether they are confessed or otherwise at the final judgement. If they confess him, it is presupposed that more than one witness will confess them in the final judgement.

At the same time, Jesus himself will be the most important witness. This is obvious in the first place from his position in the first half of the saying, in which confessing him in the present life is the crucial event which ensures that the person confessing him will be confessed in the final judgement. The same applies to the next saying, according to which denying him in the present life is the crucial event which guarantees that the person will be denied in the final judgement. Whether Jesus will himself be the judge is not actually stated. On the one hand, it is not excluded by his role as a witness, nor by the ability of other people to bear witness on the same occasion, for ancient judges could bear witness for or against people, just as other people could appear as witnesses in the court over which one or many judges presided. On the other hand, the reference to the eschatological court by means of the expression קדם מלאכיא די אלהא strongly suggests that God himself will be in charge of this court, so that Jesus will be a witness, albeit the most important witness among however many may be envisaged.

We can now consider the saying from the perspective of the translators who had to render (א)שנ(א) בר into Greek. We have seen that the translators generally operated with a strategy, according to which they normally rendered בר (א)שנ(א) with ὁ υἱὸς τοῦ ἀνθρώπου when it referred to Jesus. Luke's Christian translator has simply followed this strategy as usual, so his behaviour is unproblematic. As always, the bilingual translator will have been able to see both articles in ὁ υἱὸς τοῦ ἀνθρώπου as generic, as well as seeing the particular reference to Jesus, as was characteristic of the original Aramaic idiom.

It was however possible to see problems in this particular saying, and these problems affected Matthew's translator here, just as Mark's translator was affected at Mark 3.28 and 9.12.[20] Unlike a monoglot Greek reader of the finished Gospel,

---

the bilingual translator would be fully aware that (א)נשׁ(א) בר had a general level of meaning, and could therefore refer to many people other than Jesus. As he considered the possibility of using ὁ υἱὸς τοῦ ἀνθρώπου as usual, he might therefore be affected by the same perception as has so regrettably afflicted many modern students of the finished Gospel, and become troubled that some readers might suppose that ὁ υἱὸς τοῦ ἀνθρώπου in this saying referred to someone other than Jesus. He therefore decided to opt for expressing the most important level of meaning of (א)נשׁ(א) בר in this saying, the reference to Jesus himself. This he has done with absolute clarity by using the first person singular instead.

It follows that when this major variant is treated as a result of the behaviour of two translators, it is quite easy to explain. Both Luke's translator, following his usual strategy of rendering (א)נשׁ(א) בר with ὁ υἱὸς τοῦ ἀνθρώπου because it referred to Jesus himself, and Matthew, opting for the first person singular to avoid the usual strategy leading to misunderstanding, have behaved in entirely understandable ways. This contrasts with the difficulties which scholars have experienced in trying to explain the text of either evangelist as a result of redaction by one evangelist. We must therefore conclude that we have before us the work of two different translators.

We must therefore conclude that the proposed reconstruction and the interpretation of it given above are both approximately correct. Two regrettable arguments are however so widespread in modern scholarship that they must also be discussed. As so often, Bultmann made the main mistake with clarity: '... it appears certain to me that the distinction between Jesus and the Son of Man is primary.'[21] From this he inferred that such sayings were authentic, for Jesus distinguished himself from the Son of man. Tödt reflected the widespread acceptance of this argument, commenting 'Today most scholars agree that the form which discriminates between the "I" of Jesus and the Son of Man is the more original one. "No church would have invented at a later time a theology making a distinction so foreign to the feeling of the church, i.e. between the person of Jesus himself, and that of the future judge."'[22] This widespread argument has no validity because it is entirely a function of ignoring the Aramaic level of the tradition. As we have seen, the original saying does not have a figure 'the Son of man' who is different from Jesus, it simply has a general level of meaning in addition to its reference to Jesus.

Haenchen correctly drew Lk. 12.8 into his discussion of Mk 8.38, but in rejecting the views of Bultmann and Tödt, he made a similar mistake.[23] He suggested that Mk 8.38 was a product of the post-Easter community, and his argument implies the same for Lk. 12.8. He argued that for that community 'waren ... Jesus und der Menschensohn "futurisch identisch": Jesus wird in naher Zukunft als der

21.   Bultmann, *Synoptic Tradition*, p. 112.

22.   Tödt, *Son of Man*, p. 55, from *Menschensohn*, pp. 50–1, quoting R. Otto, *The Kingdom of God and the Son of Man* (trans. F. V. Filson and B. L. Woolf. London: Lutterworth, 1938), p. 163, and referring to Bultmann, *Synoptic Tradition*, p. 112.

23.   E. Haenchen, *Der Weg Jesu. Eine Erklärung des Markus-Evangeliums und der kanonischen Parallelen* (Berlin: de Gruyter, 2nd edn, 1968), pp. 298–300.

Menschensohn (der er jetzt noch nicht war) mit den Wolken des Himmels zurückkehren. In seinem Erdenleben war er noch nicht der Menschensohn …' Each step in this argument is wrong, because Haenchen ignored the Aramaic level of the tradition just as Bultmann and Tödt had done. Jesus was בר (א)נ(א)ש(א) throughout his earthly life because he was a human being. Accordingly, he could not become בר (א)נ(א)ש(א) after his death, so these grounds for attributing the whole of Mk 8.38 and similar sayings to the early church are not satisfactory.

Borsch made a profoundly similar mistake in producing the following form of Lk. 12.8-9, on the ground that agreement might be reached from different perspectives on something like it as 'an early saying':

> Everyone who acknowledges me before men (sons of men?) בר (א)נ(א)ש(א) will also acknowledge before the angels of God; everyone who is ashamed of me before men (sons of men?) בר (א)נ(א)ש(א) will be ashamed of before the angels of God.

He comments, 'I frankly find it difficult to hear a speaker referring to himself by different means in the same sentence'.[24] It is ironical that speakers do this in English,[25] the wrong language but one which, like all languages, provides comparative data which should warn us to examine Aramaic usage carefully without such preconceptions. It is of central importance that this apology of a reconstruction is in the wrong language, and that we have Aramaic texts in which similar switches occur (e.g. Sefire III.14–17).[26] Moreover, Borsch wrote years after I had offered reconstructions of Lk. 12.8 and Mk 8.38, from which this much should have been clear.[27] Borsch's mistake also illustrates the fact, known to some linguists for years, that abstract theorizing tends to depend on one's own idiolect rather than on standard usage.[28]

A different kind of mistake was made by Käsemann. He argued that Mk 8.38 and Mt. 10.32f. are of a form 'Sentences of Holy Law', and the same must follow for Lk. 12.8-9.[29] He argues explicitly that the Marcan and Matthean versions of the saying cannot go back to Jesus himself: 'proof of this is to be found both in the content, where the confession of Christ is estimated to be the standard of judgement at the Last Day, and also in the form of the sentence.'[30] Käsemann attributed the

24. F. H. Borsch, 'Further Reflections on "The Son of Man": The Origins and Development of the Title', in J. H. Charlesworth (ed.), *THE MESSIAH. Developments in Earliest Judaism and Christianity*, (Minneapolis: Fortress, 1992), pp. 130–44 (144).

25. Cf. Wales, '"Personal" and "Indefinite" Reference'; H. Sacks, 'Everyone Has to Lie', in M. Sanches and B. G. Blount (eds), *Sociocultural Dimensions of Language Use* (London/NY: Academic Press, 1975), pp. 57–79; catalogued with discussion by Casey, 'Jackals', pp. 10–12, with nn. 24–26.

26. See pp. 67–8 above.

27. Casey, *Son of Man*, pp. 162, 194.

28. S. Greenbaum, 'Contextual Influence on Acceptability Judgements', *Linguistics* 187 (1977), pp. 5–11.

29. E. Käsemann, 'Sätze heiligen Rechtes im Neuen Testament', *NTS* 1 (1954–5), pp. 248–60: 'Sentences of Holy Law in the New Testament', in E. Käsemann, *New Testament Questions of Today* (trans. W. I. Montague; London: SCM, 1969), pp. 66–81.

30. Käsemann, 'Sentences', p. 77.

sentences of holy law to early Christian prophets. Many scholars followed this approach. For example, Edwards declared the use of this form 'widespread', and exaggerated some of Käsemann's comments in attributing to him the view that this form had its *Sitz im Leben* in the celebration of the Eucharist. He further proposed that in Lk. 12.8, 'we have an example of the Son of Man theology leaving the eschatological correlative form to function in a similar way in another judgmental *Gattung*.'[31] Rejecting the authenticity of Lk. 12.8f. with particular reference to the work of Tödt, Gaston commented: 'The form of the saying agrees so well with the Sätze heiligen Rechtes which Käsemann has established as a form of prophetic sayings in the gospels, that it can hardly be denied that Lk 12:8f has been given its present form by early Christian prophets.'[32]

None of this should be accepted.[33] In the first place, it is not clear that the small number of sayings collected by Käsemann form a genuinely separate Gattung with a specific *Sitz im Leben*. Edwards attempted a description of the supposed *Gattung*, largely following Perrin: 'The *Sätze heiligen Rechtes* or "eschatological-judgement-pronouncement saying is composed of two parts in which the same verb is used in each part, in the first part referring to man's activity and the second referring to God's activity", usually by putting the verb in the passive voice.'[34] But some of the sayings used by Käsemann do not fit this definition. For example he uses Lev. 18.5 at Gal. 3.12, 'He who does them shall live by them', to show that 'holy Scripture provided the primitive Christian prophets with the stylistic form in which to clothe their sentences of holy law.'[35] The more precise the proposed definition of this *Gattung*, the fewer the number of examples, and Käsemann knew that examples were not 'widespread'. Gal. 3.12 also takes us to the second point: this is from a letter by Paul, not from a pronouncement by an early Christian prophet. Only one of Käsemann's examples is really from an early Christian prophet, Rev. 22.18-19, and even that closes a literary work. It follows that the proposed *Sitz im Leben* is quite unsupported, and its assertion for this small group of Gospel sayings is quite arbitrary.

We must therefore conclude that none of these widespread arguments is valid. All of them illustrate the perils of working without the use of the original language spoken by Jesus to help to locate his teaching in his original Jewish culture. We must return to the saying reconstructed above for a reasonable view of what Jesus said and meant. He declared that people who confessed him on earth in the here and

---

31.   R. A. Edwards, 'The Eschatological Correlative as a *Gattung* in the New Testament', *ZNW* 60 (1969) pp. 9–20 (14–15).

32.   L. Gaston, *No stone on another. Studies in the significance of the fall of Jerusalem in the Synoptic Gospels* (NovTSup 23. Leiden: Brill, 1970), pp. 403–4.

33.   For a full critique of Käsemann, see P. Berger, 'Zu den sogenannten Sätzen Heiligen Rechtes', *NTS* 17 (1970–71), pp. 10–40; 'Die sog. "Sätze heiligen Rechtes" im N.T. Ihre Funktion und ihr Sitz im Leben', *TZ* 28 (1972), pp. 305–30.

34.   Edwards, 'Eschatological Correlative', p. 14, quoting Perrin, *Rediscovering the Teaching of Jesus*, p. 22.

35.   Käsemann, 'Sentences', pp. 76–7.

now would for that reason be supported by people witnessing at the final judgement before the angels in God's court. Just as he was the most important person in the here and now as the leader of the Jesus movement and the final messenger from God who called upon Israel to repent, so he would also be the crucial witness among many at the final judgement.

In the next saying, Mt. 10.33//Lk. 12.9, the differences between Matthew and Luke can again be accounted for by the work of two translators, with the addition of some editing by the evangelists. The reconstruction proposed above shows extensive symmetry with the previous saying. Both evangelists have some form of δέ, for which I have reconstructed the ubiquitous ו. This gives an excellent link between the original connected sayings, and the Greek is a sound equivalent. In place of πᾶς in the previous saying, for which I naturally reconstructed כל, Matthew has ὅστις ... ἄν with the subjunctive, where Luke has ὁ with the participle ἀρνησάμενος. I have reconstructed מן ד, which is the approximate equivalent of both 'he who', and 'whoever'. It has thus been correctly translated twice, in both cases within the parameters of the normal linguistic habits of each evangelist. There is no serious difference from כל די, so this is effectively a stylistic variation which the tradition attributed to Jesus. As I noted in discussing the previous saying, Luke now has ἐνώπιον, as he does later in this verse, rather than ἔμπροσθεν which both evangelists had in the previous verse, and Matthew continues with here. This is perfectly sound Greek, and both words belong to normal Lukan Greek, whereas Matthew does not use ἐνώπιον. At the end of the first half of the saying, I have again reconstructed בני אנשא for the evangelists' τῶν ἀνθρώπων, for the same reasons as in the previous verse.

The next variation between the evangelists is central to the reconstruction and interpretation of this verse. Matthew again has the first person singular of the verb, this time ἀρνήσομαι, and again he has reinforced it with κἀγώ. Luke, who had καὶ ὁ υἱὸς τοῦ ἀνθρώπου at this point in the previous verse, has no such thing this time, preferring the future passive ἀπαρνηθήσεται. Mk 8.38, however, often thought to be an independent variant form of this same saying, does have exactly καὶ ὁ υἱὸς τοῦ ἀνθρώπου at this point. This presents a very complex problem, so I deal briefly with other details first. In each Gospel, this verse ends in a very similar way to the previous one. Matthew has ἔμπροσθεν τοῦ πατρός μου τοῦ ἐν οὐρανοῖς, exactly as before. We must regard it as secondary, for the same reasons as in the previous verse. Luke has ἐνώπιον τῶν ἀγγελεων τοῦ θεοῦ, no more than a Greek stylistic variation on the previous ἔμπροσθεν τῶν ἀγγελεων τοῦ θεοῦ. I have accordingly reconstructed מלאכיא די אלהא, just as in the previous verse.

We may now return to the opening phrase of the second half of Mt. 10.33//Lk. 12.9. Here I have again reconstructed בר אנש, with בה following the verb. Matthew has ἀρνήσομαι κἀγὼ αὐτόν. This is strongly parallel to ὁμολογήσω κἀγὼ ἐν αὐτῷ at Mt. 10.32. We have already seen that it was a bold but comprehensible translation of בר (א)נ(א)ש in that verse, so it is likely to be the same thing here. This is especially so since the idiom itself makes perfect sense as part of a saying of Jesus, and the translation process is perfectly comprehensible, as outlined above. This time, Luke has the future passive ἀπαρνηθήσεται. This is perfectly comprehensible as Lukan editing, for it is in accordance with Lukan usage in general, and in particular as an editorial response to a collection of sayings which includes Lk. 12.10. Both these points have often been made before. For example, Cadbury observed that 'Luke shows considerable freedom in the use of the passive. Especially frequent is the future passive … in his parallels to Mt. and Mark, Luke's preference for the future passive is especially striking.' Cadbury correctly listed this passage among his examples.[36] More recently, Fleddermann went further: '… the form ἀπαρνηθήσεται is Lucan, reflecting three tendencies of Luke's style. First, Luke favors compound verbs, and he frequently switches from simple to compound verbs both in Marcan and Q material. Second, he also likes the future passive, again introducing it into his sources. Third, Luke tends to lengthen the future passive forms by prefixing prepositions, even though the forms are already quite long.'[37]

On the second point, Müller comments that 'Lukas benutzt die Passivform vermutlich, weil er eine Wiederholung des Ausdrucks vermeiden wollte, da er auch im folgenden Vers ein "Menschensohn"-Wort bringt, nämlich daß es verzeihbar sei, ein Wort gegen "des Menschen Sohn" zu reden.' Beasley-Murray adds, 'Luke's passive verb in 12:9 is almost certainly attributable to an accommodation to the sentence that follows in verse 10, which appears as a Son of Man saying with passive verbs in both clauses …'.[38] All this should be accepted. If Luke received this saying either in Aramaic with (א)נשׁ(א) בר, or in Greek with ὁ υἱὸς τοῦ ἀνθρώπου, he had good reason to alter this expression. The original expression served the mechanical collection of the three sayings at Lk. 12.8-10 into one place, but it caused tension between the last two sayings. Luke therefore altered the saying in a manner fully in accordance with his own style.

It will be noted that I have *not* argued that an Aramaic reconstruction of Lk. 12.9, complete with its specific variants, would be impossible to produce, and a full discussion demands that this be illustrated.

ומן דיכפר בי קדם בני אנשא יתכפר קדם מלאכיא די אלהא

There is nothing wrong with this saying, which might potentially be thought to have a sound *Sitz im Leben* in the teaching of Jesus. There is only one significant difference from the reconstruction which I have preferred. This is that those who have denied Jesus on earth will be denied in the heavenly court by God himself, rather than by witnesses of whom Jesus himself would be the most important. There are however three basic reasons for preferring the reconstruction which I proposed at the beginning of this chapter. One is the behaviour of Jesus himself. It is difficult to see why he should have several witnesses, including most notably himself,

---

36.   H. J. Cadbury, *The Style and Literary Method of Luke* (HTS 6. Cambridge, MA: Harvard U.P., 1920), p. 164.

37.   Fleddermann, 'Q Saying on Confessing and Denying', pp. 611–12.

38.   Müller, *Ausdruck 'Menschensohn'*, pp. 131–2: G. R. Beasley-Murray, *Jesus and the Kingdom of God* (Grand Rapids: Eerdmanns, 1986), p. 225.

witnessing on behalf of those who confess him, and change to God himself as the sole being who denies those who have denied Jesus. Secondly, there is the argument of cumulative weight formed by the explanation of both the saying itself and of the editorial behaviour of the evangelists as I have just proposed. Thirdly, there is the argument from Mk 8.38.

In its present form, Mk 8.38 reads as follows:

ὃς γὰρ ἐὰν ἐπαισχυνθῇ με καὶ τοὺς ἐμοὺς λόγους ἐν τῇ γενεᾷ ταύτῃ τῇ μοιχαλίδι καὶ ἁμαρτωλῷ, καὶ ὁ υἱὸς τοῦ ἀνθρώπου ἐπαισχυνθήσεται αὐτὸν ὅταν ἔλθῃ ἐν τῇ δόξῃ τοῦ πατρὸς αὐτοῦ μετὰ τῶν ἀγγέλων τῶν ἁγίων.

At first sight, this looks very different from Mt. 10.33//Lk. 12.9, but it is intelligible as an edited version of an Aramaic saying which differs by only one letter from the reconstruction proposed above, with חפר, 'be ashamed', rather than כפר, 'deny'. This was pointed out by Jeremias, and I carried it forward.[39] I now offer an updated version of this hypothesis, beginning with a slightly modified reconstruction of a possible saying underlying Mk 8.38:

ומן דיחפר בי מדק בני אנשא אף בר אנש יחפר בה קדם מלאכיא די אלהא.

Here Mark has replaced the ubiquitous ו with the connecting particle γάρ, thereby integrating the saying into its present Marcan context. Otherwise, Mark's ὃς ... ἐὰν for מן ד is very similar to Matthew's ὅστις ... ἂν, and we have already seen that Luke's ὁ ... ἀρνησάμενος is an entirely reasonable alternative to this. The next difference is the most important point, with חפר proposed behind ἐπαισχυνθῇ where the proposed original behind Lk. 12.9 has כפר, and the same difference between the proposed versions in the next line. These words sound very similar, so that Jeremias was led to comment: 'The bifurcation of the tradition ('be ashamed'/'deny') must have taken place during the course of oral tradition in an Aramaic-speaking milieu.'[40] This is an entirely plausible suggestion, which I have accordingly used in producing the rest of the proposed reconstruction of the Marcan version, the remainder of which is identical to the proposed reconstruction of the saying underlying Lk. 12.9.

I have accordingly suggested that the simple בי was translated with με and expanded with καὶ τοὺς ἐμοὺς λόγους. This could have been done in Aramaic with ובמלי, or Jesus might have said both versions of the saying on different occasions. I have likewise suggested קדם בני אנשא, as in both the other sayings. Mark will then have edited this to produce ἐν τῇ γενεᾷ τῇ μοιχαλίδι καὶ ἁμαρτωλῷ. Again, however, it is not impossible that Jesus said בדרא דן גירא וחטיא. Next, Mark has καὶ for אף, just like Luke at 12.8 and equivalent to the same word in crasis with ἐγώ to produce κἀγώ twice in Mt. 10.32-33. The next expression is the crucial one, with בר (א)נש(א) as at Lk. 12.8, supporting the possibility that בר (א)נש(א) was also the expression in the Aramaic original of Lk. 12.9. If the short Aramaic version

---

39.   Jeremias, *New Testament Theology*, p. 7, n. 2; Casey, *Son of Man*, pp. 161–3.
40.   Jeremias, *New Testament Theology*, p. 7, n. 2.

behind Mk 8.38 proposed above be thought probable, this is a very strong argument. Finally, I have proposed that the whole of the last piece, ὅταν ἔλθη ἐν τῇ δόξῃ τοῦ πατρὸς αὐτοῦ μετὰ τῶν ἀγγελων τῶν ἁγίων, is a piece of expansive midrash taking off from the original קדם מלאכיא די אלהא.

The plausibility of this, especially its *Sitz im Leben* in the editorial activity of Mark, depends partly on the discussion of Mk 13.26 and 14.62 in Ch. 10.[41] This shows that Mark created two composite midrashim, both using Dan. 7.13 as one of the major texts. The proposed expansion at Mk 8.38 is in the same midrashic mode, and uses this same text. Mark's ἔλθη represents the Danielic אתה; δόξῃ recalls יקר; τοῦ πατρὸς αὐτοῦ is a particularly Christian description of God, whose presence as עתיק יומיא is central to Dan. 7.13; and the angels must be presupposed as the subject of הקרבוהי (as explicitly at Midr. Ps. 21,5). The interpretation of Dan. 7.13 which is presupposed at Mk 8.38 is also the same as at Mk 13.26 and 14.62: the western Christian interpretation according to which Dan. 7.13 describes the parousia of Jesus. The proposed hypothesis accordingly posits consistent behaviour by Mark, who midrashically created references to Jesus' second coming when these were absent from his sources.

It is therefore entirely plausible to suppose that both Mk 8.38 and Lk. 12.9 resulted from accidental and deliberate changes to a single saying. I have not however used the word for 'be ashamed of' which is best attested in Aramaic sources of sufficiently early date. The attestation of חפר in biblical Hebrew and in Syriac should be regarded as sufficient for the proposed corruption to have taken place, but it is worth seeing what happens if we try to reconstruct the whole of Mk 8.38 using בהת, which is found at 4Q213a frg 2 line 5, with the cognate noun in line 4 and at 4QEn^g 1 ii 25 (*1 En.* 92.2); the verb בהת is also found in later Jewish Aramaic, Christian Palestinian Aramaic, Samaritan Aramaic and Syriac. One might suggest the following, and translate it into English rather differently from the way it was translated into Greek to form Mk 8.38:

מן דיבהת בי ובמלי בדרא דן גירא וחטיא

אף בר אנש יבהת בה

כד אתא בשבח אבא עם מלאכיא קדישיא

Whoever is ashamed of me and my words in this adulterous and sinful generation, a/the son of man will be ashamed of him too when the Father comes in glory with the holy angels.

Even in this complete form, the saying understood in this way has a potentially satisfactory *Sitz im Leben* in the teaching of Jesus. The coming of God for judgement was part of Old Testament expectation: for example, at Zech. 14.5 we find God coming at the final judgement, and all the holy ones with him. This expectation was continued after the Old Testament period. For example, at *1 En.* 1.9 he comes with myriads of holy ones to execute judgement on all.

There is therefore no serious problem in attributing this expectation to the Jesus of history. The setting of this saying would be the same as that of Mt. 10.32-33//

---

41.   See pp. 242–5 below.

Lk. 12.8-9. The description בדרא דן גירא וחטיא is simply more dramatic and critical than קדם בני אנשא. Both expressions make clear that it is a person's attitude to Jesus of Nazareth during his current ministry that will determine their fate at the final judgement. Equally, the setting of their ultimate fate 'when the Father comes in glory with the holy angels' is a clear reference to their fate at the final judgement, just as at Mt. 10.32-33//Lk. 12.8-9. The proposed Aramaic is perfectly idiomatic. In particular, בר (א)נש(א) is used in the same idiomatic way as in the proposed originals of Mt. 10.32-33//Lk. 12.8-9. The saying has a general level of meaning which presupposes that there will be witnesses at the final judgement who will be ashamed of people who were ashamed of Jesus during the historic ministry. At the same time, בר (א)נש(א) is being used idiomatically because Jesus himself, the author of the saying, will be the most important witness at the judgement.

This proposal also makes excellent sense of the behaviour of the translator. As a committed Christian, he shared the belief of the rest of the New Testament in the early return of Jesus. I have noted this expressed with the use of ὁ υἱὸς τοῦ ἀνθρώπου and ἔρχομαι, with other signs of Dan. 7.13, at Mk 13.26 and 14.62.[42] This same understanding has been applied to the translation process here. Hence the translator has continued with בר (א)נש(א) as the subject of אתא , and has taken שבח as a construct before אבא. Apart from these changes, the whole of the translation is as straightforward as possible. We must therefore conclude that this proposal is just as sound as the one proposed at the beginning of this chapter. We have two alternative possibilities for understanding the origins of Mk 8.38. This makes no difference to our understanding of what the saying means in its present context in Mark, and less difference than one might expect to our understanding of the teaching of Jesus found in the two somewhat different sayings which I have reconstructed. In either case, Jesus asserted that people's attitudes to him during the historic ministry would be decisive at the final judgement, when Jesus himself and other witnesses would deny or be ashamed of them as they had denied or been ashamed of him here on earth. In either case, Jesus used the term בר (א)נש(א) in an idiomatic way to say this.

It follows that we can achieve the main purpose of this chapter in reconstructing and interpreting two or three Son of man sayings in the teaching of Jesus, even though uncertainty remains about the details of the Aramaic saying which lay behind Mk 8.38. There should be no doubt that, in two or three sayings, Jesus declared that people's attitude to him during the historic ministry would condition their fate at the last judgement. If they confessed him in the here and now, Jesus and other witnesses would confess them at the final judgement. If they denied him in the here and now, Jesus and other witnesses would deny them at the final judgement. He may also have said in somewhat more graphic terms that if people were ashamed of him in the here and now, Jesus and other witnesses would be ashamed of them at the final judgement. In that case, he would also have made clear reference to the coming of God himself for the final judgement.

42.   See pp. 192 above; 242–5 below.

Even with this degree of uncertainty, the genuine sayings which I have recovered are of central importance in understanding the significance which Jesus saw in his ministry. He regarded it as the final event of salvation history which would condition the eternal fate of everyone who was there at the time. This gives him the totally central position which led the early Christians to describe him as the Christ.

Chapter Eight

BETRAYED BY A KISS (LUKE 22.48)

There is just one authentic Son of man saying which has survived in Luke alone. It belongs to an incident which is related by Mark, and which certainly took place. The basic story of Jesus' betrayal by Judah of Kerioth is not the kind of thing that the early church had any reason to produce, and it has many signs of authenticity. The Greek ᾿Ιούδας is a straightforward version of the Hebrew and Aramaic יהודה, which is generally rendered into English as Judah. ᾿Ισκαριωθ (Mk 3.19//Lk. 6.16; Mk 14.10) and ᾿Ισκαριωτης (Mt. 10.4; 26.14; Lk. 22.3; Jn 6.71; 12.4; 13.2,26; 14.22) are transliterations into Greek, firstly without and then with Greek endings added, of the Hebrew איש קריות, 'man of Kerioth'.[1] Kerioth was a small village in the very south of Judea (Josh. 15.25). Hence the variant reading ἀπὸ Καρυώτου (Jn 6.71 א* Θ pc; 12.4 D; 13.2 D; 13.26 D). Judah was thus the only one of the twelve not to come from Galilee, which is presumably why he was known by his place of origin.

Judah's betrayal of Jesus has been a great puzzle. Mark tells us that he went to the chief priests of his own volition and offered to hand Jesus over to them (Mk 14.10-11). The incident in which Lk. 22.48 is found is part of the story of how Judah took an armed party to arrest Jesus in a garden at night (Mk 14.43-50), thereby solving the chief priests' problem of how to arrest him without a major riot.

The reason why Judah's motives have proved so difficult to understand is because of the influence of later Christian tradition. If we imagine that Judah became one of the Twelve because he realized the perfect goodness of his Incarnate Lord coming from heaven to redeem the world, and because Jesus perceived in him the personal qualities needed by an apostle who would spread this wonderful news: and if we imagine that Judah's betrayal of Jesus was a perfectly evil act, bringing about the work of the devil by betraying him to perfectly evil people: we get an overnight transition from goodness to evil which is indeed impossible to explain. We cannot get further than the most inaccurate and hostile of the Gospel writers: τότε εἰσῆλθεν εἰς ἐκεῖνον ὁ σατανᾶς (Jn 13.27, cf. Lk. 22.3).

To understand Judah's motives, we must leave Christian tradition behind and understand him as a faithful Jew. He joined the Jesus movement because he saw in

---

1.   This continues to be disputed, but it is not relevant enough for detailed discussion here. See e.g. R. E. Brown, *The Death of the Messiah. A Commentary on the Passion Narratives in the Four Gospels* (ABRL. 2 vols.; London/New York: Chapman/Doubleday, 1994), vol. 2; pp. 1410–18, with bibliography.

it a prophetic movement dedicated to the renewal of Israel. Jesus chose him because he was a faithful Jew, dedicated to God and to the renewal of Israel, and with the qualities necessary to take a leading role in a ministry of preaching and exorcism. Like other faithful Jews, he will have been troubled by Jesus' controversies with scribes and Pharisees during the historic ministry. Exactly what he objected to, we have no idea. Perhaps he tithed mint, dill and cummin, and felt the decorated monuments of the prophets were quite magnificent. Perhaps it was something else – it must have been something which did not seem contrary to the prophetic renewal of Israel. While such details are conjectural, our main point is surely secure – he will have been troubled by these controversies, and he did not undergo an overnight conversion.

Nonetheless, given the point at which he went to the chief priests and the seriousness of what he undertook to do, there should be no doubt as to which event was the final straw for him – the cleansing of the Temple. From the perspective of a faithful member of normative Jewish tradition, the will of God laid down in the Torah was that the house of God should be run by the priests. In charge were the chief priests, as God had appointed, with scribes who interpreted the scriptures so that everyone knew how the Temple was to be run. From Judah's point of view, it was accordingly quite wrong of Jesus to enter the Court of the Gentiles, and upset the arrangements duly made by the chief priests and scribes for the payment of the Temple tax and the purchase of the offerings most used by the poor. From our point of view, Judah changed sides and betrayed his master. From Judah's point of view, he did nothing of the kind. He was a faithful Jew doing the will of God from beginning to end, and when a most regrettable conflict became unacceptable, his only master was God.

Moreover, to some extent Jesus must have colluded with Judah. I have discussed in detail the sayings with which Jesus, at the Last Supper, predicted his betrayal in terms which led the disciples each to deny that they would betray him.[2] In going to the garden of Gethsemane, Jesus allowed Judah to bring an armed group of people to arrest him. He could have run for it if he had so wished. Indeed, he did not have to come to Jerusalem if he had not wished. His obligation to attend Passover, and to remain within greater Jerusalem for the night, could both be overridden by the need to save life. We have however seen that he predicted and interpreted his forthcoming death, and went to Jerusalem in order to die. Moreover, Jacob and John said they would share in his death (Mk 10.35-45), and Peter and others said after the Last Supper that they would die with him rather than deny him (Mk 14.31).[3] Jesus therefore knew full well that he would be executed if he were arrested. This is the extent of his collusion with Judah: he went where he knew that he would be found (cf. Jn 18.2). All this makes a perfectly coherent narrative, which should be accepted as historical fact.

Luke's major source for his Gospel was the Gospel of Mark, which however he often rewrote to a considerable degree. Sometimes, especially in the accurate

---

2.   See pp. 134–6 above; Casey, *Aramaic Sources of Mark's Gospel*, pp. 229–32.
3.   See further pp. 131–4 above; Casey, *Aramaic Sources of Mark's Gospel*, pp. 193–218.

parts of the passion narrative, it is difficult to tell whether he perhaps had another source which was rather like Mark. There are two points at which he certainly did, though scholars have often contested this. These are the two points where Matthew turned to the same non-Marcan source. At Mk 14.65, Mark relates how the people mocking Jesus said to him 'prophesy'. Luke, whose account differs considerably from Mark and who has the incidents in a different order, adds the words τίς ἐστιν ὁ παίσας σε; (Lk. 22.64). Matthew, whose account follows Mark more closely but by no means slavishly, adds ἡμῖν, χριστέ and then the same five words, τίς ἐστιν ὁ παίσας σε ; (Mt. 26.68). This is very strong evidence that Matthew and Luke had access to a common source for this part of the narrative, that it was written in Greek, and that it related the same incident as we find in Mark.

Similar remarks apply to Mt. 26.75//Lk. 22.62. Here, where Mk 14.72 has καὶ ἐπιβαλὼν ἔκλαιεν, Matthew and Luke have five words running in common, only the first of which is Marcan: καὶ ἐξελθὼν ἔξω ἔκλαυσεν πικρῶς. Moreover the text of Mark is quite unsatisfactory from the point of view of a monoglot speaker of Greek, since ἐπιβαλὼν means 'throwing', which does not make sense. In Syriac, however, שׁדא is used of 'throwing' threats and curses, much as in English we may 'hurl' abuse. We must therefore infer that Mark had a written source which read וּשׁרא בכא: 'And he began to weep'. He misread this as וּשׁדא בכא: 'And throwing (*sc.* more abuse), he wept'. This made sense to him because the idiomatic use of שׁדא was already present in Aramaic, and he translated with ἐπιβαλὼν because he was suffering from the double level of interference inevitable in translators.[4] Matthew and Luke, however, had in front of them the text of Mark, which does not make proper sense to anyone approaching it from a purely Greek perspective.

4.   Casey, *Aramaic Sources of Mark's Gospel*, pp. 85–6. This was rejected by Mastin, who insisted that we should use Qumran Aramaic, in which 'he began to weep' would have been וּשׁרא למבכא, which would make nonsense of my suggestion. Mastin's insistence that we should use only Qumran Aramaic to reconstruct sources from first-century Galilee is however completely unsatisfactory (see pp. 56–9 above). שׁרי may be followed by a participle in both later Jewish Aramaic and in Syriac, so it is entirely reasonable to posit it here.

A different criticism was made by P. J. Williams, in a review article full of mistakes which cannot be enumerated here: P. M. Head and P. J. Williams, 'Q Review', *TynBul* 54 (2003), pp. 119-44 (143-4). Williams argued that שׁרא could mean 'begin' only in the *pa'el*, so the form would have to be וּשׁרי, which would require two letters to have been misread, one of them (י misread as א) implausible. That שׁרא can mean 'begin' only in the *pa'el* is true in vocalized Syriac, but it is not clear that the author of Mark's source would know this, nor is it obvious in earlier unpointed texts. For example, שׁרית, 'I began', occurs at 1QapGen XII,13.15; XIX,18; XXI,15; it could be either *pe'al* or *pa'el*. It is most improbable that the author of Mark's source had been trained in Aramaic grammar. Accordingly, there is nothing wrong in supposing that he wrote שׁרא. Williams also insists that שׁדא must have been used in the *pe'al*, but he does not justify this opinion at all. If Mark's source did write וּשׁרי בכא, 'and he began weeping', it could have been misread וּשׁדי בכא, 'and he threw (*sc.* threats and curses), he wept'. A bilingual suffering from interference as s/he translated might well render this καὶ ἐπιβαλὼν ἔκλαιεν.

Moreover D Θ 565 read καὶ ἤρξατο κλαίειν, sin וּשׁרי הוא דנבכא, pesh וּשׁרי דנבכא, hark וכד שׁרי הוא בכא. Clearly the home of Semitic readings noticed what had happened, and corrected Mark's mistake. Both Mastin and Williams have created strict rules which prevent the solution of problems like this. We should not do so.

This is exactly the point at which both of them had good reason to consult another version if they knew it. Luke shows ample signs of having such evidence available to him. We should therefore infer that this included an account of Peter's denial, and that Matthew, seeing something wrong with the Marcan account which he usually follows, looked again at his alternative account, just as he had done a few verses earlier.[5]

Luke's account of the betrayal shows significant overlap with that of Mark, but not such that one can decide whether he was simply rewriting Mark or using an alternative Greek account. At Lk. 22.47, he has the following words in common with Mark: ἔτι αὐτοῦ λαλοῦντος ... Ἰούδας εἷς τῶν δώδεκα ... αὐτόν, and in a different position, ὄχλος. Similarly at Lk. 22.50: εἷς ... τις ... τὸν δοῦλον τοῦ ἀρχιερέως καὶ ἀφεῖλεν ... τὸ ... αὐτου. This strongly suggests that Luke knew Mark, but every word is also literally true, so this is consistent with Luke having access to a non-Marcan source which overlapped with Mark at ancient and accurate material. On the other hand, Lk. 22.49 looks like secondary story-telling. So is the peculiarly Lukan notion that Jesus healed the slave's ear (Lk. 22.51), a normally impossible event which produced no favourable reaction among the arresting party and was not thought worthy of mention in the Marcan tradition. Outside v. 48, there is no sign of Luke having any special Aramaic source.

Jesus' saying at Lk. 22.48 itself is nonetheless a perfectly good example of an Aramaic idiom. I reconstructed it some years ago,[6] and I see no reason to alter that reconstruction now:

יהודה, נשק לבר אנש ותמסרנה.
Judah, kissing a/the son of man and you betray him!

This example is rather near the limits of Aramaic idiom. It is a reaction of horror that Judah of Kerioth, one of the chosen members of the Twelve, should betray Jesus and should do so with a kiss. The general level of meaning which is idiomatically used is a generalization from his own personal experience, and one which has resonated with most people ever since. He was expecting to be betrayed, but he had already expressed his condemnation of the traitor. He now expressed his horror at this way of betraying him. The use of a general level of meaning should not be allowed to undermine the drama or the emotion of the moment. Jesus really meant that Judah himself was doing something horrible to Jesus himself. He expressed himself indirectly because that was a normal way of expressing oneself in Aramaic in overtly humiliating circumstances, which these were.

As at Mk 14.21, I have used the conventional English 'betray' to translate the Aramaic מסר, reconstructed behind the Greek παραδίδωμι. Klassen is prominent among scholars who have objected to this.[7] Klassen has some philology on his side

---

5.   For more detailed discussion of these two passages, with some comments on standard secondary literature, see Casey, *Aramaic Approach to Q*, pp. 26–9.

6.   Casey, 'General, Generic and Indefinite', p. 39.

7.   W. Klassen, *Judas. Betrayer or Friend of Jesus?* (London: SCM, 1996).

up to a point, but the context of these two sayings is the reason why I have not accepted his view. The main point which he has right is that παραδίδωμι has a much broader semantic area, and is basically equivalent to the English 'hand over' in a wide range of circumstances. The Aramaic and Hebrew מסר are however both used in circumstances where people would not want to be handed over. Judah handed his master Jesus over to his most serious enemies in circumstances which might well lead to his death. While there must have been a certain degree of collusion for the event to have been possible, Jesus' words at Mk 14.21 express extreme condemnation, and his saying at Lk. 22.48 expresses shock and horror. I call that 'betrayal'.

This perfectly sound example of an Aramaic idiom makes it most unlikely that Luke made the saying up on the basis of Mk 14.21 and 14.41. It is much more probable that he has picked it up from his non-Marcan source. We have seen how impossible it is to reconstruct that, at least partly because we know that Luke edited Mark heavily, and he may well have done the same to his non-Marcan source(s). I can accordingly see no plausibility, and consequently no value, in attempting to reconstruct more extensive Aramaic source material from this part of Luke. Even this son of man saying may have reached him in Greek.

The following conclusions may therefore be drawn. Judah of Kerioth betrayed Jesus with a kiss, as recorded in Mark's narrative. Luke picked up what Jesus said at the time, probably from a Greek source which was more extensive than we can recover. The saying is a sound example of an Aramaic idiom which we have seen Jesus use on other occasions. It presupposes the normal human feeling that a kiss is an especially awful way to betray a person. The saying is nonetheless nothing like a vague generality. Together with Mk 14.21, it is a dramatic record of Jesus' rejection of the man who betrayed him.

Chapter Nine

JESUS PREDICTS HIS DEATH AND RESURRECTION

I have already discussed two of Jesus' predictions of his death which used the term (א)נש(א) בר. One of these, Mk 10.45, concluded a genuine incident in the ministry of Jesus. This began with a question from Jacob and John, who asked if they could sit on his right and left in his glory. Jesus' response took it for granted that he would indeed be in glory, with people honoured by sitting on his right and left. It thus presupposed his resurrection, presumably as part of the coming of the kingdom of God and the general resurrection of the dead. The Son of man saying briefly expounds the atoning value of his death, and asserts that Jacob and John, presumably with others, would share in his death. The theology of martyrdom underlies the whole discussion.[1] I have also discussed Mk 14.21. This is part of an accurate though abbreviated account of Jesus' final Passover with his disciples. It predicts Jesus' death in accordance with scripture, and I was able to locate some passages which will have been in Jesus' mind. It also predicts his betrayal, with very severe condemnation of the traitor.[2] Despite the general level of meaning of the term (א)נש(א) רב, both sayings make clear the fundamental importance of Jesus' death in salvation history.

As part of these discussions, I have also considered more briefly Lk. 13.31-33. Here Jesus was warned that Herod was seeking to kill him. He responded by declaring his determination to continue his ministry until his death in Jerusalem. To predict this, he used a general statement with נביא rather than (א)נש(א) בר, associating his death with that of other prophets.[3] There is another prediction of his death at Lk. 12.50, albeit in such metaphorical terms that it is difficult to squeeze additional information out of it. As the final events approached, Jesus also used the occasion of his final Passover with his disciples to offer further interpretation of his forthcoming death as an atoning sacrifice (Mk 14.22-24).[4] All these predictions hold together very well. There should be no doubt that Jesus predicted his forthcoming death in Jerusalem, and interpreted it as an atoning sacrifice which would enable God to redeem Israel. His death would thus be of fundamental importance in salvation history.

---

1.   See pp. 131–4 above; Casey, *Aramaic Sources of Mark's Gospel*, pp. 193–218.
2.   See pp. 134–6 above; Casey, *Aramaic Sources of Mark's Gospel*, pp. 233–6.
3.   Casey, *Aramaic Sources of Mark's Gospel*, pp. 188–9.
4.   See further Casey, *Aramaic Sources of Mark's Gospel*, pp. 238–42.

It is against this background that we must investigate the central group of predictions of his death and resurrection which run through the middle of Mark's Gospel (Mk 8.31; 9.31; 10.33-34). They have caused a great deal of trouble to scholars. None of the standard treatments has become generally acceptable, and an earlier attempt which I made to reconstruct one possible original behind all three sayings also met with severe criticism. Rather than defend it in its original form, I propose to make a fresh attempt.[5] There is good reason to begin from Mk 8.31: the Marcan context has inalienable features of authenticity.

Καὶ ἤρξατο διδάσκειν αὐτοὺς ὅτι δεῖ τὸν υἱὸν τοῦ ἀνθρώπου πολλὰ παθεῖν καὶ ἀποδοκιμασθῆναι ὑπὸ τῶν πρεσβυτέρων καὶ τῶν ἀρχιερέων καὶ τῶν γραμματέων καὶ ἀποκτανθῆναι καὶ μετὰ τρεῖς ἡμέρας ἀναστῆναι.

Like the other sayings in this group, this cannot be turned into a satisfactory Aramaic sentence as it stands. It contains the vital term ὁ υἱὸς τοῦ ἀνθρώπου, which goes back to the Aramaic (א)שׁנ(א) בר. As we have seen, this was a general term for 'man', and while it could be used idiomatically to refer to Jesus in particular, such examples must also have some general level of meaning. Here the problem is that the saying makes precise reference to the elders and chief priests and scribes, that is, to the circumstances of Jesus' death so specific as to preclude any general level of meaning. Peter is nonetheless portrayed as understanding this saying very clearly, and reacting in an understandable way which the church would have no reason to create:

καὶ προσλαβόμενος ὁ Πέτρος αὐτὸν ἤρξατο ἐπιτιμᾶν αὐτῷ. ὁ δὲ ἐπιστραφεὶς καὶ ἰδὼν τοὺς μαθητὰς αὐτοῦ ἐπετίμησεν Πέτρῳ καὶ λέγει, Ύπαγε ὀπίσω μου, Σατανᾶ, ὅτι οὐ φρονεῖς τὰ τοῦ θεοῦ ἀλλὰ τὰ τῶν ἀνθρώπων (Mk 8.32-33).

So serious a criticism of Peter would not be found in Mark's Gospel if it did not represent approximately what Jesus said. But if Jesus' criticism of Peter is authentic, and Peter's reaction must be equally authentic, Peter must have had something like Mk 8.31 to react to. There are therefore good reasons why something like Mk 8.31 must be authentic, and good reasons why it cannot be authentic in its present form.

The solution to this puzzle lies in repeated editing by all three evangelists of one or more genuine sayings of Jesus. This can be seen most clearly in Matthew and Luke. In the central group of Marcan predictions, Jesus predicts his resurrection μετὰ τρεῖς ἡμέρας. Every single time, both Matthew and Luke alter this to τῇ τρίτῃ ἡμέρᾳ. The reason for this is obvious: they have edited the predictions in the light of their actual stories of the resurrection, in which Jesus does rise 'on the third day', not literally 'after three days'. They also add details to the predictions of Jesus' death. For example, only Mt. 20.19 predicts crucifixion (also added to the heavily reworked Lk. 24.7). It is in this light that we must consider the increasing details of the successive predictions in Mark. So we find that only Mk 10.33-34, followed by

5. For an earlier defence of my original suggestion, see Casey, 'General, Generic and Indefinite', 43–9.

Mt. 20.19 and Lk. 18.32-33, predicts that Jesus will be handed over to the Gentiles and scourged. This too must be attributed to the evangelist rewriting the prediction in the light of what he knew of the actual story of Jesus.

We must therefore go back to Mk 8.31, the first of these predictions in Mark, and see whether we can remove detailed references to the story of Jesus' death and thereby uncover a prediction with a general level of meaning. We can begin with some main points. We have already seen that some prediction of Jesus' death must have been involved for Peter to have had something to react to. With Mark's ἀποκτανθῆναι in mind we shall be tempted to think of קטל, but we should by no means exclude מות, which lends itself more readily to a general level of meaning. We must also include 'after three days', since this does not fit a literal reference to the story of Jesus' resurrection, so בתר תלתה יומין at or near the end of the saying. We shall see that it does not have to be taken literally: rather, resurrection 'after three days' could mean after a short interval. We shall also see that the Aramaic word קום need not refer to a bodily resurrection, and that going straight to heaven was a normal way to visualize the immediate fate of the suffering righteous. We can see from the story of the rich man and Lazarus (Lk. 16.19-31) that Jesus shared this view. Equally, all men die, and it was believed that everyone would rise at the general resurrection, which Jesus believed would take place before very long. All this fits beautifully so far: Jesus predicted his death and his resurrection after three days, with a general statement using the term בר (א)נש(א), which took for granted the death of everyone and the general resurrection.

How far, then, should we go? We must eliminate ὑπὸ τῶν πρεσβυτέρων καὶ τῶν ἀρχιερέων καὶ τῶν γραμματέων, because this is too specific to the fate of Jesus and has no proper general level of meaning. We must now go back to the beginning of the saying, where we obviously keep בר (א)נש(א). Mark's first word, δεῖ, has often been eliminated on the ground that it has no precise equivalent in the Aramaic of this period, but in this context it is a perfectly reasonable translation of the Aramaic חיב, which is approximately equivalent to the English 'liable to', 'guilty of'. I have previously suggested a simple future ימות, while noting also the possibility of עתיד, which is also used here by Schwarz, or indeed חיב.[6] I have also suggested that עתיד should be posited behind δεῖ at Mk 9.11.[7] I now prefer חיב here at Mk 8.31 on the ground that it makes better sense both of the general level of meaning and of the teaching of Jesus. The term חיב is used in sayings with reference to death. For example, Hillel is credited with saying that a person who does not learn is worthy of death (דילא יליף קטלה חיב, M.Aboth I,13). Similarly, R. Aqiba is credited with saying that someone who is unwilling to serve the sages is worthy of death (קטלא חייב, y. Naz. 7,1/18 (56b)). These are not the same as our passage, but there is some similarity in the use of חייב with reference to death. It is regrettable that we do not have a full context for חובה למות at 4Q536 1 ii 12. In general, human

---

6.   Casey, *Son of Man*, p. 232; 'General, Generic and Indefinite', pp. 43–6; Schwarz, *Menschensohn*, p. 277.

7.   Casey, *Aramaic Sources of Mark's Gospel*, pp. 121, 123; 'Aramaic Background of Mark 9:11'.

beings are liable to suffer rejection and death because of the fall of man. More particularly, Jesus was predicting his own suffering, rejection by Israel and death as an atoning sacrifice. We must consider each of these points in turn.

The next words, πολλὰ παθεῖν, have often been eliminated too on the ground that παθεῖν has no precise Aramaic equivalent. However we have seen that כאב, the Hebrew word for 'suffer', was used in the Aramaic of Jesus' time.[8] Moreover, in discussing Mk 9.12, I have shown that meditation on Job 14.22, where כאב is used, will have encouraged Jesus to use it.[9] Job 14 is a rather depressive account of the life of man in general (אדם, Tg בר נש). It begins with a programmatic first verse:

אדם ילוד אשה קצר ימים ושבע רגז.
Man who is born of woman is shortlived and full of turmoil.

Job 14 ends with the verse which uses כאב, which is retained in both translations into Aramaic in the rabbinical Targum, as well as in the Peshitta:

אך בשרו עליו יכאב ונפשו עליו תאבל.
Indeed his flesh suffers upon him, and his soul mourns over him.

This gives comprehensive scriptural warrant for suffering being a normal part of a man's life. This provides a general level of meaning for the suffering of a/the son of man, which Jesus used to predict the suffering which he anticipated. So we have a good start to reconstructing Jesus' prediction:

חיב בר אנשא למכאב שגיא
A/the son of man is liable to suffer much

What about ἀποδοκιμασθῆναι? It is tempting to eliminate this, because in the present form of Mk 8.31 it is closely associated with ὑπὸ τῶν πρεσβυτέρων καὶ τῶν ἀρχιερέων καὶ τῶν γραμματέων. The rejection of the Son of man is however found also, linked with his suffering much, at Mk 9.12b:

τῶς γέγραπται ἐπὶ τὸν υἱὸν τοῦ ἀνθρώπου ἵνα πολλὰ πάθῃ καὶ ἐξουδενηθῇ.

Here the suffering and rejection of the Son of man is said to be written in scripture. Moreover, we have seen that an Aramaic reconstruction of Mk 9.12b alone makes sense of it, for the general level of meaning was used to make particular reference to John the Baptist as well as to Jesus. I also showed that this rejection should be traced back to Jer. 6.27-30; 7.29, references on either side of the passage on which Jesus preached in the Temple during his last days.[10] Rejection is mentioned as follows:

לשוא צרף צרוף ורעים לא נתקו: כסף נמאס קראו להם כי מאס יהוה בהם.
Refining he refines in vain, and the wicked are not drawn off: they shall be called rejected silver, for the LORD has rejected them (Jer. 6.29-30).

8. See p. 128 above.
9. Casey, *Aramaic Sources of Mark's Gospel*, pp. 126–8; pp. 127–8 above.
10. Casey, *Aramaic Sources of Mark's Gospel*, pp. 126–30, pp. 127–9 above; 'Cleansing of the Temple'.

כי מאס יהוה ויטש את־דור עברתו.

For the LORD has rejected and abandoned the generation of his fury (Jer. 7.29).

The implication of the use of this material at Mk 8.31 is that Jesus would be rejected by God when he died, representing the rejection of Israel, for which his death would atone. This is related to how he felt when he was crucified (Mk 15.34). Moreover, the Aramaic form of the prediction was likely to be so interpreted, because the passive was commonly used to refer indirectly to the action of God. It may well have been the translator, who may in any case have been Mark himself, who added ὑπὸ τῶν πρεσβυτέρων καὶ τῶν ἀρχιερέων καὶ τῶν γραμματέων for this very reason. There was a very obvious need for such an 'explicitative' translation, one which explains what the translator takes the text to really mean. We must therefore add the Aramaic ולתבסרה, 'and be rejected', to the prediction. This has אתבסר as the word which Jesus used to pick up מאס, and which the translator rendered καὶ ἀποδοκιμασθῆναι. It has the right semantic area. It occurs before the time of Jesus at 4Q542 1 i 6, and subsequently in several dialects, including Jewish Aramaic. It is entirely reasonable that the translator rendered it with ἀποδοκιμασθῆναι, because of the similarity of the semantic area of these two words. The Greek word ἀποδοκιμάζω renders מאס six times in the LXX, and nothing else. The use of ἐξουδενηθῇ at Mk 9.12 should not be regarded as problematical. All these words had overlapping semantic areas, and ἐξουδενέω or a similar form renders מאס sixteen times in the LXX, as well as other words, notably בזה. We should not expect our translator(s) to have been uniform when the text in front of us has two different words with similar semantic areas and an intelligible linguistic and cultural background.

We can now pass to the next words, καὶ ἀποκτανθῆναι. We have seen that the original prediction must have included Jesus' death, as only this will explain Peter's reaction and Jesus' rebuke of him. The present form of Mk 8.31 in Greek, however, stretches the general level of meaning too far, precisely in its use of ἀποκτανθῆναι. Although it is literally true that we are all *liable* to be put to death, this does not produce anything like as good a general level of meaning as the obvious fact that we are all liable to die. It is therefore better to suppose that this too is an explicitative translation. Jesus will have said ולממת, 'and die', and the translator, knowing the passion story, will have translated this καὶ ἀποκτανθῆναι, a relatively early stage in clarifying Jesus' original prediction(s) in the light of subsequent events. In the LXX, the verb מות used of someone who will be put to death is similarly rendered both with ἀποκτείνω (e.g. Deut. 22.22,25) and with θανατόω (e.g. Exod. 21.14; 1 Sam. 14.45).

The obvious fact that we all die is also scripturally based. The most basic text is the narrative of the fall of man, who is consequently subject to death (Gen. 3.19,22, cf. e.g. *4 Ezra* 3.7; 7.11-16,78). I have also drawn attention to Jesus meditating on Job 14, which extensively presents the death of man. The word לממת accordingly provides an excellent general level of meaning, which Jesus used in order to predict his own death, as we have seen him do elsewhere.

We now have this:

חייב בר אנשא למכאב שגיא ולתבסרה ולממת

A/the son of man is liable to suffer much and be rejected and die.

This leaves resurrection after three days, and we have already seen that this part of the prediction must be genuine. The Aramaic word קום has a very wide range of meaning, including any sort of rising or getting up. For example, it may be used of getting up literally, as e.g. at Dan. 6.20, where יקום is used of Darius getting out of bed in the morning. This usage is found in the life of Jesus at Mk 5.41, where he takes a sick girl by the hand and tells her κουμ, the Aramaic קום, transliterated and then correctly translated ἔγειρε. It is thus a natural word for rising from sleep, as for example at y. AZ 2,3/7(41a) where a woman's husband got up from sleep: קם בעלה מן שינתיה. More generally, it may be used of coming into existence, as e.g. at Dan. 7.24, where יקמון is used of ten kings who will arise in turn to rule over the fourth kingdom. Equally, it may be used of remaining in existence, as e.g. at Dan. 2.44, where it is said of the kingdom of God תקום לעלמיא, meaning that it will remain in existence for ever. It is accordingly an obvious word to use for rising from the dead, whether what we think of as resurrection of the body or immortality of the soul is really in mind. For example, R. Joḥanan is said to have contemplated what might happpen to him, commenting אין קמית ביני צדיקיא, 'If I rise among the righteous', or on the other hand אין קמית ביני רשיעיא, 'If I rise among the wicked', (y. Kil 9,4/6(32b)). The word קום itself does not tell us the relationship of his body or soul, or whatever was left of him, to the resurrection process.

We must accordingly turn next to contemporary Jewish beliefs in survival after death.[11] Jewish documents of our period put forward more than one view of survival after death, and their comments appear to be related to the situation which they consider, rather than to concepts held by them. They tend to put forward something like a view of resurrection when they consider the general resurrection at which Israel or the righteous will finally be vindicated. When they consider the fate of individuals at death, however, they generally make comments which are more akin to our concept of immortality.

For example, Dan. 12.1-3 portrays the end of all things, and envisages the resurrection of many people at a single moment of time. The reference to their sleeping in the dusty ground implies that their graves will be empty, though this is not explicitly stated. This event is placed in the future, though in apocalyptic literature this means in the very near future. Contrast Josephus' account of the belief of the Pharisees, when he considers the fate of people at death.

ἀθάνατόν τε ἰσχὺν ταῖς ψυχαῖς πίστις αὐτοῖς ἐῖναι καὶ ὑπὸ χθονὸς δικαιώσεις τε καὶ τιμὰς οἷς ἀρετῆς ἢ κακίας ἐπιτήδευσις ἐν τῷ βίῳ γέ γονεν, καὶ ταῖς μὲν εἰργμὸν ἀίδιον προτίθεσθαι, ταῖς δὲ ῥαστώνην τοῦ ἀναβιοῦν.

---

11.   For this, I am indebted to S. H. Schagen, 'Concepts of Resurrection and Immortality in Intertestamental Judaism and in the New Testament' (unpublished doctoral dissertation, Nottingham University, 1985). Dr Schagen is not however responsible for the use which I have made of her work.

They hold a belief that souls have power to survive death, and under the earth there are rewards and punishments for those who have led lives of virtue or wickedness. Some receive eternal punishment, while others pass easily to live again (*Ant.* XVIII, 14).

Here we find no mention of the resurrection of the body, but only the continued existence of souls. There is no indication of any kind of pause after death before a final judgement: the natural interpretation is that the soul goes to its eternal fate at once.

Some documents imply both an immediate and a final judgement. *1 En.* 22 classifies the dead in terms of righteousness and wickedness, including one group of sinners in a particular compartment for those who have already been punished. There will nonetheless be a final judgement, when other sinners will enter very great torment, but those who have already been punished will not rise. Some documents introduce clear concepts to deal with specific problems. For example, *4 Ezra* has the disembodied souls of the righteous received at once by God, spend seven days contemplating their fate and the universe, and then go to chambers in the underworld to await their resurrection and vindication at the last judgement. As a document, however, *4 Ezra* is hardly consistent on its own major problem, the salvation of the chosen people. The agonizing Chs 3–10 imply the damnation of most Jews because they have not kept the Law up to orthodox standards, while the visions of Chs 11–13 resolve this problem by their vigorous portrayal of the salvation of Israel. Evidence of this kind should lead us to a more general conclusion. The concepts which Jewish people used at the time of Jesus to cope with death and with the destiny of Israel were variable, and liable to a degree of obscurity, change and inconsistency beyond those which modern scholars regard as tolerable when they see them in others.

The meagre evidence of the Gospels suggests that Jesus shared the attitude to resurrection and immortality characteristic of Jews who believed in survival after death. For example, in answer to an awkward question from the Sadducees, Jesus assumed that there will be an occasion when the dead rise. His saying may readily be reconstructed in Aramaic:

כדי יקומון מן מיתיא לא נסבין נשים ולא מתנסבן, אלא כמלאכין בשמיא אנון.

For when they rise from the dead they neither take wives nor are taken, but they are like angels in the heavens.

The natural assumption is that they rise on a particular occasion, and Jesus conspicuously fails to say that they will not have bodies at a point where such a conception would have been helpful to his argument. On the other hand, the parable of the rich man and Lazarus (Lk. 16.19-31) pictures the fate of the righteous and the wicked at death. Consequently, there is no pause in time before they pass to bliss and torment respectively, and it is clear they have not left their tombs empty. Nor presumably did father Abraham, who was already in the next world with powers to send a messenger from the dead if he wished. This process is described at Lk. 16.30, ἐάν τις ἐκ νεκρῶν πορευθῇ, and at 16.31 ἐάν τις ἐκ νεκρῶν πορευθῇ. This latter expression must represent Jesus' use of קום with respect to a dead person who has passed to his eternal fate at once returning to earth to visit people who are still alive. This further indicates how broadly קום might be used. The strength of Jesus' belief in survival after death is illustrated by his supposedly crushing argument against the Sadducees, who did not hold any belief of this kind. He argued from the nature of God himself. God is so clearly the God of the living (cf. Jer. 10.10) that his declaration to Moses 'I am the God of Abraham and the God of Isaac and the God of Jacob' (Exod. 3.6, 15, 16) is held to demonstrate the survival of Abraham, Isaac and Jacob, and thereby the raising of the dead (Mk 12.26-7).[12]

It follows that Jesus' use of קום in this prediction shows that he expected God to vindicate him by raising him from the dead. His use of קום does not however indicate when or how this would take place. Can we get more from μετὰ τρεῖς ἡμέρας?[13] We have already seen that this must be an authentic part of the prediction. Matthew and Luke consistently altered it because, if interpreted literally, it does not fit their stories of Jesus' tomb being empty earlier than that. A second reason complements this. In some passages, 'three days' seems to mean little more than a short interval. So, for example, Jonah was in the belly of a big fish for three days and three nights (Jon. 2.1), but nothing is made of so precise a measurement, which seems to indicate simply a short interval. At Acts 28.7,12,17 we might believe in three precise three-day intervals in such a short narrative, but it may be that here too we should more vaguely understand 'a short time'. Moreover, a more certainly general interpretation of 'after three days' may be deduced from midrashic sayings which declare that Israel, or the righteous, will not be left in distress for more than three days, a view supported with several passages of scripture. One such occasion is the last days, when deliverance will be by means of the resurrection. For example Gen.R. LVI,1 comments on Gen. 22.4, beginning with a quotation of Hos. 6.2, and having the following among the examples:

> … on the third day of Jonah, 'and Jonah was in the belly of the fish three days' (Jon. 2.1): on the third day of those returning from the exile, 'and we dwelt there for three days' (Ezra 8.32): on the third day of the resurrection of the dead, 'After two days he will revive us, on the third day he will raise us up and we shall live before him' (Hos. 6.2).

Similarly, Est.R. IX,2 comments on Est. 5.1:

> Israel are never left in dire distress for more than three days … of Jonah it says, 'And Jonah was in the belly of the fish three days and three nights' (Jon. 2.1). The dead also will come to life only after three days, as it says, 'On the third day he will raise us up, and we shall live before him' (Hos. 6.2).

---

12.   Cf. F. G. Downing, 'The Resurrection of the Dead: Jesus and Philo', *JSNT* 15 (1982), pp. 42–50; P. Lapide, *The Resurrection of Jesus* (London: SPCK, 1984), pp. 59–63; O. Schwankl, *Die Sadduzaerfrage (Mk 12, 18-27 parr)* (Frankfurt: Athenäum, 1987).

13.   See esp. J. Jeremias, 'Die Drei-Tage-Worte der Evangelien', in G. Jeremias *et al.* (eds) *Tradition und Glaube. Das frühe Christentum in seiner Umwelt. Festgabe für K. G. Kuhn zum 65. Geburtstag* (Göttingen: Vandenhoeck & Ruprecht, 1971); H. K. McArthur, 'On the Third Day', *NTS* 18 (1971), pp. 81–6.

If 'three days' is interpreted like this, the general resurrection could be expected 'after three days'. It is especially to be noted that these passages do not seem to mind whether scripture says 'on the third day' or 'after three days', which is natural if a short interval is really what is meant.

These midrashic passages are however of very late date. It is accordingly of particular importance that three other sayings of Jesus use the three-day interval in a similar metaphorical sense. I have noted Lk. 13.32-33:[14]

32 ואמר להון, הלכו אמרו לתעלא דנה, הא, מפק שידין אנה ומשלם אסותא יומא דן ויום אחרן ובתליתיא שלם אנה.

33 ברם עתיד אנה מהלך יומא דן ויום בתר יום, כי לא יאי לנביה דיאבד ברא מן ירושלם.

[32]And he said to them, 'Go tell that jackal, Look! I am casting out demons and performing healings to-day and tomorrow, and on the third day I am perfected.

[33]But I am going to proceed to-day and day after day, for it is not fitting for a prophet to perish outside Jerusalem.'

In the first of these sayings, Jesus used a more elaborate version of the three-day interval to look forward to his death on the third day. In the second saying, he used another more elaborate version of the three-day interval, effectively to look forward to his death after three days. This underlines the obviously metaphorical use of these three-day intervals. At Mk 14.58, a more difficult saying, both in its interpretation and in the question of its authenticity, he is reported to have said he would build a temple not made with hands διὰ τριῶν ἡμερῶν. At a more literal level, three days is just long enough to ensure that a person was really dead (cf. Jn 11.39; b. Sem VIII,1; Lev. R. XVIII,1). We may conclude that, in the original saying, Jesus probably meant that he would be vindicated in the general resurrection, which would take place after a short interval. The way in which he put it was however rather opaque, and eminently capable of reinterpretation after his death.

We must therefore conclude that Jesus said something very like this:

חיב בר אנשא למכאב שגיא ולתבסרה ולממת ולמקם בתר תלתה ימוין.

A/the son of man is liable to suffer much and be rejected and die, and rise after three days.

Given the cultural background in the Jewish scriptures sketched above, this has a perfectly good general level of meaning. The first part of the saying refers to the effects of the fall of man, and we have seen that man's suffering and rejection, as well as his death, were written in the scriptures. Jesus could also rely on widespread belief in the resurrection of the dead. His assertion that this would take place 'after three days', in the metaphorical sense of after a short interval, is of a piece with his expectation that the kingdom of God would come in the near future. This general level of meaning also helps to explain how Jacob and John might participate in his death (Mk 10.35-40), and how Peter and other disciples might contemplate dying with him (Mk 14.31).[15] At the same time, the established nature of this idiomatic use of בר (א)נש(א) was sufficient to ensure that everyone would realize that Jesus was

---

14.   Casey, *Aramaic Sources of Mark's Gospel*, pp. 188–9.
15.   See further pp. 129–36 above.

referring primarily to himself. The humiliating nature of suffering, being rejected and put to death, on the one hand, and the central importance of his death in God's plan followed by his vindication through resurrection, all this made the use of this particular idiom especially appropriate.

This primary reference to Jesus himself explains Peter's immediate reaction. He did not start complaining about the fall of man! He obviously objected to Jesus' intention to die, and there is no mention of the death of anyone else. Jesus' ferocious reaction makes the same assumption. We must therefore accept the authenticity of this prediction in something very close to the form which I have constructed. This was Jesus' first prediction of his death and resurrection, and it was very important both at the time and later.

The next major prediction is at Mk 9.31:

Ὁ υἱὸς τοῦ ἀνθρώπου παραδίδοται εἰς χεῖρας ἀνθρώπων, καὶ ἀποκτενοῦσιν αὐτόν, καὶ ἀποκτανθεὶς μετὰ τρεῖς ἡμέρας ἀναστήσεται.

The authenticity of this saying has often been defended, sometimes with reference to a partial Aramaic reconstruction. In a brief but influential treatment, Jeremias suggested a possible original:

mitmᵉsar bar ᵉnāšā līdē bᵉnē ᵉnāšā.
God will (soon) deliver up the man to men.

Jeremias described this as 'a *māšāl*, a riddle, simply because *bar ᵉnāšā* can be understood either as a title or generically.' He regarded this as 'the ancient nucleus which underlies the passion prediction'.[16] This should no be accepted. בר (א)נשׂ(א) was an ordinary term for man, and does not offer the alternative of being a title. Without a much clearer context, the general level of meaning does not make proper sense. If the above reconstruction from Mk 8.31 is even approximately correct (Jeremias did not accept that), it is difficult to see why Jesus should offer this riddle after a prediction so clear that Peter objected to it at once. It also omits the reference to resurrection, part of the prediction in common with Mk 8.31 which we have seen good reason to defend.

Lindar's attempt is even shorter:

Ithmesar bar enasha
A man may be delivered up …[17]

Here the modal 'may' is part of the English translation, not of the text, and it is difficult to see why אתמסר should be rendered with the present tense παραδίδοται. Moreover, even as an original basis for longer sayings, this is too short to be fruitful.

When we consider this saying as a whole, we should conclude that an Aramaic reconstruction is not possible.[18] The first part does not make proper sense, and καὶ

16. Jeremias, *New Testament Theology*, p. 282; similarly e.g. Hampel, *Menschensohn*, pp. 288–300.
17. Lindars, *Son of Man*, p. 68.
18. For detailed discussion of what happens if one tries, and what is wrong with the result, see Casey, 'General, Generic and Indefinite', 46–9.

ἀποκτανθείς is too Greek for an Aramaic reconstruction, especially following ἀποκτενοῦσιν αὐτόν. At the same time, Ὁ υἱὸς τοῦ ἀνθρώπου παραδίδοται, the opening of the saying at Mk 9.31, is found at Mk 14.21, the authenticity of which I have defended: καὶ ἀποκτενοῦσιν αὐτόν, καὶ ἀποκτανθείς is an elaborate version of καὶ ἀποκτανθῆναι at Mk 8.31, where I argued that it is a translation of וימיתהו: and the very end of Mk 9.31, μετὰ τρεῖς ἡμέρας ἀναστήσεται, is close to καὶ μετὰ τρεῖς ἡμέρας ἀναστῆναι, which I defended as part of a prediction underlying Mk 8.31. The remaining words, εἰς χεῖρας ἀνθρώπων, are fairly close to ביד ... אנש in another authentic Son of man saying at Mk 14.21, and to εἰς τὰς χεῖρας τῶν ἁμαρτωλῶν in another Son of man saying at Mk 14.41. We must infer that Mk 9.31 was written by Mark on the basis of existing traditions which were available to him.

We must make the same inference for Mk 9.32: οἱ δὲ ἠγνόουν τὸ ῥῆμα, καὶ ἐφοβοῦντο αὐτὸν ἐπερωτῆσαι. If the prediction of 9.31 is due to Marcan editing, the disciples' reaction to it must be likewise. On historical grounds, the incident does not make good sense. We have seen that when Jesus first predicted his death at Mk 8.31, Peter understood him immediately and reacted memorably. By 10.35-40, Jacob and John understand that their request to sit on his right and left in his glory entails that they share his death. That in the meantime Jesus made another prediction of his death and resurrection, and none of the inner circle of three nor any of the others understood him and were too afraid to ask, is not plausible. It fits very well, however, into Mark's regrettable and influential view of the disciples' lack of understanding. We must infer that Mark wished to present another prediction by Jesus of his death and resurrection, but that he rewrote the tradition because he did not have a prediction other than that underlying Mk 8.31 to present at that point.

This result is confirmed at Mk 10.33-34:

Ἰδοὺ ἀναβαίνομεν εἰς Ἱεροσόλυμα, καὶ ὁ υἱὸς τοῦ ἀνθρώπου παραδοθήσεται τοῖς ἀρχιερεῦσιν καὶ τοῖς γραμματεῦσιν, καὶ κατακρινοῦσιν αὐτὸν θανάτῳ καὶ παραδώσουσιν αὐτὸν τοῖς ἔθνεσιν καὶ ἐμπαίξουσιν αὐτῷ καὶ ἐμπτύσουσιν αὐτῷ καὶ μαστιγώσουσιν αὐτὸν καὶ ἀποκτενοῦσιν, καὶ μετὰ τρεῖς ἡμέρας ἀναστήσεται.

Here again, even more obviously than at Mk 9.31, there is no possibility of reconstructing an adequate Aramaic original of the prediction as a whole. Moreover, we can see where the details have come from. ὁ υἱὸς τοῦ ἀνθρώπου is from Mk 8.31 and 9.31. παραδοθήσεται is an improvement on παραδίδοται at 9.31. τοῖς ἀρχιερεῦσιν καὶ τοῖς γραμματεῦσιν replaces the Semitic εἰς χεῖρας ἀνθρώπων at 9.31 in light of ὑπὸ τῶν πρεσβυτέρων καὶ τῶν ἀρχιερέων καὶ τῶν γραμματέων at 8.31. The words καὶ ἀποκτενοῦσιν are from 9.31, and everything in between these last two rewrites, καὶ κατακρινοῦσιν αὐτὸν θανάτῳ καὶ παραδώσουσιν αὐτὸν τοῖς ἔθνεσιν καὶ ἐμπαίξουσιν αὐτῷ καὶ ἐμπτύσουσιν αὐτῷ καὶ μαστιγώσουσιν αὐτόν, all this is *vaticinium ex eventu* based on the actual events of the passion. μετὰ τρεῖς ἡμέρας ἀναστήσεται, is identical to the end of Mk 9.31. Once again, therefore, we must conclude that Mark wanted to present another prediction of Jesus' death and resurrection, but that he did not have a satisfactory alternative to Mk 8.31 to present.

This also makes excellent sense of context. We are told that they were on their way up to Jerusalem, and Jesus went ahead, καὶ ἐθαμβοῦντο, οἱ δὲ ἀκολουθοῦντες ἐφοβοῦντο (Mk 10.32). While there may be some truth in this, ἐφοβοῦντο is the same as at Mk 9.32, and it does not make historical sense of the behaviour of Jacob and John in the very next pericope, where they are obviously neither amazed nor frightened. Again, however, it makes excellent sense of the Marcan theme of the disciples' lack of understanding.

The following conclusions may therefore be drawn. Mk 8.31 is a somewhat explicitative translation of a genuine prediction by Jesus of his suffering, death and resurrection after a short interval. We have its original context as the first such prediction by Jesus, for it led directly to Peter's attempt to rebuke him, and that led directly to Jesus' severe rebuke of Peter. It was a very important prediction at the time, and was treated as such during the later transmission of the tradition. Mark presents Jesus as predicting his death and resurrection repeatedly. His other predictions at 9.31 and 10.33-34, however, were written by him in the light of Mark 8.31, the authentic prediction at 14.21, and the actual events of the passion. It remains possible that Jesus gave different versions of the prediction which we can reconstruct from Mk 8.31, and that what Mark did not like about them is that, like Mk 8.31 itself, they were not specific enough for the later part of his narrative. All we can be sure of is that we have one prediction which was of fundamental importance, and that it was subsequently rewritten.

Chapter Ten

OTHER SYNOPTIC SAYINGS

The purpose of this chapter is to argue that the remaining Son of man sayings in the synoptic tradition, i.e. those not discussed in Chs 4–9, are not authentic sayings of Jesus. They are the work of the early church, or the editorial contribution of the evangelists, or some combination of the two. I begin with the two largest complexes of material, which are centred on Matthew 24, and on Luke 17 and 21. Both include vigorous editorial work by these two evangelists, each of whom used some Q material.

1. Matthew 24

The first 36 verses of Matthew 24 are for the most part his edited version of Mk 13.1-32. Both chapters are rightly famous as eschatological discourses, each of which reflects to a considerable degree the interests of the early church rather than the preaching of the historical Jesus.

The first important piece of Matthean editing relevant for present purposes is at v. 3. Mark has a question put by the inner group of three, Peter, Jacob and John, together with Peter's brother Andrew: πότε ταῦτα ἔσται, καὶ τί τὸ σημεῖον ὅταν μέλλῃ ταῦτα συντελεῖσθαι πάντα; Matthew made the second part of this question, which he attributes to 'the disciples', much more precise: πότε ταῦτα ἔσται, καὶ τί τὸ σημεῖον τῆς σῆς παρουσίας καὶ συντελείας τοῦ αἰῶνος; the first expression refers to the events associated with the destruction of Jerusalem, and the last makes clear that these events are the final eschatological ones. Among them, we have Matthew's own phrase τῆς σῆς παρουσίας.

The word παρουσία is used only in Mt. 24 in the whole of the synoptic Gospels. All the other three examples refer clearly to ἡ παρουσία τοῦ υἱοῦ τοῦ ἀνθρώπου (24.27,37,39), and all four refer to Jesus' second coming at the end of all things. The expression τὸ σημεῖον τῆς σῆς παρουσίας refers forward particularly to τὸ σημεῖον τοῦ υἱοῦ τοῦ ἀνθρώπου ἐν οὐρανῷ among the final events at Mt. 24.30. The term παρουσία has no natural Aramaic equivalent, as the efforts of the Syriac versions to translate it indicate: מתיתה (sin), מאתיתה (pesh hark) or מיתיותה (palsyrlec) at 24.27, and similarly elsewhere. The underlying verb אתה is common in all kinds of Aramaic from the earliest times through to the modern period, but this noun מ(א)תיתא is specific to Syriac, which has more abstract nouns of this kind than other ancient Aramaic dialects. The possibility that מ(א)תיאת was there for Jesus to use in first-century Israel may therefore safely be excluded. What is more, the term παρουσία has an excellent *Sitz im Leben* in the Greek-speaking church. While it naturally continued to be used of the appearance of real people in the here and now (e.g. 1 Cor. 16.17), some New Testament authors use it with clear reference to the second coming of Jesus in the last days. Paul uses it at the beginning of his graphic picture of the second coming at 1 Thess. 4.15, where he refers reassuringly to himself and his audience as ἡμεῖς οἱ ζῶντες οἱ περιλειπόμενοι εἰς τὴν παρουσὰν τοῦ κυρίου. Other references are less graphic but equally clear: 1 Cor. 15.23; 1 Thess. 2.19, 3.13, 5.23; 2 Thess. 2.1. Jacob also uses the phrase ἡ παρουσία τοῦ κυρίου (Jas 5.7-8). Similar usage of παρουσία is also preserved in 2 Peter (1.16; 3.4) and 1 John (2.28). It follows that Matthew's use of παρουσία is part of his own presentation of the second coming of Jesus, which was such an important part of the belief system of the early church. We shall see that his particular expression ἡ παρουσία τοῦ υἱοῦ τοῦ ἀνθρώπου results from combining it with a term which was of central importance to Gospel traditions in particular.

Another important piece of editing is at Mt. 24.15, where Matthew elaborates the perceived prophecy and retains the request for interpretation beyond the confines of his text:῞Οταν οὖν ἴδητε τὸ βδέλυγμα τῆς ἐρημώσεως τὸ ῥηθὲν διὰ Δανιὴλ τοῦ προφήτου ἑστὸς ἐν τόπῳ ἁγίῳ, ὁ ἀναγινώσκων νοείτω .... The abomination of desolation is mentioned at Dan. 9.27; 11.31; 12.11. It has obviously been updated and interpreted eschatologically. There would be no difficulty in seeing the destruction of the Temple, foretold at Mt. 24.2, in an updated interpretation of Dan. 9.26-27. Interpretative material of this kind is covered by retaining the phrase ὁ ἀναγινώσκων νοείτω. This is the situation from which Matthew urges people in Judaea to flee. He also expands the instruction to pray that their flight does not take place in winter, with μηδὲ σαββάτῳ (Mt. 24.20). This shows what a serious part of early Christianity Judaism still was when this Gospel was written, and it is one of the indications that we should prefer an earlier date than is conventional.

As so often, Matthew amalgamates his Q material with his Marcan source, inserting vv. 26-28 in between his editing of Mk 13.23 and 13.24. By this stage, he has taken over from Mark the prediction that this would be the worst period of distress in human history (Mt. 24.21). He also retains from Mark enough of the language of Dan. 12.1 to make clear that he followed the western interpretation of that passage.[1] Its actualizing exegesis constantly updated the whole text of Dan. 7, 9-12, so that this prediction of disaster remained in the future. Matthew also follows Mark in the comment that God will shorten the days to prevent the extinction of humankind (Mt. 24.24 from Mk 13.20). This makes it clear that, apart from the destruction of Jerusalem, the last times will see large-scale human casualties. This sets up the following Q passage, Mt. 24.28 (//Lk. 21.27). Matthew takes also from Mark the prediction of false Christs and false prophets (Mt. 24.24 from Mk 13.22).

---

1.   On the western interpretation of Daniel 7, see Casey, *Son of Man*, Ch. 4.

We know from other evidence that this was a genuinely serious problem. For example, Josephus has this account of Theudas:

> When Fadus was procurator of Judaea, a certain impostor (γόης) called Theudas persuaded most of the masses to take up their possessions and follow him to the river Jordan. For he said he was a prophet, and that he would part the river by his command and provide an easy passage for them. With these words he deceived many people. Fadus, however, did not allow them to benefit from their folly, but sent out against them a troop of cavalry, which fell on them unexpectedly and killed many, and took many alive. They captured Theudas himself, cut off his head and took it to Jerusalem (*Ant.* XX. 97-8).

This has everything that Matthew was concerned about. Like Josephus, who calls him γόης, Matthew would obviously regard Theudas as a ψευδοπροφήτης. He promised signs and wonders, deceived many, and took them into the wilderness, which Matthew warns against in the following Q passage (Mt. 24.26). The result of this was disastrous for Theudas' followers, as well as for him.

Matthew's prediction of false Christs and false prophets begins with a slightly edited version of Mark's warning not to believe anyone who says where the Christ is (Mt. 24.23). This neatly sets up the opening of the Q passage (Mt. 24.26). The parallel to Mt. 24.26-28 at Lk. 17.23-24,37 is close enough for us to infer that we are dealing with common source material. The differences between Matthew and Luke are however so great that we must recognize also that there has been heavy editing. These differences are of such a kind that they cannot possibly be explained as resulting from two Greek translations of a common Aramaic source. They have resulted from extensive editing by the evangelists. Nowhere is this more obvious than with Matthew's expression ἡ παρουσία τοῦ υἱοῦ τοῦ ἀνθρώπου (Mt. 24.27). It also appears to be true of the opening Q saying: ἐὰν οὖν εἴπωσιν ὑμῖν, Ἰδοὺ ἐν τῇ ἐρήμῳ ἐστίν, μὴ ἐξέλθητε· Ἰδοὺ ἐν τοῖς ταμείοις, μὴ πιστεύσητε (Mt. 24.26). Here ἐὰν + subj. and μὴ πιστεύσητε are the same as at Mt. 24.23//Mk 13.21, from which they have presumably been taken to form a clear connecting link. Having had ὧδε ... ὧδε at Mt. 24.23, Matthew now elaborates with ἐν τῇ ἐρήμῳ: we have seen from Theudas how appropriate that is. His second elaboration is ἐν τοῖς ταμείοις, 'in the inner rooms'. This has puzzled some of the commentators, but it forms an excellent rhetorical contrast with ἐν τῇ ἐρήμῳ. It also makes perfectly good sense of people hoping that someone of royal breed would emerge from an aristocratic palace to lead the nation back to victory.

Black suggested that a translator may have misread the Aramaic *be'idrayya*, from the Aramaic *'idar, 'idra*, 'threshing floor', 'area', 'assembly', 'congregation', 'Sanhedrin', so that the original meaning behind ἐν τοῖς ταμείοις was 'in the Assemblies', 'in the Sanhedrin'. This was misread as *be'idronayya* 'in inner rooms', and this is how it came to be translated ἐν τοῖς ταμείοις.[2] This suggestion should not be accepted. In the first place, as we have seen, the text makes perfectly good sense as it stands. Secondly, Black's procedure embodies a common error of method.

---

2.   M. Black, 'The Aramaic Dimension in Q with Notes on Luke 17.22 and Matthew 24.26 (Luke 17.23)', *JSNT* 40 (1990), pp. 33–41 (39).

He did not like the text, so he posited a change of a single word. This is not enough to show that the saying ever existed in Aramaic, let alone in its present form in a passage where Matthew is editing heavily. Thirdly, the word אדר is not attested with the right meaning anything like early enough, and not certainly attested with this meaning at all. It is attested in early Aramaic, and derived from the Akkadian *adru*, with the meaning 'threshing-floor', as at Dan. 2.35. It is well attested later in Jewish Palestinian Aramaic, Samaritan Aramaic, Christian Palestinian Aramaic and Syriac, still meaning 'threshing-floor', and sometimes with the slightly extended meaning 'barn', 'granary'. Black's attempt to justify his proposed meaning from Tg. Prov. 27.22 is not satisfactory. This Targum is too late and wayward to count on its own as evidence of first-century usage in Israel. Moreover, Black does not offer the detailed discussion necessary to justify either his reading *be'idrak* or his interpretation of this difficult verse. Accordingly, Black's suggestion is methodologically and empirically unsatisfactory. We must not proceed like this.

Matthew has also elaborated the lightning saying from Q: ὥσπερ γὰρ ἡ ἀστραπὴ ἐξέρχεται ἀπὸ ἀνατολῶν καὶ φαίνεται ἕως δυσμῶν, οὕτως ἔσται ἡ παρουσία τοῦ υἱοῦ τοῦ ἀνθρώπου. Lightning is always rapid and sometimes destructive. The immediate context suggests that both features are in view. The rapidity of the Son of man's appearance makes it pointless to look in the desert or in inner rooms for him. The whole passage Mt. 24.23-27 makes sense only if we assume that the Son of man is the Christ, a point which is meant to be obvious by this stage of the Gospel, and which was stated with especial clarity and emphasis in Matthew's version of Peter's confession (Mt. 16.13-20). Accordingly, the function of this comment is to warn people that the parousia will be so rapid and visible that all the stories of the Messiah being somewhere to be found can be known to be false in the meantime. The saying also looks forward to the description of the parousia in the following verses, where the sign of the Son of man φανήσεται … ἐν οὐρανῷ (Mt. 24.30), another strong parallel with lightning. Matthew has also retained from Q the saying, 'Where the corpse is, there the vultures will gather' (Mt. 24.28). The use of ἀετοί rather than the more technical γῦπες has caused trouble, and Jeremias was led to declare a mistranslation of the Aramaic נשרא, which means both 'eagle' and 'vulture'.[3] This is not however necessary, since vultures were more generally thought of as a kind of eagle (Aristotle, *Hist. an.* 9.32; Pliny, *N.H.* 10.3), so this cannot function as evidence that the saying once existed in Aramaic. In its literal sense, the saying is obviously true. It also fits with the picture of mass destruction which I have noted at Mt. 24.22 (from Mk 13.20), and which we shall find again in the next bit of Q (Mt. 24.37-39//Lk. 17.26-27). It could possibly also be a second image indicating that the coming of the Son of man will be publicly obvious.

Matthew now moves back to Mark for his picture of the actual parousia itself. This is based on midrashic use of Old Testament texts, with the Son of man from Dan. 7.13 at its climax: καὶ ὄψονται τὸν υἱὸν τοῦ ἀνθρώπου ἐρχόμενον ἐπὶ

---

3.   J. Jeremias, *The Parables of Jesus* (trans. S. H. Hooke. London: SCM, 2nd edn, 1963), p. 162 n. 46.

τῶν νεφελῶν τοῦ οὐρανοῦ μετὰ δυνάμεως καὶ δόξης πολλῆς. Two small changes from Mk 13.26 show Matthew deliberately and consciously using the text of Dan. 7.13 himself: the replacement of ἐν with ἐπί as at LXX Dan. 7.13, and the addition of τοῦ οὐρανοῦ. Matthew has accordingly taken over the western Christian interpretation of the man-like figure of Dan. 7.13, just as he has the western interpretation of Dan. 9.26-27 at Mt. 24.15. This not only puts the event in the eschatological future, it also identifies the man-like figure as Jesus at his second coming, rather than as a symbol of the Saints of the Most High. Matthew's conscious use of Dan. 7.13 is quite crucial for understanding his view of his major title ὁ υἱὸς τοῦ ἀνθρώπου. From his point of view, it is a *scriptural* title. It is also a scriptural title with a *context*, what Matthew calls ἡ παρουσία τοῦ υἱοῦ τοῦ ἀνθρώπου (Mt. 24.27,37,39). Thirdly, it is absolutely clear from his use of Mark that in using this title in describing the parousia in scriptural terms, Matthew was working in *Greek*. We have already seen that in describing the occasion as ἡ παρουσία τοῦ υἱοῦ τοῦ ἀνθρώπου, Matthew was working in Greek. From Matthew's perspective, therefore, this is a *Greek* title. It follows that, as in the church Fathers, the uniqueness of the Greek expression ὁ υἱὸς τοῦ ἀνθρώπου was already perceived as part of the uniqueness of Jesus, not as a problem.

Matthew's love of this unique title is especially well illustrated by his insertion of it in another Son of man saying at Mt. 24.30, making midrashic use of Isa. 11.12, which does not contain this term: καὶ τότε φανήσεται τὸ σημεῖον τοῦ υἱοῦ τοῦ ἀνθρώπου ἐν οὐρανῷ ... . Isaiah 11 is a well-known messianic chapter. Already at v. 10 we find ἐπ' αὐτῷ ἔθνη ἐλπιοῦσιν. Then at v. 12 we find the phrase which was climactic for Matthew: καὶ ἀρεῖ σημεῖον εἰς τὰ ἔθνη. The phrase εἰς τὰ ἔθνη has been expanded by Matthew with κόψονται πᾶσαι αἱ φυλαὶ τῆς γῆς, using Zech. 12.10-14, of which he will have been reminded by ὄψονται at Mk 13.26. In Isa. 11, the raising of the σημεῖον is immediately followed by the gathering (συνάξει) of people from Israel and Judah from the four corners of the earth, which will have been for Matthew the same event as he describes as the gathering of the elect at Mt. 24.31, directly editing Mk 13.27. Thus the σημεῖον fits perfectly into the context of both Isa. 11 and Mt. 24, so there should be no doubt that Isa. 11.12 is the midrashic basis of the additional Son of man saying.

The σημεῖον is based on the Jewish custom of raising an ensign, or totem, on a hill, and sounding a shofar, as a call to battle.[4] The Hebrew for the ensign was נס, often translated with σημεῖον, as here at Isa. 11.12, where the Hebrew text has ונשא נס לגוים (Tg ויזקוף את לעממיא; Pesh ונשקול אתא לעממא). Matthew has added in the trumpet at Mt. 24.31, perhaps using Isa. 27.13, for in both passages the sounding of the trumpet is followed immediately by the gathering of the exiles. The same complex of hope is found in the tenth benediction:

---

4.   For detailed discussion, see J. A. Draper, 'The Development of "the Sign of the Son of Man" in the Jesus Tradition', *NTS* 39 (1993), pp. 1–21.

> Blow the great *shofar* for our freedom and raise an ensign (נס) to gather our exiles. Blessed art thou, Lord, who gathers the dispersed of his people Israel.[5]

Accordingly, Matthew's σημεῖον fits perfectly into his Jewish culture and into the scriptural sources of his creative midrash. It is doubly remarkable that he has chosen to describe it as τὸ σημεῖον τοῦ υἱοῦ τοῦ ἀνθρώπου. This further underlines the importance of the title ὁ υἱὸς τοῦ ἀνθρώπου to him.

After this graphic picture of the second coming, Matthew reproduces Mark's comments on the nearness of the end, with very little alteration (Mt. 24.32-36, editing Mk 13.28-32). He reinforces the warning that no one knows the exact time of the End, not even the angels or the Son, but only the Father, by adding the word μόνος, so ending with the very forceful εἰ μὴ ὁ πατὴρ μόνος. This has caused trouble to Christian commentators from the patristic period onwards, but it is perfectly understandable from within Matthew's first-century Jewish and Christian subculture. Some Jewish sources also say that only God knows the time of the End. For example, Baruch prays to God: 'You alone know the end of the times before they come' (*2 Bar.* 21.8). This was very natural, because a lot of people had tried to work out when the End would come, but it did not come. The Qumran community were among those disappointed, and one of them commented on Hab. 2.3:

> 'If it lingers wait for it, for it will surely come and not be late' (Hab. 2.3b). Its interpretation concerns the men of truth who do the Law, whose hands shall not relax from the service of truth when the final age is prolonged upon them. For all the ages of God shall come to their appointed end as he has decreed for them in the mysteries of his prudence (1QpHab VII, 9-14).

Matthew was in a very similar position to the author of this commentary. The parousia was a central item of his faith. It had been expected for some time, longer than when Mark wrote his Gospel, but it had not come. The teaching of Jesus himself had no actual date for the coming of the kingdom or anything like that, beyond that repeated at Mt. 24.34 from Mk 13.30, that everything would be accomplished within a generation, and one or two sayings sound suspiciously as if Jesus expected it much sooner, perhaps even before his death. Matthew therefore accepted and reinforced Mark's conclusion: like everyone else, even the angels in heaven, Jesus did not know the time of the End, complete with his parousia. Christian Christology had developed very rapidly, and was now very high, as we can see from the titles in Matthew 24 alone. It had not however yet become docetic enough for people to imagine that Jesus must have known everything.

With this made clear, Matthew now shifts back to the same block of Q that he had used before (Mt. 24.37-41//Lk. 17.26-27,34-35). Once again, the parallel passages in the two evangelists are close enough for us to infer that we are dealing with common source material. The differences between Matthew and Luke are however again so great that we must recognize also that there has been heavy editing. Here

---

5.   For the text and translation of the Eighteen Benedictions, see C. A. Evans, *Jesus and His Contemporaries. Comparative Studies* (Leiden: Brill, 1995), pp. 277–80.

too, the differences are of such a kind that they cannot possibly be explained as resulting from two Greek translations of a common Aramaic source. It is clear that the original passage compared the days of Noah with the time of the final appearance of the Son of man. Moreover, the point of the comparison has been retained by both Matthew and Luke. The generation of Noah, who are notorious in Jewish sources too as sinners (e.g. Jos. *Ant.* I, 72-6), carried on with their normal lives until the flood destroyed them. It follows that the final coming of the Son of man will involve large-scale destruction of sinners who have ignored the message of Jesus, and, by this stage, early Christianity. I have noted the destructive aspect of the final events already: this passage simply reinforces this in a picturesque rather than a blunt manner. Matthew's editing retains the meaning of the original comparison in Q. His most dramatic change is purely editorial, framing the comparison between two examples of his phrase ἡ παρουσία τοῦ υἱοῦ τοῦ ἀνθρώπου (Mt. 24.37,39). While two examples of ὁ υἱὸς τοῦ ἀνθρώπου itself evidently stood in Q (Lk. 17.26,30), Matthew's double use of ἡ παρουσία τοῦ υἱοῦ τοῦ ἀνθρώπου again shows how important belief in the parousia was to him.

Matthew concludes his use of this section of Q with two more sayings which also indicate large-scale and apparently random casualties in the last times (Mt. 24.40-41//Lk. 17.34-35). The salvation of others is likewise indicated.

Matthew now moves to another piece of Q material, with a parallel in Luke 12 (Mt. 24.43-51//Lk. 12.39-40,42-46). He has one linking verse to make yet again one of his main points, and it has made evident use of Mk 13.35: γρηγορεῖτε οὖν, ὅτι οὐκ οἴδατε ποίᾳ ἡμέρᾳ ὁ κύριος ὑμῶν ἔρχεται (Mt. 24.42). At first sight, this is a remarkable verse, because it is the only verse in the synoptic Gospels where reference is made to the second coming of Jesus with ἔρχομαι but not with ὁ υἱὸς τοῦ ἀνθρώπου. However, this is not difficult to explain. In the first place, it comes from the Marcan parable which Matthew has edited: γρηγορεῖτε οὖν· οὐκ οἴδατε γὰρ ποτε ὁ κύριος τῆς οἰκίας ἔρχεται ... (Mark 13.35). This also forms a natural link to the second parable from this next piece of Q material, in which the authoritative figure who returns unexpectedly is again ὁ κύριος. Secondly, we will recall that this is a term used by other New Testament writers in alluding to the second coming of Jesus. So Paul, for example, declares that ὁ κύριος ... καταβήσεται ἀπ᾽ οὐρανοῦ (1 Thess. 4.16); one of the deutero-Paulines urges good behaviour μέχρι τῆς ἐπιφανείας τοῦ κυρίου Ἰησοῦ Χριστοῦ (1 Tim. 6.14); Jacob declares ἡ παρουσία τοῦ κυρίου ἤγγικεν (Jas 5.8); and Revelation almost concludes with a prayer founded on the primitive *maranatha* (1 Cor. 16.22), which shows that similar usage was already derived from the early Aramaic-speaking church: Ἀμήν, ἔρχου, κύριε Ἰησοῦ (Rev. 22.20).[6] This should remind us again that Matthew's use of ὁ υἱὸς τοῦ ἀνθρώπου, vigorous though it be, is by no means exclusive of other titles,

---

6.   For *maranatha* in the light of the most recent research, see P. M. Casey, 'Monotheism, Worship and Christological Developments in the Pauline Churches', in C. C. Newman, J. R. Davila and G. S. Lewis (eds), *The Jewish Roots of Christological Monotheism*. Papers from the St Andrews Conference on the Historical Origins of the Worship of Jesus (Leiden: Brill, 1999), pp. 214–33 (223–5).

not even with reference to what he has repeatedly called ἡ παρουσία τοῦ υἱοῦ τοῦ ἀνθρώπου. The Son of man was Lord for Matthew just as much as for other New Testament writers.

The following Q passage has such a high proportion of verbal identity that we must infer that it was transmitted in Greek and reached each evangelist in Greek. Some variations, such as Luke's insertion of Lk. 12.41-42a, are obviously due to an evangelist's editing, and all should be so explained: none are due to Aramaic variants. The passage opens with a parable about the coming of a thief in the night. This short parable ends by applying its warning to the coming of the Son of man. There are no Jewish parallels to the image of the thief for any aspect of the day of the Lord or the coming of the kingdom. The image however recurs in the New Testament, and some of the parallels are especially instructive. One is at 1 Thess. 5.2: αὐτοὶ γὰρ ἀκριβῶς οἴδατε ὅτι ἡμέρα κυρίου ὡς κλέπτης ἐν νυκτὶ οὕτως ἔρχεται. This uses the traditional description 'day of the Lord', which could so easily be shifted from traditional Jewish belief in the judgement of God to the parousia of Jesus. The absence of the articles with ἡμέρα κυρίου shows close connection with the underlying Semitic tradition. The introduction shows that the Thessalonians were certainly expected by Paul to hold this belief, and strongly suggests that they were already familiar with the imagery of the thief in the night. The image is used similarly at 2 Pet. 3.10. It is reapplied to a coming of Jesus in judgement at Rev. 3.3: ἐὰν οὖν μὴ γρηγορήσῃς, ἥξω ὡς κλέπτης, καὶ οὐ μὴ γνῷς ποίαν ὥραν ἥξω ἐπὶ σέ (cf. 16.15). This material shows every sign of being early,[7] and it contains ἔρχεται but not ὁ υἱὸς τοῦ ἀνθρώπου.

We should infer that a genuine parable of Jesus underlies this Q passage. This certainly included the little story of Mt. 24.43//Lk. 12.39, and an earlier version of the warning in the following verse. The title ὁ υἱὸς τοῦ ἀνθρώπου should be regarded as secondary. The collocation of ὁ υἱὸς τοῦ ἀνθρώπου and ἔρχεται must be regarded as due to the underlying influence of Dan. 7.13. We have already seen Matthew deliberately using this text at Mt. 24.30, editing Mk 13.26, which already made midrashic use of this same text. This means that Matthew used this text in Greek, deriving both ὁ υἱὸς τοῦ ἀνθρώπου and ἔρχεται from it. Apart from Mt. 24.42, which I have already discussed, all synoptic references to Jesus' coming at his parousia use both ὁ υἱὸς τοῦ ἀνθρώπου and ἔρχομαι, as references elsewhere in the New Testament do not. The use of Dan. 7.13, which we have already seen to be conscious for both Mark and Matthew, is the only possible explanation for this.[8] Accordingly, the addition of ὁ υἱὸς τοῦ ἀνθρώπου has an excellent *Sitz im Leben* in the midrashic work of the early church, and in Greek.

It is more difficult to believe in satisfactory Aramaic, or to find a satisfactory *Sitz im Leben* for this term in the teaching of Jesus. I have attempted an Aramaic reconstruction elsewhere:[9]

---

7. The same cannot be said of the non-eschatological parallels in *Gos. Thom.* 21, 103.
8. See further Casey, *Son of Man*, pp. 162–4.
9. Casey, *Son of Man*, p. 190.

ואנתון הוו עתידין די בה שעתא די לא מסברין בר אנש אתה.

This is not quite impossible Aramaic, in the sense that the ending could be a reference to Dan. 7.13 if it was spoken to people who could be relied upon to pick this up. It is however possible only in these very restricted circumstances. We shall look at more general reasons for supposing that this did not happen in the teaching of Jesus.

Accordingly, we have a very strong argument of cumulative weight for supposing that the occurrence of the term ὁ υἱὸς τοῦ ἀνθρώπου in this saying is due to secondary editing by the early church in Greek, under the influence of Dan. 7.13.

In its present context, the saying fits perfectly into Matthew's editing. The image of the thief implies the destruction of unwary people, and we have seen that the destruction of outsiders was part of Matthew's view of the parousia. The secondary editing of ὁ υἱὸς τοῦ ἀνθρώπου with ἔρχεται recalls Matthew's use of Dan. 7.13 in his picture of the parousia just a few verses previously (Mt. 24.30). This perfect fit is presumably the reason why Matthew put this piece of Q material here.

The next piece of Q material (Mt. 24.45-51//Lk. 12.42-46) is another parable about an absent master returning suddenly and unexpectedly, so from Matthew's perspective it is another parable about the parousia. It too indicates salvation for the faithful, and punishment for the wicked, the latter emphasized by Matthew's final addition, intended to recall the final judgement: ἐκεῖ ἔσται ὁ κλαυθμὸς καὶ ὁ βρυγμὸς τῶν ὀδόντων (Mt. 24.51). At this point Matthew leaves this second piece of Q material. His interpretation of the parable of the wise and foolish maidens, which he alone has (Mt. 25.1-13), is along the same lines. The bridegroom being delayed and then coming suddenly is meant to recall the interval before the parousia and its predicted suddenness. The faithful are again rewarded and the others left outside. Matthew concludes again with a message about the parousia: Γρηγορεῖτε οὖν, ὅτι οὐκ οἴδατε τὴν ἡμέραν οὐδὲ τὴν ὥραν. Matthew has similarly interpreted his parable of the talents (Mt. 21.14-30), which has some overlap with Luke (Lk. 19.11-27), suggesting that an original parable has been much retold and re-edited. Matthew again has the Lord coming (ἔρχεται, Mt. 25.19) and rewarding the faithful. Once again the punishment of the useless slave slips over from the parable into a reminder of eternal punishment: καὶ τὸν ἀχρεῖον δοῦλον ἐκβάλετε εἰς τὸ σκότος τὸ ἐξώτερον· ἐκεῖ ἔσται ὁ κλαυθμὸς καὶ ὁ βρυγμὸς τῶν ὀδόντων (Mt. 25.30).

Thus the coming of the Son of man at his parousia has been in Matthew's mind throughout this lengthy section in which parabolic material, basically in story mode, led him to use different language. The final parable, or rather picturesque story, of the last judgement has a Matthean introduction which returns to his pre-eminent title of Jesus at the time of the final events: Ὅταν δὲ ἔλθῃ ὁ υἱὸς τοῦ ἀνθρώπου ἐν τῇ δόξῃ αὐτοῦ καὶ πάντες οἱ ἄγγελοι μετ' αὐτοῦ, τότε καθίσει ἐπὶ θρόνου δόξης αὐτοῦ ... (Mt. 25.31). Several details again recall Dan. 7.13-14. We have already seen that the collocation of ἔλθῃ with ὁ υἱὸς τοῦ ἀνθρώπου is sufficient to indicate dependence on this text. We have also seen that Matthew was aware of using this text when he edited Mk 13.26 to produce Mt. 24.30.[10] There are further parallels

10. See pp. 215–6 above.

between the two texts. δόξα is used at LXX Dan. 7.14, a wayward translation in which we cannot be certain whether it represents the Aramaic יקר. In more general terms, the whole scene is quite glorious. There are plural θρόνοι (כרסון) at Dan. 7.9. R. Aqiba saw here two thrones, one for God and one for David, by which he may or may not have meant the Messiah (b. Ḥag. 14a//San. 38b). The virulent rejection of his opinion is due to similar Christian use of the same text. Matthew may accordingly have seen the glorious throne already at Dan. 7.9. The accompanying angels may also be seen round the throne of God at Dan. 7.9-10, and bringing the Son of man at Dan. 7.13-14. πάντα τὰ ἔθνη at Mt. 25.32 could also be taken from LXX Dan. 7.14 (where it translates כל עממיא). Quite how much of this Matthew saw in Dan. 7.9-14 must remain to some degree uncertain, but his use of this text is not uncertain: it was the basis for his picture of ὁ υἱὸς τοῦ ἀνθρώπου at the last judgement. Other texts may also have been used, whether deliberately or simply through absorption in scripturally based Jewish tradition. We have seen Matthew use Zech. 12.10-14 at Mt. 24.30: Zech. 14.5 has καὶ ἥξει κύριος ὁ θεός μου καὶ πάντες οἱ ἅγιοι μετ' αὐτοῦ. Matthew might have reapplied this to the coming of ὁ υἱὸς τοῦ ἀνθρώπου. Be that as it may, the main point is clear. Matthew's picture of the Son of man coming in glory to carry out the final judgement is scripturally based, with Dan. 7.13-14 at the centre of it.

There are also a number of parallels with the *Similitudes of Enoch*. Here the central figure is also called 'Son of man', and the first time he is mentioned Dan. 7.13 has been used (*1 En.* 46.1-3). This Son of man also sits on the throne of his glory (*1 En.* 62.5; 69.29). He is moreover the eschatological judge. It has sometimes been suggested that Matthew was actually dependent on this work,[11] but this cannot be demonstrated. When a possible Aramaic substratum is reconstructed from the difficult Ge'ez text, the term 'son of man' emerges as an ordinary term for man, used to conceal Enoch's identity in the body of the work in preparation for the explicit revelation of his identity in the dénouement of the whole work (*1 En.* 71.14-17).[12] This is significantly different from the major Christological title which characterizes the work of Matthew. It may well be therefore that all the parallels are due to the common use of Jewish tradition, rather than to Matthew's specific dependence on this one document, especially as we have seen how heavily Matthew is dependent on scriptural tradition.

We have seen that the introduction to this scene of final judgement has an excellent *Sitz im Leben* in the editorial work of Matthew. In the body of the narrative, the controlling figure is called ὁ βασιλεύς. This is a very striking difference. The only reasonable explanation of it is that Matthew inherited a parable in which the eschatological judge was ὁ βασιλεύς, presumably therefore God himself.

---

11. See especially J. Theisohn, *Der auserwählte Richter. Untersuchungen zum traditionsgeschichtlichen Ort der Menschensohngestalt der Bilderreden des Äthiopischen Henoch* (SUNT 12. Göttingen: Vandenhoeck & Ruprecht, 1975), esp. pp. 149–82; D. R. Catchpole, 'The Poor on Earth and the Son of Man in Heaven. A Reappraisal of Mt. XXV.31-46', *BJRLM* 61 (1978–9), pp. 355–97 (378–83).

12. See pp. 91–111 above.

Matthew then wrote the introductory piece himself. He will not have wanted to alter ὁ βασιλεύς because he fervently believed that Jesus was βασιλεύς τῶν Ἰουδαίων (Mt. 2.2; 21.5; 27.11,29,37,42), who as χριστός fulfilled Jewish hopes of deliverance by a king (Mt. 2.4, cf. 1.21; 16.16,20; 26.63; 27.17,22). As before, the only possible conclusion is that ὁ υἱὸς τοῦ ἀνθρώπου was an important title for Matthew *in Greek*.

Matthew's editing of Chs 24–25 in general, and his use of ὁ υἱὸς τοῦ ἀνθρώπου in particular, form a coherent and consistent whole. He fully intended to give a picture of the last times, both with straightforward predictions and with picturesque parables, images and stories. At the centre of his expectation was ἡ παρουσία τοῦ υἱοῦ τοῦ ἀνθρώπου, coming on the clouds of heaven, bringing salvation and judgement. Matthew found this usage of ὁ υἱὸς τοῦ ἀνθρώπου in both Mark and in his Q material. Crucially, he also found it in scripture. This was a massively strong combination of source material, which ensured that Matthew used ὁ υἱὸς τοῦ ἀνθρώπου redactionally, with his new phrase ἡ παρουσία τοῦ υἱοῦ τοῦ ἀνθρώπου clarifying the tradition which he inherited. He felt no need to inform his readers and audiences as to what ὁ υἱὸς τοῦ ἀνθρώπου means, a matter to which we must return. He found it in scripture and tradition, and it was his ideal phrase for describing the return of Jesus, for which he urged the church to be both patient and always ready.

2. Luke 17 and 21

Luke also has four occurrences of ὁ υἱὸς τοῦ ἀνθρώπου partly dependent on the first of the two pieces of Q material used in Matthew 24, and he too shortly followed them with a fifth. He used however a very different frame of reference. In the first place, this is nowhere near the eschatological discourse of Luke 21, which I consider next. Luke put these Son of man sayings from Q further back in Luke 17. Luke 17 is part of a massive and quite static travel narrative, which consists of Q and special Lukan material, and which Luke gathered together between Lk. 9.50 (from Mk 9.39-40) and Lk. 18.15 (from Mk 10.13). There is blatant Lukan editing at various points, including for example the linking comment at Lk. 17.5: καὶ εἶπαν οἱ ἀπόστολοι τῷ κυρίῳ.

The eschatological section in Luke 17 is introduced by a small piece which has a perfect *Sitz im Leben* in the theology and general concerns of Luke:

Ἐπερωτηθεὶς δὲ ὑπὸ φαρισαίων πότε ἔρχεται ἡ βασιλεία τοῦ θεοῦ ἀπεκρίση αὐτοῖς καὶ εἶπεν, Οὐκ ἔρχεται ἡ βασιλεία τοῦ θεοῦ μετὰ παρατηρήσεως, οὐδὲ ἐροῦσιν, Ἰδοὺ ὧδε· ἤ, Ἐκεῖ· ἰδοὺ γὰρ ἡ βασιλεία τοῦ θεοῦ ἐντὸς ὑμῶν ἐστιν (Lk. 17.20-22).

This mirrors one of Luke's central concerns, to ward off any threat to Christian belief and action from the lengthy delay in the coming of the kingdom. This concern is repeated in Lukan editing at Lk. 19.11. Luke wrote considerably later than Matthew. By this time the notion of the kingdom coming within a generation, the outer limit which might be thought to be implied in the teaching of Jesus, was barely feasible. He brings forward the Pharisees, whom he portrays as maliciously hostile and sometimes as foolish.[13] We expect a silly question from them, and asking when the kingdom of God would come was in Luke's view just that. Jesus' response presents the kingdom as not really future at all. He first rejects any notion that the kingdom is a future entity which comes in such a way that one can look for signs of it, as people committed to a fairly literal apocalyptic view of the kingdom might. He then makes the positive statement that the kingdom of God is ἐντὸς ὑμῶν.

This phrase has caused a lot of discussion, because its precise meaning is not clear. Taking the commonest meaning of ἐντὸς from Greek usage as a whole, we would expect the phrase ἐντὸς ὑμῶν to mean 'within you'. From patristic times through to recent scholarship, it has often been so interpreted. This interpretation has however been subjected to two decisive objections. In its immediate context, this would mean that the kingship of God was to be found in the Pharisees, an interpretation contrary to the teaching of Jesus and to the theology of Luke. Secondly, this interpretation of the kingdom of God does not have a proper *Sitz im Leben* in the teaching of Jesus or the theology of Luke. Recent scholarship has accordingly tended to favour the interpretation 'among you'. This can then be supported from the traditional view that the kingship of God is manifest in the ministry of Jesus, a view essential for the interpretation of Lk. 11.20(//Mt. 12.28).[14] This also fits perfectly with an entirely feasible Lukan interpretation of ἡ βασιλεία τοῦ θεοῦ at Lk. 18.16,17. The Greek word ἐντὸς has a semantic area which does stretch to 'within' and hence 'among' a social group.[15] This is sufficient for ἐντὸς ὑμῶν to refer to the whole social group of which the Pharisees were a part. We should infer from the word ἐντὸς, which Luke does not use elsewhere and for which he might more clearly have preferred ἐν μέσῳ (Lk. 2.46; 8.7; 10.3; 21.21; 22.27; 24.36), that he took this part of the saying from the traditions available to him. His editing of it has ensured that it fits his needs perfectly.

The introduction of the first Son of man saying in this section also fits Luke's editorial purpose perfectly. The audience is deliberately shifted to the disciples, who are to be instructed in what the church will need to know in future years.

Ἐλεύσονται ἡμέραι ὅτε ἐπιθυμήσετε μίαν τῶν ἡμερῶν τοῦ υἱοῦ τοῦ ἀνθρώπου ἰδεῖν καὶ οὐκ ὄψεσθε (Lk. 17.22).

This straightforwardly describes the period during which the parousia was expected and did not come. It is presented as a prediction of Jesus, so that Christians of Luke's time could be reassured that Jesus knew that the parousia would not happen as soon as they had hoped, and that their predecessors had been mistaken to expect it. The saying has no parallel in Matthew, and should be regarded as a Lukan

---

13. Cf. J. T. Carroll, 'Luke's Portrayal of the Pharisees', *CBQ* 50 (1988), pp. 604–21.
14. See Casey, *Aramaic Approach to Q*, pp. 167–73.
15. J. Lebourlier, '*Entos hymôn*. Le sens "au milieu de vous" est-il possible?', *Bib* 73 (1992), pp. 259–62.

construction on the basis of the tradition which Luke inherited. It is clear from the three Matthean parallels already discussed that the three following examples of ὁ υἱὸς τοῦ ἀνθρώπου have come directly from Q (Lk. 17.24,26,30//Mt. 24.27,37,39). In all three cases, it is a title of Jesus at his parousia, the same usage that Matthew inherited and developed. Like Matthew, Luke inherited it from Mark, and he re-edited one of the passion predictions here at Lk. 17.25 (see esp. Lk. 9.22 from Mk 8.31), though without repeating the term ὁ υἱὸς τοῦ ἀνθρώπου from the previous verse.

The plural τῶν ἡμερῶν at Lk. 17.22 has caused problems to some commentators, but it has a straightforward origin in the following passage from Q and it fits in with Lukan usage much better than is usually thought. The plural is used of the days of Noah in Q at Mt. 24.37//Lk. 17.26, and where Matthew refers to Jesus in the second half of the saying with ἡ παρουσία τοῦ υἱοῦ τοῦ ἀνθρώπου, Luke has ἐν ταῖς ἡμέραις τοῦ υἱοῦ τοῦ ἀνθρώπου, very precisely parallel to ἐν ταῖς ἡμέραις Νῶε in his version of the same verse. This is quite natural, because the 'days' of a person's life was a common description of the times in which they lived (e.g. Lk. 1.5; 4.25). Luke's expression ἐν ταῖς ἡμέραις τοῦ υἱοῦ τοῦ ἀνθρώπου (Lk. 17.26) looks forward to a considerable period after the second coming. This would be a period of bliss for Jesus' followers, and this is what they are expected to look forward to at Lk. 17.22. Similar expressions do not occur earlier because earlier expectation focused on the moment of Jesus' return, as we have seen in discussing Matthew's treatment of this issue. Luke does this too at Lk. 17.24,30; 21.27. The passage of time, combined with the need for the church not to be dismayed by the delay of the single day of the Son of man's return, has led Luke to look at the whole of the later period in a different way at Lk. 17.26 and then in editing Lk. 17.22.

The perceived problem at Lk. 17.22 has led some scholars to propose an Aramaic solution. Torrey proposed that the Aramaic *laḥdā'* 'very much', had been misunderstood and hence mistranslated as the sign of the accusative *lĕ*, followed by *ḥădā'* 'one'. The original meant 'you will long very much to see the days of ...'. This explanation was enthusiastically followed by T. W. Manson.[16] It should not be accepted. It embodies a familiar error of method. The text has been deemed unsatisfactory, so an attempt has been made to alter it by guessing at the change of a single word, without even showing that the saying ever had an Aramaic original. Secondly, the change of a single word without reconstructing the whole sentence means that objections to an Aramaic original have not been faced. Another attempt was made by Black, though like Torrey he did not work it fully through.[17] He appears to suppose that the original Aramaic was חד מן יומיא דבר אנשא, which he considered to be idiomatic Aramaic for 'a certain Day of/for the Son of Man'. In the expression חד מן יומיא, however, Aramaic is not as different from Greek or English as Black suggests, nor is his English translation. To establish the supposedly idiomatic use of the Aramaic חד מן, Black quotes Dan. 7.16, where however חד מן קאמיא means

___

16.   C. C. Torrey, *The Four Gospels. A New Translation* (London/New York: Harper, 1933), p. 312, followed by Manson, *Sayings*, p. 142.

17.   Black, 'Aramaic Dimension in Q', p. 39.

'one of the bystanders': on this analogy, חד מן יומיא would mean 'one of the days', so it would not help with the perceived problem. Since they do not reconstruct the whole saying, neither Torrey nor Black considers the meaning of בר (א)נש(א) in an expression such as חד מן יומיא דבר אנשא. With בר (א)נש(א) still being a normal term for 'man', it does not have enough referring power to single out Jesus or any other particular (son of) man. Once again, we find that just at the point where we have good reason to posit creative writing by an evangelist, the saying will not make sense in any proposed Aramaic. We must accordingly reject these Aramaic proposals, and return to the view expressed above, that Lk. 17.22 is a deliberate Lukan introduction to the edited versions of Q sayings which follow.

Verse 23 begins the section of Luke 17 which is drawn from Q and Luke's special material. We have seen Matthew selecting the Marcan version of this saying (Mt. 24.23 editing Mk 13.21) and revising the Q version (Mt. 24.26). In Matthew, as in Mark, the subject of the saying is ὁ χριστός and the context is the presence of false prophets and pseudo-messiahs. In Luke, the reference is directly to the Son of man, and the context dictates that this saying refers to false expectation of the second coming of Jesus, which is warded off. This makes even better sense of the comparison of this event to lightning (Lk. 17.24//Mt. 24.26). It ensures that the visibility of the lightning is the centre of the entirely appropriate comparison, and makes its destructive force less likely to come to people's minds. The term ὁ υἱός τοῦ ἀνθρώπου must have stood in Q because it is found in both evangelists' versions of the saying, and we have seen that the specially Matthean ἡ παρουσία τοῦ υἱοῦ τοῦ ἀνθρώπου is secondary. For this part Luke has ὁ υἱός τοῦ ἀνθρώπου ἐν τῇ ἡμέρᾳ αὐτοῦ. This is likely to be the old Q tradition, since the expectation of the parousia was greatly influenced by existing traditions about the Day of the Lord. It is all the more noteworthy that this part of the saying will not make proper sense in Aramaic. We could attempt a reconstruction as follows: כדן להוא בר אנשא ביומה. Here again the term בר (א)נש(א) does not have sufficient referring power to single out Jesus or any other particular (son of) man. Consequently, the saying does not make proper sense. This is further evidence that this part of the Q material was composed as well as edited in Greek.

At 17.25, Luke inserts into the Q material his own version of a prediction which he has edited elsewhere. It is closest to Lk. 9.22, where Luke is editing Mk 8.31 (cf. also Lk. 9.44; 18.31-33; 24.7). Its major concern is to make absolutely clear that the coming of the Son of man was never regarded as imminent during the ministry, and was always to be preceded by his suffering and death. This same concern is evident close to Lk. 9.22, in the editing of Mk 9.1 at Lk. 9.27-28. In this passage, Luke altered Jesus' prediction of the coming of the kingdom in power within a generation to engineer its fulfilment in the following narrative of the Transfiguration. We have noted the similar concerns in the editing of the opening part of the eschatological section here in Luke 17, and again some way ahead at Lk. 19.11. Thus the insertion of this prediction at 17.25 is wholly in accordance with Luke's editorial concerns, and his insertion of something important to him into Q is in accordance with his normal editorial habits. Since the main point to be made was the necessity of Jesus' passion long before his second coming, an abbreviated prediction was also in accordance with Luke's needs. The precise term τῆς γενεᾶς ταύτης will also have been chosen to set up the following comparison with the days of Noah, a conspicuously righteous person chosen by God from one of the most evil generations of all.

Despite some differences in wording, partly and perhaps wholly due to the editorial activity of Matthew, the comparison with the days of Noah is basically the same in both evangelists (Lk. 17.26-27, cf. Mt. 24.37-39). As I noted above, it must mean that the final coming of the Son of man will involve large-scale destruction of sinners who have ignored the message of early Christianity.[18] The passage of time gave Luke no reason to alter this. It is reinforced with a similar comparison to the days of Lot, especially his escape from the wicked city of Sodom which was destroyed by God with fire and brimstone (Lk. 17.28-29). Whether this stood in Matthew's Q source is quite uncertain. The Son of man statement at the end certainly did, for it is found in both evangelists. Matthew has *exactly* the same form of words at Mt. 24.39 as in the two previous occurrences (Mt. 24.27,37): οὕτως ἔσται ἡ παρουσία τοῦ υἱοῦ τοῦ ἀνθρώπου. Luke is different both from Matthew and from his other comments elsewhere, so he may well be reproducing his source with little change at this point: κατὰ τὰ αὐτὰ ἔσται ᾗ ἡμέρᾳ ὁ υἱὸς τοῦ ἀνθρώπου ἀποκαλύπτεται. This is different language for the single event of Jesus' second coming. The use of the verb 'reveal' is reminiscent of the cognate noun at 1 Cor. 1.7, where Paul has the Corinthians await τὴν ἀποκάλυψιν τοῦ κυρίου ἡμῶν Ἰησοῦ Χριστοῦ. It is again striking that where Luke has another form of words for this major event, a feasible Aramaic underlay cannot be reconstructed. It follows that anything like the present form of these Son of man sayings first existed in Greek, and that Luke, like Matthew, regarded ὁ υἱὸς τοῦ ἀνθρώπου as an important title of Jesus *in Greek*.

These sayings comparing the days of the Son of man to the people of the days of Noah and Lot are followed by more sayings which imply large-scale casualties. The first one (Lk. 17.31) has a close parallel at Mk 13.15-16//Mt. 24.17-8, so it probably stood in this same section of Q material inherited by Luke, whereas Matthew preferred the Marcan version in its Marcan position. One more saying of this kind comes from the same section of Q (Lk. 17.35//Mt. 24.41). Luke then has his own introduction to his somewhat edited version of the saying about vultures:

καὶ ἀποκριθέντες λέγουσιν αὐτῷ Ποῦ, κύριε; ὁ δὲ εἶπεν αὐτοῖς, Ὅπου τὸ σῶμα, ἐκεῖ καὶ οἱ ἀετοὶ ἐπισυναχθήσονται (Lk. 17.37, cf. Mt. 24.28).

It is usually inferred that Luke moved this saying here from the Matthean position which it held in Q. This should be accepted. It makes better sense straight after several sayings which imply a lot of corpses. The collection of sayings thus ends on a note of judgement upon outsiders, and it makes it clear that the end has not yet come.

The parable of the unjust judge (Lk. 18.1-8) ends this eschatological section of Luke. There is an obvious sign of Lukan redaction in the narrative use of ὁ κύριος

18.   See pp. 213–22 above.

as a description of Jesus right at the beginning of the eschatological application of the parable (Lk. 18.6). The application as a whole (Lk. 18.1,6-8) clearly refers to the period of the church awaiting deliverance at the time of the second coming. It advocates constant prayer at this time, a significant Lukan concern, and assures the faithful that God will avenge them quickly when they are crying to him day and night. This eschatological section of Luke ends with its fifth Son of man saying:

πλὴν ὁ υἱὸς τοῦ ἀνθρώπου ἐλθὼν ἆρα εὑρήσει τὴν πίστιν ἐπὶ τῆς γῆς;

This reflects Luke's Gentile world, in which most people were not Christians. Some years ago, I explored the possibility of an Aramaic reconstruction, and the best I could produce was this:

להן בר אנש אתה הישכח המנותא בארעא

As I commented at the time, 'It is very difficult to feel any confidence that this saying existed in Aramaic before I made it up.'[19] It has a perfect *Sitz im Leben* in the early church at the time when Luke's Gospel was written. The parousia, or the coming of the kingdom, had been delayed and there was an obvious risk that some people would lose heart and slip back into the Gentile world. This is where this concept of πίστις appears to belong, something Christian which could be lost. While 'Son of man' and 'coming' together indicate some influence of Dan. 7.13, the saying itself seems very remote from those in which this influence originated. We must conclude that the saying originated in the Greek-speaking church, and is probably a Lukan construction. This is further evidence that, for Luke as for Matthew, ὁ υἱὸς τοῦ ἀνθρώπου was an important Christological title *in Greek*.

Before going on to consider Luke 21, which is an eschatological discourse and thus from a formal point of view Luke's basic parallel to Matthew 24 as a whole, we must consider how much information about the previous history of ὁ υἱὸς τοῦ ἀνθρώπου we can draw from those Q sayings which are found in Luke 17 and Matthew 24. Luke created his introduction to these sayings (Lk. 17.22), and moved the saying about vultures to the end, creating his own introduction (Lk. 17.37). In other respects, however, Luke stayed close to the Q source, notably in the three Son of man sayings which both evangelists inherited (Mt. 24.27//Lk. 17.24; Mt. 24.37//Lk. 17.26; Mt. 24.39//Lk. 17.30).

Despite some uncertainty over details, the basic interpretation of all three sayings has emerged clearly from the above discussion. In all three sayings, the term ὁ υἱὸς τοῦ ἀνθρώπου is a title of Jesus at his second coming. That much is just as clear in the Lukan versions as in the Matthean sayings, which have the stereotyped and secondary expression ἡ παρουσία τοῦ υἱοῦ τοῦ ἀνθρώπου. The first saying (Mt. 24.27//Lk. 17.24) was a comparison of the appearing of the Son of man to lightning. This was certainly intended to invoke the suddenness and visibility of lightning, and perhaps the destructive force evident in the second saying (Mt. 24.37//Lk. 17.26). This compared the time of the Son of man's coming with the days of Noah.

19. Casey, *Son of Man*, p. 196.

This had in mind the large-scale destruction of the wicked, and the salvation of the relatively righteous, who could only be identified with the Christian churches. The third saying is of exactly the same kind, and it is likely to have followed the similar comparison with the days of Lot (Lk. 17.28-29) rather than to have come at the end of the comparison with Noah as well as the beginning (Mt. 24.37,39). Be that as it may, it too could only have in mind the large-scale destruction of the wicked, as well as the salvation of Christians.

It follows that in all three Q sayings, as in Matthew and Luke, ὁ υἱὸς τοῦ ἀνθρώπου was already a title for Jesus at a second coming which would bring judgement on outsiders as well as salvation for the followers of Jesus. Moreover, we have seen that no version of any of these sayings can be effectively reconstructed in Aramaic. It follows further that in the Q source used here by both evangelists, ὁ υἱὸς τοῦ ἀνθρώπου was already a title for Jesus *in Greek*. This is an important result, which can be properly assessed only after all Son of man sayings have been discussed.

I turn next, then, to Lk. 21.5-36, Luke's parallel to Matthew 24 as a complete eschatological discourse based on Mark 13. The opening part is noteworthy for an addition to the words of those who will mislead many: they will say ὁ καιρὸς ἤγγικεν (Lk. 21.8). This intensifies Luke's rejection of the apocalyptic hopes which characterized both the ministry of Jesus and earlier Christianity. There are also some noteworthy additions to the predictions of the persecution of the disciples, which are retained and expanded as a reflection of the sufferings of Christians in the prolonged period of the church.

The most striking change is at Lk. 21.20-24, where in place of the abomination of desolation and related troubles we find the siege of Jerusalem:

Ὅταν δὲ ἴδητε κυκλουμένην ὑπὸ στρατοπέδων Ἰερουσαλήμ, τότε γνῶτε ὅτι ἤγγικεν ἡ ἐρήμωσις αὐτῆς … Ιερουσαλὴμ ἔσται πατουμένη ὑπὸ ἐθνῶν, ἄχρι οὗ πληρωθῶσιν καιροὶ ἐθνῶν.

This reflects the siege and sack of Jerusalem in 66–70 CE, which explains why Luke was so concerned about the delay in the coming of the kingdom and the parousia. A considerable time had passed since the historic ministry of Jesus. The last words leave open the possibility that there will be a significant gap after the fall of Jerusalem. Luke also omitted the prediction of Mk 13.20 according to which the Lord would shorten the days, for by the time Luke wrote the Lord had clearly not shortened the days. Only at this stage does Luke predict heavenly phenomena followed by the coming of the Son of man, omitting Mark's prediction that he would send his angels to gather the elect (Mk 13.27):

καὶ τότε ὄψονται τὸν υἱὸν τοῦ ἀνθρώπου ἐρχόμενον ἐν νεφέλῃ μετὰ δυνάμεως καὶ δόξης πολλῆς (Lk. 21.27).

Here Luke has retained the use of ὁ υἱὸς τοῦ ἀνθρώπου as a title of Jesus at his parousia. This reinforces the evidence of Luke 17 that it was very important to him as such. We can see him making one change which was important to him, the alteration of Mark's ἐν νεφέλαις to ἐν νεφέλη. This fits in with a very literal understanding of Luke's story of the Ascension (Acts 1. 9-11). He must therefore have believed this prediction in a literal way. Whether he perceived any reference to Dan. 7.13 is doubtful. He retains the term ὁ υἱὸς τοῦ ἀνθρώπου, together with ἐρχόμενον, the crucial indicators of the influence of Dan. 7.13. But we know that Luke took these, and everything else which could ultimately come from Daniel, directly from Mark. The change from νεφέλαις to νεφέλη suggests that Luke was not aware of the Danielic reference, for it is such a straightforward move away from the sacred text. If this is so, Luke will have believed that he was rewriting Mark to make his picture of the second coming more accurate, and he will have accepted from Mark the title ὁ υἱὸς τοῦ ἀνθρώπου *in Greek* as a true representation of the teaching of Jesus about his return, but not as a scriptural reference in the way that Matthew and Mark saw it.

In place of Mark's prediction that the Son of man will send out his angels and gather the elect (Mark 13.27), Luke has a prediction which again implies the passage of time before the final events begin (Lk. 21.28).This also refers to ἡ ἀπολύτρωσις ὑμῶν in such a way as to make clear that it is the deliverance of Christian disciples which is to be expected. Luke proceeds with the parabolic material from Mk 13.28-29, clarifying it by saying that when these various events have happened, ἐγγύς ἐστιν ἡ βασιλεία τοῦ θεοῦ. This is exactly what he has been at such pains to show was not due to have happened earlier, and should not have been expected then. In this light, his retention of Mk 13.30 with only slight alteration has puzzled scholars:

ἀμὴν λέγω ὑμῖν ὅτι οὐ μὴ παρέλθη ἡ γενεὰ αὕτη ἕως ἂν πάντα γένηται (Luke 21.32).

If a 'generation' is interpreted chronologically as a period of some 25–30 years, if we assume that ἡ γενεὰ αὕτη must be Jesus' own generation, and if we further assume perfect consistency between what Luke leaves in and his editorial aims, then this saying is difficult to fit into Lukan theology. Hence Nolland went so far as to claim, 'This verse is a standing embarrassment to all attempts to see the delay of the Parousia as a major Lukan preoccupation.'[20] The rest of the evidence which I have surveyed on this matter should not however be downgraded in this way. It is not surprising that some scholars have argued that ἡ γενεὰ αὕτη has been interpreted by Luke as Luke's own generation, rather than the generation of Jesus.[21] It is however difficult to fit this interpretation into a speech by Jesus edited by Luke, because he has been so careful elsewhere to distinguish between the time of the life of Jesus and the time of the eschatological events. We should rather note what has happened to the Hebrew equivalent דד in the Qumran commentary on Habakkuk. I have already pointed out the trouble caused to the community by the perceived delay in the coming of the End. Nonetheless, they still described Habakkuk's prophecies

20. Nolland, *Luke*, p. 1009.
21. E.g. Fitzmyer, *Luke*, p. 1353.

as aimed at הדור האחרון, 'the last generation' (1QpHab VII,2). They evidently did not interpret הדור האחרון chronologically as a period of some 25–30 years. We must take the same view of Luke's ἡ γενεὰ αὕτη.[22] The criticism of his 'generation' by Jesus, and his threats of judgement against them, has caused Luke to keep the term 'generation' for people from the time of Jesus right down to his own times. It is not too long for some people to have lived through both, and for all we know such people may have included Luke himself.

Luke omits the saying about the Son's ignorance (Mk 13.32). At Acts 1.7, the risen Jesus tells his apostles that it is not for *them* to know the times which the Father has set, which again reflects the disappointed expectations of earlier Christianity. By Luke's time, the whole idea of the Son himself not knowing the time had become insupportable. The shift into the Gentile world was a factor in this, as well as rising Christology. In Second Temple Judaism, Jewish people constantly revised their predictions of eschatological events, without finding fault with their predecessors for expecting events which had not taken place (yet). Greek-speaking Gentiles were however more likely to suppose that predictions of events which did not take place as expected were mistakes by the people who made the predictions. Luke's editing has carefully and consistently removed Jesus from that group of people.

Luke concludes his eschatological discourse with a warning to Christians to live properly and be on the alert for the last times, and a warning that the judgement will be universal. Christians should hope to survive these things, καὶ σταθῆναι ἔμπροσθεν τοῦ υἱοῦ τοῦ ἀνθρώπου. This is an additional Son of man saying, referring to Jesus as the eschatological judge. There are no signs of Dan. 7.13, as there were at Mt. 25.31. More simply, Luke has so completely accepted ὁ υἱὸς τοῦ ἀνθρώπου as a Greek title for Jesus in the last times that he has used it creatively as the last words of the eschatological discourse. In this respect he is just like Matthew.

We have now studied the major groups of Son of man sayings which do not go back to Jesus, and we have found that both Matthew and Luke inherited and used ὁ υἱὸς τοῦ ἀνθρώπου as a major title of Jesus seen in his role in the final events. We must consider next the remaining secondary uses in each of the synoptic evangelists, before proceeding in the next chapter to discuss the transition from Jesus' use of בר (א)נש(א) to each of the synoptic evangelists' view of this title as a whole.

3. More Son of Man Sayings in Matthew

I now proceed through the remaining secondary Son of man sayings in Matthew. The first is perhaps the strangest of all:

---

22.   Cf. E. Lövestam, *Jesus and 'This Generation'. A New Testament Study* (ConBNT 25. Stockholm: Almqvist & Wiksell, 1995), pp. 81–7.

ὅταν δὲ διώκωσιν ὑμᾶς ἐν τῇ πόλει ταύτῃ, φεύγετε εἰς τὴν ἑτέραν· ἀμὴν γὰρ λέγω ὑμῖν, οὐ μὴ τελέσητε τὰς πόλεις τοῦ Ἰσραὴλ ἕως ἂν ἔλθῃ ὁ υἱὸς τοῦ ἀνθρώπου (Mt. 10.23).

This saying appears at first sight to be placed during the historic ministry of Jesus. It is part of a missionary discourse, when the twelve were sent out on a mission to Israel, memorably defined at Mt. 10.5-6:

Εἰς ὁδόν ἐθνῶν μὴ ἀπέλπητε, καὶ εἰς πόλιν Σαμαριτῶν μὴ εἰσέλθητε· πορεύεσθε δὲ μᾶλλον πρὸς τὰ πρόβατα τὰ ἀπολωλότα οἴκου Ἰσραήλ.

This is an excellent definition of the scope of the historical ministry, and it has an excellent *Sitz im Leben* where Matthew has placed it. The end of the discourse is likewise set to perfection in the historic ministry, and it appears to be a piece of deliberate Matthean editing to this effect:

Καὶ ἐγένετο ὅτε ἐτέλεσεν ὁ Ἰησοῦς διατάσσων τοῖς δώδεκα μαθηταῖς αὐτοῦ, μετέβη ἐκεῖθεν τοῦ διδάσκειν καὶ κηρύσσειν ἐν ταῖς πόλεσιν αὐτῶν (Mt. 11.1).

It is understandable, therefore, that Schweitzer interpreted the saying in this historic context. We have seen that the coming of the Son of man in Matthew refers consistently to the parousia. Schweitzer accordingly interpreted this saying as an unfulfilled prediction that Jesus' parousia would take place during the historic ministry.[23] There are three serious problems with this interpretation. In the first place, it is difficult to fit in with Jesus' other predictions of his forthcoming death in Jerusalem. Secondly, any underlying Aramaic has to include a reference to Daniel 7. I have previously suggested a possible reconstruction of the difficult part, Mt. 10.23b:[24]

לא תהשלמון קריה די ישראל עד די בר אנש אתה

This has clear reference to Dan. 7.13, and this is what is difficult about it. We shall see good reason to believe that all such references are secondary.[25] In Aramaic or Greek, this also reinforces the point that the coming of the Son of man in Matthew always refers to the parousia of Jesus, since this is how he interpreted Dan. 7.13. Thirdly, if this is what the saying is really supposed to mean, it is extraordinary that so careful an editor as Matthew retained it, when he could so easily have left it out.

Christian scholars, in the patristic and modern periods alike, have not liked this interpretation for the dogmatic reason that it attributes to Jesus a mistaken prediction. Any mistake by Jesus does not fit in with the docetic Christology characteristic of supposedly orthodox Christianity, and these same Christian scholars, fervent in their continued belief that the Son of man will come on the clouds of heaven eventually,

---

23. A. Schweitzer, *The Quest of the Historical Jesus. First Complete Edition* (trans. W. Montgomery *et al.*; London: SCM, 2000), pp. 327–32.
24. Casey, *Son of Man*, p. 185.
25. See pp. 242–5 below.

have regarded this as an important matter. Consequently, this interpretation would make Jesus responsible for an important mistake, rather than a trivial one. Accordingly, a variety of implausible interpretations have been adopted.[26] The most mundane suggestion is that the end of the verse really means 'until I join you'.[27] This involves an impossible interpretation of the term 'Son of man' in either Aramaic or Greek, and people who thought it meant this are most unlikely to have considered it worth preserving. Matthew is especially likely to have clarified it and recorded its fulfilment, rather than omitting the end of the mission, as he has done. Another suggestion is that Jesus was referring to the fall of Jerusalem.[28] This replaces what the text says with something more convenient. If Jesus meant this, he would surely have said it, and if Matthew meant this, he would surely have written it. Interpretations of this kind can hardly be regarded as critical scholarship. They show a total lack of respect for what the text says, and assert their own meanings to avoid the conservative Christian problem that Jesus appears to have been mistaken.

For once, recent redaction criticism has come to the rescue. By the time we reach vv. 17-18, what is to us a fundamental shift of focus has clearly taken place. Some of the predictions no longer have a satisfactory *Sitz im Leben* in the historic ministry of Jesus, but belong rather to the period of the early church. Jesus predicts that the disciples will be handed over to sanhedrins, flogged in synagogues, and brought before rulers and kings for a witness to them καὶ τοῖς ἔθνεσιν. This happened in the period of the early church, but not during the historic ministry. Consistently with this, there are close parallels to some of Matthew's comments in the eschatological discourse of Mk 13, from which Matthew has notably omitted some of them (see esp. Mk 13.9-13). Matthew has shifted from the forthcoming mission of the disciples in the historic ministry to the Christian mission in the period of the early church. From his perspective, this was a reasonable thing to do. He regarded the mission of the church as a continuation of the mission of the first apostles. He also belonged to a culture which interpreted prophecy as partly fulfilled, partly referring to the present and partly referring to the future. Apocalyptic writers wrote with the same schema deliberately in mind.

Once we have got this straight, we have the correct framework for interpreting Mt. 10.23. Its *Sitz im Leben* is in the period of the early church. While the mission to the Gentiles was of central importance, and indirectly referred to at Mt. 10.18, there was also a mission to Israel. We should not forget either that in any given city, the Gentile mission normally began from the synagogue. It therefore flourished in many cities which had long-established, prosperous and successful Jewish communities. Matthew's concept of 'the cities of Israel' may therefore have been broader than

26.   For the history of scholarship up to the time when it was written, see M. Künzi, *Das Naherwartungslogion Matthäus 10,23. Geschichte seiner Auslegung* (BGBE 9. Tübingen: Mohr (Siebeck), 1970).

27.   E.g. J. Dupont, '"Vous n'aurez pas achevé les villes d'Israël avant que le Fils de l'homme ne vienne" (Mat. X.23)', *NovT* 2 (1958), pp. 228–44.

28.   E.g. A. Feuillet, 'Les origines et la signification de Mt 10,23b: Contribution à l'étude du problème eschatologique', *CBQ* 23 (1961), pp. 182–98.

ours, including cities where people of Israel dwelt, not only cities which were physically in Israel. We must interpret the saying literally. The coming of ὁ υἱὸς τοῦ ἀνθρώπου refers to the parousia of Jesus, as we have just seen throughout Mt. 24 and at 25.31. This saying reassures disciples of Jesus that the parousia will take place before the mission to Jews, and in Jewish places, is completed. This fits in completely with Matthew's editing. He believed that the parousia had been delayed, but that it was now at hand in his own time. It was this great event which would bring the persecution of the church to an end, with salvation for the disciples and judgement on outsiders. In its present form, the saying cannot go back to Jesus, for its Aramaic is problematic and it has no proper *Sitz im Leben* in his teaching. It has a perfect *Sitz im Leben* in the editorial procedures of Matthew, and no parallel in Luke. In its present form, therefore, the saying is a Matthean creation, though we cannot tell whether Matthew re-edited an older saying for his own purposes. Be that as it may, this is another example of ὁ υἱὸς τοῦ ἀνθρώπου as a title of Jesus *in Greek*, used with reference to his parousia.

Matthew took his next secondary saying from Q. It has also caused a lot of puzzlement to commentators, from the ancient period onwards. It is a response to a request for a sign. Matthew gives Jesus' response as follows:

Γενεὰ πονηρὰ καὶ μοιχαλὶς σημεῖον ἐπιζητεῖ, καὶ σημεῖον οὐ δοθήσεται αὐτῇ εἰ μὴ τὸ σημεῖον Ἰωνᾶ τοῦ προφήτου. ὥσπερ γὰρ ἦν Ἰωνᾶς ἐν τῇ κοιλίᾳ τοῦ κήτους τρεῖς ἡμέρας καὶ τρεῖς νύκτας, οὕτως ἔσται ὁ υἱὸς τοῦ ἀνθρώπου ἐν καρδίᾳ τῆς γῆς τρεῖς ἡμέρας καὶ τρεῖς νύκτας (Mt. 12.39-40, cf. Lk. 11.29-30).

To understand the origins of this midrash, we must go in the first place to a genuine incident recorded in our oldest source, the Gospel of Mark (Mk 8.11-13). Mark records that some Pharisees asked Jesus for a sign from heaven. He refused, with some considerable annoyance, complaining about 'this generation' seeking a sign. His refusal begins with one of the characteristics of his *ipsissima verba*, and continues with an idiom natural in Aramaic and in Hebrew, but not in Greek. It may be reconstructed as follows:

אמן אמר אנה לכון, אן יתיהב לדרא דן את.
Amen I say to you, a sign will certainly not be given to this generation!

It is this incident which was fastened on by a midrashist. From it comes the seeking for a sign, Jesus' criticism of the generation contemporary with him, and his declaration that a sign will not be given, a passive which refers to God at least as much as to himself. The midrashist has qualified this somewhat with his reference to Jonah. We know that Matthew took this from Q because he has so much in common with Luke. Both of them have the following:

γενεὰ πονηρὰ … σημεῖον (ἐπι)ζητεῖ, καὶ σημεῖον οὐ δοθήσεται αὐτῇ εἰ μὴ τὸ σημεῖον Ἰωνᾶ … γὰρ … Ἰωνᾶς … οὕτως ἔσται ὁ υἱὸς τοῦ ἀνθρώπου …

This is more than enough to show that there was a Q version, which Matthew and Luke each inherited in one form or another. The midrashist turned to the book of

Jonah, and produced a scripturally based piece which Matthew was happy to inherit, and which Luke felt a need to alter. The following part of the Matthean version is a straight quotation from LXX Jon. 2.1:

ἦν Ἰωνᾶς ἐν τῇ κοιλίᾳ τοῦ κήτους τρεῖς ἡμέρας καὶ τρεῖς νύκτας.

This is strong evidence that the midrashist was working in Greek. Moreover, the whole midrashic comparison makes excellent sense in Greek, provided that we understand what the three-day interval means. I have already brought forward evidence that it may refer to a short time.[29] In rabbinical literature it refers among other things to the period before the deliverance of Israel by means of the resurrection of the dead. This three-day interval was supported from scriptures such as Hos. 6.2, 'on the third day he will raise us up'. Jon. 2.1 is sometimes used in the same midrashic passages. Moreover, Jesus himself used the three-day interval with reference to a relatively short time (Lk. 13.32-33). The Q midrashist worked with a similar concept of a short time. This is what he meant by the three days and three nights, and he will not have thought that he was contradicting the teaching of Jesus. Rather, the midrashic comparison between Jonah and Jesus showed that the death and resurrection of Jesus was the only sign his generation would get, and from a Pharisaic perspective, that was not the sign from heaven for which they had asked.

The next secondary sayings in Matthew are both in the interpretation of the parable of the tares. It is generally agreed that the interpretation is completely secondary, and has been composed by Matthew. It has no satisfactory *Sitz im Leben* in the ministry of Jesus. It presupposes that the parable is an allegory so obscure that no one could understand it unless Jesus told them the interpretation. This is contrary to the aims and nature of the public teaching of Jesus. The interpretation has however a perfectly good *Sitz im Leben* in Matthew, who attached the greatest importance to the final judgement, with the salvation of the elect and the punishment of sinners. The linguistic argument for Matthean composition is especially strong, and includes some points which are difficult to understand in Aramaic rather than Greek.[30] Nowhere is this more obvious than in the first son of man saying, which identifies the original sower of the good seed in the field:

Ὁ σπείρων τὸ καλὸν σπέρμα ἐστὶν ὁ υἱὸς τοῦ ἀνθρώπου (Mt. 13.37).

Here the Greek term ὁ υἱὸς τοῦ ἀνθρώπου is a *Greek* title, considered by Matthew to be quite sufficient on its own to identify Jesus. This could not be done like this in Aramaic, for בר (א)נש(א) was a normal word for man. Consequently, it would have to be qualified to make reference to any particular person. In the light of the other passages which we have already discussed, we must further infer that Matthew regarded ὁ υἱὸς τοῦ ἀνθρώπου as especially appropriate here because of his eschatological role. This is expounded with the second occurrence of ὁ υἱὸς τοῦ ἀνθρώπου at Mt. 13.41. Here the Son of man sends out his angels, and the result

29.   See pp. 207–8 above.
30.   See especially Jeremias, *Parables*, pp. 82–5.

is the punishment of the wicked and the salvation of the righteous, points which we have seen to be central in the eschatological presentation of Matthew 24. It is evident that Matthew's knowledge of the Aramaic origins of ὁ υἱὸς τοῦ ἀνθρώπου in no way inhibited his creative use of it as a Greek title. It is also significant that ὁ υἱὸς τοῦ ἀνθρώπου is associated with βασιλεία in this passage, especially in v. 41. If Jesus had really taken 'son of man' from Dan. 7.13-14, where כבר אנש receives מלכו, this association would have been normal in his teaching. Instead, we find this association only in an evangelist who certainly did make midrashic use of Dan. 7.13, and who found ὁ υἱὸς τοῦ ἀνθρώπου as a Christological title in this very text.

Matthew's next Son of man saying has been edited into his Marcan source. In the introduction to Peter's confession at Caesarea Philippi (Mk 8.27), the Marcan Jesus asks his disciples,

τίνα με λέγουσιν οἱ ἄνθρωποι εἶναι;

This introduces genuine material recording verdicts that Jesus was really John the Baptist, Elijah or 'one of the prophets'. These are verdicts which the early church would not have the slightest interest in making up, and which have an excellent *Sitz im Leben* in the Judaism of Jesus' time. Mark then interpolated Peter's confession σὺ εἶ ὁ χριστός, and his 'messianic secret', followed by his heavily redacted version of Jesus' genuine prediction of his forthcoming death. In a detailed discussion, I have sought to establish that the genuine prediction did contain the term בר (א)נש(א), which was reasonably translated with ὁ υἱὸς τοῦ ἀνθρώπου, in accordance with a definable translator's strategy. This prediction was then subjected to secondary development.[31]

Matthew continued the editorial processes already visible in Mark. In his introduction to the actual prediction (Mt. 16.21), he supplied a subject, named as Ἰησοῦς, to which he may have added χριστός (read by א* B*). Among his many alterations to the prediction itself is the replacement of τὸν υἱὸν τοῦ ἀνθρώπου with αὐτόν, so that it is no longer a specifically Son of man prediction. In Jesus' question which introduces the whole incident, Matthew replaces με with τὸν υἱὸν τοῦ ἀνθρώπου, so that the edited question at Mt. 16.13 now reads:

τίνα λέγουσιν οἱ ἄνθρωποι εἶναι τὸν υἱὸν τοῦ ἀνθρώπου;

To understand these editorial changes, we must begin with Matthew's two main points, his revised version of Peter's confession and the extraordinary delineation of Peter's leading position in the church which follows. His version of Peter's confession has two of the church's major Christological titles:

σὺ εἶ ὁ χριστὸς ὁ υἱὸς τοῦ θεοῦ τοῦ ζῶντος.

31.   See pp. 201–9 above.

Jesus' response has Peter play the leading role in the church which he did in fact play in the years immediately succeeding Jesus' death and resurrection. It contains the famous pun with Peter being the rock on which Jesus will build his church, a pun which works as well in Aramaic with כיפא as in Greek with Πέτρος, and in American English with Rock. This is extremely coherent, for we know from Acts and the Epistles that 'Christ' and 'Son of God' were two of the three major confessional titles of the early church. Moreover, whereas κύριος has a very broad range of meaning and is frequently used by Matthew (*c.* 76 times) throughout that range, these two titles were by this stage more specific. The term χριστός tended to be used with particular reference to Jesus' role in salvation history, and he was by now 'son of God' in the special sense of being especially closely related to God and chosen by him for his outstanding role in salvation history. Peter's confession is accordingly to be regarded as a model Christian confession.

We can now see why ὁ υἱὸς τοῦ ἀνθρώπου has been removed from the first passion prediction. It is not that Matthew considered ὁ υἱὸς τοῦ ἀνθρώπου in any way unsuitable for passion predictions. He uses this term when editing Marcan passion predictions at Mt. 17.12, editing Mk 9.12; Mt. 17.22, editing Mk 9.31; Mt. 20.18, editing Mk 10.33; and Mt. 20.28, editing Mk 10.45. Of these passages Mt. 17.22 and 20.18 are especially close to the present passage, Mt. 16.21. Matthew also uses ὁ υἱὸς τοῦ ἀνθρώπου in a passion prediction of his own inserted at Mt. 26.2. It was therefore in his view an entirely suitable term for Jesus to use in passion predictions in general. He had entirely positive reasons for introducing this first prediction with Ἰησοῦς, with or without χριστός, and simply referring back to Jesus in this capacity as αὐτόν. What Matthew was determined to do was to mention Jesus personally by name in a passion prediction which immediately follows the two major confessional titles, ὁ χριστός and ὁ υἱὸς τοῦ θεοῦ. He has also replaced Mark's διδάσκειν αὐτούς with δεικνύειν τοῖς μαθηταῖς αὐτοῦ, so revelation directed personally at the disciples shortly before Peter, just presented as the Rock of the church, makes the catastrophic mistake of trying to persuade Jesus not to undergo his atoning death. This first passion prediction is the first presentation of what was for Matthew the centre of salvation history. So it is Ἰησοῦς, the human being who has to die, but who is also ὁ χριστός and ὁ υἱὸς τοῦ θεοῦ, which made his death of central importance, who is deliberately mentioned here.

It is with all this editing in mind that Matthew inserted ὁ υἱὸς τοῦ ἀνθρώπου into his introduction to the whole section at Mt. 16.13:

τίνα λέγουσιν οἱ ἄνθρωποι εἶναι τὸν υἱὸν τοῦ ἀνθρώπου;

The manuscript tradition did not like this, with most MSS interpolating με as at Mk 8.27 and Lk. 9.18, and C W having it in a different position. We must however follow ℵ B 579 al., a sound MS tradition which did not have reason to leave με out unless it was absent from their sources. We must infer that Matthew regarded ὁ υἱὸς τοῦ ἀνθρώπου as an unambiguous term for Jesus himself, in Greek. He has deliberately inserted it here as a correct reference to Jesus, preceding the false answers of uncomprehending people followed by the true confession of Peter. It forms an *inclusio* with ὁ υἱὸς τοῦ ἀνθρώπου at 16.27-28, which marks off a complete episode in which Matthew has used all three of his major Christological titles in a vigorous presentation of Jesus' forthcoming death, resurrection and second coming for salvation and judgement.

The next occurrence of ὁ υἱὸς τοῦ ἀνθρώπου, at Mt. 16.27, is an edited version of a genuine saying found at Mk 8.38, so I discuss the original saying elsewhere.[32] Matthew has omitted the first part of Mk 8.38, of which he has another version at Mt. 10.33 (//Lk. 12.9).[33] He has also developed the second part of the saying. The result is an unambiguous reference to Jesus' second coming, followed by judgement:

μέλλει γὰρ ὁ υἱὸς τοῦ ἀνθρώπου ἔρχεσθαι ἐν τῇ δόξῃ τοῦ πατρὸς αὐτοῦ μετὰ τῶν ἀγγέλων αὐτοῦ, καὶ τότε ἀποδώσει ἑκάστῳ κατὰ τὴν πρᾶξιν αὐτοῦ.

This saying also has the references to 'Son of man' and 'coming' which are crucial indicators of the influence of Dan. 7.13, and we have already seen Matthew making conscious use of this text in describing Jesus' parousia.[34] Glory, God and angels are also to be found in the Danielic context, and Matthew's addition of the final words are strongly scriptural in orientation too (cf. LXX Ps. 61.13; Prov. 24.12). These points are crucial for understanding Matthew's editing of Mk 9.1 to form Mt. 16.28. Mark's prediction of the coming of the kingdom was not quite clear enough for Matthew, so he edited it to make absolutely clear that the second coming of Jesus would take place during the lifetime of some of the disciples who were present during the historic ministry:

ἀμὴν λέγω ὑμῖν ὅτι εἰσίν τινες τῶν ὧδε ἑστώτων οἵτινες οὐ μὴ γεύσωνται θανάτου ἕως ἂν ἴδωσιν τὸν υἱὸν τοῦ ἀνθρώπου ἐρχόμενον ἐν τῇ βασιλείᾳ αὐτοῦ.

Here again we have the collocation of 'Son of man' and 'coming', the crucial indicators of the further influence of Dan. 7.13. This time we also have a reference to the kingdom, which is given to the man-like figure at Dan. 7.14. We have seen that it is a standing weakness of the theory that the Gospel term ὁ υἱὸς τοῦ ἀνθρώπου is derived primarily from Dan. 7.13-14 that ὁ υἱὸς τοῦ ἀνθρώπου and βασιλεία are not associated either frequently, or in anything which looks plausible as the earliest layer of the tradition. It is entirely appropriate that they are associated here, where Matthew's editorial activity shows awareness of his use of this text. Otherwise, the two terms are associated only at Mt. 13.41 in the whole of the synoptic tradition, and we have seen that Mt. 13.41 is entirely due to secondary Matthean editing. Moreover, the kingdom of God was central to the teaching of Jesus. If Dan. 7.13-14 had been the main source of his use of (א)שנ(א) בר, the two terms would surely have been used together more often, and in tradition which showed some signs of being primitive. Matthew's late and secondary editorial procedures are culturally perfectly in place in Jesus' environment. This is part of the evidence that this kind of use of ὁ υἱὸς τοῦ ἀνθρώπου is secondary.

32. See pp. 191–3 above.
33. See further pp. 189–92.
34. See pp. 215–6 above.

Finally, we see once again that Matthew considered ὁ υἱὸς τοῦ ἀνθρώπου an entirely natural term to use when expounding Jesus' second coming in Greek. In using it at Mt. 16.27-28 to form an *inclusio* with Mt. 16.21, in which it is used as generally as possible as a description of Jesus in particular, he further shows how much it was at home in the exposition of Gospel traditions in Greek.

There is one more secondary use of the term Son of man to discuss here, in Matthew's version of the Q saying, Mt. 19.28//Lk. 22.30. The original saying must have been very remarkable, for it had the Twelve sitting on twelve thrones in a scene which must belong somehow to the last judgement. Unfortunately, neither Matthew nor Luke seems to have been satisfied with the introduction, which we can no longer recover. The Matthean version is as follows:

Ἀμὴν λέγω ὑμῖν ὅτι ὑμεῖς οἱ ἀκολουθήσαντές μοι, ἐν τῇ παλιγγενεσίᾳ, ὅταν καθίσῃ ὁ υἱὸς τοῦ ἀνθρώπου ἐπὶ θρόνου δόξης αὐτοῦ, καθήσεσθε καὶ ὑμεῖς ἐπὶ δώδεκα θρόνους κρίνοντες τὰς δώδεκα φυλὰς τοῦ Ἰσραήλ.

The first part of this saying is reminiscent of Mt. 25.31, the only other New Testament text in which the Son of man sits on the throne of his glory. We have already seen that this is secondary, and that it was partly formed by conscious use of Dan. 7.9-14. We must make the same inference here. The introduction cannot be satisfactorily reconstructed in Aramaic, which has no proper equivalent for παλιγγενεσία. All this evidence is entirely coherent. The specifically Matthean introduction to a Q saying has a perfect *Sitz im Leben* in Matthew, and cannot be reconstructed as part of the teaching of Jesus. This is moreover Matthew's dominant use of ὁ υἱὸς τοῦ ἀνθρώπου in secondary sayings, with reference to the last times.

This concludes our study of secondary Son of man sayings in Matthew. We have seen that Matthew found the term ὁ υἱὸς τοῦ ἀνθρώπου in both scripture and tradition. He expanded freely and creatively the usage which he found at Dan. 7.13, where he saw a picture of the second coming of Jesus. In the eschatological chapters 24–25, the centre of his expectation was ἡ παρουσία τοῦ υἱοῦ τοῦ ἀνθρώπου, coming on the clouds of heaven, bringing salvation and judgement. This is also reflected in his other secondary sayings, virtually all of which also refer to the last times. These sayings were created both with and without reference to the primary text Dan. 7.13, and to other texts. The nearest to an exception is Mt. 16.13, where however Matthew is clearly editing a complex of material in which the term ὁ υἱὸς τοῦ ἀνθρώπου has been taken from Mark 8.31. It is nonetheless instructive, because in this text it is so obvious that Matthew regards ὁ υἱὸς τοῦ ἀνθρώπου as an unambiguous reference to Jesus, without any further explanation. Otherwise, all Matthew's secondary sayings refer to the last times, when Jesus would come in glory for salvation and judgement. We know from the rest of the New Testament how important the second coming was for the early church. This is the reason for Matthew's secondary use of ὁ υἱὸς τοῦ ἀνθρώπου. It does not matter that this term is virtually absent outside the Gospels (except Acts 7.56 with the articles, Heb. 2.6, Rev. 1.13 and 14.14 without them). Matthew knew nothing about that. He found ὁ υἱὸς τοῦ ἀνθρώπου in tradition and scripture, and in both of them it was already used with reference to one of his most profound needs, to portray creatively the second coming of Jesus. That is the reason for his extensive secondary usage.

4. More Son of Man Sayings in Luke

I have already considered most of Luke's secondary sayings, because they are concentrated in the eschatological sections Lk. 17–18.8, 21. I found that, like Matthew, Luke used ὁ υἱὸς τοῦ ἀνθρώπου as a major title for Jesus in his eschatological role in the last times. He differed from Matthew in making clear that these times were not imminent at the time of Jesus or soon afterwards: rather they were at hand in Luke's own day. I also found that he cannot be shown to have been aware of the derivation of ὁ υἱὸς τοῦ ἀνθρώπου from Dan. 7.13. For him it was a traditional title for Jesus, but we cannot show that he regarded it as scriptural. I also found that he did not share the extent of Matthew's creativity. He himself produced only two sayings, one of them a passion prediction based on his other passion predictions (Lk. 17.25), the other the conclusion to his final eschatological discourse (Lk. 21.36). These are the two major definable categories in which he found the term ὁ υἱὸς τοῦ ἀνθρώπου in his sources. His usage should therefore not be regarded as very innovatory.

Similar remarks apply to the majority of Luke's other secondary sayings, though not perhaps to the first. This is a Q saying, at Lk. 6.22:

μακάριοί ἐστε ὅταν μισήσωσιν ὑμᾶς οἱ ἄνθρωποι, καὶ ὅταν ἀφορίσωσιν ὑμᾶς καὶ ὀνειδίσωσιν καὶ ἐκβάλωσιν τὸ ὄνομα ὑμῶν ὡς πονηρὸν ἕνεκα τοῦ υἱοῦ τοῦ ἀνθρώπου·

Here the Son of man is obviously Jesus, a fact so obvious to Luke that he uses it without explanation at its first occurrence here. Luke's audiences will surely have thought of persecution in the days of the early church, which they may not have distinguished from the times of the historic ministry. Thus ὁ υἱὸς τοῦ ἀνθρώπου is not used with an eschatological reference here. This is perfectly in accordance with the traditions which Luke inherited. It is however very difficult to tell whether Luke himself invented or merely inherited this particular occurrence. Matthew has ἕνεκεν ἐμοῦ (Mt. 5.11). It has often been argued that Matthew is so keen on ὁ υἱὸς τοῦ ἀνθρώπου that he would not have removed it.[35] We have however seen that it was probably he who did remove it from the authentic sayings – Mt. 10.32-33 (//Lk. 12.8-9, 8.38)[36] – and he may not have liked the very mundane nature of this usage, which refers neither to Jesus' eschatological role nor to anything significant during the historic ministry.

Discussion of the Aramaic level of the tradition however suggests that ὁ υἱὸς τοῦ ἀνθρώπου is indeed secondary. One might attempt a reconstruction as follows:

35.   E.g. Fitzmyer, *Luke*, p. 635.
36.   See pp. 183–6 above.

בריכין אנתון כד סנין יתכון וחסדין ונסחין שמכון כביש בדילי

Blessed (are) you when (people) hate you and revile (you) and remove your name as evil because of me.

Luke's Greek ἐκβάλωσιν τὸ ὄνομα ὑμῶν is peculiar, and a natural Aramaic idiom can readily be reconstructed for it, while Matthew's editing has produced more fluent Greek. Black suggested the Aphel of נפק as the underlay for ἐκβάλωσιν.[37] The Aramaic word נפק has a large semantic area, it is the most obvious equivalent of ἐκβάλλω, and it is consequently used here by sin cur pesh. None of Black's parallels are however quite the same as the proposed usage in this saying, and all are of much later date. I have accordingly preferred to use נסח. This word occurs at Ezra 6.11, and in later Jewish Aramaic, so it will have been in use at the time of Jesus. It is basically a somewhat stronger word for removing, but the crucial point is that it is used in two earlier texts for removing someone's name, in a similar sense and context to the hostility of the present passage (KAI 225 9-10; 228A 14-15). In this context it would be difficult to translate, and ἐκβάλωσιν would be an entirely reasonable rendering.

I have however followed Matthew in reconstructing בדילי. The use of בר (א)נש(א) at this point would not be satisfactory, because it is indefinite just at the point where we need a clear reference to Jesus. We must therefore infer that τοῦ υἱοῦ τοῦ ἀνθρώπου is indeed secondary, and that it replaced the first person pronoun when the tradition was being transmitted in Greek. Whether it was Luke personally or a predecessor who did this must remain uncertain. The term ὁ υἱὸς τοῦ ἀνθρώπου was clearly an unambiguous term for Jesus when the tradition was being transmitted in Greek, and it was used of the earthly Jesus during his ministry. Either Luke or a predecessor may accordingly have found it appropriate here.

The next secondary saying is Lk. 11.30, which I have already discussed to some extent in considering the Q parallel at Mt. 12.40.[38] We have seen that this saying was developed from a genuine saying of Jesus, in which he refused a request for a sign from heaven (Mk 8.11-13). The Matthean version was produced by a midrashist who used the book of Jonah in Greek. Luke's version is significantly shorter than that of Matthew:

καθὼς γὰρ ἐγένετο Ἰωνᾶς τοῖς Νινευίταις σημεῖον, οὕτως ἔσται καὶ ὁ υἱὸς τοῦ ἀνθρώπου τῇ γενεᾷ ταύτῃ.

We know that the title ὁ υἱὸς τοῦ ἀνθρώπου was in the Q version, because it is reproduced by both evangelists. We should probably infer that Luke has abbreviated the Q version. As a Greek Gentile Christian, he will not have been happy with the logical implication that Jesus would be in the earth for three days and three nights. His abbreviated version does not home in on any particular feature of Jonah or Jesus, except the uniqueness of each of them in being God's only sign for their generation in their place. The use of the term ὁ υἱὸς τοῦ ἀνθρώπου does not bring

---

37.   Black, *Aramaic Approach*, p. 165.
38.   See pp. 233–4 above.

any particular implication to this. Luke has accordingly accepted it from the tradition as an unambiguous reference to Jesus, as he does elsewhere.

Apart from Lk. 17–18.8, the eschatological sayings discussed above, the next secondary saying in Luke is unique to him. It comes at the end of the story of Zacchaeus, which is unique to Luke as a whole. When Zacchaeus has repented and promised restitution, Jesus announces salvation for his house, and concludes with a saying in which Jesus explains his own function:

ἦλθεν γὰρ ὁ υἱὸς τοῦ ἀνθρώπου ζητῆσαι καὶ σῶσαι τὸ ἀπολωλός (Lk. 19.10).

This cannot be an original saying in its present form, because (א)שׁנ(א) בר would not have sufficient referring power to make clear the reference to Jesus. It makes excellent sense in Greek, for by this time ὁ υἱὸς τοῦ ἀνθρώπου was an unambiguous and unique title of Jesus. Moreover, it correctly represents a significant aspect of the ministry of the historical Jesus, and it has an excellent *Sitz im Leben* where we now find it. Whether Luke inherited it from tradition or wrote it himself as an appropriate conclusion to this story, we can no longer tell. In either case, he regarded it as an unambiguous title of Jesus, perfectly in place with reference to the historic ministry as well as to the events of the last day.

There is one final saying which is secondary in its present place, though it is obviously based on old tradition, and I have argued that the sayings on which it is based go back ultimately to at least one genuine prediction by Jesus of his death and resurrection.[39] Luke altered the Marcan tradition that the resurrection appearances were in Galilee. In preparing for his stories in which they take place in Jerusalem instead, he replaced the instruction by Mark's angel that the women should tell the disciples to go to Galilee with a reminder by his two angels of the prediction which Jesus had made when he was in Galilee (Lk. 24.7). This form of the prediction is clearly based on Luke's other predictions, and simply shows that Luke was very happy with ὁ υἱὸς τοῦ ἀνθρώπου as a title of Jesus, in passion predictions as elsewhere.

Luke's usage is accordingly less extensive than that of Matthew. Like Matthew, he has a majority of secondary sayings with an eschatological orientation. Unlike Matthew, he has very few secondary sayings outside his main eschatological sections, Luke 17–18.8 and 21. One of these sayings is from Q, one from the Marcan tradition of predictions of Jesus' passion and resurrection, and it is possible that both the other two sayings are drawn from tradition. Two conclusions follow. In the first place, Luke was entirely happy with the title ὁ υἱὸς τοῦ ἀνθρώπου, which he inherited from Mark and Q. On the other hand, Luke did not make great use of this title when he was creating new sayings.

He did so again at Acts 7.56. Here he wrote a short speech for the dying Hellenistic Christian Stephen. In it, he used ὁ υἱὸς τοῦ ἀνθρώπου, thereby showing again that from Luke's point of view it was an important title of Jesus alone *in Greek*.

---

39. See Ch. 9.

5. Mark

Apart from his development of the passion and resurrection predictions, which are derived ultimately from two genuine sayings of Jesus and hence discussed in Chapter 9, Mark has only two secondary sayings, Mk 13.26 and 14.62.[40]

The first of these two secondary sayings comes at the climax of Mark's eschatological discourse. This contains a number of features which have a natural *Sitz im Leben* in the period of the early church, rather than in the ministry of Jesus. The most striking is in a context of the predicted persecutions which in fact took place during the period of the early church. This is the prediction that the Gospel must first be preached to all the nations (Mk 13.10). The Gentile mission does not have any *Sitz im Leben* in the teaching of Jesus. He expected the kingdom to come too soon for it to take place, and consequently it does not belong within his teaching in general. Equally secondary are the predictions that people will report the presence of ὁ χριστός, and that ψευδόχριστοι will arise (Mk 13.21-22). These are dependent on the development of the title 'the Christ' in the earliest period of the church.[41] It is only after this complex of secondary events that Mark presents scripturally based predictions of heavenly phenomena such as the darkening of the sun and moon, and the falling of the stars (Mk 13.24-25). There follows the climactic moment of Jesus' second coming:

καὶ τότε ὄψονται τὸν υἱὸν τοῦ ἀνθρώπου ἐρχόμενον ἐν νεφέλαις μετὰ δυνάμεως πολλῆς καὶ δόξης.

The dependence of this verse on Dan. 7.13 is almost universally recognized. It has the crucial terms ὁ υἱὸς τοῦ ἀνθρώπου and ἔρχομαι, the distinctive clouds, and the common elements of power and glory. As in Matthew and Luke, the reference of the title ὁ υἱὸς τοῦ ἀνθρώπου, already used of Jesus several times by Mark, is taken to be unambiguous. It follows that ὁ υἱὸς τοῦ ἀνθρώπου was already a Greek title of Jesus, seen in Dan. 7.13 interpreted as a prophecy of his second coming. Moreover, it is clear that this is part of a midrash on several Old Testament passages. Some of the other ones are difficult to locate with precision, precisely because this is a midrash which utilizes passages creatively rather than quoting them. For example, the falling of the stars at Mk 13.25 may well be from Isa. 34.4, and the gathering at Mk 13.27 could be from Zech. 2.10 LXX. Since people on earth see the event of the Son of man coming, he must come from heaven to earth, as the man-like figure should be seen to do in the original text of Dan. 7.13. The passage should be interpreted literally, in accordance with the normal beliefs of the early church. It is immediately followed by the gathering of the elect, as for example at Deut. 30.4.

This passage accordingly shows ὁ υἱὸς τοῦ ἀνθρώπου already used as a title of Jesus in Greek, and seen in scripture at Dan. 7.13 in a prediction of his return. This

---

40.   For more detailed discussion of some aspects of these texts, including consideration of some of the older secondary literature, see Casey, *Son of Man*, pp. 165–83, 213–17.

41.   Casey, *From Jewish Prophet to Gentile God*, pp. 41–4, 105–6.

mirrors the belief in his second coming found abundantly outside the Gospels in the New Testament, as already in a speech of Peter at Acts 3.20. It differs precisely in its use of Dan. 7.13 and the title ὁ υἱὸς τοῦ ἀνθρώπου. This strongly suggests that the use of Dan. 7.13 in particular was due to the perception that ὁ υἱὸς τοῦ ἀνθρώπου was to be found in the authentic sayings of Jesus which form the majority of Son of man sayings in Mark.

The other secondary Son of man saying in Mark is equally clearly embedded in a secondary context, and part of a midrashic combination of scriptural texts. It comes at the climax of Jesus' trial before the high priest, Joseph Caiaphas. It is well known that the account of the trial has many peculiarities.[42] These basically begin after the disciples had fled (Mk 14.50-52), so it is a reasonable conjecture that Mark supplied information at points where his source material failed him. After problems over the question of the destruction of the Temple, the high priest asks what is, in terms of the Marcan narrative, a leading question:

Σὺ εἶ ὁ Χριστὸς ὁ υἱὸς τοῦ εὐλογητοῦ; (Mk 14.61).

There are two things wrong with this in itself. First, the term Χριστός and its Aramaic equivalent (א)משיח had not yet crystallized out into a title like this. Accordingly, the use of Χριστός must be due to the early church, or to Mark himself. Second, while τοῦ εὐλογητοῦ sounds like a circumlocution for God, it is not attested as such. Once again, therefore, we must see here the hand of the early church. But if the early church is responsible for the question, it must also be responsible for the first part of Jesus' answer:

Ἐγώ εἰμι, καὶ ὄψεσθε τὸν υἱὸν τοῦ ἀνθρώπου ἐκ δεξιῶν καθήμενον τῆς δυνάμεως καὶ ἐρχόμενον μετὰ τῶν νεφελῶν τοῦ οὐρανοῦ.

After his affirmative answer to the secondary question, Jesus continues with the same midrashic use of Dan. 7.13 as we have seen in the secondary Mk 13.26. Here again we have the crucial ὁ υἱὸς τοῦ ἀνθρώπου and ἔρχομαι, and this time also the very clear μετὰ τῶν νεφελῶν τοῦ οὐρανοῦ, five words running identical to the (perfectly accurate) translation of Theodotion.

Here too we have Dan. 7.13 in midrashic combination with at least one other Old Testament text, with ὄψεσθε probably from Zech. 12.10, and ἐκ δεξιῶν καθήμενον τῆς δυνάμεως certainly dependent on the opening of Ps. 110. This text is used more than any other in the New Testament.[43] It is also quoted in Peter's early speech at Acts 2.34-35, a speech which shows many signs of being based upon early and indeed authentic tradition. It was a very useful text because it could be interpreted

---

42. For detailed discussion of the primary sources with a full review of the secondary literature, see Brown, *Death of the Messiah*, pp. 315–560.

43. D. M. Hay, *Glory at the Right Hand. Psalm 110 in Early Christianity* (Nashville: Abingdon, 1973); W. R. G. Loader, 'Christ at the Right Hand – Ps. CX 1 in the New Testament', *NTS* 24 (1977–8), pp. 199–228; M. Gourges, *A La Droite de Dieu. Résurrection de Jésus et Actualisation du Psaume 110:1 dans le Nouveau Testament* (EBib. Paris: Gabalda, 1978).

of Jesus at the right hand of God, and consequently used, as Peter used it, as a proof that God had raised Jesus from the dead. This was especially important when the mode of resurrection was not clear, and the stories of the empty tomb had not yet been told. Consequently, the early Christians will have needed this text right from the beginning, just when Luke portrays Peter as using it. Jesus' second coming is logically secondary to this, and Dan. 7.13 did not catch on in the rest of the New Testament, as it surely would have done if Jesus had used it in this clear way at such a climactic moment. From Mark's point of view, this verse also brings the 'messianic secret' to an end, another secondary development which has an excellent *Sitz im Leben* in the Gospel of Mark, but not in the teaching of Jesus.

The high priest's reaction to Jesus' answer is equally problematical from a historical point of view. He tore his garments and accused Jesus of blasphemy, after which the whole council judged Jesus worthy of death. The high priest should tear his garments after a conviction for the legal offence of blasphemy, a conviction unjustified by what Jesus is supposed to have said. Jesus was crucified for sedition, which would be very difficult to justify from this charge of blasphemy. All this is accordingly too much to believe as a historical account. We are dealing with the creativity of the early church, and probably that of Mark himself.

There are two more general reasons for not believing in the historicity of Mk 13.26 and 14.62, apart from their obvious *Sitz im Leben* in the early church and in Mark, and the historical problems surrounding their presence in evidently secondary material. In the synoptic Gospels as a whole, Jesus never refers to his second coming except by using Dan. 7.13 and referring to the Son of man coming (except the parabolic Mk 13.35, edited at Mt. 24.42).[44] It was not characteristic of Jesus to deal with a topic only in such rigidly scriptural terms. Secondly, the resurrection of the Son of man and his coming are never combined, even though they are alternative indications of his vindication: this implies a separate origin for these two groups of sayings.

This concludes a massive argument of cumulative weight. These two sayings are certainly secondary. This is a quite fundamental result, though it is not new. It means that our oldest Gospel contains seven uses of the term Son of man in authentic sayings of Jesus, five sayings which were developed from two or more authentic predictions of his death and resurrection, and only two sayings which have resulted from the midrashic activities of the early church. It has often been argued that many Son of man sayings must be authentic sayings of Jesus because the term is so common throughout all four Gospels. We can now see that our oldest Gospel does in fact have a distribution of sayings that is entirely consistent with such inferences. It shows how the use of the term ὁ υἱὸς τοῦ ἀνθρώπου began. The Aramaic (א)שׁנ(א) בר was used in authentic sayings of Jesus. The Greek ὁ υἱὸς τοῦ ἀνθρώπου was used to translate it. It was therefore used in the expansion of the predictions of Jesus' death and resurrection, expansions which satisfied a profound need of the early church, for which Jesus' death and resurrection were of central

44.   See pp. 218–9 above.

importance. The Greek ὁ υἱὸς τοῦ ἀνθρώπου was consequently seen in Dan. 7.13, and used in midrashic combination with other texts to portray Jesus' second coming, another belief of central importance to the early church. I consider the nature of this transition process more fully in the next chapter.

6. Conclusions

The major conclusions of this chapter are extraordinary, though they are well enough known. Despite its origin as an attempt to translate the idiomatic use of an Aramaic phrase into Greek, a language which contains no such idiom, ὁ υἱὸς τοῦ ἀνθρώπου was an important title of Jesus *in Greek*, and that for all three synoptic evangelists. Mark and Matthew also found it important that the term was to be found in Dan. 7.13, which they treated as a prophecy of the second coming of Jesus. Both Matthew and Luke have a definably predominant use of the term in secondary sayings: they use it with reference to Jesus' role in the events of the last times, a usage founded on the work of Mark in his two secondary sayings (Mk 13.26; 14.62). While Luke cannot be shown to have made conscious use of Dan. 7.13 himself, its deliberate use by both Mark and Matthew shows that the influence of this text is one reason for the predominant use of ὁ υἱὸς τοῦ ἀνθρώπου with eschatological reference in secondary sayings.

The other reason for this dominant eschatological reference was the need for it. One of the church's most profound needs was to believe in the second coming of Jesus. In Matthew, we can see the creative stage of this need in full flow, and in Mark we can see its clear beginnings. Finding the term ὁ υἱὸς τοῦ ἀνθρώπου in both scripture and tradition with deliberate eschatological reference, Matthew expanded this usage creatively, inventing the expressive term ἡ παρουσία τοῦ υἱοῦ τοῦ ἀνθρώπου, which describes the churches' need so beautifully. Luke's usage was different, because he wrote so much later. In secondary sayings, he still uses ὁ υἱὸς τοῦ ἀνθρώπου predominantly with eschatological reference, because this is what his sources transmitted to him, and he was happy with it. The passage of time, however, made it essential for him to show that the second coming of Jesus should not have been expected sooner. On the other hand, like so many Christians down to the present day, he remained fervent in his belief that the Son of man would come soon.

We are now in a position to see the overall shape of the solution to the Son of man problem. The first sayings were the authentic sayings of Jesus studied in Chs 4–8. A second group resulted from the development of one or more predictions of Jesus' death and resurrection, studied in Ch. 9. A third group began from the use of Dan. 7.13 at Mk 13.26 and 14.62, and was subsequently expanded into the eschatological sayings of Matthew and Luke. There is more to say about the transition process from (א)נשׁ(א) בר to ὁ υἱὸς τοῦ ἀνθρώπου, to be considered in the next chapter.

Chapter Eleven

TRANSLATION AND THE USE OF SCRIPTURE. FROM SAYINGS OF JESUS TO THE SYNOPTIC EVANGELISTS

In Chs 4–9, I discussed authentic sayings of Jesus. All these were originally spoken in Aramaic. In all of them, Jesus used the Aramaic term (א)שׁנ(א) בר in a particular idiomatic way, which I examined in Ch. 2. In Ch. 10, I discussed secondary sayings. In these, all three synoptic evangelists used ὁ υἱὸς τοῦ ἀνθρώπου as a Greek title of Jesus, the same Greek title as they used in their Greek versions of authentic sayings of Jesus. Matthew and Mark both used ὁ υἱὸς τοῦ ἀνθρώπου with particular reference to Jesus' second coming, which they saw predicted at Dan. 7.13. The primary purpose of this chapter is to examine the transition from (א)שׁנ(א) בר to ὁ υἱὸς τοῦ ἀνθρώπου. I examine first the translation process as applied to authentic sayings, secondly the midrashic creation of new sayings, and thirdly the rewriting of authentic sayings both to modify them and effectively to create new ones. I then consider whether we can uncover an overall view of ὁ υἱὸς τοῦ ἀνθρώπου taken by each of the synoptic evangelists, and by Q.

1. The Translation Process

We saw in Ch. 1 that the question of the translation of (א)שׁנ(א) בר to produce ὁ υἱὸς τοῦ ἀνθρώπου set impossible problems for all the older scholarship. I noted for example the clear statement of Wellhausen that this translation was wrong, and that ὁ ἄνθρωπος should have been used.[1] Negative comments on ὁ υἱὸς τοῦ ἀνθρώπου itself have also been frequent. For example, in 1971 Jeremias described ὁ υἱὸς τοῦ ἀνθρώπου as 'a rather barbaric literal translation'.[2] Similar comments have continued in recent years. I have noted for example Hare arguing that the translator should have put ἄνθρωπος or υἱὸς ἀνθρώπου, A.Y. Collins ἄνθρωπος, and Ross ὁ ἄνθρωπος οὗτος, ἄνθρωπος, τις or ἄνθρωπος τις.[3] Such views have been so widespread that Burkett, writing as recently as 1999, attributed to me the view that in authentic sayings using (א)שׁנ(א) בר, 'the general reference was *misunderstood* as a title referring to Daniel 7.13', and he classified

---

1. See p. 18 above.
2. Jeremias, *New Testament Theology*, p. 260.
3. See pp. 43–4 above.

me with scholars who 'have to assume that the Aramaic has been *mistranslated*' (italics mine).[4] I have never expressed either view. On the contrary, I have argued repeatedly and at length that 'the translator should be considered to have done as well as possible'.[5] Marcus, writing in 2003 with my previous efforts to consider the translation process available to him, simply chose to cast them on one side in favour of the extraordinary assumption that ὁ υἱὸς τοῦ ἀνθρώπου somehow must mean *exactly* what the historical Jesus said.[6] It is reasonable to contrast the basic and accurate summary of one of the world's leading authorities in Translation Studies:

> Translation is a very complex activity, and anyone engaged in it knows full well that there is no such thing as equivalence conceived of as sameness across languages. The translated text will never be the same as the source text. Moreover, there is always a context in which translation takes place which influences the decisions that the translators have to take.[7]

It follows that a fresh attempt on the problems posed by the translation of בר (א)נש(א) with ὁ υἱὸς τοῦ ἀνθρώπου must now be made. I again argue that, given the subculture in which this work was done, this translation was the most natural possible. To achieve this result, I again draw on the work of our colleagues in other fields of study, especially bilingualism, translation studies and the LXX.

Bilingualism, or even multilingualism, is an inevitable result of living where more than one language is spoken. Consequently, people may be functionally bilingual without having full command of both languages. Moreover, all bilinguals suffer from interference. The most important forms of interference are those which are visible, sufficiently different from the speech and writing of monoglot users of the language for scholars to be able to measure them. One of the least obvious forms of interference is accordingly relevant when it can be measured – the use of a linguistic item more commonly than by monoglot speakers. For example, Danish students are reported using the English definite article more often than monoglot speakers of English. This reflects 'the fact that Danish and English seem to have slightly different conceptions of what constitutes generic as opposed to specific reference'.[8] More generally, a sample of the use of the English definite article in translations from Finnish showed a more frequent use than in a corresponding sample of untranslated text, even though the translations from Finnish had been checked by native English speakers.[9] Translations from German

---

4. Burkett, *Son of Man Debate*, pp. 90, 93. See further pp. 47–8 above.

5. Casey, 'Idiom and Translation', p. 177, quoting *Son of Man*, p. 231.

6. Marcus, 'Son of Man as son of Adam', pp. 43–5.

7. S. Bassnett, 'Text Types and Power Relations', in A. Trosborg (ed.), *Text Typology and Translation* (BTL 26. Amsterdam: Benjamins, 1997), pp. 87–98 (88–9). For discussion of the concept of equivalence in recent scholarship, see S. Halverson, 'The Concept of Equivalence in Translation Studies: Much Ado About Something', *Target* 9 (1997), pp. 207–33.

8. S. Larsen, 'Testing the Test: a preliminary investigation of translation as a test of writing skills', in S. Larsen (ed.), *Translation. A Means to an End* (The Dolphin 18. Aarhus: Aarhus Univ., 1990), pp. 95–108 (102).

9. A. Chesterman, *Memes of Translation. The Spread of Ideas in Translation Theory* (BTL 22. Amsterdam: Benjamins, 1997), pp. 134–6.

into Hungarian, and to a lesser extent from English and French into Hungarian, often suffer from too many indefinite articles, because these are more frequently used in English, French and German than in Hungarian.[10] This is especially important in understanding the articles in ὁ υἱὸς τοῦ ἀνθρώπου. We must make sure that we understand them in accordance with the ways that they might be understood by a Greek translator suffering interference from Aramaic, rather than simply by Greek usage, let alone the assumptions which scholars bring from their own native languages.

This reflects another major result from the modern field of Translation Studies. Whereas bilinguals suffer from interference anyway, translators suffer from it much more strongly, because the text which they are translating always reinforces the interference. Švejcer summarized the basic points:

> As a bilingual, the translator is exposed to far greater interference (other conditions being equal) than one who, in using heterolinguistic systems, produces his utterances on the basis of his own programme rather than a source-language text ... in translating it is a translation variant that is subject to choice ... The factors which determine the choice are also different: in translation the choice is 'programmed' by the content of the original, whereas in the verbal activity of a bilingual it is determined by the external conditions of the communicative event.[11]

This may result in overliteral translation. For example, the LXX translator of Gen. 6.14 put νοσσιάς for קִנִּים because it is usually the Greek equivalent for this Hebrew word. He probably did not imagine a pair of lions living in a bird's nest at the top of Noah's ark, but if he did, he put νοσσιάς all the same because literal translation was his preferred solution to that kind of difficulty. Neubert summarizes our knowledge of modern translators in a similar situation, noting that translators may read their translations with the original texts still in the back of their minds. Consequently, translations, through interference, qualify as second-rate target texts: they read differently from original texts.[12] At Gen. 6.14, the translator's use of νοσσιάς will have been controlled by קִנִּים in a way that the use of νοσσιάς in a monoglot Greek-speaker could not be. The use of ὁ υἱὸς τοῦ ἀνθρώπου as a translation of בר (א)נש(א) may fruitfully be viewed as a more extensive example of the same phenomenon: when a bilingual translator read his version of sayings such as Mk 2.28 and 14.21, he could see the original idiom which he had translated in a way that was not possible for a monoglot speaker of Greek.

These two important points, interference in bilinguals and the increase in interference among translators, show that the form of a language spoken by bilinguals

---

10.   K. Klaudy, *Languages in Translation. Lectures on the Theory, Teaching and Practice of Translation* (Trans. T. J. de Kornfeld, P. Heltai, K. Károly and K. Klaudy; Budapest: Scholastica, 2003), pp. 383–5.

11.   A. D. Švejcer, 'Literal Translation as a Product of Interference', in H. Schmidt (ed.), *Interferenz in der Translation* (Übersetzungswissenschaftliche Beiträge 12. Leipzig: Enzyklopädie, 1989), pp. 39–44 (39).

12.   A. Neubert, 'Interference between Languages and between Texts', in Schmidt, *Interferenz*, pp. 56–64 (56–7).

and produced by translators is not the same as the form of that same language spoken by monolinguals. Moreover, the form of a second or further language produced by bilinguals and translators changes as they become more competent and experienced. Consequently, some scholars who work in these fields use the term 'interlanguage'. Appel and Muysken describe it and comment as follows:

> [Interlanguage is] the version or the variety of the target language which is part of the implicit linguistic knowledge or competence of the second-language learner. He or she proceeds through a series of interlanguages on the way to complete mastery of the target language. Of course, most second-language learners never reach this stage …

Interference is one of the major features which they select for discussion.[13] This means that we cannot expect Gospel writers to produce normal koine Greek if they were bilingual, and doubly so if they were translating. This is especially important in dealing with ὁ υἱὸς τοῦ ἀνθρώπου, because this is a unique expression. It should therefore be an obvious possibility that it was produced by means of processes normal among bilingual translators.

Another major result is that translators have to deal with two cultures, not just two languages. They may then write for the target culture, and make changes accordingly. Neubert describes the difference: 'In plain words, *translation recasts the original for different people*, after an unavoidable *time lag* and, as a rule, at a *different place*. It is displaced communication.'[14] This is true of the synoptic Gospels as a whole. They were written for Christians rather than Jews. A lengthy time lag is obvious for Luke. A few years had already gone by before Mark was written, a few more before Matthew was composed. The Gospels were written in the diaspora. Some of the translating was done before the composition of the Gospels themselves, but this is still displaced communication for the benefit of the target audience. This is also a major factor in understanding the *Sitz im Leben* of ὁ υἱὸς τοῦ ἀνθρώπου in the Gospels as they now stand. We have seen that, in secondary sayings, Mark, Matthew and Luke all treat ὁ υἱὸς τοῦ ἀνθρώπου as a Christological title in Greek. We must take seriously the possibility that (א)נשׁ(א) בר changed into ὁ υἱὸς τοῦ ἀνθρώπου during the translation process partly because the Gospel writers needed Christological titles.

Deliberate changes during the translation process are sufficiently widespread to have given rise to the *skopos* theory of translation, for which the changes for the target culture form the main point.[15] For example, Séguinot studied the translation of ten articles in *Le Monde* for *The Guardian Weekly* in 1981, looking for changes

13.   R. Appel and P. Muysken, *Language Contact and Bilingualism* (London: Arnold, 1987), p. 83. Cf. L. Selinker, *Rediscovering Interlanguage* (London: Longman, 1992).

14.   A. Neubert, *Text and Translation* (Übersetzungswissenschaftliche Beiträge 8. Leipzig, Enzyklopädie, 1985), p. 8.

15.   See especially K. Reiß and H.-J. Vermeer, *Grundlegung einer allgemeinen Translationstheorie* (Linguistische Arbeiten 147. Tübingen: Niemeyer, 1984). In English, e.g. H. J. Vermeer, *A skopos theory of translation (Some arguments for and against)* (Heidelberg: TEXTconTEXT, 1996).

which 'clearly arose from a change in the communicative situation'.[16] She reckoned 175 discrepancies between the source and target versions of the texts, and classified these as increased readability/explicitness (50%), adaptation to the target audience (21%), reductions in emotive and figurative language (21%), increased objectivity (4%), and reductions in journalistic style (4%). Here the needs of the target culture have evidently been of prime importance. The same applies to translators of our period. For example, at Num. 24.17, LXX has ἄνθρωπος for שׁבט, and *Tg. Onqelos* has משׁיחא. Both these renderings are deliberately interpretative. LXX makes clear that Israel will be led to victory by a man. Targum *Onqelos*, written later when messianic expectations had crystallized round the figure of a future Davidic king, identifies the victor as the Messiah. Given the known shift in meaning in the transition from (א)בר נשׁ(א) to ὁ υἱὸς τοῦ ἀνθρώπου, and the *Sitz im Leben* of ὁ υἱὸς τοῦ ἀνθρώπου as a Christological title in all three synoptic writers, we must take seriously the possibility that it was much more welcome as a translation than the older scholarship could possibly have imagined.

More recent developments of the *skopos* theory have become known as 'functionalism'.[17] This makes no serious difference to the present study. The main concern of functionalism is still to draw attention to the ways in which translators make alterations to satisfy the needs of the target culture. It is this which is important for understanding the production of ὁ υἱὸς τοῦ ἀνθρώπου during the translation process.

Translators who have in mind the needs of their target culture are sometimes very free in handling their text. It is well known that some of the Targums come into this category. An outstanding example from the ancient world is the Greek translation of the *Testament of Ephraem*. In general, Lamy characterized this translation as follows: 'En comparant cette version au texte syriaque, il est facile de voir que le traducteur grec a rendu le sens du syriaque; mais, visant à l'élégance, il amplifie et fait une paraphrase plutôt qu'une traduction.' Duval correctly went further: 'Il est regrettable que la version grecque ne soit pas littérale et qu'elle nous offre autant une paraphrase qu'une traduction; le commentaire y recouvre le fond au point de rendre parfois méconnaissable la phrase syriaque.'[18] In line 124, for example, he rendered ברנשׁא with ἄνδρα, and for כל ברנשׁ at T. Ephraem 944 he put τῆς τοῦ θεοῦ ἐκκλησίας. The first example is free enough, and the second shows that there is no

16.　T. C. Séguinot, 'The editing function of translation', *Bulletin of the Canadian Association of Applied Linguistics* 4 (1982), pp. 151–61, as reported by Neubert, *Text and Translation*, pp. 72–3, and A. Neubert and G. M. Shreve, *Translation as Text* (Translation Studies 1. Kent, Ohio: Kent State Univ., 1992), pp. 87–8.

17.　E.g. C. Nord, 'A Functional Typology of Translations', in Trosborg (ed.), *Text, Typology and Translation*, pp. 43–66; C. Nord, *Translating as a Purposeful Activity: Functionalist Approaches Explained* (Manchester: St. Jerome, 1997); C. Schäffner (ed.), *Translation and Quality* (Clevedon: Multilingual Matters Ltd, 1998).

18.　M. Lamy, 'Le Testament de Saint Éphrem le Syrien', *Compte rendu du IVᵉ Congrès Scientifique International des Catholiques. Première Section. Sciences Religieuses* (1898) pp. 173–209 (174); R. Duval, 'Le Testament de Saint Éphrem', *Journal Asiatique* ser 9, 18 (1901), pp. 234–319 (240).

felt need to keep to the same rendering of a single expression. The second example is also highly interpretative, and vigorously directed at the target culture.

The unique nature of the expression ὁ υἱὸς τοῦ ἀνθρώπου, and those aspects of it which are literally equivalent to aspects of (א)שׁנ(א) בר, shows that the expression itself did not result from such free translation. In considering whole sayings, however, we have to take account of the fact that the Gospel writers were completely immersed in the target culture. The *skopos* theory of translation, and the practical examples of the Targums and the *Testament of Ephraem* show us how far translators might go. At this point, we must bear in mind also the nature of midrash as we find it for example in the *Genesis Apocryphon*. Here some verses of Genesis have been translated into Aramaic, and the whole story has been massively developed in accordance with the author(s)' aims of telling stories about traditional figures for Aramaic-speaking Jews. The development of the passion predictions proposed in Ch. 9 fits into the very varied picture of the possibilities available to translators who were also Gospel writers, or to Gospel writers who worked closely with translators. The editing of Mark by Matthew and Luke also illustrates how much editing could be done in Greek. All this needs to be taken into account in considering the development of Son of man sayings as a whole.

Whereas some translators are relatively or even extremely free, others are consistently literalistic. Perhaps the best known in our field is Aquila, who translated the Pentateuch into Greek very literally, even rendering the Hebrew את with the Greek σύν when את means only that the next word will be the object of a verb.[19] Other literal translations include the syrohexapla to the Old Testament and the Harklean version of the New. Such literalism is very helpful if one is trying to reconstruct an original text: it greatly increases the proportion of cases in which only one original text could have given rise to such a translation. It is fortunate that some Son of man sayings in the Gospels have been translated into Greek so literally that we can reconstruct them in Aramaic. Some of them are even embedded in contexts which have been translated equally literally. I have argued this throughout Chs 4–8. The sayings studied in these chapters, and the contexts of some of them, fit perfectly into a model of relatively literal translating. This is in no way unusual, and it is important that literal aspects of the translation of (א)שׁנ(א) בר with ὁ υἱὸς τοῦ ἀνθρώπου fit perfectly into the known habits of more literal translators.

Many translators vary in the extent of their literalism. The LXX is like this if treated as a single translation, which of course it is not. It is however a partial parallel to the Gospels, in that the later translators knew at least some of the work of the earlier ones. Looking at the rendering of בן אדם in the LXX as a whole, we find that it generally went for υἱὸς ἀνθρώπου, but that there are two exceptions, Isa. 56.2: ἄνθρωπος, and Ps. 146.3: υἱοὺς ἀνθρώπων. Of these, Isa. 56.2 is just free

19.   On the complex questions surrounding this rendering, see K. Hyvärinen, *Die Übersetzung von Aquila* (ConBOT 10. Uppsala: Almqvist & Wiksell, 1977), pp. 26–9; L. L. Grabbe, 'Aquila's Translation and Rabbinic Exegesis', *JJS* 33 (1982), pp. 527–36; A. Paul, 'La Bible grecque d'Aquila et l'idéologie du judaïsme ancien', *ANRW* II.20.1 (1987), pp. 221–45; J. Ziegler, 'Die Wiedergabe der nota accusativi *'et, 'aet* mit σύν', *ZAW* 100 (1988 Supp.), pp. 222–33.

enough to pass as normal monoglot Greek, and Ps. 146.3 is somewhat literalistic and interpretative at the same time. It is important for understanding ὁ υἱὸς τοῦ ἀνθρώπου in translated sayings in the synoptics that a translator could be both somewhat literalistic and interpretative at the same time.

A relevant habit by some translators on the literal end of the spectrum is known to some scholars as 'stereotyping'. Tov describes it as follows:

> Many translators rendered all occurrences of a given Hebrew word, element (e.g. prep), root or construction as far as possible by the same Greek equivalent, often disregarding the effect of this type of translation upon its quality. This tradition (rather than system) of consistently representing words and roots by the same equivalents probably developed in a school-type milieu and may reflect the belief that the words of the Holy Bible should be rendered consistently in order to remain as faithful as possible to the source language.[20]

When therefore we find evidence of a consistent decision by Gospel translators to render (א)בר נ(א)ש in the singular with ὁ υἱὸς τοῦ ἀνθρώπου, we find evidence of a decision wholly in accordance with the known habits of translators in their culture.

This draws attention to another major facet of the translation process. Translators may *deliberately* retain visible aspects of the source language and culture when this is what the target culture needs. The LXX is an outstanding example of this. It includes a number of expressions which are not found in monoglot Greek, such as ἐγένετο ... καί (e.g. Gen. 21.22, for ו ... ויהי). Expressions like this ensured that the Greek language of the LXX was as distinctively Jewish as its context. This was ideal for the needs of Greek-speaking Jewish communities. It meant that they could understand their sacred text in Greek, and that at the same time the language of their sacred text was distinctively their own, significantly different from the Greek of secular and pagan works. The LXX was the Bible of the early Christian churches, so that distinctively Jewish Greek was a central part of their culture. The effects of this are visible all over the New Testament. Some of the best examples are in the Gospel of Luke, who is justly famous for writing the best Greek of the three synoptic Gospels, and some of the best in the New Testament. For example, he too uses ἐγένετο ... καί (e.g. Lk. 5.17; 8.1), and it is notorious that his birth narratives are distinctively Septuagintal in style.[21] In this way, Luke faithfully served the needs of Christian communities who needed distinctively Christian Gospels. All three of the synoptic evangelists recall the Jewish culture of Jesus in language as well as in content. This made them quite unique, and marked them off from the secular and pagan culture of the Greco-Roman world, as well as from Jesus' Aramaic-speaking Judaism. This is the cultural *Sitz im Leben* of the production of the major Christological title ὁ υἱὸς τοῦ ἀνθρώπου.

This is related to another major facet of translation studies, the discussion of strategies. Translators faced with significant problems in the translation of material from one language into another may take deliberate decisions as to what they

---

20.   E. Tov, 'The Septuagint', *Mikra* (ed. M. J. Mulder and H. Sysling; CRINT II,1. Assen/Maastricht/Philadelphia: Van Gorcum/Fortress, 1988) pp. 161–88 (172).

21.   Cf. e.g. Fitzmyer, *Luke,* pp. 107–27, 'Lucan Language and Style'.

will do, either as a general approach to a particular piece of work, or as a specific approach to a particular repeated problem. Nord's appreciation of Reiß, one of the most important advocates of the *skopos* theory of translation, put the underlying situation in a nutshell: 'She knew that real life presents situations where equivalence is not possible, and in some cases not even desired.'[22] The first of these points is very well illustrated by Aquila's rendering of the Hebrew את with the Greek σύν + Accusative when את means only that the next word will be the object of a verb. This use of את has no equivalent in Greek, so this is a straightforward example of a case where equivalence is not possible. The rendering of כל ברנש at T. Ephraem 944 with τῆς τοῦ θεοῦ ἐκκλησίας illustrates the second of these points equally well, for it is such a vigorous interpretative rendering that it shows that the translator was not even desiring equivalence.

As for a definition of what a strategy is, Schäffner thought the definition which Chesterman quoted from Lörscher worth repeating:

> a potentially conscious procedure for the solution of a problem which an individual is faced with when translating a text segment from one language into another.[23]

Aquila's rendering of the Hebrew את with the Greek σύν + Accusative is a clear example of a 'conscious procedure for the solution of a problem'. Most translators have preferred to omit the Hebrew את when את means only that the next word will be the object of a verb. This is 'a potentially conscious procedure for the solution of a problem', such an obvious one that it may become automatic to the point of not always being conscious.

2. The Translation of (א)נש(א) בר with ὁ υἱὸς τοῦ ἀνθρώπου

The translation of (א)נש(א) בר with ὁ υἱὸς τοῦ ἀνθρώπου is a perfect example of a translators' strategy. To understand it fully, we need all the insights from Translation Studies sketched above, together with a complete knowledge of ancient Aramaic. First of all, we have to understand what the strategy was. One of the most outstanding features of the usage of ὁ υἱὸς τοῦ ἀνθρώπου is that it almost always refers to Jesus alone. This could not however be true of (א)נש(א) בר. This was an ordinary term for 'man', which Jesus was accordingly bound to have used with reference to other people. This supplies us with the first part of the translators' strategy: ὁ υἱὸς τοῦ ἀνθρώπου is to be used as a translation of (א)נש(א) בר when it

---

22. Nord, *Purposeful Activity*, p. 9: cf. n. 15 above, and the early work of K. Reiß, *Möglichkeiten und Grenzen der Übersetzungskritik* (München: Huebner, 1971); *Translation Criticism – The Potentials and Limitations* (Trans. E. F. Rhodes; Manchester: St. Jerome, 2000).

23. C. Schäffner, 'Strategies of Translating Political Texts', in Trosborg (ed.), *Text Typology and Translation*, pp. 119–43 (120), quoting A. Chesterman, 'From "Is" to "Ought": Laws, Norms and Strategies in Translation Studies', *Target* 5 (1993), pp. 1–20, (13), quoting W. Lörscher, *Translation Performance, Translation Process and Translation Strategies. A Psycholinguistic Investigation* (Tübingen: Narr, 1991), p. 76.

refers to Jesus, and not otherwise. Where words such as ἄνθρωπος have been used to translate בר (א)נשׁ(א), we can no longer tell. There are however passages where our Greek text has ἄνθρωπος, and בר (א)נשׁ(א) would make perfectly good idiomatic sense. For example, many Aramaic stories begin חד בר נשׁ. The parable of the Good Samaritan is one of several which begin ἄνθρωπος τις (Lk. 10.30): this might be a translation of חד בר נשׁ. At Mk 7.11, Jesus' version of a teaching of scribes and Pharisees begins ἐὰν εἴπῃ ἄνθρωπος: this could be a translation of אן אמר בר נשׁ. Of course, there will always be uncertainty about any individual example, but this should not detract from our appreciation of the strategy as a whole. As a speaker of normal Aramaic, Jesus was bound to have used בר (א)נשׁ(א) with reference to people other than himself: the translators' strategy explains why ὁ υἱὸς τοῦ ἀνθρώπου almost always refers to him.

The next part of the strategy concerns the plural בני (א)נשׁ(א). This expression was also such a normal part of Aramaic discourse that Jesus was bound to have used it too. In the Greek of the synoptic Gospels, however, the plural οἱ υἱοὶ τῶν ἀνθρώπων occurs only at Mk 3.28. We must infer that the basic strategy was not to use the plural οἱ υἱοὶ τῶν ἀνθρώπων. Natural alternatives include the straightforward plural οἱ ἄνθρωποι. As in the case of the singular ἄνθρωπος, we can no longer tell where οἱ ἄνθρωποι may have been used to render בני (א)נשׁ(א). Again, however, there are passages where our Greek text has ἄνθρωποι, and בני (א)נשׁ(א) would make perfectly good idiomatic sense. For example, at Mt. 5.16 ἔμπροσθεν τῶν ἀνθρώπων might be a translation of קדם בני (א)נשׁ(א), while at Lk. 13.4 πάντας τοὺς ἀνθρώπους could be a translation of כל בני (א)נשׁ(א). Here too, we cannot verify any individual example, but the general point should be regarded as unassailable. The almost complete absence of οἱ υἱοὶ τῶν ἀνθρώπων from the synoptic Gospels must flow from a decision not to use it as a translation of בני (א)נשׁ(א).

The three exceptions to this strategy illustrate how difficult it is to carry through a strategy for the translation of the idiomatic use of ὁ υἱὸς τοῦ ἀνθρώπου into Greek. We have seen that at Mk 9.12, Jesus used בר (א)נשׁ(א) in a reference to the deaths of both John the Baptist and himself. This meant that the translators' strategy was very difficult to apply. I have argued that they selected the level of meaning which was most important to them, the reference to Jesus.[24] Hence they decided that they would use ὁ υἱὸς τοῦ ἀνθρώπου. For monoglot Greek-speakers reading or hearing the text, it is simply not intelligible, and in the first churches to hear Mark's Gospel, the passage will have needed explaining. This is due to the lack of equivalence between the source text and the target language. It is not appropriate to blame the translator, as if they could have done something better. Moreover, the translator was necessarily bilingual, and will accordingly have been able to see the original Aramaic idiom in this Greek translation.

Another divergence from the agreed strategy was at Mk 3.28. Here I have argued that the translator was worried about the sense, for s/he did not like the idea that speaking against Jesus was forgivable. They therefore took בר (א)נשׁ(א) to be

24.   See pp. 125–31 above.

collective, and as part of a very explicitative translation, they rendered it with the plural τοῖς υἱοῖς τῶν ἀνθρώπων.[25] The third divergence from the agreed strategy was at Mt. 10.32-33. Here the translator opted for the first person pronoun ἐγώ in place of ὁ υἱὸς τοῦ ἀνθρώπου, using the emphatic κἀγώ twice, with the verb accordingly in the first person singular.[26] Whereas the use of ὁ υἱὸς τοῦ ἀνθρώπου removes the general level of meaning for uninstructed monoglot Greeks, the use of the first person singular removes the general level of meaning completely. We must infer that the translator believed that Jesus would be the only important witness for or against people at the last judgement, when he would give decisive testimony to God.

It follows that these three divergences from the translators' strategy do not cast doubt on what that strategy was. On the contrary, they illustrate the above comments on the limitations of strategies in the difficult circumstances which cause translators to adopt them. The translators of Mk 3.28 and of Mt. 10.32-33 are especially likely to have been very pleased with themselves, because their translations include explicitative alterations as a result of which the sayings mean very clearly exactly what their respective translators thought they ought to mean.

The next point to discuss is why the translators should arrive at *this* strategy, choosing ὁ υἱὸς τοῦ ἀνθρώπου in particular as their rendering of בר (א)נש(א) when it refers to Jesus, as well as having a general level of meaning. I have noted the uncomprehending criticisms of conventional scholarship at this point, with Wellhausen and A.Y. Collins among those who suppose that the translators should not have used υἱός, and Hare and A.Y. Collins among those who suppose that they should not have used the definite articles.[27] Neither verdict is justified.

I begin with υἱός in the Septuagint. The Septuagint was the Bible of the early Christian churches. It was therefore a Bible with which all the Gospel translators and evangelists were familiar, regardless of how well they also knew the Hebrew Bible and/or any available Targums. Those entrusted with the translation of Gospel traditions from Aramaic into Greek are likely to have had some knowledge of the Hebrew Bible. Any who may have undergone any kind of apprenticeship or training, or who attempted to train themselves, are likely to have used the Septuagint as a model for seeing how to translate material from a Semitic language into Greek. They are likely to have been familiar with the statement of the problem by the grandson of Jesus son of Sirach, and if they did not know this passage, they would soon encounter the same problems:

Παρακέκλεσθε οὖν μετ' εὐνοίας καὶ προσοχῆς τὴν ἀνάγνωσιν ποιεῖσθαι καὶ συγγνώμην ἔχειν ἐφ' οἷς ἂν δοκῶμεν τῶν κατὰ τὴν ἑρμηνείαν πεφιλοπονημένων τισὶν τῶν λέξεων ἀδυναμεῖν· οὐ γὰρ ἰσοδυναμεῖ αὐτὰ ἐν ἑαυτοῖς Ἑβραϊστὶ λεγόμενα καὶ ὅταν μεταχθῇ εἰς ἑτέραν γλῶσσαν· οὐ μόνον δὲ ταῦτα, ἀλλὰ καὶ αὐτὸς ὁ νόμος καὶ αἱ προφητεῖαι καὶ τὰ λοιπὰ τῶν βιβλίων οὐ μικρὰν ἔχει τὴν διαφορὰν ἐν ἑαυτοῖς λεγόμενα.

---

25. See pp. 140–3 above.
26. See further pp. 183–6 above.
27. See pp. 18, 43–4 above.

> Be encouraged therefore to conduct the reading with goodwill and attention, and to be
> indulgent in cases where we may seem to have fallen short in the interpretation of some
> words, despite the great efforts spent on the translation. For what is expressed in Hebrew
> does not have the same meaning when it is translated into another language. And not only
> this work, but the Law itself and the prophets and the rest of the books differ not a little when
> read in the original (Sir. *Prol.* 15-26).

The problems posed by translating Aramaic into Greek are very similar to the
problems posed by translating Hebrew into Greek. They will have been very obvious
to the translators, who will certainly have been familiar with the results in the Greek
Bible, even if they varied in the extent to which they understood the processes of its
production. Moreover, even in the case of translators less familiar with the process
of translation from the Hebrew Bible to the Septuagint, the translations of υἱός
produce patterns which were always liable to be repeated in fresh translations from
Aramaic into Greek which had to cope with phrases including the Aramaic בר.

We must consider next, therefore, the translation of בן and בר with υἱός in the
Septuagint, with a sample of Targumic equivalents. The first point is that these three
words are very precise equivalents in the majority of instances, when a man or boy
is the biological son of another person. This usage is very common, as for example
when 2 Kgs 15.1 describes Azariah as בן אמציה, LXX υἱὸς Ἀμεσσιου (IV Kgdms
15.1), Tg. בר אמציה. Likewise in natural Aramaic, Zechariah is described as בר עדוא
(Ezra 6.14), LXX υἱοῦ Ἀδδου (2 Esd. 6.14), Pesh. בר עדו. The plural is common in
the same sense of people's biological sons, as when we are told that Noah fathered
שלשה בנים (Gen. 6.10), LXX τρεῖς υἱούς, Onq. תלתה בנין. The same terms are used
when a mother is said to have given birth to a son, as for example at Gen. 30.23,
where Rachel תלד בן, LXX ἔτεκεν … υἱόν, Neof. ילידת בר. They are also used when
the behaviour of sons in general is discussed, as when Prov. 10.1 contrasts בן חכם
with בן כסיל, LXX υἱός σοφός and υἱός ἄφρων, Tg. בר חכימא and ברא סכלא. These
are not however merely facts about the sacred text, which our translators must have
known. They should alert us to the fact that every single bilingual translator of
Gospel sources used and heard בר and υἱός as precise equivalents thousands of
times during the course of their daily lives, not only when considering the act of
translation. This sets up a massive disposition within a bilingual to regard these
terms as equivalents for purposes of translation.

Another very common usage is in descriptions of nations. Num. 20.1 is one
of many passages in which the Israelites are described as בני ישׂראל, LXX οἱ υἱοὶ
Ἰσραηλ, Onq. בני ישׂראל. Natural Aramaic has the same expression, as at Ezra 6.16
בני ישׂראל, LXX 2 Esd. 6.16 οἱ υἱοὶ Ἰσραηλ, Pesh. בני איסראיל. At Ps. 77.16, they
are described as בני יעקב ויוסף, LXX τοὺς υἱοὺς Ἰακωβ καὶ Ἰωσηφ (Ps. 76.16),
Pesh. בני יעקוב ויוסף. The Jewish people may be addressed as בני עמך, as for example
at Ezek. 37.18, LXX οἱ υἱοὶ τοῦ λαοῦ σου, Tg. בני עמך. After the disappearance
of the twelve tribes, and the exile from Judaea, the Jewish group are described at
Dan. 1.6 as בני יהודה, Theod. τῶν υἱῶν Ἰουδα, Pesh. בני יהודה. Other nations are
described in a similar way, as are tribal groups within Israel. Examples include the
following: Num. 2.25 בני דן, LXX τῶν υἱῶν Δαν, Onq. בני דן; Deut. 2.19 בני עמון

(bis) and בני לוט, LXX υἱῶν Ἀμμαν (bis) and τοῖς υἱοῖς Λωτ, Sam. בני עמון (bis)
and בני לוט; Josh. 19.23 בני יששכר, LXX υἱῶν Ἰσσαχαρ, Tg. בני יששכר; Amos 9.7
בני כשיים, LXX υἱοὶ Αἰθιόπων, Pesh. בני כושיא; Ezek. 16.26 בני מצרים, LXX τοὺς
υἱοὺς Αἰγύπτου, Tg. בני מצרים; and Ezek. 23.7 בני אשור, LXX υἱοὶ Ασσυρίων, Tg.
בני אתור.

This is a natural extension of the primary usage, since there were widespread
stories that these groups were descended from single individuals. Educated Greeks
would also be reminded of the Homeric description of the Greeks as υἶες Ἀχαιῶν,
an alternative for Ἀχαιοί. There were similar expressions with παῖς, such as
παῖδες Ἑλλήνων (A. *Pers.* 403) for the Greeks, and Λυδῶν παῖδας (Hdt. I.
27) for the Lydians. All this means that bilingual translators would find all such
expressions entirely natural in their Greek translations, and that this would also
massively dispose them to regard בן, בר and υἱός as precise equivalents.

Priestly groups could be described in similar terms. So we find for example at Lev.
21.1 בני אהרן, LXX τοῖς υἱοῖς Ἀαρων, Neof. בנוי דאהרן; at Num. 18.21 בני לוי, LXX
τοῖς υἱοῖς Λευι, Ps-J בנוי דלוי; and at Ezek. 40.46 בני צדוק, LXX οἱ υἱοὶ Σαδδουκ,
Tg. בני צדוק. These groups were also believed to descend from the individual named
in each one. With all this established within the range of normality, it is natural
that there should be a somewhat broader range of descriptions of social groups. An
especially notable one is found for example at IV Kgdms 2.3: οἱ υἱοὶ προφητῶν,
for בני הנביאים (2 Kgs 2.3), Pesh. בני נביא. This term simply means 'prophets', so it is
analogous to some Greek terms which have παῖδες rather than υἱοί. For example,
at Plato, *Laws* VI, 769b, οἱ ζωγράφων παῖδες are simply painters, and Lucian
describes doctors as ἰατρῶν παῖδες (*Dips.* 5). The presence of such terms in natural
Greek will have helped to ensure that bilingual translators would simply assume
that their formally similar expressions were perfectly satisfactory Greek. Similarly,
at 2 Esd. 22.28 we find οἱ υἱοὶ τῶν ᾀδόντων for בני המשררים (Neh. 12.28), and
they are simply the singers. Such examples typify further the precise equivalence
between בן, בר and υἱός which is the major factor affecting less direct examples in
the Septuagint and fundamental to understanding our Gospel translators.

The Septuagint has further examples of somewhat less straightforward social
groups. For example, at Judg. 6.3 we find οἱ υἱοὶ ἀνατολῶν for בני קדם, Tg. בני מדנחא;
at 2 Kgdms 22.45 υἱοὶ ἀλλότριοι for בני נכר (2 Sam. 22.45), Tg. בני עממיא; at 2 Esd.
4.1 οἱ υἱοὶ τῆς ἀποικίας for בני הגולה (Ezra 4.1), Pesh. בני שביתא; at 2 Esd. 6.16 υἱῶν
ἀποικεσίας for בני גלותא (Ezra 6.16); at Ezek. 44.7 υἱοὺς ἀλλογενεῖς for בני נכר, Tg.
בני עממיא; at Ezek. 44.9 πᾶς υἱὸς ἀλλογενής for כל בן נכר, Tg. כל בני עממיא; at Dan.
2.25 Theod. τῶν υἱῶν τῆς αἰχμαλωσίας τῆς Ἰουδαίας for בני גלותא די יהוד, Pesh.
בני שביתא דיהוד; and at Dan. 11.14 Theod. οἱ υἱοὶ τῶν λοιμῶν τοῦ λαοῦ σου for
בני פריצי עמך, Pesh. בני עולא עמך. These examples illustrate again the precise perceived
equivalence between בן, בר, and υἱός.

It is this precise perceived equivalence which explains the use of υἱός for בן in more
metaphorical examples too. For instance, at 1 Kgdms 20.31 we find υἱὸς θανάτου for
בן מות (1 Sam. 20.31), Pesh. בר מתוא; at 1 Kgdms 26.16 υἱοὶ θανατώσεως for בני מות (1
Sam. 26.16), Pesh. בנו מותא; at 2 Kgdms 2.7 υἱοὺς δυνατούς for בני חיל (2 Sam. 2.7),

Pesh. בני חילא; at 2 Kgdms 7.10 υἱὸς ἀδικίας for בני עולה (2 Sam. 7.10), Tg. בני רשעא; at 2 Kgdms 17.10 υἱὸς δυνάμεως for בן חיל and υἱοὶ δυνάμεως for בני חיל (2 Sam. 17.10), Pesh. גנבר חילא and גנברי חילא; at 3 Kgdms 20.10 υἱοὺς παρανόμων for בני בליעל (1 Kgs 21.10), Tg. בני רשעא; and at Ps. 88.23 υἱὸς ἀνομίας for בן עולה (MT Ps. 89.23), Tg. בר רישעא. The more these examples appear to be somewhat different from normal monoglot Greek usage, the more they underline the precise perceived equivalence between בן, בר, and υἱός natural to bilingual translators.

Another idiom must be noted, the use of בן, בר, and υἱός to describe a person's age. For example, at 2 Kgdms 5.4 David is described as υἱὸς τριάκοντα ἐτῶν for בן שלשים שנה (2 Sam. 5.4), Tg. בר תלתין שנין; and at 4 Kgdms 14.2 Amaziah is described as υἱὸς εἴκοσι καὶ πέντε ἐτῶν for בן עשרים וחמש שנה (2 Kgs 14.2), Tg. בר עסרין וחמיש שנין. This is not normal monoglot Greek usage, but it is conventional in the Septuagint, and this further underlines the precise perceived equivalence between בן, בר, and υἱός natural to bilingual translators.

All this provides the cultural context for the conventional renderings of בן אדם with υἱὸς ἀνθρώπου and of בני (ה)אדם with (οἱ) υἱοὶ τῶν ἀνθρώπων. The 106 examples of the singular υἱὸς ἀνθρώπου are in effect fewer than they appear at first sight, because the 93 examples of the vocative υἱὲ ἀνθρώπου in the book of Ezekiel resulted from a single decision. In addition to this, however, there are still a dozen examples spread over six different books: Num. 23.19; Isa. 51.12; Jer. 49.18 (LXX 30.12); 49.33 (LXX 30.28); 50.40 (LXX 27.40); 51.43 (LXX 28.43); Ps. 8.5; 80.18 (LXX 79.16); Job 16.21; 25.6; 35.8; Dan. 8.17 LXX and Theod.. There is one minor adjustment in the addition of ὡς at Num. 23.19 (some doubts about the text of Job 16.21 and 35.8 do not affect the main point at issue). There is also an alteration at Ps. 146.3, where the plural υἱοὺς ἀνθρώπου (LXX Ps. 145.3) has been used: in this case בן אדם is obviously collective, and parallel to the plural נדיבים/ἄρχοντας. At Dan. 7.13, the Aramaic בר אנש has also been rendered with υἱὸς ἀνθρώπου, by both LXX and Theodotion. We should also note υἱοῦ ἀνθρώπου at Dan. 10.16 Theod., where however there is a textual problem in the MT; and the rendering of the analogous בן אנוש at Ps. 144.3 with υἱὸς ἀνθρώπου (LXX Ps. 143.3). The only genuine exception to the normal rendering is accordingly at Isa. 56.2, where בן אדם has been rendered with ἄνθρωπος, making good parallelism with ἀνήρ (MT אנוש). The main message from these renderings should therefore be clear. The precise perceived equivalence between בן, בר, and υἱός natural to bilingual translators has caused several different translators to use υἱός for בן in בן אדם, and likewise for בר in the single example of בר אנש.

The Peshitta and the Targums normally render the singular בן אדם with בר (א)נש(א). The major exception is the Targum to Ezekiel, which notoriously has בר אדם. It is important to count this correctly. Although there are 93 examples, they resulted from a single decision. Accordingly the majority and natural translation should be regarded as בר (א)נש(א). Apart from the Ezekiel Targum, the only major disruption to the norm is at Num. 23.19, where the translators were clearly concerned about the sense. So for example the Samaritan Targum has בר אדם, Onqelos כעובדי בני בסרא, and Pseudo-Jonathan has a massive expansion, including the words לא דמיין עובדוי לעובדי בני ביסרא. Only the Peshitta rendered simply with ברנשא. All these examples illustrate the main point. From the perspective of translators into Aramaic, the natural perceived equivalent of אדם בן אדם was בר (א)נש(א). As always, however, a deliberate strategy to the contrary could be adopted, as with בר אדם in the Targum to Ezekiel. Equally, the normal perceived equivalent could be departed from if the translators found the sense of a biblical verse problematic, as with most translators of Num. 23.19.

There are also 48 examples of the plural בני (ה)אדם in the Hebrew Bible. It is normally translated into Greek with (οἱ) υἱοὶ (τῶν) ἀνθρώπων, some 32 times. This figure would be much higher but for the abnormal behaviour of the exceptionally literal Greek translator of Ecclesiastes, who used (οἱ) υἱοὶ τοῦ ἀνθρώπου *c.*11 times. The standard translation with (οἱ) υἱοὶ (τῶν) ἀνθρώπων usually has both articles even for the anarthrous בני אדם, though each possible variation is found somewhere. For example, at Mic. 5.6 we find υἱοῖς ἀνθρώπων for בני אדם; this is a generic reference to humankind, so the addition of the articles in Greek was not necessary. The Peshitta and Targum both prefer the singular בר אנש, which gives a simpler parallel to the singular איש, Tg. אנש, Pesh. גבר. At LXX Ps. 10.4, we find τοὺς υἱοῖς τῶν ἀνθρώπων for בני אדם (MT Ps. 11.4): this is another generic reference to humankind, and here the generic articles have been added in Greek, as happens several times. The Peshitta and the Targum both use the definite state בני (א)נשא generically. At 1 Kgdms 26.19, on the other hand, we find the anarthrous υἱοὶ ἀνθρώπων for בני האדם (1 Sam. 26.19). Here the translator may have felt that an article with υἱοὶ would have made the expression too definite. Although the expression could be interpreted as a generic reference to men as opposed to God, it is also a reference to an indefinite group of real people, and that might be the main point. No such problem affected Tg. Pesh. בני אנשא, because the Aramaic definite state does not necessarily have the same implications as the Greek definite articles. At LXX Ps. 32.13, we find πάντας τοὺς υἱοὺς τῶν ἀνθρώπων for כל בני האדם (MT Ps. 33.13). Here the generic reference to the whole of humankind is retained by using the Greek articles to represent the Hebrew article. The same effect is achieved by the definite state בני נשא (Tg., Pesh). Thus the main point from the majority of examples reinforces the results which I have already put forward: the precise perceived equivalence between בן, בר, and υἱός natural to bilingual translators caused several different translators to use υἱοὶ for בני in בני (ה)אדם.

I have noted that the translator of Ecclesiastes was unusual in using (οἱ) υἱοὶ τοῦ ἀνθρώπου *c.*11 times: the exact figure is slightly uncertain due to textual problems with the first two examples, but the rationale for his view makes it probable that he was consistent, and that some scribes interfered with the expression until they realized that it was not a mistake. We may consider two examples. At Eccl. 9.3 we find υἱῶν τοῦ ἀνθρώπου for בני האדם; here there is no article with υἱῶν equivalent to ה, though the generic article would have made perfect sense. At Eccl. 9.12, we find οἱ υἱοὶ τοῦ ἀνθρώπου for בני האדם; here he has kept the generic article, which he used in rendering האדם with ὁ ἄνθρωπος earlier in the same verse. The use of the singular τοῦ ἀνθρώπου should be ascribed to exceptional literalism. This translator was so literalistic that he has been compared to Aquila, and sometimes even thought to *be* Aquila.[28] He has Aquila's best known characteristic, rendering the Hebrew את with σύν + acc. when את means only that the next word will be the object of a verb (e.g. Eccl. 1.14; 7.29). The Hebrew אדם is of course literally singular, and the Greek singular ὁ ἄνθρωπος on its own may be generic, as for example for האדם at Eccl. 3.11; 6.1; 8.9, and for אדם preceded by an inseparable preposition at Eccl. 1.3; 6.11; 8.15. It is this view of אדם in בני (ה)אדם that caused him to use the singular τοῦ ἀνθρώπου in the expression (οἱ) υἱοὶ τοῦ ἀνθρώπου. This reminds us of how literalistic a translator can be, but we do not suppose that the translators of Gospel material were this literalistic because they do not have any phenomena comparable to σύν + acc. The Peshitta is perfectly straightforward, with בני (א)נשא all but once (the sg. ברנשא at Eccl. 9.3). Despite its massive midrashic expansions, the Targum is also relatively straightforward, with בני (א)נשא the normal rendering.

The Hebrew Bible also has two examples of the Aramaic בני אנשא, both of them generic. At Dan. 2.38, the maverick LXX translator has ἀνθρώπων, while Theodotion has the normal οἱ υἱοὶ τῶν ἀνθρώπων (Pesh. בני אנשא, unchanged from MT). At Dan. 5.21, Theodotion has τῶν ἀνθρώπων, while LXX has nothing resembling this verse (Pesh. has the conventional בנינשא).

We must consider also the exceptional renderings of the Hebrew בני (ה)אדם. At Deut. 32.8, we find υἱοὺς Ἀδαμ for בני אדם. Here the context of the Song of Moses has moved from creation (32.6) to the separation of people into different nations. The narrative account of this in Gen. 10 is carried through in genealogical terms, and this context has caused the translator to think of the Adam story and accordingly transmit אדם as Adam. The Samaritan translator was similarly affected and put בני אדם, just like the MT, whereas other Aramaic translations (Neof., Onq., Pesh., Ps-J.) have some form of בני (א)נשא. Isa. 52.14 is part of an exceptionally difficult passage to translate. It is concerned with the appearance of the suffering servant, which is compared unfavourably to that of human beings in general. The translator put ἀπὸ ἀνθρώπων for מאיש, and ἀπὸ τῶν ἀνθρώπων for מבני אדם. We should infer that he thought especially carefully about what he was doing, and came up with something perfectly satisfactory. The fact that the majority rendering is with υἱός shows how *naturally* that came to most translators, not that they were incapable of taking different decisions. At Ps. 49.3, the translator had to render both בני אדם and, immediately after it, בני איש. For גם בני אדם גם בני איש, he came up with οἵ τε γηγενεῖς καὶ οἱ υἱοὶ τῶν ἀνθρώπων (LXX Ps. 48.3). Here the translator has evidently not wanted to use οἱ υἱοὶ τῶν ἀνθρώπων twice (unlike the translator of Ps. 62.10, see LXX Ps. 61.10). The Targum went for בני אדם קדמאה, with בנוי דיעקב for the following בני איש. The Peshitta is very close to the LXX with בני ארעא for בני אדם, and the more conventional בנינשא for the following בני איש. Finally, at Dan.

28.   Cf. A. H. McNeile, *An Introduction to Ecclesiastes with Notes and Appendices* (Cambridge: CUP, 1904), pp. 115–68; S. Holm-Nielsen, 'The Book of Ecclesiastes and the Interpretation of it in Jewish and Christian Theology', *ASTI* 10 (1975–6), pp. 38–96 (57–65); Hyvärinen, *Aquila*, pp. 88–99; R. Beckwith, *The Old Testament Canon of the New Testament Church and its Background in Early Judaism* (London: SPCK, 1985), pp. 302–4, 472–7; Ziegler, 'Wiedergabe'; J. Jarick, 'Aquila's *Koheleth*', *Textus* 15 (1990), pp. 131–9.

10.16 there are problems with the text. The LXX χειρὸς ἀνθρώπου presumably read יד אדם, as the fragmentary 6Q Dan, with the feminine form נג[עה just about surviving, presumably did too. Whether Theodotion's υἱοῦ ἀνθρώπου altered בני אדם or read בן אדם we cannot tell, but in either case the use of υἱός is conventional. In such circumstances, nothing significant can be squeezed from the Peshitta's אנשא.

The Peshitta and the Targums normally render the plural בני אדם with בני (א)נשא. One or two exceptions have been noted above. They do not in any way upset the obvious fact that the Hebrew בני in the expression בני אדם was generally rendered with the Aramaic בני in the expression בני (א)נשא because of perceived precise equivalence.

All these examples point in the same direction. The precise perceived equivalence between בן, בר, and υἱός natural to bilingual translators has caused several different translators to use υἱός for בן in בן אדם, and the plural υἱοί for בני in בני (ה)אדם. This is the natural and normal rendering. Its underlying cause was the perceived precise equivalence between בן, בר, and υἱός throughout normal usage in these three languages. It follows that the use of υἱός in the transformation of בר (א)נשא (א) into ὁ υἱὸς τοῦ ἀνθρώπου is entirely natural. From the perspective of the translators, it was hardly even literalistic, just normal to the point of being almost universal.

The whole range of the usage of בן, בר, and υἱός is accordingly reflected in the synoptic Gospels. The Greek υἱός is found in its most literal usage, when men and boys are said to be son of another person. So for example, we find Ἰάκωβος καὶ Ἰωάννης οἱ υἱοὶ Ζεβεδαίου (Mk 10.35). When Elizabeth came to the conclusion of her pregnancy, ἐγέννησεν υἱόν (Lk. 1.57). This is the basic usage, which established the precise perceived equivalence between בן, בר, and υἱός. The use with reference to nations is also found, as when the angel of the Lord predicts that John the Baptist will bring back to the Lord πολλοὺς τῶν υἱῶν Ἰσραηλ (Lk. 1.16). More metaphorical uses are also found. At Mk 2.19, a parable of Jesus refers to οἱ υἱοὶ τοῦ νυμφῶνος (//Mt. 9.15//Lk. 5.34). Jesus' nickname for the sons of Zebedee is correctly translated υἱοὶ βροντῆς (Mk 3.17).[29] Matthew contrasts the righteous and the wicked as οἱ υἱοὶ τῆς βασιλείας and οἱ υἱοὶ τοῦ πονηροῦ (Mt. 13.38). Luke similarly contrasts οἱ υἱοὶ τοῦ αἰῶνος τούτου with τοὺς υἱοὺς τοῦ φωτός (Lk. 16.8). He also refers to a decent kind of person as υἱὸς εἰρήνης (Lk. 10.6).

All this is entirely normal and relatively consistent. The precise perceived equivalence between בן, בר, and υἱός was natural to bilingual translators because of the extensive use of these words as equivalents. It follows that the use of υἱός in the transformation of בר (א)נשא (א) into ὁ υἱὸς τοῦ ἀνθρώπου was also entirely natural.

I turn next to the articles in ὁ υἱὸς τοῦ ἀνθρώπου. We have seen that this has also caused endless trouble to conventional scholarship. It has been inferred that בר (א)נשא (א) in sayings of Jesus must have always been in the definite state, which is not consistent with Aramaic evidence about its idiomatic usage. It has also been supposed that, if the idiom had a general level of meaning, which we have seen

---

29. Casey, *Aramaic Sources of Mark's Gospel*, pp. 197–8.

that it did, the articles would not have been necessary. The solution to all these problems is to pay careful attention once again to the translators' strategy. I have already worked out what this strategy was: ὁ υἱὸς τοῦ ἀνθρώπου is to be used as a translation of (א)נשׁ(א) בר when it refers to Jesus, and not otherwise, and the plural is not to be used. I consider next the effects of this strategy, from the perspective of bilingual translators and then of Gospel writers.

The first notable effect of this strategy is to produce a major new Christological title, which clearly refers to Jesus alone. This is just what the church needed. The negative aspects of the strategy helped to ensure that the new title was unique, as nothing like υἱὸς ἀνθρώπου was used with reference to anyone other than Jesus. The positive aspects of the strategy, keeping υἱός and using the articles, ensure that the reference to Jesus himself is always clear. This is why the use of the articles is of such central importance. Some reference to Jesus himself is always clear from the context, and the article is a normal way of making clear a reference to a particular, previously known person. There was therefore no chance that the first article could be taken as simply generic. It is also important at this point to keep in mind that the original idiom could not be exactly reproduced in Greek. Whereas the original Aramaic had both a general level of meaning and a particular reference to Jesus himself, the Greek translators had to opt for one meaning or the other being clear to monoglot Greek-speaking Christians. The use of the articles ensures that the primary reference to Jesus himself is retained clearly for everyone to see. Bilingual translators could themselves perceive the original idiom by interpreting the first article as generic as well as particular. They will therefore have thought that in translating examples of this idiom in this way, they had done as well as possible. From the perspective of both bilingual translators and monoglot Greek-speaking Christians, they were quite right. The original idiom could be perceived by bilinguals, and the most important level of meaning, the reference to Jesus himself, could be seen by everyone.

The second article is simply generic. The generic article was very common in Greek. Consequently, statements about humankind could be made using the article with ἄνθρωπος, without there being any risk of confusion over which man was being referred to. For example, in commenting on a Spartan embassy, Pericles made a very general reference to the plans of human beings, τὰς διανοίας τοῦ ἀνθρώπου (Thuc.I,140,1). Here τοῦ ἀνθρώπου is obviously generic, and there is no possibility of a particular man being thought of. Again, Paul opens Romans 7 by reminding his audience that the law has jurisdiction over people only as long as they are alive: ὁ νόμος κυριεύει τοῦ ἀνθρώπου ἐφ᾽ ὅσον χρόνον ζῇ. Here τοῦ ἀνθρώπου clearly refers to people in general, and once again there is no possibility of a particular man being thought of.

The same applies to the translation Greek of the Septuagint and the synoptic Gospels. I have noted some very general examples in Ecclesiastes.[30] Some examples refer to a smaller social subgroup as human beings. For example, at Deut. 8.3 Moses tells Israel that people (האדם) do not live by bread alone. Here the Israelites are

---

30.   See p. 260 above.

referred to as human beings, with the generic article used with the singular noun, האדם. The Septuagint follows, translating האדם with ὁ ἄνθρωπος. Here too there is a general reference to the Israelites as human beings, and there is no possibility of a particular man being thought of. At Mk 2.27, a saying organically linked to the Son of man saying at Mk 2.28, ὁ ἄνθρωπος refers to the situation of the primordial creation of the sabbath for humankind, even as everyone knew that it was kept by Israel: τὸ σάββατον διὰ τὸν ἄνθρωπον ἐγένετο καὶ οὐχ ὁ ἄνθρωπος διὰ τὸ σάββατον.[31] Here both τὸν ἄνθρωπον and ὁ ἄνθρωπος are generic, and there is no possibility of a single person being exclusively thought of, even though the story of Adam may have come to many people's minds.

These factors ensure that ὁ υἱὸς τοῦ ἀνθρώπου would effectively be interpreted as 'the son of humankind', so the most important person on earth, appropriately described also as ὁ υἱὸς τοῦ θεοῦ (Mk 3.11; Mt. 16.16; Lk. 4.41 etc.). This fits almost all Son of man sayings perfectly, since they generally refer to Jesus himself, and the early church regarded him as the most important person who had been on earth. Let us consider for example Mk 2.28: ὥστε κύριός ἐστιν ὁ υἱὸς τοῦ ἀνθρώπου καὶ τοῦ σαββάτου. This makes it quite clear that Jesus himself was in charge of the sabbath. This makes perfect sense of the narrative as a whole. When Jesus' disciples were accused of doing something unlawful on the sabbath, they did not defend themselves, Jesus defended them, with two decisive arguments. This was because he was in charge, as everyone knew. From the point of view of Mark and of his audiences in the early church, this is a perfect end to the pericope. It is an unambiguous declaration of Jesus' authority, just what the early church needed. Moreover, from their perspective it follows on perfectly from Mk 2.27. This recalls the original creation of the sabbath, when God himself rested on the sabbath and made it holy (Gen. 2.3), together with the fourth commandment, which gives this as the reason why people, together with their guests and animals, should rest on the sabbath (Exod. 20.8-11). It therefore follows that the son of humankind, the most important person to be on earth, was in charge of interpreting the observance of the sabbath by his disciples.

The effectiveness of this translation in producing a Christological title may be further clarified by contrasting the other suggestions which scholars have made. Wellhausen argued that the translators should have used ὁ ἄνθρωπος.[32] Let us see what effect this has on the interpretation of Mk 2.27-28:

τὸ σάββατον διὰ τὸν ἄνθρωπον ἐγένετο καὶ οὐχ ὁ ἄνθρωπος διὰ τὸ σάββατον, ὥστε κύριός ἐστιν ὁ ἄνθρωπος καὶ τοῦ σαββάτου.

Here ὁ ἄνθρωπος would naturally be interpreted generically in v. 28, an obvious interpretation already guaranteed by the two examples of the generic ὁ ἄνθρωπος in v. 27. Thus there is no particular reference to Jesus at all. This is accordingly quite disastrous, and not remotely comparable with the successful production of the

---

31. For detailed discussion, see pp. 121–5 above.
32. Wellhausen, *Israelitische und Jüdische Geschichte*, p. 312 n.1. See p. 18 above.

important Christological title ὁ υἱὸς τοῦ ἀνθρώπου. It is also difficult to see the force of καὶ before τοῦ σαββάτου, since humankind has not previously been said to be lord of anything else. We have seen that it really refers back to Mk 2.10, but ὁ ἄνθρωπος at Mk 2.10 would make no better sense than at Mk 2.28.

Hare argued that, if I were right about the idiomatic use of (א)שׁנ(א) בר, the translators should have used the simple ἄνθρωπος.[33] Let us therefore try this at Mk 2.27-28:

τὸ σάββατον διὰ τὸν ἄνθρωπος ἐγένετο καὶ οὐχ ὁ ἄνθρωπος διὰ τὸ σάββατον, ὥστε κύριός ἐστιν ἄνθρωπος καὶ τοῦ σαββάτου.

Here ἄνθρωπος would naturally be interpreted in an indefinite and generic way. In view of God's creation of the sabbath for the benefit of humankind, any man, by virtue of his position as a human being, is lord of the sabbath. This is very little different from the previous suggestion, and equally disastrous, because there is no particular reference to Jesus himself. This too is not remotely comparable with the succesful production of the important Christological title ὁ υἱὸς τοῦ ἀνθρώπου.

Hare made an alternative suggestion, again on the supposition that I might be right about the idiomatic use of (א)שׁנ(א) בר. If 'they wished to be more literal or more poetic', the translators might have used υἱὸς ἀνθρώπου.[34] Let us therefore try this at Mk 2.27-8.

τὸ σάββατον διὰ τὸν ἄνθρωπον ἐγένετο καὶ οὐχ ὁ ἄνθρωπος διὰ τὸ σάββατον, ὥστε κύριός ἐστιν υἱὸς ἀνθρώπου καὶ τοῦ σαββάτου.

This is more Semitic, but not in any significant way different from Hare's other suggestion. Here υἱὸς ἀνθρώπου would naturally also be interpreted in an indefinite and generic way. In view of God's creation of the sabbath for the benefit of humankind, any son of man, by virtue of his position as a human being, is lord of the sabbath. Once again, there is no particular reference to Jesus himself. This too is not remotely comparable with the succesful production of the important Christological title ὁ υἱὸς τοῦ ἀνθρώπου.

Similar comments apply to all scholarly suggestions that (א)שׁנ(א) בר in this idiom might reasonably have been translated by anything other than ὁ υἱὸς τοῦ ἀνθρώπου. This illustrates by contrast how sensible the translators were to produce this major Christological title out of the translation process.

A few genuine Son of man sayings would have been more amenable to alternative translations, and for all we know might once have been translated differently. Perhaps the best example of this is Lk. 22.48. This is from the moment at which Judah of Kerioth identified Jesus as the man whom the thugs from the chief priests should arrest. Here Luke's special source informed him that Judah approached Jesus to kiss him. I reconstructed the original saying of Jesus in Ch. 8:

33.   Hare, *Son of Man*, pp. 249–50.
34.   Hare, *Son of Man*, pp. 249–50.

יהודה, נשק לבר אנש ותמסרנה.

Judah, kissing a/the son of man and you betray him!

Let us try out a translation of this with Wellhausen's view that the translator should have used ὁ ἄνθρωπος to translate בר (א)נש(א).

Ἰησοῦς δὲ εἶπεν αὐτῷ, Ἰούδα, φιλήματι υἱὸν ἀνθρώπου παραδίδως;

This is uncomfortable Greek, but at least the reference to Jesus could not be avoided because of the narrative context. Moreover, it could be improved by omitting the article, which the translator might well have done if the saying did in fact use בר אנש in the indefinite state. In this case, ἄνθρωπον could be understood as indefinite rather than generic. Although there was no established Greek idiom for using the indefinite ἄνθρωπος with reference to a particular person, in this case such a reference could not be avoided because of the narrative context, in which Judah had just identified Jesus with a kiss, thereby handing him over to his enemies.

Similar remarks apply to Hare's view that, if I were right about the idiomatic use of בר (א)נש(א), the translators might have used υἱὸς ἀνθρώπου.[35] Let us suppose again that the saying did in fact use בר אנש in the indefinite state, and that this led a translator to put the following:

Ἰησοῦς δὲ εἶπεν αὐτῷ, Ἰούδα, φιλήματι υἱὸν ἀνθρώπου παραδίδως;

This would also be sufficiently clear, given the narrative context. Although there was no established Greek idiom for using the indefinite υἱὸν ἀνθρώπου with reference to a particular person, the expression could not mean anything other than a person, and the reference to Jesus is guaranteed in this version too by the fact that Judah had just identified Jesus with a kiss, thereby handing him over to his enemies.

At this point it becomes important that we do not have before us the work of several different translators. We have the work of three Gospel writers, two of whom, Matthew and Luke, finished their Gospels and used the work of their predecessor, Mark. The relative consistency of usage which we now find can be verified only as the result of a combined effort which was completed by these three editors. If, for example, Luke inherited one of the above alternative translations of Lk. 22.48, he would be very strongly motivated to put the Christological title ὁ υἱὸς τοῦ ἀνθρώπου in place of whichever alternative he found. We have seen that he was very happy with this title, for he uses it no less than 25 times. None of these possible alternative versions is a proper example of previously known monoglot Greek idiom. Much the most important aspect of the meaning of the saying to Luke could only be the reference to Jesus himself. No alternative version could survive this combination of circumstances. Moreover, such alternative versions would be most unlikely to be created for most genuine sayings because, as we have seen for Mk 2.28, they would generally create unwelcome nonsense. It is only in the few cases where such a version is feasible that a change of this kind may have taken place.

35. Hare, *Son of Man*, pp. 249–50.

There are two more reasons why we should not imagine Gospel translators working too independently of each other. One is the widespread communications between different churches. Christianity originally spread through networking based on the existing framework of Jewish communities throughout the Greco-Roman diaspora.[36] We know from Acts and the epistles that major figures in the early church travelled around this network, and we know from Jewish sources that travel from diaspora communities to Jerusalem for major festivals was a regular and common event in which many people from many different communities participated. Any significant material from Jesus' historic ministry will have had to go along these routes. The number of bilinguals available to carry through the translation process is likely to have been very limited, because, by the standards of Jewish/Christian/Greco-Roman culture, translation from Aramaic into Greek was a relatively specialist activity. It is therefore entirely plausible to suppose that the translators of Gospel source materials consulted each other, even before the evangelists themselves made the translated material relatively uniform.

Finally there is the relative uniformity of the actual results. All three synoptic evangelists were very happy with ὁ υἱὸς τοῦ ἀνθρώπου as a Christological title. Two of the three exceptions to the translators' strategy, Mk 3.28 and Mt. 10.32-33, are the only signs in the whole of the synoptic tradition of translation of בר (א)נש(א) with anything other than ὁ υἱὸς τοῦ ἀνθρώπου. We must infer that the tradition was genuinely uniform in translating בר (א)נש(א) with ὁ υἱὸς τοῦ ἀνθρώπου.

3. The Creation of New Son of Man Sayings

We have seen abundantly in Chapter 10 that the synoptic evangelists also created new Son of man sayings in which they used ὁ υἱὸς τοῦ ἀνθρώπου as an important Christological title *in Greek*. I now reconsider major aspects of this, before putting together the evangelists' overall view of this title.

We have seen that only two sayings in our oldest Gospel are completely secondary, Mk 13.26 and 14.62.[37] Both these sayings make evident midrashic use of Dan. 7.13, and both use it in combination with other biblical texts. At Mk 14.62, Ps. 110.1 has clearly been employed with Dan. 7.13, and Zech. 12.10 has probably been used as well. At Mk 13.26, the midrashic process is equally evident, but the precise texts are more difficult to determine: I noted among the possibilities Deut. 30.4; Isa. 34.4; Zech. 2.10 LXX. In both sayings, Daniel's כבר אנש, LXX Theod. υἱὸς ἀνθρώπου, has been replaced with the new Christological title ὁ υἱὸς τοῦ ἀνθρώπου. This can only be deliberate. It presupposes the interpretation of the man-like figure as Jesus, and the location of the incident as his second coming.

---

36.   Full discussion of this cannot be offered here. See especially W. A. Meeks, *The First Urban Christians. The Social World of the Apostle Paul* (London/New Haven: Yale University, 1993); R. Stark, *The Rise of Christianity. A Sociologist Reconsiders History* (Princeton: Princeton U.P., 1996).

37.   See pp. 242–5 above.

Moreover, while Christians learned in the scriptures would pick up the reference to Dan. 7.13, the major reference from everyone's perspective was to Jesus himself. It was his coming on the clouds of heaven for which the early church profoundly hoped.

We must infer that Mark was aware of the use of ὁ υἱὸς τοῦ ἀνθρώπου in the translation process. As we have seen, the production of this title was a natural outcome of the translation of genuine sayings of Jesus from Aramaic into Greek. It would not however be entailed in the same way by midrashic use of Dan. 7.13, because the midrashic use of biblical texts is too loose a process to necessitate this. We have seen this in the context of Mk 13.26, where other biblical texts have evidently been employed, but so loosely that we cannot tell which ones with any degree of certainty. We should note also Rev. 1.7, where Dan. 7.13 has been employed together with Zech. 12.10-14, but the title ὁ υἱὸς τοῦ ἀνθρώπου is not used. If Mark did not know ὁ υἱὸς τοῦ ἀνθρώπου from the translation process, he would have had no reason to invent it here. It follows that Mark regarded ὁ υἱὸς τοῦ ἀνθρώπου as an important Christological title used by Jesus himself in his teaching. This is how Mark came to see it in Dan. 7.13, and thus use it with reference to Jesus' parousia.

This also explains how the pattern according to which Jesus used ὁ υἱὸς τοῦ ἀνθρώπου with reference to himself, and without any explanation, came to be established. From Mark's point of view, this was already a feature of genuine sayings of Jesus, and the fact that ὁ υἱὸς τοῦ ἀνθρώπου referred to Jesus himself was too obvious for Mark to feel any need for a special explanation of it.

With all this in mind, we can see how natural it was for Mark to use ὁ υἱὸς τοῦ ἀνθρώπου in his development of Jesus' predictions of his death. We have seen Jesus discussing his forthcoming death with two genuine uses of 'Son of man' at Mk 14.21, and we have seen that the prediction of his death in the Son of man saying at Mk 8.31 is largely genuine. We have also seen his death referred to, together with that of others, in genuine Son of man sayings at Mk 9.12 and 10.45, where the use of the major Christological title ὁ υἱὸς τοῦ ἀνθρώπου would be obvious to everyone, and the general level of meaning lost on uninstructed monoglot Greeks. This means that Mark already knew the major Christological title ὁ υἱὸς τοῦ ἀνθρώπου as a feature of sayings in which Jesus looked forward to his atoning death predicted in the scriptures. This explains why Mark used ὁ υἱὸς τοῦ ἀνθρώπου in the major predictions at Mk 9.31 and 10.33-34. We have seen in Chapter 9 that Mk 9.31 was formed on the basis of existing traditions, especially those found in Mk 8.31 and 14.21. We have seen further that 10.33-34 resulted from creative rewriting of these same traditions in the light of the events of the passion. Mark had every reason to retain the Christological title ὁ υἱὸς τοῦ ἀνθρώπου as he rewrote these traditions. From his point of view it was both characteristic of bedrock tradition in the sayings of Jesus, and perfectly adapted to the needs of the church.

Similar comments apply to Mk 9.9. This is in a very late context, with the secrecy motif prominent following the secondary narrative of the Transfiguration. It appears to be based on the immediately preceding reference to the resurrection of the Son of man at Mk 8.31. Mk 14.41 is more difficult to deal with, owing to some disturbance in the text. It is not however the Son of man saying which is difficult, and Mark may have added it in order to clarify something which he knew was difficult. The term παραδίδοται is found with ὁ υἱὸς τοῦ ἀνθρώπου in the previous Son of man saying at Mk 14.21, and Mark will surely have had this in mind as he sought to describe the situation clearly.

Mark's handling of the tradition is accordingly quite clear. He inherited ὁ υἱὸς τοῦ ἀνθρώπου as a major Christological title in the Greek versions of sayings of Jesus. He therefore continued to use it when he needed to rewrite these traditions as he put together a whole Gospel. He also found it in scripture at Dan. 7.13, and used it in two midrashically composed passages which employ other scriptures as well. It is especially important to note that secondary uses of ὁ υἱὸς τοῦ ἀνθρώπου are to a large extent due to its use in the Greek translations of genuine sayings of Jesus. It follows that we must be very careful not to infer that most Son of man sayings are genuine simply on the grounds that they are largely confined to sayings attributed to Jesus. The distribution of ὁ υἱὸς τοῦ ἀνθρώπου in Mark is partly due to genuine sayings of Jesus, but it is also due to his own secondary use of this term.

The patterns of the usage of ὁ υἱὸς τοῦ ἀνθρώπου established by Mark were inherited and continued by Matthew, with much further development. We have seen that Matthew recognized the use of Dan. 7.13 at Mk 13.26, and developed the saying much further. This development included a second Son of man saying, which made midrashic use of Isa. 11.12, as well as material from Zech. 12.10-14 (Mt. 24.30). Matthew carried much further the eschatological reference of ὁ υἱὸς τοῦ ἀνθρώπου. He notably created the expression ἡ παρουσία τοῦ υἱοῦ τοῦ ἀνθρώπου in his editing of secondary Q sayings (Mt. 24.27,37,39). He then proceeded to use ὁ υἱὸς τοῦ ἀνθρώπου quite freely in creating more sayings with an eschatological reference. This resulted in a high proportion of secondary sayings in Matthew. As in Mark, however, the major cause of the use of ὁ υἱὸς τοῦ ἀνθρώπου in secondary sayings is that it was already a well-established Christological title, and the reason for this was its use in the translation of genuine sayings of Jesus.

Matthew also continued the development of the passion predictions, notably altering Mark's accurate and figurative μετὰ τρεῖς ἡμέρας to τῇ τρίτῃ ἡμέρᾳ, now understood as a literal reference to the inaccurate stories of Jesus' bodily resurrection (Mt. 16.21; 17.23; 20.19). He also re-edited completely Mk 9.11-13, which became quite incoherent for monoglot Greeks as a result of the difficult process of translating it from its original Aramaic source.[38] Matthew's version is entirely coherent, and in it ὁ υἱὸς τοῦ ἀνθρώπου is a title of Jesus alone, whereas the incoherence in Mark's account was due to the original reference of בר (א)נש(א) to John the Baptist as well. This shows the major shift of meaning characteristic of the translation process to be fully in accordance with the needs of the evangelists' editing. Like Mark, Matthew also produced a new prediction, on the basis of existing tradition, when he felt his narrative needed it (Mt. 26.2). This has ὁ υἱὸς τοῦ ἀνθρώπου and παραδίδοται

---

38. See pp. 125–31 above.

from the tradition, with a reference to crucifixion added in from the passion narrative, as already in Matthew's editing of the third major passion prediction (Mt. 20.19, editing Mk 10.34).

Matthew's editorial procedures also explain how the pattern according to which Jesus used ὁ υἱὸς τοῦ ἀνθρώπου with reference to himself, and without any explanation, was continued. Matthew inherited this pattern from Mark, and probably also from Q material. We have seen that he considered it to be a major Christological title in Greek, and he knew it from sayings of Jesus himself. It was blindingly obvious to him that ὁ υἱὸς τοῦ ἀνθρώπου referred to Jesus himself. He therefore had no reason to alter the basic pattern.

The patterns of the usage of ὁ υἱὸς τοῦ ἀνθρώπου established by Mark were also inherited and continued by Luke, with developments in some ways very similar to those of Matthew, but with some important differences too. Luke continued to use ὁ υἱὸς τοῦ ἀνθρώπου as a Christological title in editing sayings with an eschatological reference. We have however seen that in so doing, Luke was careful to remove the impression given by some Marcan sayings that the second coming of Jesus should have taken place relatively soon after the historic ministry. So, for example, before editing Mk 13.26 at Lk. 21.27, Luke made clear reference to the fall of Jerusalem, and his comments are consistent with seeing a considerable gap between the fall of Jerusalem and the coming of the Son of man. Again, in editing Q sayings at Lk. 17.24,26,30, Luke retains the eschatological reference of all three sayings. However, he introduces them with clear sayings to the effect that the kingdom will not come soon (Lk. 17.20-21), and that there will be a significant time during which Jesus' disciples will hope for one of the days of the Son of man and will *not* see any such (Lk. 17.22). This also puts the retained eschatological reference in perspective. It is striking that Luke has chosen to postpone rather than remove this eschatology, and that in so doing he has retained the title ὁ υἱὸς τοῦ ἀνθρώπου. It is even more striking that he has used it in his opening declaration of the interim period in which people will not be able to see one of the days of the Son of man (Lk. 17.22), and that he has used a pronoun to refer back to the use of ὁ υἱὸς τοῦ ἀνθρώπου at 17.24 in the passion prediction which he has inserted on the basis of tradition at 17.25.

Luke did remove the eschatological orientation of the important saying at Mk 14.62 when he edited it at Lk. 22.69. He omitted ὄψεσθε, and with it the notion that Jesus' judges would see the Son of man, and he omitted the coming on the clouds of heaven, so the second coming has been removed altogether from this passage, and with it all trace of Dan. 7.13. In its place, Luke declares that *from now onwards* (ἀπὸ τοῦ νῦν) the Son of man will be sitting on the right hand of God. This replaces a supposedly future event which had not happened with an exalted present state which cannot be falsified. It is all the more remarkable that Luke has retained the title ὁ υἱὸς τοῦ ἀνθρώπου. He evidently considered it to be an important title of Jesus, and not one which was especially associated with eschatological events which had not occurred. Nonetheless, just as we have seen him use it in eschatological contexts where he makes clear that the coming of the

Son of man was never intended to take place as soon as it was expected, so we find him producing a new Son of man saying with reference to the situation when all the final earthly events are completed (Lk. 21.36). Here the believer will finally stand ἔμπροσθεν τοῦ υἱοῦ τοῦ ἀνθρώπου, a significantly modified version of the earlier eschatological and judgemental reference of ὁ υἱὸς τοῦ ἀνθρώπου. Luke's continued use of this title shows how important it was to him.

Luke also continued the development of the passion predictions. Like Matthew, he notably altered Mark's accurate and figurative μετὰ τρεῖς ἡμέρας to τῇ τρίτῃ ἡμέρᾳ, now understood as a literal reference to the inaccurate stories of Jesus' bodily resurrection (Lk. 9.22; 18.33, omitted from the much abbreviated Lk. 9.44). He also produced another prediction on the basis of tradition and edited it in at Lk. 17.25, using αὐτόν to refer back to ὁ υἱὸς τοῦ ἀνθρώπου in the Q saying reproduced in the previous verse. He interpolated a flashback prediction at Lk. 24.7, where he recalls the tradition of Jesus' predictions of his death and resurrection, using ὁ υἱὸς τοῦ ἀνθρώπου as in the traditions which he inherited, as well as τῇ τρίτῃ ἡμέρᾳ, now actually placed in the resurrection story. These passages show Luke entirely happy with ὁ υἱὸς τοῦ ἀνθρώπου as a major Christological title in Jesus' predictions of his death and resurrection, to the point where he edited in fresh predictions at points where he felt he needed them.

I have noted two more secondary occurrences of ὁ υἱὸς τοῦ ἀνθρώπου in Luke.[39] One is at Lk. 6.22, where the term ὁ υἱὸς τοῦ ἀνθρώπου clearly refers to Jesus as central to the life of persecuted Christians, and the term is absent from the parallel at Mt. 5.11. The other is at Lk. 18.8, where a purely Lukan conclusion to a parable looks forward to the eventual return of ὁ υἱὸς τοῦ ἀνθρώπου during the period of the church.

Luke's editorial procedures, like those of Matthew, further explain how the pattern according to which Jesus used ὁ υἱὸς τοῦ ἀνθρώπου with reference to himself, without any explanation, was continued. Like Matthew, Luke inherited this pattern from Mark, and probably also from Q material. We have seen that he considered it to be a major Christological title in Greek, and he knew it from sayings of Jesus himself. It was blindingly obvious to him, as it was to Mark and Matthew, that ὁ υἱὸς τοῦ ἀνθρώπου referred to Jesus himself. He therefore had no reason to alter the basic pattern.

It would be good if we could infer the position of Q in these matters, but it is difficult to do so because Q in itself does not exist, and its contents and nature have to be inferred from two very vigorous editors, Matthew and Luke. We have seen that Q contained four genuine Son of man sayings of Jesus. Two of these, Mt. 8.20//Lk. 9.58 and Mt. 11.19//Lk. 7.34, came to the evangelists in a single Greek translation, which used ὁ υἱὸς τοῦ ἀνθρώπου as a translation of בר (א)נש(א). Here, therefore, we certainly find the translators' strategy in Q material. One Q saying, Mt. 12.32//Lk. 12.10, either reached the evangelists in two separate translations both of which used ὁ υἱὸς τοῦ ἀνθρώπου as a translation of בר (א)נש(א), again showing

---

39.   See pp. 239–41 above.

the translators' strategy in Q material: or it was translated by or for the evangelists, in which case we simply have the translators' strategy operating in the finished documents of two evangelists both of whom loved ὁ υἱὸς τοῦ ἀνθρώπου as a major Christological title.

One genuine saying, Mt. 10.33//Lk. 12.8, survives in two different translations. The later one, Lk. 12.8, follows the established strategy of rendering (א)נשׁ(א) בר with ὁ υἱὸς τοῦ ἀνθρώπου. The earlier one, Mt. 10.32, however, does not: it has ἐγώ, in the form κἀγώ so as to translate אף as well. Even more remarkable is Mt. 10.33//Lk. 12.9. Here we might reasonably infer from Mk 8.38 that Jesus used (א)נשׁ(א) בר in the original saying, and Mk 8.38 itself follows the translators' strategy of rendering it with ὁ υἱὸς τοῦ ἀνθρώπου.[40] Mt. 10.33, however, has κἀγώ again, while Luke has used the future passive instead. It is very interesting that genuine sayings in Q, necessarily the oldest because they are genuine, and only the third saying in Mark's Gospel (Mk 3.28-29), provide all the exceptions to the translators' strategy of rendering (א)נשׁ(א) בר with ὁ υἱὸς τοῦ ἀνθρώπου. We should infer that this strategy took some time to become firmly established. Extensive connections between the churches, based originally on extensive connections between Jewish communities in the Greco-Roman world, form the general framework within which an agreement was eventually reached. It did not however give Matthew, Mark and Luke sufficient reason to alter this small proportion of initial exceptions.

The remaining Son of man sayings in Q use ὁ υἱὸς τοῦ ἀνθρώπου as a Christological title in Greek. One of them, Mt. 24.44//Lk. 12.40, ends with a reference to the second coming of Jesus with the words ὁ υἱὸς τοῦ ἀνθρώπου ἔρχεται. This has the collocation of 'Son of man' and 'coming' at the last times which is a clear indication of the midrashic use of Dan. 7.13. We have seen that this usage is secondary. In this passage, it applies a probably genuine parable of Jesus (Mt. 24.43//Lk. 12.39) to the situation of Christians who believed they were living in the last times and who fervently hoped for the second coming of Jesus. We must infer that the midrashic use of Dan. 7.13 which we have already noted in Mark and much developed by Matthew was also known to those Christians who were responsible for this secondary addition to a saying of Jesus.

One further Son of man saying in Q, Mt. 12.40//Lk. 11.30, is clearly based on another scriptural episode, the fate of Jonah. Despite the enthusiastic expansion of it now found in Matthew, with a quotation from Jonah 2.1, there is so much verbal overlap in Greek that we must infer that the Q saying reached Matthew and Luke in Greek. This is further evidence that, for some of the Q material, ὁ υἱὸς τοῦ ἀνθρώπου was an important Christological title in Greek. It also continues the use of scripture which we have seen already in Mark and carried further in Matthew. The remaining Son of man sayings in Q, Mt. 24.27//Lk. 17.24 and Mt. 24.37, cf.39// Lk. 17.26, clearly use ὁ υἱὸς τοῦ ἀνθρώπου as a Christological title in Greek, as we have seen at length.[41] Moreover, despite evident editorial activity by Matthew, it is clear that both sayings reached both evangelists in Greek.

40. For full discussion, including an alternative view, see pp. 179–94 above.
41. See pp. 215–8, 225–8 above.

It follows that the Q material basically supports the view of Matthew, Mark and Luke that ὁ υἱὸς τοῦ ἀνθρώπου is an important Christological title in Greek.

4. Conclusions

The following conclusions should therefore be drawn. The Greek title ὁ υἱὸς τοῦ ἀνθρώπου emerged in the first place from the translation of genuine sayings of Jesus from Aramaic into Greek. All these genuine sayings used the Aramaic term (א)נש(א) בר in a particular idiomatic way. In all cases Jesus said something about himself, but the idiom also included a more general level of meaning. The importance of this level of meaning varied. In a few cases, it was of genuine importance, as in the proposed death of the sons of Zebedee (Mk 10.45), or the practical conditions to be endured by a potential disciple on a migratory mission (Mt. 8.20//Lk. 9.58). In many cases, however, it was not of particular importance, since most people did not forgive sins (Mk 2.10) or expect to rise shortly from the dead (Mk 8.31).

The idiom itself could not be translated into Greek, because Greek has no such idiom. The translators therefore adopted a strategy. Up to a point, they proceeded literally, rendering בר with its precise perceived equivalent υἱός, and (א)נש(א) with its precise perceived equivalent ἀνθρώπου. They also had to take a decision about whether to use Greek articles, because the original Aramaic might use either state of (א)נש(א). They decided to use both definite articles, to give them the Christological title ὁ υἱὸς τοῦ ἀνθρώπου. This was a wonderful creative outburst, not some sort of mistake. It selected in the target language the most important reference of the original idiom, the reference to Jesus himself. Any other decision would have been a failure, because the reference to Jesus himself would have been lost, and that would not have been in accordance with the needs of the earliest Christians. Bilingual translators suffering from interference could continue to see both original levels of meaning in their translation, because the articles could both be interpreted generically, as the second one always must be. It was however much more important that all Greek-speaking Christians could see the reference to Jesus, for this was what was most important to all those Christians who heard the Gospels read. To avoid confusion, the translators also decided not to use (ὁ) υἱὸς (τοῦ) ἀνθρώπου, with or without the Greek articles, when an original (א)נש(א) בר referred to anyone other than Jesus, and not to use the plural.

The result of this major creative outburst was a Christological title ὁ υἱὸς τοῦ ἀνθρώπου. Mark liked it so much that he used it 14 times, Matthew used it 30 times, and Luke 25. In addition to the translation of simply genuine sayings, all three evangelists continued to use it in expanding and developing Jesus' predictions of his death and resurrection. Mark also found this term at Dan. 7.13, and constructed two major predictions of Jesus' second coming by combining his use of this text in midrashic manner with other texts (Mk 13.26; 14.62). This accounts for all Mark's Son of man sayings. Matthew continued this midrashic creativity, using other texts to amplify his picture of Jesus' second coming in the near future. He went further, using ὁ υἱὸς τοῦ ἀνθρώπου on its own as a title of Jesus, especially in sayings with an eschatological reference. Luke, writing somewhat later, was careful to make it clear that the second coming of Jesus should not have been expected too soon after his earthly life. In the process, he removed verifiable reference to Dan. 7.13 from both Mk 13.26 (Lk. 21.27) and 14.62 (Lk. 22.69). He nonetheless retained ὁ υἱὸς τοῦ ἀνθρώπου as an important Christological title in eschatological as well as other contexts.

It follows that ὁ υἱὸς τοῦ ἀνθρώπου was a major Christological title for all three synoptic evangelists. They did not need to explain that it always referred to Jesus himself because this was blindingly obvious to everyone from the first. This usage and reference continued in the Johannine community.

Chapter Twelve

THE JOHANNINE SAYINGS

1. Introduction:
The Origin and Meaning of ὁ υἱὸς τοῦ ἀνθρώπου *in the Fourth Gospel*

The thirteen Johannine Son of man sayings belong for the most part to a different world from those in the synoptic Gospels. The Johannine Son of man does not do earthly things such as come eating and drinking (Mt. 11.19//Lk. 7.34). Nor is he flogged and put to death (Mt. 20.19//Mk 10.34//Lk. 18.33), though Jesus suffers this fate without its being associated with this term (Jn 19.1,16-30). Nor does the Johannine Son of man rise from the dead (Mt. 16.21//Mk 8.31//Lk. 9.22; Mt. 17.9// Mk 9.9; Mt. 17.23//Mk 9.31; Mt. 20.19//Mk 10.34//Lk. 18.33; Lk. 24.7), though Jesus most certainly does rise and appear to the disciples through closed doors and the like (Jn 20–21). Nor does the Johannine Son of man do anything like come on the clouds of heaven (Mt. 24.30//Mk 13.26, cf. Lk. 21.27; Mt. 26.64//Mk 14.62). The Johannine Son of man does unsynoptic things such as descend and ascend (Jn 3.13; 6.62). When his death is referred to, the authors tell us that he will be lifted up or exalted (Jn 3.14; 8.28; 12.34), or even glorified (Jn 12.23). Unless you eat the flesh of the Son of man and drink his blood, you have no life in you, whereas people who do eat his flesh and drink his blood have eternal life, and Jesus promises to raise them at the last day (Jn 6.53-54).

These differences are extreme, and scholars have been right to try to explain them. Taking these differences seriously has however had an unfortunate side-effect. It has combined with other factors to cause scholars to look outside Christian tradition for the origin and meaning of this term. I surveyed the major theories in Ch. 1, and some main points must be recalled here. Some scholars attempted to construct an ancient figure of a Heavenly Man, who had features such as ascending and descending in common with the Johannine Son of man. One influential attempt was by Bultmann. He drew on Mandean, Manichean and Gnostic material to form this picture.[1] Another major attempt was by Borsch, who also drew on a massive range of texts to put forward a mythical picture of a primaeval Man-King. All such

---

1.   R. Bultmann, 'Die Bedeutung der neuerschlossenen mandäischen und manichäischen Quellen für das Verständnis des Johannesevangeliums', *ZNW* 24 (1925), pp. 100–46; repr. R. Bultmann (ed. E. Dinkler), *Exegetica. Aufsätze zur Erforschung des Neuen Testaments* (Tübingen: Mohr (Siebeck), 1967), pp. 55–104.

attempts have two major faults.[2] In the first place, they are all modern constructs. Each supposed myth occurs nowhere. It is a conglomerate drawn in small pieces from a wide range of texts, many of them from a later period than the Fourth Gospel. Secondly, no such theory led to a proper explanation as to why this Gospel uses the term ὁ υἱὸς τοῦ ἀνθρώπου rather than ὁ ἄνθρωπος ὁ οὐράνιος or the like as a major Christological title.

The second major scholarly resource outside the Gospels has been the Son of Man Concept. We have seen in Ch. 1 that this also has major faults.[3] In the first place, it too is a modern construct, amalgamated from a few texts. Secondly, it relied too heavily on German or English translations of the corrupt Ge'ez translation of the *Similitudes of Enoch*. Thirdly, the Son of Man Concept is an eschatological being, in many ways quite different from the Son of man in the Fourth Gospel. Attempts to get round this by pointing out eschatological features of the Fourth Gospel miss the main point completely. They do not explain why the authors of this document, apparently in search of a major Christological title, should draw on a source so inappropriate for their purposes. Finally the notion that this would produce exactly the same term as the synoptics, ὁ υἱὸς τοῦ ἀνθρώπου, was always dubious. Some of these difficulties were sometimes mitigated by seeing the influence of Jesus and/or the synoptic Gospels as well as this figure. All of them could not however be resolved, and acknowledgement of the influence of Jesus and/or the synoptic Gospels takes us back to the real origin of this term.

I have argued that the origins of the use of ὁ υἱὸς τοῦ ἀνθρώπου go right back to the use of the Aramaic (א)שׁנ(א) בר by the historical Jesus. The idiomatic use of the Aramaic (א)שׁנ(א) בר was difficult to translate, so the translators had a strategy, to use ὁ υἱὸς τοῦ ἀνθρώπου when the reference was to Jesus, and not otherwise. They found this term in scripture at Dan. 7.13, which Mark and Matthew already used in combination with other scriptural texts. The Gospels of Matthew and Mark, and just possibly Luke, must be the source of the Fourth Gospel's use of ὁ υἱὸς τοῦ ἀνθρώπου, because this term is unique. Other features common to all four Gospels are the use of ὁ υἱὸς τοῦ ἀνθρώπου with reference to Jesus alone, almost entirely by Jesus alone, and the employment of scriptures with it in midrashic mode. These arguments should be regarded as decisive. Whether the Johannine community had other sources or not, they cannot have failed to know the Gospels of Matthew and Mark.

How then do we explain the major differences between the Johannine Son of man sayings and those of the synoptics, as indicated above? By paying attention to the most central feature of the Fourth Gospel: it consists almost entirely of rewritten history. This has been basically known for more than a century, and taking full advantage of recent work on the rewriting of history, I have mapped it out in a single book, for the arguments were not readily available in a single place.[4] This is the key to the massive differences between sayings using ὁ υἱὸς τοῦ ἀνθρώπου

2.   See further pp. 23–8 above.
3.   See pp. 23–30 above.
4.   P. M. Casey, *Is John's Gospel True?* (London: Routledge, 1996).

in the synoptic Gospels on the one hand, and in the Fourth Gospel on the other. The authors of the Fourth Gospel fully intended to rewrite the story of Jesus in accordance with the needs of the Johannine community at Ephesus in the late first century. They have rewritten sayings using ὁ υἱὸς τοῦ ἀνθρώπου with everything else. They have rewritten sayings using the other major Christological titles with everything else too.

Three other points from recent scholarship are worthy of initial mention. One is the contention, associated especially with the work of E. D. Freed, that ὁ υἱὸς τοῦ ἀνθρώπου is little more than a stylistic variation on other ways of writing about Jesus.[5] This is not true, but Freed's article was part of a process of clarifying some important points. It is notable that, with the exception of Jn 1.51, what is said of Jesus with the term ὁ υἱὸς τοῦ ἀνθρώπου is also said without it. It follows that this document does not have a 'Son of man Christology' which is separate from the rest of its Christology. This is a great improvement on the various attempts in traditional scholarship to uncover a specific Son of man Christology understood against a particular cultural background reconstructed from other documents. It also follows that we should not expect any particular distribution of the term ὁ υἱὸς τοῦ ἀνθρώπου. This is good, because there is no obvious logic to its distribution, which is natural if this document was written by people who wrote things about Jesus as naturally without ὁ υἱὸς τοῦ ἀνθρώπου as they did with it.

A second major point has been the revival of the traditional patristic view that ὁ υἱὸς τοῦ ἀνθρώπου is a particular reference to Jesus' humanity. In recent scholarship, the work of Moloney has been especially notable in presenting this view.[6] There is truth in this opinion too. Unlike λόγος and υἱός, ὁ υἱὸς τοῦ ἀνθρώπου is for the most part used with reference to the incarnate Jesus. Once again, however, we must be careful not to exaggerate. At the climax of the prologue the λόγος becomes σάρξ, not ὁ υἱὸς τοῦ ἀνθρώπου, and the term is not used once in the passion narrative. Moreover, Moloney gets into terrible tangles at 3.13-14, where the term is used with reference to Jesus' pre-existence, ascension and subsequent presence in heaven.[7] Nonetheless, the way in which ὁ υἱὸς τοῦ ἀνθρώπου is used for the most part is genuinely significant. I shall conclude that it has its natural meaning, 'the son of humankind' and hence the most important person there has ever been on earth.

The third point is perhaps the most remarkable of all. There has been hardly any work on the Aramaic level of the tradition. I have shown elsewhere that large-scale claims that this document was translated from Aramaic are spurious. I also noted that there are problems with the use of ὁ υἱὸς τοῦ ἀνθρώπου in particular.[8] Smalley, on the contrary, claimed much earlier that these Son of man sayings go back to an authentic Aramaic tradition. Yet apart from (א)נש(א) בר, his discussion

---

5.   E. D. Freed, 'The Son of Man in the Fourth Gospel', *JBL* 86 (1967), pp. 402–9.

6.   F. J. Moloney, *The Johannine Son of Man* (BSRel 14. Rome: LAS, 1976, 2nd edn 1978).

7.   Moloney, *Johannine Son of Man*, pp. 53–67.

8.   Casey, *Is John's Gospel True?*, pp. 87–97.

of Johannine sayings notes only two Aramaic words, both taken from Black, who subsequently dropped one of them.[9]

I now proceed to work through the Johannine Son of man sayings in the order in which they occur.

2. John 1.51

This first saying occurs right at the end of a section. The witness of John the Baptist is followed by the introduction of Jesus' first disciples. The last of these disciples is Nathanael, a Johannine character who is absent from the synoptic Gospels. He hails Jesus as Son of God, a centrally important Johannine confession, and as king of Israel. Jesus' reply ends with the Son of man saying:

Ἀμὴν ἀμὴν λέγω ὑμῖν, ὄψεσθε τὸν οὐρανὸν ἀνεῳγότα καὶ τοὺς ἀγγελους τοῦ θεοῦ ἀναβαίνοντας καὶ καταβαίνοντας ἐπὶ τὸν υἱὸν τοῦ ἀνθρώπου.

The double ἀμὴν is distinctively Johannine, the community's rewritten version of a hallmark of the speech of the historical Jesus. The saying is widely recognised to be a midrash on Gen. 28.12, another distinctively Johannine feature. We have seen that Mark, followed by Matthew, found ὁ υἱὸς τοῦ ἀνθρώπου in Dan. 7.13, and used it midrashically with other texts. One of the two most striking examples is Mt. 26.64//Mk 14.62. Here ὄψεσθε is found with τὸν υἱὸν τοῦ ἀνθρώπου, the verse also contains ὁ οὐράνος, and the Matthean version also uses ἐπί. This is a massive overlap with Jn 1.51. The use of ὄψεσθε, perhaps derived originally from Zech. 12.10,[10] is especially striking because Jesus has just addressed Nathanael in the singular, ending with the very word ὄψῃ (Jn 1.50). While Jesus' shift to the plural ὄψεσθε at Jn 1.51 makes perfectly good Johannine sense (cf. Jn 3.10-11), it is well explained by the use of Mt. 26.64. Moreover, most of the rest of each saying consists of the midrashic use of other biblical texts. So does the other synoptic text which combines ὄψομαι with τὸν υἱὸν τοῦ ἀνθρώπου, together with the angels, the Matthean version again using ὁ οὐράνος and ἐπί, and both authors adding additional biblical texts (Mt. 24.30-31//Mk 13.26-27).[11] There are other significant features of Mt. 26.64 which are relevant to the immediate context of Jn 1.51. The most important is the high priest's demand that Jesus should say εἰ σὺ εἶ ὁ χριστὸς ὁ υἱὸς τοῦ θεοῦ (Mt. 26.63). Jesus' response is σὺ εἶπας (Mt. 26.64). This means that Joseph Caiaphas has unwittingly declared Jesus' true status while in the midst of an act of extreme treachery. Contrast the open confession of Nathanael, Ῥαββί, σὺ εἶ ὁ υἱὸς τοῦ θεοῦ, σὺ βασιλεὺς εἶ τοῦ Ἰσραήλ (Jn 1.49). That is the proper

---

9.   S. S. Smalley, 'The Johannine Son of Man Sayings', *NTS* 15 (1968–9), pp. 278–301. He notes על for ἐπί at Jn 1.51 from Black, *Aramaic Approach* (2nd edn 1954), p. 85, not retained in the third edition; and Jn 3.14, where Black, *Aramaic Approach* (3rd edn 1967), p. 141, noting the work of previous scholars, has ὑψωθῆναι be an Aramaism, reflecting זקף.

10.   See further pp. 243–4 above.

11.   See further pp. 215–7, 242–3 above.

response of Ἰσραηλίτης ἐν ᾧ δόλος οὐκ ἔστιν (Jn 1.47), a striking contrast to Joseph Caiaphas, as well as the better known contrast to Jacob/Israel (Gen. 27.35).

All these points, taken together, form an overwhelming argument of cumulative weight. The Johannine community rewrote Mt. 26.64, in light of the problems surrounding Mk 14.61-62 and Mt. 24.30-31//Mk 13.26-27 (cf. Lk. 21.27; 22.67-70).

They had devastating reasons for doing so. The midrashically constructed texts of Mt. 26.64//Mk 14.62 are taken from Ps. 110.1 and Dan. 7.13. Both are conditioned by the introductory ὄψεσθε, perhaps originally from Zech. 12.10. The first thing that Jesus' hostile judges were supposed to see was Jesus himself at the right hand of God, which would only be possible if they saw God himself. By the time that the Fourth Gospel was written, everyone knew that this had not happened. Luke altered the beginning of the prediction, so that it read:

ἀπὸ τοῦ νῦν δὲ ἔσται ὁ υἱὸς τοῦ ἀνθρώπου καθήμενος ἐκ δεξιῶν τῆς δυνάμεως τοῦ θεοῦ (Lk. 22.69).

This the whole of the early church firmly believed. It solves the same problem in a different way. The Johannine solution is more radical, partly because the Johannine community had an even more serious problem. As the prologue put it programmatically: θεὸν οὐδεὶς ἑώρακεν πώποτε (Jn 1.18). This is repeated in the body of this work (Jn 5.37; 6.46), as well as at 1 Jn 4.12. It follows that the belief that no one had seen God was very important to the community. This is a second reason why Jesus should not predict that his hostile judges should see God.

The second thing which the hostile judges were to see was Jesus coming on/with the clouds of heaven (Mt. 26.64//Mk 14.62). This was even worse. The second coming of Jesus had been vigorously expected throughout the period of the early church. It had not taken place, as everyone, including hostile Jews in Ephesus, knew full well. Luke's countermeasures included the omission of ὄψεσθε and ἐρχόμενον μετὰ τῶν νεφελῶν τοῦ οὐρανοῦ from his version of Mk 14.62 (Lk. 22.69).[12] The Johannine solution to this problem was also much more radical. It included the invention of the Paraclete, who represented the presence of God with the community after Jesus' death and resurrection.[13] The exposition of this is somewhat ambiguous, for experience of the presence of God is a matter of experience rather than of logic. It includes the presence of Jesus, as well as of the Father and the Paraclete: Οὐκ ἀφήσω ὑμᾶς ὀρφανούς, ἔρχομαι πρὸς ὑμᾶς (Jn 14.18). The expectation of the parousia has only just been retained in the appendix to the Gospel (21.22-23). This also tells in story form of the death of all the first disciples, as if the expectation of the beloved disciple surviving until the parousia had been a misunderstanding. That is how the Johannine community saw it. They knew that Jesus had not come, and they restructured their religious experience and understood it as Jesus' renewed presence in the activity of the Holy Spirit. This gave them a decisive reason for rewriting Mt. 26.64.

12.   See pp. 222–30, 239–41 above.
13.   Casey, *Is John's Gospel True?*, pp. 151–4, with bibliography.

At this point, we must consider also the other major synoptic passage in which the Son of man is associated with the angels (Mt. 16.27-28//Mk 8.38–9.1//Lk. 9.26-27). The Marcan version is bad enough. This has the coming of the Son of man with the holy angels in one verse, followed in the next by the prophecy that some people standing there would not see death until they had seen the kingdom of God come in power. Everyone in the Johannine community knew that this had not happened. Once again, Luke already took countermeasures. He removed all mention of the 'generation' from Mk 8.38, dropped ἐληλυθυῖαν ἐν δυνάμει from Mk 9.1, and linked the prophecy of the kingdom closely to the following narrative of the Transfiguration with the introductory words ἐγένετο δὲ μετὰ τοὺς λόγους τούτους ὡσεὶ ἡμέραι ὀκτώ. For Luke's readers, the coming of the Son of man had no indication of time, and Jesus' prophecy that some of those standing with him would not see death until they had seen the kingship of God was fulfilled in the presence of Peter, Jacob and John at the Transfiguration.

Matthew took a diametrically opposed view. He cut the opening of Mk 8.38 and thereby made the coming of the Son of man the substantive centre of the prediction. He added midrashically the final judgement of the Son of man, in words reminiscent of Ps. 61.13 (MT 62.13) and Prov. 24.12. He also edited the Son of man into Mk 9.1. Matthew's readers would not be left in any doubt. Jesus predicted that some of the people standing with him would live to see the Son of man coming with the angels to carry out the final judgement. The only other mention of the Son of man coming with the angels (Mt. 25.31) introduces a more extensive picture of the final judgement. The vigorous presentation of the final coming of the Son of man at Mt. 16.27-28 follows shortly after Peter's confession. The Matthean version of this is fuller than those of Mark and Luke: σὺ εἶ ὁ χριστὸς ὁ υἱὸς τοῦ θεοῦ τοῦ ζῶντος (Mt. 16.16). Nathanael's confession at Jn 1.49 is another version of this, as much as of Caiaphas's question. In Matthew alone, Jesus responds to Peter's confession with a dramatic declaration, the opening of which refers to him as Σίμων Βαριωνά (Matt. 16.17). The Aramaic Βαριωνά, or בר יונא, 'son of John', is translated into Greek at Jn 1.42, where Jesus also addresses him: σὺ εἶ Σίμων ὁ υἱὸς Ἰωάννου. The Matthean Jesus addresses him a second time, σὺ εἶ Πέτρος (Mt. 16.18). The correct Aramaic, with a Greek ending which reflects the name by which Peter was frequently known in the early church (e.g. Gal. 1.18), followed by a correct translation, is supplied at Jn 1.42: σὺ κληθήσῃ Κηφᾶς, ὃ ἑρμηνεύεται Πέτρος.

All this is far too extensive to be coincidental. When the authors of Jn 1.51 rewrote Mt. 26.64, they had in mind the set of problems derived from sayings of Jesus predicting events which had not taken place. The two most notable events predicted were the coming of the kingdom of God, the central concept of the teaching of Jesus, and the parousia of the Son of man, which appears central to people who read the synoptic Gospels as if they were a record of the life and teaching of Jesus. We know also that the Johannine community's reaction to these problems as a whole was quite drastic. They virtually wrote the kingdom of God out of the teaching of Jesus, taking the parables with it.[14] Apart from the one mention of the second

14. Casey, *Is John's Gospel True?*, pp. 81–3.

coming in the appendix to the Gospel (Jn 21.22-23), it has been replaced with the presence of God in the church. This is why the rewriting of Mt. 26.64 has been so drastic that scholars have not seen it for what it is. Faced with a midrash of ὄψεσθε from Zech. 12.10, and the substance of the saying from Ps. 110.1 and Dan. 7.13, the community have retained ὄψεσθε from Zech. 12.10, together with τὸν υἱὸν τοῦ ἀνθρώπου and heaven from Dan. 7.13. For the rest, they have retained the form of the midrash, but replaced these texts by midrashic use of Gen. 28.12.

In the original Hebrew text of Gen. 28.12, the angels evidently go up and down on the ladder, since this is what ladders are for. This interpretation is also explicit in the LXX, where αὐτῆς is feminine and can only refer back to κλίμαξ. From a purely grammatical point of view, however, בו in the Hebrew text could refer to Jacob, rather than to the ladder. This interpretation is found in later Jewish sources. It is best known from Gen. R. 68.12. We must not pre-date the details of such a late source, but the grammatical ambiguity in the Hebrew text is undeniable, and the Johannine community made use of it. The Johannine context has further evidence of midrashic use of a text about Israel. In the rewriting of the witness of John the Baptist, which replaces the synoptic account of him actually baptising Jesus, we find John attributing to God the revelatory words which enabled him to identify Jesus as the one on whom the Spirit descended. He also identifies Jesus as ὁ ἐκλεκτός τοῦ θεοῦ, as we must surely read at 1.34 with P[5vid] א*, rather than the easier reading ὁ υἱὸς τοῦ θεοῦ.[15] This shows midrashic use of Isa. 42.1, where the LXX has the following: Ἰσραηλ ὁ ἐκλεκτός μου ... ἔδωκα τὸ πνεῦμα μου ἐπ' αὐτόν.

The Johannine context also has further evidence of the midrashic use of the Genesis narrative. I have noted Jesus' comment on Nathanael at 1.47, Ἴδε ἀληθῶς Ἰσραηλίτης ἐν ᾧ δόλος οὐκ ἔστιν. This is an obvious contrast with Jacob at Gen. 27.35. We should also note John the Baptist's double declaration, κἀγὼ οὐκ ᾔδειν αὐτόν (Jn 1.31,33). This is strongly reminiscent of Gen. 28.16, where Jacob/Israel, having awoken from his dream, declares, 'The LORD (LXX κύριος) is in this place, and I did not know' (LXX ἐγὼ δὲ οὐκ ᾔδειν). This is further evidence of the way in which our authors were inspired by the scriptural texts.

After all this, what was Jn 1.51 actually intended to mean? The commentators are largely in agreement on one main point, which should be accepted. As R. H. Lightfoot put it, 'the meaning of this important verse is like that of I[14] and I[18]; it is a description of the coming ministry in which His disciples will witness their Lord's unbroken communion with the Father and will themselves partake in it. This unrestricted commerce (cf. 5[17], 8[29]) between the Father and the Son of man is here pictured as a never-ceasing activity.'[16] This is not only correct in itself, it also fits this verse into the Gospel as a whole. It enables us to see that, when properly understood, this verse is unique only in being a midrash: its meaning is perfectly

15.   So e.g. A. T. Hanson, *The Prophetic Gospel. A Study of John and the Old Testament* (Edinburgh: T&T Clark, 1991), p. 36.

16.   R. H. Lightfoot (ed. C. F. Evans), *St. John's Gospel. A Commentary* (Oxford: Clarendon, 1956), p. 99.

Johannine. The actual term ὁ υἱὸς τοῦ ἀνθρώπου clearly refers to Jesus during his earthly ministry.

Many commentators have endeavoured to draw much more out of this verse, with largely disastrous results. For example, Brown, arguing that the verse was originally an isolated saying, used as his fourth argument, 'there is nothing in what follows 51 to indicate that its promise was ever fulfilled, if the vision promised is to be taken literally.' Sanders and Mastin infer that Jesus 'is the second Jacob, i.e. the true Israel in his own person'. Burkett, heading for his view that '1.51 parallels the Son of Man with the ladder', objects to the equation of the Son of man with Jacob, commenting that 'the Gospel puts Nathanael and the other disciples in the place of Jacob as the recipients of the vision, not the Son of Man'.[17] No comments of this kind should be regarded as acceptable. Every one of them presupposes that Jn 1.51 and its background are pieces of information from which logically ordered deductions may be drawn. It is nothing of the kind. It is an inspired midrash which takes off from its sources and leaves them behind. Its present interpretation must be inferred from its context. The problems which it sought to solve may be inferred from its background, and we can find the texts from which it took off, but these texts do not control it.

It remains to comment on ἀνεῳγότα, which is not found at Gen. 28.12, Mt. 26.64, or any other of the texts which I have so far discussed. Different forms of this verb are found in the accounts of the heavens opening at Jesus' baptism, ἠνεῴχθησαν at Mt. 3.16 and ἀνεῳχθῆναι at Lk. 3.21, and there are angels ministering to Jesus in the following account of the temptation in both Matthew and Mark (Mt. 4.11//Mk 1.13). We should infer that this is what inspired the author of Jn 1.51. He rewrote the synoptic narratives of John the Baptist's encounter with Jesus at Jn 1.26-36, and he still had this in mind when he concluded the further revelations of this chapter.

We have seen that Jn 1.51 originated as a rewrite of Mt. 26.64, in the light of the serious problems posed for the Johannine community by this and other similar passages of Matthew and perhaps Mark. The rewriting was done largely by removing Ps. 110.1 and some aspects of Dan. 7.13, leaving however the important term ὁ υἱὸς τοῦ ἀνθρώπου. In its present form, Jn 1.51 has been carefully integrated into its context, which shows many signs of being written with constant aims and constant attention to passages of both the Old Testament and of other Gospels, especially Matthew. It concludes the story of the witness of John the Baptist and the call of the first disciples. It brings all these to a climax by predicting in midrashic form the constant contact between Jesus and his heavenly Father throughout his earthly ministry. For this purpose the title ὁ υἱὸς τοῦ ἀνθρώπου is especially appropriate. It is a Greek title, which unquestionably refers to Jesus alone. It particularly refers to Jesus as a human being during his incarnate ministry on earth.

---

17. Respectively, R. E. Brown, *The Gospel According to John*, vol. 1; (AB 29. London: Cassell, 1966), p. 89; J. N. Sanders and B. A. Mastin, *The Gospel According to St John* (BNTC. London: Black, 1968), p. 105; D. Burkett, *The Son of Man in the Gospel of John* (JSNTSup 56. Sheffield: Sheffield Academic), pp. 116–18.

3. John 3.13-15

The next two Son of man sayings occur together, and the second of them is clearly another midrash:

καὶ οὐδεὶς ἀναβέβηκεν εἰς τὸν οὐρανὸν εἰ μὴ ὁ ἐκ τοῦ οὐρανοῦ καταβάς, ὁ υἱὸς τοῦ ἀνθρώπου, ὁ ὢν ἐν τῷ οὐρανῷ. ¹⁴καὶ καθὼς Μωυσῆς ὕψωσεν τὸν ὄφιν ἐν τῇ ἐρήμῳ, οὕτως ὑψωθῆναι δεῖ τὸν υἱὸν τοῦ ἀνθρώπου, ¹⁵ἵνα πᾶς ὁ πιστεύων ἐν αὐτῷ ἔχη ζωὴν αἰώνιον.

The easily verifiable use of scripture in this passage is the employment of Num. 21.9 at Jn 3.14, so it is convenient to begin with it. In the wilderness, Moses made a bronze serpent, and set it on a pole, so that people bitten by deadly serpents could look at the bronze serpent and live (ζήσεται, LXX Num. 21.8; ἔζη, 21.9). In real life, the serpent was a cult object, and Hezekiah had it destroyed (2 Kgs 18.4). In the Numbers narrative, it might also be taken as a magical object. Later Jewish tradition shows sensitivity to this issue, as already in the Wisdom of Solomon. This says of the person who, being bitten, turned to the bronze serpent: οὐ διὰ τὸ θεωρούμενον ἐσώζετο, ἀλλὰ διὰ σὲ τὸν πάντων σωτῆρα (Wis. 16.7). We must infer that this kind of tradition was inherited by the Johannine community. This has helped with the comparison between Jesus and the serpent, and has been developed in the light of the community's beliefs into v. 15: ἵνα πᾶς ὁ πιστεύων ἐν αὐτῷ ἔχη ζωὴν αἰώνιον.

What about τὸν υἱὸν τοῦ ἀνθρώπου? At Jn 1.51, where it was preceded by ὄψεσθε, I traced it back to Mt. 26.64, where the ultimate source was Dan. 7.13. Here it is preceded by δεῖ. This has rightly sent scholars to the major passion prediction Mk 8.31//Lk. 9.22 (cf. Mt. 16.21), which also has δεῖ and τὸν υἱὸν τοῦ ἀνθρώπου. The Matthean version, which has δεῖ in the actual prediction but τὸν υἱὸν τοῦ ἀνθρώπου moved to 16.13, is in the same Matthean context as Peter's confession and the problematic Son of man sayings at Mt. 16.27-28. We have seen that this passage of Matthew was also important in the rewriting process which led to Jn 1.51. We must infer that this synoptic passion prediction was the source of δεῖ τὸν υἱὸν τοῦ ἀνθρώπου at Jn 3.14. The prediction was already a rewritten version of a genuine saying of Jesus. It has now been rewritten in classic Johannine manner. The mundane details of the event have been removed, for these are merely the story, to be told later (Jn 18–19). In the prediction they have been replaced with the theological term ὑψωθῆναι. This was important enough to the authors for them to repeat it elsewhere (Jn 8.28; 12.32,34), and to use it earlier in this verse in their description of how Moses displayed the bronze serpent.

Its origin is to be seen in further midrashic work, using Isa. 52.13, where it is said of the servant of the Lord, ὑψωθήσεται καὶ δοξασθήσεται σφόδρα. I have noted the midrashic use of Isa. 42.1 at Jn 1.32-34, where the chosen one is Israel, and the midrashic use of Jacob/Israel at Jn 1.51. A further connection is to be seen at Isa. 49.3, where δοξασθήσομαι is used of the servant, identified as Israel. δοξάζω is also used of ὁ υἱὸς τοῦ ἀνθρώπου at Jn 12.23 and 13.31-32. This is sufficient for us to have to put it all together: Isa. 52.13 is the origin of ὑψωθῆναι at Jn 3.14. The reference is clearly to Jesus' death. This is explicit in the explanation of Jesus' use of ὑψωθῶ with reference to himself at Jn 12.32-33: τοῦτο δὲ ἔλεγεν σημαίνων ποίῳ θανάτῳ ἤμελλεν ἀποθνῄσκειν. Thus Jn 3.14 continues the tradition of Mt. 16.21//Mk 8.31//Lk. 9.22 in predicting Jesus' passion, only it does so in theological rather than literal terms. In Acts, the word ὑψόω is used with reference to Jesus' ascension to the right hand of God (Acts 2.33; 5.31; cf. ὑπερύψωσεν at Phil. 2.9). This is likely to be in mind too. Jesus was not *merely* crucified. From a Johannine perspective, he was raised from the dead and returned to the Father, necessary events to complete the salvific nature of his work so that πᾶς ὁ πιστεύων ἐν αὐτῷ ἔχῃ ζωὴν αἰώνιον (Jn 3.15). We shall also see that the ascension is referred to at Jn 3.13.

The use of ὁ υἱὸς τοῦ ἀνθρώπου in this saying is completely appropriate. We have seen that it is derived ultimately from one of Jesus' genuine predictions of his death, one that has been much rewritten. It is also a proper reference to Jesus' genuine humanity, for it is characteristic of human beings that they die. At the same time, this is not the only way for the authors to refer to Jesus' death. I have particularly noted Jn 12.32-33, where Jesus uses ὑψωθῶ with reference to himself, and there is an explanation that this refers to his death. The following verse goes further, for faith in him leading to eternal life might well be predicated of a divine being. This is precisely what is expounded at Jn 3.16, using the term τὸν υἱὸν τὸν μονογενῆ. This illustrates perfectly the overlap in usage between these two major titles.

It has often been suggested that the use of ὑψόω in this verse reflects the Aramaic זקף.[18] The Aramaic word זקף is widely attested with the general meaning 'lift', 'raise up', a meaning found already in the Akkadian *zakapu*. In Syriac, it is also a normal word for 'crucify'. It is already used with reference to impalement at Ezra 6.11, and it is found with reference to crucifixion in late Jewish Aramaic as well. The possibility that ὑψωθῆναι is an Aramaism is accordingly feasible. The older scholarship did not however work this suggestion properly through. I have already given good reason to suppose that this saying was dependent both on synoptic predictions in Greek, and on LXX Isa. 52.13. This particular Aramaic suggestion is therefore probably unnecessary. A possible Aramaic original of the whole saying is moreover difficult to envisage, and a possible Aramaic original of the whole discourse is out of the question. There were however bilingual people in the Johannine community, and people who could read the Bible in Hebrew. It is possible that this verse was created in Greek by someone who was familiar with both meanings of the Aramaic זקף and who accordingly suffered from interference. This might have prompted them to use the Greek ὑψωθῆναι with this double meaning.

McNamara suggested the use of the Aramaic סלק.[19] This is widely attested with the semantic area of 'go up', 'ascend', and in the Aphel 'lift', 'take up', 'raise', as

---

18. E.g. Black, *Aramaic Approach*, p. 141.

19. M. McNamara, *The New Testament and the Palestinian Targum to the Pentateuch* (AnBib 27A. Rome: Biblical Institute, 2nd edn, 1978), pp. 145–9, with bibliography to previous scholarship.

already in the Haphel at Dan. 3.22; 6.24. McNamara noted its use with reference to death in Targum Neofiti I and other late sources. This is not as good a suggestion as זקף, because of the later date of these sources. It is also less precise.

The proposed double sense has also been reported for the Greek ὑψόω itself, but the passages concerned are too specialized to illuminate normal usage. For example, Artemidorus claims that if someone dreams he is dancing high up (ὑψηλός), he will fall into fear and apprehension, but if he is a criminal he will be crucified (σταυρωθήσεται) (Artemidorus Daldianus, *Oneirocriton* I,76). He also claims that if someone dreamt he was crucified (ἐσταυρῶσθαι), this would indicate glory (δόξα) because of the high position of the crucified (διὰ τὸ ὑψηλότατον εἶναι τὸν ἐσταυρωμένον) (IV, 49). These passages are however specific to the subculture of dream interpretation, in which many things in dreams are held to indicate something quite different in daily life. Such interpretations are not relevant to the normal usage of words.[20]

I turn now to Jn 3.13. I have printed above the longer text, in which the term ὁ υἱὸς τοῦ ἀνθρώπου is qualified by the expression ὁ ὢν ἐν τῷ οὐρανῷ. This is read by the majority of manuscripts, including A (with the original omission of ὢν, reinserted by a corrector). This puts the Son of man in heaven even as Jesus is talking about him here on earth. This has caused endless trouble to the commentators, many of whom regard the reading as impossible rather than as the more difficult.[21] We shall see however that it is already implied by ἀναβέβηκεν earlier in the verse, and that it makes excellent Johannine sense of a kind unwelcome to some of the commentators. The other readings should be regarded as corrections of it by scribes who had the same concerns as some of the commentators. The best attested is the short reading, which simply omits ὁ ὢν ἐν τῷ οὐρανῷ. At first sight this seems well attested, for Greek manuscripts which attest it include the apparently strong and early combination P⁶⁶ P⁷⁵ ℵ B. These manuscripts are however all Alexandrian. The shorter reading should therefore be regarded as a deliberate correction by Alexandrian scribes who did not like the natural sense of the text.

The concerns of the Alexandrian scribes are well illustrated by the two poorly attested readings. In place of ὁ ὢν ἐν τῷ οὐρανῷ, 0141 80 syr^sin read ὁ ὢν ἐκ τοῦ οὐρανοῦ. This solves the perceived problem. According to this reading, the earthly Jesus looks back to his descent from heaven at his incarnation, the event which enabled him to be the Revealer. This is perfectly Johannine, expounded programmatically in the prologue (Jn 1.14-18), and assumed in the present context. It is too weakly attested to be taken seriously as the original reading. It shows rather that ὁ ὢν ἐν τῷ οὐρανῷ was found to be too difficult by some scribes in the ancient period. The other reading is not even attested in Greek. The Old Latin and some of the Syriac (cur pal) presuppose ὃς ἦν ἐν τῷ οὐρανῷ. This is effectively the same solution to the perceived problem. According to this reading too, the earthly Jesus

---

20.   P. Létourneau, *Jésus Fils de l'Homme et Fils de Dieu. Jean 2,23-3,36 et la double christologie johannique* (Montréal/Paris: Bellarmin/Cerf, 1993) p. 176 n. 155 adds Homer, *Batrachomomyachia*, 81, and Artemidorus II, 53, but these are no more convincing.

21.   E.g. D. A. Carson, *The Gospel According to John* (Leicester; IVP, 1991), p. 203.

looks back to his descent from heaven at his incarnation, the event which enabled him to be the Revealer. Accordingly, this is also perfectly Johannine, and will have satisfied the scribes responsible for it.

The perceived problem with the longer reading lies in Jesus' apparent reference to his ascension as a past event, and his current presence in heaven, while he is still speaking here on earth. This is already implied by the use of ἀναβέβηκεν earlier in this verse. In accordance with the classical use of the Greek perfect, this ought to mean that no one has gone up to heaven and is still there, except for the Son of man. The addition ὁ ὢν ἐν τῷ οὐρανῷ then simply brings out what the text must mean in any case. With the shorter text in mind, but taking ἀναβέβηκεν with its proper force, Burkett put the perceived problem of this verse as wrongly as possible:

> According to one view, the statement anachronistically refers to Jesus' post-resurrection ascension. It was a slip of the Evangelist from whose perspective the ascension had already occured. This explanation is not satisfactory, since nowhere else does the Evangelist speak anachronistically. It requires the unlikely hypothesis that the Evangelist writes from Jesus' perspective in 3.1-12, abruptly shifts to his own perspective in 3.13, then reverts to Jesus' perspective in 3.14.[22]

Here, even the use of the word 'anachronistically' is anachronistic. It firstly presupposes that the evangelist could not possibly write from the perspective of late first-century Ephesus and attribute his words to Jesus, placed in a historical setting during the historic ministry. Yet this was a normal habit in the culture from which the Johannine community emerged. For example, Jubilees 50 presents the sabbath *halakhah* of its orthodox community, including prohibitions of sex and of war, which were not part of the normative *halakhah* of the Jewish community. It presents these prohibitions together with standard ones as if all were delivered to Moses on Mt Sinai. We may feel this is anachronistic, but they behaved otherwise. Accordingly, even the description 'anachronistically' is prejudicial, since it sounds as if the authors have done something wrong. The term 'slip' is equally prejudicial, since it too presupposes that the evangelist has unintentionally done something which even he would regard as unfortunate.

Most centrally, the notion that 'nowhere else does the Evangelist speak anachronistically' is completely incorrect if we accept Burkett's use of the term 'anachronistically', and with this Burkett's attribution to him of abrupt shifts in perspective is inaccurate. The perspective of the whole chapter, and indeed the whole document, is that of the Johannine community in late first-century Ephesus, written within the historical framework of Jesus' ministry.[23] It begins with a visit

---

22. Burkett, *Son of Man in John*, p. 82.

23. For the chapter as an intended unity, see D. Rensberger, *Overcoming the World. Politics and Community in the Gospel of John* (London: SPCK, 1988), Ch. 3; for literary perspectives on this, see D. A. Lee, *The Symbolic Narratives of the Fourth Gospel. The Interplay of Form and Meaning* (JSNTSup 95. Sheffield: Sheffield Academic, 1994), Ch. 2; D. Tovey, *Narrative Art and Act in the Fourth Gospel* (JSNTSup 151. Sheffield: Sheffield Academic, 1997), Ch. 5; and for the placement of the whole chapter within the perspective of the Johannine community, see Casey, *Is John's Gospel True?*, pp. 75–8, 127–32.

from Nicodemus, a character absent from the synoptic Gospels. Jesus' exposition begins with the concept of rebirth, a Hellenistic concept which is not found in the Judaism of this period. This is used to rewrite the teaching of Jesus about the kingdom of God.

The kingdom of God has almost been written out of the Fourth Gospel. We have seen one of its problems at Mk 9.1, where some of those present would not see death until they had seen the kingdom of God come in power, a prophecy rewritten to include the coming of the Son of man at Mt. 16.28. This event had still not occurred when members of the Johannine community completed their Gospel. We have seen some of the rewriting caused by this and other synoptic texts at Jn 1.51. In this text, the parousia of the Son of man has been midrashically replaced with symbolic comment on the contact between the Son of man and heaven.[24] At Jn 3.3, further rewriting has made seeing the kingdom of God dependent on being born again/from above (ἄνωθεν), which was perceived to take place at Christian baptism. This is further clarified at Jn 3.5, where 'entering' the kingdom of God is dependent on being born of water and the Spirit. There are synoptic Son of man sayings in which 'entering' the kingdom of God is presented as a future event, and at least some of them can readily be interpreted eschatologically, just like Mk 9.1 and Mt. 16.28: see Mt. 5.20; 7.21; 18.3; Mt. 19.23-24//Mk 10.23-25//Lk. 18.24-25; Mk 9.47, cf. Mt. 18.9; Mk 10.15//Lk. 18.17. This evidently constituted a problem for the Johannine community. The majority of these sayings use some form of εἰσέλθειν, and can readily be interpreted of the single moment of entering the kingdom when it is established at the last day. Those which use the future can be interpreted in the same way.

The closest to Jn 3.5 are Mt. 18.3 and Mk 10.15//Lk. 18.17. Both have the concept of becoming like a child, which could be rewritten as rebirth, introduced with Nicodemus' question at Jn 3.4. Both have a clear negative with εἰσέλθειν, used of not entering the kingdom if a condition of entry is not fulfilled. Both begin ἀμὴν λέγω, for which ἀμὴν ἀμὴν λέγω is the conventional Johannine rewrite. Mt. 18.3 has the precise conditional introduction ἐὰν μή, and the form γένησθε, which is the more readily rewritten with γεννηθῇ, since it could be interpreted as 'be born' as well as 'become'. Mk 10.15//Lk. 18.17 is expressed in the third person, and has the precise form τὴν βασιλείαν τοῦ θεοῦ. We must conclude that these sayings provide us with the tradition which the Johannine community have rewritten. From their perspective, they have solved the problems posed by the perception that Jesus' predictions about the coming of the kingdom had not been fulfilled. They have removed the unwelcome time element in the concepts of 'seeing' and 'entering' the kingdom of God, and made both of them dependent on Christian baptism interpreted as being born again from above. It follows that the opening part of the discourse is not written from anything like the perspective of Jesus: it is written from the perspective of the Johannine community.

The discourse continues with Jesus' exposition of rebirth through the Spirit. Nicodemus has one final word to ask the uncomprehending question, Πῶς δύναται

24.   See pp. 277–81 above.

ταῦτα γενέσθαι; Jesus replies to him personally, addressing him in the singular: εἰ ὁ διδάσκαλος τοῦ Ἰσραὴλ καὶ ταῦτα οὐ γινώσκεις; This is profoundly ironical, for no teacher of Israel knew about the Hellenistic concept of rebirth used in the reinterpretation of Christian baptism. There is no further mention of Nicodemus in this discourse, which clarifies the fact that the discourse does not come from the ministry of Jesus. This is made even clearer as Jesus proceeds to shift from addressing Nicodemus in the singular to address people in the plural:

ἀμὴν ἀμὴν ἔγω σοι ὅτι ὃ οἴδαμεν λαλοῦμεν καὶ ὃ ἐωράκαμεν μαρτυροῦμεν, καὶ τὴν μαρτυρίαν ἡμῶν οὐ λαμβάνετε (Jn 3.11).

The people addressed are evidently the Jewish community, and Jesus' use of οἴδαμεν and ἐωράκαμεν prepares the way for the presentation of him as the Revealer who reveals what he knows because he is from heaven. This is carried further in the following verse:

εἰ τὰ ἐπίγεια εἶπον ὑμῖν καὶ οὐ πιστεύετε, πῶς ἐὰν εἴπω ὑμῖν τὰ ἐπουράνια π ιστεύσετε;

This prepares for the presentation of Jesus in Jn 3.13 as the only person fit to reveal τὰ ἐπουράνια, for he alone has come from heaven. There is therefore no question of an abrupt shift from Jesus' perspective to the evangelist's perspective at 3.13: the perspective of the Johannine community has been presented all along, and the pronouncement of 3.13 has been carefully prepared for.

Similar comments apply to the remainder of the discourse. We have seen that the immediate continuation is a midrash using Num. 21.9 and Isa. 52.13, with which some of Jesus' passion predictions have been rewritten. This shifts into the presentation of him as the only-begotten Son. This implies his deity, a concept quite alien to Jesus of Nazareth and of central importance to the Johannine community. Faith in him, whether as Son of man (3.14-15) or as the only-begotten Son (3.16-18) is necessary for eternal life. Accordingly, there is no question of reverting to Jesus' perspective at 3.14: the authors continue to expound Johannine theology from their own perspective. They continue with their transmuted eschatology, according to which salvation or judgement takes place in the here and now, depending on whether one has faith in the only-begotten Son of God (Jn 3.18).

With all these points clarified, the authors put John the Baptist's baptism in its place: he is to be completely eclipsed by Jesus, to whom he finally bears witness (3.22-36). At this point Jesus baptizes, and more successfully than John (3.22,26; 4.1), and this is corrected to baptism by Jesus' disciples (4.2), two ways of making the point that Christian baptism is essential for salvation. This is again the perspective of the Johannine community, and just as strikingly remote from the ministry of Jesus as Jn 3.13. John the Baptist concludes the discourse by reiterating the main points of the basic shift in covenantal nomism, attributing the whole matter to the Father, having the Son at the centre, with faith in him vital for salvation, and the eschatology transmuted to express the need for immediate decision: ὁ πατὴρ ἀγαπᾷ τὸν υἱόν, καὶ πάντα δέδωκεν ἐν τῇ χειρὶ αὐτοῦ. ὁ πιστεύων εἰς τὸν υἱὸν ἔχει ζωὴν αἰώνιον· ὁ δὲ ἀπειθῶν τῷ υἱῷ οὐκ ὄψεται ζωήν, ἀλλ' ἡ ὀργὴ τοῦ θεοῦ μένει ἐπ' αὐτόν (3.35-36). This full Christian witness is also the perspective of the Johannine community.

It follows that many scholars, represented in the above quotation from Burkett, have completely misconstrued the nature of this discourse. It is a presentation of the perspective of the Johannine community from beginning to end. In this profound sense, Jn 3.13 fits into its context perfectly, when that context is properly appreciated. I therefore proceed to more detailed exegesis of Jn 3.13 and its background in the conflict between the Johannine community and the Jewish community.

The verse begins with the very strong statement that no-one has gone up to heaven except for the Son of man. Scholars have naturally thought of Enoch and other sages who were widely believed to have gone up to heaven and indeed to still be there. So for example the book of Jubilees tells us that Enoch was with the angels of God for six jubilees of years. They showed him everything, and he wrote down everything (*Jub.* 4.21-22). *1 En.* 14 has a graphic account of Enoch's ascent to heaven, where he sees God. At *1 En.* 81.5, after receiving revelations, Enoch is brought to his house by the seven holy ones, and subsequently he writes his revelations for Methuselah to preserve and pass on to future generations. He is the central revelatory figure in the whole of *1 Enoch*, and at *1 En.* 71 he is finally translated permanently to heaven. Scholars have accordingly been right to associate with the denial of Jn 3.13 the repeated comments, already noted above, that no one has seen God. The prologue put it programmatically: θεὸν οὐδεὶς ἑώρακεν πώποτε· μονογενὴς θεὸς ὁ ὢν εἰς τὸν κόλπον τοῦ πατρὸς ἐκεῖνος ἐξηγήσατο. Putting this all together, we have a very strong commitment to Jesus as the only Revealer. He has seen God, he came down from heaven, and he has ascended to heaven and he is still there. No one else has done so.

The revelations of Enoch and other sages are not however likely to have been a conspicuous threat to the Johannine community. A minority of scholars have accordingly been right to look further at chariot mysticism.[25] The foundational chapter for chariot mysticism was Ezek.1. We have known for a long time that this was meditated on during the rabbinical period, and that people who meditated on it were thought to have gone up to heaven, and come down again with revelations. This was a dangerous process. Orthodox rabbis like R. Aqiba might go up and come down safe and sound. When Elisha ben Abuya ascended and saw Metatron, however, he thought that there might be two powers in heaven (b. Ḥag 15//*3 En.* 16). He became apostate, his revelations as serious a danger to Judaism as could be. We now know from the Dead Sea scrolls that this chariot mysticism did not begin in the rabbinical period. It was a continuous tradition from the time of Ezekiel onwards, and passages such as the ascent of Enoch in *1 Enoch* 14 were written in light of it.[26]

---

25.   See especially J. J. Kaganaraj, *'Mysticism' in the Gospel of John. An Inquiry into its Background* (JSNTSup 158. Sheffield: Sheffield Academic, 1998).

26.   For a summary of relevant Dead Sea material, see J. R. Davila, 'The Dead Sea Scrolls and Merkavah Mysticism', in T. H. Lim *et al.* (eds), *The Dead Sea Scrolls in Their Historical Context* (Edinburgh: T&T Clark, 2000), pp. 249–64.

We must infer that there were chariot mystics in the Jewish community at Ephesus. The Jewish community believed that they had gone up to heaven, had seen God, and had come down again with revelations. It follows from the strength of the Johannine denials that these revelations were most unwelcome to the Johannine community. This is not difficult to envisage. The chariot mystics were faithful members of the Jewish community. Accordingly they will not have seen Jesus at the right hand of God, or preparing places for the members of the Johannine community. Possible revelations would be that he was a false prophet, and that his supposed deity was a blasphemous violation of the oneness of God. Such revelations are the only kind of reason which could cause the Johannine community to produce such strong denials of any means of revelation except through Jesus.

This also explains the order of events in Jn 3.13. Sages such as Enoch, and chariot mystics alike, had to go up to heaven from earth before they could come back with revelations of heavenly things. Hence the first point of the denial is that no one has gone up to heaven. This denies the reality of chariot mysticism, and with it the stories of Enoch and others. This is sufficient to exclude the possibility that anyone could have come down with revelations of heavenly things. We are then given the exception, the Son of man who came down from heaven. This is a reference back to the incarnation, which was expounded programmatically in the prologue, ending with the position of Jesus as the only Revealer. His heavenly origin is explicit again for example at 3.31-32, where he who is from heaven bears witness to what he has seen and heard; likewise at 8.23, Jesus declares ἐγὼ ἐκ τῶν ἄνω εἰμί. He also refers to the glory which he had with God πρὸ τοῦ τὸν κόσμον εἶναι (Jn 17.5). We shall see that he uses καταβαίνω of his descent from heaven again in Ch. 6. When this frame of reference is taken seriously, Jesus' position as the one who descended from heaven in the incarnation and who is the Revealer can be seen to permeate the whole Gospel. Significant passages include the immediately following piece, in which God 'gave' and 'sent' his 'only-begotten Son', an event alternatively described as the light coming into the world (Jn 3.16,17,19).

We can now see the fundamental importance of the longer text of this verse to the authors of this document. In Freed's terms, ὁ υἱὸς τοῦ ἀνθρώπου, ὁ ὢν ἐν τῷ οὐρανῷ (Jn 3.13) is another way of saying μονογενὴς θεὸς ὁ ὢν εἰς τὸν κόλπον τοῦ πατρὸς (Jn 1.18). In fact the two statements are not the same, but they are very closely related. Both present Jesus as having returned to his position in heaven with God the Father, the position which enabled him to descend to earth as the only valid Revealer. The importance of Jesus' return to the Father is stressed elsewhere in this document. Narratively, it comes towards the end of the original document, where Jesus tells Mary Magdalene to stop holding on to him (Jn 20.17, cf. Mt. 28.9): οὔπω γὰρ ἀναβέβηκα πρὸς τὸν πατέρα· πορεύου δὲ πρὸς τοὺς ἀδελφούς μου καὶ εἰπὲ αὐτοῖς, Ἀναβαίνω πρὸς τὸν πατέρα μου καὶ πατέρα ὑμῶν καὶ θεόν μου καὶ θεὸν ὑμῶν. We shall see Jesus' return presented in another Son of man statement at Jn 6.62-63: ἐὰν οὖν θεωρῆτε τὸν υἱὸν τοῦ ἀνθρώπου ἀναβαίνοντα ὅπου ἦν τὸ πρότερον, τὸ πνεῦμά ἐστιν τὸ ζῳοποιοῦν.

Jesus' return to the Father also permeates the final discourses. It is sometimes stated straightforwardly: νῦν δὲ ὑπάγω πρὸς τὸν πέμψαντά με (Jn 16.5). It involves more complex presentation of the Johannine community's experience of God, including his continued revelations to them. God's presence may be presented as Jesus' continued presence with them, as at 14.18: Οὐκ ἀφήσω ὑμᾶς ὀρφανούς, ἔρχομαι πρὸς ὑμᾶς. Equally, it may be presented as the presence of both Jesus and the Father, as at 14.23: Ἐάν τις ἀγαπᾷ με τὸν λόγον μου τηρήσει, καὶ ὁ πατήρ μου ἀγαπήσει αὐτόν, καὶ πρὸς αὐτὸν ἐλευσόμεθα καὶ μονὴν παρ' αὐτῷ ποιησόμεθα. Most commonly in the final discourses, this is presented as the work of the Paraclete. The first presentation of this is at Jn 14.16-17: κἀγὼ ἐρωτήσω τὸν πατέρα καὶ ἄλλον παράκλητον δώσει ὑμῖν ἵνα μεθ' ὑμῶν εἰς τὸν αἰῶνα ᾖ, τὸ πνεῦμα τῆς ἀληθείας, ὃ ὁ κόσμος οὐ δύναται λαβεῖν, ὅτι οὐ θεωρεῖ αὐτὸ οὐδὲ γινώσκει· ὑμεῖς γινώσκετε αὐτό, ὅτι παρ' ὑμῖν μένει καὶ ἐν ὑμῖν ἔσται. The immediate explanation of this includes both 14.18 and 14.23, which should make it clear that these are three different ways of looking at the presence of God within the community. It is the presence of God as this can be only after Jesus' death, resurrection and ascension. This is put in negative form, but with great clarity, at 16.7: ἀλλ' ἐγὼ τὴν ἀλήθειαν λέγω ὑμῖν, συμφέρει ὑμῖν ἵνα ἐγὼ ἀπέλθω. ἐὰν γὰρ μὴ ἀπέλθω, ὁ παράκλητος οὐκ ἐλεύσεται πρὸς ὑμᾶς· ἐὰν δὲ πορευθῶ, πέμψω αὐτὸν πρὸς ὑμᾶς.

A central facet of the role of the Paraclete is his teaching function. This is clearly presented at Jn 14.26, where he is also described as τὸ πνεῦμα τὸ ἅγιον: ἐκεῖνος ὑμᾶς διδάξει πάντα καὶ ὑπομνήσει ὑμᾶς πάντα ἃ εἶπον ὑμῖν ἐγώ. Seen in its proper context, this evidently means that words of Jesus may be supplied by people in the Johannine community who felt themselves inspired by the Holy Spirit. This is expanded at Jn 16.13: ὁδηγήσει ὑμᾶς ἐν τῇ ἀληθείᾳ πάσῃ· οὐ γὰρ λαλήσει ἀφ' ἑαυτοῦ, ἀλλ' ὅσα ἀκούσει λαλήσει, καὶ τὰ ἐρχόμενα ἀναγγελεῖ ὑμῖν. The immediately following comments attribute all this new material to both the Father and to Jesus himself, speaking, as at 3.13, from within the narrative framework of this historic ministry: ἐκεῖνος ἐμὲ δοξάσει, ὅτι ἐκ τοῦ ἐμοῦ λήμψεται καὶ ἀναγγελεῖ ὑμῖν. πάντα ὅσα ἔχει ὁ πατὴρ ἐμά ἐστιν· διὰ τοῦτο εἶπον ὅτι ἐκ τοῦ ἐμοῦ λαμβάνει καὶ ἀναγγελεῖ ὑμῖν (Jn 16.14-15). This legitimates new material via the Holy Spirit via Jesus to God himself. Christological development, which is such a notable feature of this document, is included here. As well as ἐκεῖνος ἐμὲ δοξάσει at 16.14, the community declares at 15.26, ἐκεῖνος μαρτυρήσει περὶ ἐμοῦ.[27]

We can now put the long text of 3.13 in its proper place, as part of an exposition characteristic of the Johannine community and necessary to its being. The position of the Son of man in heaven, where he was before, is essential to his position as the only Revealer. Through the incarnation, when he became ὁ ἐκ τοῦ οὐρανοῦ καταβάς, he alone became the Revealer of τὰ ἐπουράνια. This process of revelation continues in the church. Now in heaven, he remains the Revealer, a role

---

27.   On the Paraclete, see further Casey, *Is John's Gospel True?*, pp. 151–4, with bibliography.

which he plays from his position εἰς τὸν κόλπον τοῦ πατρός. This process may be perceived as carried out through the Paraclete, the Holy Spirit, who remains God in action, in accordance with Jewish tradition. It required Jesus' death and his ascension, both referred to in Jn 3.14 as his exaltation. As a result of this, everyone who believes in him has eternal life (3.15).

From a Johannine perspective, the term ὁ υἱὸς τοῦ ἀνθρώπου was perfectly in order at 3.13 as well as 3.14. At 3.14, it refers to Jesus' death, a characteristically human experience not shared by heavenly beings. At 3.13, it refers to Jesus' incarnation, for which his humanity was essential. It also fits the strong denials, since it was human beings who were believed by some Jews to have gone up to heaven and come down again with important revelations. Jesus' position as the only Revealer was dependent on the incarnation. At the same time, he was the only-begotten Son, so that the shift to this title for the exposition at Jn 3.16-18 is also entirely appropriate.

So far, then, ὁ υἱὸς τοῦ ἀνθρώπου is a Greek title used with special reference to the incarnation.

4. John 5.27

The next saying is the only Son of man saying in all the Gospels to be used without the definite articles:

καὶ ἐξουσίαν ἔδωκεν αὐτῷ κρίσιν ποιεῖν, ὅτι υἱὸς ἀνθρώπου ἐστίν.

The absence of the articles has caused a great deal of controversy. Some of this controversy has centred on the question of dependence on Dan. 7.13, where both the LXX and Theodotion have ὡς υἱὸς ἀνθρώπου, also without the articles. A great deal of trouble has also been caused by attributing some parts of the passage to a redactor whose efforts to edit an earlier source have resulted in a text which is supposedly not consistent. I therefore begin by discussing this saying in its present Johannine context, and then consider what we may infer about its origins.

This saying belongs to a Johannine discourse, the most relevant part of which is the opening verses, Jn 5.19-30. This takes off from 'the Jews' wanting to kill Jesus, ὅτι οὐ μόνον ἔλυεν τὸ σάββατον ἀλλὰ καὶ πατέρα ἴδιον ἔλεγεν τὸν θεόν, ἴσον ἑαυτὸν ποιῶν τῷ θεῷ (Jn 5.18). Jesus' response begins with a very strong subordinationist statement, according to which the Son can do nothing except what he sees the Father doing. This gradually becomes more specific, with the Son giving life (ζῳοποιεῖ) as the Father does (Jn 5.21). There follows a significant parallel to 5.27, but with the major Johannine title 'the Son' rather than Son of man: οὐδὲ γὰρ ὁ πατὴρ κρίνει οὐδένα, ἀλλὰ τὴν κρίσιν πᾶσαν δέδωκεν τῷ υἱῷ, ἵνα πάντες τιμῶσι τὸν υἱὸν καθὼς τιμῶσι τὸν πατέρα (Jn 5.22-23). This theme of judgement recurs throughout the Gospel. It is an effect of the ministry of Jesus, which splits the world into those who believe and do not come to judgement, and those who do not believe and hence have already been judged (Jn 3.18). This transmuted eschatology follows immediately at Jn 5.24, where the believer already has eternal life and does not come to judgement, but has passed from death to life. This is amplified in the immediately following verses, with the Son having life in himself as a result of the Father's gift. It is this which leads to the crucial verse, in which the Father has given him (*sc.* the Son) power to exercise judgement, ὅτι υἱός ἀνθρώπου ἐστίν. These words explain why judgement is exercised by the Son rather than by the Father himself. That is because he is a man. There is a partial parallel at *T.Abr.* XIII, where God, in delegating the function of Judgement to Abel, comments: 'I will not judge you, but every man shall be judged by a man.'

The specifically Johannine context is however more important than this. We have seen that ὁ υἱὸς τοῦ ἀνθρώπου refers particularly to the humanity of the incarnate Jesus. This is essential in interpreting Jn 5.27 too. God did not send the Son into the world to judge the world (Jn 3.17). Nonetheless, judgement was the effect of the incarnate ministry, because some people did not believe in the Son (Jn 3.18-20). It follows that judgement must be exercised by the incarnate Jesus, because it was his earthly ministry which was decisive in bringing salvation and judgement. The anarthrous phrase υἱὸς ἀνθρώπου at Jn 5.27 accordingly has the same meaning and reference as ὁ υἱὸς τοῦ ἀνθρώπου in the other Johannine Son of man sayings.

It follows that the debate about whether υἱὸς ἀνθρώπου is really titular and really the same as ὁ υἱὸς τοῦ ἀνθρώπου is less important than has often been thought. Colwell's Law[28] has often been invoked in attempts to equate the two phrases, but this application of it is dubious. It is supposed to explain the absence of the articles from the fact that υἱὸς is a predicative nominative noun which precedes the verb. While this might explain the absence of the article with υἱὸς, it is doubtful whether it explains its absence before ἀνθρώπου. Moreover, it does not explain why the evangelist expressed himself like this. If he intended to repeat an important Christological title, he would have done better to have placed it after the verb, complete with articles, or to have expressed himself quite differently. We must infer that he intended to draw attention to the centrality of the incarnate ministry of Jesus as a human being to the function of judgement. This is absolutely clear from the context, and does not require the use of the articles.

This brings us to the question of the origins of this verse. It fits perfectly where it is, but should we follow scholars who have argued that it has come from somewhere else? The immediately following verses are important in considering this question. They present a traditional eschatology, with people emerging from their tombs, those who have done good to the resurrection of life, and those who have done evil to the resurrection of judgement (Jn 5.28-29). This traditional eschatology is the kind of setting from which the term 'Son of man' is familiar from the synoptic Gospels. It is associated with judgement especially clearly at Mt. 16.27-28, where ὁ υἱὸς τοῦ ἀνθρώπου ... ἀποδώσει ἑκάστῳ κατὰ τὴν πρᾶξιν αὐτοῦ. This is

---

28.   E. C. Colwell, 'A Definite Rule for the Use of the Article in the Greek New Testament', *JBL* 52 (1933), pp. 12–21, citing this example on p. 14.

also the case with the opening of the massive picture of the final judgement at Mt. 25.31. We have been here before! We have seen that Mt. 16.27-28 was central to the complex of passages which were rewritten to form Jn 1.51, and that it belongs to the same context as the passion prediction which was rewritten to form Jn 3.14.[29] Mt. 25.31 is an obviously related passage. We must infer that these passages were also formative in the origin of Jn 5.27.

Both these passages and Mk 8.38, the source of Mt. 16.27, have the collocation of 'Son of man' and 'coming' which reveals midrashic use of Dan. 7.13. The Johannine community's knowledge of the scriptures, as revealed in their Gospel, was so extensive and profound that they must have been aware of this use of Dan. 7.13. Moreover, once we know that the authors had in mind the term ὁ υἱὸς τοῦ ἀνθρώπου, which they themselves used in no less than twelve Son of man sayings, we need a particular reason for them not to have used the articles in this saying. It is not sufficient that the result makes excellent sense, both linguistically and theologically. We must accordingly infer that the absence of the articles in this passage is due to their awareness of Dan. 7.13. Equally, however, the authors have not drawn attention to Dan. 7.13 when they could easily have done so, much as they did draw the attention of those learned in the scriptures to Gen. 28.12 (Jn 1.51) and Num. 21.8-9 (Jn 3.14). We should infer that, like Matthew and Mark, they held the western Christian interpretation of Dan. 7.13 as a prediction of the second coming of Jesus on the clouds of heaven. They did not however wish to draw attention to this, because of the trouble caused by predictions which had not been fulfilled.

We must also infer that this saying was written in Greek. It is part of a Greek document which shows no signs of having been written in Aramaic, and has some clear indications that it was originally written in Greek.[30] In itself, it has partly resulted from careful study of synoptic sayings in their Greek form, and of the foundational text Dan. 7.13, probably in Greek form too. It is accordingly ironical that, as far as it goes, it makes perfectly good sense in Aramaic. The following reconstruction may be suggested:

ויהב לה שלטן למעבד דין דבר אנש הוא.

In its present context in this discourse, this saying makes sound sense, not seriously different from the Greek of Jn 5.27. Moreover, it does require this context to make good sense. Since the discourse itself does not lend itself to an Aramaic reconstruction as a whole, and makes perfect sense in Greek, we should infer that this Aramaic does not represent an original source. It is not however an amazing coincidence. There were bilingual people in the community, and people who read the scriptures in the original languages. The text goes back ultimately to an Aramaic scripture which uses בר אנש, and there will have been people in the community who knew that this was an ordinary term for 'man'. Some such people were involved in the writing of this discourse, and they will have suffered from interference both from Aramaic and

29. See pp. 277–81, 282–3 above.
30. Casey, *Is John's Gospel True?*, pp. 87–97.

from biblical texts. These factors have all combined to enable them to write υἱὸς ἀνθρώπου without articles as a deliberate reference to the humanity of Jesus.

The following conclusions should therefore be drawn. The expression υἱὸς ἀνθρώπου at Jn 5.27 refers particularly to the humanity of the incarnate Jesus, as ὁ υἱὸς τοῦ ἀνθρώπου does elsewhere. In the context, we have already been told that the Father has given all judgement to the Son. Jn 5.27 explains that this is because he is a human being as well as God, whose earthly ministry was decisive in bringing salvation and judgement. The absence of the articles makes no significant difference to the interpretation of this verse. It was due ultimately to recognizing the influence of Dan. 7.13 at Mt. 16.27 and elsewhere, but the authors were not deliberately using this text in order to make a point.

5. John 6.27,53,62

The next three Son of man sayings all belong to the same discourse. This takes off from rewritten versions of the synoptic stories of the feeding of the 5,000 and of Jesus walking on the sea (Mt. 14.13-33//Mk 6.32-52, cf. Lk. 9.10b-17, Mk 8.1-21). Aus has shown that the walking on the sea is a midrash, inspired by Exod. 14-15 and other biblical texts.[31] The feeding of the 5,000 is a midrash on Exod. 16 and other texts.

The Johannine discourse is also a midrash on Exod. 16 and other texts.[32] Pss 77–8 are among other texts which have been used in the creation of both the Marcan stories and the Johannine discourse. It follows that the Johannine community knew not only Mt. 14.13-33//Mk 6.32-52, they also knew the Old Testament texts which had been used in writing them. They have expanded the story with further texts. For example, at the end of the feeding story, people say οὗτός ἐστιν ἀληθῶς ὁ προφήτης ὁ ἐρχόμενος εἰς τὸν κόσμον (Jn 6.14), referring to the prophet like Moses promised by God at Deut. 18.15-19. The discourse contains a scriptural quotation primarily from Isa. 54.13: καὶ ἔσονται πάντες διδακτοὶ θεοῦ (Jn 6.45).[33] The opening of Isa. 55 has the kind of metaphorical references to eating, thirst, bread and wine which seem to have helped to inspire the opening of this Johannine discourse. Similar metaphorical expressions are found with reference to Wisdom, an important being influential in the creation of Johannine Christology in general. For example, at Prov. 9.5, Wisdom calls on people to eat of her bread, and drink of the wine which she has mixed.

---

31.   R. D. Aus, *'Caught in the Act', Walking on the Sea, and the Release of Barabbas Revisited* (Atlanta: Scholars, 1998), pp. 53–133.

32.   See the classic discussion of P. D. Borgen, *Bread from Heaven. An Exegetical Study of the Concept of Manna in the Gospel of John and the Writings of Philo* (NovTSup 10. Leiden: Brill, 1965).

33.   See especially M. J. Menken, 'And They Shall All Be Taught by God', *ETL* 64 (1988), pp. 164–72, reprinted in M. J. Menken, *Old Testament Quotations in the Fourth Gospel. Studies in Textual Form* (Kampen: Pharos, 1996), pp. 67–77.

The discourse reaches its climax with the interpretation and significance of the Johannine Eucharist. Unfortunately, even reference to the Eucharist has been denied in a tradition of Protestant scholarship imbued with Protestant rejection of the Catholic Eucharist. It is therefore necessary to consider the reasons why a Eucharistic interpretation of this chapter should be followed. At the Last Supper, Jesus of Nazareth interpreted bread and wine as his body and blood, thereby looking forward to his atoning death. His disciples took part in this meal, eating the bread and drinking the wine which Jesus interpreted. An account of this meal is preserved from an eyewitness account in the Gospel of Mark. It is incomplete, but perfectly accurate as far as it goes.[34] It includes Jesus' use of the term ὁ υἱὸς τοῦ ἀνθρώπου, at Mk 14.21. This is used twice with reference to Jesus' forthcoming betrayal, which is also predicted at Jn 6.64,71, using the same verb, παραδίδωμι. The genuine prediction of his betrayal at Mk 14.21 also refers to scripture. The equally genuine prediction Mk 14.18 also uses παραδίδωμι, and shows that Ps. 41.10 was among the scriptures which Jesus had in mind.[35] Jesus quotes this verse and predicts its forthcoming fulfilment at Jn 13.18, adding a prediction with the verb παραδίδωμι at Jn 13.21. The Marcan account was somewhat rewritten by Matthew. He retained the interpretation of the bread and wine as Jesus' body and blood, the eating and drinking of the bread and wine, the predictions which use παραδίδωμι, and the double use of the expression ὁ υἱὸς τοῦ ἀνθρώπου. Neither Mark nor Matthew records that Jesus instituted the Eucharist. He does not do so in John either.

A very strong connection between the Last Supper and the 'Lord's Supper' was made by St Paul. He was trying to control riotous Corinthian meals, from which we must infer that the Corinthian Christians were meeting for common meals already, and that Paul expected them to do this. Luke records common meals among Jewish Christians in the very earliest period (Acts 2.42,46), making no connection with the Last Supper or the Eucharist. We should therefore infer that the connection between the Last Supper and the 'Lord's Supper' was the work of St Paul. In rewriting relevant aspects of the story at 1 Cor. 11.23-25, he omits reference to the Passover, so that there is no need to imagine the event as an annual one, or the bread being unleavened. He retains one central point, the interpretation of the bread as Jesus' body. Paul also adds the first rubric, τοῦτο ποιεῖτε εἰς τὴν ἐμὴν ἀνάμνησιν. The reference to Jesus' blood is still found in the interpretation of the cup, but altered somewhat to make it more fruitful to the new situation: τοῦτο τὸ ποτήριον ἡ καινὴ διαθήκη ἐστὶν ἐν τῷ ἐμῷ αἵματι. The command to repeat the rite is even more carefully focused than before, since it has ὁσάκις ἐὰν πίνητε, pushing all fellowship meals into the Pauline frame of reference. We are not told how often these meals were to take place, but they were clearly meant to be part of the normal framework of the Christian life.

Some further information is available from 1 Cor. 10.16-17: τὸ ποτήριον τῆς εὐλογίας ὃ εὐλογοῦμεν, οὐχὶ κοινωνία ἐστὶν τοῦ αἵματος τοῦ

---

34. Casey, *Aramaic Sources of Mark's Gospel*, Ch. 6.
35. See pp. 134–6 above.

Χριστοῦ; τὸν ἄρτον ὄνκ λῶμεν, οὐχὶ κοινωνία τοῦ σώματος τοῦ Χριστοῦ ἐστιν; ὅτι εἷς ἄρτος, ἓν σῶμα οἱ πολλοί ἐσμεν, οἱ γὰρ πάντες ἐκ τοῦ ἑνὸς ἄρτου μετέχομεν. This clearly refers to the Pauline Eucharist, with the bread interpreted of the body of Christ and the cup interpreted with reference to his blood. Moreover, without the polemical context of 1 Cor. 11.17-34, which arose from the Corinthians not behaving as Paul thought they should, this passage also makes it clear that the Eucharist was an established community event. It stresses very strongly the significance of the Eucharist as a community fellowship event, and it does not make sense unless this event was reasonably frequent in the community's life.

This epistle was written by Paul and Sosthenes *c.*54 CE. This is the latest possible date for the Pauline eucharist being an established community event. It included interpretation of the bread and wine with reference to the body and blood of the Lord Jesus, and a rubric for it to be a repeated event. It was written from Ephesus (1 Cor. 16.8), during Paul's lengthy ministry there. Luke has this ministry last more than two years, and to be the centre of a generally successful ministry in Asia (Acts 19.8,10). This is natural in view of the position of Ephesus as the outstanding metropolis in the Roman province of Asia. It follows that, by *c.*55 CE at the latest, Eucharistic worship was a normal part of Ephesian Christianity. It must have included interpretation of the bread and wine with reference to the body and blood of the Lord Jesus.

This was a whole generation before the composition of the Gospel attributed to John. During this period, the Christian community had every reason to continue with its Eucharistic celebrations, because they were important community events which reinforced the community's identity. The nature of this document as a whole, however, suggests that they might well rewrite their thoughts about it creatively. Accordingly, the historical situation behind this document is one in which the Eucharist had been celebrated continuously for more than a generation. It is in this light that the language of Jn 6 must be interpreted.

For this reason, some people are bound to have begun to think of the Eucharist fairly early on in the discourse, perhaps even as early as the feeding narrative. Jesus describes himself as the bread of God already at v. 33, and as the bread of life at v. 35. Since the Eucharistic bread was regularly interpreted as his body at a major community event, some people will have thought of the Eucharist already even the first time they heard the discourse. More will have done so when they had become familiar with the crucial verses later in the discourse. At v. 51, the bread which Jesus gives, which he has already defined as himself, and which one can eat, is further described as 'my flesh'. By this stage, everyone who attended the Eucharist at all frequently was bound to think of the Eucharistic bread, always interpreted as Jesus' body. At v. 52, 'the Jews' ask how he can give them his flesh to eat. The question does not receive a literal answer, which correctly reflects the fact that everyone in the Johannine community will by this stage have known the answer: in the Eucharist. It also reflects the perfectly correct delineation of 'the Jews' as the people who did not know this: the Jewish community did not accept the Johannine Eucharist.

Accordingly, the answer actually given to this question includes very strong intensification of the Eucharistic imagery. At v. 53, anyone who does not eat the Son of man's flesh and drink his blood, has no life in them: correspondingly at v. 54, he who eats Jesus' flesh and drinks his blood has eternal life, and Jesus will raise him up at the last day. This very strong imagery, especially that of drinking blood, reflects the community's complete security with its own Eucharistic imagery. This in turn reflects the lengthy period during which the Eucharist had been an important and fruitful repeated event in the Johannine community's life. Moreover, the whole idea of drinking blood is in general so revolting to all decent people that it has no other *Sitz im Leben*. It is *only* because the Eucharist is in mind that such a strong expression could be used. It is also a boundary marker over against the Jewish community. Jewish people drain blood from meat in obedience to the biblical injunctions not to eat blood. The requirement that they should drink blood, even symbolically, shows that the Eucharist has been rewritten to be offensive to 'the Jews', as well as fruitful for the Johannine community. It is therefore appropriate that after further discussion, including further references to the great significance of eating Jesus' flesh and drinking his blood, many of his disciples in the Capernaum synagogue declare this unacceptable, and after some further discussion, they leave (Jn 6.59-66).

These arguments should be regarded as decisive. The whole of John 6 is directed at the imagery of the Johannine Eucharist. Many Protestant scholars have argued otherwise. I have refuted the main arguments of the most important secondary literature elsewhere,[36] and I do not repeat them here. With the background of the Johannine Eucharist in mind, I turn to the three Son of man sayings, beginning with Jn 6.27:

ἐργάζεσθε μὴ τὴν βρῶσιν τὴν ἀπολλυμένην ἀλλὰ τὴν βρῶσιν τὴν μένουσαν εἰς ζωὴν αἰώνιον, ἣν ὁ υἱὸς τοῦ ἀνθρώπου ὑμῖν δώσει· τοῦτον γὰρ ὁ πατὴρ ἐσφράγισεν.

The saying begins with τὴν βρῶσιν τὴν ἀπολλυμένην, which people are not to work for. In its context, this refers to any normal food, including the loaves and fishes in the feeding of the 5,000, referred to in the previous verse. The mention of food which perishes also prepares the way for discussion of the manna in the wilderness. It is contrasted with the main theme of the discourse, τὴν βρῶσιν τὴν μένουσαν εἰς ζωὴν αἰώνιον, ἣν ὁ υἱὸς τοῦ ἀνθρώπου ὑμῖν δώσει. It is natural that, in the narrative context, the audience do not understand what Jesus means. For those who do, it begins an exposition which reaches its climax in the Eucharist. This is τὴν βρῶσιν τὴν μένουσαν εἰς ζωὴν αἰώνιον. This food remains (τὴν μένουσαν) rather than perishes, the permanent Johannine Eucharist providing a contrast with perishable food. This food also leads to eternal life, for Johannine Christians who perceived the nature of the Eucharist had already passed from death to life, and Jesus would raise them up at the last day (cf. e.g. Jn 5.24; 6.40). This

36. Casey, *Is John's Gospel True?*, pp. 46–51.

food also remains until eternal life because it is Jesus himself, as explicitly stated already at 6.35, and the Son is a being of the eternal Godhead.

We are next told that the Son of man will give this food. Once again, the use of ὁ υἱὸς τοῦ ἀνθρώπου is especially appropriate because it refers to the humanity of the incarnate Jesus. Jesus' death was essential to the Last Supper and the Lord's Supper alike, and death is characteristic of human beings as opposed to deities. The Greek term ὁ υἱὸς τοῦ ἀνθρώπου had also been associated with Jesus' death from the time of the translation of Gospel traditions into Greek. I have noted it in predictions of Jesus' death, and in the prediction of his betrayal at the Last Supper. At the same time, in this document Jesus' death is significant because it is the death of the pre-existent Son. There are several references to Jesus' heavenly origin in the discourse, and they make an excellent contrast to the heavenly origin of the perishable manna in the wilderness. For example, the true bread from heaven is mentioned already at v. 32, and Jesus says in the first person καταβέβηκα ἀπὸ τοῦ οὐρανοῦ at v. 38. The crowd turn into grumbling Jews at v. 41, which precisely isolates the offence to them as Jesus saying ἐγώ εἰμι ὁ ἄρτος ὁ καταβὰς ἐκ τοῦ οὐρανοῦ. This has his pre-existence, which in this document entails his deity, just what the Jewish community rejected.

It is a consequence of this, rather than a peculiarity, that what is said here of ὁ υἱὸς τοῦ ἀνθρώπου is also said without the use of this term. As the discourse builds to its climax, Jesus says in the first person, ὁ ἄρτος δὲ ὃν ἐγὼ δώσω ἡ σάρξ μού ἐστιν ὑπὲρ τῆς τοῦ κόσμου ζωῆς (Jn 6.51). At v. 55, ἡ γὰρ σάρξ μου ἀληθής ἐστιν βρῶσις. It is precisely because Jesus is God incarnate that Johannine terminology is fruitful at its most flexible. Jesus' deity needs to be made plain, and Jesus must talk and act like a human being. The term ὁ υἱὸς τοῦ ἀνθρώπου refers to this basic aspect of the humanity of the incarnate Jesus, but everything else is needed for a complete exposition.

Jn 6.27 concludes: τοῦτον γὰρ ὁ πατὴρ ἐσφράγισεν ὁ θεός. The aorist is timeless, and the statement means that God guarantees the validity and authenticity of Jesus' earthly ministry. Thus it belongs with the subordinationist element which is integral to Johannine Christology and attributes the whole of Jesus' ministry to God himself. This was especially important in conflict with 'the Jews', who should have accepted Jesus because he was sent by God. Analogous comments include 5.37a: καὶ ὁ πέμψας με πατὴρ ἐκεῖνος μεμαρτύρηκεν περὶ ἐμοῦ. This also declares the Father's complete support of the validity of Jesus' earthly mission.

In the following verses, Jesus is repeatedly identified as the bread of life. As early as v. 33, the bread of God gives life, and at vv. 40 and 47 the believer has eternal life. There are repeated references to descent from heaven, as of the bread of God already at v. 33, and of Jesus himself at v. 38. I have noted the particular importance of v. 41, where 'the Jews' object to Jesus' identifying himself as the bread which came down from heaven. This is because descent from heaven implies his pre-existence and hence his deity, as does the description of him as the Son in the immediately preceding verse. This prepares for the use of ὁ υἱὸς τοῦ ἀνθρώπου at v. 53, because this term always has reference to the incarnation. It also prepares for the divisive effect of whether one eats his flesh and drinks his blood, both at vv. 53-54 and in the final quarrel of vv. 60-66. There are positive references to the need for and positive effects of believing, and as early as v. 36 there is also a reference to the fact that some of Jesus' audience do not believe. These pave the way both for the possible perception of the Eucharist at vv. 53-54, and for the rejection and departure of those who do not believe at vv. 60-66.

As the discourse builds towards its climax, references to eating the bread which descended from heaven, already identified as Jesus, begin at v. 50. At v. 51, Jesus also identifies this bread as his σάρξ, and declares that it is for the life of the world. The final lead-in to the discussion is a quarrel among οἱ Ἰουδαῖοι, who do not understand how Jesus can give his flesh to eat (v. 52). This is very appropriate, because the Jewish community did not accept the Eucharist, and consequently they did not believe that Jesus could give his flesh to eat. This is followed at once by the climactic Son of man saying at Jn 6.53, which must be taken together with the immediately following verse:

εἶπεν οὖν αὐτοῖς ὁ Ἰησοῦς, Ἀμὴν ἀμὴν λέγω ὑμῖν, ἐὰν μὴ φάγητε τὴν σάρκα τοῦ υἱοῦ τοῦ ἀνθρώπου καὶ πίητε αὐτοῦ τὸ αἷμα, οὐκ ἔχετε ζωὴν ἐν ἑαυτοῖς. ⁵⁴ὁ τρώγων μου τὴν σάρκα καὶ πίνων μου τὸ αἷμα ἔχει ζωὴν αἰώνοιν, κἀγὼ ἀναστήσω αὐτὸν τῇ ἐσχάτῃ ἡμέρᾳ.

This begins with the solemn introduction Ἀμὴν ἀμὴν λέγω ὑμῖν, the Johannine version of a peculiarity of Jesus' own speech, used to underline the importance of the saying. The imagery of these two verses is extremely strong, with blunt references to eating the flesh and drinking the blood of the Son of man. From the point of view of the internal needs of the Johannine community, this is to be explained with reference to the Eucharist. It is only because this important, traditional and frequent occasion is referred to that such strong terminology was safe. Equally, as the whole context shows, this was a boundary marker which distinguished the community from 'the Jews'.

The use of σάρξ in place of the original and traditional σῶμα will have been partly suggested by the traditional Hebrew phrase בשׂר ודם. This is frequently used in rabbinical literature to denote humankind, especially humankind as different from God. That it is much older is shown by the two earliest occurrences at Sir. 14.18 and 17.31. The LXX, which was done in the second century BCE by the author's grandson, has σαρκὸς καὶ αἵματος (14.18), and σάρξ καὶ αἷμα (17.31), for σάρξ is the obvious rendering of בשׂר, and consequently common in the LXX, and the same applies to the rendering of דם with αἷμα. We must infer that the combination σὰρξ καὶ αἷμα was available to the Johannine community to represent humankind. From their point of view, it helped to tie the Eucharist closely to the incarnation.

This is also presented by means of the use of the term ὁ υἱὸς τοῦ ἀνθρώπου. This again evokes the humanity of Jesus as found in the incarnation. Jesus became σάρξ at the incarnation (Jn 1.14), and αἷμα points particularly to his death, as it did in the Last Supper and in the Pauline Lord's Supper. As before, ὁ υἱὸς τοῦ ἀνθρώπου refers especially to Jesus as a human being who dies, as human beings must and God the Father does not. At the same time, the Eucharist which brings eternal life can do so only because this particular human being is the incarnate Son. Hence the use of ὁ υἱὸς τοῦ ἀνθρώπου is not the only way of putting the matter, and it is replaced with the first person in v. 54. It is precisely because he is incarnate as a human being that the pre-existent and eternal Son can speak about 'my' flesh and blood.

We can now see how these verses really function. First, 'unless you eat the flesh of the Son of man and drink his blood, you do not have life in yourselves'. There were two ways of not doing what this verse requires. First, one might not attend the Eucharist at all. This is very simple, and excludes everyone who does not belong to the Johannine community, or to a similar Christian community elsewhere. The primary reference is however to the more complex situation of people who did attend Eucharistic worship, but who did not believe that they were eating the flesh of the Son of man or drinking his blood, however symbolically. These are a later and more complex version of those whom Paul accused of 'not discerning the body' (1 Cor. 11.29). They may not have got drunk before others arrived, but from a Johannine perspective they failed to realize what they should believe they were doing on these occasions. Exactly what they did believe we are not told, but we can infer the kind of beliefs which they must have held from the background culture. They will have attended a community fellowship meal, at which they ate bread and drank wine as a memorial to Jesus of Nazareth. They will have commemorated his death, and recalled his final Passover with his disciples when he interpreted the bread and wine as symbols of his body and blood, thus looking forward to his forthcoming death. Such an approach fits perfectly well into the culture of those of 'the Jews' (6.52) who were also 'his disciples' (6.60). This explains their response σκληρός ἐστιν ὁ λόγος οὗτος (6.60). From their point of view it was just that, a piece of gross overinterpretation which was associated with the deity of Jesus and which was expressed in imagery quite alien to their view of God's commandments.

Such people are excluded by v. 53. The positive group are described in v. 54, only one group but they have to do two things. All good Johannine Christians not only went to the Eucharist, they also believed Johannine theology about what they were doing when they were there. ὁ τρώγων μου τὴν σάρκα καὶ πίνων μου τὸ αἷμα is not just someone who attends Eucharistic worship: it is someone who has a complete Johannine faith, and who thus believes that they are in fact eating Jesus' flesh and drinking his blood. It is such Johannine Christians who are defined as having eternal life, so that Jesus will raise them up at the last day.

It should therefore be clear that there is no question of the Eucharist having an automatic effect, as if participation in it granted eternal life regardless of a person's faith. Even Ignatius should not be brought into this discussion, let alone the later Catholic Eucharist. These two verses are moreover in dialectical relationship with Jn 6.60-66, which discuss further the fate of Jewish Christians who left the Johannine community. Leading up to this is some further exposition of the Eucharist in vv. 55-58. This grants the believing participant in the Eucharist mutual indwelling with Jesus (v. 56), and has further references to life. The discourse ends by contrasting the bread which came down from heaven with the manna eaten by the wilderness generation, thus recalling the early part of the discourse. Whereas the fathers ate and died, the person who eats the bread which came down from heaven 'will live for ever' (6.58). This further reinforces the message that Johannine Christians who believe in their fully developed Eucharistic theology already possess eternal life.

At the end of the discourse, we are informed that it took place in a synagogue in Capernaum. It follows that as the description of Jesus' interlocutors changes from 'the Jews' (6.41,52) to 'his disciples' (6.60, likewise 6.61,66), we should infer that the authors mean Jewish disciples. The rationale for this is that we are to be presented next with some of Jesus' Jewish disciples leaving the Johannine community (6.61-66). We should not confuse this group with hostile outsiders, often described in this document as 'the Jews'. We have seen that their reaction to the discourse is a natural Jewish reaction to the very high Eucharistic theology in the discourse, including the implication of Jesus' deity: σκληρός ἐστιν ὁ λόγος οὗτος· τίς δύναται αὐτοῦ ἀκούειν; this means that, as we are told in the following verses, many of his disciples did not believe in the Johannine theology of the previous discourse.

Jesus responds with the remaining Son of man saying of this discourse. It has caused endless trouble to commentators. Moloney comments, 'Interpreters have difficulty with v. 62 because it is an aposiopesis, that is, a conditional clause which has the protasis, but lacks the apodosis'.[37] They presuppose a translation like that of RSV: 'Then what if you were to see the Son of man ascending where he was before?' They then discuss whether this would remove the offence, or make the disciples' difficulties even worse, or ensure that they have to take a decision. None of this is properly Johannine, because it is only those who already have a full Johannine faith who could possibly perceive the Son of man ascending where he was before. Others do not believe he was pre-existent with God in heaven before his earthly ministry, and at his death they see at most the crucifixion of a prophet, not the exaltation and subsequent resurrection and ascension of the Son of man. I therefore punctuate and translate this verse, and its immediate context, as follows:

τοῦτο ὑμᾶς σκανδαλίζει. ⁶²ἐὰν οὖν θεωρῆτε τὸν υἱὸν τοῦ ἀνθρώπου ἀναβαίνοντα ὅπου ἦν τὸ πρότερον, ⁶³τὸ πνεῦμά ἐστιν τὸ ζῳοποιοῦν. ἡ σὰρξ οὐκ ὠφελεῖ οὐδέν. τὰ ῥήματα ἃ ἐγὼ λελάληκα ὑμῖν πνεῦμά ἐστιν καὶ ζωή ἐστιν.
This scandalizes you. If therefore you see the Son of man going up where he was before, it is the Spirit which is giving life. The flesh is no help at all. The words which I have spoken to you are spirit and life.

This makes excellent Johannine sense. Jesus begins with a blunt reaction to his disciples' rejection of his teaching: 'This scandalizes you.' So it obviously does, and it will shortly lead to 'many' of them leaving. The 'if' clause follows on logically. The many who leave have no hope of seeing the Son of man going up where he was before, in their current unregenerate state. In the complex dispute with the Jewish community, however, it was important in practical terms to leave the door open for

37. Moloney, *Johannine Son of Man*, p. 120.

them to convert into a full Johannine faith and rejoin the Johannine community. This verse offers a theological understanding of such an event. If some of them do come to believe that Jesus was the pre-existent λόγος, and see him ascending to be with the Father where he was before, that can only be because the Holy Spirit gives them life. Moreover, if 'many' leave, some, shortly symbolized by the faithful eleven of the Twelve, do not leave. They should eventually reach a full Johannine faith, if they have not yet done so. When this happens, the Spirit gives them life, and when the Spirit gives them life, they too can perceive the Son of man going up where he was before. This is therefore a genuine conditional sentence, in which the protasis and apodosis are properly related to each other.

It also contains standard Johannine theology about the Son of man. This term refers to Jesus' humanity as God incarnate. In discussing the fairly close parallel at Jn 3.13, I have noted that this document has several passages which are concerned with Jesus' pre-existence or his return to the Father, which is effectively his ascent.[38] Once again, therefore, what is said with the term 'Son of man' is said without it. This is because of the great mystery of the incarnation, which needs to be presented in different ways.

This brings us to another comment which has caused endless trouble to exegetes, ἡ σάρξ οὐκ ὠφελεῖ οὐδέν. This statement about the σάρξ has more than one possible meaning. In general, σάρξ without πνεῦμά represents ordinary human life without the influence of God, so in a general sense σάρξ is of no help to anyone who does not have the Spirit. At the incarnation, however, the λόγος became σάρξ, and we beheld his δόξα. Only in the σάρξ can we see his δόξα, for no one has ever seen God. To see the σάρξ of the incarnation, however, we need a full Johannine faith, inspired by the Spirit. Otherwise even the σάρξ of the incarnation is of no help, for without the Spirit we cannot see that it is the σάρξ of the incarnate λόγος. Thirdly, this comment about the σάρξ is a reference back to Jesus' flesh in the Eucharist. From the point of view of the Johannine community, Johannine Christians who eat the flesh and drink the blood of the Son of man in the Eucharist already have eternal life. Jewish Christians who eat bread and drink wine on the same occasion, however, do not receive life. We already know that Jesus is speaking to Jewish disciples who do not accept the Eucharistic theology which he has just expounded. What the Johannine community regards as the σάρξ of the Eucharist is accordingly of no help to them.

It is therefore appropriate that Jesus should continue: τὰ ῥήματα ἃ ἐγώ λελάληκα ὑμῖν πνεῦμά ἐστιν καὶ ζωή ἐστιν (6.63). From a Johannine perspective, this is just what was needed by the Jewish Christians who were about to leave. They should believe the Eucharistic theology which Jesus has just expounded. His words are spirit and bring life. If they believe what Jesus has said, they will eat his flesh and drink his blood in the Eucharist, and they too will have eternal life. They will also see the Son of man going up where he was before. But some do not believe, and many leave (6.64-66). The concluding narrative includes Peter's confession, ῥήματα ζωῆς αἰωνίου ἔχεις (6.68).

---

38.   See pp. 282–91 above.

This again emphasizes the importance of the Eucharistic theology of this chapter. It is a boundary marker over against the Jewish community, and it is essential for eternal life.

All three Son of man sayings in this chapter use the term ὁ υἱὸς τοῦ ἀνθρώπου with the same reference. It refers to Jesus' humanity as God incarnate. Only as a human being could he die, and his death is central to the symbolism of the Eucharist (6.53). Only in this way could he provide food which remains unto eternal life (6.27). Equally, his death could only be significant and lead to the provision of the Eucharist because he was pre-existent with the Father, and subsequently ascended to him (6.62-63). The use of ὁ υἱὸς τοῦ ἀνθρώπου in this chapter accordingly fits perfectly with the way in which it is used in the Son of man sayings earlier in the Gospel.

6. John 8.28

The next Son of man saying is an integral part of the second discourse at Tabernacles, which begins with Jesus' declaration 'I am the light of the world' (Jn 8.12). Light was one of the great symbolic features of Tabernacles, and Jesus in effect replaces Tabernacles and achieves more than it ever could by bringing life to the whole world rather than merely to 'the Jews'. 'The Pharisees' are brought forward to offer a detailed legal objection to the validity of his witness. In addition to his witness to himself, Jesus asserts μαρτυρεῖ περὶ ἐμοῦ ὁ πέμψας με πατήρ (8.18). This attributes the whole responsibility for Jesus' ministry to the Father, whose purpose and witness the Pharisees should have accepted. In the concluding altercation, the Pharisees do not know who Jesus' father is, as he affirms, thereby accusing them of not knowing their own God. This sets up the ferocious polemic which characterizes the rest of the chapter.

Jesus sets off the second part of the discourse by telling 'them' that they will die in their sins, ὅπου ἐγὼ ὑπάγω ὑμεῖς οὐ δύνασθε ἐλθεῖν (Jn 8.21). 'The Jews' have just one tiny glimmer of what he might mean by supposing that he might kill himself. The dispute moves towards the Son of man saying with another significant declaration: ἐὰν γὰρ μὴ πιστεύσητε ὅτι ἐγώ εἰμι, ἀποθανεῖσθε ἐν ταῖς ἁμαρτίαις ὑμῶν (8.24). This uses the divine revelatory formula 'I am' from Deutero-Isaiah.[39] These three aspects of the first part of the discourse, the attribution of complete responsibility for the ministry to the Father himself, the reference to Jesus' death, and the divine revelatory formula, set up the Son of man saying.

The immediate reaction to the Son of man saying is equally important. While he was still speaking, πολλοὶ ἐπίστευσαν εἰς αὐτόν (8.30). This means that a response of faith must be taken seriously in the interpretation of the Son of man saying at 8.28. It is confirmed by the description of the people to whom Jesus speaks

---

39. For detailed discussion, see C. Williams, *I am He. The Interpretation of 'Anî Hû' in Jewish and Early Christian Literature* (WUNT 2.113. Tübingen: Mohr Siebeck, 2000), esp. pp. 266–75.

as τοὺς πεπιστευκότας αὐτῷ Ἰουδαίους (8.31). This is further confirmed by Jesus' declaration to them: Ἐὰν ὑμεῖς μείνητε ἐν τῷ λόγῳ τῷ ἐμῷ, ἀληθῶς μαθηταί μού ἐστε ... (8.31). This takes for granted the reality of their existing faith. This position is not maintained in the subsequent narrative, in which they become the children of the devil who seek to kill Jesus. At the end of the chapter, their reaction to another use of the divine revelatory formula ἐγώ εἰμι, in circumstances which imply his pre-existence, leads them to seek to stone him (8.58-59), the standard Jewish penalty for blasphemy. Accordingly, at 8.48 they become οἱ Ἰουδαῖοι without qualification, and so they remain (8.52,57). This must not lead us to underestimate the narrators' intention to present a faith response at 8.30-31, essential as this is to understanding the Son of man saying at 8.28. Rather it reflects the gravity of the situation in late first-century Ephesus, where some Jews who did share the Johannine community's faith left the Johannine community because of their unshakable allegiance to the Jewish community. The same situation is presented at the end of the narrative of the public ministry, at 12.42-43. It is more serious than the situation at the end of Ch. 6, when many disciples who never had shared a full Johannine faith left the community.

I now turn to the Son of man saying at Jn 8.28, understood in its literary context:

> ὅταν ὑψώσητε τὸν υἱὸν τοῦ ἀνθρώπου, τότε γνώσεσθε ὅτι ἐγώ εἰμι, καὶ ἀπ᾽ ἐμαυτοῦ ποιῶ οὐδέν, ἀλλὰ καθὼς ἐδίδαξέν με ὁ πατὴρ ταῦτα λαλῶ.

This is a further development of the material at 3.14. In that passage, ὁ υἱὸς τοῦ ἀνθρώπου was derived from genuine and secondarily developed passion predictions, a usage continued here. I also noted the midrashic use of scripture, with Num. 21.9 being obvious and Isa. 52.13 being the source of ὑψωθῆναι. This is continued here, with Isa. 52.13 still the source of ὑψώσητε, and the use of the divine revelatory formula ἐγώ εἰμι from Deutero-Isaiah. Further midrashic use of Deutero-Isaiah is evident in the Johannine context.[40] At Jn 3.15, the purpose of the Son of man being lifted up was given: ἵνα πᾶς ὁ πιστεύων ἐν αὐτῷ ἔχῃ ζωὴν αἰώνιον. Here we find a faith response in the context, and in this saying a reference to having knowledge of something which can be known only by faith.

The ὅταν clause accordingly refers to the crucifixion and exaltation of the Son of man. The second person plural is deliberately used to lay the responsibility for the crucifixion on the Jewish people as a whole. The passion narrative also seeks to do this in a literal sense, while the final discourses never lose sight of the responsibility of the κόσμος. The exaltation is of equal importance, not least because it is only those who perceive the exaltation of the Son of man in the crucifixion who can possibly know ὅτι ἐγώ εἰμι. This divine revelatory formula implies a full Johannine faith, including the deity of Jesus as well as the importance of his death. The rest of the verse attributes to these people the realization that God the Father is completely responsible for the whole of Jesus' ministry, including his teaching.

40.   Hanson, *Prophetic Gospel*, pp. 119–22.

The group in mind here are Jewish converts to Christianity. That they crucified the Son of man should not be taken literally. They are held responsible for the crucifixion as members of the Jewish people, just as other people have been held responsible as members of the sinful human race. The use of ὅταν with the subjunctive is especially appropriate for the perception of Jesus' exaltation, a perception repeated many times over a long period of time. We might translate overliterally, to bring out one aspect of the meaning: 'Whenever you exalt the Son of man, then you will know that I AM (he) …' From a Johannine perspective, this is obviously true. It is only when people perceive the exaltation of the Son of man in his crucifixion that they can go further and appreciate the divine revelatory formula, and the classic Johannine paradox that God incarnate was entirely dependent on the Father throughout his earthly ministry.

The Johannine community will have been acutely aware that many converts to Christianity had been Jewish. They included all the first Christians, and many of the most important known evangelists: Paul, Andronicus, Apollos, Aquila, Joseph Barnabas, Junia, perhaps Priscilla, Silvanus and Timothy. Of these, Apollos, Aquila, Priscilla and Timothy all worked in Ephesus, and Paul was the outstanding known evangelist in the history of the Ephesian church. After persecuting the church, he saw the exalted Christ on the Damascus road, and the crucified Christ was central to the message which he preached with extraordinary success. From a Johannine perspective, Paul was the most wonderful example of Jn 8.28 that anyone could ask for. The most woeful examples are portrayed later in this chapter, where those Jews who believed in him at 8.31 turn so rapidly back into the hostile outsiders οἱ Ἰουδαῖοι, as in this document as a whole. It is this wonderful and then disastrous situation which has led to the description, unique in this document, 'the Jews who believed in him'.

Accordingly, the term ὁ υἱὸς τοῦ ἀνθρώπου has the same meaning at Jn 8.28 as in the other Son of man sayings which I have discussed. It refers firstly to the humanity of Jesus, which was essential for him to be able to die. At the same time, it refers to his humanity as God incarnate who can appropriately use the divine revelatory formula 'I am'. As long as we recognize this formula and give it its full weight, it does not matter whether we take Son of man a second time as the complement of εἰμι. If we choose to do so, it is obviously true that if you exalt the Son of man by recognizing the real importance of his crucifixion, and accept his use of the divine revelatory formula ἐγώ εἰμι, you will know that Jesus is that person. The rest of the verse, which declares his complete dependence on God the Father during his earthly ministry, again underlines his humanity.

7. John 9.35

The next Son of man saying is also embedded in a narrative and discourse setting. It is still set at Tabernacles, and dominated by the light imagery which was such a conspicuous feature of that festival. It begins with the healing of a man born blind. This is a deliberate writing up of synoptic events, for healing blind people lies within the parameters of what a traditional healer can do and the historical Jesus did, whereas healing a man born blind is a normally impossible event. It is therefore suitable to be a σημεῖον (9.16) which should lead to faith but which actually leads to division. After putting mud on the man's eyes, Jesus sends him to wash in the pool of Siloam, the source of the water-drawing ceremony, the other central piece of symbolism characteristic of Tabernacles.

The light/darkness imagery begins already at vv. 4-5, where Jesus repeats that he is the light of the world (9.5, cf. 8.12). When the man goes and washes in the pool of Siloam, at once he came 'seeing' (9.7). The subsequent narrative has several references to the man having his eyes opened and seeing. When he is taken to the Pharisees (9.13), there is a division of opinion about the supposed event, and people ask the man what he thinks of the man who 'opened' his 'eyes'. He responds 'he is a prophet' (9.17). This is the first step towards a fuller faith, a step prompted by the miracle. On the other hand, 'the Jews' 'did not believe' that he had been blind and gained his sight (9.18), and they conclude their interrogation by throwing him out (9.34). During the proceedings, they contrast Moses to whom God spoke with 'this man', saying they do not know πόθεν ἐστιν (9.29). From the reader's point of view, this recalls Jesus' heavenly origin. The man finds it remarkable that they do not know πόθεν ἐστιν, 'and he opened my eyes' (9.30). This associates Jewish ignorance of Jesus with the dominant imagery of the chapter. The man himself then goes further than before and announces that the person who healed him is παρὰ θεοῦ (9.33), a genuinely Johannine answer to the question implied by πόθεν ἐστιν.

After Jesus' meeting with the man, he announces that he came into the world for judgement, ἵνα οἱ μὴ βλέποντες βλέπωσιν καὶ οἱ βλέποντες τυφλοὶ γένωνται (Jn 9.39). This presents the imagery of this chapter as a whole. It leads some of the Pharisees to ask whether they are blind. Jesus' somewhat ironical reply finds fault with them for saying that they see, and informs them that their sin remains. In effect, therefore, they are symbolically blind while the formerly blind man can now see.

Jesus' meeting with the man (9.35-38) charts his further coming to faith, over and above his initial belief that the man who healed him was a prophet (9.17), and going further than the declaration that he was παρὰ θεοῦ (9.32). Jesus found him, and began with the Son of man saying:

σὺ πιστεύεις εἰς τὸν υἱὸν τοῦ ἀνθρώπου;

This use of the expression ὁ υἱὸς τοῦ ἀνθρώπου in what is effectively a request for a confession has caused more trouble than it should, and has led to some strange suggestions. For example, Higgins suggested that it was based on a confession from a baptismal ceremony in the Johannine community.[41] This is just what should *not* be inferred from a text of this kind. The term ὁ υἱὸς τοῦ ἀνθρώπου is notoriously absent from all confessions in the New Testament period. We should not construct one from a narrative. Nor is the later ecclesiastical association of this story with baptism

41.   Higgins, *Jesus and the Son of Man*, pp. 155, 175.

any excuse for uncontrolled imagination. We must keep closer to the text which we have got. Problems are already evident in the ancient period, where some scribes altered ἀνθρώπου to θεοῦ. This reading cannot possibly be right, because weight of attestation clearly favours ἀνθρώπου, and so does transcriptional probability. Scribes have altered ἀνθρώπου to θεοῦ to produce the more exalted title: the possibility of the opposite alteration being made is simply incomprehensible.

The association between πιστεύω and ὁ υἱὸς τοῦ ἀνθρώπου is close already at Jn 3.14-15:

¹⁴καὶ καθὼς Μωϋσῆς ὕψωσεν τὸν ὄφιν ἐν τῇ ἐρήμῳ, οὕτως ὑψωθῆναι δεῖ τὸν υἱὸν τοῦ ἀνθρώπου, ¹⁵ἵνα πᾶς ὁ πιστεύων ἐν αὐτῷ ἔχῃ ζωὴν αἰώνιον.

Here it is precisely everyone who has faith in the Son of man who is to have eternal life.[42] This makes faith in the Son of man one way of putting what is central to the process of salvation. As we have seen, it is especially closely associated with his death and exaltation. This feature in turn associates it with the Son of man saying at Jn 8.28, where the believer requires the kind of knowledge that is dependent on faith. It follows that ὁ υἱὸς τοῦ ἀνθρώπου is a perfectly natural phrase for the Johannine Jesus to use in asking whether the healed man has faith in him. It refers especially to his humanity as God incarnate, so it implies a full Johannine faith.

This is at first too much for the man, who asks who this is (9.36). The Revealer then reveals himself, and that is enough, despite the fact that the man cannot be expected to know what ὁ υἱὸς τοῦ ἀνθρώπου actually means. The way it is expressed is interesting: καὶ ἑώρακας αὐτὸν καὶ ὁ λαλῶν μετὰ σοῦ ἐκεῖνός ἐστιν (9.37). The first point, 'you have seen him' uses the imagery central to the chapter, and lets us know that the man has sight, both literal and metaphorical. The second is a more straightforward identification. The man at once reacts by declaring his faith: πιστεύω, κύριε (9.38). Furthermore, προσεκύνησεν αὐτῷ. This verb does not necessarily denote worship of a deity, but it is enough to indicate that the man has taken another step in the right direction. Jesus next declares that he has come into the world for judgement, and the divisive effect of his ministry is indicated by his criticism of the effectively blind Pharisees following his acceptance of the man. We have seen that judgement was given to the Son on the ground that he is Son of man (Jn 5.27). This gave the evangelist another reason to use ὁ υἱὸς τοῦ ἀνθρώπου here.

I therefore conclude that this Son of man saying fits perfectly into Johannine usage. It refers to the humanity of God incarnate who reveals himself through his σάρξ. Faith in him is required, as at 3.14-15 (cf. 8.28), and his ministry brings judgement as at 5.27.

---

42. See further pp. 287–8 above.

8. John 12.23,34

The next three Son of man sayings belong to the final discourse of the public ministry. Six days before Passover (Jn 12.1), Jesus is anointed at Bethany, and looks forward to his burial (12.7). The next day he enters Jerusalem, and is hailed by the crowd as king of Israel, with scriptural references which at least include Ps.118. 25-26, one of the Hallel psalms set for singing at Passover, and Zech. 9.9.[43] We are told that the disciples 'remembered' that this was written of him ὅτε ἐδοξάσθη Ἰησοῦς (Jn 12.16). Here ἐδοξάσθη clearly looks forward to Jesus' death and exaltation.

Some Greeks, the group of Gentiles among whom the Gospel spread with extraordinary effectiveness, come to see Jesus. They do not see him. Instead, Jesus looks forward to his death, the major event which must happen to enable the conversion of Gentiles to take place. As Jesus puts it in the first person at Jn 12.32, κἀγὼ ἐὰν ὑψωθῶ ἐκ τῆς γῆς, πάντας ἑλκύσω πρὸς ἐμαυτόν. His exposition of his forthcoming death begins with the Son of man saying at 12.23:

ἐλήλυθεν ἡ ὥρα ἵνα δοξασθῇ ὁ υἱὸς τοῦ ἀνθρώπου.

I have already noted the derivation of the term ὁ υἱὸς τοῦ ἀνθρώπου from the synoptic tradition, and the derivation of ὑψόω at Jn 3.14 and 8.28 from Isa. 52.13, ὑψωθήσεται καὶ δοξασθήσεται σφόδρα.[44] As well as the use of ὑψωθῶ at 12.32, the Son of man saying at 12.34 has δεῖ ὑψωθῆναι τὸν υἱὸν τοῦ ἀνθρώπου, almost a quotation from 3.14. Moreover, Isa. 53.1 is quoted at Jn 12.38. Once again we have an overwhelming argument of cumulative weight: midrashic use of Isa. 52.13 is the major source of the use of δοξασθῇ in the Son of man saying at Jn 12.23.

Furthermore, several Son of man sayings in the synoptic Gospels use the term δόξα. They include Mt. 16.27-28//Mk 8.38–9.1, and Mt. 24.30//Mk 13.26, both among the passages which the Johannine community needed to replace because of the problems which they posed by way of their unfulfilled predictions. Both passages are already based on midrashic use of scripture, and the Johannine community replaced them with Son of man sayings which make midrashic use of different passages of scripture.[45] The community cannot have been much happier with Mt. 24.44//Lk 12.40: καὶ ὑμεῖς γίνεσθε ἕτοιμοι, ὅτι ᾗ οὐ δοκεῖτε ὥρα ὁ υἱὸς τοῦ ἀνθρώπου ἔρχεται. Here too the use of ὁ υἱὸς τοῦ ἀνθρώπου is inspired by Dan. 7.13, and an unfulfilled prediction of the second coming may reasonably be perceived: the use of ὥρα is central to it.[46]

We have also seen that some of the passion predictions in John originated as replacements of synoptic passion predictions, including Jn 3.14 with its use of

43.   Cf. E. D. Freed, *Old Testament Quotations in the Gospel of John* (NovTSup 11. Leiden: Brill, 1965), pp. 66–81; B. G. Schuchard, *Scripture within Scripture. The Interrelationship of Form and Function in the Explicit Old Testament Citations in the Gospel of John* (SBLDS 133. Atlanta: Scholars, 1992), pp. 71–84; Menken, *Old Testament Quotations*, pp. 79–97.

44.   See pp. 275–80, 282–3, 304 above.

45.   See pp. 277–80, 282–3 above.

46.   On the interpretation of this verse, see pp. 219–20 above.

Isa. 52.13.[47] There is an important comment on the moment of Jesus' betrayal in the Matthean and Markan passion narratives. The Matthean version is lucid: ἰδοὺ ἤγγικεν ἡ ὥρα καὶ ὁ υἱὸς τοῦ ἀνθρώπου παραδίδοται εἰς χεῖρας ἁμαρτωλῶν. This is Mt. 26.45, rewriting Mk 14.41, part of which has not been correctly preserved. Most MSS of Mk 14.41 read ἦλθεν ἡ ὥρα, followed by ἰδού, and it may be this which helped inspire Jn 12.23. Jesus also prayed that ἡ ὥρα might pass from him at Mk 14.35, a prayer which the Johannine community found problematic enough to rewrite at Jn 12.27, again using ὥρα. It may be this which ensured that they used the Marcan version of the story.

While some of the details of this process must remain uncertain, the main points are not. The Son of man saying at Jn 12.23 has resulted from the community's rewriting synoptic Son of man sayings by means of the midrashic use of scripture, and the use of δοξάζω is due to the influence of Isa. 52.13. The resulting saying is perfectly Johannine. Jesus announces that his death is about to take place, and does so in a way which implies that he is really in charge of it. While his δόξα was revealed at other points in his ministry (e.g. 2.11), and the faithful could see it all the time (1.14), his death was a moment central to his glorification, as to his exaltation. As elsewhere, the use of ὁ υἱὸς τοῦ ἀνθρώπου is especially appropriate because it is characteristic of human beings that they die. At the same time, Jesus' glorification in death is only possible because he is God incarnate. This is also the reason why his death was fundamental to the mission to the Gentiles, the essential point of this Johannine context. For the same reasons, the narrator may refer to Jesus being glorified, using his proper name rather than the term ὁ υἱὸς τοῦ ἀνθρώπου (Jn 7.39; 12.16).

Burney suggested that ἵνα was a mistranslation of the Aramaic דביה, 'in which', a suggestion which would support the view that the Son of man sayings in this Gospel go back to an Aramaic tradition, and might seem to open up the possibility that the historical Jesus said them. As we have seen, however, John's Greek makes excellent sense as it stands: 'The hour has come for the Son of man to be glorified'. Burney found John's use of ἵνα to be unsatisfactory because it is in accordance with ordinary Hellenistic Greek, not with classical excellence.[48] Moreover, it is not possible to reconstruct a convincing Aramaic original. One might suggest the following:

אתת שעתא דיתהדר רב אנשא.

Here we must suppose that the Aramaic הדר, 'glorify', underwent a change of semantic field identical to that of the Greek δοξάζω, 'glorify', so that it could refer to Jesus' death. That is not impossible, but we should be aware that postulating too many developments in Aramaic to account for John's Greek would become more

47. See pp. 282–3 above.
48. Burney, *Aramaic Origin*, p. 78. Cf. E. C. Colwell, *The Greek of the Fourth Gospel. A Study of its Aramaisms in the Light of Hellenistic Greek* (Chicago: University of Chicago, 1931), pp. 99–100; Black, *Aramaic Approach*, p. 79.

and more dicey if we had to increase the number of examples. The major problem with this verse, however, is the term בר אנשא itself. It does not have enough referring power to mean Jesus himself with any clarity. Nor is it an example of the traditional idiom which the historical Jesus in fact used to refer to himself. It would accordingly have been a very unsatisfactory choice as a means of predicting Jesus' death.

We must therefore conclude that the whole idea of an Aramaic origin for this saying is unsatisfactory. This is entirely coherent with its having a perfect *Sitz im Leben* in Johannine theology, and in the process of rewriting synoptic Son of man sayings which the community found in Greek.

The narrative continues to develop in Greek. I have noted especially 12.32-33, where Jesus refers to his forthcoming exaltation, using ὑψωθῶ, and the narrator interprets this as a reference to the kind of death he would die, so a reference to his forthcoming crucifixion. The crowd produce the next two examples of ὁ υἱὸς τοῦ ἀνθρώπου:

Ἡμεῖς ἠκούσαμεν ἐκ τοῦ νόμου ὅτι ὁ Χριστὸς μένει εἰς τὸν αἰῶνα, καὶ πῶς λέγεις σὺ ὅτι δεῖ ὑψωθῆναι τὸν υἱὸν τοῦ ἀνθρώπου; τίς ἐστιν οὗτος ὁ υἱὸς τοῦ ἀνθρώπου;

This is a remarkable breakdown of one of the major patterns of the usage of ὁ υἱὸς τοῦ ἀνθρώπου in the Gospels. It is the only occasion when the term is not used by Jesus himself. We have seen that the model for Johannine Son of man sayings was the synoptic tradition of Son of man sayings. This explains why they have mostly been used in the rewriting of the teaching of Jesus. Once they were divorced from their origins, however, the Johannine community had no reason to maintain this pattern. They chose to write much of their theology in the form of discourses attributed to Jesus. These discourses are often carried forward by questions from other people, and some of the questions are not very bright by our standards. These are two such questions.

The crowd first express part of their messianic beliefs, which they claim to know from scripture:

ἡμεῖς ἠκούσαμεν ἐκ τοῦ νόμου ὅτι ὁ χριστὸς μένει εἰς τὸν αἰῶνα.

We should follow those scholars who see a reference to Ps. 88.37 LXX: τὸ σπέρμα αὐτοῦ εἰς τὸν αἰῶνα μενεῖ. The seed referred to here is that of David, and later Jewish sources interpret this text with reference to the Messiah.[49] We must infer that this is the scriptural exegesis which the crowd are supposed to have in mind. The term νόμος is used in its broadest sense to include any passage of scripture. The crowd then refer to Johannine theology which has been attributed to Jesus and which does not fit with their view of the coming of the Messiah:

πῶς λέγεις σὺ ὅτι δεῖ ὑψωθῆναι τὸν υἱὸν τοῦ ἀνθρώπου;

---

49. W. C. van Unnik, 'The Quotation from the Old Testament in John 12.34', *NovT* 3 (1959), pp. 174–9.

This has caused great trouble to literally minded scholars because it is not what Jesus has *just* said. For example, Hare declares that this 'of course, is inaccurate (assuming that the crowd has not learned from Nicodemus what was said at 3:14!)'.[50] But the authors could not use Jesus' comment at Jn 12.23, because the glorification of the Son of man could be identified with the permanence of the Messiah. Nor could they use Jn 12.32, which is conditional and clearly refers to Jesus. They have therefore used the formulation of Jn 3.14, for this enables them to present with clarity the *theological* point, the crowd's lack of understanding. They believe in the permanence of the Messiah, and they know that Jesus has said δεῖ ὑψωθῆναι τὸν υἱὸν τοῦ ἀνθρώπου. They do not understand how both can be true. They choose the stupidest option:

τίς ἐστιν οὗτος ὁ υἱὸς τοῦ ἀνθρώπου;

This is the crowd's demise in darkness. If they do not even know that Jesus is the Christ and the Son of man who must be crucified and thereby exalted, they truly haven't the foggiest notion. Jesus gives up on their knowledge of the Christ and the Son of man, and responds with the simplest and most appropriate imagery possible. He invites them to believe in the light, having already presented himself as the light of the world. Then he hid himself from them, for they did not believe. The Johannine theologians reflect on the prophecies of Isaiah, which predicted the Jewish crowd's incomprehension and lack of belief.

The use of ὁ υἱὸς τοῦ ἀνθρώπου in these sayings presupposes that we as readers or audience share the conventional Johannine understanding of this expression.

9. John 13.31-32

The final Son of man saying in this document begins Jesus' discourse after the Last Supper. As we must infer from the synoptic accounts, Jesus expects to be betrayed by Judas Iscariot, and knows that this is predicted in Ps. 41. But the Johannine account goes further. Jesus actually tells Judas to go and do his deed (Jn 13.27). When he has gone out, Jesus begins his discourse:

νῦν ἐδοξάσθη ὁ υἱὸς τοῦ ἀνθρώπου, καὶ ὁ θεὸς ἐδοξάσθη ἐν αὐτῷ· ³²εἰ ὁ θεὸς ἐδοξάσθη ἐν αὐτῷ, καὶ ὁ θεὸς δοξάσει αὐτὸν ἐν αὐτῷ, καὶ εὐθὺς δοξάσει αὐτόν.

We have already seen that the use of δοξάζω originated in midrashic use of Isa. 52.13, and that δοξάζω may refer especially to Jesus' glorification in his death. Some of the commentators have been very puzzled by the aorist tenses here, and even by the opening νῦν. We should take the aorists in a standard way as references to a single past event, and the νῦν qualifies this as a reference to the immediately past event of the Last Supper. Jesus has just been glorified by effectively bringing about his own death. In this document, Jesus is fully in charge of the events of his

50.   Hare, *Son of Man*, p. 108.

own passion. He has just shown that he was fully aware that he was to be betrayed by Judas Iscariot, and that this was predicted in Ps. 41. In this knowledge, he has given the decisive order himself at 13.27, and Judas has obeyed him. It is precisely in giving that order that the Son of man was now glorified, and God was glorified in him.

I have printed the longer reading, which must be read, despite its omission by some good and early MSS, notably P⁶⁶ ℵ* B. The omission should be ascribed to homoioteleuton, perhaps assisted by scribes who found the longer reading redundant or difficult. The longer reading also makes excellent sense. 'If God was glorified in him' refers again to the immediately preceding event, in which Jesus ordered Judas to go and carry out his deed quickly (13.27). It follows from this that God will also glorify him in himself, since the Father is in overall control of the whole ministry, and therefore glorifies Jesus in the passion, as Jesus asks him to in the prayer of Ch. 17. As Jesus has ordered Judas to act quickly, so God will glorify him at once, and does so after the final discourses and that prayer.

The use of ὁ υἱὸς τοῦ ἀνθρώπου in this saying is accordingly particularly closely related to the saying at 12.23, and is thus in complete accordance with Johannine usage. It refers especially to the humanity of Jesus as God incarnate. Since this is a pervasive feature of the document, the glorification of Jesus can also be referred to without this term (cf. Jn 7.39; 12.16; 16.14; 17.1,5).

10. Conclusions

In the Gospel attributed to John, the term ὁ υἱὸς τοῦ ἀνθρώπου is a title of Jesus. Its origin is to be found in the synoptic Gospels, most probably those of Matthew and Mark. In particular, Jn 1.51 originated as a deliberate replacement of Mt. 26.64, because of the serious problems caused by the unfulfilled predictions in this and similar passages of Matthew and Mark. The Johannine community continued with the midrashic use of scripture found in Mt. 26.64 and other Son of man sayings in the synoptic tradition. They created a new Son of man saying by replacing Ps. 110.1 and Dan. 7.13 with creative use of Gen. 28.12. They integrated it into its present context by careful and creative use of these and other passages of the Old Testament and of the synoptic Gospels. Jn 5.27 resulted likewise from the replacement of Mt. 16.27-28 and similar sayings. Both Mt. 16.27-28 and Mk 8.38, the source of Mt. 16.27, show clear signs of the deliberate use of Dan. 7.13. Jn 5.27 was written by someone who was aware of this. This is the limit of the influence of Dan. 7.13 in the Son of man sayings of this Gospel. Even Jn 5.27 was not a deliberate reference to this text, and otherwise it has been removed rather than used, because its deliberate use in the synoptic tradition was in predictions which had not been fulfilled.

Jn 3.14 resulted similarly from rewriting synoptic passion predictions, especially Mk 8.31 (cf. Mt. 16.13,21). Here mundane details were replaced with more theological comments also based on the midrashic use of scripture, in this case Num. 21.9 and Isa. 52.13. Some other Johannine Son of man sayings have also resulted from rewriting synoptic material with midrashic use of scripture. Synoptic sayings which seem to have been in mind include the genuine Mk 14.21, which seems to be in the background of Jn 6 and 13, and sayings such as Mk 8.31 which are partly genuine and have to some extent already been rewritten in the synoptic tradition. This is as near as Johannine Son of man sayings ever get to the Aramaic level of the tradition. Not one of them is a translation of an Aramaic saying. Some of them have been formed from rewriting synoptic Son of man sayings which are ultimately derived from genuine Aramaic sayings of Jesus.

The term ὁ υἱὸς τοῦ ἀνθρώπου in this document is accordingly a Greek title of Jesus. It refers particularly to his humanity as God incarnate. The incarnation is a central feature of this Gospel as a whole. Consequently, Son of man sayings are also used in passages such as Jn 6, where there is no direct sign of them being rewritten versions of synoptic Son of man sayings (though synoptic material has been rewritten in this chapter, and midrashic use of scripture was important in its composition). The three Son of man sayings in this chapter (6.27,53,62) are used to clarify the Johannine community's view of the Eucharist, to which the incarnation was essential. A second consequence of the use of ὁ υἱὸς τοῦ ἀνθρώπου as a deliberate reference to the humanity of God incarnate is that almost everything written about ὁ υἱὸς τοῦ ἀνθρώπου is also written of Jesus without the use of this term. This indicates how completely the authors have integrated their use of ὁ υἱὸς τοῦ ἀνθρώπου into their theology as a whole. This explains why there is no apparent pattern to the distribution of this term in this document as a whole. The authors used it when they wished to refer to the humanity of God incarnate in this particular way. They could however write about this in different terms, and they had no reason to impose a particular pattern of distribution on the term ὁ υἱὸς τοῦ ἀνθρώπου.

Chapter Thirteen

CONCLUSIONS

The purpose of this chapter is to summarize the proposed solution to the Son of man problem which has been the subject of this book. Previous scholars have been handicapped by lack of the knowledge necessary for solving this problem, a massive degree of ignorance compounded by ideological bias. This regrettable combination manifested itself in frequently reading primary sources in translation, rather than in the languages in which they have survived. It also led to the almost complete domination of the study of this problem by Christian scholars committed to the study of the Gospels in Greek, without any proper appreciation of the study of Aramaic, the language which Jesus spoke. I isolated the sorry consequences of this situation in Ch. 1.

Given that Jesus spoke Aramaic, the next task was to discuss the use of the Aramaic term which Jesus used when the Gospels attribute to him the Greek term ὁ υἱὸς τοῦ ἀνθρώπου. There has not been much doubt that this was the Aramaic term (א)שנ(א) בר. Accordingly, Ch. 2 investigated the ways in which this term was used, bringing to bear much more primary evidence than had previously been used. To do this effectively, I first had to discuss the basic development of the Aramaic language, since this has not generally been known to New Testament scholars. The central point is that it was an exceptionally stable language. Consequently, it is perfectly legitimate to use both early and late sources to illuminate the Aramaic background of sayings of the historical Jesus. The development of generic expressions is especially important. In general, generic nouns may be used in either the definite or indefinite state, because the use of one state or the other cannot make any difference to their meaning. Now (א)שנ(א) בר is such a term, especially in a particular idiomatic usage which is central to appreciating the use of this term by the historical Jesus.

In this idiom, a speaker may use the term (א)שנ(א) בר in a sentence which has both a general and a specific level of meaning. The general level of meaning varies greatly in both extent and significance. Sayings using this idiom may be intended to be true of all human beings. At the other end of the spectrum, a person may generalize from their own experience, and the generalization may be false. Equally, the general level of meaning may be very important, or it may have no significance beyond its application to the speaker. The intended reference may be to the speaker, or to the speaker and a group of associates, or to another person made obvious by the context. This massive degree of variation is important in assessing sayings of the historical Jesus, not least because contrary assumptions have been widespread in scholarship.

I have found over 30 examples of general statements using בר (א)נשׁ(א) with reference to the speaker, or a group of people including the speaker, or someone else made obvious by the context. The majority of examples are in Jewish Aramaic from Israel, and most of these concern rabbis who have some connection with Galilee. There is also one very early example, which is important because it establishes the use of this idiom long before the time of Jesus. There is also one Babylonian example, and a handful of examples have been noted in Syriac. It follows that when examples of this idiomatic usage emerge from the reconstruction of Aramaic sources from our Gospel sayings, they should be accepted as genuine examples of this idiom.

The third chapter was devoted to a modern construct, the Son of Man Concept. I showed that this was a major scholarly mistake. In the foundational source for this Concept, Dan. 7.13, כבר אנשׁ, 'one like a son of man', is a pure symbol of the Saints of the Most High, a description of the people of Israel. He is not a separate figure, and he is merely likened to a man. The study of the *Similitudes of Enoch* has been made very difficult by the fact that it has survived only in Ge'ez, and in a very corrupt textual tradition at that. Careful study of Aramaic source material which can be recovered from the oldest manuscripts has shown that בר (א)נשׁ(א) was used in the original text of this work in the same way as it is used in extant Aramaic texts, as a normal term for 'man'. Other sources studied either do not use the term 'son of man', or use it normally. Accordingly, this scholarly construct is ignored in the remaining chapters of this book.

The next few chapters studied genuine sayings of the historical Jesus. In Ch. 4, I recapitulated previously published work on six genuine Son of man sayings, each of which belongs in the context of a literally translated Aramaic source which can be recovered: Mk 2.28; 9.12; 10.45; 14.21 (where the term occurs twice); Mt. 11.19//Lk. 7.34; and Mt. 12.32//Lk. 12.10. In each case there is some general level of meaning, as well as a particular reference to Jesus. At Mk 2.28, there is a general level of meaning referring to the poor disciples who had been taking Peah on the sabbath, but the position of Jesus was nonetheless pre-eminent. The use of the idiom is due to that pre-eminent position, which led Jesus to speak of himself indirectly.

Mk 9.12 is unusual in that there is an important reference to John the Baptist, as well as a very general level of meaning referring perhaps to humanity as a whole, or at least to the Jewish people. The importance of John the Baptist set a problem for the translator, who decided to use ὁ υἱὸς τοῦ ἀνθρώπου on the grounds that Jesus was more central. The result has been very difficult for scholars to understand, and it has only become really clear since I reconstructed the original Aramaic. At Mk 10.45, there is a particular reference to Jacob and John, as well as a more general reference to any disciples who might share in Jesus' death and an underlying theology of martyrdom. At the same time, there is a reference to the pre-eminent position of Jesus himself, who was in fact the only one to die an atoning death on the way to his pre-eminent position in glory. At Mk 14.21 there is a general meaning referring to the fate of humanity as subject to death, and a second general level of meaning of a much more restricted kind, referring to people who are betrayed. In both sayings, the major reference is to Jesus himself. At Mt. 11.19//Lk. 7.34 there is a general level of meaning referring to people who are falsely accused of being rebellious sons, and a pre-eminent reference to Jesus himself, who is compared and contrasted with John the Baptist. At Mt. 12.32//Lk. 12.10, there is an underlying reference to humanity in general, and a pre-eminent reference to Jesus himself. In each of the last five sayings, the use of this indirect idiom is due to the humiliating circumstances surrounding the experiences of Jesus and the other people particularly referred to.

In Ch. 5, I offered an Aramaic reconstruction of the story of the healing of a paralytic, omitting a few pieces as glosses. Here too the Son of man saying (Mk 2.10) fits perfectly into the context of an incident which really took place. The healing used the biblical model of sin as the cause of illness, and in this context Jesus twice declared that the man's sins were forgiven before he used a third such declaration as part of the healing process. The Son of man saying has a general level of meaning, but it is one which is very much at the limit of usage in this idiom. Most people cannot heal, and do not declare God's forgiveness of the sins of others. The saying is basically about Jesus, who did. He generalized from his own experience, in declaring that in undoing this man's sins by healing him from his paralysis, he was using a power which God had made available to people. He will also have been aware that there were other healers who could do so too, whether or not there were any in Galilee at the time. The use of this indirect idiom was due to Jesus' declaration of his very high position in declaring the forgiveness of sins and healing the man. In other words, this idiom is used here because the saying is not remotely true of everyone, not because it somehow might be.

In Chs 6–8, I discussed more isolated sayings, carrying further discussions which I had previously published. At Mt. 8.19-20, a saying with a very short contextual introduction, the Son of man saying has a general level of meaning which includes the disciple who asked the question and any other disciples who might go on a migratory ministry and have nowhere to stay. At the same time, it refers especially to Jesus, who was in charge of the ministry. The indirect idiom was used because he was in the humiliating position of pointing out that anyone who went on this ministry was liable to have to sleep rough. In Ch. 7, I discussed two or three complex sayings which comment on the situation at the final judgement. All of them make clear that people's attitude to Jesus during the historic ministry will determine their fate at the judgement before the heavenly court. The sayings have a general level of meaning, in that there will be witnesses other than Jesus, as in an earthly court. At the same time, Jesus will be the most important witness, and his extraordinarily high position is underlined by the way in which people's eternal fate is sealed by their attitude to him during the historic ministry. It is this extraordinarily high position which caused him to use this indirect idiomatic way of expressing himself. In Ch. 8 I discussed the only genuine Son of man saying not to be found in Mark or Q. It comes from the historically certain incident of Jesus' betrayal by Judah of Kerioth. Luke picked up the sentence in which he expressed his horror of Judah's identification of him with a kiss, so that he could be arrested. The saying does have a general level of meaning, in that such behaviour does happen elsewhere. At the same time, it refers very particularly to Jesus himself, to the point where it is almost another generalization from his own experience. He was in an extremely humiliating situation, which accounts for his use of this indirect idiom.

In Ch. 9, I offered a fresh discussion of the central group of predictions of Jesus' death and resurrection (Mk 8.31; 9.31; 10.33-34). I found it relatively easy to remove some secondary glossing and reconstruct one genuine prediction from Mk 8.31. Here there was again some general level of meaning, in that all people die, and the saying presupposes belief in the general resurrection. Moreover, there is evidence that disciples, including the inner circle of three, expected to die with Jesus. At the same time, the prediction is primarily about Jesus himself. His death and resurrection were already of central importance during the historic ministry, and became even more central in early Christianity. Hence the need of all three evangelists to gloss the original prediction, and to create further ones on the same lines. Mk 9.31 and 10.33-34 are not separate original predictions. Both were created by the evangelist on the basis of Mk 8.31, the genuine prediction at Mk 14.21, and the actual events of the passion. He may well have received a tradition that Jesus predicted his death and resurrection repeatedly.

In Ch. 10, I discussed all the other Son of man sayings in the synoptic Gospels, and argued that none of them were authentic. In these secondary sayings, ὁ υἱὸς τοῦ ἀνθρώπου is uniformly used by all three evangelists as an important title of Jesus alone *in Greek*. Accordingly, Ch. 11 is devoted to the transition process from (א)נשׁ(א) בר to ὁ υἱὸς τοῦ ἀνθρώπου, and the use of the latter term in secondary sayings. There are three main points. The first is the entirely natural nature of the translation process, which was an excellent creative outburst, not some kind of mistake. The authentic sayings of Jesus, using the term (א)נשׁ(א) בר, cannot be translated into Greek in such a way as to retain the original idiom, because there is no such idiom in Greek. The translators accordingly adopted a strategy. They used ὁ υἱὸς τοῦ ἀνθρώπου in the singular when they thought that the primary reference was to Jesus. Whenever they encountered (א)נשׁ(א) בר referring to anyone else, they used a different term such as ἄνθρωπος, and when they encountered (א)נשׁ(א) בני in the plural, they did not use the plural (οἱ) υἱοὶ τῶν ἀνθρώπων, but preferred other terms, such as ἄνθρωποι.

This was an excellent strategy at three different levels. First of all, it is a literal translation, fully in accordance with literal translations which were normal in the culture of the translators. Secondly, it retained the most important level of meaning of all the original sayings, the primary reference to Jesus himself. Thirdly, it created a major Christological title, and thereby satisfied the need of the target culture to express the centrality of Jesus.

The importance of this third factor is especially well shown by the next point, finding this title in scripture. The two earliest examples are in our oldest gospel. Both Mk 13.26 and 14.62 have clearly made midrashic use of Dan. 7.13 in combination with other scriptural texts. In addition to carrying further the creation of a new Christological title, both passages also predict the Second Coming, which we know from the epistles to have been a major concern of the early church. Moreover, I have now accounted for *all* the Son of man sayings in Mark. This means that our oldest Gospel was completely involved in the processes of the original production of ὁ υἱὸς τοῦ ἀνθρώπου as a major Christological title. All its sayings are accounted for as translations of genuine sayings, secondary development of the translations of two genuine sayings, and midrashic use of Dan. 7.13.

This process was carried further by Matthew. His further midrashic developments of Mk 13.26 and 14.62 show that he was fully aware of the use of Dan. 7.13, with its eschatological context. He also inherited some Q sayings, some of which are genuine sayings of Jesus, and some of which carry further the use of ὁ υἱὸς τοῦ ἀνθρώπου in eschatological contexts. Matthew carried this use further in creating new Son of man sayings.

Luke was also very happy with ὁ υἱὸς τοῦ ἀνθρώπου as a major Christological title. He even continued to use it in eschatological contexts. In so doing, he made quite clear that the End should not have been expected as soon as it had been, and would not come until after the fall of Jerusalem, and perhaps not for some time after that. This makes it the more remarkable that he continued to use ὁ υἱὸς τοῦ ἀνθρώπου in eschatological contexts. He must have felt that it was exceptionally well established in Gospel traditions for him to do this. Like Matthew, he also inherited Son of man sayings from Q material. Like some Marcan sayings, some of these are not set in an eschatological context. Luke accordingly proceeded to create some new sayings which were not eschatologically orientated.

In Ch. 12, I examined the 13 Johannine Son of man sayings. Not one of these is a genuine saying of Jesus, so there is no sign of the idiomatic use of בר (א)נשׁ(א). At the same time, ὁ υἱὸς τοῦ ἀνθρώπου as a major Christological title was derived directly from the synoptic tradition, especially the Gospel of Matthew. A trace of the use of Dan. 7.13 remained in one saying (Jn 5.27), where however it referred to Jesus' judgemental function, not to the Second Coming. The delay of the Parousia was a very serious problem for the Johannine community, locked as it was in severe conflict with 'the Jews'. The first saying in John (1.51) continued the midrashic tradition of Mark and Matthew, but rewrote it completely to replace the Second Coming of the Son of man with the presence of God with him during his earthly ministry. The second saying (Jn 3.13-14) continued midrashic development, using new texts and at the same time rewriting Jesus' predictions of his death. Some of the other sayings are within a loose midrashic context, others are not. All of them fit perfectly into the cultural context of Johannine theology. One example (Jn 12.34) is attributed to 'the crowd' rather than to Jesus himself. This further measures the massive distance between the historical Jesus and the Fourth Gospel. Otherwise, all examples of ὁ υἱὸς τοῦ ἀνθρώπου in this Gospel refer to the humanity of the incarnate Son. This further indicates the success of the production of the Christological title ὁ υἱὸς τοῦ ἀνθρώπου, which was henceforth for centuries to be a major title which indicated the humanity of the incarnate Lord.

I have accordingly proposed a complete solution to the Son of man problem. I hope that it recommends itself to the judgement of others.

BIBLIOGRAPHY

1. Primary Sources

The Hebrew Bible and Versions

תורה נביאים וכתובים *Biblia Hebraica Stuttgartensia* (ed. K. Elliger and W. Rudolph. Stuttgart: Deutsche Bibelstiftung, 1967–77).

Η ΠΑΛΑΙΑ ΔΙΑΘΗΚΗ ΚΑΤΑ ΤΟΥΣ Ο´ Septuaginta: Id est Vetus Testamentum Graece iuxta LXX interpretes (ed. A. Rahlfs; Stuttgart: Deutsche Bibelgesellschaft, 1935).

Septuaginta: Vetus Testamentum Graecum Auctoritate Societatis Litterarum Gottingensis Editum (ed. J. Ziegler *et al.*; Göttingen: Many vols, 1936–).

The Old Testament in Syriac according to the Peshitta Version (ed. P. A. H. de Boer *et al.*; many vols; Leiden: Brill, 1966–).

Translatio Syra Pescitto Veteris Testamenti ex Codice Ambrosiano Sec. fere vi photolithographice edita (curante et adnotante A. M. Ceriani. 2 vols; Milan: Croce, 1876–83).

Biblia sacra iuxta Vulgatam versionem (ed. R. Weber *et al.*; 2 vols; Stuttgart: Württembergische Bibelanstalt, 1969).

Löfgren, O. (ed. & trans.), *Die äthiopische Übersetzung des Propheten Daniel* (Paris: Guethner, 1927).

Dillmann, A. (ed.), *Veteris Testamenti aethiopici tomus quintus, quo continentur Libri Apocryphi* (Berolini: Asher et Socios, 1894).

Sperber, A. (ed.), *The Bible in Aramaic* (5 vols; Leiden: Brill, 1959–73).

Clarke, E. G. *et al.*, *Targum Pseudo-Jonathan of the Pentateuch: Text and Concordance* (Hoboken: Ktav, 1984).

Díez Macho, A. *et al.* (eds and trans.), *Neophyti 1. Targum Palestinense Ms de la Biblioteca Vaticana* (6 vols; Madrid: Consejo Superior de Investigaciones Cientificas, 1968–79).

Lagarde, P. de (ed.), *Hagiographa Chaldaice* (Lipsiae: Teubner, 1873).

Le Déaut, R., and Robert, R., *Targum des Chroniques* (AnBib 51, 2 vols; Rome: Biblical Institute, 1971).

Stec, D. M., *The Text of the Targum of Job: an Introduction and Critical Edition* (AGJU 20. Leiden: Brill, 1994).

Stenning, J. F. (ed.), *The Targum of Isaiah* (Oxford: Clarendon, 1949).

Tal, A. (ed.), התרגום השומרוני לתורה *The Samaritan Targum of the Pentateuch* (3 vols; Tel-Aviv: Tel-Aviv University, 1980–3).

Other Jewish Sources

Joseph Albo, *Sepher Ha-'Ikkarim, Book of Principles*. Critically edited ... with a translation and notes by I. Husik (5 vols; Philadelphia: Jewish Publication Society of America, 1929–30).

Baillet, M., *et al.* (eds), *Les 'Petites Grottes' de Qumran* (DJD III. Oxford: Clarendon, 1962).

Bensly, R. L., with M. R. James, *The Fourth Book of Ezra* (Cambridge: CUP, 1892).

Beyer, K., *Die aramäischen Texte vom Toten Meer* (Göttingen: Vandenhoeck & Ruprecht, 1984).

——*Die aramäischen Texte vom Toten Meer. Ergänzungsband* (Göttingen: Vandenhoeck &

Ruprecht, 1994).

Blackman, P., *Mishanyoth* (7 vols; London: Mishna, 1951–6).

Bogaert, P., *Apocalypse de Baruch: introduction, traduction du syriaque et commentaire* (2 vols; SC 144–5. Paris: Cerf, 1969).

Brooke, G., *et al.*, *Qumran Cave 4. XVII. Parabiblical Texts, Part 3* (DJD XXII. Oxford: Clarendon, 1996).

Broshi, M., *et al.* (eds), *Qumran Cave 4. XIV. Parabiblical Texts, Part 2* (DJD XIX. Oxford: Clarendon, 1995).

Charles, R. H., *The Book of Enoch Translated from Professor Dillmann's Ethiopic Text, emended and revised* ... (Oxford: Clarendon, 1893; 2nd edn., 1912).

——*The Ethiopic Version of the Book of Enoch Edited from Twenty-three mss. together with the fragmentary Greek and Latin Versions* (Oxford: Clarendon, 1906).

——*The Greek Versions of the Testaments of the Twelve Patriarchs* (Oxford: Clarendon, 1908).

Charlesworth, J. H. (ed.), *The Old Testament Pseudepigrapha* (2 vols; New York: Doubleday, 1983–5).

Charlesworth, J. H., *et al.* (eds), *Miscellaneous Texts from the Judaean Desert* (DJD XXXVIII. Oxford: Clarendon, 2000).

Chyutin, M., *The New Jerusalem Scroll from Qumran. A Comprehensive Reconstruction* (trans. R. Fiantz; JSPSup 25. Sheffield: Sheffield Academic, 1997).

Cohen, A. (ed. and trans.), *Hebrew-English Edition of the Babylonian Talmud Minor Tractates* (London: Soncino, 1984).

Cohn, L., *et al.* (eds), *Philonis Alexandrinis opera quae supersunt* (6 vols + index; Berlin: Reimer (index de Gruyter) 1896–1926).

Colson, F. H. *et al.* (eds), *Philo, with an English Translation* (12 vols; LCL; Cambridge, MA/ London: Harvard UP/Heinemann, 1929–62).

Cotton, H. M., and A. Yardeni, *Aramaic, Hebrew and Greek Documentary Texts from Naḥal Ḥever and Other Sites* (DJD XXVII. Oxford: Clarendon, 1997).

De Jonge, M., *et al.* (eds), *The Testaments of the Twelve Patriarchs: A Critical Edition of the Greek Text* (PVTG; Leiden: Brill, 1978).

Dillmann, A., *Liber Enoch aethiopice ad quinque codicum fidem editus* (Leipzig: Vogel, 1851).

——*Das Buch Henoch übersetzt und erklärt* (Leipzig: Vogel, 1853).

Epstein, I., (ed.), תלמוד בבלי *Hebrew-English Edition of the Babylonian Talmud* (32 vols; London: Soncino, 1952–90).

Evans, C. A., *Jesus and His Contemporaries. Comparative Studies* (Leiden: Brill, 1995), pp. 277–80 (18 Benedictions).

Fitzmyer, J. A., *The Genesis Apocryphon of Qumran Cave I: A Commentary* (BibOr 18. Rome, Pontifical Biblical Institute, 1966; BibOr 18A, 2nd edn; 1971).

García Martínez, F., E. J. C. Tigchelaar, and A. S. van der Woude, *Qumran Cave 11. II. 11Q2–18, 11Q20–31* (DJD XXIII. Oxford: Clarendon, 1998).

García Martinez, F., and E. J. C. Tigchelaar (eds), *The Dead Sea Scrolls Study Edition* (2 vols; Leiden: Brill, 1997–8).

Geffcken, J. (ed.), *Die Oracula Sybillina* (GCS VIII. Leipzig: Hinrichs, 1902).

Gropp, D. M. (ed.), *Wadi Daliyeh II. The Samaria Papyri from Wadi Daliyeh* (DJD XXVIII. Oxford: Clarendon, 2001).

Gry, L., *Les dires prophétiques d'Esdras* (2 vols. Paris: Geuthner, 1938).

Hoffmann, A. G., *Das Buch Henoch in vollständiger Übersetzung mit fortlaufenden Kommentar* ... (2 vols; Jena: Croeker, 1833–8).

Jacobson, H. (ed.), *The Exagoge of Ezekiel* (Cambridge: CUP, 1983).

Klein M. L. (ed. and trans.), *Genizah Manuscripts of the Palestinian Targum to the Pentateuch* (2 vols; Cincinatti: Hebrew Union College, 1986).

Knibb, M. (ed. and trans.), *The Ethiopic Book of Enoch. A New Edition in the Light of the Aramaic Dead Sea Fragments* (2 vols; Oxford: Clarendon, 1978).

Laurence, R., *The Book of Enoch the Prophet* ... *now first translated from an Ethiopic manuscript in the Bodleian Library* (Oxford: Parker, 1821).

——*Libri Enoch versio ethiopica* (Oxford: Parker, 1838).

Lauterbach, J. Z. (ed. and trans.), *Mekilta de-Rabbi Ishmael* (3 vols; Philadelphia: Jewish Publication Society of America, 1933–5).

Margulies, M., *Midrash Wayyikra Rabbah: A Critical Edition Based on Manuscripts and Genizah Fragments with Variants and Notes* (5 vols; Jerusalem: Epstein, 1953–60).

Midrash Rabbah, with full commentaries (2 vols; Vilna: Rom, 1878–87).

Milik, J. T., *The Books of Enoch. Aramaic Fragments of Qumrân Cave 4* (Oxford: Clarendon, 1976).

Odeberg, H. (ed.), *3 Enoch, or The Hebrew Book of Enoch* (Cambridge: CUP, 1928).

Puech, E., (ed.), *Qumrân Grotte 4. XXII. Textes Araméens Première Partie. 4Q529–549* (DJD XXXI. Oxford: Clarendon, 2001).

Schäfer, P. and H-J. Becker with G. Reeg *et al.* (eds), *Synopse zum Talmud Yerushalmi.* סינופסיס לתלמוד הירושלמי (7 vols; TSAJ 31, 33, 35, 47, 67, 82, 83. Tübingen: Mohr Siebeck, 1991–2001).

Schmidt, F. (ed. and trans.), *Le Testament grec d'Abraham* (TSAJ 11. Tübingen: Mohr, 1986).

Stuckenbruck, L. T., *The Book of Giants from Qumran. Texts, Translation, and Commentary* (TSAJ 63. Tübingen: Mohr Siebeck, 1997).

Thackeray, H. St.J., *et al.* (eds), *Josephus, with an English Translation* (9 vols; LCL; Cambridge, MA/London: Harvard UP/Heinemann, 1929–53).

Theodor, J., and Ch. Albeck, *Bereschit Rabbah* (3 vols: Berlin: Akademie, Itzkowski & M. Poppelauer, 1903–29).

Uhlig, S. (ed. and trans.), *Das Äthiopische Henochbuch* (JSHRZ V,6. Gütersloh: Gütersloher, 1984).

Vanderkam. J. C. (ed. and trans.), *The Book of Jubilees* (2 vols; CSCO 510–511, SA 87–8; Leuven: Peeters, 1989).

New Testament

Novum Testamentum Graece (ed. B. Aland *et al.* Stuttgart: Deutsche Bibelgesellschaft, 27th edn, 1993).

The New Testament in Syriac (London: British and Foreign Bible Society, 1955).

Aland, K. (ed.), *Synopsis Quattuor Evangeliorum* (Stuttgart: Württembergische Bibelanstalt, 5th edn, 1968).

Kiraz, G. A. (ed.), *Comparative Edition of the Syriac Gospels, Aligning the Sinaiticus, Curetonianus, Peshîttâ and Harklean Versions* (4 vols; NTTS XXI. Leiden: Brill, 1996).

Lewis, A. S. and Gibson, M. D. (eds), *The Palestinian Syriac Lectionary of the Gospels, re-edited from two Sinai MSS. and from P. de Lagarde's edition of the 'Evangeliarium Hierosolymitanum'* (London: Kegan Paul, 1899).

Zuurmond, R., (ed.), *Novum Testamentum Aethiopice: The Synoptic Gospels.* Vol. 1, *General Introduction, Edition of the Gospel of Mark* (Aethiopistiche Forschungen 27; Stuttgart: Steiner, 1989). Pt 3, *The Gospel of Matthew* (Aethiopistiche Forschungen 55; Wiesbaden: Harrassowitz, 2001).

Other Christian Sources

Hennecke, E., *New Testament Apocrypha* (ed. and trans. R. Mc.L. Wilson; 2 vols; London: Lutterworth, 1963–5).

Lightfoot, J. B., *The Apostolic Fathers*, Pt I vol. II (London: Macmillan, 1890).

Robinson, J. M. (ed.), *The Nag Hammadi Library in English* (4th edn, Leiden: Brill, 1996).

Layton, B. *et al.* (eds), *Nag Hammadi Codex II,2–7...* vol. 1; *Gospel according to Thomas* ... (NHS 20. Leiden: Brill, 1989).

Aphrahat, *Demonstrations*, ed. and trans. I. Parisot, in R. Graffin (ed.), *Patrologia Syriaca* vol. I (Paris: Firmin-Didot et Socii, 1894).

Ps-Athanasius, *On the Incarnation of Our Lord Jesus Christ, Against Apollinaris*, *PG* XXVI, cols 1094–1166.

Bardesanes, *Liber Legum Regiorum*, cuius textum syriacum vocalium signis instruxit, latine vertit F.Nau, annotationibus locupletavit Th.Nöldeke, in F. Graffin (ed.), *Patrologia Syriaca* vol. 2 (Paris: Firmin-Didot et Socii, 1907), pp. 490–657.

Ephraem: Assemanus J. S., P. Benedictus and S. E. Assemanus, *Sancti Ephraem Opera Omnia Quae Exstant*, vol. 5 (Rome: Ex Typographia Vaticana, 1740).

Saint Éphrem. Commentaire de L'Evangile Concordant. Texte Syriaque (Ms Chester Beatty 709) (ed. and trans. L. Leloir. CBM 8. Dublin: Hodges Figgis, 1963).

Saint Éphrem. Commentaire de L'Evangile Concordant. Texte Syriaque (Ms Chester Beatty 709). Folios Additionels (ed. and trans. L. Leloir. CBM 8. Leuven/Paris: Peeters, 1990).

Grégoire de Nazianze. Discours 27–31 (Discours Théologiques) (ed. and trans. P. Gallay. SC 250. Paris: Cerf, 1978).

Gregory of Nyssa, *Contra Eunomium Libri*, ed. W. Jaeger, in W. Jaeger (ed.), *Gregorii Nysseni Opera*, vol. II (Leiden: Brill, 1960).

Hippolytus, *Commentaire sur Daniel*. Introduction de G. Bardy, Texte établi et traduit par M. Lefèvre (SC 14. Paris: Cerf, 1947).

——*Refutatio Omnium Haeresium* (ed. M. Marcovich. PTS 25; Berlin: de Gruyter, 1986).

Isho'dad, *The Commentaries of Isho'dad of Merv, Bishop of Ḥadatha (c. 850 A.D.) in Syriac and English* (ed. and trans. M. D. Gibson). Vol. II. *Matthew and Mark in Syriac* (Horae Semiticae VI. Cambridge: CUP, 1911).

Iustini Martyris Dialogus cum Tryphone (ed. M. Marcovich. PTS 47. Berlin: de Gruyter, 1997).

Jacques de Saroug. Homélies Contre les Juifs, ed. and trans. M. Albert, *PO* 38 (Turnhout: Brepols, 1976), pp. 3–242.

Jerome: *S. Hieronymi Presbyteri Opera*. Pars I. *Opera Exegetica*. 5. F. Glorie (ed.), *Commentariorum in Danielem Libri III (IV)* (*CChr. SL* LXXVA. Turnhout: Brepols, 1964).

John of Dalyatha, 'La Collection des Lettres de Jean de Dalyatha. Édition Critique du Texte Syriaque Inédit, Traduction Française, Introduction et Notes', par R. Beulay, *PO* 39 (Turnhout: Brepols, 1978), pp. 254–538.

Narsai's Metrical Homilies on the Nativity, Epiphany ..., ed. and trans. F. G. McLeod, *PO* 40 (Turnhout: Brepols, 1979), pp. 4-193.

J. Frishman, 'The Ways and Means of the Divine Economy. An Edition, Translation and Study of Six Biblical Homilies by Narsai' (Diss., Leiden, 1992).

Philoxeni Mabbugensis, *Dissertationes decem de Uno e Sancta Trinitate... V. Appendices: Tractatus ...*, ed. and trans. M. Brière and R. Graffin, *PO* 41 (Turnhout: Brepols, 1982), pp. 3–143.

Tertullian, *Adversus Marcionem*, ed. and trans. E. Evans (2 vols; Oxford: Clarendon, 1972).

Q. S. F. Tertulliani Opera (2 vols CChr, SL I–II. Turnhout: Brepols, 1954).

Tertullian's Treatise against Praxeas, ed. and trans. E. Evans, with Commentary (London: SPCK, 1948).

ΤΟΥ ΜΑΚΑΡΙΟΥ ΘΕΟΔΩΡΗΤΟΥ ...ΥΠΟΜΝΗΜΑ ΕΙΣ ΤΑΣ ΟΡΑΣΕΙΣ ΤΟΥ ΠΡΟΦΗΤΟΥ ΔΑΝΙΗΛ, *PG* LXXXI, cols 1255–1546.

Theodorus bar Kōnī – Liber Scholium (ed. A. Scher. 2 vols; CSCO 55 and 69: SS 19 and 26. Louvain: Peeters, 1910–12).

Other Primary Sources

Balme, D. M. (ed. and trans.), *Aristotle. History of Animals, Books VII–X* (Cambridge, Massachusetts: Harvard University, 1991).

Baumeister, A. (ed.), *Hymni Homerici*, accedentibus *Epigrammatis* et *Batrachomyamachia*, Homero vulgo attributis (Lipsiae: Teubner, 1838).

Cowley, A., *Aramaic Papyri of the Fifth Century B.C.* (Oxford: Clarendon, 1923).

Donner, H. and W. Röllig, (eds and trans), *Kanaanäische und Aramäische Inschriften* (Wiesbaden: Harrassowitz, 1962–4; 2nd edn, 1966–9).

Edelstein, E. J., and L. Edelstein, *Asclepius. A Collection and Interpretation of the Testimonies* (2 vols; Baltimore: Hopkins, 1945).

England, E. B., (ed.), *The Laws of Plato* (2 vols; Manchester: Manchester Univ., 1921).

Fitzmyer, J. A., 'The Aramaic Letter of King Adon to the Egyptian Pharaoh', *Bib* 46 (1965), pp. 41–55.

Hall, E. (ed. and trans.), *Aeschylus: Persians* (Warminster: Aris & Phillips, 1996).

Hude, C. (ed.), *Herodoti Historiae* (OCT, 2 vols; 3rd edn; Oxford: Clarendon, 1927).

Iacobita, C., *Luciani samosatensis opera* (3 vols; Lipsiae: Teubner, 1853–67).

Jones, S. H., and Powell, J. E. (eds), *Thucydidis Historiae* (OCT, 2 vols; Oxford: Clarendon, 1900–1; emended reprints to 1963).

LiDonnici, L. R., *The Epidaurian Miracle Inscriptions. Text, Translation and Commentary* (Scholars: Atlanta, 1995).

Lindenberger, J. M., *The Aramaic Proverbs of Ahiqar* (Baltimore: Johns Hopkins Univ., 1983).

Pack, R. A. (ed.), *Artemidori Daldiani Onirocriticon Libri V* (Lipsiae: Teubner, 1963).

Peck, A. L., (ed. and trans.), *Aristotle. Historia Animalium* (LCL 3 vols. London/Cambridge, Massachusetts: Heinemann/Harvard University, 1965).

Perrin, B., (ed. and trans.), *Plutarch's Lives* (LCL, 11 vols; London/Cambridge, Massachusetts: Heinemann/Harvard University, 1914–26).

Porten, B., and A. Yardeni, *Textbook of Aramaic Documents from Ancient Egypt, Newly Copied, Edited and Translated into Hebrew and English* (4 vols; Jerusalem: Hebrew University, 1986–99).

Rackham, H., *et al.* (eds and trans), *Plinius Secundus, Caius, Naturalis Historia* (LCL, 10 vols; London/Cambridge, Massachusetts: Heinemann/Harvard University, 1938–62).

2. Secondary Literature: The Son of Man Problem

Abbott, E. A., *Notes on New Testament Criticism* (Diatessarica VII. London: A & C Black, 1907), pp. 140–52, 'The Son of Man'.

——*The Message of the Son of Man* (London: Black, 1909).

——*The 'Son of Man' or Contributions to the Study of the Thought of Jesus* (Cambridge: CUP, 1910).

Angel, A., *Chaos and the Son of Man: The Hebrew Chaoskampf Tradition in the Period 515 BCE to 200 CE* (London: T&T Clark, 2005).

Annus, A., 'Ninurta and the Son of Man', in R. M. Whiting (ed.), *Mythology and Mythologies* (Helsinki: Neo-Assyrian Text Corpus Project, 2001), pp. 7–17.

Appel, H., *Die Selbstbezeichnung Jesu: Der Sohn des Menschen* (Stavenhagen: Beholtz, 1896).

Ashby, E., 'The Coming of the Son of Man', *ExpT* 72, 1960–1, pp. 360–3.

Ashton, J., *Understanding the Fourth Gospel* (Oxford: Clarendon, 1991), Ch. 9.

Aufrecht, W. E., 'The Son of Man Problem as an Illustration of the *techne* of NT Studies', in B. H. McLean (ed.), *Origins and Method. Towards a New Understanding of Judaism and Christianity.* Essays in Honour of John C. Hurd (JSNTSup 86. Sheffield: JSOT, 1993), pp. 282–94.

Bacon, B. W., 'The "Son of Man" in the Usage of Jesus', *JBL* 41 (1922), pp. 143–82.

Badham, F. P. 'The Title "Son of Man"', *TT* 45 (1911), pp. 395–448.

Balz, R. H., *Methodische Probleme der neutestamentlichen Christologie* (WMANT 25. Neukirchen-Vluyn: Neukirchener, 1967).

Barrett, C. K., 'The Background of Mark 10:45', in A. J. B. Higgins (ed.), *New Testament Essays: Studies in Memory of Thomas Walter Manson 1893–1958* (Manchester: Manchester U.P., 1959), pp. 1–18.

——'Stephen and the son of man', in W. Eltester and F. H. Kettler (eds.), *Apophoreta*. Festschrift
     E. Haenchen (BZNW 30. Berlin: Töpelmann, 1964), pp. 32–8.
——'Mark 10.45: a Ransom for Many', *New Testament Essays* (London: SPCK, 1972), pp. 20–6.
Bauckham, R. J., 'The Son of Man: "A Man in my Position" or "Someone"?', *JSNT* 23 (1985), pp.
     23-33.
Bayer, H. F., *Jesus' Predictions of Vindication and Resurrection* (WUNT 2.20. Tübingen: Mohr
     (Siebeck), 1986).
Berger, K., *Die Auferstehung des Propheten und die Erhöhung des Menschensohnes* (SUNT 13.
     Göttingen: Vandenhoeck & Ruprecht, 1976).
Betz, O., *Jesus und das Danielbuch*. Vol 2, *Die Menschensohnworte Jesu und die Zukunftserwartung
     des Paulus (Daniel 7,13-14)* (Frankfurt am Main: Lang, 1985).
Beyschlag, W., *Die Christologie des Neuen Testaments. Ein biblisch-theologischer Versuch* (Berlin:
     Rauh, 1866), pp. 9–34, 'Die Idee des Menschensohns'.
Bietenhard, H., '"Der Menschensohn" – ὁ υἱὸς τοῦ ἀνθρώπου. Sprachliche und
     religionsgeschichtliche Untersuchungen zu einem Begriff der synoptischen Evangelien. I.
     Sprachlicher und religionsgeschichtlicher Teil', *ANRW* II.25.1 (1982), pp. 265–350.
Billerbeck, P., 'Hat der alte Synagoge einen präexistenten Messias gekannt', *Nathanael* 21 (1905),
     pp. 89–150.
Black, M., 'The "Son of Man" in the Old Biblical Literature', *ExpT* 60 (1948-9), pp. 11–15.
——'The "Son of Man" in the Teaching of Jesus', *ExpT* 60 (1948–9), pp. 32–6.
——'The Eschatology of the Similitudes of Enoch', *JTS* NS 3 (1952), pp. 1–10.
——'Servant of the Lord and Son of Man', *SJT* 6 (1953), pp. 1–11.
——'The Son of Man Problem in Recent Research and Debate', *BJRL* 45 (1963), pp. 305–18.
——'The "Son of Man" Passion Sayings in the Gospel Tradition', *ZNW* 60 (1969), pp. 1–8.
——'The Throne-Theophany Prophetic Commission and the "Son of Man": A Study in Tradition-
     History', in R. Hamerton-Kelly and R. Scroggs (eds), *Jews, Greeks and Christians: Essays in
     Honor of W. D. Davies* (Leiden: Brill, 1976), pp. 57–73.
——'The "Parables" of Enoch (1 En 37-71) and the "Son of Man"', *ExpT* 88 (1976–7), pp. 5–8.
——'Jesus and the Son of Man', *JSNT* 1 (1978), pp. 4–18.
——'Aramaic Barnâshâ and the "Son of Man"', *ExpT* 95 (1983–4), pp. 200–6.
——'The Aramaic Dimension in Q with Notes on Luke 17.22 and Matthew 24.26 (Luke 17.23)',
     JSNT 40 (1990), pp. 33–41.
——'The Messianism of the Parables of Enoch: Their Date and Contributions to Christological
     Origins', in J. H. Charlesworth (ed.), *THE MESSIAH. Developments in Earliest Judaism and
     Christianity* (Minneapolis: Fortress, 1992), pp. 145–68.
Bleibtreu, W., 'Jesu Selbstbenennung als der Menschensohn', *Theologische Studien und Kritiken*
     99 (1926), pp. 164–211.
Bock, D. L., 'The Son of Man Seated at God's Right Hand and the Debate over Jesus' "Blasphemy"',
     in J. B. Green and M. Turner, *Jesus of Nazareth: Lord and Christ. Essays on the Historical
     Jesus and New Testament Christology* (Eerdmanns/Paternoster: Grand Rapids/Carlisle, 1994),
     pp. 181–91.
Boers, H., 'Where Christology is Real. A Survey of Recent Research on New Testament Christology',
     Interpretation 26 (1972), pp. 300–27 (302–15).
Bolten, J. A., *Der Bericht des Matthäus von Jesu dem Messia* (Altona: Staben, 1792).
Boobyer, G. H., 'Mk II,10a and the Interpretation of the Healing of the Paralytic', *HTR* 47 (1954),
     pp. 115–20.
Borgen, P., 'Some Jewish Exegetical Traditions as Background for Son of Man Sayings in John's
     Gospel (Jn 3,13-14 and context)', in M. de Jonge (ed.), *L'Evangile de Jean: Sources, rédaction,
     théologie* (BETL 44. Gembloux/Leuven: Duculot/Leuven U.P., 1977), pp. 243–58.
Borsch, F. H., 'The Son of Man', *ATR* 45 (1963), pp. 174–90.
——*The Son of Man in Myth and History* (London: SCM, 1967).
——'Mark XIV.62 and 1 Enoch LXII.5', *NTS* 14 (1968), pp. 565–7.
——*The Christian and Gnostic Son of Man* (SBT ²14. London: SCM, 1970).

——'Further Reflections on "The Son of Man": The Origins and Development of the Title', in J. H. Charlesworth (ed.), *THE MESSIAH. Developments in Earliest Judaism and Christianity* (Minneapolis: Fortress, 1992), pp. 130–44.

Bowker, J., 'The Son of Man', *JTS NS* 28 (1977), pp. 19–48.

——*The Religious Imagination and the Sense of God* (Oxford: Clarendon, 1978), Ch. II.2.

Bowman, J. W., 'The Background of the Term "Son of Man"', *ExpT* 59 (1947–8), pp. 283–8.

——'David, Jesus Son of David and Son of Man', *Abr-Nahrain* 27 (1989), pp. 1–22.

Broadhead, E. K., *Naming Jesus: Narrative Christology in the Gospel of Mark* (Sheffield: Sheffield Academic, 1999), Ch. 13.

Brown, J. P., 'The Son of Man: "This Fellow"', *Bib* 58 (1977), pp. 361–87.

Bruce, F. F., 'The Background to the Son of Man Sayings', in H. H.Rowdon (ed.), *Christ the Lord. Studies in Christology presented to Donald Guthrie* (Leicester: IVP, 1982), pp. 50–70.

Bulcock, H., 'Was the Double Use of "Son of Man" a Factor in the Deification of Jesus?', *Congregational Quarterly* 17 (1939), pp. 44–55.

Burkett, D., *The Son of Man in the Gospel of John* (JSNTSup 56. Sheffield: Sheffield Academic, 1991).

——'The Nontitular Son of Man: A History and Critique', *NTS* 40 (1994), pp. 504–21.

——*The Son of Man Debate. A History and Evaluation* (SNTSMS 107. Cambridge: CUP, 1999).

Burkill, T. A., 'The Hidden Son of Man in St. Mark's Gospel', *ZNW* 52 (1961), pp. 189–213, reprinted in T. A. Burkill, *New Light on the Earliest Gospel: Seven Markan Studies* (Ithaca: Cornell, 1972), pp. 1–38.

Buth, R., 'A More Complete Semitic Background for בר־אנשא, "Son of Man"', in C. A. Evans and J. A. Sanders (eds), *The Function of Scripture in Early Jewish and Christian Tradition* (JSNTSup 154. Sheffield: Sheffield Academic, 1998), pp. 176–89.

Cadoux, A. T., 'The Son of Man', *The Interpreter* 18 (1921–2), pp. 202–14.

Campbell, J. Y., 'The Origin and Meaning of the Term Son of Man', *JTS* 48 (1947), pp. 145–55.

Caquot, A., 'Remarques sur les chapitres 70 et 71 du livre éthiopien d'Hénoch', in *Apocalypses et Théologie de l'Espérance. Congrès de Toulouse (1975)* (LD 95. Paris: Cerf, 1977), pp. 111–22.

Caragounis, C. C., *The Son of Man. Vision and Interpretation* (WUNT 38; Tübingen: Mohr (Siebeck), 1986).

——'Kingdom of God, Son of Man and Jesus' Self-Understanding', *TynBul* 40 (1989), pp. 3–23, 223–38.

Casey, P. M., 'The Son of Man Problem', *ZNW* 67 (1976), pp. 147–54.

——'The Use of the Term "son of man" in the Similitudes of Enoch', *JSJ* 7 (1976), pp. 11–29.

——'The Corporate Interpretation of "one like a son of man" at the time of Jesus', *NovT* 18 (1976), pp. 167–80.

——*Son of Man. The Interpretation and Influence of Daniel 7* (London: SPCK, 1980).

——'Aramaic Idiom and Son of Man Sayings', *ExpT* 96 (1984–5), pp. 233–6.

——'The Jackals and the Son of Man (Matt. 8.20//Luke 9.58)', *JSNT* 23 (1985), pp. 3–22.

——'General, Generic and Indefinite: The Use of the Term "Son of Man" in Aramaic Sources and in the Teaching of Jesus', *JSNT* 29 (1987), pp. 21–56.

——*From Jewish Prophet to Gentile God. The Origins and Development of New Testament Christology* (The Cadbury Lectures at the University of Birmingham, 1985–6. Cambridge/ Louisville: James Clarke/Westminster/John Knox, 1991), pp. 46–56.

——'Method in our Madness, and Madness in their Methods. Some Approaches to the Son of Man Problem in Recent Scholarship', *JSNT* 42 (1991), pp. 17–43.

——'The Use of the Term (א)נש(א) בר in the Aramaic Translations of the Hebrew Bible', *JSNT* 54 (1994), pp. 87–118.

——'Idiom and Translation. Some Aspects of the Son of Man Problem', *NTS* 41 (1995), pp. 164-82.

——*Aramaic Sources of Mark's Gospel* (SNTSMS 102. Cambridge: CUP, 1998), pp. 111–121, 130–2, 163–6, 211–18, 233.

——*An Aramaic Approach to Q: Sources for the Gospels of Matthew and Luke* (SNTSMS 122. Cambridge: CUP, 2002), pp. 133–42, 177–82.

——'Aramaic Idiom and the Son of Man Problem: a Response To Owen and Shepherd', *JSNT* 25 (2002), pp. 3–32.

—— 'The Aramaic Background of Mark 9:11: A Response to J. K. Aitken, *JTS NS* 55 (2004), pp. 92–102.

Catchpole, D. R., 'The Son of Man's Search for Faith (Luke xviii 8b)', *NovT* 19 (1977), pp. 81–104.

——'The Poor on Earth and the Son of Man in Heaven. A Re-appraisal of Matthew xxv.31-46', *BJRLM* 61 (1979), pp. 355–97.

——'The Angelic Son of Man in Lk 12.8', *NovT* 24 (1982), pp. 255–65.

Ceroke, C. P., 'Is Mk 2,10 a Saying of Jesus?', *CBQ* 22 (1960), pp. 369–90.

Chilton, B. D., 'The Son of Man: Human and Heavenly', in *The Four Gospels 1992*. Festschrift Frans Neirynck, ed. F. van Segbroeck *et al.* (3 vols; Leuven: Leuven U.P./Peeters, 1992), vol. I, pp. 203–18.

——'The Son of Man – Who Was He?', *Bible Review* 12 (1996), pp. 34–48.

——'(The) Son of (the) Man, and Jesus', in B. Chilton and C. A. Evans (eds), *Authenticating the Words of Jesus* (Leiden: Brill, 1999), pp. 259–87.

Christensen, J., 'Le fils de l'homme s'en va, ainsi qu'il est écrit de lui', *ST* 10 (1957), pp. 28–39.

Chronis, H. L., 'To Reveal and to Conceal: A Literary-Critical Perspective on "the Son of Man" in Mark', *NTS* 51 (2005), pp. 159–81.

Ciholas, P., '"Son of Man" and Hellenistic Christology', *RevExp* 79 (1982), pp. 487–501.

Coke, P. T., 'The Angels of the Son of Man', in A. Fuchs (ed.), *Probleme der Forschung* (SUNT 3. Vienna/Munich: Herold, 1978), pp. 91–8.

Collins, A.Y., 'The Origin of the Designation of Jesus as "Son of Man"', *HTR* 80 (1987), pp. 391–407.

——'Daniel 7 and Jesus', *Journal of Theology* 93 (1989), pp. 5–19.

——'The Son of Man Sayings in the Sayings Source', in M. P. Horgan and P. J. Kobelski (eds), *To Touch the Text. Biblical and Related Studies in Honor of J. A. Fitzmyer S.J.* (New York: Crossroad, 1989), pp. 369–89.

——'Daniel 7 and the Historical Jesus', in H. W. Attridge *et al.* (eds), *Of Scribes and Scrolls: Studies on the Hebrew Bible, Intertestamental Judaism and Christian Origins presented to John Strugnell* (Lanham/New York/London: University Press of America, 1990) pp. 181–93.

——'The Apocalyptic Son of Man Sayings', in B. Pearson *et al.* (eds), *The Future of Early Christianity: Essays in Honor of Helmut Koester* (Minneapolis: Fortress, 1991), pp. 220–8.

——'The "Son of Man" Tradition and the Book of Revelation', in J. H. Charlesworth (ed.), *THE MESSIAH. Developments in Earliest Judaism and Christianity* (Minneapolis: Fortress, 1992), pp. 536–68.

Collins, J. J., 'The Heavenly Representative: The "Son of Man" in the Similitudes of Enoch', in J. J. Collins and G. W. E. Nickelsburg (eds), *Ideal Figures in Ancient Judaism: Profiles and Paradigms* (Chico: Scholars, 1980), pp. 111–33.

——'The Son of Man in First Century Judaism', *NTS* 38 (1992), pp. 448–66. Repr. J. J. Collins, *The Scepter and the Star: The Messiahs of the Dead Sea Scrolls and Other Ancient Literature* (New York: Doubleday, 1995), pp. 173–94.

Colpe, C., 'Der Begriff "Menschensohn" und die Methode der Erforschung messianischer Prototypen', *Kairos* 11 (1969), pp. 241–63; 12 (1970), pp. 81–113; 13 (1971), pp. 1–17; 14 (1972), pp. 241–57.

——ὁ υἱὸς τοῦ ἀνθρώπου, *TWNT* VIII (1969), pp. 400–77: Trans. G. W. Bromiley, *TDNT* VIII (1972), pp. 400–77.

——'Neue Untersuchungen zum Menschensohn-Problem', *TRev* 77 (1971), cols 353–72.

Coppens, J., *La Relève apocalyptique du Messianisme royal*: vol. III, *Le Fils de l'homme néotestamentaire* (BETL 55. Leuven: Leuven UP/Peeters, 1981): vol. II, *Le Fils d'homme vétéro- et intertestamentaire* (BETL 61. Leuven: Leuven U.P./Peeters, 1983).

Cortés, J. B., and Gatti, F. M., 'The Son of Man or the Son of Adam', *Bib* 49 (1968), pp. 457–502.

Creed, J. M., 'The Heavenly Man', *JTS* 26 (1925), pp. 113–36.

Cullmann, O., Die Christologie des Neuen Testaments (Tübingen: Mohr (Siebeck), 1957): *The Christology of the New Testament* (trans. S. C. Guthrie and C. A. M. Hall; London: SCM, 1959), Ch. 6, 'Jesus the Son of Man'.

Dalman, G. H., *Die Worte Jesu; mit Berücksichtigung des nachkanonischen jüdischen Schrifttums und der aramäischen Sprache.* Bd I. *Einleitung und wichtige Begriffe* (Leipzig, 1898. There was no second volume. 2nd edn, 1930): *The Words of Jesus Considered in the Light of Post-Biblical Jewish Writings and the Aramaic Language. I. Introduction and Fundamental Ideas* (trans. D. M. Kay; Edinburgh: T&T Clark, 1902).

Davies, M., Rhetoric and Reference in the Fourth Gospel (JSNTSup 69. Sheffield: JSOT Press, 1992), Ch. 8, 'Jesus, the Son of Man'.

Dhanis, 'De filio hominis in Vetere Testamento et in Judaismo', *Gregorianum* 45 (1964), pp. 5–59.

Díez Macho, A., 'L'usage de la troisième personne au lieu de la première dans le Targum', in P. Casseti, O. Keel and S. Schenker (eds), *Mélanges Dominique Barthélemy* (Fribourg/Göttingen: Universitas/Vandenhoeck & Ruprecht, 1981), pp. 61–90.

——'La Christologia del Hijo del Hombre y el uso de la tercera persona en vez de la primera', *Scripta Theologica* 14 (1982), pp. 189–201.

Doble, P., 'The Son of Man Saying in Stephen's Witnessing: Acts 6.8–8.2', *NTS* 31 (1985), pp. 68–84.

Donahue, J. R., 'Recent Studies on the Origin of "Son of Man" in the Gospels', *CBQ* 48 (1986), pp. 484–98.

Doran, R., 'The Divinisation of Disorder: The Trajectory of Matt. 8:20//Luke 9:58//Gos. Thomas 86', in B. Pearson *et al.* (eds), *The Future of Early Christianity: Essays in Honor of Helmut Koester* (Minneapolis: Fortress, 1991), pp. 210–19.

Draper, J. A., 'The Development of "the Sign of the Son of Man" in the Jesus Tradition', *NTS* 39 (1993), pp. 1–21.

Dreyer, Y., 'The institutionalization of Jesus' charismatic authority': "Son of Man" as case study', *Hervormde Teologiese Studies* 56 (2000), pp. 1057–78.

Driver, S. R., 'Son of Man', in J. Hastings (ed.), *A Dictionary of the Bible*, vol. iv (Edinburgh: T&T Clark, 1902), pp. 579–89.

Drummond, J., 'The Use and Meaning of the Phrase "The Son of Man" in the Synoptic Gospels', *JTS* 2 (1901), pp. 350–8, 539–71.

Duncan, G. S., *Jesus, Son of Man. Studies Contributory to a Modern Portrait* (London: Nisbet, 1947), chs xi-xiii.

Dunn, J. D. G., *Christology in the Making* (London: SCM, 1980), Ch. III, 'The Son of Man'.

——'"Son of God" as "Son of Man" in the Dead Sea Scrolls? A Response to John Collins on 4Q246', in S. E. Porter and C. A. Evans (eds), *The Scrolls and the Scriptures: Qumran Fifty Years After* (JSPSup 26. Sheffield: Sheffield Academic, 1997), pp. 198–210.

——'The Danielic Son of Man in the New Testament', in J. J. Collins and P. W. Flint (eds), *The Book of Daniel. Composition and Reception* (VTSup 83. 2001), vol. 2; pp. 528–49.

Dupont, G., *Le Fils de l'Homme: Essai Historique et Critique* (Paris: Fischbacher, 1924).

Dupont, J., '"Vous n'aurez pas achevé les villes d'Israël avant que le Fils de l'homme ne vienne" (Mt 10.23)', *NovT* 2 (1958), pp. 228–44.

Edwards, R. A., 'The Eschatological Correlative as a *Gattung* in the New Testament', *ZNW* 60 (1969), pp. 9–20.

Eerdmans, B. D., 'De oorsprong van de uitdrukking "Zoon des Menschen" als Evangelische Messiastitel', *TT* 28 (1894), pp. 153–76.

——'De uitdrukking "Zoon des menschen" in het boek "Henoch"', *TT* 29 (1895), pp. 48–71.

Eggler, J., *Influences and Traditions Underlying the Vision of Daniel 7:2-14* (OBO 177. Fribourg/Göttingen: Universitätsverlag Freibourg/, Vandenhoeck & Ruprecht, 2000).

Elliott, J. H., 'Man and the Son of Man in the Gospel According to Mark', in T. Rendtorff and A.

Rich (eds), *Humane Gesellschaft: Beiträge zu ihrer sozialen Gestaltung. Zum 70.Geburtstag von Prof. D. Heinz-Dietrich Wendland* (Zurich: Zwingli, 1970), pp. 47–59.

Emerton, J. A., 'The Origin of the Son of Man Imagery', *JTS NS* 9 (1958), pp. 225–42.

Ferch, A. J., *The Son of Man in Daniel 7* (Berrien Springs: Andrews Univ., 1983).

Feuillet, A., 'Le Fils de l'homme de Daniel et la Tradition Biblique', *RB* 60 (1953), pp. 170–202, 321–46.

——'L'*Exousia* du Fils de l'Homme', *RevScRel* 42 (1954), pp. 161–92.

——'Les origines et la signification de Mt 10.23b: Contribution à l'étude du problème eschatologique', *CBQ* 23 (1961), pp. 182–98.

——'Le Triomphe du Fils de l'homme d'après la déclaration du Christ aux Sanhédrites (Mc., XIV,62; Mt., XXVI,64; Lc., XXII,69)', in E. Massaux (ed.), *La venue du Messie* (Bruges: Desclée de Brouwer, 1962), pp. 149–71.

Fiebig, P., *Der Menschensohn: Jesu Selbstbezeichnung* (Tübingen: Mohr (Siebeck), 1901).

Fitzmyer, J. A., 'Another View of the "Son of Man" Debate', *JSNT* 4 (1979), pp. 58–68.

——'The New Testament Title "Son of Man" Philologically Considered', in J. A. Fitzmyer, *A Wandering Aramean. Collected Aramaic Essays* (SBLMS 25. Missoula: Scholars, 1979), pp. 143–60.

Fleddermann, H. T., 'The Q Saying on Confessing and Denying', *SBL Seminar Papers* 26 (Atlanta: Scholars, 1987), pp. 606–16.

Fletcher-Louis, C. H. T., *Luke-Acts: Angels, Christology and Soteriology* (WUNT 2.94. Tübingen: Mohr Siebeck, 1997).

——'The High Priest as Divine Mediator in the Hebrew Bible: Dan 7:13 as a Test Case', *SBLSP* 36 (Atlanta: Scholars, 1997), pp. 161–93.

——'The Revelation of the Sacral Son of Man. The Genre, History of Religions Context and the Meaning of the Transfiguration', in F. Avemarie and H. Lichtenberger (eds), *Auferstehung – Resurrection: the Fourth Durham-Tübingen Research Symposium: Resurrection, Transfiguration and Exaltation in Old Testament, Ancient Judaism and Early Christianity* (Tübingen: Mohr-Siebeck, 2001), pp. 247–98.

Ford, J. M., '"The Son of Man" – A Euphemism?', *JBL* 87 (1968), pp. 257–66.

Formesyn, R. E. C., 'Was There a Pronominal Connection for the "Bar Nasha" Self-designation?', *NovT* 8 (1966), pp. 1–35.

Freed, E. D., 'The Son of Man in the Fourth Gospel', *JBL* 86 (1967), pp. 402–9.

Fuller, R., 'The Son of Man: A Reconsideration', in D. E. Groh and R. Jewett (eds), *The Living Text: Essays in Honor of Ernest W. Saunders* (Lanham: University Press of America, 1985), pp. 207–17.

Gaillardus, J., *Specimen Quaestionum in Novum Instrumentum de Filio Hominis* (Lugduni-Batavorum: Lopez, 1684).

Gathercole, S., 'The Justification of Wisdom (Matt 11.19b/Luke 7.35)', *NTS* 49 (2003), pp. 476–88.

——'The Son of Man in Mark's Gospel', *ExpT* 115, 2003–4, pp. 366–72.

—Geist, H., *Menschensohn und Gemeinde. Eine redaktionskritische Untersuchung zur Menschensohnsprädikation im Matthäusevangelium* (FzB 57. Würzburg: Echter, 1986).

Gelston, A., 'A Sidelight on the "Son of Man"', *SJT* 22 (1969), pp. 189–96.

Gerleman, G., *Der Menschensohn* (Leiden: Brill, 1983).

Gese, H., 'Die Weisheit, der Menschensohn und die Ursprünge der Christologie als konsequente Entfaltung der biblischen Theologie', *SEÅ* 44 (1979), pp. 77–114.

Glasson, T. F., 'The Ensign of the Son of Man (Matt. xxiv.30)', *JTS NS* 15 (1964), pp. 299–300.

Goppelt, L., 'Zum Problem des Menschensohns. Das Verhältnis von Leidens- und Parusieankündigung', in H. Sierig (ed.), *Mensch und Menschensohn. Festschrift für Bischof Professor D. Karl Witte* (Hamburg: Wittig, 1963), pp. 20–32.

Goulder, M., 'Psalm 8 and the Son of Man', *NTS* 48 (2002), pp. 18–29.

Grelot, P., 'Jésus, Fils de l'homme', *RevThom* 105 (2005), pp. 89–103.

Grotius, H., *Annotationes in quatuor Evangelia & Acta Apostolorum* in H. Grotii *Opera Omnia*

Theologica (Amsterdam: Blaev, 1679), Tom II vol. I.

Guillet, J., 'Le Fils de l'homme. Titre eschatologique ou mission prophétique?', *RSR* 88 (2000), pp. 615–38.

Hahn, F., *Christologische Hoheitstitel* (FRLANT 83. Göttingen: Vandenhoeck & Ruprecht, 1963): *The Titles of Jesus in Christology* (trans. H. Knight and G. Ogg; London: Lutterworth, 1969), Ch. 1.

Ham, C., 'The Title "Son of Man" in the Gospel of John', *Stone-Campbell Journal* 1 (1998), pp. 67–84. (n.v.)

Hampel, V., *Menschensohn und historischer Jesus. Ein Rätselwort als Schlüssel zum messianischen Selbstverständnis Jesu* (Neukirchen-Vluyn: Neukirchener, 1990).

Hare, D. R. A., *The Son of Man Tradition* (Minneapolis: Fortress, 1990).

Haufe, G., 'Das Menschensohn-Problem in der gegenwärtigen wissenschaftlichen Diskussion', *EvT* 26 (1966), pp. 130–41.

Haupt, P., 'Hidalgo and Filius Hominis', *JBL* 40 (1921), pp. 167–70.

——'The Son of Man = hic homo = ego', *JBL* 40 (1921), p. 183.

Hay, L. S., 'The Son of Man in Mark 2.10 and 2.28', *JBL* 89 (1970), pp. 69–75.

Hayman, A. P., 'The "Man from the Sea" in 4 Ezra 13', *JJS* 49 (1998), pp. 1–16.

Higgins, A. J. B., 'Son of Man – *Forschung* since "The Teaching of Jesus"', in A. J. B. Higgins (ed.), *New Testament Essays: Studies in Memory of Thomas Walter Manson 1893–1958* (Manchester: Manchester U.P., 1959), pp. 119–35.

——*Jesus and the Son of Man* (London: Lutterworth, 1964).

——'Is the Son of Man Problem Insoluble?', in E. E. Ellis and M. Wilcox (eds), *Neotestamentica and Semitica: Studies in Honour of Matthew Black* (Edinburgh: T&T Clark, 1969), pp. 70–87.

——*The Son of Man in the Teaching of Jesus* (SNTSMS 39. Cambridge: CUP, 1980).

Hill, D., '"Son of Man" in Psalm 80 v. 17', *NovT* 15 (1973), pp. 261–9.

Hodgson, P. C., 'The Son of Man and the Problem of Historical Knowledge', *JR* 41 (1961), pp. 91–108.

Hoffmann, P., 'Mk 8,31. Zur Herkunft und markinischen Rezeption einer alten Überlieferung', in P. Hoffmann (ed.), *Orientierung an Jesus. Zur Theologie der Synoptiker. Für Josef Schmid* (Freiburg/Basel/Wien: Herder, 1973), pp. 170–204.

——'Der Menschensohn in Lukas 12.8', *NTS* 44 (1991), pp. 357–79.

——'Jesus versus Menschensohn. Mt 10,32f und die synoptische Menschensohnüberlieferung', in L. Oberlinner and P. Fiedler (eds), *Salz der Erde – Licht der Welt. Exegetische Studien zum Matthäusevangelium.* Festschrift für Anton Vögtle zum 80. Geburtstag (Stuttgart: Katholisches Bibelwerk, 1991), pp. 165–202.

——'QR und der Menschensohn. Eine vorläufige Skizze', in *The Four Gospels 1992.* Festschrift Frans Neirynck, ed. F. van Segbroeck *et al.* (3 vols; Leuven: Leuven U.P./Peeters, 1992), vol I; pp. 421–56.

Hooker, M. D., *The Son of Man in Mark* (London: SPCK, 1967).

——'Is the Son of Man problem really insoluble?', in E. Best and R. McL. Wilson (eds), *Text and Interpretation. Studies in the New Testament presented to Matthew Black*, (Cambridge: CUP, 1979), pp. 155–68.

——'The Son of Man and the Synoptic Problem', in *The Four Gospels 1992.* Festschrift Frans Neirynck, ed. F. van Segbroeck *et al.* (3 vols; Leuven: Leuven U.P./Peeters, 1992), vol. I; pp. 189–201.

Horbury, W., 'The Messianic Associations of "The Son of Man"', *JTS NS* 36 (1985), pp. 34–55.

Howard, J. Keir, *Disease and Healing in the New Testament: An Analysis and Interpretation* (Lanham: Univ. Press of America, 2001).

Jackson, D. R., 'The Priority of the Son of Man Sayings', *WTJ* 47 (1985), pp. 83–96.

Jacobson, A. D., 'Apocalyptic and the Synoptic Sayings Source Q', in F. van Segbroeck *et al.* (eds), *The Four Gospels 1992.* Festschrift Frans Neirynck (3 vols; Leuven: Leuven U.P./Peeters, 1992), vol. I, pp. 403–19.

Järvinen, A., 'The Son of Man and His Followers: A Q Portrait of Jesus', in D. Rhoads and K.

Syreeni (eds), *Characterization in the Gospels. Reconceiving Narrative Criticism* (JSNTSup 184. Sheffield: Sheffield Academic, 1999), pp. 180–222.

James, J. C., 'The Son of Man: Origin and Uses of the Title', *ExpT* 36 (1924–5), pp. 309–14.

Jansen, H. L., *Die Henochgestalt. Eine vergleichende religionsgeschichtliche Untersuchung* (Oslo: Dybwad, 1939).

Jay, E. G., *Son of Man/Son of God* (London: SPCK, 1965), Ch. 4.

Jennings, T. W., 'The Martyrdom of the Son of Man', in T. W. Jennings (ed.), *TEXT AND LOGOS. The Humanistic Interpretation of the New Testament* (Atlanta: Scholars, 1990), pp. 229–43.

Jeremias, J., 'Die älteste Schicht der Menschensohn-Logien', *ZNW* 58 (1967), pp. 159–72.

——*New Testament Theology.* Vol. I. *The Proclamation of Jesus* (trans. J. Bowden; London: SCM, 1971), pp. 250–99.

——'Die Drei-Tage-Worte der Evangelien', in G. Jeremias *et al.* (eds) *Tradition und Glaube. Das frühe Christentum in seiner Umwelt. Festgabe für K.G. Kuhn zum 65. Geburtstag* (Göttingen: Vandenhoeck & Ruprecht, 1971).

Kearns, R., *Vorfragen zur Christologie.* Vol. 1. *Morphologische und Semasiologische Studie zur Vorgeschichte eines christologischen Hoheitstitels* (Tübingen: Mohr (Siebeck), 1978); Vol. 2. *Überlieferungsgeschichtliche und Rezeptionsgeschichtliche Studie zur Vorgeschichte eines christologischen Hoheitstitels* (Tübingen: Mohr (Siebeck), 1980); Vol. 3. *Religionsgeschichtliche und Traditionsgeschichtliche Studie zur Vorgeschichte eines christologischen Hoheitstitels* (Tübingen: Mohr (Siebeck), 1982).

——*Das Traditionsgefüge um den Menschensohn. Ursprünglicher Gehalt und älteste Veränderung im Urchristentum* (Tübingen: Mohr (Siebeck), 1986);

——*Die Entchristologisierung des Menschensohnes. Die Übertragung des Traditionsgefüges um den Menschensohn auf Jesus* (Tübingen: Mohr (Siebeck), 1988).

——*Mutmaßungen zur Christologie.* Part 1, *Der gewaltsam getötete und nach dem Tod verherrlichte Gerechte* (Tübingen: Gulde-Druck Gmbh, 2002); Part 2. Ὁ υἱὸς τοῦ ἀνθρώπου *als hoheitstitulares Wortgebilde* (Tübingen: Gulde-Druck Gmbh, 2003); Part 3. *Die Epiphanie des Menschensohnes in der Welt: Die transzendent-eschatologische Epiphanie des Menschensohnes* (Tübingen: Gulde-Druck Gmbh, 2003); Part 4. Ὁ κύριος *als Hoheitstitel* (Tübingen: Gulde-Druck Gmbh, 2004); Part 5. *Der Allherr und die Übrigbleibenden* (Tübingen: Gulde-Druck Gmbh, 2004).

Kertelge, K., 'Die Vollmacht des Menschensohnes zur Sündenvergebung (Mk 2,10)', in P. Hoffmann (ed.), *Orientierung an Jesus. Zur Theologie der Synoptiker. Für Josef Schmid* (Freiburg/Basel/ Wien: Herder, 1973), pp. 205–13.

Kim, S., *'The "Son of Man'" as the Son of God* (WUNT 30. Tübingen: Mohr Siebeck, 1983).

Kingsbury, J. D., 'The Title "Son of Man" in Matthew's Gospel', *CBQ* 37 (1975), pp. 193–202.

Kinniburgh, E., 'The Johannine "Son of Man"', *SE* 4 (1968), pp. 64–71.

Klöpper, A., 'Der Sohn des Menschen in den synoptischen Evangelien', *ZWT* 42 (1899), pp. 161–86.

Kmiecik, U., *Der Menschensohn im Markusevangelium* (FzB 81. Würzberg: Echter, 1997).

Kraeling, C. H., *Anthropos and Son of Man: A Study in the Religious Syncretism of the Ancient Orient* (*Columbia University Oriental Studies* 25. New York: Columbia U.P., 1927).

Kümmel, W. G., 'Jesusforschung seit 1965. V. Der persönliche Anspruch Jesu ... Die Menschensohnfrage', *TRu* 45 (1980), pp. 40–84.

——'Jesus der Menschensohn?' *Sitzungsberichte der Wissenschaftlichen Gesellschaft an der Johann Wolfgang Goethe-Universität Frankfurt am Main XX,3* (Stuttgart: Steiner, 1984).

Künzi, M., *Das Naherwartungslogion Matthäus 10,23. Geschichte seiner Auslegung* (BGBE 9. Tübingen: Mohr (Siebeck), 1970).

Kvanvig, H. S., 'Henoch und der Menschensohn. Das Verhältnis von Hen 14 zu Dan 7', *ST* 38 (1984), pp. 101–33.

——*Roots of Apocalyptic. The Mesopotamian Background of the Enoch Figure and of the Son of Man* (WMANT 61. Neukirchen-Vluyn: Neukirchener, 1988).

Legasse, S., 'Jésus historique et le Fils de l'Homme: Aperçu sur les opinions contemporaines', in

M. Delcor *et al.*, *Apocalypses et Théologie de l'Espérance. Congrès de Toulouse (1975)*, (LD 95. Paris: Cerf, 1977), pp. 271–98.

Leivestad, R., 'Der apokalyptische Menschensohn ein theologisches Phantom', *ASTI* 6 (1967–8), pp. 49–105.

——'Exit the Apocalyptic Son of Man', *NTS* 18 (1971–2), pp. 243–67.

Lemcio, E. E., '"Son of Man", "Pitiable Man", "Rejected Man": Equivalent Expressions in the Old Greek of Daniel', *TynBul* 56 (2005), pp. 43–60.

Létourneau, P., *Jésus Fils de l'Homme et Fils de Dieu. Jean 2,23–3,36 et la double christologie johannique* (Montréal/Paris: Bellarmin/Cerf, 1993).

Levy, B. B., 'Why *Bar-nash* Does Not Mean "I"', in B.Walfish (ed.), *The Frank Talmage Memorial Volume I* (Haifa: Haifa Univ., 1993), 85–101.

Lietzmann, H., *Der Menschensohn. Ein Beitrag zur neutestamentlichen Theologie* (Freiburg i.B./ Leipzig: Mohr (Siebeck), 1896).

Lindars, B., 'The Son of Man in the Johannine Christology', in B. Lindars and S. S. Smalley (eds), *Christ and the Spirit in the New Testament. Studies in honour of C. F. D. Moule* (Cambridge: CUP, 1973), pp. 43–60.

——'The Apocalyptic Myth and the Death of Christ', *BJRLM* 57 (1974–5), pp. 366–87.

——'Re-Enter the Apocalyptic Son of Man', *NTS* 22 (1975–6), pp. 52–72.

——'Jesus as Advocate: A Contribution to the Christology Debate', *BJRLM* 62 (1979–80), pp. 476–97.

——'The New Look on the Son of Man', *BJRLM* 63 (1980–1), pp. 437–62.

——*Jesus Son of Man. A Fresh Examination of the Son of Man Sayings in the Gospels in the Light of Recent Research* (London: SPCK, 1983).

——'Response to Richard Bauckham: The Idiomatic Use of Bar Enasha', *JSNT* 23 (1985), pp. 35–41.

Lindeskog, G., 'Das Rätsel des Menschensohnes', *ST* 22 (1968), pp. 149–75.

Loba-Mkole, J. C., 'Une synthèse d'opinions philologiques sur le Fils de l'homme', *Journal of North-West Semitic Languages* 22 (1996), pp. 107–23.

——'"Son of Man" and exegetical myths', *Hervormde Teologiese Studies* 59 (2003), pp. 837–58.

Luz, U., 'The Son of Man in Matthew: Heavenly Judge or Human Christ', *JSNT* 48 (1992), pp. 3–21.

McArthur, H. K., 'Mark XIV.62', *NTS* 4 (1957–8), pp. 156–8.

——'On the Third Day', *NTS* 18 (1971–2), pp. 81–6.

McDermott, J., '*Luke*, XII, 8-9: Stone of Scandal', *RB* 84 (1977), pp. 523–37.

——'*Luc*, XII, 8-9: Pierre angulaire', *RB* 85 (1978), pp. 381–401.

——'Mt. 10:23 in Context', *BZ* 28 (1984), pp. 230–40.

McNeil, B., 'The Son of Man and the Messiah: A Footnote', *NTS* 26 (1979–80), pp. 419–21.

Maddox, R., 'The Function of the Son of Man according to the Synoptic Gospels', *NTS* 15 (1968–9), pp. 45–74.

——'The Quest for Valid Methods in "Son of Man" Research', *AusBR* 19 (1971), pp. 36–51.

——'The Function of the Son of Man in the Gospel of John', in R. Banks (ed.) *Reconciliation and Hope. New Testament Essays on Atonement and Eschatology presented to L. L. Morris on his 60th birthday*, (Exeter: Paternoster, 1974), pp. 186–204 .

Malbon, E. S., 'Narrative Christology and the Son of Man: What the Markan Jesus Says Instead', *BibInt* 11 (2003), pp. 373–85.

Manson, T. W., 'The Son of Man in Daniel, Enoch and the Gospels', *BJRL* 32, 1949–50, pp. 171–93. Reprinted in T. W. Manson (ed. M.Black), *Studies in the Gospels and Epistles* (Manchester: Manchester U.P., 1962), pp. 123–45.

Marcus, J., 'Son of Man as son of Adam', *RB* 110 (2003), pp. 38–61, 370–86.

Marshall, I. H., 'The Synoptic Son of Man Sayings in Recent Discussion', *NTS* 12 (1965–6), pp. 327–51.

——'The Son of Man in Contemporary Debate', *EvQ* 42 (1970), pp. 67–87.

——*The Origins of New Testament Christology* (Leicester: IVP, 1976), pp. 63–82.

——'The Son of Man and The Incarnation', *Ex Auditu* 7 (1991), pp. 29–43.

——'The "Son of Man" Sayings in the Light of Linguistic Study', in T. E. Schmidt and M. Silva (eds), *To Tell the Mystery. Essays on New Testament Eschatology in Honor of R. H. Gundry* (JSNTSup. 100 Sheffield: JSOT Press, 1994), pp. 72–94.

Martin de Viviés, P. de, *Jésus et le Fils de l'Homme. Emplois et significations de l'expression 'Fils de l'Homme' dans les Évangiles* (Lyons: Profac, 1995).

Meadors, E. P., *Jesus the Messianic Herald of Salvation* (WUNT 2,72. Tübingen: Mohr (Siebeck), 1995), pp. 97–145.

Mearns, C., 'The Son of Man Trajectory and Eschatological Development', *ExpT* 97 (1985–6), pp. 8–12.

Meeks, W. A., 'The Man from Heaven in Johannine Sectarianism', *JBL* 91 (1972), pp. 44–72.

Messel, N., *Der Menschensohn in den Bilderreden des Henoch* (BZAW 35. Giessen: Töpelmann, 1922).

Meyer, A., *Jesu Muttersprache. Das galiläische Aramäisch in seiner Bedeutung für die Erklärung der Reden Jesu und der Evangelien überhaupt* (Freiburg i.B./Leipzig: Mohr (Siebeck), 1896).

Michaelis, W., 'Joh. 1,51, Gen. 28,12 und das Menschensohn-Problem', *TLZ* 85 (1960), pp. 561–78.

Michel, O., 'Der Menschensohn. Die eschatologische Hinweisung. Die apokalyptische Aussage. Bemerkungen zum Menschensohnverständnis des Neuen Testaments', *TZ* 27 (1971), pp. 81–104.

——'Der Menschensohn in der Jesusüberlieferung', *TBei* 2 (1971), pp. 119–28.

——'Der Umbruch: Messianität = Menschensohn. Fragen zu Markus 8,31', in G. Jeremias *et al.* (eds), *Tradition und Glaube: Das frühe Christentum in seiner Umwelt. Festgabe für K. G. Kuhn zum 65. Geburtstag* (Göttingen: Vandenhoeck & Ruprecht, 1971), pp. 310–16.

Moloney, F. J., 'The Targum on Ps. 8 and the New Testament', *Salesianum* 37 (1975), pp. 326–36.

——*The Johannine Son of Man* (BSRel 14. Rome: LAS, 1976, 2nd edn 1978).

——'The End of the Son of Man?', *Downside Review* 98 (1980), pp. 280–90.

——'The Re-Interpretation of Psalm VIII and the Son of Man Debate', *NTS* 27 (1980–81), pp. 656–72.

Moule, C. F. D., 'From Defendant to Judge – and Deliverer', *BSNTS* 3 (1952), pp. 40–53. Reprinted in C. F. D. Moule, *The Phenomenon of the New Testament* (SBT II,1. London: SCM, 1967), pp. 82–99.

——'Neglected Features in the Problem of "The Son of Man"', in J. Gnilka (ed.), *Neues Testament und Kirche*. Für Rudolf Schnackenburg, (Freiburg: Herder, 1974), pp. 413–28.

——*The Origin of Christology* (Cambridge: CUP, 1977), pp. 11–22.

——'"The Son of Man": Some of the Facts', *NTS* 41 (1995), pp. 277–9.

Mowinckel, S., *Han som kommer* (Copenhagen: Gad, 1951): *He That Cometh* (trans. G. W. Anderson; Oxford: Blackwell, 1956).

Muilenberg, J., 'The Son of Man in Daniel and the Ethiopic Apocalypse of Enoch', *JBL* 79 (1960), pp. 197–209.

Müller, K., 'Beobachtungen zur Entwicklung der Menschensohnvorstellung in den Bilderreden des Henoch und im Buche Daniel', *Östliche Christentum* 25 (1971), pp. 253–61.

——'Menschensohn und Messias. Religionsgeschichtlichen Vorüberlegungen zum Menschensohnproblem in den synoptischen Evangelien', *BZ* 16 (1972), pp. 161–87; 17 (1973), pp. 52–66.

Müller, M., 'Über den Ausdruck "Menschensohn" in den Evangelien', *ST* 31 (1977), pp. 65–82.

——*Der Ausdruck 'Menschensohn' in den Evangelien. Vorausset zen und Bedeutung* (Acta Theologica Danica XVII. Leiden: Brill, 1984).

——'The Expression "the Son of Man" as Used by Jesus', *ST* 38 (1984), pp. 47–64.

——'"Have you Faith in the Son of Man?" (John 9.35)', *NTS* 37 (1991), pp. 291–4.

——'Schleiermacher und der Ausdruck "Menschensohn". Ein typisches Beispiel und ein Ausdruck', in D. Lange and P. Widmann (eds), *Kirche zwischen Heilsbotschaft und*

Lebenswirklichkeit. Festschrift für Theodor Jorgensen zum 60 Geburtstag (Frankfurt am Main: Lang), pp. 69–80.

Müller, U. B., *Messias und Menschensohn in jüdischen Apokalypsen und in der Offenbarung des Johannes* (Gütersloh: Mohn, 1972).

——'Parusie und Menschensohn', *ZNW* 92 (2001), pp. 1–19.

Mussner, F., 'Die Skepsis des Menschensohnes. Zu Lk 18,8b', in C. Niemand (ed.), *Forschungen zum Neuen Testament und seiner Umwelt. Festschrift für Albert Fuchs* (Frankfurt/M.: Lang, 2002), pp. 271–5.

Naluparayil, J. C., *The Identity of Jesus in Mark. An Essay On Narrative Christology* (SBF 49. Jerusalem: Franciscan, 2000).

Nebe, G., 'The Son of Man and the Angels: Reflections on the Formation of Christology in the Context of Eschatology', in H. G. Reventlow (ed.), *Eschatology in the Bible and in Jewish and Christian Tradition* (JSOTSup 243. Sheffield: Sheffield Academic, 1997), pp. 111–31.

Neugebauer, F., *Jesus der Menschensohn: ein Beitrag zur Klärung der Wege historischer Wahrheitsfindung im Bereich der Evangelien* (Stuttgart: Calwer, 1972).

——'Die Davidssohnfrage (Mark 12.35-7 parr.) und der Menschensohn', *NTS* 21 (1974–5), pp. 81–108.

Olson, D. C., 'Enoch and the Son of Man in the Epilogue of the Parables', *JSP* 18, 1998, pp. 27–38.

O'Neill, J. C., 'Son of Man, Stone of Blood (John 1:51)', *NovT* 45 (2003), pp. 374–81.

Orlando, L., 'Il Figlio dell'Uomo. Percorso Teologico', *Antonianum* 80 (2005), pp. 207–44.

Otto, R., *Reich Gottes und Menschensohn* (Munich: Beck, 1934, 2nd edn 1940): *The Kingdom of God and the Son of Man* (trans. F. V. Filson and B. L.Woolf; London: Lutterworth, 1938, 2nd edn 1943).

Owen, P. and Shepherd, D., 'Speaking up for Qumran, Dalman and the Son of Man: Was *Bar Enasha* a Common Term for "Man" in the Time of Jesus?', *JSNT* 81 (2001), pp. 81–122.

Painter, J., 'The Enigmatic Johannine Son of Man', in F. van Segbroeck *et al.* (eds), *The Four Gospels 1992. Festschrift Frans Neirynck* (3 vols; Leuven: Leuven U.P./Peeters, 1992), vol III, pp. 1869–87.

Pamment, M., 'The Son of Man in the First Gospel', *NTS* 29 (1983), pp. 116–29.

——'The Son of Man in the Fourth Gospel', *JTS NS* 36 (1985), pp. 56–66.

Parker, P., 'The Meaning of "Son of Man"', *JBL* 60 (1941), pp. 151–7.

Pazdan, M. M., *The Son of Man. A Metaphor for Jesus in the Fourth Gospel* (Collegeville: Liturgical, 1991).

Peake, A. S., 'The Messiah and the Son of Man', *BJRL* 8 (1924), pp. 52–81.

Perrin, N., 'Mark 14:62: The End Product of a Christian Pesher Tradition?', *NTS* 12 (1965–6), pp. 150–5.

——'The Son of Man in Ancient Judaism and Primitive Christianity: A Suggestion', *BR* 11 (1966), pp. 17–28.

——'The Creative Use of the Son of Man Traditions by Mark', *USQR* 23 (1967–8), pp. 237–65.

——*A Modern Pilgrimage in New Testament Christology* (Philadelphia: Fortress, 1974).

Pesch, R., 'Über die Autorität Jesu. Eine Rückfrage anhand des Bekenner und erleugnerspruchs Lk 12,8f par.', in R. Schnackenburg *et al.* (eds), *Die Kirche des Anfangs. Für Heinz Schürmann* (Leipzig: St Benno, 1978), pp. 25–55.

Pesch, R., and Schnackenburg, R., in zusammenarbeit mit O. Kaiser (eds), *Jesus und der Menschensohn: Für Anton Vögtle* (Freiburg i.B.: Herder, 1975).

Preiss, T., *Le Fils de l'Homme* (Montpellier, 1951).

——'Le Fils de l'Homme dans le IVᵉ Evangile', *ETR* 28 (1953), pp. 7–61.

Procksch, O., 'Der Menschensohn als Gottessohn', *Christentum und Wissenschaft* 3 (1927), pp. 425–43, 473–81.

Rhea, R., *The Johannine Son of Man* (ATANT 76. Zürich: Theologischer, 1990).

Robinson, J. M., 'The Son of Man in the Sayings Gospel Q', in C. Elsas *et al.* (eds), *Tradition und Translation: Zum Problem der interkulturellen Übersetzbarkeit religiöser Phänomene:*

Festschrift für Carsten Colpe zum 65 Geburtstag (Berlin: De Gruyter 1994), pp. 315–35.

Rochais, G., 'Jésus et le Fils de l'Homme', in J. L. D'Aragon *et al.* (eds), *Jésus? De l'histoire à la foi* (CTHP 9. Montreal: Fides, 1974), pp. 83–122.

Rose, R. P., 'Études Évangeliques. III. Fils de l'homme et Fils de Dieu', *RB* 9 (1900), pp. 169–99.

Ross, J. M., 'The Son of Man', *IBS* 13 (1991), pp. 186–198.

Roth, W., 'Jesus as the Son of Man: the Scriptural Identity of a Johannine Image', in D. E. Groh and R. Jewett (eds), *The Living Text: Essays in Honor of Ernest W. Saunders* (Lanham: University Press of America, 1985), pp. 11–26.

Sahlin, H., 'Wie wurde ursprünglich die Benennung "Der Menschensohn" verstanden?', *ST* 37 (1983), pp. 147–79.

Sandmel, S., 'Son of Man', in D. J. Silver (ed.), *In the Time of Harvest: Essays in Honor of Abba Hillel Silver* (New York: Macmillan, 1963), pp. 355–67.

Sänger, D. (ed.), *Gottessohn und Menschensohn. Exegetische Studien zu zwei Paradigmen biblischer Intertextualität* (Biblisch-Theologische Studien 67. Neukirchen-Vluyn: Neukirchener, 2004).

Sasse, M., *Der Menschensohn im Evangelium nach Johannes* (Texte und Arbeiten zum neutestamentlichen Zeitalter 35. Tübingen: Francke, 2000).

Schaberg, J., 'Daniel 7,12 and the New Testament Passion-Resurrection Predictions', *NTS* 31 (1985), pp. 208–22.

Schenk, W., *Das biographische Ich-Idiom 'Menschensohn' in den frühen Jesus-Biographien* (FRLANT 177. Göttingen: Vandenhoeck & Ruprecht, 1997).

Schippers, R., 'The Son of Man in Matt. xii.32 = Lk. xii.10, compared with Mk. iii.28', *SE* IV (TU 102, 1968), pp. 231–5.

Schmid, H., 'Daniel, der Menschensohn', *Judaica* 27 (1971), pp. 192–220.

Schmidt, N. A., 'Was בר נשא a Messianic Title?', *JBL* 15 (1896), pp. 36–53.

——'The Son of Man in the Book of Daniel', *JBL* 19 (1900), pp. 22–8.

——'Son of Man', in T. K. Cheyne and J. S. Black (eds), *Encyclopaedia Biblica* vol. 4 (London: A & C Black, 1903), cols. 4705–40.

——'Recent Study of the Term "Son of Man"', *JBL* 45 (1926), pp. 326–49.

Schmiedel, P. W., 'Der Name "Menschensohn" und das Messiasbewusstsein Jesu', *PM* 2 (1898), pp. 252–67.

——'Bezeichnet Jesus den Menschen als solchen durch "Menschensohn"?', *PM* 2 (1898), pp. 291–308.

——'Die neuesten Auffassungen des Namens "Menschensohn"', *PM* 5 (1901), pp. 333–51.

Schmithals, W., 'Die Worte vom leidenden Menschensohn. Ein Schlüssel zur Lösung des Menschensohn-Problems', in C. Andresen and G. Klein (eds), *Theologia Crucis – Signum Crucis*. Festschrift für E. Dinkler zum 70 Geburtstag (Tübingen: Mohr, 1979), pp. 417–45.

Schnackenburg, R., 'Der Menschensohn im Johannesevangelium', *NTS* 11 (1964–5), pp. 123–37.

Scholten, W., *Specimen hermeneutico-theologicum: De appellatione* τὸν υἱὸν τοῦ ἀνθρώπου *qua Jesus se Messiam professus est* (Paddenburg & Schoonhoven: Trajecti ad Rhenum, 1809).

Schröter, J., 'The Son of Man as the representative of God's kingdom: On the Interpretation of Jesus in Mark and Q', in M. Labahn and A. Schmidt (eds), *Jesus, Mark and Q. The Teaching of Jesus and its Earliest Records* (JSNTSup 214. Sheffield: Sheffield Academic, 2001), pp. 34–68.

Schulz, S., *Untersuchungen zur Menschensohn-Christologie im Johannesevangelium* (Göttingen: Vandenhoeck & Ruprecht, 1957).

Schulze, L. Th., *Vom Menschensohn und vom Logos: Ein Beitrag zur biblischen Christologie* (Gotha: Perles, 1867).

Schwarz, G., *Jesus 'der Menschensohn'. Aramaistische Untersuchungen zu den synoptischen Menschensohnworten Jesu* (BWANT 119, = VI, 19; Stuttgart: Kohlhammer, 1986).

Schweizer, E., 'Der Menschensohn (Zur eschatologischen Erwartung Jesu)', *ZNW* 50 (1959), pp. 185–209.

——'The Son of Man', *JBL* 79 (1960), pp. 119–29.

——'The Son of Man Again', *NTS* 9 (1962–3), pp. 256–61.

Scott, R. B. Y., '"Behold, He Cometh with the Clouds"', *NTS* 5 (1958–9), pp. 127–32.

Seitz, O. J. F., 'The Future Coming of the Son of Man: Three Midrashic Formulations in the Gospel of Mark', *SE* VI (TU 112, 1973), pp. 478–94.

Sharman, H. B., *Son of Man and Kingdom of God* (New York: Harper, 1943).

Sidebottom, E. M., *The Christ of the Fourth Gospel in the Light of First-Century Thought* (London: SPCK, 1961).

Sjöberg, E., *Der Menschensohn im äthiopischen Henochbuch* (Lund: Gleerup, 1946).

——'בן אדם und בר אנש im Hebräischen und Aramäischen', *Acta orientalia* 21 (1953), pp. 57–65, 91–107.

——*Der verborgene Menschensohn in den Evangelien* (Lund: Gleerup, 1955).

Slater, T. B. 'One Like a Son of Man in First-Century CE Judaism', *NTS* 41 (1995), pp. 183–98.

——'Comparisons and the Son of Man', *Biblebhashyam* 24 (1998), pp. 67–78.

Smalley, S. S., 'The Johannine Son of Man Sayings', *NTS* 15 (1969), pp. 278–301.

Smith, M. H., 'No Place for a Son of Man', *Forum* 4 (1988), pp. 83–107.

——'To Judge the Son of Man. The Synoptic Sayings', *Forum* 7 (1991), pp. 207–42.

Stauffer, E., 'Messias oder Menschensohn', *NovT* 1 (1956), pp. 81–102.

Stott, W., '"Son of Man" – A Title of Abasement', *ExpT* 83 (1971–2), pp. 278–81.

Stowasser, M., 'Mk 13,26f und die urchristliche Rezeption des Menschensohns', *BZ* 39 (1995), pp. 246–52.

Strecker, G., 'Die Leidens- und Auferstehungsvoraussagen im Markusevangelium', *ZTK* 64 (1967), pp. 16–39.

Sturch, R. L., 'The Replacement of "Son of Man" by a Pronoun', *ExpT* 94 (1982–3), p. 333.

Svedlund, G., 'Notes on *bar nash* and the Detrimental Effects of its Transformation into the Title "The Son of Man"', *Orientalia Suecana* 33–5 (1984–6), pp. 401–13.

Talbert, C. H., 'The Myth of a Descending-Ascending Redeemer in Mediterranean Antiquity', *NTS* 22 (1975–6), pp. 418–40.

Taylor, V., 'The "Son of Man" Sayings Relating to the Parousia', *ExpT* 58 (1946–7), pp. 12–15.

——*The Names of Jesus* (London: Macmillan, 1953), Ch. 7, 'The Son of Man'.

Teeple, H. M., 'The Origin of the Son of Man Christology', *JBL* 84 (1965), pp. 213–50.

Theisohn, J., *Der auserwählte Richter. Untersuchungen zum traditionsgeschichtlichen Ort der Menschensohngestalt der Bilderreden des äthiopischen Henoch* (SUNT 12. Göttingen: Vandenhoeck & Ruprecht, 1975).

Thompson, G. H. P., 'The Son of Man – Some Further Considerations', *JTS NS* 12 (1961), pp. 203–9.

Tillmann, F., *Der Menschensohn: Jesu Selbstbezeugnis für seine messianische Würde* (Freiburg i.B.: Herder, 1907).

——'Hat die Selbstbezeichnung Jesus "der Menschensohn" ihre Wurzeln in Dn 7,13?', *BZ* 5 (1907), pp. 35–47.

Tödt, H. E., *Der Menschensohn in der synoptischen Überlieferung* (Gütersloh: Mohn, 1959); *The Son of Man in the Synoptic Tradition* (trans. D. M. Barton; London: SCM, 1965).

Tödt, I., 'Der "Menschensohn" und die Folgen', in C. Frey and W. Huber (eds), *Schöpferische Nachfolge: Festschrift für H. E. Tödt* (Heidelberg, 1978).

Toll, C., 'Zur Bedeutung des aramäischen Ausdruckes bar nāš', *Orientalia Suecana* 33–5 (1984–6), pp. 421–28.

Tuckett, C. M., 'The Present Son of Man', *JSNT* 14 (1982), pp. 58–81.

——'The Son of Man in Q', in M. C. De Boer (ed.), *From Jesus to John. Essays on Jesus and New Testament Christology in Honour of Marinus de Jonge* (JSNTSup 84. Sheffield: JSOT Press, 1993), pp. 196–215.

——'Q 12,8 Once Again – "Son of Man" or "I"?', in J. M. Asgeirsson, K. de Troyer and M. W. Meyer (eds), *From Quest to Q. Festschrift James M. Robinson*, (*BETL* CXLVI. Leuven: Leuven & Peeters, 2000), pp. 171–88.

——'The Son of Man and Daniel 7: Q and Jesus', in A. Lindemann (ed.), *The Sayings Source Q and the Historical Jesus* (*BETL* CLVIII. Leuven: Leuven UP/Peeters, 2001), pp. 371–94.

Vaage, L. E., 'The Son of Man Sayings in Q: Stratigraphical Location and Significance', *Semeia* 55 (1992), pp. 103–29.

VanderKam, J. C., 'Righteous One, Messiah, Chosen One and Son of Man in 1 Enoch 37–71', in J. H. Charlesworth (ed.), *THE MESSIAH. Developments in Earliest Judaism and Christianity* (Minneapolis: Fortress, 1992), pp. 169–91.

Vermes, G., 'The Use of בר נש/בר נשא in Jewish Aramaic', App.E in M. Black, *An Aramaic Approach to the Gospels and Acts* (Oxford: OUP, 3rd edn, 1967), pp. 310–28; reprinted in G. Vermes, *Post-Biblical Jewish Studies* (Leiden: Brill, 1975), pp. 147–65.

——*Jesus the Jew* (London: Collins, 1973), pp. 160–6.

——'The Present State of the "Son of Man" Debate', *JJS* 29 (1978), pp. 123–34. Reprinted in G. Vermes, *Jesus and the World of Judaism* (London: SCM, 1983), pp. 89–99.

——'The "Son of Man" Debate', *JSNT* 1 (1978), pp. 19–32.

Vielhauer, P., 'Gottesreich und Menschensohn in der Verkündigung Jesu', in W. Schneemelcher (ed.), *Festschrift für Günther Dehn zum 75. Geburtstag*, pp. 51–79. Reprinted in P. Vielhauer, *Aufsätze zum Neuen Testament* (TBü 31. Munich: Kaiser, 1965).

——'Jesus und der Menschensohn: Zur Diskussion mit Heinz Eduard Tödt und Eduard Schweizer', *ZTK* 60 (1963), pp. 133–77. Reprinted in Vielhauer, *Aufsätze*, pp. 92–140.

Vögtle, A., 'Bezeugt die Logienquelle die authentische Redeweise Jesu vom "Menschensohn"?', in J. Delobel (ed.), *Logia: les paroles de Jésus – The Sayings of Jesus* (BETL 59. Leuven: Leuven U.P./Peeters, 1982), pp. 77–99.

——'Eine überholte "Menschensohn" Hypothese?', in K. Aland und S. Meurer (eds), *Wissenschaft und Kirche. Festschrift für Eduard Lohse* (Bielefeld: Luther, 1989), pp. 70–95.

——*Die 'Gretchenfrage' des Menschensohnproblems. Bilanz und Perspective* (Quaestiones Disputatae 152. Freiburg/Basel/Wien: Herder, 1994).

Völter, P., *Die Menschensohn-Frage neu untersucht* (Leiden: Brill, 1916).

Walker, W. O., 'The Origin of the Son of Man Concept as applied to Jesus', *JBL* 91 (1972), pp. 482–90.

——'The Son of Man: Some Recent Developments', *CBQ* 45 (1983), pp. 584–607.

——'John 1.43-51 and "The Son of Man" in the Fourth Gospel', *JSNT* 56 (1994), pp. 31–42.

Wellhausen, J., *Israelitische und Jüdische Geschichte* (Berlin: Reimer, 1894), p. 312 n.1.

——*Skizze und Vorarbeiten* VI (Berlin: Reimer, 1899), pp. 187–215, 'Des Menschen Sohn'.

——*Einleitung in die drei ersten Evangelien* (Berlin: Reimer, 2nd edn, 1911), pp. 95–8, 123–30.

Wifall, W., 'Son of Man – A Pre-Davidic Social Class?', *CBQ* 37 (1975), pp. 331–40.

Wilson, F. M., 'The Son of Man in Jewish Apocalyptic Literature', *Studia biblica et theologica* 8 (1978), pp. 28–52.

Wink, W., '"The Son of Man" in the Gospel of John', in R. T. Fortna and T. Thatcher (eds), *Jesus in Johannine Tradition* (Louisville: Westminster John Knox, 2001), pp. 117–23.

——*The Human Being. Jesus and the Enigma of the Son of Man* (Minneapolis: Fortress, 2002).

Witherington, B. III, *The Christology of Jesus* (Minneapolis: Fortress, 1990), pp. 233–62.

Xeravits, G., 'Does the Figure of the "Son of Man" Have a Place in the Eschatological Thinking of the Qumran Community?', *LouvStud* 26 (2001), pp. 334–45.

Zehrer, F., 'Jesus, der Menschensohn', *BLit* 47 (1974), pp. 165–76.

Zorn, R. O., 'The Significance of Jesus' Self-Designation, "The Son of Man"', *Vox reformata* 34 (1980), pp. 1–21.

3. Other Secondary Literature Cited

Anderson, H., *The Gospel of Mark* (NCB. London: Oliphants, 1976).

Appel R., and P. Muysken, *Language contact and bilingualism* (London: Arnold, 1987).

Aus, R. D., *'Caught in the Act', Walking on the Sea, and the Release of Barabbas Revisited* (Atlanta: Scholars, 1998).

Avalos, H., *Illness and Health Care in the Ancient Near East. The Role of the Temple in Greece, Mesopotamia and Israel* (HSM 54. Atlanta: Scholars, 1995).

Baker, J. H., and J. R. Silver, 'Hysterical paraplegia', *Journal of Neurology, Neurosurgery and Psychiatry* 50 (1987), pp. 375–82.

Barr, J., '"Determination" and the Definite Article in Biblical Hebrew', *JSS* 34 (1989), pp. 307–35.

Bass, C. (ed.), *Somatization: Physical Symptoms and Psychological Illness* (Oxford: Blackwell, 1990).

Bassnett, S., 'Text Types and Power Relations', in A. Trosborg (ed.), *Text Typology and Translation* (BTL 26. Amsterdam, Benjamins, 1997), pp. 87–98.

Beasley-Murray, G. R., *Jesus and the Kingdom of God* (Grand Rapids: Eerdmanns, 1986).

Beckwith, R., *The Old Testament Canon of the New Testament Church and its Background in Early Judaism* (London: SPCK, 1985).

Berger, P., 'Zu den sogenannten Sätzen Heiligen Rechtes', *NTS* 17 (1970–1), pp. 10–40.

——'Die sog. "Sätze heiligen Rechtes" im N.T. Ihre Funktion und ihr Sitz im Leben', *TZ* 28 (1972), pp. 305–30.

Black, M., *An Aramaic Approach to the Gospels and Acts* (Oxford: OUP, 3rd edn, 1967).

Borgen, P. D., *Bread from Heaven. An Exegetical Study of the Concept of Manna in the Gospel of John and the Writings of Philo* (NovTSup 10. Leiden: Brill, 1965).

Brown, R. E., *The Gospel According to John* (2 vols; AB 29 and 29A. London: Cassell, 1966).

——*The Death of the Messiah. A Commentary on the Passion Narratives in the Four Gospels* (ABRL. 2 vols; London/New York: Chapman/Doubleday, 1994).

Bultmann, R., 'Die Bedeutung der neuerschlossenen mandäischen und manichäischen Quellen für das Verständnis des Johannesevangeliums', *ZNW* 24 (1925), pp. 100–46; repr. R. Bultmann (ed. E. Dinkler), *Exegetica. Aufsätze zur Erforschung des Neuen Testaments* (Tübingen: Mohr (Siebeck), 1967), pp. 55–104.

——*Die Geschichte der synoptischen Tradition* (FRLANT 29, N.F.12. Göttingen: Vandenhoeck & Ruprecht, 1921): *The History of the Synoptic Tradition* (trans. J. Marsh; Oxford: Blackwell, 1963).

——*Theology of the New Testament* (2 vols; Trans. K. Grobel; London: SCM, 1952).

Burney, C. F., *The Poetry of Our Lord* (Oxford: Clarendon, 1925).

Cadbury, H. J., *The Style and Literary Method of Luke* (HTS 6. Cambridge, MA: Harvard U.P., 1920).

Cansdale, F. S., *Animals of Bible Lands* (Exeter: Paternoster, 1970).

Caquot, A., 'La Double Investiture de Lévi (Brèves remarques sur *Testament de Lévi, VIII*)', in C. J. Bleeker *et al.* (eds), *Ex orbe religionum. Studia Geo Widengren* (2 vols; NumenSup 21–2. Leiden: Brill, 1972), vol. 1, pp. 156–61.

Carmignac, J., 'Studies in the Hebrew Background of the Synoptic Gospels', *ASTI* 7 (1968–9), pp. 64–93.

Carroll, J. T., 'Luke's Portrayal of the Pharisees', *CBQ* 50 (1988), pp. 604–21.

Carson, D. A., *The Gospel According to John* (Leicester: IVP, 1991).

Casey, P. M., 'Porphyry and the Origin of the Book of Daniel', *JTS* NS 27 (1976), pp. 15–33.

——'The Fourth Kingdom in Cosmas Indicopleustes and the Syrian Tradition', *Rivista di Storia e Letteratura Religiosa* 25 (1989), pp. 385–403.

——'Porphyry and Syrian Exegesis of the Book of Daniel', *ZNW* 81 (1990), pp. 139–42.

——'The Original Aramaic Form of Jesus' Interpretation of the Cup', *JTS* NS 41 (1990), pp. 1–12.

——*From Jewish Prophet to Gentile God. The Origins and Development of New Testament Christology* (The Cadbury Lectures at the University of Birmingham, 1985–6. Cambridge/ Louisville: James Clarke/Westminster/John Knox, 1991).

——*Is John's Gospel True?* (London: Routledge, 1996).

——'Culture and Historicity: the Cleansing of the Temple,' *CBQ* 59 (1997), pp. 306–32.

——'Monotheism, Worship and Christological Developments in the Pauline Churches', in C. C. Newman, J. R. Davila and G. S. Lewis (eds), *The Jewish Roots of Christological Monotheism. Papers from the St Andrews Conference on the Historical Origins of the Worship of Jesus* (Leiden: Brill, 1999), pp. 214–33.

Chesterman, A., 'From "Is" to "Ought": Laws, Norms and Strategies in Translation Studies', *Target* 5 (1993), pp. 1–20.

——*Memes of Translation. The Spread of Ideas in Translation Theory* (BTL 22. Amsterdam: Benjamins, 1997).

Colwell, E. C., *The Greek of the Fourth Gospel. A Study of its Aramaisms in the Light of Hellenistic Greek* (Chicago: University of Chicago, 1931).

——'A Definite Rule for the Use of the Article in the Greek New Testament', *JBL* 52 (1933), pp. 12–21.

Crossley, J. G., *The Date of Mark's Gospel. Insight from the Law in Earliest Christianity* (JSNTSup 266. London: T&T Clark International, 2004).

Davies, W. D., and Dale Allison, C., *The Gospel According to Saint Matthew* (ICC. 3 vols; Edinburgh, T&T Clark, 1988–97).

Davila, J. R., 'The Dead Sea Scrolls and Merkavah Mysticism', in T. H. Lim *et al.* (eds), *The Dead Sea Scrolls in Their Historical Context* (Edinburgh: T&T Clark, 2000), pp. 249–64.

De Jonge, M., 'Jesus' death for others and the death of the Maccabean martyrs', in T. Baarda *et al.* (eds), *Text and Testimony. Essays on New Testament and Apocryphal Literature in Honour of A. F. J. Klijn* (Kampen: Kok, 1988), pp. 142–51.

Downing, F. G., 'The Resurrection of the Dead: Jesus and Philo', *JSNT* 15 (1982), pp. 42–50.

Downing, J., 'Jesus and Martyrdom', *JTS* NS 14 (1963), pp. 279–93.

Dupont-Sommer, A., 'Exorcismes et guérisons dans les récits de Qoumrân', in G. W. Anderson *et al.* (eds), *Congress Volume Oxford 1959* (VTSup 7. Leiden: Brill, 1960), pp. 246–61.

Duval, R., 'Le Testament de Saint Éphrem', *Journal Asiatique* ser 9, 18 (1901), pp. 234–319.

Edwards, R. A., 'The Eschatological Correlative as a *Gattung* in the New Testament', *ZNW* 60 (1969) pp. 9–20.

Fitzmyer, J. A., 'The Languages of Palestine in the First Century A.D.', *CBQ* 32 (1970), pp. 501–31, rev. *Wandering Aramean*, pp. 29–56.

——*The Gospel According to Luke. A New Translation with Introduction and Commentary* (2 vols; AB 28 and 28A. New York: Doubleday, 1981–5).

Fleddermann, H. T., *Mark and Q. A Study of the Overlap Texts* (BETL 122. Leuven: Leuven University Press, 1995).

Freed, E. D., *Old Testament Quotations in the Gospel of John* (NovTSup 11. Leiden: Brill, 1965).

Gaston, L., *No stone on another. Studies in the significance of the fall of Jerusalem in the Synoptic Gospels* (NovTSup 23. Leiden: Brill, 1970).

J. Gnilka, *Das Evangelium nach Markus* (EKKNT. 2 vols. Düsseldorf/Neukirchen-Vluyn: Benziger/Neukirchener, 4th edn, 1994).

Gourges, M., *A La Droite de Dieu. Résurrection de Jésus et Actualisation du Psaume 110:1 dans le Nouveau Testament* (EBib. Paris: Gabalda, 1978).

Grabbe, L. L., 'Aquila's Translation and Rabbinic Exegesis', *JJS* 33 (1982), pp. 527–36.

Greenbaum, S., 'Contextual Influence on Acceptability Judgements', *Linguistics* 187 (1977), pp. 5–11.

Grotius, H., *Annotationes in libros evangeliorum* (Amsterdam/Paris, 1641), in *Annotationes in quatuor Evangelia & Acta Apostolorum* in H. Grotii *Opera Omnia Theologica* (Amsterdam: Blaev, 1679), Tom II vol. I.

Gundry, R. H., *Mark. A Commentary on His Apology for the Cross* (Grand Rapids: Eerdmans, 1993).

Haenchen, E., *Der Weg Jesu. Eine Erklärung des Markus-Evangeliums und der kanonischen Parallelen* (Berlin: de Gruyter, 2nd edn, 1968).

Hagner, D. A., *Matthew 1-13,* (WBC 33A. Dallas: Word Books, 1993).

Hallévi, J., 'Recherches sur la langue de la rédaction primitive du Livre d'Énoch', *Journal Asiatique*, Sixième Série, 9 (1867), pp. 352–95.

Halligan, P. W., and A. S. David (eds), *Conversion Hysteria: Towards a Cognitive Neuropsychological Account* (Hope: Psychology Press, 1999).

Halverson, S., 'The Concept of Equivalence in Translation Studies: Much Ado About Something', *Target* 9 (1997), pp. 207–33.

Hanson, A. T., *The Prophetic Gospel. A Study of John and the Old Testament* (Edinburgh: T&T Clark, 1991).

Harvey, A. E., *Jesus and the Constraints of History* (BaL 1980. London: Duckworth, 1982).

Hay, D. M., *Glory at the Right Hand. Psalm 110 in Early Christianity* (Nashville: Abingdon, 1973).

Hilgenfeld, A., *Die jüdische Apokalyptik in ihrer geschichtlichen Entwicklung* (Jena: Mauche, 1857).

Hogan, L. P., *Healing in the Second Temple Period* (NTOA 21. Freiburg/Göttingen: Universitätsverlag/Vandenhoeck & Ruprecht, 1992).

Hönig, H. G., 'Holmes' "Mapping Theory" and the Landscape of Mental Translation Processes', in K. M. van Leuven-Zwart and T. Naaijkens (eds), *Translation Studies: The State of the Art.* Proceedings of the First James S. Holmes Symposium on Translation Studies (Amsterdam, 1991), pp. 77–89.

Holm-Nielsen, S., 'The Book of Ecclesiastes and the Interpretation of it in Jewish and Christian Theology', *ASTI* 10 (1975–6), pp. 38–96.

Hooker, M. D., *Jesus and the Servant* (London: SPCK, 1959).

——*The Gospel According to St Mark* (BNTC. London: Black, 1991).

Huehnergard, J., 'What is Aramaic?', *Aram* 7 (1995), pp. 261–82.

Hyvärinen, K., *Die Übersetzung von Aquila* (ConBOT 10. Uppsala: Almqvist & Wiksell, 1977).

Jablensky, A., 'The Concept of Somatoform Disorders: A Comment on the Mind-Body Problem in Psychiatry' in Y. Ono *et al.* (eds), *Somatoform Disorders. A Worldwide Perspective* (Tokyo: Springer, 1999), pp. 3–10.

Jarick, J., 'Aquila's *Koheleth*', *Textus* 15 (1990), pp. 131–9.

Jeremias, J., *The Parables of Jesus* (trans. S. H. Hooke. London: SCM, 2nd edn, 1963).

——*The Prayers of Jesus* (London: SCM, 1967).

——*New Testament Theology* (vol. I; trans. J.Bowden; London: SPCK, 1971).

Kaganaraj, J. J., *'Mysticism' in the Gospel of John. An Inquiry into its Background* (JSNTSup 158. Sheffield: Sheffield Academic, 1998).

Käsemann, E., 'Sätze heiligen Rechtes im Neuen Testament', *NTS* 1 (1954–5), pp. 248–60: 'Sentences of Holy Law in the New Testament', in E. Käsemann, *New Testament Questions of Today* (trans. W. I. Montague; London: SCM, 1969), pp. 66–81.

Keir Howard, J., *Disease and Healing in the New Testament. An Analysis and Interpretation* (Lanham: University Press of America, 2001).

Kingsbury, J. D., 'On Following Jesus: the "Eager" Scribe and the "Reluctant" Disciple (Matthew 8.18-22)', *NTS* 34 (1988), pp. 45–59.

Klassen, W., *Judas. Betrayer or Friend of Jesus?* (London: SCM, 1996).

Klaudy, K., *Languages in Translation. Lectures on the Theory, Teaching and Practice of Translation* (Trans. T. J. de Kornfeld, P. Heltai, K. Károly and K. Klaudy; Budapest: Scholastica, 2003).

Klein, M. L., 'Converse Translation: A Targumic Technique', *Bib* 57 (1976), pp. 515–37.

Kleinman, A., *Patients and Healers in the Context of Culture. An Exploration of the Borderland between Anthropology, Medicine and Psychiatry* (Berkeley/L.A.: Univ. of California, 1980).

Kümmel, W. G., *Promise and Fulfilment: The Eschatological Message of Jesus* (trans. D. M. Barton; SBT 23; London: SCM, 2nd edn, 1961).

Lamy, M., 'Le Testament de Saint Éphrem le Syrien', *Compte rendu du IVᵉ Congrès Scientifique International des Catholiques. Première Section. Sciences Religieuses* (1898) pp. 173–209.

Lane, W. L., *The Gospel of Mark* (London: Marshall, Morgan & Scott, 1974).

Lapide, P., *The Resurrection of Jesus* (London: SPCK, 1984).

Larsen, S., 'Testing the Test: a preliminary investigation of translation as a test of writing skills', in S. Larsen (ed.), *Translation. A Means to an End* (The Dolphin 18. Aarhus: Aarhus Univ., 1990), pp. 95–108.

Lebourlier, J., '*Entos hymôn*. Le sens "au milieu de vous" est-il possible?', *Bib* 73 (1992), pp. 259–62.

Lee, D. A., *The Symbolic Narratives of the Fourth Gospel. The Interplay of Form and Meaning* (JSNTSup 95. Sheffield: Sheffield Academic, 1994).

Lightfoot, R. H. (ed. C. F. Evans), *St. John's Gospel. A Commentary* (Oxford: Clarendon, 1956).

Lipiński, E., *The Aramaeans. Their Ancient History, Culture, Religion* (OLA 100. Leuven: Peeters, 2000).

Loader, W. R. G., 'Christ at the Right Hand – Ps. CX 1 in the New Testament', *NTS* 24 (1977–8), pp. 199–228.

Loisy, A., under the pseudonym of J. Lataix, 'Le Commentaire de s. Jérôme sur Daniel', *Revue d'histoire et de littérature religieuses* II (1897), pp. 164–73, 268–77.

Lörscher, W., *Translation Performance, Translation Process and Translation Strategies. A Psycholinguistic Investigation* (Tübingen: Narr, 1991).

Lövestam, E., *Jesus and 'this Generation'. A New Testament Study* (ConBNT 25. Stockholm: Almqvist & Wiksell, 1995).

McNamara, M., *The New Testament and the Palestinian Targum to the Pentateuch* (AnBib 27A. Rome: Biblical Institute, 2nd edn, 1978).

McNeile, A. H., *An Introduction to Ecclesiastes with Notes and Appendices* (Cambridge: CUP, 1904).

Manson, T. W., *The Teaching of Jesus* (Cambridge: CUP, 1931; 2nd edn, 1935).

——*The Sayings of Jesus* (1937, as Part II of *The Mission and Message of Jesus*, ed. H. D. A. Major et *al.* Reprinted separately, London: SCM, 1949).

Marcus, J., *Mark 1-8. A New Translation with Introduction and Commentary* (AB 27. New York: Doubleday, 2000).

Marshall, J. T., 'The Aramaic Gospel', *The Expositor*, 4th series, 3 (1891), pp. 1–17, 109–24, 275–91.

Meeks, W. A., *The First Urban Christians. The Social World of the Apostle Paul* (London/New Haven: Yale University, 1993).

Menken, M. J., *Old Testament Quotations in the Fourth Gospel. Studies in Textual Form* (Kampen: Pharos, 1996).

Metzger, B. M., *A Textual Commentary on the Greek New Testament* (Swindon: UBS, 1971).

Micklem, E. R., *Miracles and the New Psychology* (London: OUP, 1922).

Murphy, M. R., 'Classification of the Somatoform Disorders', in C. Bass (ed.), *Somatization: Physical Symptoms and Psychological Illness* (Oxford: Blackwell, 1990), pp. 10–39.

Neubert, A., *Text and Translation* (Übersetzungswissenschaftliche Beiträge 8. Leipzig: Enzyklopädie, 1985).

——'Interference between Languages and between Texts', in H. Schmidt (ed.), *Interferenz in der Translation* (Übersetzungswissenschaftliche Beiträge 12. Leipzig: Enzyklopädie, 1989), pp. 56–64.

Neubert, A., and G. M. Shreve, *Translation as Text* (Translation Studies 1. Kent, Ohio: Kent State Univ., 1992).

Nöldeke, Th., *Compendious Syriac Grammar* (trans. J. A. Crichton; London: Williams & Norgate, 1904).

Nolland, J., *Luke 9:21–18:34* (WBC 35B. Dallas: Word Books, 1993).

——*Luke 18:35–24:53* (WBC 35C. Dallas: Word Books, 1993).

Nord, C., *Translating as a Purposeful Activity: Functionalist Approaches Explained* (Manchester: St Jerome, 1997).

——'A Functional Typology of Translations', in A. Trosborg (ed.), *Text Typology and Translation* (BTL 26. Amsterdam, Benjamins, 1997), pp. 43–66.

Owen, A. R. G., *Hysteria, hypnosis and healing: the work of J.-M. Charcot* (London: Dobson, 1971).

Pattison, E. M., N. A. Lapins and H. A. Doerr, 'Faith Healing. A Study of Personality and Function', *Journal of Nervous and Mental Disease* 157 (1973), pp. 397–409.

Paul, A., 'La Bible grecque d'Aquila et l'idéologie du judäisme ancien', *ANRW* II.20.1 (1987), pp. 221–45.

Reed, J. L., *Archaeology and the Galilean Jesus. A Re-examination of the Evidence* (Harrisburg: Trinity Press International, 2000).

Reiß, K., *Möglichkeiten und Grenzen der Übersetzungskritik* (München: Huebner, 1971); *Translation Criticism – The Potentials and Limitations* (Trans. E. F. Rhodes; Manchester: St Jerome, 2000).

Reiß, K., and H.-J. Vermeer, *Grundlegung einer allgemeinen Translationstheorie* (Linguistische Arbeiten 147. Tübingen: Niemeyer, 1984).

Rensberger, D., *Overcoming the World. Politics and Community in the Gospel of John* (London: SPCK, 1988).

Rogerson, J. W., 'The Hebrew Conception of Corporate Personality: a Re-examination', *JTS NS* 21 (1970), pp. 1–16.

Rose, L., *Faith Healing* (London: Penguin, 1971).

Sacks, H., 'Everyone Has to Lie', in M. Sanches and B. G. Blount (eds), *Sociocultural Dimensions of Language Use* (London/NY: Academic Press, 1975), pp. 57–79.

Sanders, J. N., and B. A. Mastin, *The Gospel According to St John* (BNTC. London: Black, 1968).

Schäffner, C., 'Strategies of Translating Political Texts', in A. Trosborg (ed.), *Text Typology and Translation* (BTL 26. Amsterdam, Benjamins, 1997), pp. 119–43.

Schäffner C., (ed.), *Translation and Quality* (Clevedon: Multilingual Matters Ltd, 1998).

Schagen, S. H., 'Concepts of Resurrection and Immortality in Intertestamental Judaism and in the New Testament' (unpublished doctoral dissertation, Nottingham University, 1985).

Schmidt, N., 'The Original Language of the Parables of Enoch', in R. F. Harper *et al.* (eds), *Old Testament and Semitic Studies in Memory of W. R. Harper* (2 vols; Chicago: Univ. of Chicago, 1908), vol. 2; pp. 327–49.

Schuchard, B. G., *Scripture within Scripture. The Interrelationship of Form and Function in the Explicit Old Testament Citations in the Gospel of John* (SBLDS 133. Atlanta: Scholars, 1992).

Schulthess, F., *Grammatik des christlich-palästinischen Aramäisch* (Tübingen: J. C. B. Mohr (Paul Siebeck), 1924).

Schwankl, O., *Die Sadduzaerfrage (Mk 12, 18-27 parr)* (Frankfurt: Athenäum, 1987).

Schwarz, G., '*Und Jesus sprach'. Untersuchungen zur aramäischen Urgestalt der Worte Jesu* (BWANT 118 = VI,18. Stuttgart: Kohlhammer, 1985, 2nd edn 1987).

Schweitzer, A., *The Quest of the Historical Jesus. First Complete Edition* (trans. W. Montgomery *et al.*; London: SCM, 2000).

Séguinot, T. C., 'The editing function of translation', *Bulletin of the Canadian Association of Applied Linguistics* 4 (1982), pp. 151–61.

Selinker, L., *Rediscovering Interlanguage* (London: Longman, 1992).

Shorter, E., *From Paralysis to Fatigue. A History of Psychosomatic Illness in the Modern Era* (New York: Free Press, 1992).

Stark, R., *The Rise of Christianity. A Sociologist Reconsiders History* (Princeton: Princeton U.P., 1996).

Staub, U., 'Das Tier mit den Hörnern: Ein Beitrag zu Dan 7.7f', *FZPT* 25 (1978), pp. 382–96.

Stone, M. E., *Fourth Ezra. A Commentary on the Book of Fourth Ezra* (Hermeneia. Minneapolis: Fortress, 1990).

Švejcer, A. D., 'Literal Translation as a Product of Interference', in H. Schmidt (ed.), *Interferenz in der Translation* (Übersetzungswissenschaftliche Beiträge 12. Leipzig: Enzyklopädie, 1989), pp. 39–44.

Taylor, V., *The Gospel According to St. Mark* (London: Macmillan, 1959).

Toone, B. K., 'Disorders of Hysterical Conversion', in Bass (ed.), *Somatization*, pp. 207–34.

Torrey, C. C., *The Four Gospels. A New Translation* (London/New York: Harper, 1933).

Totman, R., *Social Causes of Illness* (London: Souvenir, 2nd edn, 1987).

Tov, E., 'The Septuagint', in M. J. Mulder and H. Sysling (eds), *Mikra* (CRINT II,1. Assen/ Maastricht/Philadelphia: Van Gorcum/Fortress, 1988) pp. 161–88.

Tovey, D., *Narrative Art and Act in the Fourth Gospel* (JSNTSup 151. Sheffield: Sheffield Academic, 1997).

Tristram, H. B., *The Natural History of the Bible* (London: Christian Knowledge Society, 1867; 10th edn, 1911).

Tropper, J., 'Die Herausbildung des bestimmten Artikels im Semitischen', *JSS* 46 (2001), pp. 1–31.

Van Unnik, W. C., 'The Quotation from the Old Testament in John 12.34', *NovT* 3 (1959), pp. 174–9.

Vermeer, H. J., *A skopos theory of translation (Some arguments for and against)* (Heidelberg: TEXTconTEXT, 1996).

Vos, L. A., *The Synoptic Traditions in the Apocalypse* (Kampen: Kok, 1965).

Wales, K., '"Personal" and "Indefinite" Reference: The uses of the pronoun *ONE* in Present-day English', *Nottingham linguistic circular* 9 (1980), pp. 93–117.

Wellhausen, J., *Israelitische und Jüdische Geschichte* (Berlin: Reimer, 1894).

——*Das Evangelium Marci* (Berlin: Reimer, 1903).

——*Einleitung in die drei ersten Evangelien* (Berlin: Reimer, 2nd edn, 1911).

Wilcox, M., 'Semitisms in the New Testament', ANRW II.25.2 (1984), pp. 978–1029.

Williams, C., *I am He. The Interpretation of 'Anî Hû' in Jewish and Early Christian Literature* (WUNT 2.113. Tübingen: Mohr Siebeck, 2000).

Wrede, W., 'Zur Heilung des Gelähmten (Mc 2,1ff)', *ZNW* 5 (1904), pp. 354–8.

J. Ziegler, 'Die Wiedergabe der nota accusativi *'et, 'aet* mit σύν', *ZAW* 100 (1988 Supp), pp. 222–33.

Index of Scripture and Ancient Literature

INDEX OF MODERN AUTHORS